Business and Society

Corporate Strategy, Public Policy, Ethics

Tenth Edition

Business and Society

Corporate Strategy, Public Policy, Ethics

James E. Post
Boston University

Anne T. Lawrence
San Jose State University

James Weber
Duquesne University

Boston   Burr Ridge, IL   Dubuque, IA   Madison, WI   New York   San Francisco   St. Louis
Bangkok   Bogotá   Caracas   Kuala Lumpur   Lisbon   London   Madrid   Mexico City
Milan   Montreal   New Delhi   Santiago   Seoul   Singapore   Sydney   Taipei   Toronto

McGraw-Hill Higher Education

A Division of The McGraw-Hill Companies

Business and Society: Corporate Strategy, Public Policy, Ethics
Published by McGraw-Hill, an imprint of The McGraw-Hill Companies, Inc. 1221 Avenue of the Americas, New York, NY, 10020. Copyright © 2002, 1999, 1996, 1992, 1988, 1984, 1980, 1975 by The McGraw-Hill Companies, Inc. All rights reserved. No part of this publication may be reproduced or distributed in any form or by any means, or stored in a database or retrieval system, without the prior written consent of The McGraw-Hill Companies, Inc., including, but not limited to, in any network or other electronic storage or transmission, or broadcast for distance learning.

Some ancillaries, including electronic and print components, may not be available to customers outside the United States.

This book is printed on acid-free paper.

domestic   1 2 3 4 5 6 7 8 9 0 FGR/FGR 0 9 8 7 6 5 4 3 2 1
international 1 2 3 4 5 6 7 8 9 0 FGR/FGR 0 9 8 7 6 5 4 3 2 1

ISBN   0-07-244506-8

Publisher: *John E. Biernat*
Sponsoring editor: *Andy Winston*
Editorial coordinator: *Sara E. Strand*
Marketing manager: *Lisa Nicks*
Project manager: *Anna M. Chan*
Production associate: *Gina Hangos*
Media producer: *Jennifer Becka*
Freelance design coordinator: *Mary L. Christianson*
Interior textures freelancer: *Sheilah Barrett Design*
Cover image: © *Stone*
Supplement producer: *Susan Lombardi*
Printer: *Quebecor World Fairfield Inc.*
Typeface: *10/12 Times Roman*
Compositor: *GTS Graphics, Inc.*

Library of Congress Cataloging-in-Publication Data

Post, James E.
    Business and society : corporate strategy, public policy, ethics.—10th ed. / James E. Post, Anne T. Lawrence, James Weber.
        p. cm.
    Frederick's name appears first on the earlier editions.
    Includes bibliographical references and indexes.
    ISBN 0-07-244506-8 (alk. paper)
    1. Social responsibility of business. I. Lawrence, Anne T. II. Weber, James. III. Title.
HD60 .F72 2002
658.4'08—dc21

                                                                              2001030661

INTERNATIONAL EDITION ISBN 0-07-112112-9
Copyright © 2002. Exclusive rights by The McGraw-Hill Companies, Inc. for manufacture and export. This book cannot be re-exported from the country to which it is sold by McGraw-Hill. The International Edition is not available in North America.

www.mhhe.com

About the Authors

James E. Post is a professor of management at Boston University. His primary areas of teaching and research are business and public affairs management, public policy, and corporate citizenship. He is the author or coauthor of such books as *Private Management and Public Policy* (with Lee E. Preston), *Managing Environmental Issues: A Casebook* (with Rogene Buchholz and Alfred Marcus), and *Redefining the Corporation: Stakeholder Management and Organizational Wealth* (with Lee Preston and Sybille Sachs). He has been an adviser to business, nongovernmental organizations, and government agencies on a range of issues involving business practices and responsibilities. He has been an expert witness before the U.S. Congress and regulatory agencies and served as a research director of the Conference Board's business and society program. He has been chairperson of the Social Issues in Management division of the Academy of Management, served as a reviewer and member of editorial boards for many management journals, and published articles in leading business journals. His book *Private Management and Public Policy* was cited by the Academy of Management for "its lasting contribution to the study of business and society."

Anne T. Lawrence is a professor of organization and management at San Jose State University. She holds a Ph.D. from the University of California, Berkeley, and completed two years of postdoctoral work at Stanford University. Her articles, cases, and reviews have appeared in many journals, including the *Academy of Management Review, Administrative Science Quarterly, Journal of Management Education, Case Research Journal, Business and Society Review,* and *Research in Corporate Social Performance and Policy*. Her cases in business and society have also been reprinted in many textbooks and anthologies. She has served as associate editor of the *Case Research Journal* and as president of both the North American Case Research Association and of the Western Casewriters Association. She was the recipient of the outstanding case of the year award from NACRA, and at San Jose State University, she was named Outstanding Undergraduate Instructor in the College of Business and received the Dean's Award for Faculty Excellence.

James Weber is a professor of management and business ethics and the director of the Beard Center for Leadership in Ethics at Duquesne University. He has a Ph.D. from the University of Pittsburgh and has taught at the University of San Francisco, University of Pittsburgh, and Marquette University. His areas of interest and research include managerial and organizational values, cognitive moral reasoning, business ethics, ethics training and education, and corporate social audit and performance. He has conducted corporate training workshops in the areas of ethical decision making and corporate–community relations for various businesses and professional associations. He has published works in numerous management and ethics journals, such as *Organization Science, Business and Society, Human Relations,* the *Journal of Business Ethics, Teaching Business Ethics,* and *Research in Corporate Social Performance and Policy.* He was recognized by the Social Issues in Management division of the Academy of Management with the Best Paper Award in 1989 and 1994. He is a member of and has served as division and program chair of the Social Issues in Management division of the Academy of Management; he has also served as president and program chair of the International Association of Business and Society (IABS). In addition, he is a member of and has served in various leadership roles in the Society for the Advancement of Socio-Economics (SASE) and the Society for Business Ethics.

Brief Contents

Preface xv
Acknowledgments xviii
Introduction and Overview xix

PART ONE
The Corporation in Society

1 The Corporation and Its Stakeholders 2
2 Business and Public Issues 29

PART TWO
Business and the Social Environment

3 Corporate Social Responsibility 56
4 Socially Responsive Management 79

PART THREE
Business and the Ethical Environment

5 Ethical Dilemmas in Business 100
6 Ethical Reasoning and Corporate Programs 125

PART FOUR
Business and Government in a Global Society

7 Business and Public Policy 152
8 Managing Business–Government Relations 184
9 Antitrust, Mergers, and Global Competition 210

PART FIVE
The Corporation and the Natural Environment

10 Ecology, Sustainable Development, and Global Business 234
11 Managing Environmental Issues 258

PART SIX
Business and Technological Change

12 Technology: An Economic–Social Force 284
13 Managing Technological Challenges 305

PART SEVEN
Responding to Stakeholders

14 Stockholders and Corporate Governance 328
15 Consumer Protection 352
16 The Community and the Corporation 374
17 Employees and the Corporation 402

PART EIGHT
Social Issues

18 Managing a Diverse Workforce 428
19 Business and the Media 452
20 Global Social Issues for a New Century 475

Case Studies in Corporate Social Policy

Odwalla, Inc., and the E. Coli Outbreak 504
Salt Lake City and the Olympics Bribery Scandal 515
Columbia/HCA and the Medicare Fraud Scandal 524
The Tobacco Deal 536
The Antitrust Case against Microsoft 548
Dow Corning and the Silicone Breast Implant Controversy 558
Nike's Dispute with the University of Oregon 570
Shell Oil in Nigeria 581
The Transformation of Shell 593

Glossary 604
Bibliography 620
Name Index 625
Subject Index 630

Contents

Preface xv
Acknowledgments xviii
Introduction and Overview xix

PART ONE
The Corporation in Society

1

The Corporation and Its Stakeholders 2

Business-Government-Society: An Interdependent System 5
A Systems Perspective 5 • The Stakeholder Concept 8 • Primary and Secondary Stakeholders 10 • Stakeholder Interests and Power 13 • Stakeholder Coalitions 14

Forces Shaping Business-Society Relations 15
Economic Competition: Strategic and Social Challenges 15 • Ethical Expectations and Public Values 19 • The Changing Role of Government and Public Policy 20 • Ecological and Natural Resource Concerns 22 • Technology and New Knowledge 23

Corporate Strategy for the Twenty-First Century 25

Summary Points of This Chapter 25

Key Terms and Concepts Used in This Chapter 26

Internet Resources 26

Discussion Case Inland National Bank 26

2

Business and Public Issues 29

Why Public Issues Matter 31
The Macroenvironment of Business 31 • Emergence of

Public Issues 34 • The Performance-Expectations Gap 34

The Public Issue Life Cycle 35
Phases of the Public Issue Life Cycle 36 • Continuing Issues 41

The Public Affairs Function 41
Public Affairs Management 41

Issues Management 44
Managing a Single Issue 46 • Managing Multiple Issues 47 • Managing Crisis 47

Creating a Strategic Approach to Public Issues 48
Strategies of Response 50

Summary Points of This Chapter 51

Key Terms and Concepts Used in This Chapter 52

Internet Resources 52

Discussion Case McDonald's in the McSpotlight 52

PART TWO
Business and the Social Environment

3

Corporate Social Responsibility 56

The Meaning of Corporate Social Responsibility 58
The Many Responsibilities of Business 58 • Social Responsibility and Corporate Power 59

How Corporate Social Responsibility Began 60
The Charity Principle 61 • The Stewardship Principle 63

The Corporate Social Responsibility Debate 64
Arguments for Corporate Social Responsibility 64 • Arguments against Corporate Social Responsibility 67

Balancing Economic, Legal, and Social
   Responsibilities   69
   Enlightened Self-Interest   69 • Economic Obligations and
   Social Responsibility   70 • Legal Requirements versus
   Corporate Social Responsibility   71 • Stockholder
   Interests versus Other Stakeholder Interests   72

Corporate Social Responsibility around the World   72

Summary Points of This Chapter   75

Key Terms and Concepts Used in This Chapter   76

Internet Resources   76

Discussion Case   Aaron Feuerstein—A Socially
   Responsible Owner   76

4

Socially Responsive Management   79

The Corporate Social Climate   80

Implementing Social Responsiveness   83
   A Model of Corporate Social Responsiveness   83 •
   Framework for Social Policy   86

Becoming a Socially Responsive Firm   87
   Top Management Philosophy   87 • Socially Responsive
   Strategy   88 • Socially Responsive Structure   88 • Line
   Manager Involvement   89

Socially Responsive Management in Practice   89
   Corporate Philanthropy   89 • Corporate Employee
   Volunteerism   90 • Corporate Awards for Social
   Responsibility   91

Corporate Social Audits   93
   Audit Standards   94

Summary Points of This Chapter   96

Key Terms and Concepts Used in This Chapter   96

Internet Resources   96

Discussion Case   Social Auditing at VanCity   96

PART THREE
**Business and the Ethical
Environment**

5

Ethical Dilemmas in Business   100

The Meaning of Ethics   102
   What Is Business Ethics?   103 • Why Should Business Be
   Ethical?   103

Business Ethics across Organizational Functions   106
   Accounting Ethics   106 • Financial Ethics   107 •
   Marketing Ethics   109 • Information Technology Ethics
   111 • Other Functional Areas   112

Why Ethical Problems Occur in Business   112
   Personal Gain and Selfish Interest   112 • Competitive
   Pressures on Profits   113 • Business Goals versus Personal
   Values   114 • Cross-Cultural Contradictions   115

Ethics in a Global Economy   116
   Efforts to Curtail Unethical Practices   117

Ethics, Laws, and Illegal Corporate Behavior   120
   Corporate Lawbreaking and Its Costs   121

Summary Points of This Chapter   122

Key Terms and Concepts Used in This Chapter   122

Internet Resources   122

Discussion Case   Viagra—Wonder Drug or Ethical
   Irresponsibility?   123

6

Ethical Reasoning and Corporate Programs   125

The Core Elements of Ethical Character   126
   Managers' Goals and Values   127 • Virtue Ethics   128 •
   Personal Character, Spirituality, and Moral Development
   129 • Corporate Culture and Ethical Climates   132

Analyzing Ethical Problems in Business   134
  Utility: Comparing Benefits and Costs   134 • Rights:
  Determining and Protecting Entitlements   135 • Justice:
  Is It Fair?   136 • Applying Ethical Reasoning to Business
  Activities   137

Making Ethics Work in Corporations   139
  Building Ethical Safeguards into the Company   140 • Top
  Management Commitment and Involvement   140 • Codes
  of Ethics   140 • Ethics Committees   142 • Ethics Officers
  142 • Ethics Ombudspersons   143 • Ethics Hot Lines
  144 • Ethics Training Programs   144 • Ethics Audits   145
  • Comprehensive Ethics Programs   146 • Corporate Ethics
  Awards   146

Summary Points of This Chapter   147

Key Terms and Concepts Used in This Chapter   147

Internet Resources   147

Discussion Case   PPG's Corporate Ethics Program
  148

PART FOUR
Business and Government in a Global Society

7
Business and Public Policy   152

The Role of Government and Public Policy   154
  Powers of Government   155 • Elements of Public
  Policy   155

Public Policy and Business   158
  National Economic Growth   159 • Taxation Policy   160 •
  Trade Policy   162 • Industrial Policy   163

Social Welfare Policies   163
  Health Policy   164 • Social Security   166 •
  Entitlements   167

Government Regulation of Business   167
  Goals and Objectives   167 • Types of Regulation   168 •
  Costs of Regulation   173 • Effectiveness of
  Regulation   174 • Reinventing Government   177

International Regulation   177
  Regulation of Imported Products   177 • Regulation of
  Exported Products   178 • Regulation of International
  Business Behavior   179

The Future   180

Summary Points of This Chapter   180

Key Terms and Concepts Used in This Chapter   180

Internet Resources   181

Discussion Case   Protecting Human Food Supplies
  181

8
Managing Business–Government Relations   184

Strategic Management of Government Relations   185
  Techniques of Political Action   186 • Political
  Involvement   188 • Managing the Political Agenda   189 •
  Corporate Political Strategy   190

American Politics in a New Century   191
  Conflict and Cooperation   192 • Political
  Cynicism   192 • Coalition Politics   193

Critical Problems   194
  Money and Campaign Financing   194 • Lobbying and the
  Power of Special Interests   198

Responsible Business Politics   204

Summary Points of This Chapter   206

Key Terms and Concepts Used in This Chapter   207

Internet Resources   207

Discussion Case   Coca-Cola's Civic Action
  Network   208

9
Antitrust, Mergers, and Global Competition   210

The Dilemma of Corporate Power   211

Antitrust Regulation   214
  Objectives of Antitrust   214 • The Major Antitrust
  Laws   216 • Enforcing the Antitrust Laws   219 • Key
  Antitrust Issues   220

Corporate Mergers   223
  The Consequences of Corporate Mergers   225

Global Competition and Antitrust Policy   226
  Antitrust Enforcement and National Competitiveness   227 •
  Enforcing Antitrust Laws against Foreign Firms   228 •
  Harmonizing International Antitrust Policies   228

Summary Points of This Chapter   229

Key Terms and Concepts Used in This Chapter   229

Internet Resources   230

Discussion Case   The AOL–Time Warner Merger   230

Summary Points of This Chapter   279

Key Terms and Concepts Used in This Chapter   280

Internet Resources   280

Discussion Case   Common Sense in Arizona   280

PART FIVE
The Corporation and the Natural Environment

PART SIX
Business and Technological Change

10
Ecology, Sustainable Development, and Global Business   234

Ecological Challenges   236
  The Global Commons   236 • Sustainable Development
  237 • Threats to the Earth's Ecosystem   238 • Forces of
  Change   240 • The Limits to Growth   242

Global Environment Issues   243
  Ozone Depletion   244 • Global Warming   245 •
  Biodiversity   247

Response of the International Business Community
  250
  World Business Council for Sustainable Development
  250 • Voluntary Business Initiatives   251

Summary Points of This Chapter   254

Key Terms and Concepts Used in This Chapter   255

Internet Resources   255

Discussion Case   Damming the Yangtze River   255

11
Managing Environmental Issues   258

Role of Government   260
  Major Areas of Environmental Regulation   260 •
  Alternative Policy Approaches   267

Costs and Benefits of Environmental Regulation   271

The Greening of Management   273
  Stages of Corporate Environmental Responsibility   273 • The
  Ecologically Sustainable Organization   274 • Elements of
  Effective Environmental Management   275 • Environmental
  Management as a Competitive Advantage   278

12
Technology: An Economic–Social Force   284

The Explosive Force of Technology   285
  Technology Defined   286 • Phases of Technology in
  Society   287 • Fueling Technological Growth   287

The Emergence of High-Technology Business   289
  Technology and E-Commerce   289 • Businesses'
  Technological Innovations   292 • Technology
  Superpowers   293 • Emerging Global Participation   293

Technology in Our Daily Lives   296
  Medical Information via the Internet   298

Special Issue: The Digital Divide   299

Summary Points of This Chapter   301

Key Terms and Concepts Used in This Chapter   302

Internet Resources   302

Discussion Case   Ethical Principles for
  E-Commerce   302

13
Managing Technological Challenges   305

Businesses Protecting Privacy   306
  Industry and Government Efforts to Manage
  Privacy   309

The Management of Information Security   310
  Businesses' Responses to Invasions of Information Security
  311 • The Chief Information Officer   312 • Government
  Efforts to Protect Information Security   313

The Management of Adult-Oriented Information   313

Protecting Intellectual Property   314
  Software Piracy and Business Responses   315 • Pirating
  Copyrighted Music and Business Responses   317

Managing Scientific Breakthroughs   318
  Human Genome   318 • Biotechnology   319 • Cloning
  320 • Genetically Engineered Foods   321

Summary Points of This Chapter   323

Key Terms and Concepts Used in This Chapter   324

Internet Resources   324

Discussion Case   Napster—Free Access or Musical
  Piracy?   324

PART SEVEN
Responding to Stakeholders

14
Stockholders and Corporate Governance   328

Stockholders   330
  Who Are Stockholders?   330 • Objectives of Stock
  Ownership   330

Stockholders' Legal Rights and Safeguards   333
  Stockholder Lawsuits   333 • Corporate Disclosures   334

Corporate Governance   334
  The Board of Directors   335 • Top Management   336 •
  Creditors   337 • The Process of Corporate Governance   338

Current Trends in Corporate Governance   339
  The Rise of Institutional Investors   339 • Changing Role
  of the Board of Directors   341 • Social Responsibility
  Shareholder Resolutions   342 • Employee Stock
  Ownership   343

Special Issue: Executive Compensation   344

Government Protection of Stockholder Interests   346
  Securities and Exchange Commission   346 • Insider
  Trading   346

Stockholders and the Corporation   348

Summary Points of This Chapter   348

Key Terms and Concepts Used in This Chapter   349

Internet Resources   349

Discussion Case   Shareholders Demand Reforms at
  Archer Daniels Midland   349

15
Consumer Protection   352

Pressures to Promote Consumer Interests   353
  The Anatomy of Consumerism   354 • Reasons for the
  Consumer Movement   355 • Consumer Advocacy Groups
  356

How Government Protects Consumers   356
  Goals of Consumer Laws   357 • Major Consumer
  Protection Agencies   359

Consumer Privacy in the Internet Age   362

Special Issue: Product Liability   365
  Strict Liability   365 • Business Efforts to Reform the
  Product Liability Laws   366

Positive Business Responses to Consumerism   367
  Total Quality Management   367 • Voluntary Industry
  Codes of Conduct   369 • Consumer Affairs Departments
  369 • Product Recalls   370

Consumerism's Achievements   370

Summary Points of This Chapter   371

Key Terms and Concepts Used in This Chapter   371

Internet Resources   371

Discussion Case   Smith & Wesson's Gun Deal   372

16
The Community and the Corporation   374

Community Relations   376
  Social Capital and Civic Engagement   377 • Limited
  Resources Face Unlimited Community Needs   378 •
  Community Involvement and Firm Size   378 •
  Community Acceptance and Support of Business   380

Strengthening the Community   383
  Improving Economic Development   384 • Housing
  385 • Education Reform   387 • Jobs, Training, and
  Welfare Reform   388 • Technical Assistance to
  Government   388 • Aid to Minority Enterprise   389 •
  Environmental Programs   389 • Disaster Relief   391

Corporate Giving   391
  Corporate Giving in a Strategic Context   393 • Priorities
  in Corporate Giving   394

The Role of Volunteerism   396

The Need for Partnerships   397

Summary Points of This Chapter   398

Key Terms and Concepts Used in This Chapter   399

Internet Resources   399

Discussion Case   Walt Disney and the License to Operate   400

17

Employees and the Corporation   402

The Employment Relationship   403

Workplace Rights   405
The Right to Organize and Bargain Collectively   405 • The Right to a Safe and Healthy Workplace   406 • The Right to a Secure Job   409

Privacy in the Workplace   411
Electronic Monitoring   412 • Romance in the Workplace   413 • Employee Drug Use and Testing   414 • Alcohol Abuse at Work   415 • Employee Theft and Honesty Testing   416

Whistle-Blowing and Free Speech in the Workplace   416

Working Conditions around the World   419
Fair Labor Standards   419

Employees as Corporate Stakeholders   422

Summary Points of This Chapter   422

Key Terms and Concepts Used in This Chapter   423

Internet Resources   423

Discussion Case   Smoking in the Workplace   423

PART EIGHT
Social Issues

18

Managing a Diverse Workforce   428

The Changing Face of the Workforce   429

Gender and Race in the Workplace   430
Women and Minorities at Work   431 • The Gender and Racial Pay Gap   432 • Where Women and Persons of

Color Manage   433 • Breaking the Glass Ceiling   434 • Women and Minority Business Ownership   435

Government's Role in Securing Equal Employment Opportunity   436
Equal Employment Opportunity   437 • Affirmative Action   439 • Sexual and Racial Harassment   440

What Businesses Can Do: Diversity Policies and Practices   442

Balancing Work and Life   444
Child Care and Elder Care   444 • Work Flexibility   446

Summary Points of This Chapter   448

Key Terms and Concepts Used in This Chapter   449

Internet Resources   449

Discussion Case   Coca-Cola Faces Charges of Racial Discrimination   449

19

Business and the Media   452

The Media Industry   453
Media's Ethical and Social Responsibilities   455 • The Image Issue   455 • The Values Issue   457 • The Fairness and Balance Issue   459 • The Free Speech Issue   460

Special Issue: Government Regulation of Tobacco Advertising   464

How Businesses Influence Their Public Image   465
Public Relations Society of America   466 • Public Relations, Public Affairs   466 • Crisis Management   467 • Media Training of Employees   470

Summary Points of This Chapter   471

Key Terms and Concepts Used in This Chapter   471

Internet Resources   471

Discussion Case   Same Crisis, Two Different Responses—Bridgestone/Firestone and Ford   472

20

Global Social Issues for a New Century   475

Global Commerce Today   477
Dominant Trends   477 • Scope and Scale   478 • Global Business Models   479

Global Social Issues   480
   Pros and Cons of Globalization   480 • Nongovernmental
   Organizations   481 • Cultural Distance   482 •
   Anti-Americanism   483 • "Affluenza"   484

Political Issues   486
   International Cooperation   486 • Repressive Political
   Regimes   486 • Global Standards   488

Global Corporate Citizenship   488
   Citizenship Strategies and Business Strategies   489

New Tools for a New Century   492
   Reputation Management   493 • Triple Bottom Line   494
   • Stakeholder Communication   495 • The Quest for
   Sustainability   496

Summary Points of This Chapter   497

Key Terms and Concepts Used in This Chapter   498

Internet Resources   498

Discussion Case   The Battle of Seattle   498

Case Studies in Corporate Social Policy

Odwalla, Inc., and the E. Coli Outbreak   504

Salt Lake City and the Olympics Bribery Scandal
   515

Columbia/HCA and the Medicare Fraud Scandal   524

The Tobacco Deal   536

The Antitrust Case against Microsoft   548

Dow Corning and the Silicone Breast Implant
   Controversy   558

Nike's Dispute with the University of Oregon   570

Shell Oil in Nigeria   581

The Transformation of Shell   593

Glossary   604
Bibliography   620
Name Index   625
Subject Index   630

Preface

The relationship between business and society continues to change in new and significant ways. In 2002, the global economy is an intricate web of social, political, and economic entities: advanced industrial nations, such as the United States, Japan, and Germany; emerging economies that are rapidly developing in Asia and Latin America; Eastern European economies that are free after decades of political repression; and countries that are still struggling to devise economic strategies that will help produce prosperity and an improved quality of life for their citizens.

The prosperity that accompanies economic growth is not shared equally among the countries in each group, however. Income, access to information, and quality of life are unevenly distributed. People with education tend to gain a larger share of wealth than those who lack schooling. Knowledge commands a premium in a world of new and powerful technologies, and education is a powerful source of economic advantage. People who understand the complex interplay of economic, political, and social forces are better able to comprehend the impact of globalization of markets, advances in science, and the changing relationships between humans and nature. We are called on to understand a complicated and rapidly changing world that would seem quite foreign to our grandparents and even our parents. In the midst of this social change, the realities of managing a business are also changing. Businesses have new roles and new responsibilities in the modern economy. Decisions are not made in the same ways as they were 10 or 20 years ago. The impact of business decisions is felt by more people, in more ways than in an earlier time. And because so many other things have changed in the new global economy, business leaders are required to think more carefully than ever about the effects of their actions on their company's employees, customers, suppliers, and investors. The actions of business are watched carefully by the media, government officials, and the communities in which business is conducted. In a very real sense, the world is watching as business executives chart their companies' future direction.

This new edition of *Business and Society* is about how we as stakeholders—managers, consumers, employees, and community members—try to understand, influence, and shape business behavior and social change. Consider these factors:

- Businesses in the United States and other nations are transforming the employment relationship, abandoning practices that once provided job security to employees, in favor of highly flexible but less secure forms of employment. This historic shift in the social contract is driven by complex economic, technological, and social factors.

- The restructuring and redesign of businesses has been driven by vigorous competition in global markets, pressure to improve the quality of products and services, and the creation of information networks that facilitate rapid transfer of economic, social, and political information. Geography, technology, and time once protected companies and people from change. Today, those buffers are disappearing.

- Government policies toward individual industries and sectors of the economy have reshaped markets for goods and services. International trade policies are now critical to the competitive future of businesses everywhere and to the welfare of more than 6 billion people who inhabit the earth.

- Ecological and environmental problems have forced businesses and governments to take action. Crises, accidents, and better understanding of how human activities affect natural resources are producing a consensus that environmental protection must be achieved *with* economic growth if development is to be sustainable.

- Public concern is growing about the ethical and moral behavior of business executives and government officials. As standards change, businesses are challenged to understand new public standards and norms, adjust business practices, and reconcile sometimes conflicting ethical messages. Social values differ from country to country, a fact that challenges accepted notions of the moral order. Businesses often operate in nations whose people hold different values about the workplace and the marketplace.

- The challenge of corporate responsibility and ethical behavior is made more complex when companies conduct business in countries with different social and political cultures. Companies are challenged to function in a world community where great differences still exist between the wealthy and the poor.

- A host of new technologies has become part of the everyday lives of billions of the world's population. Advances in basic sciences—physics, biology, and chemistry—are stimulating extraordinary changes in agriculture, telecommunications, and pharmaceuticals. The media uses phrases such as *new economy*, *biotechnology revolution*, and the *information age* to convey some of the exciting possibilities that these scientific and technological developments promise. New industries emerge, and new approaches to living and working follow from these advances. But serious public issues also arise, as with genetically modified foods, cloned animals, or use of the Internet for pornographic and exploitative purposes.

This Book

This edition of *Business and Society* addresses this complex agenda of issues and their impact and influence on business and its stakeholders. The authors bring a broad background of business and society teaching, research, and case development to this endeavor. The development of this edition began by asking current users of the book to share their suggestions and insights with the author team. Many recommended changes are integrated into this new edition.

Since the 1960s, when Professors Keith Davis and Robert Blomstrom wrote the first edition of this book, *Business and Society* has maintained a position of leadership by discussing central issues of business performance in a form that students and faculty have found engaging and stimulating. The leadership of Professor Davis and Professor

William C. Frederick helped *Business and Society* to consistently achieve a high standard of quality and market acceptance in the field. Thanks to the authors' remarkable eye for the emerging issues that shape the organizational, social, and public policy environments in which students will soon live and work, the book has added value to the business education of many thousands of students.

The tenth edition of *Business and Society* builds on this legacy of market leadership by reexamining such central issues as the role of business in society, the nature of corporate responsibility, business ethics practices, and the complex roles of government and business in the global economic community. Examples of individuals and companies of all sizes illustrate the concepts, theories, and ideas for action in each topical area.

New Themes

The tenth edition also addresses important new themes in modern business and management education.

- The rise of *cross-disciplinary* teaching has created a need for books that span the breadth of business activity, including strategic and operational management. *Business and Society* helps meet this need by illustrating how all types of business decisions impact stakeholders within and outside the firm.

- Business schools are teaching today's students how to *manage across business functions*. This edition presents examples of companies that have managed social issues across the business functions in a strategic, stakeholder-oriented manner.

- The growth of the *Internet* and proliferation of *websites* create new opportunities for students and faculty to enrich courses with information drawn from a nearly infinite universe of sources. A list of useful websites is included at the end of each chapter, and many text references include Internet references.

Finally, *this is a book with a vision.* It is not simply a compendium of information and ideas. This edition of *Business and Society* articulates the view that in a global community, where traditional buffers against change no longer protect business from external change, managers *can* create strategies that integrate stakeholder interests, respect personal values, support community development, and are implemented fairly. Most important, these goals can be achieved while also being economically sound and successful. Indeed, they may be the *only* way to do so over the long term.

Acknowledgments

We are grateful for the assistance of many colleagues at universities in the United States and abroad who have made suggestions and shared ideas for this edition. We also note the feedback from students in our classes and from other colleges and universities that have helped make this book as user-friendly as possible.

A number of research assistants and former students have made contributions throughout this project for which we are grateful. Among the special contributors to this project were research assistants Sarah Cruz, Peter Graham, and Jennifer Meyers, Boston University; Stephanie Glyptis and David Wasieleski, formerly of Duquesne University, who also assisted in preparing the instructor's resource manual; and Timothy Reif, formerly of San Jose State University.

We also wish to acknowledge the assistance of several colleagues who provided sage advice and imaginative ideas for this book: Drs. Barbara W. Altman, University of North Texas; Jeanne Logsdon, University of New Mexico; and Sandra Waddock, Boston College. We also wish to thank Joel V. Copeland, president of Cinergy Media Communication, who produced multimedia versions of the two Shell cases.

We also appreciate the efforts of the following reviewers: Eric J. Akers, Ashland University; Virginia W. Gerde, University of New Mexico; Kathleen Getz, American University; Glenn M. Gomes, California State University, Chico; Robert Hogner, Florida International University; Patrice Luoma, Quinnipiac College; Diane S. McNulty, University of Texas at Dallas; and Joseph A. Petrick, Wright State University.

We are grateful to the excellent editorial and production team at McGraw-Hill. Special thanks to Andy Winston, sponsoring editor, for his leadership throughout the long months of this project. We also wish to recognize the assistance of Sara Strand, editorial coordinator, who never met a problem she couldn't solve; Anna M. Chan, project manager, whose ability to keep us on track and on time has been critical; Sue Lombardi, supplements coordinator; Steve Gomes, copy editor; and Mary Christianson, who designed the book cover. Each of these people has provided professional contributions that we deeply value and appreciate.

Finally, we wish to express a continuing debt of gratitude to Professors Keith Davis and William C. Frederick, who invited us into this project many years ago. Writing a textbook requires many different skills. Keith and Bill have been role models whose friendship, professionalism, and faith in each of us provides a continuing source of inspiration.

James E. Post
Anne T. Lawrence
James Weber

Introduction and Overview

The book is divided into parts that are organized around major themes. In this introduction, we explain the overall design of the book. Each chapter contains a number of pedagogical features designed to enhance student learning, including learning objectives, updated case examples, an end-of-chapter summary of key points, and new or updated discussion cases with questions. Additional materials are included in the Instructor's Resource Manual.

Part One: The Corporation in Society

Readers are introduced to the basic conceptual themes and ideas of the interaction of business and society. Chapter 1 introduces the corporation and its stakeholders and provides a focused way of understanding and mapping the relationships between an organization and its stakeholders. The chapter also discusses the central forces that are shaping business and society relations as we move into the new century. The role of the firm in its social, economic, political, and technological setting is discussed.

Chapter 2 introduces a strategic management approach that executives and organizations actually use in dealing with public issues. By understanding the distance, or gap, between corporate performance and stakeholder expectations, it is possible to follow the evolution of public issues through a normal life cycle. Business responses to public issues are discussed, with a close look at the corporate public affairs function and the development of issues management systems. The chapter concludes with a discussion of four basic strategies of response and how to manage an organization's stakeholder relations as a core part of a company's strategy.

Part Two: Business and the Social Environment

Chapter 3 discusses societal expectations that business will be successful and act in a socially responsible manner. This chapter looks at the evolution of corporate social responsibility and how the doctrine of corporate social responsibility is practiced by businesses around the world. The chapter also examines various limits to a firm's social obligations. Striking a balance among its economic, legal, and social responsibilities is a major challenge for today's business.

Chapter 4 describes how a socially responsive firm manages its relations with stakeholders. Firms must develop a social strategy that responds to environmental forces and expectations. This chapter provides a model for determining if a firm is acting in a socially responsive manner.

Part Three: Business and the Ethical Environment

Chapters 5 and 6 introduce the concept of business ethics. Learning how to recognize ethical issues and understanding their importance to business are emphasized in Chapter 5.

International efforts to curtail unethical practices are described. Chapter 6 focuses on business efforts to promote an ethical environment in the workplace. An ethical decision-making framework and ethical safeguards are discussed in this chapter.

Part Four: Business and Government in a Global Society

Chapter 7 discusses the changing role of government in the global economy. In many nations, government is a strategist for national economic growth and social welfare. The many roles and responsibilities of government in advanced industrial nations are examined, including regulatory processes and activities. The tactics of managing business–government relationships, in the regulatory and political arenas, are discussed in Chapter 8.

Chapter 9 revisits the century-old issue of antitrust in the context of today's rapid technological change and the globalization of markets. As the world economy has changed, policymakers have confronted new challenges in promoting free competition and curbing monopoly power.

Part Five: The Corporation and the Natural Environment

Chapters 10 and 11 address the ecological and natural resource issues that will reshape entire industries as the next century unfolds. Rapid population growth and the explosive development of many of the world's economies have placed new pressures on scarce resources. Water, air, and land pollution have created new constraints for business around the globe. These chapters explore both the challenges and the opportunities presented by the need to move to a more sustainable business model.

Part Six: Business and Technological Change

Business and society will be profoundly affected by a new age of scientific and technological change in the twenty-first century. We have expanded our coverage of these issues to two chapters to more thoroughly frame the issues for students.

Chapter 12 examines technology as a social force in our daily lives. The complex relationships between science, technology, business, and society are creating numerous ethical and political issues. The revolution in information management and the emergence of high-technology businesses will shape the careers of future managers in many powerful ways.

Chapter 13 focuses on how managers can address these complicated decisions. The sound management of technological change involves an understanding of the stakeholder impacts and risks, and the ethical, social, and political consequences that follow.

Part Seven: Responding to Stakeholders

The central concepts and themes discussed in earlier chapters are applied to managing relations with the corporation's primary stakeholders and to a number of emerging social issue areas.

Chapter 14 explores the changing roles and responsibilities of stockholders, managers, boards of directors, and other stakeholders in contemporary corporate governance. It also takes up the controversial debate over executive compensation.

Chapter 15 focuses on consumer protection, including such current topics as consumer privacy in the information age and product liability reform.

Chapter 16 examines the role of the corporation in the community. This chapter looks at business's role in the community, including new models of strategic philanthropy and community involvement. The role of business in education reform and community development is also discussed, as is the importance of corporate charitable giving and employee volunteerism to community life.

Chapter 17 focuses on the evolving employee–employer relationship. Governmental influences on this relationship from countries around the world are described in this chapter. Ethical challenges concerning employees' and employers' rights in the workplace are discussed.

Part Eight: Social Issues

This part focuses on three areas in which change has been, and seems likely to be, of long-term importance to business and society.

Chapter 18 addresses the special issue of diversity in the workplace. What does diversity mean in the modern workplace? What are its benefits, and how is it best achieved? This chapter also explores programs companies have developed to support working parents and eliminate sex discrimination.

Chapter 19 examines the role of media in society, the way that it has shaped business practice in the twenty-first century, and how we characterize groups of people in society. Examples of successful and unsuccessful business interaction with the media are discussed.

Chapter 20 focuses on the powerful long-term global changes that are reshaping the business world. The positive and negative influence of multinational corporations is addressed, as is the rising tide of antibusiness sentiment. The growth of ethnic, religious, and radical forces is shaping the global processes of commerce. The business challenge of acting responsibly, managing issues well, and living by ethical norms is the ultimate long-term challenge for today's students.

Cases

The tenth edition of this book features nine full-length case studies, including a number of new cases prepared especially for this edition. The cases are written to provide rich discussion material and present a variety of opportunities for instructors to connect topics raised in individual chapters.

PART ONE

The Corporation in Society

1

The Corporation
and Its Stakeholders

Businesses develop complex relationships with individuals, organizations, and various segments of society. These relationships require careful management attention and action. Every organization is affected—positively and negatively—by its stakeholders. Stakeholder relationships shape how businesses behave in both market and nonmarket environments. In a world of new technologies, competition, shifting public attitudes, ecological concerns, and government policies, managers are challenged to achieve economic results while meeting the needs and requirements of their business's stakeholders.

This chapter focuses on these key questions and objectives:

- Why are business, government, and society an interactive system?

- What kind of involvement does business have with other segments of society?

- Who are a corporation's primary and secondary stakeholders?

- Why are stakeholders important to a corporation, and how can they affect its success?

- What forces of change are reshaping the business environment in the twenty-first century?

E ach day, hundreds of newsworthy stories are made by businesses and managers making decisions about new products, employment policies, advertising, locations for production and manufacturing, marketing strategies, and future research and development activities. The face of business in modern society is dynamic, diverse, and continuously changing. Some events are exciting, others depressing. But many of the most important decisions made in business reflect trends and underlying forces that are shaping business and society around the world, as illustrated by the following examples.[1]

- Summer is a time for vacations, travel, and relaxation. In recent years, it has also been a time for labor contract negotiations in the airline industry. Increasingly, those relations have shown serious signs of strain. Pilots at United Airlines, for example, were working without a contract while negotiations between the Airline Pilots Union and United Airlines' management dragged on. During the summer of 2000, frustrated pilots refused to work overtime at United. This affected the airline's schedule, which was made worse by bad weather and airport congestion. The result was a nightmare for the company and its passengers. United eventually canceled more than 2,500 scheduled flights per month, losing hundreds of millions of dollars of revenue. Worse, its customers began defecting to other airlines for their travel, vowing not to fly "the friendly skies" in the future.

- The news was a shock to investors. Government officials in the United States and Europe had turned down the application of MCI/WorldCom to acquire Sprint, a leading cellular telephone service provider. MCI/WorldCom was, itself, the product of an earlier merger in which WorldCom, a smaller, but more prosperous, global communications firm, acquired MCI, for $34 billion.[2] In rejecting the Sprint acquisition proposal, the U.S. Department of Justice and the European Union officials cited "competition policy" and the anticompetitive effects it would have on telecommunications services in the United States and Europe. Consumer groups and competitors had objected to the deal and raised serious questions about MCI/WorldCom's failure to live up to promises made during the earlier merger. In light of this history, government officials expressed doubt that the company could be trusted to honor commitments not to compete unfairly against other firms in the United States and Europe.

- Warner-Lambert, a global pharmaceutical company with headquarters in Morris Plains, New Jersey, was fined $3 million after pleading guilty to falsifying reports on the levels of pollutants released from a wastewater treatment plant in Puerto Rico, according to the U.S. Justice Department. The company also had to pay a $670,000 civil penalty for releasing excessive levels of pollutants during a three-year period and violating its wastewater discharge permit 347 times. The plant's supervisor pleaded guilty to charges of failing to

---

[1] Based on published material in the *Wall Street Journal,* the *New York Times,* and *Business Week.* See also, company websites.

[2] These figures were eclipsed by the $100 billion ExxonMobil merger in 1999 and the proposed $125 billion merger of DeutscheTelekom and Vodafone in 2000.

properly collect and analyze wastewater samples for 34 pollutants, including fecal coliform, metals, oil, and grease. As a result, he faced a prison sentence of up to 27 months in jail.

- When officials at Eastman Kodak Company announced a reorganization, citizens worried in Rochester, New York. "Big Father Yellow," as Kodak is called in Rochester, has long been the city's largest employer, taxpayer, and purchaser of goods and services. Kodak is one of the world's best-known companies; its photographic film and imaging equipment are sold throughout the world. Kodak dominated the photographic film business for many decades and used its market power to charge high prices and earn high profits. But this pricing strategy also provided an incentive to new competition. Fuji, a Japanese firm, entered the U.S. market with low-cost, high-quality film. Kodak lost market share to Fuji, and as the company's problems worsened, top management announced a new emphasis on global operations and a major restructuring that would eliminate 10,000 jobs. Kodak promised benefits and job assistance for workers. Rochester's mayor expressed confidence that unemployed workers would find jobs in the local economy and spoke appreciatively of Kodak's commitment to the community. In year 2000, China was the second-largest market in the world for Kodak products.

These examples highlight some of the powerful forces affecting business firms in the modern economy. Why did MCI/WorldCom want to merge with Sprint, and what led regulators to object to the deal? Why did Kodak have to reorganize its business and look to China as a market? The changing shape of business competition is reflected in the plans of companies such as WorldCom and Kodak. New technology produces many benefits but also makes some products obsolete, forcing companies to close operations. Competition creates pressure for new and better products, but it can also pose ethical issues if those products or services violate customer rights, such as personal privacy. The intersecting, and sometimes conflicting, interests of employees, investors, and other constituencies are illustrated in the problems at United Airlines and Kodak. Such conflict complicates the challenge of doing the right thing. The importance of the natural environment, and the need for government regulation to protect the public against unlawful action by companies and managers, is clearly illustrated in the Justice Department's lawsuits against Warner-Lambert. All of these examples highlight the complicated and challenging relationships that exist between businesses and the society in which they operate.

Every business has complex relationships with many people, groups, and organizations in society. Some are intended and desired; others are unintentional and not desired. Whether desired or not, voluntary or involuntary, the people and organizations with which a business is involved have an interest, or stake, in the decisions, actions, and practices of the firm. Customers, suppliers, employees, owners, creditors, and local communities are affected by the economic performance of the business. They have a stake in the business, and their support can be critical to its success or failure.

The modern company, whether small or large, is part of a vast global business system. As the Internet expands communication, companies are more knowledgeable and aware of the social issues, events, and conflicts that take place around the world. Whether a company has 50 employees or 50,000, its links to customers, suppliers, employees, and communities are certain to be numerous, diverse, and vital to its success. This is why the relationship between business, government, and society is important to understand as both a citizen and a manager. Whether viewed as a citizen of the local community or as a manager, employee, or entrepreneur, each of us needs to recognize that the business environment affects the fortunes of companies in powerful ways. Successful businesses learn to blend their economic and social activities together, and successful managers learn to build businesses and create value with minimum conflict and maximum benefits for all.

Business-Government-Society: An Interdependent System

As the examples above illustrate, business, government, and other elements of society are highly interdependent. Business activities impact others in society, and many decisions by government have direct or indirect effects on business. And, of course, both business and government decisions continuously affect other segments of society. To manage these interdependencies, managers need an understanding of their company's key relationships and how the social and economic system of which they are a part affects, and is affected by, their decisions.

A Systems Perspective

Management thinking has been greatly influenced by general systems theory. According to this theory, all living organisms (systems) interact with, and are affected by, other forces in their host environments. The key to survival is the ability to adapt—to be responsive to the changing conditions in the environment. For an organism such as the modern corporation, systems analysis provides a powerful tool to help managers appreciate the relationships between their companies and the rest of the world.

Figure 1-1 illustrates the systems connections between broad, abstract ways of thinking about business-government-society relationships and specific, practical ways of doing so. The broadest view of that relationship is a societal perspective that emphasizes the systems connections between a nation's economic activity, its political life, and its culture. Every society is a mixture of economic, political, and cultural influences. This mix of factors shapes the roles that business, government, and community organizations play in a society and the expectations generated by its people, institutions, and ideas.[3] In other words, the "reality" all of us operate in is a mixture of economic, political, and cultural influences.

A somewhat narrower perspective is illustrated in the middle panel of Figure 1-1. Business is composed of many segments, industries, and sectors; government involves political life at the local, national, and, increasingly, international levels; and society is composed of many segments, groups, and stakeholders. Once, it was believed that

---

[3] This is developed in Robert D. Putnam, *Bowling Alone: The Collapse and Revival of American Community* (New York: Simon and Schuster, 2000). See also, Amitai Etzioni, *The New Golden Rule* (New York: Basic Books, 1996); and Amitai Etzioni, *The Spirit of Community* (New York: Crown Publishers, 1993).

Figure 1-1

A range of levels for understanding business-government-society relationships.

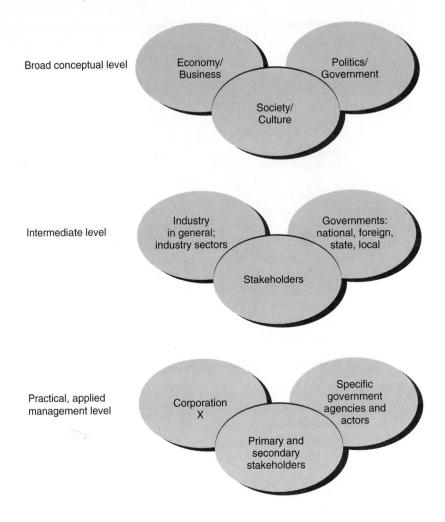

Broad conceptual level

Economy/Business

Politics/Government

Society/Culture

Intermediate level

Industry in general; industry sectors

Governments: national, foreign, state, local

Stakeholders

Practical, applied management level

Corporation X

Specific government agencies and actors

Primary and secondary stakeholders

business interacted with others only through the marketplace. But that view has long since been replaced by an understanding that business and society have many nonmarket interactions as well. Business decisions are shaped by cultural and political forces, as well as economic factors, and business also affects the political life and culture of a society.

> *About a decade ago, Bell Atlantic (now named Verizon), a telecommunications company, formed a joint venture with the national telecommunications company of New Zealand. The joint venture expanded telecommunications services for citizens and businesses in New Zealand. Faxes between New Zealanders and others throughout the Pacific grew rapidly, and the number of international telephone calls exploded. New Zealanders quickly became more connected to the rest of the world. Despite great geographic distances, New Zealand businesses were*

EXHIBIT 1-A

Internet Usage in 2005

The *Computer Industry Almanac* reports that the number of Internet users is growing around the world. In 2000, the top 15 countries account for more than 80 percent of users, including business, educational, and home users. The United States has an estimated 135 million users, which is 36 percent of approximately 375 million worldwide users. This percentage is expected to decline, however, as Internet use grows in other parts of the world. The United States is expected to account for only about 25 percent of users in 2005 when it is expected that more than 10 percent, or 600 million, of the world's 6 billion people will have Internet access.

Top Nations in Internet Use at Year-End 2000

	Users in Millions	Percentage of Total
1. United States	135.7	36.20%
2. Japan	26.9	7.80
3. Germany	19.1	5.10
4. UK	17.9	4.77
5. China	15.8	4.20
6. Canada	15.2	4.05
7. South Korea	14.8	3.95
8. Italy	11.6	3.08
9. Brazil	10.6	2.84
10. France	9.0	2.39
11. Australia	8.1	2.16
12. Russia	6.6	1.77
13. Taiwan	6.5	1.73
14. Netherlands	5.4	1.45
15. Spain	5.2	1.39
Worldwide total	374.9	

Source: eTForecasts.

connected to important markets in the global economy in ways that had not previously been possible.

What happened in New Zealand in the 1990s is happening in many other countries today because of the Internet and wireless communications. As shown in Exhibit 1-A, a significant portion of the world's 6 billion people is likely to have access to the Internet by 2005. The people of China, for example, are rapidly adopting modern communications technology. Culture, business, and community life are undergoing great change as millions of Chinese citizens use technology to expand their own horizons. Most important, this phenomenon is happening in nearly every country in the world. Technology has pervasive effects on cultures and societies everywhere. From automobiles to computers to jet airplanes to the Internet, cultural effects are inevitable when companies introduce new technology, sell it to many types of customers, and encourage the public to use it for work and entertainment.

One result of this close, inseparable relationship between business and society is that many business decisions have a social impact, much as a pebble thrown into a pond creates ever-widening ripples. Another result is that the prosperity of business depends on society's actions and attitudes. Business can be smothered under a heavy blanket of social demands. Taxes can be set at levels that limit available funds for capital investment or encourage relocation to communities in countries with lower tax burdens. Environmental regulations may prove too costly or technically impossible to allow certain industries to continue operating, leading to plant closings and job losses. Labor unions can demand wages or working conditions that exceed a company's ability to pay or damage its ability to compete in the marketplace. So, while business decisions can have both positive and negative impacts on society, the actions of a society also influence and affect whether a business firm will prosper or fail.[4]

That is why business and society, taken together, form an *interactive social system*. Each needs the other, and each influences the other. They are entwined so completely that any action taken by one will surely affect the other. They are both separate and connected. Business is part of society, and society penetrates far and often into business decisions. In a world where global communication is rapidly expanding, the connections are closer than ever before. At the beginning of the twentieth century, most travel was done by horse-drawn vehicles, trains, and ships. Fifty years later, autos and airplanes were transforming society. Today, early in the twenty-first century, equally momentous changes are occurring through the Internet, wireless communications, and other technologies. The effects are felt throughout business, politics, and culture. Throughout this book are examples of organizations and people who are grappling with the challenges and shaping business-society relationships of the twenty-first century.

The Stakeholder Concept

When business interacts so often and so closely with society, a shared interest and interdependence develops between a company and other groups—the organization is interacting with its stakeholders.[5] **Stakeholders** are those people and groups that affect, or can be affected by, an organization's decisions, policies, and operations. The number of stakeholders and the variety of their interests can be quite large, making a company's decisions very complex. Some stakeholders share in the benefits a company creates; others bear the risks generated through the company's activities. Of course, those who

---

[4] William C. Frederick, *Values, Nature, and Culture in the American Corporation* (New York: Oxford University Press, 1995).

[5] R. Edward Freeman, *Strategic Management: A Stakeholder Approach* (Marshfield, MA: Pitman, 1984); and Thomas Donaldson and Lee E. Preston, "The Stakeholder Theory of the Corporation: Concepts, Evidence, Implications," *Academy of Management Review,* January 1995, pp. 71–83.

EXHIBIT **1-B**	**IBM: No Longer a Three-Legged Stool?**

IBM is an interesting example of how the stakeholder concept has evolved in one of the world's most successful business organizations.

- Thomas J. Watson, Sr., chairman of IBM in the 1950s, described management's role as one of balancing a three-legged stool whose legs were employees, customers, and shareholders. To emphasize their equality, he routinely changed the order in which he mentioned the three groups in his talks and speeches. In those days, it could be assumed that these were the stakeholders who mattered.

- In contrast, the 1990 book about IBM by Thomas J. Watson, Jr., son of the senior Watson, emphasized the large number and variety of other stakeholders—communities, arts organizations, colleges and universities, foreign governments, and many more—with which the company interacted during the era of the younger Watson's leadership.

- John Akers was deposed as IBM's chief executive officer in 1993 because he was unable to meet expectations of critical stakeholders such as shareholders and creditors. The multilegged stool had become unbalanced; investors reasserted their power and it cost Akers his job.

- Louis V. Gerstner, Jr., Akers's successor, emphasized IBM's interdependence with all of the company's stakeholders and led a dramatic turnaround in IBM's fortunes at the end of the 1990s. The results benefited all of IBM's stakeholders, including investors, employees, customers, communities, and the many educational institutions the company supports through its corporate-giving programs.

benefit are not always those who bear the risks. Good decisions are made when attention is given to the effects of those decisions—pro and con—on the people and interests that are affected. Weighing conflicting considerations is an important part of any manager's job.

The relationships between companies and their stakeholders have changed over the years. (See Exhibit 1-B for an example of how the stakeholder concept has evolved at IBM.) In the past, managers could simply keep their focus on those stakeholders that made and bought their products, concentrating on bringing products and services to market as efficiently and effectively as possible. The number of relevant stakeholders was described as a *three-legged stool* and limited to employees, investors, and customers. Today, business is more complicated and the number of relevant stakeholders has grown. Managers have the challenge of weighing and balancing the interests of *all* of corporate stakeholders. If legitimate concerns are disregarded, stakeholders may damage the company's operations or refuse to do business with it.

On the positive side, a corporation's stakeholders are an asset that can be enlisted to aid and support a company in trouble.

For example, when Malden Mills, a textile manufacturer located in Methuen, Massachusetts, suffered a devastating fire that destroyed its mill, employees, community officials, the governor, state legislative leaders, and prominent business leaders were ready to help. When the company's owner, Aaron Feuerstein, announced his desire to rebuild, the Malden Mills stakeholder network was concerned and eager to help the company. The state's congressional representatives and senators urged the secretary of labor and president of the United States to invoke federal law to help the company. In the end, the company did reopen and virtually all employees were offered jobs at the new facility. Feuerstein was hailed as a business hero and received many prizes, honorary degrees, and commendations. He insisted the credit belonged to others and always thanked the company's many friends and supporters.

On the negative side, there are many examples of companies that disregard stakeholders' wishes, either out of the belief that the stakeholder is wrong or out of the misguided notion that an unhappy customer, employee, or regulator doesn't matter. Such attitudes are foolish and often prove costly to the company involved. Today, for example, builders know that they cannot locate a plant in a community that strongly objects. To build a power plant, incinerator, or new housing requires working with the community, responding to concerns, and creating and maintaining a relationship of trust. John deButts, a former chairman of AT&T, once commented about stakeholders as a three-legged stool this way: "The only image which recurs with uncomfortable persistence is not a piece of furniture at all. It is a porcupine, with quills reversed!"[6]

Today, many stakeholders have the ability to stick quills into business. But as the Malden Mills example suggests, stakeholder relationships are also a vital part of the company's assets. According to a growing number of experts and executives, networks of stakeholder relationships are the source of organizational wealth for today's companies.[7] To create that wealth, and protect it against loss, companies need managers and decision-making approaches that take into account the needs of a larger and more diverse group of stakeholders. Business cannot be done in a social and political vacuum, and good management planning must take into account this web of stakeholder considerations.

Primary and Secondary Stakeholders

Business interacts with society in a variety of different ways, and a company's relations differ with different stakeholders. Figure 1-2 shows business interacting with groups that affect its ability to carry out its primary purpose of providing society with goods and services. Investors (stockholders) and creditors provide financial resources to the

---

[6] John deButts, "A Strategy of Accountability," in William Dill, ed., *Running the American Corporation* (Englewood Cliffs, NJ: Prentice Hall, 1978), quoted at p. 141.
[7] James E. Post, Lee E. Preston, and Sybille Sachs, *Redefining the Corporation: Stakeholder Management and Organizational Wealth* (Palo Alto: Stanford University Press, 2001).

Figure 1-2

Relations between a
business firm and its
primary stakeholders.

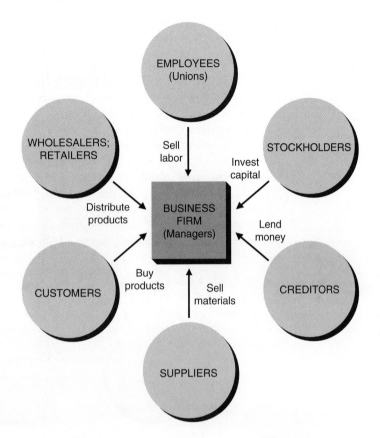

company; employees contribute their work skills and knowledge; suppliers provide raw materials, energy, and other supplies; and wholesalers, distributors, and retailers help move the product from plant to sales offices to customers. All businesses need customers who are willing to pay for the products or services being produced, and most companies compete against others offering similar products and services in the marketplace. These are the fundamental interactions every business has with society, and they help us define the primary economic mission of the company.

A business's primary involvement with society includes all the direct relationships necessary for it to perform its major mission of producing goods and services for customers. These interactions normally occur in the marketplace and involve processes of buying and selling. These primary involvements shape a company's strategy and the policy decisions of its managers and reveal the importance of its **primary stakeholders.** These stakeholders, who are critical to the company's existence and activities, include customers, suppliers, employees, and investors.

However, as Figure 1-3 reveals, a business's relationships go beyond those primary involvements to others in society. Secondary interactions and involvements occur when other groups express interest in or concern about the organization's activities. **Secondary**

Figure 1-3

Relations between a
business firm and
some of its other
(secondary)
stakeholders.

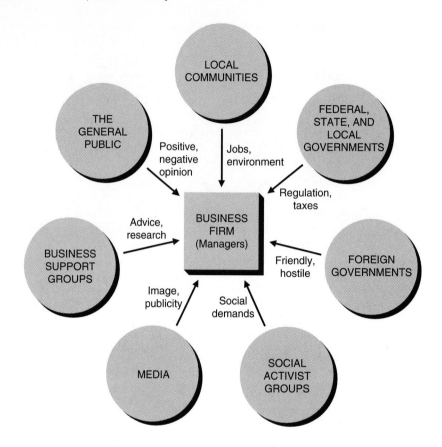

stakeholders are those people and groups in society who are affected, directly or indirectly, by the company's primary activities and decisions. They include the general public, various levels of government, social activist groups, and others.

Calling these interactions and stakeholders "secondary" does not mean that they are less important than business's primary relationships with society. It means that they occur as a *consequence* of the normal activities of conducting business. Primary and secondary areas of involvement are not always sharply distinguished; often, one area shades into the other. For example, while the safety or environmental effect of a product (e.g., an automobile) is a primary concern to a customer, the cumulative effect of the use of the product may represent a secondary safety or environmental concern for the entire community (e.g., smog from automobile emissions).

By combining a business's primary and secondary interactions, we can see how business and society form an interactive model. The interactive model of business and society recognizes the fundamental role of business as an economic contributor to society. But it also suggests that managers must make decisions and take actions that benefit the society as a whole as well as the company's economic interests. The net effect is to enhance the quality of life in the broadest possible way, as that quality of life is defined by society.

Business acts to produce the goods and services that society wants, recognizes the social effects of its activities, and is concerned with the social and economic effects on society.

Stakeholder Interests and Power

Stakeholder groups exist in many forms, some well organized, others much less so. This variety makes it more difficult for a company's managers to understand and respond to stakeholder concerns. Each stakeholder has a unique connection with the organization, and managers must understand these relationships and respond accordingly. For example, stockholders have an ownership interest in the firm. The economic health and success of the corporation affects these people financially; their personal wealth is at stake. Customers, suppliers, and retailers have different interests. Owners are most interested in realizing a return on their investment; customers and suppliers are most interested in gaining fair value in the exchange of goods and money. Neither has a great interest in the other's stake. And when we recognize that there are different kinds of owners, ranging from pension funds with large holdings to individual owners with only a few shares of stock, the picture is more complicated.

Governments, public interest groups, and local communities have another sort of relationship with the company. In general, their stake is broader than the financial stake of owners or persons who buy products and sell services to the company. They may wish to protect the environment, assure human rights, or advance other broad social interests. Managers need to track these stakeholder interests with great care.

Different stakeholders also have different types and degrees of power. Stakeholder power, in this instance, means the ability to use resources to make an event happen or to secure a desired outcome. Most experts recognize three types of stakeholder power: voting power, economic power, and political power.

Voting power means that the stakeholder has the legitimate right to cast a vote. For example, each stockholder has a voting power proportionate to the percentage of the company's stock he or she owns. Stockholders typically have an opportunity to vote on such major decisions as mergers, acquisitions, and other extraordinary issues. Through the exercise of informed, intelligent voting, they may influence company policy so that their investment is protected and produces a healthy return.

Customers, suppliers, and retailers have *economic power* with the company. Suppliers can withhold supplies or refuse to fill orders if a company fails to meet its contractual responsibilities. Customers may refuse to buy a company's products if the company enacts an improper policy. Customers can boycott products if they believe the goods are too expensive, poorly made, unsafe, or inappropriate for consumption.

Governments exercise *political power* through legislation, regulations, or lawsuits. Whereas government agencies act directly, other stakeholders use their political power indirectly by urging government to use its powers by passing new laws or enacting regulations. In this way, we can see that government agencies also have stakeholders, including business itself.

The interplay of different types of stakeholder power can be illustrated by two real-life situations that became the subject of popular movies. In A Civil Action, *starring John Travolta, a group of citizens in Woburn,*

Massachusetts, sued W.R. Grace and Company and Beatrice Foods for allegedly dumping toxic chemicals that leaked into underground wells used for drinking water. The deaths and illnesses of family members led the survivors to mobilize political power against the two companies. Investigations were conducted by private groups and government agencies. The lawsuits and public pressure made toxic dumping and the protection of water supplies an important political issue. A similar story was portrayed in Erin Brockovich, starring Julia Roberts. The disposal practices of a large California utility were associated with higher than normal rates of disease in local neighborhoods. Again, citizens were mobilized to sue the company and discovered the scientific data that the company had collected many years before.

A single stakeholder is capable of exercising more than one type of power. In both cases, families of victims sued the companies involved (political power), but they had other types of power as well. They could have boycotted the companies' products (economic power), or they could have purchased shares of stock in the companies and used voting power as owners to oust the directors and management through a proxy fight. (Stockholder power is further discussed in Chapter 14.)

Stakeholder Coalitions

Groups are always changing their relationships to one another in society. **Stakeholder coalitions** are the temporary unions of stakeholder groups that come together and share a common point of view on a particular issue or problem. Some coalitions are quite local or narrowly focused on one issue or problem. But there are also many broad coalitions whose members are organizations that span the nation and the world. Movements to protect the natural environment or advance human rights involve hundreds of state, national, and international organizations and may operate with little formal coordination and policy making. Other movements may be very diverse but operate in a coordinated manner through a central policy-making board or group.

Stakeholder coalitions are not static. Groups that are highly involved with a company today may be less involved tomorrow. Controversial issues that are highly salient at one time may be replaced by other issues; stakeholders who are most dependent on an organization at one time may be less so at another. To make matters more complex, the process of shifting coalitions does not occur uniformly in all parts of a large corporation. Stakeholders involved with one part of a large company often have little or nothing to do with other parts of the organization.

Coalitions of stakeholders have become increasingly international in recent times. Communications technology has enabled like-minded people to interact quickly, irrespective of political boundaries. Wireless telephones, the Internet, computers, and fax machines have become powerful tools in the hands of groups that monitor how multinational businesses are operating in different locations around the world.

For example, when the Scott Paper Company, a U.S. multinational corporation headquartered in Philadelphia, negotiated an agreement with the government of Indonesia to build a new paper mill and pulp-processing plant on Sumatra, one of Indonesia's principal islands, Indonesian environmental activists were outraged. They vowed to fight the proposal and stop construction of the new mill. They feared that the paper mill would inevitably lead to destruction of Sumatra's rain forest. Since pulp and paper mills are notorious for producing air and water pollution, the Indonesian environmentalist groups contacted friends in the United States, including the Natural Resources Defense Council (NRDC). NRDC staff focused on what kind of pressure they could apply against Scott. They concluded that a national boycott of Scott paper products, including such highly visible consumer products as Scotties tissues, was possible. This threat was communicated to Scott Paper's executives, who recognized the company's vulnerability to a boycott and decided to withdraw from the Indonesia project. The Indonesian government was disappointed, having anticipated tax revenues and new jobs. The government eventually turned to a Japanese company to build and operate the pulp and paper mill.[8]

This example illustrates how national and international networks of activists, coupled with the media's interest in such business and society issues, make coalition development and issue activism an increasingly powerful strategic factor for companies. As business issues become more global in nature, the solutions and approaches must become more global as well. Nongovernmental organizations regularly meet to discuss problems such as global warming,[9] human rights, and international trade just as their business counterparts do. In the twenty-first century, stakeholder coalitions are more numerous and important to every industry and company.

Forces Shaping Business-Society Relations

Businesses do not operate in a social or political vacuum. In fact, most companies operate in a swirl of social, economic, technological, and political change that produces both opportunities and threats. Even small businesses that serve mostly local markets are affected by price fluctuations, disruptions in supply, and uncertainty stemming from political events. Figure 1-4 illustrates some of the critical forces that are shaping business-society relations. Each of these forces is introduced below. These themes will reappear throughout the chapters of this book.

Economic Competition: Strategic and Social Challenges

Economic competition is a powerful force for change in business and in society. Competition motivates companies to serve customers efficiently and to identify and meet new needs. Businesses continuously reassess their assumptions about how and where to compete. As the Eastman Kodak example at the beginning of this chapter illustrates,

---

[8] Based on an interview conducted by one of the authors with the head of the Indonesian Environmental Federation.
[9] See Andrew Revkin, "Treaty Talks Fail to Find Consensus in Global Warming," *New York Times,* November 26, 2000, pp. A1, 16.

Figure 1-4

Forces that shape the business and society relationship.

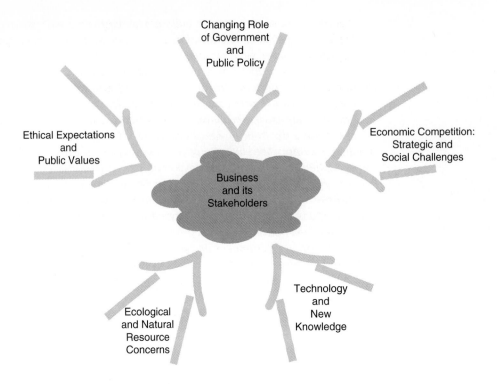

strategic rethinking may lead to restructuring of business operations. Reorganization of business operations occurs as companies try to improve the quality of their products and services, reduce costs, and improve the speed with which they respond to customers. This redesign of business operations is known as **reengineering.**

Traditional ideas about a corporation's responsibility to its stakeholders may be challenged when a company begins to rethink its strategy. Repositioning the business can have significant effects on people and communities. Facilities may be closed; employees may be dismissed from jobs eliminated in the redesigned manufacturing or service-delivery system. People who made long-term career commitments to the firm may be pressured to take early retirement or face dismissal.

The relationship between a business and its stakeholders often creates an implied understanding, or **social contract,** as to how they will act toward one another. These implied understandings are, in words of two leading scholars, the "ties that bind."[10] Social contracts are inevitably affected when a company's business strategy changes. Commitments to employees change; a company's community involvement and charitable contributions may also decline when it encounters severe economic problems. Changes in these social contracts occurred frequently during the 1990s, with American companies eliminating more than 5 million jobs, leading some observers to conclude that

---

[10] Thomas Donaldson and Thomas Dunfee, *Ties That Bind* (Boston: Harvard Business School Press, 1998).

the "good corporation" is dead.[11] This downsizing occurred across nearly every sector of the economy. Manufacturing, financial services, retailing, and transportation were among the industries most severely affected.

Companies often try to smooth the process and minimize the negative effects of workforce reductions. Benefits packages are offered to departing employees, including compensation based on years of service, continuation of health care benefits for a period of time (ranging from 30 days to one year), and support for retraining or education. At Kodak, for example, job losses were tempered by severance payments to workers, job training, and efforts to place employees in new jobs. But the overwhelming sense of loss that people feel in such circumstances is reflected in social indicators such as increased suicide, alcoholism, mental illness, and child and spouse abuse. Changes in a company's business strategy affect other social relationships as well. External stakeholders are hurt when a business closes: suppliers, wholesalers, and other businesses (restaurants, retailers, banks, and movie theaters) all suffer. A "multiplier effect" leaves the community short on jobs, tax revenues, and morale. Research shows that *surviving* employees also feel the psychological impact of staff reductions, including fears of how management will act in the future. Some companies (e.g., Levi Strauss) recognized these concerns by stating in writing the commitments continuing employees could count on receiving. These statements of commitment are called *compacts, covenants,* or *social contracts,* signifying the special nature of the employee-employer relationship.

Some observers believe that a **new social contract** has emerged between the corporation and its stakeholders.[12] Because stakeholder relationships will inevitably change as business realities change, a company's responsibilities and behavior must be built on new assumptions. The new social contract implies that managers and companies will recognize relationships with all of their stakeholders, acknowledge the company's impact on them, and engage in stakeholder management practices that minimize harm and maximize positive contributions through the corporation's activities (see Chapter 17). This approach is built on the premise that it is possible for managers and companies to do the right thing and do it in the right way.

Reinventing corporate strategy along these lines is a matter of mind and managerial attitude. It takes a business executive who is willing to recognize that employees, customers, and others are people first and economic actors second. Typically, a company's employees are evaluated on the quality of their work performance. But they are also family members, citizens of communities, members of churches, political adherents, and individuals with aspirations, problems, hopes, and desires. Wise managers understand that people are productive assets—sometimes called **human capital**—but also emotional beings.

---

[11] John W. Houck and Oliver Williams, eds., *Is the Good Corporation Dead?* (South Bend, IN: University of Notre Dame Press, 1996). The phrase was first used by Robert J. Samuelson, "R.I.P.: The Good Corporation," *Newsweek,* July 5, 1993, p. 41.

[12] Post, Preston, and Sachs, *Redefining the Corporation.* See also, James E. Post, "The New Social Contract," in Oliver Williams and John Houck, eds., *The Global Challenge to Corporate Social Responsibility* (New York: Oxford University Press, 1995); and Severyn T. Bruyn, *A Future for the American Economy: The Social Market* (Stanford, CA: Stanford University Press, 1991).

Research shows that companies with the positive social reputations and good social performance records have top management teams that develop a broad view of their company's place in society.[13] In fact, these managers often believe that their companies should take the lead in helping society solve its problems. Managers with this attitude take a long-run view of the business rather than focusing exclusively on short-run gains. Social goals, as well as economic goals, are given a high priority in planning the company's future. This attitude will not inoculate the company from the pressures of economic competition or enable the managers to avoid difficult business issues (e.g., restructuring or reorganizing), but it will help ensure that corporate strategy *integrates* the interests of all of its stakeholders.

There are many companies, large and small, that are committed to finding ways to turn this philosophy into reality. Business for Social Responsibility, an organization of member companies that share a commitment to be *both* economically and socially successful, has grown to include more than 1,000 member-companies in less than a decade.[14] One of the leaders in developing this network is the Body Shop International, a company that manufactures and markets natural cosmetics, soaps, and toiletries through franchise stores. The Body Shop's founder and managing director, Anita Roddick, describes her vision in this way:

> [O]ver the past decade, while many businesses have pursued what I call
> "business as usual," I have been part of a different, smaller business
> movement—one that has tried to put idealism back on the agenda. We
> want a new paradigm, a whole new framework, for seeing and understand-
> ing [that] business can and must be a force for positive social change. It
> must not only avoid hideous evil—it must actively do good.[15]

Interestingly, many of the new, technology-oriented companies formed in recent years ("dot com" companies) have values that are similar to those espoused by the Body Shop. Their employees work very hard, but they believe in a work environment that is enjoyable and in which people are treated with respect. Living these values is as important to many people working in these companies as are the stock options and chance to become wealthy. The success of these companies puts pressure on other companies to change their ways and become more competitive by becoming more socially oriented and successful.

Whether or not this attitude will yield consistent, high levels of economic performance is not yet clear. What is clear is that the business-society relationship is always dynamic; it has been changing rapidly in recent years and is likely to continue doing so in the next decade. Successful business strategy requires managers who ensure that the

[13] Charles J. Fombrun, *Reputation: Realizing Value from the Corporate Image* (Boston, MA: Harvard Business School Press, 1996). See also *Corporate Reputation Review,* a journal that focuses on the role and management of reputation as a strategic asset of the organization.

[14] See Business for Social Responsibility at www.BSR.org.

[15] Anita Roddick, "Corporate Responsibility: Good Works Not Good Words," speech to the International Chamber of Commerce, October 21, 1993; reprinted in *Vital Speeches of the Day* 60, no. 7 (January 15, 1994), pp. 196–99. See also, Anita Roddick, *Business As Unusual,* New York: Thorsons/HarperCollins, 2001.

business continues to perform a positive role in society. These issues are discussed further in Chapters 3 and 4.

Ethical Expectations and Public Values

Ethical expectations are a vital part of the business environment. The public expects business to be ethical and wants corporate managers to apply ethical principles—in other words, guidelines about what is right and wrong, fair and unfair, and morally correct—when they make business decisions.

Ethical standards can vary from one society to another. In spite of differences in ethical meanings—and even what is meant by *ethics*—cultural variation does not rule out common ethical agreement being reached among people of different societies. For example, the European Union's Social Charter promotes common job rights and humane workplace treatment among member-nations. The 29 nations of the Organization for Economic Cooperation and Development (OECD), including the world's leading industrial economies, have adopted a treaty banning bribery of foreign officials in international commerce.[16] These kinds of problems and how to deal with them are discussed in Chapters 5 and 6.

Human rights issues have become more prominent and important for business. For many years, international pressure was exerted on South Africa's political leaders to halt racially discriminatory practices of apartheid and its business leaders to challenge the South African government's enforcement of the policy. More recently, pressures from many sources have focused on alleged abuses of human rights in countries such as China, Burma (Myanmar), and Nigeria. And religious organizations in the United States, Canada, and Britain proposed Principles for Global Corporate Responsibility. In 2000, Secretary-General Kofi Annan announced the United Nations Global Compact with leading corporations that have committed to honoring basic ethical principles everywhere they do business (see discussion in Chapters 5, 7, and 20).

The question is not, Should business be ethical? Nor is it, Should business be economically efficient? Society wants business to be both at the same time. Ethical behavior is a key aspect of corporate social performance. To maintain public support and credibility—that is, business legitimacy—businesses must find ways to balance and integrate these two social demands: high economic performance and high ethical standards. When a company acts ethically toward its stakeholders, it improves its contribution to society. When a company fails to act ethically, however, it faces the risk of losing the public support needed to be both credible and successful.

Business leaders face the challenge of meeting **public expectations** that continue to change with the times. Yesterday's acceptable behavior may not be tolerated today. Many forms of harassment and discrimination were once common. Today, social standards make such actions unacceptable, and managers who permit such behavior can be held liable. The expectations of ethical behavior that the public holds are as relevant to a business as are expectations of customers for its products. A business cannot be successful without satisfying both.

---

[16] Edmund Andrews, "29 Nations Agree to Outlaw Bribing Foreign Officials," *New York Times,* November 21, 1997, pp. A1, C2.

The Changing Role of Government and Public Policy

The role of government has changed dramatically in the United States and many other nations in the past two decades. The winds of reform began to blow through many of the world's economic, political, and social institutions in the late 1970s. Demands were made to disperse power more widely within many societies and nations. "Power to the people" became a slogan that captured the essence of this new social force. Leaders discovered that their grip on institutional power was not as secure as it had been in earlier times. The public, less trusting of political leaders, wanted more influence and control over government policy and practice. Believing that too much power had been concentrated at the top of society's major institutions, the public demanded democratic reforms. This has been called the *devolution* of governmental power.

In the United States, these political changes generated two key ideas affecting business: industry *deregulation* and *privatization.* In the Soviet Union, the key ideas affecting business and society were *glasnost* (openness) and *perestroika* (reform, reconstruction); in China, the key ideas were freer markets and a more decentralized economic system. In each instance, centralized governmental power was forced to give way toward more decentralized power. During the past 10 years, many countries in Eastern Europe, Latin America, and Asia have undergone some degree of reform based on these models. The net effect has been a redefinition of the role of government and business in modern society.

What does this global reform of government mean for business? First and foremost, it creates more freedom and business opportunities. When free markets open up where none existed before, corporations can take advantage of profit opportunities. For example, European, Japanese, and American business firms flocked to China in the 1990s. But they became cautious when government authorities showed signs of reinstalling centralized power over business decisions, such as restricting what content could be broadcast over the Internet. Reform poses business risks, as well as opportunities. When the Eastern European nations relaxed government controls and welcomed economic ties with Western nations, many corporations moved in, seeking profitable opportunities. But the business risks were considerable, and some companies suffered heavy losses because of unstable currencies, corruption, and cultural complexities. As Eastern European nations struggled to transform economic and political institutions, governments faced problems of inflation, unemployment, and declining national income. In the early 1990s, one political scientist predicted, "The cold war is over, but this will be a very dangerous peace. . . . Conflicts are growing between nationalities, between rich people and poor, between the government and street protesters, between industrialists and laborers."[17] This view was prophetic: Ethnic, ideological, and economic conflicts have raged in Bosnia, Serbia, and Kosovo, and the political winds have often blown in different, contradictory directions.

The movement from centralized government toward democracy and freedom carries both pluses and minuses for business. Corporations have often found themselves facing large measures of uncertainty and risk.

---

[17] "East Europe Offers Investors Big Profits and Big Perils," *Wall Street Journal,* January 11, 1991, p. A6. For a current assessment of Eastern Europe's prospects, see *The Economist.*

> *Russia is one of the largest and most resource-abundant countries in the world. Since the fall of communism, it has suffered political convulsions as Mikhail Gorbachev, Boris Yeltsin, Vladimir Zhiranovsky, and Vladmiri Putin have contested for power. The political uncertainty has affected how Central Asia's oil industry has been developing. Chevron Corporation, a U.S. multinational oil company, has invested heavily in Kazhakstan, a former Soviet republic. As the political fortunes of the republics have ebbed and flowed, Chevron's political risk has also grown. Its traditional multinational oil competitors—Royal Dutch Shell (Anglo/Dutch) and Total (France)—are trying to acquire drilling rights in the area where Chevron has conducted explorations. Each company has political friends. New state oil companies from Russia (Gazprom) and Malaysia (Petronas) are work-ing to foreclose U.S. companies. Billions of dollars of oil are at stake, and Chevron executives know it can be very risky. In the 1980s, Chevron invested—and lost—$1 billion in Sudan. Although Chevron sees business potential in Kazhakstan and Central Asia, its executives also recognize that political risk may overwhelm the business opportunity.*[18]

Volatile political and ideological forces are important business risks in the world economic climate. Corporations and their managers cannot ignore them; to do so could be fatal. Learning how to integrate changing political realities into a corporate business strategy has become a basic requirement for companies and managers. Stakeholder management can be an important way of doing so.

> *Royal Dutch Shell, for example, developed a sophisticated stakeholder analysis to assess its prospects for successfully developing potential oil and gas resources in the Camisea region of Peru. Despite the area's com-mercial potential, the company concluded that the full range of stakeholder interests—including ecological protection and the interests of native people—could not be properly safeguarded if drilling was started. The company withdrew from the project.*[19]

This type of stakeholder analysis seems likely to become more important in the future. In some countries, the risk may involve the collapse of an old political system and the problems of establishing a new system. In other countries, such as the United States today, the challenge may be one of understanding where a new administration or "new politics" is leading.

The role of government has changed significantly in the United States in recent decades. (These issues are discussed in Chapters 7, 8, and 9.) Government has moved away from much of the old-style, "command and control" regulation that once governed the airline, trucking, and communications industries. The federal government is still engaged in major legal actions, such as those involving the tobacco industry (discussed

---

[18] Sheila N. Heslin, "The New Pipeline Politics," *New York Times,* November 10, 1997, p. A37.
[19] Post, Preston, and Sachs, *Redefining the Corporation,* chap. 6.

in a case study at the end of the book), the Microsoft antitrust case (discussed in another case study), and situations such as the proposed MCI/WorldCom merger. Many efforts have been made to pass responsibility to state and local government for meeting public needs, yet federal spending remains at record high levels. In recent presidential campaigns, the candidates have disagreed about the role of the federal government in education, health care, environmental protection, and the economy. As political pundit Chris Matthews suggested, "Americans like political gridlock."

Humor aside, the importance of these issues was well expressed by economist Milton Friedman, who argued that government should not interfere with free markets:

> *It is today possible, to a greater extent than at any time in the world's history, for a company to locate anywhere, to use resources from anywhere to produce a product that can be sold anywhere. . . . [The challenge] is to use our influence to make sure governments are not short-sighted and do not short-circuit the process.*[20]

Ecological and Natural Resource Concerns

One of the most important social challenges to business is to strike a balance between economic activity and what is ecologically sustainable. Farming, mining, and industrial production produce waste and pollution along with needed goods and services. Waste and pollution are the side-effects that extract a price from society for rising populations, urbanization, and more goods and services. Industrial societies—whether the United States, Japan, Germany, Russia, or South Korea—create a disproportionate (relative to population) share of the world's pollution and waste because these are the by-products of a high level of economic activity. The emerging nations of the third world, with their rapid growth rates and limited pollution controls, also contribute to global ecological problems as their economies become more industrialized.

At the individual level, consumers bear responsibility for much of the solid waste and pollution because we demand, buy, and use pollution-generating products such as automobiles, refrigerators, air conditioners, and computers. The widespread use of product packaging and the proliferation of toxic products such as cleaners, lawn chemicals, batteries, and antifreeze all contribute to global pollution issues.

Ecological impacts extend far beyond national boundaries. Stratospheric ozone depletion threatens health and agriculture on a worldwide basis. The industrial accident at the Chernobyl nuclear power station spread dangerous radiation across several European nations and sent a radiation cloud around the globe. Oil spills have fouled the oceans and beaches of many nations. The cutting and burning of tropical rain forests has the potential to affect weather climates throughout the world.

Environmental protection, involving pollution control, waste minimization, and natural resource conservation, has become a high priority for all nations. International agreements have been negotiated to address the most pressing issues, such as ozone depletion, biodiversity, and global warming. But government and industry leaders

---

[20] Milton Friedman, quoted in Lindley H. Clark, Jr., "The New Industrial Revolution," *Wall Street Journal,* November 23, 1993, p. A16.

recognize that this is just the beginning of what must be done to achieve a sustainable balance between economic activity, which requires the use of resources, and global environmental protection, which requires the preservation of resources. Business leaders and managers at every level of business activity from corporate headquarters to the local retail outlet are being challenged by the need to integrate ecological thinking into their decision making. These issues are discussed in Chapters 10 and 11.

Today, companies are learning how to adjust their products, manufacturing processes, purchasing activities, and business strategies to the need for sustainable economic and ecological practices. Although much has already been improved, there is no doubt that reducing harmful ecological effects will continue to be a major social challenge for corporate managers. Pollution and waste cannot be stopped entirely, but their volume can be reduced through improved product designs, better controls, and the recycling of reusable materials. Environmental accidents can be prevented and cleanup efforts can be pursued vigorously with new techniques and technologies. The basic goal is to achieve a livable balance between human needs and nature's limits.[21]

Technology and New Knowledge

Technology is one of the most dramatic and powerful forces affecting business and society. Technology includes machines of all sizes, shapes, and functions; processes that enable business to produce goods at faster speeds, lower costs, and with less waste; and software that incorporates new forms of learning into formats that speed activities and are more reliable. Technology involves harnessing human imagination to create new devices and new approaches to the needs, problems, and concerns of a modern society. Indeed, government statistics show that computing and telecommunications industries grew by 57 percent during the 1990s to more than $866 billion in 1999 and more than $1 trillion by 2000, making these businesses the nation's largest industry, ahead of construction, food products, and automotive manufacturing.[22]

Technology also brings together different fields of knowledge to create new ways to solve problems or perform tasks. In telecommunications, for example, the transmission of three types of information—voice, data, and video—is becoming available on a single broadband receiving device. Wireless transmission and receiving devices will enable people to access all types of information virtually anywhere.

As the Internet has transformed many business activities, absence of a fail-safe means of personal identification has prevented people from using a computer signature for legal documents. In 2000, the U.S. Congress passed a law permitting a person's "digital signature" to be used for legal documents. This was made possible because the science of "biometrics" had created a new technology of personal identification.

---

[21] Andrew J. Hoffman, *Competitive Environmental Strategy: A Guide to the Business Landscape* (Washington, DC: Island Press, 2000); Andrew J. Hoffman, *From Heresy to Dogma* (San Francisco: New Lexington Press, 1997); and Andrew J. Hoffman, ed., *Global Climate Change* (San Francisco: New Lexington Press, 1998).

[22] "How to Bring E-Business into Your Business" (Special Report), *The Economist,* November 11–17, 2000. See also, Steve Lohr, "Information Technology Field Is Rated Largest U.S. Industry," *New York Times,* November 18, 1997, p. D12.

Biometrics is a field that integrates biological science and computer science. One application of this new field of knowledge involves identification procedures. Scientists know that no two persons have the same fingerprint. This makes fingerprints a nearly foolproof method of identification. In the past, an individual's fingers were coated with ink, and impressions were made on paper, then compared with impressions made by others. Laboratories such as the Federal Bureau of Investigation (FBI) kept files containing thousands of fingerprints. Computers now enable researchers to digitize fingerprints and reproduce them on computer screens. This enables searches to occur much faster once fingerprints are on file.

Biometrics has now made possible the next step in this evolution of identification science. New scanners enable a person to place his or her finger on an imaging surface and instantaneously receive confirmation that the fingerprint matched that of the owner of an identification card. This technology of identification has been used to speed health care identification, eligibility for welfare benefits, and credit-card approvals.[23]

New technologies may also have a negative effect on some people. For example, if biometric scanners are generally adopted, ink-based print systems will be rendered obsolete, costing manufacturers of inkpads and employees of inkpad companies their livelihood. Still, for society as a whole, biometric identification may prove to be a highly efficient and productive use of resources. In this way, new technologies put pressure on today's companies to understand and respond to new knowledge and its applications.

Many technologies have broad social impacts as well as competitive effects. As discussed in Chapters 12 and 13, the development of new technologies should lead managers and organizations to examine the ethical implications of their use.

For example, as medical experts learned how to transplant living organs such as kidneys and hearts from one person to another, ethical concerns emerged about the criteria that hospitals would follow in deciding when, and under what conditions, transplants would occur. These decisions affect both the donors and the recipients. When is a person really dead? Should some organs be removed before the donor is dead but after a medical team is certain that death will soon occur? Is it safe for a living donor to give up a kidney, eye, lung, or other organ?

As new technologies become available, the challenges to ethical decision making become more complicated. Experiments with fetal tissues show that it is possible to regenerate cells that once were thought to be dead. Hospitals and medical staffs struggle to decide whether the tissue of aborted fetuses can be used to treat people with strokes, spinal cord injuries, and health problems once thought to be beyond hope.

Technology is creating what experts call the **knowledge economy.** This is an economy in which new knowledge, in its many forms, reshapes and transforms old

---

[23] "Biometrics: The Next New Thing," *The Economist,* September 9–15, 2000, pp. 85–91. Also, Rolf Boone, "Biometrics Making an Impression in Identification," www.dbusiness.com, July 18, 2000.

industries and businesses, creating new industries and businesses and ultimately affecting individuals, families, communities, and institutions throughout the world. For these reasons, technology must be understood as one of the major drivers of change in both business and society.

Corporate Strategy for the Twenty-First Century

Business, government, and society are interdependent with complex relations in every nation. Systems theory makes clear that all organisms—whether biological or social (such as organizations)—are affected by their host environments. An organization must learn how to be responsive to changes and conditions in its environment if it is to survive and succeed. That requires good leadership.

This web of interactions between business, government, and society creates a system of stakeholders—groups affected by and influential in corporate decisions and actions. The analysis of these stakeholders—who they are, what power they hold, and the ways in which they interact with one another—helps managers understand the nature of their concerns and needs and how these relationships are changing. If the creation of stakeholder networks is a natural process, managers must learn how to understand and utilize these relationships. The business of the twenty-first century must have managers who understand the importance of creating business strategies that include these considerations.

The relationship between business and society is continuously changing. People, organizations, and social issues change; inevitably, new issues will arise and challenge managers to develop new solutions. To be effective, corporate strategy must respond to the biggest and most central questions in the public's mind. People expect businesses to be competitive, to be profitable, and to act responsibly by meeting the reasonable expectations of stakeholders. The corporation of the twenty-first century is affected by new technologies, economic competition, political trends, and stakeholders who expect their interests to be involved in the decision making of companies from whom they buy goods and services, contribute labor and ideas, and extend the hospitality of their communities.

Summary Points of This Chapter

- Business, government, and society form an interactive system because each affects and influences the others and because none can exist without the others. Economic, political, and cultural life are entwined with one another in every nation. Together, they define the uniqueness of a society.
- Every business firm has economic and social involvements and relationships with others in society. Some are intended, some unintended; some are positive, others negative. Those related to the basic mission of the company are its primary involvements; those that flow from those activities but are more indirect are secondary involvements.
- The people, groups, and organizations that interact with the corporation and have an interest in its performance are its stakeholders. Those most closely and directly

involved with a business are its primary stakeholders; those who are indirectly connected are its secondary stakeholders.

- Stakeholders can exercise their economic, political, and other powers in ways that benefit or challenge the organization. Stakeholders may also act independently or create coalitions to influence the company.
- A number of broad forces are affecting the business-society relationship as companies move into the twenty-first century. These include economic competition and strategic refocusing of businesses; changing ethical expectations and public values; redefinition of the role of government; ecological and natural resource concerns; and the transformational role of technology.

Key Terms and Concepts Used in This Chapter

- Stakeholders
- Primary stakeholders
- Secondary stakeholders
- Stakeholder coalitions
- Reengineering
- Social contract

- New social contract
- Human capital
- Public expectations
- Environmental protection
- Knowledge economy

Internet Resources

• www.businessweek.com	*Business Week*—broad range of business topics
• www.economist.com	*The Economist*—strong international coverage
• www.fortune.com	*Fortune*—useful profiles of large corporations
• www.ethics.org	Ethics Resource Center
• www.whitehouse.gov/fsbr/ssbr.html	Executive Office of the President of the United States

Discussion Case: *Inland National Bank*

Amy Miller, manager of strategic planning for retail banking operations at Inland National Bank (INB), was facing a problem. Inland recently acquired another local bank, Home Savings Bank. INB's senior management was reorganizing the company's retail banking operations, and some of the branches were sure to be closed. Located in a medium-sized city in the midwestern United States, INB has earned a good reputation for community involvement and solid financial performance. The decision to reorganize the bank's branches made economic sense, but Amy was troubled by how it would affect a number of local neighborhoods. She was especially concerned about two retail branches.

Rockdale Branch

This was a small Home Savings branch. The problem here was obvious: The neighborhood was old and on the decline. Home Savings had not modernized the facility for many years, and a major investment was needed to improve the facility. Amy thought the cost would be about $500,000. It was unclear whether the financial potential of the neighborhood warranted such an investment. Home Savings had been the last bank with a branch in Rockdale; all of the other banks had closed their branches at least five years ago. If the local office was closed, Rockdale customers could use INB's branch in Culver Heights, about a 10-minute auto or bus ride from Rockdale. The Culver Heights branch was conveniently located on a local bus route.

North Madison Branch

Miller was also concerned about a branch office located in North Madison, a neighborhood adjacent to Rockdale. North Madison was a poor neighborhood, with average income that was $2,000 per household below that of any other neighborhood in the city. Many of North Madison's residents were on welfare and public assistance. Home Savings Bank had a branch office on the main street of North Madison's commercial district. INB had closed its local branch in North Madison more than a decade ago.

The senior executive in charge of INB's business strategy had talked about replacing branches with automatic teller machines in convenient locations such as the North Madison shopping district. The move would eliminate a total of 20 jobs at the branch. Only a few of these employees were likely to find other jobs within the bank. INB's CEO had given a number of speeches in which he discussed how technology could better serve customers. The bank had announced that it would soon introduce new online banking services for its customers.

Other Factors

Rockdale residents had organized a group of picketers in front of the Home Savings branch a few days after the merger announcement was made. A local television station sent a crew to cover the story. One local resident who was interviewed said, "INB just hates old people, and old people is all that lives in Rockdale! They care more about money than people."

INB had also received angry telephone calls from several city officials. Sheila Thomas was an elected member of the city council whose district included both the Rockdale and North Madison neighborhoods. She was outspoken about the bank's plan and questioned whether the bank was acting in good faith toward all of the city's residents. During a television interview Thomas said, "It's wrong for this bank to cut the heart out of neighborhoods by replacing people with ATMs." Amy Miller respected Sheila Thomas, but she also recognized that the council member was an ambitious politician with a talent for media coverage.

Inland National Bank operated under the regulatory supervision of several federal and state banking agencies. The bank had a good record with these authorities, but the branch reorganization plan clouded the picture. Under the federal Community Reinvestment Act (CRA), INB had to disclose where its deposits came from and where they were invested. This was to help ensure that money was being fairly reinvested in the communities where depositors lived and worked. The law gave banking officials some leverage to force banks to pay attention to local community needs.

The protests from residents and merchants had gotten the attention of the state banking officials who had to approve INB's branch closings. The traditional test for banking officials was whether the financial solvency of the bank would be improved or harmed by the proposed action. The governor had recently appointed a new state banking commissioner who had given a number of speeches urging banks to "invest at home," and "in people, as well as technology." Rockdale and North Madison were raising tough new issues.

The Decision

At a recent meeting with INB's CEO and senior management committee, Miller learned that the state banking officials had told INB to submit a plan that responded to the issues raised by the residents of Rockdale and North Madison. She was named to a team that had to recommend a course of action to INB's CEO by the end of the week. The team's leader had called a meeting for this afternoon. He had suggested that one way for INB to get out of this problem was to close just one of the branches. Miller had been asked to bring her analysis of the Rockdale and North Madison branches to the meeting.

Discussion Questions

1. Who are the stakeholders in this case? Which are primary, and which are secondary? What influence do they have? How are they related to each other? Draw a diagram of the stakeholder relationships to INB.
2. If INB decides to close one or both of the branch banks, how will the business-government-society relationship come into play? How might the issue develop? What considerations must be weighed by INB's management?
3. What should Amy Miller recommend to her team? Does the "close one branch" option solve the problem for the bank or the community? Which branch would you recommend be closed?
4. What steps can, or should, the bank take to soften the impact of a closing?

2

Business and Public Issues

Businesses face a large number of public and social issues. Each firm must deal with a unique set of stakeholder relationships and public issues connected to its activities. Senior executives often spend large amounts of time managing stakeholder relationships and public issues. Many organizations designate specific managers to the job of public affairs management; others believe that managing public and social issues is a job that all managers must perform.

This chapter focuses on these key questions and objectives:

- Why does strategic management depend on sound macro environmental analysis?
- Why do stakeholder expectations matter to managers and organizations?
- What is the life cycle through which public issues evolve?
- What is the mission and purpose of a company's public affairs function?
- What strategies can an organization use to cope with specific public issues?
- What activities make up an issues management system?
- What must a company do to strategically manage its stakeholder relations?

he Ford Motor Company is one of the world's most successful manufacturers of motor vehicles. The company has earned a reputation as an innovative designer and manufacturer of cars and trucks for customers throughout the world. Still, there are times when Ford vehicles fail to meet customer expectations. This may be the result of the manufacturer's mistake or perhaps the fault of other companies that supply key parts, such as tires. In 2000, Ford encountered a major problem when its popular sports utility vehicles, or SUVs, were found to have unsafe tires. The tires were manufactured by Bridgestone/Firestone, an established tire manufacturer and long-time Ford supplier. The two companies were thrust into the public spotlight when it was disclosed that more than 60 deaths and hundreds of accidents involved Ford SUVs with Firestone tires. The case was reminiscent of other crises the company had faced in the past.

Ford has sold automobiles and light trucks for more than 80 years and now sells millions of vehicles in North America each year. During one five-year period in the early 1990s, for example, Ford sold 26 million cars and light trucks in North America. Unfortunately, these vehicles have sometimes proved to be unsafe and dangerous to drivers and passengers. Ford has endured three serious experiences that have shattered public confidence in the company's products and forced it to develop a strategic management approach to public issues. One of the earliest major examples of product design problems occurred with the Pinto automobile. The Pinto had a poorly designed fuel tank that could explode when hit by another vehicle, producing an instantaneous fire. Critics argued that an inexpensive protection device could have prevented many of these fires. Many lawsuits were filed against the company before it eventually recalled the Pinto and settled liability claims with the families of victims.

In the mid-1990s, Ford faced what was called the case of the Flaming Fords.[1] In this instance, the problem involved an ignition system that experienced an internal short circuit, overheating and creating smoke and fire in the steering column of the vehicle. By 1993, Ford had received reports of at least 300 such fires among Canadian owners and more than 800 from owners in the United States. In many of these cases, the entire vehicle had been engulfed and the driver injured. Ford denied the ignition system was defective and defended its overall safety. To advance their case, lawyers for some victims tried to locate other Ford owners who experienced such problems in the hope of joining forces in a class-action lawsuit. The lawyers created a website entitled "Association of Flaming Ford Owners." One page on the site showed a burnt-out truck and asked, "Are you one of the 26 million owners of a Ford manufactured vehicle that contains an ignition switch that starts fires?" The reader was prompted to click onto the model and year of Ford vehicle owned for information in the database. This website provided current information about the ignition system, pending lawsuits, and other plaintiffs. The website made it possible for customers to proceed much faster and with more complete information than in the past. The power of the Internet was not a complete surprise to Ford, because the company was developing web-based marketing strategies. But Ford executives seemed to be surprised that customers and critics would also use the Internet to challenge commercial practices.

---

[1] See www.flamingfords.com/flaming1/cgi. Also see www.ford.com.

By 2000, when the Firestone tire problem became known, the Internet was a basic part of everyone's strategy. Ford owners received information about the product recall via the Internet; Ford and Firestone issued bulletins and explained procedures using e-mail and company websites. The National Highway Safety Transportation Agency (NHSTA) used the Internet to monitor public information and reaction.

Technology is changing the way *both* commercial transactions and social issues are managed. The Pinto case took years to develop because information was hard to assemble; the Flaming Fords case developed faster with some use of the Internet; and the SUV tire problem became public knowledge very quickly because of communications technology. Many companies now use the Internet to improve their dealings with suppliers, vendors, and customers. At the same time, lawyers, activists, and the public use the Internet to learn about public issues and to organize others into a powerful force for action. The Internet is, therefore, a tool for both promoting commerce and for promoting public awareness of problems involving products, business practices, and social impacts.

In terms of the forces discussed in Chapter 1, Ford's response to the defective tires on its sport utility vehicles shows how technology is forcing ethics and business strategy closer together. In modern business, there is no hiding from a world of stakeholders who are capable of closely observing every decision and every mistake a company makes.

Why Public Issues Matter

As Ford's experience illustrates, companies cannot afford to ignore their stakeholders. Customers, suppliers, and competitors are capable of quickly organizing forces to pressure a company's managers. Of course, not every claim is legitimate, and not every stakeholder has a request that is reasonable. But managers who ignore the concerns of their company's stakeholders do so at their peril and may place the company at risk.

In the modern business environment, no organization can long ignore legitimate stakeholders whose lives are entwined with the activities of the business. First, many stakeholders (e.g., owners, employees, suppliers) have a legitimate connection to the business, often sacrificing something of value for the success of the enterprise. Second, to ignore stakeholders is to risk the kind of campaign that Ford faced with the Flaming Fords. For this reason, many organizations have created systematic ways of responding to stakeholder issues as they arise and have developed more strategic, longer-term business approaches to their key stakeholder relationships.

The Macroenvironment of Business

To formulate a strategy that will be economically and socially effective, a firm needs a framework of environmental information. Environmental analysis provides managers with the information about issues and trends (see Chapter 1) that enable an organization to develop a strategy that minimizes threats and takes advantage of new opportunities.

Managers must understand what is occurring in many sectors of the external world. According to two authorities, the environment that is relevant for businesses and their managers consists of four distinct segments: social, economic, political, and

Figure 2-1

The macro-
environment
of business.

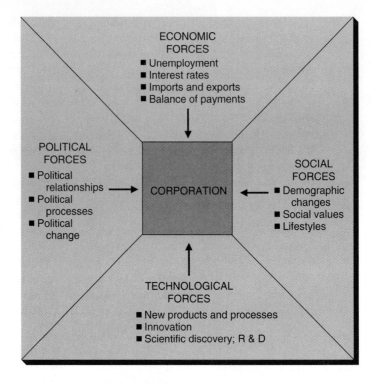

technological.[2] This macroenvironment of business consists of an almost unlimited amount of information, including facts, trends, issues, and ideas; and each of these segments represents a focused area of information, some of it important and relevant to the business. Figure 2-1 illustrates each of the four segments of the macroenvironment of business.

As shown in the figure, the *social segment* focuses on information about (1) demographics, (2) lifestyles, and (3) social values of a society. Managers have a need to understand changes in population (e.g., baby boom), characteristics of the population (e.g., average age), emergence of new lifestyles, and social values that are in or out of favor with the population.

The *economic segment* focuses on the general set of economic factors and conditions confronting industries in a society. For example, information about interest rates, unemployment, foreign imports, and many other such factors is relevant to virtually all businesses. The economic segment has a major impact on all business organizations.

The *political segment* deals with specific political relationships in society, changes in them, and the processes by which society makes political decisions. Changes in the tax code, for example, redistribute income and tax burdens. This involves political relationships between various segments of society. The creation and dissolution of

[2] Liam Fahey and V.K. Narayanan, *Macroenvironmental Analysis for Strategic Management* (St. Paul, MN: West, 1986), pp. 28–29.

regulatory institutions that set standards for business behavior are examples of changes in the political process.

The *technological segment* is concerned with the technological developments and potential hazards that are taking place in society. New products, processes, or materials, including any negative social impacts; the general level of scientific activity; and advances in science are the key concerns in this area. Problems such as Firestone's defective tires or the Ford ignition switches are one aspect of the technological analysis that goes on in many businesses.

The **macroenvironment,** as presented in Figure 2-1, is a system of interrelated segments, each one connected to and influencing the others. At the Ford Motor Company, for example, managers had to integrate their knowledge of social, economic, political, and technological factors to formulate a successful response to the problems of the defective tires. The company needed a technological solution to the problem that was also economical, plus an understanding of the legal and regulatory effects of the consumer campaign against the company. Managers learn about these factors when the problem becomes a crisis for the company. The preferable approach however, is to understand each segment and their interrelationships *before* they affect the organization.

Environmental Scanning

Environmental scanning is a managerial process of analyzing the external social, economic, political, and technological environments. Scanning may be done informally or as a formal management process. However it is done, scanning involves collecting, analyzing, and processing information. Done well, it can help an organization avoid crises and spot opportunities. Environmental scanning is done in one or more of the following ways: trend analysis of developments in government, society, or segments of each; issues analysis of concerns that are emerging in the company's industry or sector of the economy or in nations where it conducts business; and stakeholder analysis of the individuals, groups, and organizations that are important to the company.

- *Trend analysis* attempts to understand and project the implications and consequences of current trends into the future. Companies whose products or services have particularly long life spans have a special need for understanding long-term trends. The life insurance industry, for example, enters into many long-term contracts that may continue for 30, 40, or 50 years. A policyholder may pay premiums on life insurance for decades before the insurer is required to pay a benefit. Trends such as increasing life spans and more active lifestyles also can alter the calculation of how many years an insurer may have to pay out on a pension plan or annuity. The failure to understand such trends and their implications can result in poor financial planning that injures the company and the insurance beneficiary or pension recipient.

- *Issues analysis* involves a careful assessment of specific concerns that are having, or may have, an impact on the company. In many companies, public affairs managers do detailed tracking and monitoring of numerous social issues, seeking opportunities for economic and social benefit. Warner-Lambert, for example, believes that responding to critical social issues enhances the company's image, builds company pride among its employees, and helps those in need. The firm addresses various social issues such as hospice care for the terminally ill and the problem of domestic violence. The company has created educational and community outreach programs in response to these emerging social issues.[3]

- *Stakeholder analysis* (see Chapter 1) focuses on the people, groups, and organizations that populate the external environment. By trying to understand what concerns the company's primary and secondary stakeholders, managers are better able to predict what types of demands are going to be made in the future. There are many ways to collect such information, ranging from opinion polls to focus groups and professional reporting services. Informal discussions with union leaders or local environmentalists can go a long way toward providing managers with an understanding of what is critical to these groups and why.

Companies do not become socially responsive overnight. New attitudes have to be developed, new routines learned, and new policies and action programs designed. Many obstacles must be overcome in implementing socially responsive strategies. Some are structural, such as the reporting relationships between groups of managers; others are cultural, such as changing traditional ways of doing things.

Emergence of Public Issues

One reason companies are exploring new ways to build positive relationships with stakeholders is that other, more adversarial approaches have often failed. The first sign of a problem may be a complaint, objection, or protest from a stakeholder or stakeholder group whose expectations are not being met. For example, a group of residents may object to the odor or smoke from a local plant. Citizens may protest the use of monkeys or mice for scientific research at a local university. Employees may claim that they became ill after eating food prepared in a company's cafeteria or breathing fumes from chemicals used in a manufacturing process. In each case, the complaint is an early warning of a problem the company's management should examine more closely.

The Performance-Expectations Gap

In each of the instances described above, a gap has developed between the actual performance of the corporation and the expectations of the stakeholder organization or group (see Figure 2-2). Stakeholder expectations are a mixture of peoples' opinions, attitudes, and beliefs about what constitutes reasonable business behavior. For example, local neighbors do not believe that noxious air emissions from a plant are acceptable. People who care about animals do not believe it is morally responsible to inflict pain on animals in the name of scientific research; employees who get sick from food or choke on fumes do not believe it is ethically responsible for a company to endanger their health in this way. The following example illustrates how one company has read the signs of stakeholder sentiment and decided to act before the **performance-expectations gap** grew any wider.[4]

---

[3] "Warner-Lambert's World, Social Responsibility," www.warner-lambert.com/info/social.html, July 9, 1997.
[4] "Child Guidance Toy Recall," *Los Angeles Times,* July 22, 2000, p. C1.

Figure 2-2

The performance-expectations gap.

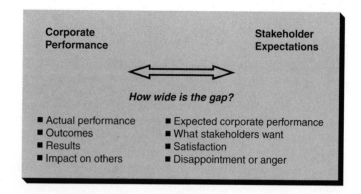

Corporate Performance | Stakeholder Expectations

How wide is the gap?

- Actual performance
- Outcomes
- Results
- Impact on others

- Expected corporate performance
- What stakeholders want
- Satisfaction
- Disappointment or anger

In June 2000, Child Guidance, a toy manufacturer, recalled more than 900,000 of the Wiggle Waggle Caterpillar toys that were sold under the Child Guidance name and made by Jakks Pacific Inc., a corporation head-quartered in California. The recall occurred after a five-month-old El Paso, Texas, girl choked to death on a small plastic ball from the musical caterpil-lar toy. The company worked with the Consumer Product Safety Commis-sion, a federal agency, to ensure a full recall. The toy was sold from May 1998 through June 2000. The 10-inch toy, which plays four songs and makes various sounds, also caused two other children to start to choke. Parents were encouraged to exchange it for another toy of similar value by calling the company. Although the girl who suffocated and a child in another incident were five months old or younger, the caterpillar toy was designed for children one year and older and was labeled accordingly, said Stephen Berman, president and chief operating officer of Jakks. The toy passed all relevant safety tests before and after the complaints were received. "But we were being prudent, and to make sure there were no other instances, we did the recall," Berman said.

Managers and organizations have good reason to understand the expectations and beliefs of their stakeholders as early as possible. Failure to understand safety concerns, for example, and to respond appropriately, as Child Guidance did in the previous exam-ple, will permit the performance-expectations gap to grow. As illustrated in Figure 2-2, this gap points to the difference between what stakeholders expect and the firm's actual performance. The larger the gap, the greater the risk of stakeholder backlash.

The Public Issue Life Cycle

Effective management of stakeholder concerns begins with the understanding that public issues often develop in predictable ways. In other words, it is possible for managers to *anticipate* how pressures will build around an issue and possibly turn it into a high profile problem that attracts the atten-tion of media and political figures.

A **public issue** exists when there is a gap between the stakeholder expectations of what an institution should do and the actual performance of those businesses,

Figure 2-3

The public issue life cycle.

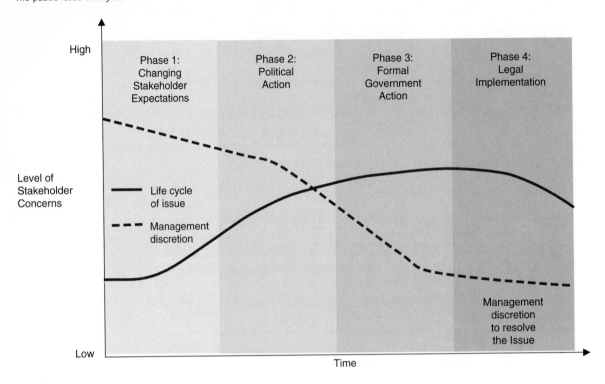

government agencies, or nonprofit organizations. Ford executives could have anticipated how the Flaming Ford members would act and responded to problems with the defective ignition issue when they were first recognized. One way companies can do so is to study the **public issue life cycle,** shown in Figure 2-3. This model illustrates the basic phases through which a public issue passes as it matures.

Phases of the Public Issue Life Cycle

Social concerns generally evolve through a series of phases that, because of their natural evolution, can be thought of as a life cycle. By recognizing the pattern through which issues evolve and spotting the early warning signs, managers can anticipate problems and work to resolve them before they reach crisis proportions. As shown in Figure 2-3, the public issue life cycle contains four phases: the changing of stakeholder expectations; political action; formal government action; and legal implementation. Each phase is discussed below.

Phase 1: Changing Stakeholder Expectations

Public issues begin when stakeholder expectations are not met. This failure can take many forms, ranging from small groups of residents objecting to a local manufacturer's air pollution, to the concern of animal lovers for the welfare of monkeys being used in scientific research in a laboratory, to the anger of voters at officials who raise taxes. As discussed above, once a gap develops, the seeds of a public issue have been sown.

Few industries have faced as large a legitimacy gap as the American tobacco industry. The industry has fought many battles in an increasingly antismoking climate. Until the 1960s, smoking was seen as a glamorous and sophisticated activity. Advertising in the 1940s featured movie stars dressed in military uniforms, which gave the impression that smoking was glamorous and patriotic. Advertising also portrayed women smokers as liberated and independent.

Today, the public perception of smoking is very different. Smoking has become unacceptable because it is so dangerous to the smoker and those nearby. Health experts argue that the public has a right to live free from smoke and its negative health effects. Cities, states, and even the federal government have taken steps to ensure that nonsmokers were free of unwanted smoke. In 1993, for example, antismoking advocates proposed legislation (the Smoke-Free Environment Act) in both houses of Congress to prohibit smoking in any building (other than private homes) that is regularly used by 10 or more workers a week.[5] In 1998, California started implementing a law that banned smoking in bars and nightclubs. Other states have followed.

Cigarette manufacturers, such as Philip Morris and R. J. Reynolds, have lived with the health effects issue for many years. As criticism mounted, the companies identified segments of the population that both oppose and support smoking restrictions. Although nonsmokers want restrictions, the companies have argued that smokers also have rights. By emphasizing this theme, the companies have tried to frame the debate in terms of balancing the rights of smokers and nonsmokers, setting reasonable expectations, and finding ways to create common ground for compromise.

Interest groups may signal the emergence of an issue by advocating government action to protect members. Managers must understand what others are asking government to do and be prepared to ask government to act on behalf of their business. International trade conflicts, for example, prompted American companies to ask the federal government to challenge the unfair trade practices of foreign competitors.

U.S. auto manufacturers sought the assistance of the federal government in getting Japan to allow more U.S. vehicles to be sold in that country. The unwillingness of Japan to open its domestic market to the sale of

---

[5] See Richard McGowan, *Business, Politics, and Cigarettes* (Westport, CT: Praeger/Quorum Books, 1995). During the 1990s, Philip Morris and R.J. Reynolds developed advertising campaigns using the accommodation theme. In one RJR-sponsored advertisement, three picture captions read: "The Berlin Wall Crumbles," "Russia Approves New Constitution," and "Democracy's Victory in South Africa." The fourth caption provided the point of contrast: "Nationwide, Reins on U.S. Smokers' Freedom Tightens." The title to the ad read, "Where, Exactly, Is the Land of the Free?" See *New York Times,* October 25, 1994, p. A17. In 2000, the company began a new campaign that emphasized the volunteer activities of the "People of Philip Morris."

*more General Motors, Ford, and Chrysler automobiles contrasted
sharply with the U.S. market, where Japanese auto companies have
established major market positions with their Toyota, Nissan, and Honda
vehicles. U.S. firms claimed Japanese governmental policy was behind
the closed market. Hence, only the U.S. government could move Japan
to change.*[6]

Phase 2: Political Action

What does it take to put a problem on the agenda for action by government? The agenda
of public issues on which officials are asked to act is enormous; not all public issues
warrant government action. Of the many issues a state or federal government is asked
to respond to each year, most fail to draw needed support. That is why political advocates (sometimes called *policy entrepreneurs*) are part of the culture wherever government bodies are located.

Strong and effective leadership is always needed to capture enough public attention to lead a reform movement. The American civil rights movement, for example, had
charismatic leadership in Dr. Martin Luther King, Jr., during the 1960s. Other movements have had leaders with very different personalities. Long before he became a
candidate for U.S. president, Ralph Nader led a fight for automobile safety by building
public support with detailed technical analyses of dangerous products, including his
famous book *Unsafe at Any Speed*.[7] Gloria Steinem and Betty Friedan were effective
advocates for women's rights. Cesar Chavez, now deceased, drew public attention to
the plight of farmworkers through hunger strikes and product boycotts. Marion Wright
Edelman provided a powerful voice for children through her leadership of the Children's
Defense Fund. Each of these leaders used his or her personality and knowledge to keep
issues in front of the public and its political leaders. A reform movement's leadership
may also come from within the political system itself. In the mid-1990s, for example,
Congressman Newt Gingrich led a political crusade to reduce the power of the federal
government. In the late 1990s, Senator John McCain led a campaign to change the rules
surrounding the political financing of elections.

Dramatic events can also prompt government to act. Environmental crises such as
the explosion at Union Carbide's chemical plant in Bhopal, India, or the more recent discovery of genetically modified corn in tacos both served to generate public pressure for
government to strengthen laws to protect people and the environment (see Chapters 10
and 11). It may take months or years for people to build a base of support sufficient to
challenge a corporation. If an issue persists, however, the group may organize formally
and campaign for its point of view through pamphlets, newsletters, web pages, and other
forms of print and electronic communication. They may attract the attention of the media,
which will result in newspaper, television, or radio coverage. This moves the issue from
one of citizen concern to one of political importance.

---

[6] This experience is discussed in Chapter 5 of James E. Post, Lee E. Preston, and Sybille Sachs, *Redefining
the Corporation: Stakeholder Management and Organizational Wealth* (Palo Alto: Stanford University Press,
2001).
[7] Ralph Nader, *Unsafe at Any Speed* (New York: Grossman, 1965).

The political drive against passive smoking took off when the Civil Aeronautics Board ruled that smokers had to be separated from nonsmokers on airline flights. Political developments included the formation of various antismoking groups, including Group Against Smoking Pollution (GASP). GASP received calls from people complaining of illness caused by passive smoke—smoke from other people's cigarettes. They assisted companies that wished to establish smoking restrictions. Antismoking activists attribute corporate willingness to set up such policies to dozens of legal cases in which nonsmokers have sued companies for failing to protect them from passive smoke. The Environmental Protection Agency issued statistics that showed passive smoke kills thousands of people each year, and courts increasingly sided with nonsmokers in passive smoking lawsuits.

In 1997, 60,000 airline attendants sued tobacco companies to recover damages for injuries from passive smoke. Trial of the case began, but it ended when the companies negotiated a settlement with the airline attendants. The attendants claimed victory. Pressure has continued to build on passive smoking issues. In 2000, for example, the town of Friendship Heights, Maryland, banned all outdoor smoking because it could affect anyone in the community. Tobacco companies claimed the restriction was unconstitutional, and the case headed for court.[8]

The battle against smoking has continued on other fronts as well. In 2000, three individual plaintiffs won a $145 billion jury verdict against tobacco companies for compensation and punitive damages. Governments have also sued tobacco companies for the costs of smoking-related disease. Florida, for example, was the first state to sue tobacco product manufacturers to recover the costs of treating tobacco-related illnesses of Florida Medicaid patients. Other states followed, and the financial risk of such lawsuits led the industry to negotiate with states' attorneys general. (See "The Tobacco Wars" case study at the end of the book.)

Politicians are interested in citizens' concerns and often are anxious to advocate action on their behalf. The government officials become new stakeholders with different types of power to use in closing the gap between public expectations and business performance. The tobacco lobby once had the support of a powerful coalition of elected representatives and senators in Washington. But as antismoking pressures have grown, more elected officials and political candidates have spoken in favor of antismoking laws. Some have also become outspoken critics of the tobacco lobby. The involvement of political actors creates more stakeholders and, hence, makes the issue more complex for the company and its executives to deal with.

Phase 3: Formal Government Action

As more people are drawn into a political conflict, ideas may emerge about how to use laws or regulations to solve the problem. When legislative proposals or draft regulations emerge, the public issue moves to a new level of action.

---

[8] "Nation's Toughest Smoking Ban Is Adopted," *New York Times*, December 13, 2000, nytimes.com.

Much legislative action has been taken in favor of antismoking activists during the past decade. Antismoking legislation has been enacted nationally and in many states and cities. The federal government has required that health warnings on cigarette labels be in larger print and that messages be rotated quarterly to provide more effective warnings. Many communities set limits on the areas in restaurants that can be used by smokers, and nonsmokers in the workplace can legally declare their immediate work area a no-smoking zone. Some cities have even outlawed smoking entirely in office buildings, restaurants, and public buildings.

Companies are normally represented by lawyers, lobbyists, and professional political consultants when dealing with the creation or amendment of legislation. Top management may be called to testify before government committees or regulatory agencies; corporate lawyers and lobbyists decide what proposals are best and worst for the company, and they make efforts to slow or alter legislative proposals that work against the company's interests.

Tobacco companies have hired hundreds of lobbyists, lawyers, and political advisers to fight antismoking efforts. The tobacco industry has been estimated to spend more than $650 million dollars per year in legal and lobbying fees. Individually and through the Tobacco Institute, an industry association, they have challenged scientific findings and worked to defeat antismoking proposals. Two powerful arguments have been used: first, that 50 million U.S. smokers are citizens who also have rights, including the personal freedom to smoke; and second, that taxes on tobacco products are an important source of revenue for cities and states, accounting for many millions of dollars. Legislators who might vote for an antismoking law are sometimes stopped by fears of what it will mean for government to lose tobacco tax revenue or to have angry smokers campaigning against them in the next election.

Phase 4: Legal Implementation

Making a public policy decision does not mean that the policy will be carried out automatically. The validity of new laws and regulations is often challenged through legal actions. Once the legal issues are settled, however, the company must comply with the law.

Stakeholder interest in an issue tends to plateau or even decline as a new law or regulation is implemented. New laws often spark lawsuits to test the interpretation and limits of the statute. Once the test cases are over, affected parties will normally abide by the law and compliance will reduce public interest in the issue. If the law is violated or ignored, however, the issue may reemerge, as a new gap develops between stakeholder expectations and the corporation's actual performance.

Business still has a chance to influence how government policy is implemented at this stage of the process. A company may negotiate with a regulatory agency for extending compliance deadlines, as steel companies have done regarding pollution controls and auto manufacturers have done in introducing air bags and other safety devices. Legal steps can also be taken by appealing to a court to review the law or regulation's constitutionality. Or an industry may play off one branch of government against another. For example, presidential decisions can sometimes be overridden by congressional votes.[9]

Continuing Issues

Debates about some public issues may continue long after the implementation of policy. Advocacy groups may keep the issue alive, knowing that new government officials may be receptive to changing the law or interpreting it differently. Groups opposed to a policy may work to document its negative effects, whereas supporters work to document the positive effects. Government officials may try to find out whether the benefits have been worth more than the costs and whether the policy goals could have been achieved in other, more efficient or less expensive ways.

Public issues often overlap and interweave with one another, creating a complex web of advocacy groups, coalitions, government policies, programs, laws, regulations, court orders, and political maneuvers. Something is always happening in each stage, often involving issues of concern to the company and its management. Thus, the business, or any other interest group, must anticipate and respond to issues in a timely way. That is the essence of good management.

The Public Affairs Function

The pressures on business firms that arise from public issues, plus the increasingly complex relationships organizations have with stakeholders, have led many companies to create specialized staff departments to manage external affairs. The emergence of the corporate public affairs function has been a major innovation in recent decades, especially as the number of stakeholder issues has grown and issues have become both more complex and more important to business.[10]

Public Affairs Management

Public affairs management refers to the active management of a company's external relations, especially its relations with external stakeholders such as government, regulatory agencies, and communities. Other names that are sometimes used to describe the function are *external affairs* or *corporate relations*. Some companies have also created separate departments for *community relations, government relations,* and *media relations*. The creation of public affairs units appears to be a global trend as well, with many companies in Canada, Australia, and Europe developing sophisticated public affairs operations.

Despite the diverse names used to describe the function, there is broad agreement among companies as to what activities have to be managed if an organization is to effectively address its external stakeholders. Exhibit 2-A presents the profile of activities

---

[9] Useful examples of typical legal and political lobbying are discussed in Haynes Johnson and David S. Broder, *The System: The American Ways of Politics at the Breaking Point* (Boston: Little, Brown, 1996).
[10] See James E. Post and Jennifer J. Griffin, "Corporate Reputation and External Affairs Management," *Corporate Reputation Review* 1 (1997), pp. 165–71. The global patterns of public affairs practice are documented in the *Journal of Public Affairs,* published by Henry Stewart Publishing beginning in 2001.

EXHIBIT
2-A

Corporate Public Affairs Activities of 250 Companies

- Federal government relations (87%)
- State government relations (83%)
- Community relations (61%)
- Trade association relations (84%)
- Local government relations (79%)
- Corporate contributions (73%)
- Grassroots management (81%)
- Issues management (83%)
- Political action committee (75%)
- Public interest group relations (58%)
- Regulatory affairs (55%)

- Public relations (54%)
- Media relations (54%)
- Employee communications (49%)
- Educational relations (35%)
- Volunteer programs (40%)
- Advertising (28%)
- International public affairs (43%)
- Environmental affairs (22%)
- Stockholder relations (18%)
- Institutional investor relations (13%)
- Consumer affairs (13%)

Sources: See Foundation for Public Affairs, *State of Public Affairs, 2000* (Washington, DC: FPA, 2000), and J. E. Post and J. J. Griffin, *State of Corporate Public Affairs, 1996* (Washington, DC: FPA, 1997).

performed by public affairs units in more than 250 large and medium-sized companies in the United States.

These activities may seem quite different, but they are all linked to an organization's need to relate to its many stakeholders. Notice how many of the activities refer to a named stakeholder group (e.g., federal, state, and local government relations; community relations; media relations; employee communications; and investor relations). Others refer to activities that are clearly connected to one stakeholder or more (e.g., political action committees, grassroots programs, environmental affairs). As one group of scholars has written,

> [T]he essential role of public affairs units appears to be that of a window out of the corporation through which management can perceive, monitor, and understand external change, and simultaneously, a window in through which society can influence corporate policy and practice. This boundary spanning role primarily involves the flow of information to and from the organization. In many firms it also involves the flow of financial resources in the form of political contributions to various stakeholder groups in society.[11]

[11] Boston University Public Affairs Research Group, *Public Affairs Offices and Their Functions: A Summary of Survey Results* (Boston: Boston University School of Management, 1981), p. 1.

Figure 2-4

The value-added derived from public affairs management.

Public Affairs: Three elements

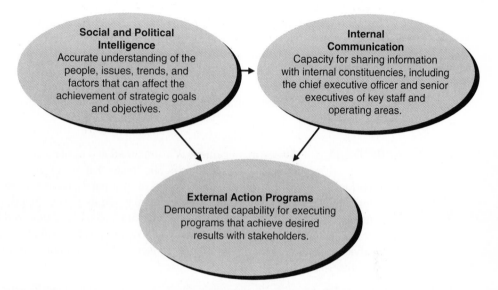

Social and Political Intelligence
Accurate understanding of the people, issues, trends, and factors that can affect the achievement of strategic goals and objectives.

Internal Communication
Capacity for sharing information with internal constituencies, including the chief executive officer and senior executives of key staff and operating areas.

External Action Programs
Demonstrated capability for executing programs that achieve desired results with stakeholders.

As shown in Figure 2-4, three critical elements help define the responsibility of public affairs in relating to stakeholder issues and concerns. These include social and political intelligence, internal communication, and external action programs. Each is discussed below.

- *Social and political intelligence.* Public affairs is responsible for collecting, analyzing, and preparing social and political intelligence for other managers. Issues are identified, trends forecasted, and activists in the external environment are studied. If there is no public affairs unit or staff, the organization must develop alternative ways to gather such information.

- *Internal communication.* Public affairs must communicate what it learns to other managers throughout the company. Public affairs units typically produce daily reports for the CEO and senior executives. Special reports are frequently prepared for the board of directors, strategic planners, heads of business units, and operating managers. Many public issues require that the interests and ideas of managers in many different parts of the organization be coordinated. This coordination is vital to the development of sound positions on complex issues.

- *External action programs.* Public affairs units are responsible for developing and executing action programs that target key external stakeholders. A company will often have a media contacts program for building regular interaction with the press; a local community affairs program for strengthening contacts with the local community; and state and federal government lobbying operations that ensure the company's voice will be heard by legislators or other government officials.

Most companies have a public affairs plan and a senior manager or executive to lead the public affairs department. This person is often a member of the company's senior management committee, providing expertise into the company's major strategy and policy decisions. The size of the department and the support staff vary widely among companies. Many companies assign employees from other parts of the business to work on public affairs issues and to help plan, coordinate, and execute public affairs activities. In this way, the formulation and implementation of the policies and programs developed by a company's public affairs unit are closely linked to the primary business activities of the firm.

Issues Management

Issues management is a structured and systematic process through which companies respond to public issues that are of greatest importance to the business. Companies rarely have full control of a public issue because of the many factors involved. But it is possible for an organization to create a management system that monitors issues as they emerge and involves managers in action to minimize the negative effects of a public issue or to maximize the positive effects to the organization's advantage. One of the foremost practitioners of a systematic approach to issues management is the Dow Chemical Company.

> *According to its executives, Dow Chemical first created an issues management system in the 1990s to provide an early warning/early response capability. The goal, according to company managers, was to anticipate issues so that a public issue's positive potential could be encouraged and enhanced and its negative potential be discouraged or inhibited. As one manager said, "The objective is to identify issues in the early stages of development before options are narrowed and liabilities expanded. The difference between issues management and crisis management is* timing.*"* [emphasis added]

Managers have less influence on a public issue as it evolves. That is another way of saying that the sooner a company can become involved in managing an issue, the more likely it can shape an outcome that is acceptable to the organization and others. The so-called issues management process is a basic tool used to achieve this objective. Figure 2-5 illustrates the components of a typical issues management system.

- *Issues identification.* This involves the active scanning of newspapers, other media, experts' views, and community concerns to identify issues of concern to the public. Because there are many ways to spot emerging issues, managers must decide how best to focus their efforts. Companies often use electronic databases, including the Internet, to track ideas, themes, and issues that may be relevant to their public policy interests.

- *Issues analysis.* Once identified, the facts and implications of the issue must be analyzed. For example, an analysis of the dioxin issue would show that there is much discussion among scientists as to the chemical process of dioxin exposure and much debate as to whether, or how, dioxin contamination can be cleaned up. Similarly, tobacco companies have invested in having researchers examine every

Figure 2-5

The issues management process.

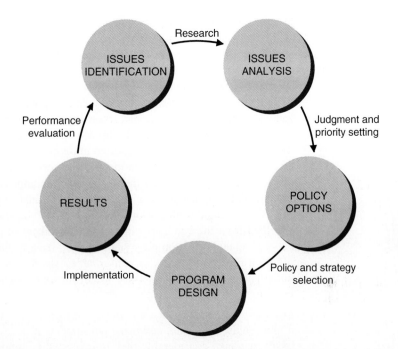

study that claims a link between passive smoking and health effects. Issue analysis is guided by management's need to answer two basic questions: (1) What impact can this issue have on our business? and (2) What is the probability that this issue will evolve into later stages of the public issue life cycle?

- *Policy options.* An issue's impact and probability of occurrence tell managers how significant the issue is for the company; but they do not tell management what to do. Developing policy options involves creating choices. It requires complex judgments that incorporate ethical considerations, the company's reputation and good name, and other nonquantifiable factors. Management may decide to change internal practices, operating procedures, or even the product itself. Companies in the pulp and paper industry, for example, have invested in developing new bleaching technologies to eliminate chlorine from their manufacturing processes. Management may also focus on changing the views of officials, the public, or the media. Doing nothing may also be an option if an issue is not ripe for immediate action. Research organizations, such as think tanks, can be useful sources of ideas about alternative policy options. These groups issue papers on many public policy topics, including environmental practices, taxation, minimum wages, and regulation.

- *Program design.* Once the policy option has been chosen, the company must design and implement an appropriate program. For example, tobacco companies made a policy choice to fight antismoking proposals in every city, state, and political district in which such proposals are made. Their program was designed to ensure that no antismoking law is created without efforts by the industry to shape, influence, or kill the proposal. This "fight on every front" policy requires a very expensive program, but it has been an integral part of the tobacco companies' strategy for years.

Early issues identification enables a company to build political capital before it is needed. Often, a company creates goodwill by helping other organizations, which, in time, can lead those organizations into becoming the company's allies. For many years, Philip Morris has been a patron of the arts. Millions of its dollars have supported museums, art galleries, and performing arts organizations across the nation. Philip Morris, which has its corporate headquarters in New York, faced the prospect of a complete ban on cigarettes in restaurants and other public places under an ordinance proposed by the New York City Council. Philip Morris executives telephoned arts institutions that had benefited from the company grants and asked them to put in a good word with the city council. The company said it would have to move away from New York if such a ban were passed, with inevitable loss of support for the arts organizations. The arts groups were asked to tell the city council how much that would mean to their organizations.[12]

- *Evaluation of results.* Once a company has tried an issues management program, it must study the results and make adjustments if necessary. Because political issues may take considerable time to evolve, it is important that the manager entrusted with a particular issue regularly update senior managers as to the actions and effectiveness of other stakeholders. The company may reposition or even rethink its approach to the issue.

Managing a Single Issue

Traditionally, public issues are managed by the company's public affairs or government relations staff. A new trend is for responsibility of managing an issue to be placed in the hands of managers from the area of the business most affected by the problem. For example, an issue involving tax rates or depreciation schedules would be assigned to an issues manager from the company's tax department; an issue involving local protests of truck traffic at a plant in Tulsa, Oklahoma, would properly be assigned to the plant manager of the Tulsa facility. TRW, a global manufacturer of defense and industrial products, pioneered the management of issues by operating managers when it created its "quarterback system," in which one manager coordinates the efforts of a team of people from across the company.

When an issue involves several areas of a company's business, an issues management team may be created to deal with the problem. Building on the quarterback concept, these teams are led by a manager from the area most directly affected by the issue. She or he will "own" the issue and be responsible for ensuring that the company is acting

---

[12] "Hooked on Tobacco Sponsorships," *New York Times,* January 13, 1998, p. A22. This pattern has been nurtured over many years. See, for example, Maureen Dowd, "Philip Morris Calls in I.O.U.'s in the Arts," *New York Times,* October 5, 1994, pp. A1, C4. The company's current pattern of support for arts organizations is presented at www.philipmorris.com

appropriately to manage the problem. Experts from other areas within the company will be included in the team as needed. Through the use of electronic mail and other technologies, teams can be organized from personnel at different locations.

> *For example, Dow Chemical created a global issues management team to deal with public issues surrounding chlorine. As one of the world's largest producers of chlorine, Dow had a very large stake in proposals to ban or regulate the use of chlorine, a widely used chemical in modern manufacturing. Members of the global issues management team were drawn from the United States, Europe, and Asia-Pacific and included scientists, plant managers, and managers from Dow's manufacturing businesses that would be affected by any changes in the availability of chlorine. The global issues management team analyzed scientific studies of chlorine, tracked government actions across the world, coordinated research into various aspects of the problem, and worked with company government relations staff to ensure that Dow spoke with one voice when talking about chlorine.*

Issues management teams usually exist only as long as the issue is a high priority for the company. This mirrors the modern management trend toward using task forces and other temporary team assignments to manage issues in companies. Rather than create large staffs and costly bureaucracies, companies have learned that flexibility is the key to managing public issues as well as other aspects of the business.

Managing Multiple Issues

Companies facing many public issues need to set priorities about which ones will receive the most attention. Many companies use an issues priority matrix such as that shown in Figure 2-6. The number of issues that a company can actively work on is affected by available resources, especially people. If resources are limited, only high-priority issues (those with the greatest impact on the firm and highest chance of occurring) will be assigned for managers to work on; the company may use trade associations or consultants to follow less important issues or issues better suited to industrywide actions.

Managing Crisis

Every organization is likely to face a crisis at some time that forces its employees to act on a difficult issue quickly and without perfect information. **Crisis management** is the process companies use to respond to short-term and immediate shocks, such as accidents, disasters, catastrophes, and injuries. Industrial accidents (e.g., explosions), oil spills, shipwrecks, airline crashes, and recalls of defective products are among the typical crises confronting companies. The problem races through the public issue life cycle, producing intense pressures and many suggestions about what the company should do or not do from outside experts, politicians, and observers. Large organizations normally develop crisis management plans to train their personnel for such conditions. But a crisis, by its nature, imposes heavy emotional pressure on people to make decisions under fire. One of the major challenges of managing crises effectively involves dealing with the media. This is further discussed in Chapter 19.

Figure 2-6

The issues priority matrix.

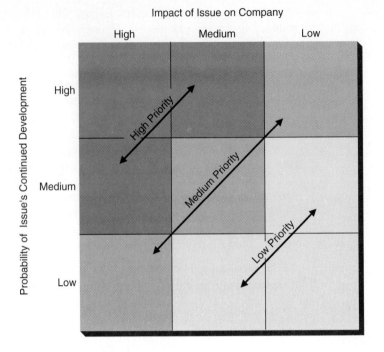

Impact of Issue on Company

Creating a Strategic Approach to Public Issues   Figure 2-7 summarizes the three settings in which managers and companies deal with external issues. When a problem erupts as a *crisis,* managers are forced to make decisions under intense pressure. Crises often require that managers deal with the media, government officials, employees, and concerned community members. *Issues management* involves important problems, but the company and its managers have more time to think about a course of action. It is possible for the organization to anticipate, interact with stakeholders, and "get ahead" of the issue. *Strategic planning* provides the organization and its managers with significant time to collect information, talk with stakeholders, and consider alternative action plans. To manage stakeholder relations and public issues effectively, the company and its executives must be prepared to address key issues in any of these situations. There are some guidelines to help prepare for this challenge.

First, managers must be aware of the company's stakeholders and acknowledge their right to participate in decisions affecting them through information sharing, consultation, and discussion. Second, the company must think proactively about how its plans will affect, positively and negatively, its many stakeholders. Plans should be developed to create stakeholder support whenever possible and creatively address negative impacts when they occur. Third, the firm should manage issues carefully and consistently, recognizing the possibility that issues may explode if mishandled, possibly creating other unanticipated and unforeseen problems.

Figure 2-7

Strategic management approach to managing external relations.

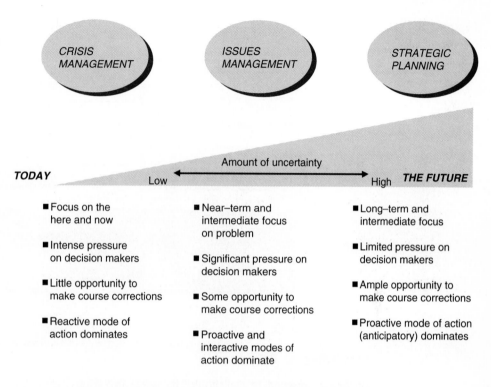

CRISIS MANAGEMENT   ISSUES MANAGEMENT   STRATEGIC PLANNING

Amount of uncertainty

TODAY   Low ←————————————————→ High   *THE FUTURE*

- Focus on the here and now

- Intense pressure on decision makers

- Little opportunity to make course corrections

- Reactive mode of action dominates

- Near–term and intermediate focus on problem

- Significant pressure on decision makers

- Some opportunity to make course corrections

- Proactive and interactive modes of action dominate

- Long–term and intermediate focus

- Limited pressure on decision makers

- Ample opportunity to make course corrections

- Proactive mode of action (anticipatory) dominates

For example, Ford Motor Company has developed important relationships with suppliers, dealers, and customers. The company regularly surveys purchasers of its products, for example, to determine customer satisfaction with the automobiles and trucks, service problems, and other concerns. This approach helps the company meet the second principle of anticipating the impact of decisions on stakeholders and the reaction of those stakeholders. When the Firestone tire problem erupted in 2000, Ford knew who its customers were and how to reach them. Unexpected surprises will inevitably occur. But as Ford learned, it is important to anticipate the reactions of customers and other stakeholders. It failed to effectively anticipate when it refused to settle the ignition fire cases; it was much more effective in dealing with its customers during the months of the Firestone tire recall.

Truly *strategic* management of stakeholder relations and external issues requires that managers link the organization's actions to its values and its performance to its commitments. The expectations of stakeholders form a framework for action in both the present and the future. Through effective strategic planning and management of issues across their entire life cycle, a company can develop stakeholder relationships that will benefit the organization and its employees, customers, suppliers, and other stakeholders.

Figure 2-8

Four basic strategies of response to stakeholder issues.

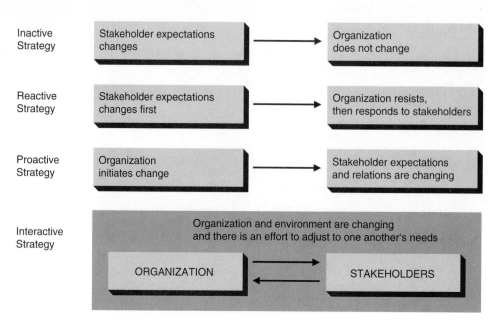

Strategies of Response

Businesses respond to stakeholder pressures in various ways. Some firms steadfastly adhere to their plans, no matter how strong the opposition or pressure from others. Some firms change only when forced to do so by strong outside pressures. Others actively attempt to move stakeholders in directions that will be to the company's advantage. And some try to find ways to harmonize the company's goals and objectives with the changing needs, goals, and expectations of the public. These approaches are respectively referred to as inactive, reactive, proactive, and interactive **strategies of response,** as illustrated in Figure 2-8.

Companies may use any of these strategies in responding to a particular issue or problem. Sometimes a company will quite deliberately be slow to respond (reactive) to an issue. At other times, the same company may be deliberately proactive in trying to head off an issue before it develops into a major problem. Some companies display a general preference for one or another of these strategies in dealing with many types of issues, although it is unclear whether this is just a style of management or a conscious strategy for use in responding to a particular issue. As the following example suggests, today's strategy may have to change—perhaps dramatically—if the business environment changes.

> *Petroleum companies have long explored for oil in remote and difficult-to-reach places. Offshore exploration has been one great challenge, as companies have sought to build and operate drilling rigs in deep ocean waters amid hurricane winds, blizzard storms, and waves the size of high-rise buildings. And in the remote jungles of African, Asian, and Latin American*

nations, another kind of problem has arisen. Having long been accused of operating with disregard for the enormous environmental impact of drilling and production activities and running roughshod over the rights of native peoples, companies such as Royal Dutch/Shell and Mobil have been the target of boycotts and other protests by global activist organizations. Stymied by such protests, Shell and Mobil pursued a different approach in developing the rich gas resources of Camisea, a remote area in Peru with enormous potential. Working with government officials, local environmental groups, and international advisers, the companies made an effort to work with local Indian tribes and critics. Plans have been adapted to local conditions, and the companies are earning respect for listening and changing their traditional practices. The process led to a stoppage of Camisea's development. It may be started in the future when conditions are more favorable.[13]

Summary Points of This Chapter

- The macroenvironment generates economic, social, technological, and political issues for organizations. Managers must learn to look outward to understand key developments and anticipate their impact on the business.
- Stakeholder expectations can, if unmet, trigger action to transform social concern into pressure on business and government. The existence of a gap between performance and expectations stimulates the formation of a public issue.
- The public issue life cycle describes the evolution of a social concern through stages of politicalization, formal government action, and implementation of legally mandated change. Every public issue passes through these stages, and managers can predict what will happen if the performance-expectations gap is not closed.
- An organization's public affairs function is charged with collecting and analyzing information about the social and political environment, communicating with internal audiences, and interacting with stakeholders to achieve the organization's objectives.
- Issues management includes identification and analysis of issues; development of policy options; program design; implementation; and evaluation of the results of such activities.
- Strategic management of stakeholder relations involves awareness of stakeholders and their interests, proactive planning of relationship development with them, and readiness to respond quickly and effectively to issues and crises.
- Companies can develop reactive, proactive, or interactive strategies to respond to public issues. Some steadfastly adhere to inactive strategies. Most organizations develop separate strategies for each issue they are trying to manage.

---

[13] See Post, Preston, and Sachs, *Redefining the Corporation,* chap. 6.

Key Terms and Concepts Used in This Chapter

- Macroenvironment
- Environmental scanning
- Performance-expectations gap
- Public issue
- Public issue life cycle

- Public affairs management
- Issues management
- Crisis management
- Strategies of response

Internet Resources

- allpolitics.com

- *nationaljournal.com*

CNN/*Time* review of emerging social-political issues

National Journal index of current events

Discussion Case: *McDonald's in the McSpotlight*

Dave Morris and Helen Steel didn't seem to be capable of challenging a great multinational corporation in the court of world opinion. But that's just what they did and are continuing to do. In doing so, they have succeeded in their battle against one of the world's best marketing organizations.

The Problem

Dave Morris (age 43) and Helen Steel (age 31) were accused of libeling McDonald's by passing out leaflets on London streets that charged the company with exploiting underpaid workers, despoiling the environment, and endangering human health. The leaflet—entitled "What's Wrong with McDonald's?"—claimed that McDonald's sells products that are high in fat, sugar, and salt and low in fiber, vitamins, and minerals, all factors associated with breast cancer and bowel and heart disease. It also charged that the company exploits children by using gimmicks to get them to eat junk food, underpays its staff, creates mountains of waste through discarded packaging, is cruel to animals, and helps destroy South American rain forests to make way for cattle ranches.

 Following its worldwide strategy of defending its brand name and reputation, McDonald's decided to go to court to secure an injunction to stop the leafleteers. To do so, it was necessary to sue Morris and Steel for damages to get a court hearing. The London media publicized the controversy and quickly christened the case, "McLibel." The David-and-Goliath imagery was enhanced when it was disclosed that Morris and Steel were a $105-a-week welfare recipient and a part-time bartender.

Strategy and Counterstrategy

British libel law is relatively restrictive, unlike that of the United States, where free-speech protections have created a broad immunity to libel suits. McDonald's decided to press its case in the British courts and hired Richard Rampton, a libel specialist, to head its legal team. Rampton, it was later disclosed, charges more than $3,285 (U.S.) per day. The proceedings involved 313 days of hearings and the testimony of more than 130 witnesses (some testified for as long as two weeks). The trial produced 40,000 documents and more than 20,000 pages of transcripts.

If McDonald's thought the lawsuit would discourage criticism of its business activities, it was badly mistaken. The McLibel Support Campaign raised donations for the defense and conducted a public campaign against the company by handing out more than 2 million leaflets in Britain since the controversy began. The group also created a website (www.mcspotlight.org) and used the Internet to post such documents as the transcript of the trial, McDonald's 500-page summing-up document, film clips, and other documentation in 15 different languages. The website became a global organizing tool for the campaign to generate support for Morris and Steel and to oppose McDonald's. McDonald's tried to shut down the website, but Morris and Steel's supporters threatened to start other sites to carry on the campaign.

Morris and Steel were unable to afford lawyers and chose to fight their own case. They flew in witnesses from around the world with donations from supporters. They cross-examined McDonald's executives in court and filed a countersuit for libel against McDonald's after the company issued leaflets that accused them of spreading lies.

Negotiations

McDonald's tried to reach a negotiated settlement with Morris and Steel. A McDonald's spokesperson said there were two separate attempts to reach a mutually acceptable resolution. Morris and Steel said that McDonald's asked them for between $130,000 and $190,000 damages; but McDonald's stated it only wanted to ensure that the pair does not continue to libel the company, calling the claim for damages a legal formality. Morris and Steel claimed that McDonald's executives from corporate head-quarters (Oak Brook, Illinois) tried on three occasions to persuade them to agree to an out-of-court settlement. They said they refused to do so unless McDonald's guaranteed to refrain from suing other people who make similar allegations, a condition the company rejected.

The Verdict

Morris and Steel said that if they lost the court proceeding to McDonald's they would exercise their right to appeal the case. They also threatened to bring the case before the European Court of Human Rights. A McDonald's spokesperson said that if the company lost the first round to Morris and Steel, it would appeal the decision to a higher court.

The trial took over three years, making it the longest-running case in British history. When Judge Rodger Bell handed down his verdict, he found that Morris and Steel had libeled McDonald's by making certain untrue statements regarding environmental damage in third world countries and claims that the company's food was unhealthy and dangerous for public consumption. But the judge also found that Morris and Steel had not libeled McDonald's on such issues as child labor, wages rates, and some food-related claims. Finally, the judge ordered that Morris and Steel pay McDonald's the sum of $100,000 in damages.

Morris and Steel declared victory, refused to pay damages to McDonald's, and launched an appeal. Their supporters vowed to carry on the fight. McDonald's has learned to live with the criticisms of its detractors. The website—www.mcspotlight.org—has become a worldwide vehicle for challenging a host of McDonald's policies and practices. An "Issues" page on the site focuses on problems of nutrition, advertising, employment, environment, animals, free speech, expansion, and capitalism.

Sources: mcspotlight.org and www.mcdonalds.com. See also, John Vidal, *Burger Culture on Trial* (New York: New Press, 1997); and Ray Moseley, "Three-Year Trial Pits Burger Giant against a Pair of Leafleteers," *Boston Globe,* June 15, 1997, p. A23. See also, Eric Schlosser, *Fast Food Nation* (Boston: Houghton Mifflin, 2001).

Discussion Questions

1. Who were the original stakeholders? What were their expectations? Who are the stakeholders today, 10 years after Morris and Steel handed out their leaflets?
2. What actions could McDonald's have taken to close the performance-expectations gap?
3. How did this issue evolve through the public issues life cycle? What were the drivers?
4. Assume you were an executive at McDonald's and asked to assemble an issues management team when the trial began. What skills would you want on your team?
5. What steps can McDonald's now take to deal with Morris and Steel?

PART TWO

Business and the Social Environment

3

Corporate Social Responsibility

Corporate social responsibility challenges businesses to be accountable for the consequences of their actions affecting the firm's stakeholders while they pursue traditional economic goals. The general public expects businesses to be socially responsible, and many companies have responded by making social goals a part of their overall business operations. Guidelines for acting in socially responsible ways are not always clear, thus producing controversy about what constitutes such behavior, how extensive it should be, and what it costs to be socially responsible.

This chapter focuses on these key questions and objectives:

- What is the basic meaning of corporate social responsibility?

- Where and when did the idea of social responsibility originate?

- What are the critical arguments for and against corporate social responsibility?

- How does business meet its economic and legal obligations while being socially responsible?

- How is corporate social responsibility practiced by businesses around the world?

Do managers have a responsibility to their stockholders? Certainly, for the owners of the business have invested their capital in the firm. Do managers also have a responsibility, a social responsibility, to their employees and the community? Since worker satisfaction and community development appear closely related to productivity, being socially supportive of employees and the local community seems to make good economic sense. What happens when these, and other, responsibilities seem to clash?

When Boeing announced the elimination of an additional 20,000 jobs in 1998, that brought the total number of jobs cut that year to 48,000. Management explained that Boeing was suffering from severe global competition and increased labor costs, necessitating these reductions in the company's workforce. In 1998 the firm lost $178 million. Yet in that same year, Boeing made $51.3 million in philanthropic contributions to various charities, partnering with communities in 27 states and two countries where Boeing had major operations. Education was a priority for Boeing, which contributed $19 million to schools in communities where many of the laid-off employees lived. Boeing also gave nearly $10 million to the United Way, over $7 million to the arts, and over $3 million to environmental causes. Boeing's 1998 Citizenship Report stated: "Wherever we have a presence, we endeavor to be good corporate citizens, and to work for the betterment of the communities where Boeing people live and work."

Joyce Bender had a rather peculiar hobby: she enjoyed finding jobs for computer specialists. This was a critical issue in western Pennsylvania since many firms in the region were suffering from the lack of technically qualified computer technicians. With her entrepreneurial spirit, Bender decided to address this economic need, but with a hint of being socially responsible in her endeavor. She was so successful in the pursuit of her hobby that she ended up creating Bender Consulting Services, a nonprofit business that employed computer experts and leased them to clients' firms. But these were not your typical job applicants. Bender sought out and placed individuals that had computer skills as well as physical disabilities. Her motto was "Competitive jobs mean freedom." "You cannot be independent or free in this country unless you can go to the bank, unless you have money to buy what everyone else does," said Bender. Thanks to Joyce Bender and her vision of social responsibility, these previously unemployable college and trade school graduates were now receiving paychecks, going to the bank, and purchasing items just like everyone else.[1]

Was Boeing practicing social responsibility when making significant donations to charities while laying off thousands of employees? Was Joyce Bender showing the true meaning of social responsibility by locating jobs for technically qualified, physically disabled job applicants through her firm? Are both examples of corporate social responsibility, practiced in different ways and in varying degrees?

In this chapter we discuss the advantages and drawbacks of being socially responsible. Most of all, though, we argue that social responsibility is an inescapable demand made by society. Whether businesses are large or small, make goods or provide services, operate at home or abroad, willingly try to be socially responsible or fight against

---

[1] Marianne Jennings and Craig Cantoni, "An Uncharitable Look at Corporate Philanthropy," *Wall Street Journal,* December 22, 1998, p. A18; Boeing 1998 Citizenship Report, www.boeing.com; and Jim McKay, "Doing Well and Doing Good," *Pittsburgh Post-Gazette,* October 18, 1998, p. E5.

it all the way—there is no doubt about what the public expects.[2] Many business leaders also subscribe to the idea of social responsibility.

> *This commitment is evident in the widespread corporate membership in three business organizations: the U.S. Business for Social Responsibility (BSR), Japan's Council for Better Corporate Citizenship (CBCC), and the Canadian Business for Social Responsibility (CBSR).*
>
> *The BSR, the largest of the three, was founded in 1992 and serves as "a U.S.-based global resource for companies seeking to sustain their commercial success in ways that demonstrate respect for ethical values, people, communities and the environment."[3]*
>
> *Businesses joined the BSR, the CBCC, and the CBSR because they believed that balancing the interests of all corporate stakeholders resulted in better-informed decisions, built organizational and customer loyalty, enhanced corporate and brand reputation, and contributed measurably to long-term profitability.*

Other organizations supporting businesses seeking to demonstrate corporate social responsibility can be found in Exhibit 3-A.

The Meaning of Corporate Social Responsibility

As these businesses recognized, **corporate social responsibility** means that a corporation should be held accountable for any of its actions that affect people, their communities, and their environment. It implies that harm to people and society should be acknowledged and corrected if at all possible. It may require a company to forgo some profits if its social impacts seriously hurt some of its stakeholders or if its funds can be used to have a positive social impact.

The Many Responsibilities of Business

However, being socially responsible does not mean that a company must abandon its other primary missions. As discussed later in this chapter, a business has many responsibilities: economic, legal, and social. The challenge for management is the blending of these responsibilities into a comprehensive corporate strategy while not losing sight of any of its obligations. At times these responsibilities will clash; at other times they will work together to better the firm. Thus, having multiple and sometimes competing responsibilities does not mean that socially responsible firms cannot be as profitable as others less responsible; some are and some are not.

Social responsibility requires companies to balance the benefits to be gained against the costs of achieving those benefits. Many people believe that both business and society gain when firms actively strive to be socially responsible. Others are doubtful, saying that taking on social tasks weakens business's competitive strength. The arguments on both sides of this debate are presented later in this chapter.

---

[2] See the special issue of the *Academy of Management Journal,* October 1999, reporting on research investigating stakeholders, social responsibility, and performance.

EXHIBIT
3-A

Organizations Supporting Corporate Social Responsibility

- *Centre for Innovation in Corporate Responsibility (CSER)*—www.cicr.net
  CSER's mission is to lead and assist businesses in redefining and realizing responsible international business practices. Through partnerships, sound corporate citizenship leads to sustainable human development.

- *Global Futures Foundation*—www.globalff.org
  Global Futures works with major corporations, governments, and advocacy groups to resolve conflict and create opportunity.

- *International Chamber of Commerce (ICC)*—www.iccwbo.org
  ICC promotes international trade investment and the market economy system worldwide and makes rules to govern the conduct of business across borders.

- *Management Institute for Environment and Business (MEB)*—www.wri.org/wri/meb
  MEB was founded in 1990 to help companies improve environmental quality through business success. The MEB promotes opportunities for sustainable development to businesses, works with business schools to integrate environmental issues into the core curricula, and provides industry outreach and training.

- *SustainAbility Ltd*—www.sustainability.co.uk
  SustainAbility is a strategic management consultancy and think tank. Founded in 1987, their mission is to help create a more sustainable world by encouraging socially responsible, environmentally sound and economically viable sustainable development.

- *World Business Council for Sustainable Development (WBCSD)*—www.wbcsd.ch
  WBCSD is a coalition of 125 international companies united by a shared commitment to the environment and to the principles of economic growth and sustainable development.

Source: California Global Corporate Accountability Project, www.nautilus.org/cap/orgs/bus.html.

Social Responsibility and Corporate Power

The social responsibilities of business grow directly out of two features of the modern corporation: (1) the essential function it performs for a variety of stakeholders and (2) the immense influence it has on the lives of the stakeholders. We count on corporations for job creation, much of our community well-being, the standard of living we enjoy, the tax base for essential municipal, state, and national services, and our needs

---

[3] Additional information about these organizations can be found at www.bsr.org, www.keidanren.or.jp/CBCC, and www.cbsr.bc.ca.

for banking and financial services, insurance, transportation, communication, utilities, entertainment, and a growing proportion of health care. These positive achievements suggest that the corporate form of business is capable of performing a great amount of good for society, such as encouraging economic growth, expanding international trade, and creating new technology.

The following well-known quotation, frequently appearing in journals for business executives, challenges the readers to assume a responsible role for business in society:

> *Business has become, in the last half century, the most powerful institution on the planet. The dominant institution in any society needs to take responsibility for the whole. . . . Every decision that is made, every action that is taken, must be viewed in light of that kind of responsibility.*[4]

In 1999, most of the 100 largest economies in the world were global corporations. The combined sales of the 200 largest companies was greater than one-third of the world's economic activity. The largest 200 businesses had twice the economic clout of the poorest four-fifths of humanity. One-third of world trade was simply transactions among units of the same company.[5]

Many people are concerned about potential corporate influence. The focused power found in the modern business corporation means that every action it takes could affect the quality of human life—for individuals, for communities, and for the entire globe. This obligation is often referred to as the iron law of responsibility. The **iron law of responsibility** says that in the long run, those who do not use power in ways that society considers responsible will tend to lose it.[6] With such technology as global computer networks, instantaneous e-commerce transactions, and exponentially increasing collection and storage of information drawing the world into a tighter and tighter global village, the entire Planet Earth has become a stakeholder of all corporations. All societies are now affected by corporate operations. As a result, social responsibility has become a worldwide expectation.

How Corporate Social Responsibility Began

In the United States, the idea of corporate social responsibility appeared around the turn of the twentieth century. Corporations at that time came under attack for being too big, too powerful, and guilty of antisocial and anticompetitive practices. Critics tried to curb corporate power through antitrust laws, banking regulations, and consumer-protection laws.

Faced with this kind of social protest, a few farsighted business executives advised corporations to use their power and influence voluntarily for broad social purposes rather than for profits alone. Some of the wealthier business leaders—steelmaker Andrew Carnegie is a good example—became great philanthropists who gave much of their

---

[4] David C. Korten, "Limits to the Social Responsibility of Business," The People-Centered Development Forum, article no. 19, June 1, 1996.

[5] The Business Week Global 1,000, *Business Week,* July 10, 2000, pp. 108–44.

[6] This concept first appeared in Keith Davis and Robert Blomstrom, *Business and Its Environment* (New York: McGraw-Hill, 1966).

Figure 3-1

Foundation principles of corporate social responsibility.

	Charity Principle	Stewardship Principle
Definition	▪ Business should give voluntary aid to society's needy persons and groups.	▪ Business, acting as a public trustee, should consider the interests of all who are affected by business decisions and policies.
Type of activity	▪ Corporate philanthropy ▪ Voluntary actions to promote the social good	▪ Acknowledging business and society interdependence ▪ Balancing the interests and needs of many diverse groups in society
Examples	▪ Corporate philan-thropic foundations ▪ Private initiatives to solve social problems ▪ Social partnerships with needy groups	▪ Enlightened self-interest ▪ Meeting legal requirements ▪ Stakeholder approach to corporate strategic planning

wealth to educational and charitable institutions. Others, like automaker Henry Ford, developed paternalistic programs to support the recreational and health needs of their employees. The point to emphasize is that these business leaders believed that business had a responsibility to society that went beyond or worked in parallel with their efforts to make profits.[7]

As a result of these early ideas about business's expanded role in society, two broad principles emerged; they are described in Figure 3-1 and in the following sections of this chapter. These principles have shaped business thinking about social responsibility during the twentieth century and are the foundation stones for the modern idea of corporate social responsibility.

The Charity Principle

The **charity principle,** the idea that the wealthier members of society should be charitable toward those less fortunate, is a very ancient notion. Royalty through the ages has

---

[7] Harold R. Bowen, *Social Responsibility of the Businessman* (New York: Harper, 1953); and Morrell Heald, *The Social Responsibility of Business: Company and Community, 1900–1960* (Cleveland: Case Western Reserve Press, 1970). For a history of how some of these business philanthropists acquired their wealth, see Matthew Josephson, *The Robber Barons: The Great American Capitalists* (New York: Harcount Brace, 1934).

been expected to provide for the poor. The same is true of those with vast holdings of property, from feudal times to the present. Biblical passages invoke this most ancient principle, as do the sacred writings of other world religions. When Andrew Carnegie and other wealthy business leaders endowed public libraries, supported settlement houses for the poor, gave money to educational institutions, and contributed funds to many other community organizations, they were continuing this long tradition of being "my brother's keeper."

> *Andrew Carnegie and John D. Rockefeller are usually credited with pioneering the path of the giant givers of modern philanthropy. For some years, the world's newspapers kept score on the giving. The* London Times *reported that in 1903 Carnegie had given away $21 million, Rockefeller $10 million. In 1913, the* New York Herald *ran a final box score: Carnegie, $332 million; Rockefeller, $175 million. All this was before the income tax and other tax provisions had generated external incentives to giving. The feeling of duty to the public good arose from inner sources.*[8]

This kind of private aid to the needy members of society was especially important in the early decades of the last century. At that time, there was no Social Security system, no Medicare for the elderly, no unemployment pay for the jobless, and no United Way to support a broad range of community needs. There were few organizations capable of counseling troubled families, sheltering women and children who were victims of physical abuse, aiding alcoholics, treating the mentally ill or the physically handicapped, or taking care of the destitute. When wealthy industrialists reached out to help others in these ways, they were accepting some measure of responsibility for improving the conditions of life in their communities. In doing so, their actions helped counteract critics who claimed that business leaders were uncaring and interested only in profits.

Before long, these community needs outpaced the riches of even the wealthiest persons and families. When that happened, beginning in the 1920s, much of the charitable load was taken on by business firms themselves rather than by the owners alone. The symbol of this shift from individual to corporate philanthropy was the Community Chest movement of the 1920s, the forerunner of today's widespread United Way drives. Business leaders gave vigorous support to this form of corporate charity, urging all firms and their employees to unite their efforts to extend aid to the poor and the needy. Business leaders established pension plans, employee stock ownership and life insurance programs, unemployment funds, limitations on working hours, and higher wages. They built houses, churches, schools, and libraries, provided medical and legal services, and gave to charity.

For some of today's business firms, corporate social responsibility means participating in community affairs by making similar kinds of charitable contributions. The American Association of Fundraising Council (AAFC) reported that corporate giving to charities topped $11 billion in 1999, up 14 percent from the previous year. Similarly, personal donations rose 7 percent to nearly $144 billion, and gifts by foundations to

---

[8] Michael Novak, *Business as a Calling: Work and the Examined Life* (New York: Free Press, 1996, p. 197).

charities showed the greatest percentage increase in 1999—up 17 percent to nearly $20 billion. Under the leadership of actor-businessman Paul Newman, a group of CEOs from the largest U.S. businesses formed the Committee to Encourage Corporate Philanthropy. This group—comprised of two dozen CEOs, including top executives from Citicorp, Johnson & Johnson, and Chase Manhattan—committed to increase its members' personal charitable contributions to prod corporate America into giving $15 billion annually to charities. Despite this encouraging news, the AAFC reported that charitable contributions in 2000 were not keeping pace with business profitability and accounted for only 1.2 percent of pretax earnings.[9] However, charitable giving is not the only form that corporate social responsibility takes.

The Stewardship Principle

Many of today's corporate executives see themselves as stewards, or trustees, who act in the general public's interest. Although their companies are privately owned and they try to make profits for the stockholders, business leaders who follow the **stewardship principle** believe they have an obligation to see that everyone—particularly those in need—benefits from their firms' actions. According to this view, corporate managers have been placed in a position of public trust. They control vast resources whose use can affect people in fundamental ways. Because they exercise this kind of crucial influence, they incur a responsibility to use those resources in ways that are good not just for the stockholders alone but for society generally. In this way, they have become stewards, or trustees, for society. As such, they are expected to act with a special degree of social responsibility in making business decisions.[10]

This kind of thinking eventually produced the modern theory of stakeholder management, which was described in the opening chapter of this book. According to this theory, corporate managers need to interact skillfully with all groups that have a stake in what the corporation does. If they do not do so, their firms will not be fully effective economically or fully accepted by the public as a socially responsible corporation. As one former business executive declared, "Every citizen is a stakeholder in business whether he or she holds a share of stock or not, is employed in business or not, or buys the products and services of business or not. Just to live in American society today makes everyone a stakeholder in business."[11] Stewardship responsibility is illustrated by the following two examples.

The Prince of Wales Business Leaders Forum launched an environmental responsibility program called the International Hotel Environmental

---

[9] *Wall Street Journal,* May 25, 2000, p. A1; Monica Langley, "CEOs' Crusade to Raise Corporate Gifts," *Wall Street Journal,* November 18, 1999, pp. B1, B6; and Christopher H. Schmitt, "Corporate Charity: Why It's Slowing," *Business Week,* December 18, 2000, pp. 164–66.

[10] Two early statements of this stewardship-trustee view are Frank W. Abrams, "Management's Responsibilities in a Complex World," *Harvard Business Review,* May 1951; and Richard Eells, *The Meaning of Modern Business* (New York: Columbia University Press, 1960).

[11] James E. Liebig, *Business Ethics: Profiles in Civic Virtue* (Golden, CO: Fulcrum, 1990), p. 217. For stakeholder theory, see R. Edward Freeman, *Strategic Management: A Stakeholder Approach* (Boston: Pitman, 1984).

Initiative. The program created a web-based environmental benchmarking tool by which hotels around the world could assess their organization's usage of natural resources and minimize waste in areas such as water and energy consumption. The program provided suggestions on how hotels could cut costs by recycling wastewater and making it ready for use in other applications.

Novo Nordisk, a biotechnology company based in Denmark, showed a commitment to the stewardship principle by regularly consulting with its stakeholders on matters of business operations. The company formed stakeholder teams at each facility, which talked with the local community about how company operations affected the neighborhoods around the plant. Novo Nordisk also consulted with its suppliers and consumer groups and regularly distributed employee surveys to get feedback on what the company was doing well or poorly. Annually the firm invited environmental groups in for additional talks.[12]

The Corporate Social Responsibility Debate

There are strong arguments on both sides of the debate about business's social responsibilities. When a person is exposed to arguments on both sides of the debate, she or he is in a better position to judge business actions in the social environment and to make more balanced business judgments.

Arguments for Corporate Social Responsibility

Who favors corporate social responsibility? Many business executives believe it is a good idea. So do activist groups that seek to preserve the environment, protect consumers, safeguard the safety and health of employees, prevent job discrimination, oppose invasions of privacy through Internet use, and maintain a strong return on their investment. Government officials also ensure corporate compliance with laws and regulations that protect the general public from abusive business practices. In other words, both the supporters and critics of business have reasons for wanting businesses to act in socially responsible ways. The major arguments they use are listed in Figure 3-2.

Balances Power with Responsibility

Today's business enterprise possesses much power and influence. Most people believe that responsibility must accompany power, whoever holds it. This obligation, presented earlier in this chapter, is called the iron law of responsibility. Businesses committed to social responsibility are aware that if they misuse the power they have, they might lose it. The sensational Microsoft antitrust case, discussed later in the book, is one example of where society determined that a business abused its monopoly power, and the Department of Justice took action to reduce Microsoft's dominance in the competitive marketplace.

---

[12] See The Prince of Wales Business Leaders Forum and www.csrforum.com, and Mark Lee, "Digging Out rather than Digging In," *Business Ethics,* January–February 2000, p. 12, for additional company information.

Figure 3-2

The pros and cons of corporate social responsibility.

Arguments for Corporate Social Responsibility	Arguments against Corporate Social Responsibility
■ Balances corporate power with responsibility.	■ Lowers economic efficiency and profit.
■ Discourages government regulation.	■ Imposes unequal costs among competitors.
■ Promotes long-term profits for business.	■ Imposes hidden costs passed on to stakeholders.
■ Responds to changing stakeholders' demands.	■ Requires social skills business may lack.
■ Corrects social problems caused by business.	■ Places responsibility on business rather than individuals.

Discourages Government Regulation

One of the most appealing arguments for business supporters is that voluntary social acts may head off an increased amount of government regulation. Some regulation may reduce freedom for both business and society, and freedom is a desirable public good. In the case of business, regulations tend to add economic costs and restrict flexibility in decision making. From business's point of view, freedom in decision making allows business to maintain initiative in meeting market and social forces. This view also is consistent with political philosophy that wishes to keep power as decentralized as possible in a democratic society. It is said that government is already a massive institution whose centralized power and bureaucracy threaten the balance of power in society. Therefore, if business by its own socially responsible behavior can discourage new government restrictions, it is accomplishing a public good as well as its own private good.

> *For example, the natural juice producer, Odwalla, described in a case study later in the book, sought to improve the safety of its fresh juice drinks by pasteurizing (heat-treating) them voluntarily. The company hoped that by doing so it would avoid strict and often more costly government regulations of its production processes.*

Promotes Long-Term Profits for Business

At times, social initiatives by business produce long-run business profits. A New Jersey judge ruled in *Barlow et al.* v. *A.P. Smith Manufacturing* that a corporate donation to Princeton University was an *investment* by the firm, thus an allowable business expense. The rationale was that a corporate gift to a school, though costly in the present, might in time provide a flow of talented graduates to work for the company. The court ruled that top executives must take "a long-range view of the matter" and exercise "enlightened

leadership and direction" when it comes to using company funds for socially responsible programs.[13]

> *A similar example was seen in the classic Johnson & Johnson Tylenol
> incident. In the 1980s, the firm absorbed millions of dollars in short-term
> costs by recalling all of its Extra-Strength Tylenol capsules. Johnson &
> Johnson took this radical action to ensure the safety of its consumers after
> the product was linked to several consumer deaths from cyanide poisoning,
> even though the company's production processes were never found defec-
> tive. Customers rewarded Johnson & Johnson's responsible actions by
> continuing to buy its products, and in the long run the company once
> again became profitable.*

Responds to Changing Stakeholders' Demands

Social expectations have increased dramatically over the past decades; demands for a
cleaner environment, safe products, fairness in the workplace, privacy protection, and
similar social issues and concerns have placed business in the social spotlight. The public, now more than ever, expects higher levels of social performance from business.
Moreover, groups representing society's point of view on these issues are better organized, funded, and able to state their case in the media and in the legislature. Businesses
clearly are challenged to more quickly and accurately respond to these changing demands
made by their stakeholders. Addressing economic performance is no longer enough, since
many investors link economic performance to social issues, as discussed in Chapter 14.
Society's demands are business's demands in the complex and dynamic business
environment.

Corrects Social Problems Caused by Business

Many people believe business has a responsibility to compensate society for the harm it
has sometimes caused. When a business pollutes the environment, the cleanup of the
mess is the responsibility of that firm. If consumers are injured due to a product defect,
the manufacturer is responsible. If a business does not voluntarily recognize its responsibility, the courts will often step in to represent society and its interests, as seen in the
following example.

> *Four major pharmaceuticals companies agreed to pay $350 million to
> settle a class-action suit brought by thousands of independent pharmacies
> and drugstore chains alleging discriminatory setting of prices for drugs.
> The four pharmaceutical firms were accused of creating a two-tiered pric-
> ing system, where lower prices offered to a preferred list of large
> customers were not available to smaller, independent retail stores. The
> higher cost of drugs to the smaller stores was passed along to the
> consumers.*[14]

---

[13] *Barlow et al.* v. *A.P. Smith Manufacturing Company* (1951, New Jersey Supreme Court), discussed in
Clarence C. Walton, *Corporate Social Responsibility* (Belmont, CA: Wadsworth, 1967), pp. 48–52.
[14] Thomas M. Burton and Elyse Tanouye, "Drug Giants Agree to Settle Pricing Suit," *Wall Street Journal*,
July 14, 1998, pp. A3, A8.

Arguments against Corporate Social Responsibility

Who opposes corporate social responsibility? Many people in the business world do. They believe that business should stick strictly to making profit and leave social matters to other groups in society. Some economists fear that the pursuit of social goals by business will lower firms' economic efficiency, thereby depriving society of important goods and services. Others are skeptical about trusting business with social improvements; they prefer governmental initiatives and programs. According to some of the more radical critics of the private business system, social responsibility is nothing but a clever public relations smokescreen to hide business's true intentions to make as much money as possible. Figure 3-2 summarizes many of the arguments against corporate social responsibility, discussed next.

Lowers Economic Efficiency and Profits

According to one argument, any time a business uses some of its resources for social purposes, it risks lowering its efficiency. For example, if a firm decides to keep an unproductive factory open because it wants to avoid the negative social effect that a plant closing would have on the local community and its workers, its overall financial performance may suffer. The firm's costs may be higher than necessary, resulting in lower profits. Stockholders may receive a lower return on their investment, making it more difficult for the firm to acquire additional capital for future growth. In the long run, the firm's efforts to be socially responsible by keeping the factory open may backfire.

Alternatively, business managers and economists argue that the business of business is business. Businesses are told to concentrate on producing goods and services and selling them at the lower competitive price. When these economic tasks are done, the most efficient firms survive. Even though corporate social responsibility is well intended, such social activities lower business's efficiency, thereby depriving society of higher levels of economic production needed to maintain everyone's standard of living.[15]

Imposes Unequal Costs among Competitors

Another argument against social responsibility is that it imposes unfair costs on more responsible companies. Consider the following scenario.

> *A manufacturer wishes to be more socially responsible and decides to install more safety equipment than the law requires protecting its employees. Other manufacturers in competition with this company do not take similar socially responsible steps. As a result, their costs are lower and their profits are higher. In this case, the socially responsible firm penalizes itself and even runs the risk of going out of business, especially in a highly competitive market.*

This kind of problem becomes acute when viewed from a global perspective, where laws and regulations differ from one country to the next. If one nation requires higher and more costly pollution control standards, or stricter job safety rules, or more

---

[15] This argument is most often attributed to Milton Friedman, "The Social Responsibility of Business Is to Increase Its Profits," *New York Times Magazine,* September 13, 1970, pp. 33, 122–26.

stringent premarket testing of consumer drugs than other nations, it imposes higher costs on business. This cost disadvantage means that competition cannot be equal. Foreign competitors who are the least socially responsible will actually be rewarded because they will be able to capture a bigger share of the market.

Imposes Hidden Costs Passed on to Stakeholders

Many social proposals undertaken by business do not pay their own way in an economic sense; therefore, someone must pay for them. Ultimately, society pays all costs. Some people may believe that social benefits are costless, but socially responsible businesses will try to recover all of their costs in some way. For example, if a company chooses to install expensive pollution-abatement equipment, the air may be cleaner, but ultimately someone will have to pay. Stockholders may receive lower dividends, employees may be paid less, or consumers may be charged higher prices. If the public knew that it would eventually have to pay these costs, and if they knew how high the true costs were, it might not be so insistent that companies act in socially responsible ways. The same might be true of government regulations intended to produce socially desirable business behavior. By driving up business costs, these regulations often increase prices and lower productivity, in addition to making the nation's tax bill higher.

Requires Skills Business May Lack

Businesspeople are not trained primarily to solve social problems. They may know about production, marketing, accounting, finance, information technology, and personnel work, but what do they know about inner-city issues or world poverty or violence in schools? Putting businesspeople in charge of solving social problems may lead to unnecessarily expensive and poorly conceived approaches. Business analysts might be tempted to believe that methods that succeed in normal business operations will also be applicable to complex social issues, even though social analysts have discovered that different approaches may work better in the social arena. For example, management methods appropriate to an auto manufacturing plant might be ill-suited to running a school or drug-treatment agency.

A related idea is that public officials who are duly elected by citizens in a democratic society should address societal problems. Business leaders are not elected by the public and therefore do not have a mandate to solve social issues. In short, businesspeople do not have the expertise or the popular support required to address what are essentially issues of public policy.

Places Responsibility on Business Rather than Individuals

The entire idea of *corporate* responsibility is misguided, according to some critics. Only *individual persons* can be responsible for their actions. People make decisions; organizations do not. An entire company cannot be held liable for its actions, only those individuals who are involved in promoting or carrying out a policy. Therefore, it is wrong to talk about the social responsibility of *business* when it is the social responsibility of *individual businesspersons* that is involved. If individual business managers want to contribute their own personal money to a social cause, let them do so; but it is wrong for them to contribute their company's funds in the name of corporate social responsibility.[16]

---

[16] This argument, like the "lowers economic efficiency and profits" argument, often is attributed to Milton Friedman. See Friedman, "The Social Responsibility of Business Is to Increase Its Profits."

Together, these arguments claim that corporate social responsibility places added burdens on both business and society without producing the intended effect of social improvement or does so at excessive cost.

Balancing Economic, Legal, and Social Responsibilities

Any organization and manager must seek to juggle multiple responsibilities. The belief that the business of business is solely profit making is no longer widely held. According to a 1997 *Business Week*/Harris poll, 95 percent of the American adults surveyed rejected the idea that corporations' only role was to make money. As shown in Figure 3-3, a business must manage its economic responsibilities to its stockholders, its legal requirements to societal laws and regulations, and its social responsibilities to various stakeholders. Although these obligations may conflict at times, a successful firm is one for which management finds ways to meet each of its critical responsibilities and develops strategies to enable these obligations to help each other.

Enlightened Self-Interest

Being socially responsible by meeting the public's continually changing expectations requires wise leadership at the top of the corporation. Companies with an ability to recognize profound social changes and anticipate how they will affect operations have proven to be survivors. They get along better with government regulators, are more open to the needs of the company's stakeholders, and often cooperate with legislators as new laws are developed to cope with social problems.

> *In response to social protests at the 1999 World Trade Organization meetings in Seattle, a number of large and small businesses reaffirmed their belief that corporate profitability is not sacrificed, in fact it may be enhanced by exhibiting a social conscience. "There's no question companies can be responsible on the environmental front and be responsive to workers' rights and still be competitive," said David Schilling, director of the Interfaith Center for Corporate Responsibility.*[17]

Figure 3-3

The multiple responsibilities of business.

Economic Responsibility

Legal Responsibility

Social Responsibility

---

[17] "Some Firms Tout Benefits of a Social Conscience," *Wall Street Journal,* December 3, 1999, p. A6.

Companies with this outlook are guided by **enlightened self-interest,** which means that they are socially aware without giving up their own economic self-interest. According to this view, profits are the reward for the firm as it continues to provide true value to its customers, to help its employees to grow, and to behave responsibly as a corporate citizen.[18] These goals are reflective of the fastest-growing, most-profitable firms in the United States.

> *An emphasis on social responsibility can attract customers. A poll conducted by Opinion Research Corporation showed that 89 percent of purchases by adults were influenced by a company's reputation. Social responsibility also benefits companies by enabling them to recruit a high-quality labor force. The reputation of the firm and the goodwill associated with socially responsible actions attract talented people seeking an employer for which they would be proud to work.*

Economic Obligations and Social Responsibility

Do socially responsible companies sacrifice profits by working conscientiously to promote the social good? Do they make higher profits, better-than-average profits, or lower profits than corporations that ignore or flout the public's desires for a high and responsible standard of social performance? Efforts to discover an observed relationship between a company's financial performance and its social performance have produced mixed results.

Some studies seem to discover that good social performers also tend to have good records of profit making, which could be an example of enlightened self-interest. Scholars generally have found "a positive association between social and financial performance in large U.S. corporations." A scholarly review of numerous studies focusing on this relationship concluded:

> *Our classification of past studies provides evidence that the correlation between CSP [corporate social performance] and CFP [corporate financial performance] may, in fact, be positive. We found 33 studies that suggest a positive relationship between CSP and CFP, 14 studies that found no effects or were inconclusive, and only 5 studies that found a negative CSP/CFP relationship.[19]*

---

[18] Jeff Frooman, "Socially Irresponsible and Illegal Behavior and Shareholder Wealth," *Business & Society,* September 1997, pp. 221–49; he argues that the negative effects on shareholder wealth when a firm acts irresponsibly support the enlightened self-interest view: act responsibly to promote shareholders' interests.

[19] The "positive social-financial performance" relationship was reported in Lee E. Preston and Douglas P. O'Bannon, "The Corporate Social-Financial Performance Relationship," *Business & Society,* December 1997, pp. 419–29; and the quotation and comprehensive review of past studies are found in Ronald M. Roman, Sefa Hayibor, and Bradley R. Agle, "The Relationship between Social and Financial Performance: Repainting a Portrait," *Business & Society,* March 1999, pp. 109–25. Prior studies investigating this relationship were summarized in Jennifer J. Griffin and John F. Mahon, "The Corporate Social Performance and Corporate Financial Performance Debate," *Business & Society,* March 1997, pp. 5–31, with different conclusions drawn than the Roman, et al. review.

Any social program—for example, an in-company child care center, a drug education program for employees, or the lending of company executives as advisers to community agencies—will usually impose immediate monetary costs on the participating company. These short-run costs certainly have a potential for reducing the company's profits unless the social activity is designed to make money, which is not usually the purpose of these programs. Therefore, a company may sacrifice short-run profits by undertaking social initiatives. But what is lost in the short run may be gained back over a longer period. For example, if a drug education program prevents and reduces on-the-job drug abuse, then resulting lower employee turnover, fewer absences from work, a healthier workforce, and fewer accidents and injuries may increase the firm's productivity and lower health insurance costs. In that case, the company may actually experience an increase in its long-run profits, although it had to make an expensive outlay to get the program started.

Legal Requirements versus Corporate Social Responsibility

Accompanying a firm's economic responsibility to its stockholders are its **legal obligations.** As a member of society, a firm must abide by the laws and regulations governing the society. How are a firm's legal obligations related to its social responsibilities? Laws and regulations are enacted to ensure socially responsible conduct by businesses. The standards of behavior expected by society are embodied in that society's laws. Can't businesses voluntarily decide to be socially responsible? Of course, but legal rules set minimum standards for businesses to follow. Some firms go beyond the law; others seek to change the law to require its competitors to be more socially responsible.

Laws and regulations help create a level playing field for businesses that compete against one another. By requiring all firms to meet the same social standards—for example, the safe disposal of hazardous wastes—government prevents one firm from gaining a competitive advantage over its rivals by acting irresponsibly. If a company dumped its wastes carelessly, it would risk lawsuits, fines, and possible jail terms for some of its managers and employees and unfavorable publicity for its actions.

Businesses that comply with laws and public policies are meeting a minimum level of social responsibility expected by the public. According to one leading scholar of corporate social performance, even legal compliance is barely enough to satisfy the public:

> *The traditional economic and legal criteria are necessary but not sufficient conditions of corporate legitimacy. The corporation that flouts them will not survive; even the mere satisfaction of these criteria does not ensure the corporation's continued existence. . . .*
>
> *Thus, social responsibility implies bringing corporate behavior up to a level where it is in congruence with currently prevailing social norms, values, and performance expectations. . . . [Social responsibility] is simply a step ahead—before the new societal expectations are codified into legal requirements.*[20]

---

[20] S. Prakash Sethi, "A Conceptual Framework for Environmental Analysis of Social Issues and Evaluation of Business Response Patterns," in S. Prakash Sethi and Cecilia M. Falbe, eds., *Business and Society: Dimensions of Conflict and Cooperation* (Lexington, MA: Lexington Books, 1987), pp. 42–43.

Stockholder Interests versus Other Stakeholder Interests

Top-level managers, along with a corporation's board of directors, are generally expected to produce as much value as possible for the company's owners and investors. This can be done by paying high dividends regularly and by running the company in ways that cause the stock's value to rise. Not only are high profits a positive signal to Wall Street investors that the company is being well run—thereby increasing the stock's value—but those profits make possible the payment of high dividends to stockholders. Low profits have the opposite effect and put great pressure on managers to improve the company's financial performance.

However, stockholders are not the only stakeholder group that management must keep in mind. The leaders of the world's largest organizations from Europe, Asia, and North America recognize that all the stakeholders must be considered; none can be ignored. As some of them stated in the publications of the Caux Roundtable, a top manager's job is to interact with the totality of the company's stakeholders, including those groups that advocate high levels of social responsibility by business. Management's central goal is to promote the interests of the entire company, not just any single stakeholder group, and to pursue multiple company goals, not just profit goals. This view and a contrasting view of corporate social responsibility are shown in Exhibit 3-B.

This broader and far more complex task tends to put more emphasis on the long-run profit picture rather than an exclusive focus on immediate returns. When this happens, dividends paid to stockholders may be less than they desire, and the value of their shares may not rise as rapidly as they would like. These are the kinds of risks faced by corporate managers who have a legal responsibility to produce high value for the company's stockholder-owners but who also must try to promote the overall interests of the entire company. Putting all of the emphasis on short-run maximum profits for stockholders can lead to policies that overlook the interests and needs of other stakeholders. Managers may also downgrade social responsibility programs that increase short-run costs, although it is well known that the general public strongly approves socially responsible companies.

As a response to the conflict between long- and short-term profit making, an enlightened self-interest point of view may be the most useful and practical approach. That means that incurring reasonable short-run costs to undertake socially responsible activities that benefit both the company and the general public in the long run is acceptable.

Corporate Social Responsibility around the World

Social responsibility reflects cultural values and traditions and takes different forms in different societies. What may be the accepted custom in the United States, Japan, or Indonesia may not be in Germany, Brazil, or the Ukraine. Determining what is socially acceptable around the world often is a difficult process. Yet, corporate social responsibility has become a global concept reflected in global business practices, particularly in the areas of environmental responsibility and community relations.

Japanese firms have proven themselves to be model citizens on many dimensions of corporate social responsibility. Their support of local community activities

**EXHIBIT
3-B**

Two Views of Corporate Social Responsibility

The Shareholder View

In a market-based economy that recognizes the rights of private property, the only social responsibility of business is to create shareholder value and to do so legally and with integrity. Yet we do have important unresolved social challenges—from drug abuse to education and the environment—that require collective action. Corporate management, however, has neither the political legitimacy nor the expertise to decide what is in the social interest. It is our form of government that provides the vehicle for collective choice via elected legislators and the judicial system.

Whether corporate social responsibility is advocated by political activists or the chief executive officer, the costs of these expenditures, which don't increase the value of the company or its stock, will be passed on to consumers by way of higher prices, or to employees as lower wages, or to shareholders as lower returns.

Source: Alfred Rappaport, "Let's Let Business Be Business," *New York Times,* February 4, 1990, p. F13. Reprinted with permission.

The Multiple Stakeholders View

We believe in treating all customers with dignity irrespective of whether they purchase our products and services directly from us or otherwise acquire them in the market. . . .

We believe in the dignity of every employee and in taking employee interests seriously. . . .

We believe in honoring the trust our investors place in us. . . .

Our relationship with suppliers and subcontractors must be based on mutual respect. . . .

We believe that fair economic competition is one of the basic requirements for increasing the wealth of nations and, ultimately for making possible the just distribution of goods and services. . . .

We believe that as global corporate citizens, we can contribute to such forces of reform and human rights . . . at work in the communities [where we operate]. . . .

Source: "The Caux Roundtable Principles for Business," Section 3: Stakeholder Principles, www.cauxroundtable.org. Reprinted with permission.

and other philanthropic endeavors has led to increased goodwill in the communities where they operate. The firms help society in areas directly related to the operations of the business. Thus, Japanese firms clearly help themselves while helping others, showing a strong commitment to the harmonious relations between the corporation and society.

From a U.S. perspective, however, Japanese firms sometimes seem to show a narrow understanding of corporate social responsibility. Victims of environmental disasters have been treated as outcasts when seeking compensation for harm caused by Japanese business. Employment practices that may favor certain groups have been generally accepted in Japan. However, as Japanese firms have become more integrated with the international community, a broader view of corporate social responsibility has begun to emerge.[21]

> *The Japan External Trade Organization (JETRO) conducted a survey of Japanese philanthropy in the United States. They reported that approximately 80 percent of Japanese-affiliated operations in the United States responding to their survey engaged in corporate philanthropy. Making cash contributions was the most common form of philanthropy (91 percent), followed by participation in community organizations (57 percent). Community development and education were the primary beneficiaries of cash donations, and encouragement of employee volunteerism was up 36 percent from 1992. Over 95 percent of responding organizations maintained or increased both cash donations and other philanthropic activities since the last survey in 1992.[22]*

The practice of corporate social responsibility has also spread to other Asian countries. In Indonesia, for example, the notion of social action is deeply rooted in the country's rich history. Philanthropic practices are aligned with Confucian teachings of family and the proper relationship between family and state.

> *In Indonesia, the concept of mutual aid pervades the country's rural traditional communities. The notion of* gotong royong *involves contributions of goods and services in case of disasters, sickness, or accident, and cash donations for marriages, burials, and other forms of celebrations. Despite the absence of tax incentives in Indonesian commercial law, many corporations are becoming engaged in social development activities. These come in various forms, such as the collective pooling of funds for the environment and support of small enterprises and sponsorship of community forestry projects.[23]*

Corporate social responsibility has assumed a different form in European countries. There, governments have provided many social services often received as benefits from private employers in the United States. For example, debate by government representatives over social responsibility issues resulted in the adoption of a social policy for the European Union countries, called the Social Charter. Rather than relying on private

---

[21] For a more thorough discussion of corporate social responsibility Japanese style, see Richard E. Wokutch and Jon M. Shepard, "The Maturing of the Japanese Economy: Corporate Social Responsibility Implications," *Business Ethics Quarterly,* July 1999, pp. 527–40.

[22] See Japan External Trade Organization, Executive Summary, at www.jetro.go.jp/jetroinfo/survey/philan.

[23] For a more thorough discussion of the historical traditions and current practices of social responsibility in Indonesia, see Onny Preijono, "Organized Private Philanthropy in Indonesia," in Barnett Baron, ed., *Philanthropy and the Dynamics of Change in East and Southeast Asia* (New York: Columbia University, 1991), pp. 17–39; and Andra L. Corrothers and Estie W. Suryatna, "Support for Indonesian NGO Programs through Corporate Philanthropy," in Tadashi Yamamoto, *Emerging Civil Society in the Asia Pacific Community* (Tokyo: Japan Center for International Exchange, 1995), pp. 539–45.

corporate initiatives, governments represented in the EU drafted a public policy that provided incentives and rewards for corporate social actions.

Embodied within the Social Charter is the Social Action Programme (SAP). Created in 1995, the SAP established workplace guidelines, a vision for economic development, and a social policy that linked economic development with social policy. The SAP objectives for 2000 included creating jobs and preventing unemployment, modernizing work and seizing the opportunity of the Information Society, and achieving equality while encouraging a healthy society.[24] Thus, European businesses' response toward social responsibility is actually often a matter of compliance with various governmental policy guidelines and program initiatives.

In many of the world's developing nations where poverty is widespread or civil strife is frequent, economic goals and military activities tend to be given a higher priority than the pursuit of social goals. Environmental protection, for example, may be considered less critical than having a polluting steel plant that creates jobs. In these countries, social responsibility initiatives by business may be slow in coming.

Summary Points of This Chapter

- Corporate social responsibility means that a corporation should be held accountable for any of its actions that affect people, their communities, and their environment. Businesses must recognize their vast power and wield it to better society.
- The idea of corporate social responsibility in the United States was adopted by business leaders in the early twentieth century. The central themes of social responsibility have been charity—which means giving aid to the needy—and stewardship—acting as a public trustee and considering all corporate stakeholders when making business decisions.
- Corporate social responsibility is a highly debatable notion. Some argue that its benefits include discouraging government regulation and promoting long-term profitability for the firm. Others believe that it lowers efficiency, imposes undue costs, and shifts unnecessary obligations to business.
- Socially responsible businesses should attempt to balance economic, legal, and social obligations. Following an enlightened self-interest approach, a firm may be economically rewarded while society benefits from the firm's actions. Abiding by legal requirements can also guide businesses in serving various groups in society. Managers should consider all of the company's stakeholders and their interests.
- Examples of corporate social responsibility are increasing around the world. While some companies in some nations historically have taken a more limited view of social responsibility, companies elsewhere, particularly in North America, Asia, and Europe, are demonstrating socially responsible principles in their business activities.

[24] Social Action Programme, www.eubusiness.com/social.

Key Terms and Concepts Used in This Chapter

- Corporate social responsibility
- Iron law of responsibility
- Charity principle

- Stewardship principle
- Enlightened self-interest
- Legal obligations

Internet Resources

- www.bsr.org
- www.responsibility.com/news

- www.ijprn.org/english/projects/csr

- www.irrc.org

Business for Social Responsibility
PricewaterhouseCoopers Responsibility,
   Inc.
Corporate Social Responsibility Project,
   Japan Pacific Resource Network
Investor Responsibility Research Center

Discussion Case: *Aaron Feuerstein—A Socially Responsible Owner*

The evening of December 11, 1995, was a special time for Aaron Feuerstein, CEO of Malden Mills. A small surprise 70th birthday party quietly was held in his honor at a local Boston restaurant. But Feuerstein's life took a dramatic turn that evening for a different reason: A boiler at his company's plant exploded, setting off a fire that injured 33 employees and destroyed three of the factory's century-old buildings. Malden Mills was a privately owned firm, with Feuerstein owning a majority share. The firm was located in a small Massachusetts town, Methuen, and employed nearly 3,000 people in the economically depressed area. The fire was a devastating blow for the community. According to Paul Coorey, local union president, "I was standing there seeing the mill burn with my son, who also works there, and he looked at me and said, 'Dad, we just lost our jobs.' Years of our lives seemed gone."

Unexpected tragedies happen all too often, and the aftermath is frequently devastating to the owners, employees, suppliers, local community, and customers of the firm. But the December 1995 tragedy at Malden Mills had a different outcome than most, primarily due to the owner of the factory—Aaron Feuerstein—and the deep sense of corporate social responsibility he showed through his actions following the tragedy at Malden Mills.

Aaron Feuerstein typically awoke at 5:30 A.M. and began each day by memorizing passages from the scriptures and Shakespeare. He firmly believed in loyalty and fairness to his workers. He often said that the average American wanted businesses and their owners to treat workers as human beings, with consideration and thoughtfulness. Feuerstein tried to meet these expectations. "I have to be worthy," he told his wife over and over again. "Too many people depend on me." He simply could not let anyone down—even after the unexpected and devastating tragedy of the December 1995 fire at his plant.

Aaron Feuerstein knew he had many options after the fire. He could close the factory and walk away with tens of millions of dollars in fire insurance. He could turn over to his industry rivals his profitable, flagship product, Polartec. This synthetic fiber was in great demand by the sport outerwear industry. Its production required a highly skilled, experienced workforce, and Malden Mills basically held a market monopoly. Many of the company's competitors would have paid a high price for the rights to produce Polartec.

Yet, Feuerstein's commitment to his employees led him to a different strategy. As he later recalled, "I was telling myself I have to be creative. Maybe there's some way out of this." In an announcement to his employees at a local high school gymnasium four days after the tragic fire, Feuerstein explained that he would keep all the nearly 3,000 employees on the payroll for a month while he started to rebuild the family business. One month later, as the rebuilding process continued at a slow pace, Feuerstein extended the salary offer to his employees for another month; a month later, he extended it for yet a third month. "What I did was merely the decent thing to do," he insisted. "The worker is not just a cuttable expense, a pair of hands. I consider the employees the most valuable asset Malden Mills has."

With the first announcement of guaranteed salaries just days before Christmas, the reactions from employees were understandably positive. "When he did it the first time, I was surprised," said Bill Cotter, a 49-year-old Malden Mills employee. "The second time was a shock. The third . . . well, it was unrealistic to think he would do it again." Nancy Cotter finished her husband's thought: "It was the third time that brought tears to everyone's eyes." By March 1996, most of the company's employees were back to work. Those who were not were offered assistance in making other arrangements or finding other employment in the area.

Malden Mills' customers and other local organizations responded to Feuerstein's actions with an extraordinary outpouring of support. An apparel company, Dakotah, sent Feuerstein a $30,000 check after the fire. The Bank of Boston donated $50,000, the company's union sent $100,000, and the Chamber of Commerce in nearby Lawrence, Massachusetts, contributed $150,000. Many of Malden Mills' customers promised to stick with the company and wait for them to rebuild and regain their production capacity rather than switch to a competitor.

Just eight months after the fire, three of the four production lines at Malden Mills were fully operational and all but 500 of the nearly 2,400 employees were back to work in the factory. But unexpected downturns in the apparel industry challenged the wisdom of Feuerstein's actions. By 1998, employees at Malden Mills experienced steady layoffs and the firm acquired $120 million in debt. Under the leadership of new chief operating officer Gerald Bowe, following the values of the company's founder, Malden Mills experienced a turnaround in 1999. Hourly employee recalls numbered 1,500, bringing the total number of employees back to the level at the time of fire. Government and overseas contracts countered the decline in sales in the competitive domestic market, and Malden Mills appeared to be recovering from its financial setbacks as the firm entered the twenty-first century. Aaron Feuerstein's commitment to both the company's economic and social mission and goals appeared to have emerged from the ashes intact.

Sources: Tom Mitkowski, "A Glow from a Fire," *Time,* January 8, 1996, www.pathfinder.com; Mitchell Owens, "A Mill Community Comes Back to Life," *New York Times,* December 26, 1996, p. B12; Louis Uchitelle, "The Risks of Keeping a Promise," *New York Times,* July 4, 1996, pp. C1, C3; Bruce D. Butterfield, "What Flames Could Not Destroy," *Boston Globe,* September 8, 1996, p. A28; Michael Ryan, "They Call Their Boss a Hero," *Parade Magazine,* September 8, 1996, pp. 4–5; Alison S. Lebwohl, "Rising from the Ashes," www.afscme.org/afscme/press; and Shona Crabtree, "The Future Looks Brighter at Malden Mills," July 28, 1999, www.eagletribune.com.

Discussion Questions

1. Which principle of social responsibility—the charity principle or the stewardship principle—was the basis of Aaron Feuerstein's actions in the case? Give some examples from the case.
2. Which arguments for corporate social responsibility support Feuerstein's actions, and which arguments against corporate social responsibility raise questions regarding his actions?
3. Was Feuerstein being responsible to his multiple stakeholders in this case? Explain.

4

Socially Responsive Management

Socially responsive corporations consider and carefully seek to foster mutually beneficial relationships with their stakeholders. They also seek to identify emerging issues emanating from the corporate social climate and to transform these issues into responsive corporate policies and programs. This chapter identifies the processes, practices, and evaluation criteria relevant to socially responsive management.

This chapter focuses on these key questions and objectives:

- What groups and social forces changed the way management responds to the social environment?
- What are the stages in the model of social responsiveness?
- What elements are critical for a business to effectively manage the corporate social environment?
- How are the principles of corporate social responsibility practiced in today's business environment?
- How can a business or society assess the effectiveness of corporate social strategies?

B y the year 2000, the AIDS crisis had reached epidemic proportions throughout most of the African continent. It was estimated that 23 million people were infected with HIV, the virus that causes AIDS. Compounding the crisis was the fact that most Africans could not afford to purchase the life-prolonging but extremely costly drugs to combat their disease. In May of that year, the world's five largest pharmaceutical manufacturers agreed to slash the prices of their AIDS combating drugs by 85 to 90 percent below U.S. prices, or about one-fifth lower than the already discounted prices then charged in some African nations. In addition, millions of dollars in grants were available to African groups combating AIDS. For example, Bristol-Myers committed $100 million over five years to help fight AIDS in southern Africa. "The companies' initiative is an excellent idea, long overdue," said Jose Zuniga, executive director of the International Association of Physicians In AIDS Care.

This corporate generosity was praised by the media but soon became a social program nightmare for the drug companies. Those entrusted with combating AIDS in many African nations were disappointed at the still-too-expensive drugs offered by the pharmaceutical manufacturers. Some African government officials began discussions with generic-drug producers in Brazil and India as leverage in their negotiations with U.S. and European pharmaceutical firms. Some African health officials discovered that the corporate donations to African AIDS programs came with restrictions on how the grant money could be used, which severely limited their fight against the fatal virus. Edward Baralengwa, founder of an AIDS counseling center in Botswana, complained when he was ordered to spend $1,500 to purchase a locked file cabinet for storage of grant-related documents. "I told them that . . . if I had $1,500, I'd pay my phone bill, not buy a file cabinet."

It became clear that the good intentions of the world's largest pharmaceutical companies needed to be linked with the culture and practices of the African health programs seeking to combat Africa's AIDS epidemic. After months of protracted negotiations, Pfizer decided to simply give away $50 million of its expensive AIDS medicine, Diflucan, to the South African government. Boehringer Ingelheim provided Nevirapine, another anti-AIDS drug, free to the Republic of Congo to help prevent the transmission of the virus from pregnant mothers to their babies. Glaxo Wellcome agreed to provide two AIDS drugs to Senegal at a tenth of their original price. Other pharmaceutical companies followed these trends to provide their AIDS drugs free or at a minimal price to those Africans in need.[1]

Why did the manufacturers of the anti-AIDS drugs find it so difficult to implement their expressions of corporate social responsiveness? What helped them become successful with their programs? What changes in the corporate social climate might have triggered new ways of conducting business in a socially responsive manner?

The Corporate Social Climate

Decades of challenges by corporate stakeholders seeking social control of business, most evident during the 1960s and 1970s in the United States, created a corporate social environment filled with

---

[1] Michael Waldholz, "Makers of AIDS Drugs Agree to Slash Prices for Developing World," *Wall Street Journal,* May 11, 2000, pp. A1, A12; Michael Waldholz, "Bristol-Myers Finds Pledging AIDS Aid Is Easier than Giving It," *Wall Street Journal,* July 7, 2000, pp. A1, A6; and Rachel Zimmerman, "Pfizer Offers AIDS Drug to South Africa," *Wall Street Journal,* November 29, 2000, pp. A3, A8.

opportunities for socially responsive strategies. Challenges by corporate stakeholders came from many diverse groups.

- Consumer advocates, spearheaded by Ralph Nader's fight against the U.S. automobile industry for safer vehicles, demanded safe products, accurate information, and competitive pricing of products.

- Environmentalists held the first Earth Days in the 1970s, calling for businesses to be accountable for air and water quality.

- Anti–Vietnam War activists demanded that businesses participating in what they termed the military-industrial complex abandon conventional and chemical weapons production and convert to the manufacture of peacetime goods.

- African-American groups, organized during the civil rights movement, pressed for an end to discriminatory practices in the hiring, promotion, and training of employees.

- Women's groups accused businesses of gender bias and discrimination.

- Workers, of all races and both genders, pushed for safer working conditions.

- Communities protested both the use and transportation of toxic materials by businesses and the construction and operation of nuclear energy plants.

These and other corporate stakeholders dramatically altered the business environment within which managers attempted to perform their tasks. Most of the groups mentioned will be discussed in greater detail in the following chapters of the book. The overall contribution of these groups to the collective social movements demanded a different response from businesses in addition to those embodied in the notions of corporate social responsibility. Firms were now required to develop a sense of corporate social responsiveness.

As discussed in the previous chapter, corporate social responsibility is based on the principles of charity and stewardship. Expressions of these concepts are seen in corporate philanthropy and the care of the public's resources. However, the basis for corporate social responsiveness does not rely on the generosity of a firm's senior management or their awareness of their role as trustees of the public's interests. **Corporate social responsiveness** is seen in the processes a firm establishes to address social demands initiated by corporate stakeholders or in the social actions taken by the firm that affect its stakeholders. The contrast between corporate social responsibility and what has been labeled corporate social responsiveness is highlighted in Figure 4-1.

More recently, the term *corporate citizenship* has been used to refer to businesses acting responsibly toward their stakeholders. **Corporate citizenship,** also discussed in chapters 16 and 20, involves proactively addressing business and society issues, building stakeholder partnerships, discovering business opportunities through social strategic goals, and transforming a concern for financial performance into a vision of corporate financial and social performance.[2] Principles of corporate citizenship are shown in Exhibit 4-A.

---

[2] See Barbara W. Altman and Deborah Vidaver-Cohen, "A Framework for Understanding Corporate Citizenship," *Business and Society Review,* Spring 2000, pp. 1–7. Also see *Journal of Corporate Citizenship* for additional articles on this topic.

EXHIBIT
4-A

Principles of Corporate Citizenship

Good corporate citizens strive to conduct all business dealings in an ethical manner, make a concerned effort to balance the needs of all stakeholders, while working to protect the environment. The Principles of Corporate Citizenship include:

Ethical Business Behavior

1. Engages in fair and honest business practices in its relationship with stakeholders.
2. Sets high standards of behavior for all employees.
3. Exercises ethical oversight of the executive and board levels.

Stakeholder Commitment

4. Strives to manage the company for the benefit of all stakeholders.
5. Initiates and engages in genuine dialogue with stakeholders.
6. Values and implements dialogue.

Community

7. Fosters a reciprocal relationship between the corporation and community.
8. Invests in the communities in which corporation operates.

Consumers

9. Respects the rights of consumers.
10. Offers quality products and services.
11. Provides information that is truthful and useful.

Employees

12. Provides a family-friendly work environment.
13. Engages in responsible human-resource management.
14. Provides an equitable reward and wage system for employees.
15. Engages in open and flexible communication with employees.
16. Invests in employee development.

Investors

17. Strives for a competitive return on investment.

Suppliers

18. Engages in fair trading practices with suppliers.

Environment Commitment

19. Demonstrates a commitment to the environment.
20. Demonstrates a commitment to sustainable development.

Source: The "Social Auditing Teaching Packet," Kim Davenport, 1999.

Figure 4-1

Contrast between corporate social responsibility, corporate social responsiveness and corporate citizenship.

	Corporate Social Responsibility	Corporate Social Responsiveness	Corporate Citizenship
Origin	1920s	1960s	1990s
Basis	Principles of charity and stewardship	Demands made by numerous social stakeholder groups	Building collaborative partnerships with stakeholder groups
Focus	Moral obligations to society at large	Practical responses by businesses to corporate stakeholders	Discovering business opportunities through partnerships
Action	Philanthropy, trustee of the public's interests	Social programs	Managing corporate social and financial performance

Central to the practice of corporate citizenship are **collaborative partnerships,** where businesses join together and with their key stakeholders (government agencies, community or special interest groups, schools, etc.) to respond to the complex social problems.

> *Haunted by a persistently high crime rate, Minneapolis acquired the unfortunate nickname "Murderopolis." In response, several local companies, including Honeywell, General Mills, and Allina Health Systems, came together to form Minnesota HEALS (Hope, Education, Law, and Safety). Besides working on various community issues, the firms also addressed employee recruitment and retention concerns.*[3]

Implementing Social Responsiveness

Companies do not become socially responsive overnight. The process takes time. New attitudes have to be developed, new routines learned, and new policies and action programs designed. Once a company is prepared to implement a social strategy, it must follow specific guidelines to achieve its social objectives. Many obstacles must be overcome in implementing socially responsive strategies. Some are structural, such as the reporting relationships between groups of managers; others are cultural, such as a historical pattern of only men or women in a particular job category.

A Model of Corporate Social Responsiveness

An early model of how large corporations effectively implement socially responsive policies is illustrated in Figure 4-2. There are three stages to the responsiveness process depicted in this model. Each is discussed below.

---

[3] Other partnership examples can be found in Bradley K. Googins and Steven A. Rochlin, "Creating the Partnership Society: Understanding the Rhetoric and Reality of Cross-sector Partnerships," *Business and Society Review,* Spring 2000, pp. 127–44, especially Table 1, p. 134.

Figure 4-2

A three-stage model of corporate social responsiveness.

Source: Adapted from Robert W. Ackerman and Raymond A. Bauer, *Corporate Social Responsiveness: The Modern Dilemma* (Reston, VA: Reston, 1976).

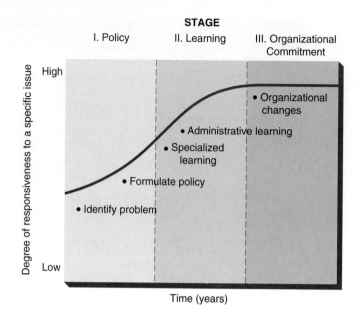

The Policy Stage

In the first stage of social responsiveness, the company becomes aware of those parts of the surrounding environment to which it needs to respond and act on. Awareness may occur after stakeholder expectations change, as repeatedly seen in the changing social climate in the 1960s and 1970s. Whether or not stakeholder pressure exists, a company's management may think, based on sensitivity to the corporate social environment, that it should respond to emerging issues, concerns, or social trends.

> *Lucent Technologies placed a high priority on a diverse, global workforce and the importance of technology-based education. To this end, the company, through the Lucent Technologies Foundation, contributed about $32 million annually to help young people around the world to realize their potential. The foundation supported such programs as Project GRAD (Graduation Really Achieves Dreams), which aimed to raise student achievement in reading, writing, and math in the Newark, New Jersey, school system, increasing the number of high school and college graduates. Outreach grants for colleges and universities seeking to improve kindergarten through twelfth grade education, identifying best practices for teacher development through peer mentoring relationships, and Lucent Links, creating opportunities for young people of diverse backgrounds to work together, were all supported by Lucent Technologies Foundation.*[4]

A company's social responses need to be guided by policies that are carefully and deliberately developed by its top management and board of directors. Those policies

[4] See Lucent Technologies *Annual Report* at www.lucent.com/news/pubs/annual.

provide a framework for shaping other aspects of the organization's response. New production policies, for example, may result in better quality control for consumer products,
may remove job hazards, and may reduce water pollution all at the same time.

The Learning Stage

Once it has identified a social problem—for example, illiteracy in the local community—and adopted a general policy, the company must learn how to tackle the problem
and make the new policy work. Two kinds of learning are needed: specialized learning
and administrative learning.

   Specialized learning occurs when a sociotechnical expert—for example, someone
trained in educational reading techniques effective with adults and children—is
employed to advise company officers and managers. The kind of specialized knowledge
that the sociotechnical expert can provide is particularly helpful in the early stages of
social responsiveness when the company is dealing with an unfamiliar social problem,
whether it is community illiteracy, prejudice against minorities in hiring practices, school
violence, or disposal of toxic chemicals.

   Administrative learning occurs when a company's supervisors and managers—
those who administer the organization's daily affairs—become familiar with new routines that are necessary to cope with a social problem. A technical expert can assist the
company in taking its first steps to solve a problem but cannot do the whole job alone.
Social responsiveness requires the full cooperation and knowledge of line managers and
staff experts. Personal involvement is essential.

> *The AT&T Learning Network was a $150 million, five-year program
> designed to assist America's youth in electronic communication. AT&T
> provided three months of free voice-messaging service and free voice mail-
> boxes to thousands of students, who the company saw as potential cus-
> tomers. To fully implement this program, online mentoring was essential.
> The mentoring aspect of the program involved AT&T managers, technical
> experts, and other employees across the corporate organization.*[5]

The Organizational Commitment Stage

A final step is needed to achieve full social responsiveness: An organization must institutionalize its new social policy.[6] The new policies and routines learned in the first two stages
should become so well accepted throughout the entire company that they are considered
to be a normal part of doing business. In other words, they should be a part of the company and its standard operating procedures. For example, when managers respond to the
needs of the local education system or to the students without having to rely on special
directives from top management, the socially responsive policy has been institutionalized.

   The normal organizational pressures to resist change mean that both effort and
time are needed to improve a corporation's responsiveness. In the past, it took large

---

[5] The AT&T Learning Network program is described in Gautan Naik, "AT&T to Give 110,000 Schools Free
Services," *Wall Street Journal,* November 1, 1995, pp. A3, A12.
[6] Robert Ackerman, "How Companies Respond to Social Demands," *Harvard Business Review,* July–August
1973, pp. 88–98.

corporations an average of six to eight years to progress from the first stage to the third stage on any given social issue or problem such as equal employment opportunity or pollution control. Yet some firms are more flexible than others, and some social problems are easier to handle than others, so the time involved may vary considerably. It is clear, however, that a combination of internal factors, especially management willpower, and external factors, especially continued stakeholder action on the problem, is necessary for effective change to occur.

Framework for Social Policy

After reaching the organizational commitment stage, the company must develop specific guidelines to direct the strategic social policy. Two scholars in the strategic management field have created a set of guidelines to enhance the success of a business's social policy.[7] They believe that social policies should:

- *Concentrate action programs on limited objectives.* No company can take significant action in every area of social responsibility. It can achieve more if it selects areas in which to concentrate its efforts. Rowley-Schlimgen, a Wisconsin-based office furniture and supplies retailer, encouraged its employees to volunteer in the local communities in which it operated, and it acknowledged community volunteers at an annual, company-sponsored Real Heroes Awards Dinner. The benefits from the event supported the Badger Chapter of the American Red Cross.

- *Concentrate action programs related to the firm's products or services.* Citibank created the Foundations in Finance program in collaboration with Singapore Management University (SMU). Bank officials volunteered to lecture business students at SMU on finance, banking, and economics based on their real-life experiences. The goals of the program were to produce graduates from SMU that understood the risk-taking strategies needed for Singapore's new emerging economy and support Citibank's investment in Singapore's new global enterprises.[8]

- *Begin action programs close to home.* The program should address local issues or social needs before spreading out or acting in far-distant regions. Rachel's Bus Company, a Chicago-based school transportation company, targeted inner-city Chicago and its economic devastation when developing its social program guidelines. Rachel Hubka, the company's president, located the company headquarters in the inner city and hired qualified applicants from the local community. The company's practices aimed to foster a stronger pride in the inner-city area that the company serves.

- *Facilitate employee action.* Programs in which employees can become involved as individuals rather than as representatives of the company encourage future

---

[7] From Archie B. Carroll and Frank Hoy, "Integrating Corporate Social Policy into Strategic Management," *Journal of Business Strategy,* Winter 1984, pp. 48–57.
[8] Sheila McNulty, "Banking on Experience," in *Responsible Business: A Financial Times Guide,* December 2000, p. 16.

participation and commitment. As part of its ongoing commitment to Habitat for Humanity, Coldwell Banker selected sales employees to travel to various sites to help build homes for deserving families. In 1997, four Coldwell Banker employees were flown to Godollo, Hungary, for the project. In past years, employees assisted Habitat for Humanity in various cites located in the United States.

Becoming a Socially Responsive Firm

How does a firm become more socially responsive? In a classic statement, Robert Miles, American scholar and consultant, observed that:

> *Executive leaders of America's largest corporations have been confronted . . . during the last two decades with an unprecedented increase in the social issues impinging upon their business policies and practices. Not only have a variety of social regulations been developed that apply universally to all industries, but each industry has also experienced to varying degrees a proliferation of industry-specific challenges for the corporate social environment.*[9]

In response to these pressures, businesses have increased their efforts to manage the corporate social environment. The social environment encompasses business activities influenced by various community and government groups. Many chief executives spend more time on the external affairs of the business than any other activity. Most executives allocate significant personnel, time, and budget to the creation of elaborate staff groups to help them understand and manage this environment and its challenges.

Some firms may be more vulnerable to social group pressure and social regulation than others. A number of factors have been identified as contributing to this vulnerability. A firm may be more vulnerable to social forces if the firm is:

- A large-sized or well-known company, thus presenting a big target.
- Located in an urban area and under increased scrutiny by the media and social groups.
- Producing a consumer-oriented product viewed as a necessity by the public.
- Providing a product or service that may cause harm or injury to the user.
- Part of a heavily regulated industry that is expected to meet high public expectations.

Top Management Philosophy

How a firm addresses its exposure to the corporate social environment heavily depends on the values and beliefs of the company managers—the philosophy they hold about the role of the corporation in society. This is called the **top management philosophy.**

---

[9] Robert H. Miles, *Managing the Corporate Social Environment* (Englewood Cliffs, NJ: Prentice Hall, 1987). Miles develops a corporate social strategy similar to the one presented in this chapter.

Managers sensitive to the impact of social forces and seeking to strategically manage their stakeholders will adopt the view that the firm is a social as well as an economic institution. They embrace the view that the firm has a duty to adapt to a changing social environment. In response to emerging social issues, these managers are more likely to modify their business policies and practices than managers who understand their responsibilities to the firm only in an economic context. Managers in socially responsive firms recognize and consider not only the interests of their immediate, core stakeholders but the interests of all of the firm's stakeholders. They see corporate social performance in broad terms extending over the long term and having an impact on their industry. Most important, these managers merge the economic and social goals of their company into the firm's planning, measurement, and reward systems developed to guide and monitor business operations and managers' performance.

> *IBM's Strategy for Corporate Citizenship states, "In our view technology is as valuable in addressing social needs, such as education or job training, as it is in business. And we apply the same careful planning, implementation, and support in the contributions we make as we do with our customers." A similar integration between business and social strategies is found in PaineWebber's Value Statement: "We believe that responsible and involved corporate citizenship is fundamental to the lasting success of the company and the entire community."*

Socially Responsive Strategy

Using a socially responsive top management philosophy as a foundation, a firm must develop a **socially responsive strategy.** This strategic orientation tends to emphasize a collaborative and problem-solving approach, as opposed to one that emphasizes only the firm's interests and is adversarial in nature.

Collaborative, problem-solving strategies are distinguished by their emphasis on maintaining long-term relationships based on trust and open communication with all of the company's stakeholders. Managers demonstrate this collaborative characteristic by participating in regulatory advisory committees and trade associations that seek mutually beneficial compromises. However, these managers are quick to explain that their strategy is not purely altruistic. They acknowledge that maintaining ongoing relationships with their stakeholders and seeking mutually beneficial problem-solving strategies will ensure the company's long-term survival. An example of the importance of collaboration and long-term thinking in a socially responsive strategy was shown at the beginning of this chapter, when the world's largest pharmaceutical manufacturers attempted to address Africa's AIDS epidemic.

Socially Responsive Structure

The next step in becoming a socially responsive organization is to change the organizational structure to be more responsive to external social challenges and better able to implement socially responsive strategies. This **socially responsive structure** evolves from the values and beliefs held by the company's top managers and expressed through socially responsive business strategies.

Nissan North America created a Philanthropic Steering Committee that guided corporate giving to prioritized social areas that included safe driving, youth-oriented programs, values education, science and technology, culture and the arts, and community improvement. Members of the Steering Committee included Nissan's public affairs manager, four division managers, and representatives from the company's legal and human resources departments, which reviewed all requests of more than $10,000. Requests for corporate contributions of less than $10,000 were reviewed and approved by Nissan's public affairs manager.

Line Manager Involvement

The final element in becoming a socially responsive firm is the extent to which line managers are involved in the strategic process. The degree of **line manager involvement** depends on the sophistication of the company's socially responsive strategy process. The more elaborate the process, the more essential is involvement by line managers.

A high degree of line manager involvement often is difficult to achieve. Initially staff units develop the strategic process, but line managers must quickly become involved and assume responsibility for the implementation of the company's socially responsive strategies. For example, if a firm develops a strategy that includes a highly integrated philanthropic contribution and employee volunteerism program with local charities, line managers often are in the best position to screen worthy recipients, determine appropriate levels of contributions, and assign employee volunteers.

For example, Cooper Industries believed in giving cash support where their employees lived, worked, and volunteered. To that end, the local human resource manager or plant manager reviewed and prioritized proposals for contributions targeting their employees' communities at each facility before forwarding the requests to the company's foundation board for approval.

In contrast, corporations that rely on staff personnel and do not foster line manager involvement will tend to exhibit a narrow, defensive, and protective socially responsive posture. This approach will buffer the company's line managers and line operations from corporate social environment influences. The degree of line manager involvement is heavily influenced by top management philosophy and generally is consistent with the socially responsive strategy and structure adopted by the company.

Socially Responsive Management in Practice

Grounded in the two basic principles of corporate social responsibility discussed in Chapter 3—the charity principle and the stewardship principle—socially responsive management and its practice can be found in many facets of modern business operations.

Corporate Philanthropy

Corporate philanthropy is the modern expression of the charity principle. The stewardship principle is given meaning today when corporate managers recognize that business and society are intertwined and interdependent, as explained in Chapter 1. This

**EXHIBIT
4-B**

Significant Philanthropic Contributions

Corporate foundations, individuals, and groups of businesses have demonstrated a clear commitment to social philanthropy, as shown by the following examples:

- Bill Gates, cofounder of Microsoft Corporation, along with his wife, Melinda, pledged $22 billion to the Bill and Melinda Gates Foundation, which finances international vaccination and children's health programs.

- George Soros, investment manager, pledged $2 billion to the Soros Foundations Network supporting children's and public health programs, contemporary artistic and cultural programs, and small-enterprise development.

- Ted Turner, founder of CNN and vice chairman of Time Warner, pledged nearly $1.5 billion to the United Nations Foundation and Turner Foundation to support international children's health and environmental programs.

- James E. Stowers, Jr., founder of American Century, a mutual-fund company, along with his wife, Virginia, pledged $360 million to the Stowers Institute for Medical Research, which supports biomedical research projects.

- Paul Allen, cofounder of Microsoft Corporation, pledged $350 million to the Allen Foundations and the Experience Music Project, a Seattle-based non-profit music museum.

- Jon Huntsman, chairman of the Huntsman Group, a chemical company, pledged $350 million to the University of Utah, the Wharton School of Finance at the University of Pennsylvania, Brigham Young University, and the Huntsman Cancer Institute.

- Patrick J. McGovern, founder of International Data Group, along with his wife, Lore Harp-McGovern, pledged $350 million to the Massachusetts Institute of Technology and the McGovern Institute for Brain Research.

- Martha R. Ingram, chairperson of Ingram Industries, a holding company, pledged $300 million to Vanderbilt University for cancer research, scholarship programs, athletics, and programs for the business and music schools.

Source: Karl Taro Greenfeld, "A New Way of Giving," *Time,* July 24, 2000, pp. 49–59.

mutuality of interests places a responsibility on business to exercise care and social concern in formulating policies and conducting business operations. Some examples of significant philanthropic giving are described in Exhibit 4-B.

Corporate Employee Volunteerism

Corporate employee volunteerism, also discussed in Chapter 16, is a relatively new phenomenon. Many large corporations developed charitable contribution programs but left employee involvement in community service up to the individual. More recently, companies began to see community service as a way to improve their images—internally and externally—as well as to serve the communities in which the business operated. According to the Points of Light Foundation, 56 percent of American adults, an estimated 109 million people, annually volunteered a total of 19.9 billion hours. The volunteer workforce represented more than 9 million full-time employees at a value of $225 billion.

> *BankBoston Corporation (now FleetBoston) used its e-mail system to post volunteer opportunities for its employees, designed by community groups so employees could locate agencies needing volunteers where they lived. Management at Enron, Corp. in Houston saw volunteerism as a benefit to the company by helping with employee recruitment and aiding in team building; and while not a criterion for promotion, one executive commented, "it couldn't hurt." At KPMG Peat Marwick, community service was seen as a key aspect of leadership training.*[10]

Employee volunteerism helps develop characteristics such as creativity, trust, teamwork, and persistence. It builds skills and attitudes that foster commitment, company loyalty, and job satisfaction. Morale is as much as three times higher in companies with volunteer programs. Research has found a positive association between employee involvement in corporate volunteer programs and better physical health, mental health, and social interaction. An example of an employee volunteer program is described in Exhibit 4-C. A study conducted by IBM and the Graduate School of Business at Columbia University showed a clear link between volunteerism and return on assets, return on investment, and employee productivity. A company with a strong community involvement program is likely to score high in profitability and employee morale.

Corporate Awards for Social Responsibility

Recognition of socially responsible behavior by business has increased dramatically. The Council on Economic Priorities (CEP) sponsored one of the first award programs. The CEP is a corporate watchdog organization that reports periodically on the social behavior of large corporations. In 1987, the council began to accentuate the positive by citing companies that had demonstrated an outstanding record of socially responsible behavior. A list of the 2000 CEP award recipients is provided in Exhibit 4-D. In addition, companies have been given dishonorable mentions for a variety of socially irresponsible actions.

The Business Enterprise Trust, founded in 1989 by prominent leaders in business, academia, labor, and the media, recognizes business leaders and other individuals who have significantly advanced the cause of social responsibility through "acts of courage, integrity, and social vision." The Trust's annual awards have been presented to Merck &

---

[10] "Volunteer Programs Are Being Fine-Tuned to Help Corporate Goals," *Wall Street Journal,* December 24, 1998, p. A1. For an electronic clearinghouse for volunteerism and community service, see www.service.org/vv/vonline4.html.

EXHIBIT
4-C

Community Service Improves Employee Job Skills

Helene Curtis, a Chicago-based personal care company, integrated community volunteerism into its management development program. The results benefited both the
employees and the business. "The program gives employees the chance to learn and
apply experiences gained through community service to their personal and professional growth," explained Ann Schwartz, manager of community relations at Helene
Curtis. "Our goal is to help employees identify the skills they want to develop and
then work with them to identify ways and venues in which to practice those skills."

The goals of the program are to formally recognize the value of business skills
gained through community service, transfer practical skills from community work to
business application, provide managers and employees with alternative ways to
develop business skills, provide a low-risk learning experience for both the employees and the corporation, and contribute to the betterment of the organization and
community. Managers at Helene Curtis see employee volunteerism as reinforcing the
values at the firm. As one employee pointed out, "This program is such a natural
fit with the Helene Curtis culture and reflects the values of our CEO."

Source: "Using Community Service Projects to Improve Employee Job Skills," *Issues in Corporate Social Responsibility,* Barnes and Associates publication, Spring 1996, p. 9.

EXHIBIT
4-D

America's Corporate Conscience Awards, 2000

- **Diversity Award**   Denny's Restaurants, "one of the most successfully diverse
  places of work in America," according to the Council on Economic Priorities.
- **Global Ethics Award**   Bristol-Myers Squibb, global pharmaceutical
  manufacturer.
- **Employee Empowerment Award**   Carris Reels, Rutland, Vermont, maker of
  industrial spools that is in the process of becoming an employee-owned
  company.
- **Environmental Stewardship Award**   Collins & Aikman Floorcoverings, Dalton, Georgia; Ricoh Corporation, West Caldwell, New Jersey; and Horizon
  Organic Holding Corporation, Longmont, Colorado.

Source: Wall Street Journal, April 27, 2000, p. A1.

Company for developing a drug to combat river blindness, McKay Nursery Company
for their employee stock ownership plan that included 60 migrant workers hired for eight
months a year, DAKA International—a restaurant and food service business—for
pioneering an aggressive AIDS education program, and Julia Stasch for developing

the Female Employment Initiative to assist women in the pursuit of careers in the construction industry.[11]

> *In a U.S. survey of more than 26,000 people in 2001, companies were acknowledged for having the "best reputations." Corporate reputation included more than being profitable; it involved successfully addressing the demands or expectations coming from the businesses' multiple stakeholders. This term was understood to include businesses that were attractive to customers, employees, or investors. Among the best were Johnson & Johnson, Maytag, Sony, Home Depot, and Intel. Specifically recognized for their "social responsibility reputation" were Home Depot, Johnson & Johnson, Daimler-Chrysler, Anheuser-Busch, and McDonald's.[12]*

Corporate Social Audits

Introduced in 1953, **social auditing** challenges businesses to be socially responsive:

> *Today, a social audit examines the social and ethical impact of the business from two perspectives: from the inside, assessing performance against the company's mission statement of objectives; and from the outside, using comparisons with other organizations' behavior and social norms.[13]*

Recently, the demand for social auditing has gained momentum in Europe as well as in the United States. A British scholar, George Goyder, made the following passionate plea:

> *Has the time come for the country which led the first industrial revolution to lead the industrialized nations a second time, by returning to those mutual aid principles which are also the principles of the natural law? For Britain, time is running out. We need the responsible company now.[14]*

Throughout the 1970s, managers remained unconvinced that financial measures involved in social auditing could be used in business decision making. They believed that social costs and benefits were too removed from the firm's mainstream functions, especially from its profits. As a result, they argued that financial accounting for social impacts was not helpful in the quest for developing socially responsible strategies or in the assessment of such strategies.[15]

In response to this skepticism, researchers have tried to develop a **social performance audit** or corporate ratings approach, such as the 20 principles developed by

---

[11] A thorough analysis of the Business Enterprise Trust program can be found in James O'Toole, "Do Good, Do Well: The Business Enterprise Trust Awards," *California Management Review,* Spring 1991, pp. 9–24.

[12] For a complete listing of the corporations with the best reputations, see Ronald Alsop, "Survey Rates Companies' Reputations, and Many Are Found Wanting," *Wall Street Journal,* February 7, 2001, pp. B1, B6.

[13] Howard R. Bowen, *Social Responsibilities of the Businessman* (New York: Harper, 1953).

[14] George Goyder, *The Just Enterprise—A Blueprint for the Responsible Company* (London: Adamantine Press, 1993). See Rob Gray, "Thirty Years of Social Accounting, Reporting and Auditing: What (If Anything) Have We Learnt?" *Business Ethics: A European Review,* January 2001, pp. 9–15.

[15] This argument was originally presented in William C. Frederick, "Auditing Corporate Social Performance: The Anatomy of a Social Research Project," in Lee E. Preston, ed., *Research in Corporate Social Performance and Policy,* vol. 1, 1978, pp. 123–137. See the special issue of *Business Ethics: A European Review,* January 2001, featuring numerous views on social auditing.

Kim Davenport and listed in Exhibit 4-A. This type of audit involves measuring a firm's corporate activities on an ideal socially responsible scale or comparing the resulting rating of a firm's actions against those of other, similar organizations. For example, if a company supports a tutorial program at a local school, the performance audit might look at not only the number of hours of employee volunteerism but also assess the change in student test scores as an indicator of the program's social impact.

As businesses entered the twenty-first century, interest in social auditing increased significantly. Global attention to corporate performance in the areas of environmental responsibility, employee and customer safety and health, community and regional development, and information privacy triggered concerns that businesses often tried to address and evaluate through a social audit. Social performance audits were used by Shell, BP Amoco, Natwest Group, Camelot, and United Utilities. One such example of a social audit involved the Body Shop.

> *A social audit was commissioned by Body Shop executives to provide an independent assessment of the company's social and ethical achievements. In the report, high marks were given to the Body Shop in areas such as the quality of its mission statement, corporate philanthropy, and environmental and animal welfare. But according to Stanford professor Kirk Hanson, who conducted the audit, the company was weak in accepting outside criticism and had a poor relationship with the public and the media.[16]*

The Mattel Toy Company began a series of social audits to assess its performance worldwide. As part of a continuing company commitment to monitor its manufacturing facilities worldwide, Mattel formed the Mattel Independent Monitoring Council (MIMCO), consisting of representatives from academia and nonprofit organizations. MIMCO audits investigated Mattel operations in Mexico and Asia concerning the company's working conditions, onsite medical facilities, worker training, wages, and overtime hours. MIMCO member Dr. Murray L. Weidenbaum, economist, international trade expert, and critic of social responsive programs, said "the new MIMCO audit . . . illustrates the opportunities that U.S. companies doing business in developing countries can utilize in enhancing local wages and working conditions."[17]

Audit Standards

Standards to judge corporate performance were developed by a number of other organizations. These included the Coalition for Environmentally Responsible Companies' (CERES) Global Reporting Initiative, the International Organization for Standardization's (ISO) 14001 standard, and the Institute of Social and Ethical Accountability's (ISEA) AccountAbility, or AA 1000. The major characteristics of these audit standards are summarized in Figure 4-3.

---

[16] See Kim Davenport, "Social Auditing: The Quest for Corporate Social Responsibility," in James Weber and Kathleen Rehbein, eds., *IABS 1997 Proceedings 8th Annual Conference,* pp. 196–201.
[17] *AOL News,* PRNewswire, May 25, 2000.

Figure 4-3

Summary of audit standard characteristics.

Sources: Global Reporting Initiative, www.globalreporting. org; ISO14001, www.iso14000.org; and AA 1000, www.accountability. org.uk.

	CERES Global Reporting Initiative	ISO 14001	ISEA AA 1000
Origin	1997	1996	1999
Focus	Link economic, environmental, and social sustainability	Support environmental protection in balance with socioeconomic needs	Quality social and ethical accounting, auditing, and reporting
Self-reported benefits	1. Internal vehicle for evaluating policy versus performance 2. Structure for effective dialogue with stakeholders 3. Framework for sharing and promoting dialogue with stakeholders	1. Identify areas for energy reduction 2. Reduce environmental risk 3. Maintain compliance with legislation and regulation 4. Receive environmental leadership rewards 5. Prevent pollution and reduce waste 6. Improve stakeholder relations 7. Receive more favorable insurance rates 8. Gain a competitive advantage	1. Support effective stakeholder relations 2. Effective in diverse global operations 3. Build synergy with emerging businesses 4. Link planning tools to quality models 5. Build accountability in public sector 6. Enhance overall performance

These audit standards are in their infancy, and the sponsoring organizations have pledged their commitment toward continuous improvement of the standards. While the ISEA AA 1000 emphasizes a more general social and ethical audit standard and is attractive to service-based organizations, the CERES Global Reporting Initiative and the ISO 14001 heavily target environmental responsibility in balance with the organization's social and economic obligations. All three standards promote a combination of internally focused economic benefits for the firm, as well as externally focused social benefits for the environment and key stakeholders.

Companies committed to socially responsive practices have used these and other standards and have made their reports available online for their stakeholders and the general public. *Online Corporate Disclosure* reported that "there are so many online reports now, it's becoming difficult to keep up with it all. Rather . . . only listed here [are] some unusually 'good' examples . . . for UK companies and European companies."[18] These examples included online reports from Reebok, British Telecom, British Airways, Traidcraft plc, Norsk Hydro, Volvo, and Daimler-Benz. A discussion case of a corporate social audit and report is provided at the end of this chapter, featuring Vancouver City Savings Credit Union.

---

[18] From www.dundee.ac.uk/accountancy/csear/corporat.html.

Summary Points of This Chapter

- In response to the numerous social challenges facing businesses, managers have recognized the need to develop formal social response strategies and programs and aggressively address the notion of corporate citizenship.
- The model of social responsiveness includes the policy stage, the learning stage, and the organizational commitment stage.
- A framework for managing the corporate social environment includes four critical elements: top management philosophy, socially responsive strategy, socially responsive structure, and line manager involvement.
- Socially responsive management in practice takes the forms of corporate philanthropy and employee volunteerism.
- Corporate social auditing is used to assess a firm's management of the corporate social environment.

Key Terms and Concepts Used in This Chapter

- Corporate social responsiveness
- Corporate citizenship
- Collaborative partnerships
- Top management philosophy
- Socially responsive strategy

- Socially responsive structure
- Line manager involvement
- Corporate philanthropy
- Social auditing
- Social performance audit

Internet Resources

- www.hbsp.harvard.edu   Business Enterprise Trust teaching material
- www.cepnyc.org   Council for Economic Priorities
- www.bsr.org   Businesses for Social Responsibility
- www.pointsoflight.org   Points of Light Foundation

Discussion Case: *Social Auditing at VanCity*

> *Vancouver City Savings Credit Union is a democratic, ethical and innovative provider of financial services to its members. Through strong financial performance, we serve as a catalyst for the self-reliance and economic well-being of our membership and community.*
>
> VanCity mission statement

On the basis of its mission statement, Vancouver City Savings Credit Union (VanCity) embarked on a strategy of corporate social responsibility that led to the company's conducting a corporate social audit and publishing its "Social Report." The path to social auditing began in 1992, when VanCity created a social accounting section in its annual report. This section provided information on the company and its impact on members, staff, community, and the environment. In 1997, VanCity created the Social Report and turned to two independent organizations as external auditors to monitor and verify its social audit process. The firms felt that this audit process helped achieve VanCity's goal of increasing the "transparency and accountability" of its operations. (The audit process followed the AccountAbility 1000 guidelines, discussed earlier in this chapter.)

VanCity is a member-owned, full-service financial institution headquartered in Vancouver, British Columbia. In 1999, the organization had $6.4 billion in consolidated assets, 261,000 member-owners, and more than 1,700 employees. During the 1990s, VanCity management believed that a social audit would provide the company's managers and stakeholders with information needed to track and set benchmarks for social and environmental performance. In a sense, the Social Report became a barometer to measure how well VanCity was meeting its commitment to corporate responsibility. At VanCity, social responsibility goes beyond donating dollars or volunteering time to worthy causes. For this organization, it is about operating in a way that is responsible to its members and staff, respectful of the environment, and supportive of the communities in which the organization operates.

VanCity is committed to being a leader in social responsibility. Its commitment is found in the following strategic goals:

- Offer business products that are socially and environmentally responsible.

- Invest in the well-being of the communities it serves through grants, scholarships, awards, fund-raising, and community service.

- Adopt business practices that are socially and environmentally responsible.

- Advocate for social and environmental responsibility with the aim of making a positive difference to the individuals and communities around it.

To identify the relevant issues and areas of concern, key organizational stakeholders (defined by VanCity as "all those people or groups that are either affected by or who can affect the activities of the organization") included VanCity members, staff, and various community organizations. In addition, stakeholder information was drawn from past organizational surveys, tracking studies, internal company documents, and interviews with VanCity managers.

The Social Report was structured around various VanCity stakeholders and subsidiaries, including members, staff, credit unions, community, environment, suppliers, business alliances, Citizens Bank of Canada, VanCity Enterprises Ltd., and the VanCity Community Foundation. The Social Report contained both VanCity's strengths and areas of weakness. For example, while more than 80 percent of its members were satisfied with VanCity's service, only 43 percent were "totally satisfied." The business established a target of 50 percent totally satisfied members by 2001.

Highlights from the 1997 and 1998–1999 VanCity Social Report include:

- 64 percent of its board members were female, compared to 30 percent in Canadian credit unions and 14 percent in Canadian banks.

- More than $34 million in loans were made for social housing programs and to nonprofit organizations.
- A Family of Ethical Funds is offered to VanCity members for investment in ethically screened mutual funds; nearly $292 million was invested by 1997.
- The VanCity EnviroFund VISA card was used by 35,000 VanCity members, with 5 percent of the VISA profits invested in local environmental projects.
- 87 percent of VanCity staff members would "recommend VanCity to others as a good place to work."
- On the basis of findings from a risk assessment survey, VanCity revised its no discrimination/no harassment policy assessing workplace issues.
- After identifying that VanCity did not have an overarching ethics policy, it committed to develop and promulgate an ethics policy companywide, identifying for others the company's set of values.
- 4.7 percent of VanCity's pretax earnings were donated to the community, with extensive staff involvement to determining where money is donated to the community.
- Concerns with environmental responsibility led to the commitment to implement an energy-efficient policy, conduct a waste audit, and design an environmental reporting format unique for the financial industry.

Source: For more information, see VanCity's 1997 and 1998–1999 Social Report, available at www.vancity.com/socialreport.

Discussion Questions

1. Do you believe organizations like VanCity are capable of meeting their economic obligations while also addressing a variety of social and environmental issues? Why or why not?
2. How far along on the three-stage model of corporate social responsiveness are VanCity's social audit efforts?
3. Does VanCity address most of the corporate citizenship issues presented in Davenport's 20 principles listed in Exhibit 4-A? Which principles appear to be omitted?

PART THREE

Business and the Ethical Environment

5

Ethical Dilemmas in Business

People who work in business—managers and employees alike—frequently encounter and must deal with on-the-job ethical issues. Learning how to recognize the different kinds of ethical dilemmas and knowing why they occur are important business skills. The costs to business and to society of unethical and illegal behavior are very large. A business firm is more likely to gain public approval and social legitimacy if it adheres to basic ethical principles and society's laws.

This chapter focuses on these key questions and objectives:

- What is ethics? What is business ethics?
- Why should business be ethical?
- Why do ethics problems occur in business?
- What efforts are being made to curtail unethical practices around the world?
- Are ethical behavior and legal behavior the same?

R oger Worsham had just graduated as an accounting major with a business degree and had landed a job with a small regional accounting firm. He, his wife, and their two small children settled in to enjoy small-town life. Roger's employer was experiencing tough competition from large accounting firms that were able to offer more varied services, including management consulting and financial advice. Losing a big client could mean the difference between staying open or closing down one of the local offices.[1]

During one of his first audit assignments of a local savings and loan (S&L) company, Roger uncovered evidence of fraud. Law restricted the S&L at that time to mortgages based on residential property, but it had loaned money to a manufacturing company. To conceal this illegal loan from Roger, someone had removed the file before he began the audit. Roger suspected that the guilty party might have been the S&L president, who, in addition to being the largest owner of the manufacturing firm, was also a very influential lawyer in town.

Roger took the evidence of wrongdoing to his boss, expecting to hear that the accounting firm would include it in the audit report, as required by standard accounting practices. Instead, he was told to put the evidence and all of his notes through a shredder. His boss said, "I will take care of this privately. We simply cannot afford to lose this client." When Roger hesitated, he was told, "You put those papers through the shredder, or I'll guarantee that you'll never get a CPA in Michigan or work in an accounting office in this state for the rest of your life."

Question: If you were Roger, what would you do? If you were Roger's boss, would you have acted differently? What is the ethical thing to do?

Chris Brown and Lee Samson had worked together for 15 years for Runner Manufacturing, primarily as system analysts. They designed, tested, and brought to operational status software that automated all functions of business management. While working at Runner's corporate headquarters, Chris and Lee collaborated on many projects and developed a close friendship. They often discussed how they felt that they had reached the upper limit of their career growth at Runner.

It was Lee who first brought up the subject of "going off on their own." At first, it was only a dream. Then Chris and Lee began to recognize that they did indeed have the skills for a start-up information technology consulting business for small and medium-sized firms. They decided to follow their dream and resign from the firm as soon as they had acquired the necessary hardware and software.

The new venture required the partners to convert space in Lee's home into an office for their computer equipment. While inspecting new file servers (data storage equipment), Chris was surprised to find the latest, most sophisticated software already loaded onto their systems at the home office. Closer scrutiny proved the software was similar to what Runner had recently purchased for use at the corporate headquarters. When questioned by Chris, Lee hedged at first but finally admitted to systematically copying Runner's systems since they would be essential for their new business. Copying was a simple procedure, since the new office was linked to Runner's corporate mainframe. Lee assured

---

[1] For more details about this episode, see LaRue Tone Hosmer, *The Ethics of Management,* 3d ed. (Homewood, IL: Irwin, 1991), pp. 164–68.

Chris that great care had been taken to avoid copying any actual data, as this would have been theft of company proprietary information and a violation of Runner's code of ethics.

Seeing Chris's dismay at the explanation, Lee said: "Look, Chris, we've worked our tails off for 15 years at Runner making these systems work for other firms. If anyone owns these systems and the right to their use, it's you and me. Runner loses nothing in this, no product or customer data, absolutely nothing."

Question: If you were Lee, what would you do? Do Chris and Lee really own the software systems? Was it ethical for Lee to copy the software for their new business?

Ethical puzzles like this occur frequently in business. They are troubling to the people involved. Sometimes, a person's most basic ideas of fairness, honesty, and integrity are at stake. This chapter explores the meaning of ethics, identifies the different types of ethical problems that occur in business, and tells why these dilemmas arise. A discussion of corporate crime illustrates the relationship of law and ethics. Chapter 6 then tells how ethical performance in business can be improved by providing some tools for grappling with on-the-job ethical dilemmas.

The Meaning of Ethics

Ethics is a conception of right and wrong conduct. It tells us whether our behavior is moral or immoral and deals with fundamental human relationships—how we think and behave toward others and how we want them to think and behave toward us. **Ethical principles** are guides to moral behavior. For example, in most societies lying, stealing, deceiving, and harming others are considered to be unethical and immoral. Honesty, keeping promises, helping others, and respecting the rights of others are considered to be ethically and morally desirable behavior. Such basic rules of behavior are essential for the preservation and continuation of organized life everywhere.

These notions of right and wrong come from many sources. Religious beliefs are a major source of ethical guidance for many. The family institution—whether two parents, a single parent, or a large family with brothers and sisters, grandparents, aunts, cousins, and other kin—imparts a sense of right and wrong to children as they grow up. Schools and schoolteachers, neighbors and neighborhoods, friends, admired role models, ethnic groups—and of course, the ever-present electronic media—influence what we believe to be right and wrong in life. The totality of these learning experiences creates in each person a concept of ethics, morality, and socially acceptable behavior. This core of ethical beliefs then acts as a moral compass that helps to guide a person when ethical puzzles arise.

Ethical ideas are present in all societies, organizations, and individual persons, although they may vary greatly from one to another. Your ethics may not be the same as your neighbor's; one particular religion's notion of morality may not be identical to another's; or what is considered ethical in one society may be forbidden in another society. These differences raise the important and controversial issue of **ethical relativism,** which holds that ethical principles should be defined by various periods of time in history, a society's traditions, the special circumstances of the moment, or personal opinion. In this view, the meaning given to ethics would be relative to time, place, circumstance, and the person involved. In that case, there would be no universal ethical standards on which people around the globe could agree. For companies conducting business in several societies at one time, whether or not ethics is relevant can be vitally important, and we discuss those issues in more detail later in this chapter.

For the moment, however, we can say that in spite of the diverse systems of ethics that exist within our own society and throughout the world, all people everywhere do depend on ethical systems to tell them whether their actions are right or wrong, moral or immoral, approved or disapproved. Ethics, in this sense, is a universal human trait, found everywhere.

What Is Business Ethics?

Business ethics is the application of general ethical ideas to business behavior. Business ethics is not a special set of ethical ideas different from ethics in general and applicable only to business. If dishonesty is considered to be unethical and immoral, then anyone in business who is dishonest with its stakeholders—employees, customers, stockholders, or competitors—is acting unethically and immorally. If protecting others from harm is considered to be ethical, then a company that recalls a dangerously defective product is acting in an ethical way. To be considered ethical, business must draw its ideas about what is proper behavior from the same sources as everyone else. Business should not try to make up its own definitions of what is right and wrong. Employees and managers may believe at times that they are permitted or even encouraged to apply special or weaker ethical rules to business situations, but society does not condone or permit such an exception. Evidence of unethical behavior at work is shown in Figure 5-1.

Why Should Business Be Ethical?

Why should business be ethical? What prevents a business firm from piling up as many profits as it can, in any way it can, regardless of ethical considerations? For example, what is wrong with Roger Worsham's boss telling him to destroy evidence of a client's

Figure 5-1

Observations of unethical behavior at work.

Source: 2000 Organizational Integrity Survey: A Summary, Integrity Management Services, KPMG LLP.

Percentage of type of observed misconduct	
Unsafe working conditions	56%
Deceptive sales practices	56%
Mishandling proprietary or confidential information	50%
Violations of privacy rights	38%
Shipping low-quality or unsafe products	37%
Employment discrimination	36%
Sexual harassment	34%
Altering product quality or safety test results	32%
Antitrust violations or unfair competitive practices	32%
Environmental breaches	31%

Figure 5-2

Why should business
be ethical?

- Fulfill public expectation for business.
- Prevent harming others.
- Improve business relations and employee productivity.
- Reduce penalties under the U.S. Corporate Sentencing Guidelines.
- Protect business from others.
- Protect employees from their employers.
- Promote personal morality.

fraudulent conduct? Why not just shred the papers, thereby keeping a good customer happy (and saving Roger's job, too)? Or why shouldn't Chris look the other way when Lee acquired the needed software from their soon-to-be former employer? Figure 5-2 lists the major reasons business firms should promote a high level of ethical behavior.

We mentioned one reason when discussing social responsibility in Chapter 3. Corporate stakeholders, described in Chapter 1, expect business to exhibit high levels of ethical performance and social responsibility. Companies and employees that fail to fulfill this public demand can expect to be spotlighted, criticized, curbed, and punished.

> *For example, Prudential Insurance Company of America was ordered to pay out over $1 billion to more than a quarter of a million policyholders in retribution for past deceptive sales practices. Many policyholders received a full refund on their policy with interest or a paid-in-full policy. Prudential was accused of misleading customers during the 1980s and 1990s about what they were buying or how long they would have to pay premiums on a policy.*

> *Yasuo Hamanaka, a Sumitomo Corporation trader, cost his firm $2.6 billion in losses through illicit copper deals. The courts found that Hamanaka forged documents to hide massive losses and had a secret Swiss bank account in which he received millions of dollars for helping third-party dealers benefit from copper trades. Hamanaka was sentenced to eight years in prison for fraud and forgery.[2]*

A second reason businesses and their employees should act ethically is to prevent harm to the general public and the corporation's many stakeholders. One of the strongest ethical principles is stated very simply: Do no harm. A company that is careless in disposing of toxic chemical wastes that cause disease and death is breaking this ethical injunction. Many ethical rules operate to protect society against various types of harm, and businesses are expected to observe these commonsensical ethical principles.

Some people argue that another reason for businesses to be ethical is that it pays. A study conducted by a DePaul University accounting professor found "a statistically

---

[2] Deborah Lohse, "Prudential Has Paid Out over $1 Billion to Policyholders So Far in Class Action," *Wall Street Journal,* June 7, 1999, p. B14; and Norihiko Shirouzu, "Former Sumitomo Trader Sentenced to Eight Years for Fraud and Forgery," *Wall Street Journal,* March 26, 1998, p. A16.

significant linkage between a management commitment to strong controls that emphasize ethical and socially responsible behavior on one hand and favorable corporate financial performance on the other." Further support for the relationship between being ethical and being profitable was found in a study conducted by Rutgers University. Researchers found that investors in firms that fostered an ethical work environment realized an annual shareholder rate of return that was about 45 percent higher than firms that ignored ethics.[3]

Being ethical imparts a sense of trust, which promotes positive alliances among business partners. If this trust is broken, the unethical party may be shunned and ignored. This situation occurred when Malaysian government officials gave the cold shoulder to executives of a French company. When asked why they were being unfriendly, a Malaysian dignitary replied, "Your chairman is in jail!" The nurturing of an ethical environment and the development of ethical safeguards, discussed in the next chapter, can be critical incentives for improving business relations and employee and organizational productivity.

The **U.S. Corporate Sentencing Guidelines** provide a strong incentive for businesses to promote ethics at work.[4] The sentencing guidelines come into play when an employee of a firm has been found guilty of a criminal wrongdoing. To determine sentencing, a federal judge computes a culpability (degree of blame) score using the equations contained in the guidelines. The score is significantly reduced if a firm's ethics program monitors and aggressively responds to reported criminal violations at work. Under the sentencing guidelines, corporate executives found guilty of criminal activity could receive lighter penalties if their firm has developed a strong ethics program.

> *The impact of the Sentencing Guidelines was felt by Hoffman-LaRoche. The multinational pharmaceutical company pled guilty to a price-fixing conspiracy in the vitamins market that spanned nine years and was fined $500 million in May 1999. Although this represented the largest criminal fine in the history of American law to date, the government noted that the Sentencing Guidelines permitted a fine as high as $1.3 billion against Hoffman-LaRoche. The sentence was reduced because Hoffman-LaRoche had an ethics program in place.*

Another reason for promoting ethical behavior is to protect business firms from abuse by unethical employees and unethical competitors. Security experts estimate that employee pilferage (stealing) has caused more businesses to go into bankruptcy than any other crime. Stealing by employees accounts for $15 to $25 billion in business losses per year. The average theft per employee is estimated at over $1,000 per incident, five times the average cost of a shoplifting incident. A study by the U.S. Department of

---

[3] Curtis C. Verschoor, "A Study of the Link between a Corporation's Financial Performance and Its Commitment to Ethics," *Journal of Business Ethics* 17 (1998), pp. 1509–16; and Dale Kurschner, "Five Ways Ethical Busine$$ Creates Fatter Profit$," *Business Ethics,* March–April 1996, pp. 20–23.

[4] For a thorough discussion of the U.S. Corporate Sentencing Guidelines, see Dan R. Dalton, Michael B. Metzger, and John W. Hill, "The 'New' U.S. Sentencing Commission Guidelines: A Wake-Up Call for Corporate America," *Academy of Management Executive* 8 (1994), pp. 7–13; and Dove Izraeli and Mark S. Schwartz, "What Can We Learn from the U.S. Federal Sentencing Guidelines for Organizational Ethics?" *Journal of Business Ethics,* 1998, pp. 1045–55.

Commerce showed that employee theft in manufacturing plants alone amounted to $8 million a day nationwide.[5] Since detection of employee stealing is often difficult, storeowners admit that they are often at the mercy of employees to act honestly.

> *A startling example of employee theft was discovered involving an MCI Communications employee. U.S. Secret Service agents arrested the employee after it was alleged that he stole more than 60,000 telephone-card numbers, which were sold on the international black market. The four major telephone carriers lost more than $50 million in revenues.*[6]

High ethical performance also protects people who work in business. Employees resent invasions of privacy (such as obtrusive video surveillance in workplace restrooms) or being ordered to do something against their personal convictions (such as falsifying an accounting report) or being forced to work in hazardous conditions (such as entering unventilated coal mines or being exposed to dangerous agricultural pesticides in the fields). Businesses that treat their employees with dignity and integrity reap many rewards in the form of high morale and improved productivity. It is a win-win-win situation for the firm, its employees, and society. The ethical obligations of employers to their employees are further discussed in Chapter 17.

A final reason for promoting ethics in business is a personal one. Most people want to act in ways that are consistent with their own sense of right and wrong. Being pressured to contradict their personal values creates much emotional stress. Knowing that one works in a supportive ethical climate contributes to one's sense of psychological security. According to an Ethics Resource Center report, 79 percent of employees said that "their organization's concern for ethics and doing the right thing" was an important reason why they continued to work there.[7]

Business Ethics across Organizational Functions

Not all ethics issues in business are the same. Because business operations are highly specialized, ethics issues can appear in any of the major functional areas of a business firm. **Functional-area ethics** tends to have its own particular brand of ethical dilemmas, as discussed next.

Accounting Ethics

The accounting function is a critically important component of every business firm. Company managers, external investors, government regulators, tax collectors, and labor unions rely on accounting data to make key decisions. Honesty, integrity, and accuracy are absolute requirements of the accounting function. No other single issue is of greater

---

[5] National Food Service Security Council report, www.assessments.ncs.com; and www.napa.ufl.edu/98news/theft98.htm.

[6] "MCI Worker Charged in U.S. Investigation of Phone-Card Fraud," *Wall Street Journal,* October 4, 1994, p. B7.

[7] Joshua Joseph, *2000 National Business Ethics Survey Volume I: How Employees Perceive Ethics at Work* (Washington, DC: Ethics Resource Center, 2000), p. 39.

concern to accountants in industry and public accountancy than ethics, as evident in this response to violations of accounting ethics.

> *In 2000, the Securities and Exchange Commission notified dozens of PricewaterhouseCoopers's clients that it had discovered thousands of violations by the accounting firm of the SEC's auditor-independence rules. These rules stipulate that audit-firm partners or their relatives (such as spouses, dependent children, or grandparents among others) cannot own investments in audit clients. PricewaterhouseCoopers auditors or their relatives, the SEC discovered, owned investments in two-thirds of the corporate audit clients, at the same time they were directly providing services to the companies. Based on the firm's pledge to improve its internal systems to avoid potential conflicts of interest, the SEC provided amnesty for these violations.*[8]

Professional accounting organizations—such as the American Institute of Certified Public Accountants and the Financial Accounting Standards Board—have developed generally accepted accounting principles whose purpose is to establish uniform standards for reporting accounting and auditing data. In 1993, the American Institute for Certified Public Accountants (AICPA) dramatically changed its professional code by requiring CPAs to act as whistle-blowers when detecting "materially misstated" financial statements or face losing their license to practice accounting.

Roger, the accountant facing the ethical dilemma at the beginning of this chapter, is required to report the discovered accounting irregularity, according to the AICPA Code of Professional Conduct. Examples of this profession's efforts toward promoting ethics are shown in Exhibit 5-A. Spurred by the increasing threat of liability suits filed against accounting firms and the desire to reaffirm professional integrity, these standards go far toward ensuring a high level of honest and ethical accounting behavior.[9]

Financial Ethics

Finance has produced some of the most spectacular ethics scandals of recent times. Wall Street financiers have been found guilty of insider trading, illegal stock transactions, and various other financial abuses. Examples of ethical abuses within the financial community follow.

> *In the late 1990s, the Securities and Exchange Commission launched investigations into the practices of two of the three largest stock exchanges in the United States. The New York Stock Exchange received numerous federal indictments regarding alleged improper trading by floor brokers. NASDAQ also was punished for a microcap scandal, and accusations were made regarding an alleged conspiracy to fix prices. An investigation conducted by*

---

[8] Elizabeth MacDonald, "Accountant Faces Salvo from SEC," *Wall Street Journal*, February 28, 2000, pp. A3, A8; and Michael Schroeder, "SEC, Accounting Firms Reach Pact on Conflicts," *Wall Street Journal*, June 8, 2000, pp. A2, A8.

[9] For several excellent examples of ethical dilemmas in accounting, see Leonard J. Brooks, *Business and Professional Ethics for Accountants,* 2d ed. (Cincinnati: South-Western College Publishing, 2000).

EXHIBIT
5-A

Professional Codes of Conduct in Accounting and Finance

American Institute of Certified Public Accountants (AICPA)

Code of Professional Conduct

These Principles of the Code of Professional Conduct of the American Institute of Certified Public Accountants express the profession's recognition of its responsibilities to the public, to clients, and to colleagues. They guide members in the performance of their professional responsibilities and express the basic tenets of ethical and professional conduct. The Principles call for an unswerving commitment to honorable behavior, even at the sacrifice of personal advantage. . . .

- Responsibilities—In carrying out their responsibilities as professionals, members should exercise sensitive professional and moral judgments in all their activities. . . .
- The Public Interest—Members should accept the obligation to act in a way that will serve the public interest, honor the public interest, and demonstrate commitment to professionalism. . . .
- Integrity—To maintain and broaden public confidence, members should perform all professional responsibilities with the highest sense of integrity. . . .
- Objectivity and Independence—A member should maintain objectivity and be free of conflicts of interest in discharging professional responsibilities. A member in public practice should be independent in fact and appearance when providing auditing and other attestation services. . . .
- Due Care—A member should observe the profession's technical and ethical standards, strive continually to improve competence and the quality of services, and discharge professional responsibility to the best of the member's ability. . . .
- Scope and Nature of Services—A member in public practice should observe the Principles of the Code of Professional Conduct in determining the scope and nature of services to be provided.

Source: Reprinted with permission from the AICPA Code of Professional Conduct, copyright 1997 by the American Institute of Certified Public Accountants, Inc. For a full text of the professional code for American Certified Public Accountants, see www.aicpa.org.

Association for Investment Management and Research (AIMR)®

Code of Ethics and Standards of Professional Conduct

Members of the Association for Investment Management and Research shall:

1. Act with integrity, competence, dignity, and in an ethical manner when dealing with the public, clients, prospects, employers, employees, and fellow members.
2. Practice and encourage others to practice in a professional and ethical manner that will reflect credit on members and their profession.

Exhibit 5-A continued

3. Strive to maintain and improve their competence and the competence of others in the profession.

4. Use reasonable care and exercise independent professional judgment.

The Standards of Professional Conduct include:

- Fundamental responsibilities—knowing all applicable laws, rules and regulations.

- Relationships with and responsibilities to a profession—includes not engaging in professional misconduct and prohibition against plagiarism.

- Relationships with and responsibilities to the employer—includes disclosure of conflicts and additional compensation arrangements.

- Relationships with and responsibilities to clients and prospects—includes reasonable representation, independence and objectivity, fair dealings and fiduciary responsibilities, preservation of confidentiality, and disclosure of conflicts and referral fees.

- Relationships with and responsibilities to the public—includes prohibition against the use of nonpublic information and prohibition against misrepresentation of investment performance.

Source: Copyright 1998, Association for Investment Management and Research. Reproduced and republished from *Standards of Practice Handbook* with permission from the Association for Investment Management and Research. All Rights Reserved. For full text, see www.aimr.org/ethics. The Association for Investment Management and Research does not endorse, promote, review, or warrant the accuracy of the products or services offered by the authors of this book.

Business Week magazine reported that the American Stock Exchange (AMEX) exhibited similar problems with self-governance of its brokers. Accusations of alleged price-fixing, illegal trading, and inadequate punishment by the AMEX when discovering wrongdoing were at the core of the investigation's report.[10]

These lapses in ethical conduct were evident despite efforts by the finance professions to foster an ethical environment, as shown in Exhibit 5-A.

Marketing Ethics

Relations with customers tend to generate many ethical problems. Pricing, promotions, advertising, product information, relations between advertising agencies and their clients, marketing research—all of these are potential problem areas. Some marketing ethics

---

[10] Gary Weiss, "Scandal on Wall Street," *Business Week,* April 26, 1999, pp. 96–98. For several good examples of other financial ethics issues, see Larry Alan Bear and Rita Maldonado-Bear, *Free Markets, Finance, Ethics, and Law* (Upper Saddle River, NJ: Prentice Hall, 1994); and John R. Boatright, ed., *Ethics in Finance* (Malden, MA: Blackwell Publishers, 1999).

EXHIBIT
5-B

Professional Codes of Conduct in Marketing and Information Technology

American Marketing Association (AMA)

Code of Ethics

Members of the American Marketing Association (AMA) are committed to ethical professional conduct. They have joined together in subscribing to this Code of Ethics embracing the following topics: . . .

- Responsibilities . . . —Marketers must accept responsibility for the consequences of their activities and make every effort to ensure that their decisions, recommendations, and actions function to identify, serve, and satisfy all relevant publics: customers, organizations, and society. . . .

- Honesty and Fairness—Marketers shall uphold and advance the integrity, honor, and dignity of the marketing profession. . . .

- Rights and Duties of Parties . . . —Participants in the marketing exchange process should be able to expect that: (1) products and services offered are safe and fit for their intended uses; (2) communications about offered products and services are not deceptive; (3) all parties intend to discharge their obligations, financial and otherwise, in good faith; and, (4) appropriate internal methods exist for equitable adjustment and/or redress of grievances concerning purchases. . . .

- Organizational Relationships—Marketers should be aware of how their behavior may influence or impact on the behavior of others in organizational relationships. They should not demand, encourage or apply coercion to obtain unethical behavior in their relationships with others. . . .

Any AMA members found to be in violation of any provision of this Code of Ethics may have his or her Association membership suspended or revoked.

Source: Reprinted with permission from the American Marketing Association's Code of Ethics, published by the American Marketing Association. For a full text of the professional marketing code, see www.ama.org.

Association for Computing Machinery (ACM)

Code of Ethics and Professional Conduct

Preamble. Commitment to ethical professional conduct is expected of every member (voting members, associate members, and student members) of the Association for Computing Machinery (ACM).

This Code, consisting of 24 imperatives formulated as statements of personal responsibility, identifies the elements of such a commitment. It contains many, but not all, issues professionals are likely to face. . . . The code and its supplemented Guidelines are intended to serve as a basis for ethical decision making in the conduct of professional work. Secondarily, they may serve as a basis for judging the merit of a formal complaint pertaining to violation of professional ethical standards.

Exhibit 5-B continued

The general imperatives for ACM members include contribute to society and human well-being, avoid harm to others, be honest and trustworthy, be fair and take action not to discriminate, honor property rights, including copyrights and patents, give proper credit for intellectual property, respect the privacy of others, and honor confidentiality.

Adherence of professionals to a code of ethics is largely a voluntary matter. However, if a member does not follow this code by engaging in gross misconduct, membership in ACM may be terminated.

Source: Courtesy of the Association for Computing Machinery, Inc. A full text of the ACM code of ethics can be found at www.acm.org/constitution/code.

issues affect the public through an organization's advertising practices, which are discussed later in Chapter 19.

To improve the marketing profession, the American Marketing Association (AMA) adopted a code of ethics for its members, as shown in Exhibit 5-B. The AMA code advocates professional conduct guided by ethics, adherence to applicable laws, and honesty and fairness in all marketing activities. The code also recognizes the ethical responsibility of marketing professionals to the consuming public and specifically opposes such unethical practices as misleading product information, false and misleading advertising claims, high-pressure sales tactics, bribery and kickbacks, and unfair and predatory pricing. These code provisions have the potential for helping marketing professionals translate general ethical principles into specific working rules.[11]

Information Technology Ethics

One of the fastest-growing areas of business ethics is in the field of information technology. Exploding in the 1990s and early 2000s were ethical challenges involving invasions of privacy; the collection, storage, and access of personal and business information, especially through e-commerce transactions; confidentiality of electronic mail communication; copyright protection regarding software, music, and intellectual property; and numerous other related issues. As described in the introductory case at the beginning of this chapter, Lee felt that years of employee service justified downloading company software systems for the new business with Chris. Chris, however, was ethically correct in challenging the ownership of this intellectual and physical property, and Lee's actions were equivalent to stealing from Runner Manufacturing.

---

[11] The AMA Code for Market Researchers and a discussion of numerous marketing ethics issues can be found in Gene R. Laczniak and Patrick E. Murphy, *Ethical Marketing Decisions* (Boston: Allyn and Bacon, 1993); and Lawrence B. Chonko, *Ethical Decision Making in Marketing* (Thousand Oaks, CA: SAGE Publications, 1995).

As discussed in later chapters of this book, the explosion of information technology raised serious questions of trust between individuals and businesses. In response to calls by businesspeople and academics for an increase in ethical responsibility in the information technology field, professional organizations have developed or revised professional codes of ethics, as shown in Exhibit 5-B.[12]

Other Functional Areas

Production and maintenance functions, which may seem to be remote from ethics considerations, can be at the center of some ethics storms. Dangerously defective products can injure or kill innocent people, and toxic production processes may threaten the health of workers and the general public. Flawed manufacturing and lack of inspection of aircraft fuse pins, which hold the engines to the wing on Boeing 747 jet airplanes, were suspected in some accidents, endangering the lives of passengers as well as innocent bystanders. Union Carbide's pesticide plant in Bhopal, India, was allegedly not properly maintained, and this failure was believed to be a contributing cause of the tragic leak that killed more than 2,000 people.

Ethics issues also arise in purchasing and supply management departments. Kmart Corporation launched a formal investigation involving many of its real estate purchasing officials after allegations of corruption and bribery. This investigation followed a federal grand jury indictment of a former Kmart real estate executive on taking more than $750,000 in bribes.

These examples make one point crystal clear: All areas of business, all people in business, and all levels of authority in business encounter ethics dilemmas from time to time. Ethics issues are a common thread running through the business world.

Why Ethical Problems Occur in Business

Obviously, ethics problems in business appear in many different forms. Although not common or universal, they occur frequently. Finding out just what is responsible for causing them is one step that can be taken toward minimizing their impact on business operations and on the people affected. Some of the main reasons are summarized in Figure 5-3 and are discussed next.

Personal Gain and Selfish Interest

Personal gain, or even greed, causes some ethics problems. Businesses sometimes employ people whose personal values are less than desirable. They will put their own welfare ahead of all others, regardless of the harm done to other employees, the company, or society.

A manager or an employee who puts his or her own self-interest above all other considerations is called an **ethical egoist.** Self-promotion, a focus on self-interest to the point of selfishness, and greed are traits commonly observed in an ethical egoist. The

---

[12] For further discussion of ethics in information technology, see M. David Ermann, Mary B. Williams, and Michele S. Shauf, *Computers, Ethics, and Society,* 2d ed. (New York: Oxford University Press, 1997); Richard Spinello, *Case Studies in Information and Computer Ethics* (Upper Saddle River, NJ: Prentice Hall, 1997); and the ISWorld Net Professional Ethics web page at www.cityu.edu.hk/is/ethics.

Figure 5-3

Why ethical problems occur in business.

Reason	Nature of Ethical Problem	Typical Approach	Attitude
Personal Gain and Selfish Interest	Selfish interest vs. others' interests	Egoistical mentality	"I want it!"
Competitive Pressures on Profits	Firm's interest vs. others' interests	Bottom–line mentality	"We have to beat the others at all costs!"
Business Goals vs. Personal Values	Boss's interests vs. subordinates' values	Authoritarian mentality	"Do as I say, or else!"
Cross-Cultural Contradictions	Company's interests vs. diverse cultural traditions and values	Ethnocentric mentality	"Foreigners have a funny notion of what's right and wrong"

ethical egoist tends to ignore ethical principles accepted by others, believing that ethical rules are made for others. Altruism—acting for the benefit of others when self-interest is sacrificed—is seen to be sentimental or even irrational. "Looking Out for Number One" is the ethical egoist's motto.[13]

> The world watched the unfolding of the Martin Frankel story in 1999, as the fugitive financier avoided an international manhunt for over four months. The search began when firefighters were called to Frankel's $3 million mansion, finding an abandoned home and a "to do" list with a note that included: "launder money." Regulators alleged that at least $215 million of small-time investors' money was missing rather than invested by Frankel. Some of these funds were found in a Swiss bank account; other funds had been used by Frankel to purchase cars, real estate, gold, and $8 million in diamonds and to finance his efforts to elude prosecution. Finally, in the fall of 1999, Frankel was apprehended and indicted on 36 counts of fraud, money laundering, racketeering, and conspiracy.[14]

Competitive Pressures on Profits

When companies are squeezed by tough competition, they sometimes engage in unethical activities to protect their profits. This may be especially true in companies whose financial performance is already substandard. Research has shown that poor

---

[13] For a compact discussion of ethical egoism, see Tom L. Beauchamp and Norman E. Bowie, *Ethical Theory and Business,* 5th ed. (Upper Saddle River, NJ: Prentice Hall, 1997), pp. 14–19.

[14] Ellen Joan Pollack, Mitchell Pacelle, and Christopher Rhoads, "Frankel's Life on the Lam Ends in Arrest," *Wall Street Journal,* September 7, 1999, pp. C1, C4; and Mitchell Pacelle, "Federal Grand Jury Indicts Frankel on 36 Counts," *Wall Street Journal,* October 8, 1999, pp. A2, A8.

financial performers and companies with lower profits are more prone to commit illegal acts.

However, a precarious financial position is only one reason for illegal and unethical business behavior, because profitable companies also can act contrary to ethical principles. In fact, it may be simply a single-minded drive for profits, regardless of the company's financial condition, that creates a climate for unethical activity.

> *Competition for profits may have been the motivation for two new practices in the telecommunications industry: slamming and cramming.* Slamming *is when a customer is switched to a new telephone company without her or his knowledge or permission. Nearly half of all consumer complaints received by telephone companies in 1999 were about slamming.* Cramming *occurs when customers are billed for services that they did not order. Both practices have become commonplace. One customer in Great Neck, New York, complained, "I'm sick of all the competition. I just want to make a simple phone call and not worry about it."*[15]

Price-fixing is a practice that often occurs when companies vigorously engage in a market with limited growth potential. Besides being illegal, price-fixing is unethical behavior toward customers, who pay higher prices than they would if free competition set the prices. Companies fix prices to avoid fair competition and to protect their profits, as happened in the following cases.

> *The former president of Ucar International, one of the world's largest makers of graphite electrodes, pled guilty to price-fixing, and agreed to serve 17 months in jail and pay a $1.25 million fine. These actions were in addition to the $110 million criminal fine assessed to his company a year earlier for the same charges. Other price-fixing convictions were made against Showa Denko KK of Japan, which paid $29 million in fines for its involvement in the graphite electrode price-fixing scheme, and Chinook Group of Canada, assessed a $5 million fine for fixing prices on bulk vitamins.*[16]

Business Goals versus Personal Values

Ethical conflicts in business sometimes occur when a company pursues goals or uses methods that are unacceptable to some of its employees. Whistle-blowing may be one outcome, if an employee goes public with a complaint after failing to convince the company to correct an alleged abuse. (This employee behavior is also discussed in Chapter 17.) Another recourse for employees caught in these situations is a lawsuit. This option has become less of a financial and professional risk for employees in recent years as a result of various governmental protection acts.

---

[15] John J. Keller, "It's Hard Not to Notice Phone-Service Leaves a Lot to Be Desired," *Wall Street Journal,* April 17, 1998, pp. A1, A4.

[16] Gordon Fairclough, "Ucar to Pay Record $110 Million in Federal Probe of Price Fixing," *Wall Street Journal,* April 8, 1998, p. B8; and "Ex-Ucar President Set to Plead Guilty in Price-Fixing Case," *Wall Street Journal,* September 30, 1999, p. A10.

Paul Blanch blew the whistle on his employer, Connecticut's Northeast Utilities. Blanch identified safety lapses in plant operations. Shortly after his complaints, Blanch was subjected to negative job evaluations and harassing internal audits. After Blanch sought government protection, the Nuclear Regulatory Commission imposed a $100,000 fine on Northeast Utilities for its actions against him. Five years later, Blanch was Northeast Utilities' ombudsman—his role was to hear and investigate complaints of corporate wrongdoing on behalf of the company.[17]

This protesting employee was not a troublemaker. He tried to work through internal company procedures to get the problems corrected. The ethical dilemmas arose because the company's goals and methods required the employee to follow orders that he believed would harm himself, other employees, customers, the company, and the general public. As far as Blanch and other whistle-blowers were concerned, they were being asked or ordered to do something unethical. Their own internal ethical compass was at odds with the goals and methods of their company. Another opportunity for a whistle-blower to correct a systemic injustice is seen in the following case.

Ven-A-Care Inc., a small Florida wholesaler, purchased drugs from pharmaceutical manufacturers and sold them to patients in their homes. A Ven-A-Care employee, Zachary Bentley, noticed that his firm paid $10 for a 50-milligram dose of a drug that Medicare reimbursed the drug manufacturer at $56 a dose. After a decade of federal and state investigations and threatening litigation against the drug makers, more than 20 companies engaged in a dialogue with government groups to eliminate these practices, promising to save consumers hundreds of millions of dollars.[18]

Cross-Cultural Contradictions

Some of the knottiest ethical problems occur as corporations do business in other societies where ethical standards differ from those at home. Today, the policymakers and strategic planners in all multinational corporations, regardless of the nation where they are headquartered, face this kind of ethical dilemma. Consider the following situations:

U.S. sleepwear manufacturers discovered that the chemicals used to flameproof children's pajamas might cause cancer if absorbed through the child's skin. When these pajamas were banned from sale in the United States, some manufacturers sold the pajama material to distributors in other nations where there were no legal restrictions against its use.

Question: Although the foreign sales were legal, were they ethical? Is dumping unsafe products ethical if it is not forbidden by the receiving nation?

---

[17] Matthew L. Ward, "Regulator Says Connecticut's Largest Power Company Harassed Worker," *New York Times,* May 5, 1993, p. B6; and Ross Kerber, "Two Pals Whose Work Closed a Nuclear Plant Come to a Bitter Parting," *Wall Street Journal,* March 12, 1998, pp. A1, A10.

[18] David S. Cloud and Laurie McGinley, "How a Whistle-Blower Spurred Pricing Case Involving Drug Makers," *Wall Street Journal,* May 12, 2000, pp. A1, A8.

When Honda began building automobile plants in Ohio, it located them in two mostly white rural areas and then favored job applicants who lived within a 30-mile radius of the plant. This policy excluded African-Americans who lived in Columbus, the nearest big city. Earlier, Honda also had agreed to pay nearly half a million dollars to settle an age-discrimination suit brought by older job applicants who had been refused work there.

Question: Were Honda's job-hiring policies, which would have caused few problems in Japan, unethical in Ohio?

These episodes raise the issue of ethical relativism, which was defined earlier in this chapter. Should ethical principles—the ones that help chart right and wrong conduct—take their meaning strictly from the way each society defines ethics? Are Japanese attitudes toward job opportunities for minorities, older workers, and women as ethically valid as U.S. attitudes? Were the children's pajama makers on solid or shaky ethical ground when they sold the cancer-risky pajama cloth in countries where government officials did not protect children from this possible health risk? Who should assume the ethical responsibility? What or whose ethical standards should be the guide?

As business becomes increasingly global, with more and more corporations penetrating overseas markets where cultures and ethical traditions vary, these questions will occur more frequently. Employees and managers need ethical guidance from clearly stated company policy if they are to avoid the psychological stresses mentioned earlier.

Ethics in a Global Economy

Examples of unethical conduct by business employees are reported from nearly every country. One example of unethical activity is **bribery,** a questionable or unjust payment often to a government official to ensure or facilitate a business transaction. It is found in nearly every sector of the global marketplace.

A Berlin-based watchdog agency, Transparency International, annually publishes a survey that ranks corruption by country according to perceptions of executives and the public. Countries where having to pay a bribe is least likely included Denmark, Finland, New Zealand, Sweden, Canada, and Iceland. At the other end of the index—countries most likely to demand or accept bribes—were Azerbaijan, Indonesia, Nigeria, and Cameroon. Of the world's 19 leading exporters, Sweden received the best ranking from Transparency International, followed by Australia and Canada. At the bottom of this list were Taiwan, South Korea, and China, including Hong Kong. The United States ranked ninth out of 19 leading export countries, with Germany, France, Japan, and Italy ranking lower on the list.[19]

Examples of bribery and corruption in business have been frequently reported. Companies in Eastern Europe, for example, reported that 30 to 60 percent of all business

---

[19] Harry Dunphy, "Bribery Prevalent in Emerging Markets," *Pittsburgh Post-Gazette,* October 27, 1999; for a comprehensive look at the state of ethics around the globe, see "Special Issue: Region- and Country-Related Reports on Business Ethics," *Journal of Business Ethics,* October 1997.

transactions in the region involved paying bribes and these firms paid from 2 to 8 percent of annual revenues in bribes. The average cost of bribery in the former Soviet Union was reported to range from 4 to more than 8 percent of company revenue. Globally, bribery occurred most often in public works contracts and construction, arms and defense industry exchanges, and business dealings in the petroleum and energy industries, according to a Transparency International report.[20]

Executives representing U.S.-based companies are prohibited by the **U.S. Foreign Corrupt Practices Act** (FCPA) from paying bribes to foreign government officials, political parties, or political candidates. To achieve this goal, the FCPA requires U.S. companies with foreign operations to adopt accounting practices that ensure full disclosure of the company's transactions. A 1999 U.S. government study looking at international competition from 1994 to 1998 reported that there were 239 instances where American-based firms were unable to compete for a contract since they were prohibited from offering a bribe. Bribery was a significant influence in securing these international contracts involving more than $108 billion.[21]

> *In 2000, accusations surfaced that several global construction firms had paid bribes in Lesotho, South Africa, in order to win portions of an $8 million water dam project. Tractebel, recently bought out by the French multi-utility Suez Lyonnaise, was investigated by Belgian and Swiss prosecutors for payments totaling 30 million euros (nearly $50 million) to three unnamed executives representing companies in Kazakstan. In another case, allegations were lodged against IBM's Argentinean subsidiary that reportedly paid out $37 million in kickbacks and bribes to land a $250 million computer network contract with the state-run Banco de la Nacion.[22]*

Efforts to Curtail Unethical Practices

Numerous efforts are underway to curb unethical business practices throughout the world. The most common control is through government intervention and regulation. Efforts to address unethical business behavior often begin with national governments, which can enact stiff legislative controls. Examples of these multinational and national efforts are presented in Exhibit 5-C. In past years, various international organizations, such as the International Labor Organization or the United Nations, have attempted to develop an international code of conduct for multinational corporations. These efforts

---

[20] John Reed and Erik Portanger, "Bribery, Corruption Are Rampant in Eastern Europe, Survey Finds," *Wall Street Journal,* November 9, 1999, p. A21; Hugh Pope, "Corruption Stunts Growth in Ex-Soviet States," *Wall Street Journal,* July 5, 2000, p. A17; and "Chronikos," *Ethikos,* March–April 2000, p. 10.

[21] Jack G. Kaikati et al., "The Price of International Business Morality: Twenty Years under the Foreign Corrupt Practices Act," *Journal of Business Ethics* 26 (2000), pp. 213–22; and Glenn R. Simpson, "Foreign Deals Rely on Bribes, U.S. Contends," *Wall Street Journal,* February 23, 1999, pp. A3, A13.

[22] "Corruption and Bribery," *Financial Times,* June 5, 2000, p. 4; John Carreyrou, "Suez Lyonnaise Unit in Bribery Probe," *Wall Street Journal,* December 28, 1999, p. A13; and "IBM's Latest Tangle in Argentina," *The Economist,* August 1, 1998, p. 31.

EXHIBIT
5-C

Global Anticorruption and Bribery Efforts

- By the end of 1998, the United States, United Kingdom, Canada, Germany, and Japan had ratified the Organization for Economic Cooperation and Development (OECD) treaty on combating the bribery of foreign public officials. Bulgaria, Finland, Hungary, Iceland, Korea, and Norway soon followed. The central provision of the treaty required each signatory to establish as a criminal offense anyone intentionally offering, promising, or giving any undue pecuniary or other advantage to a foreign public official or to a third party, in an effort to have the public official act or refrain from acting in the performance of her or his official duties, in order to obtain or retain business or an improper advantage in the conduct of international business.

- On November 4, 1998, the Council of Europe, which included Central and Eastern European countries, adopted the Criminal Law Convention on Corruption. This law went beyond the OECD treaty by addressing the demand side, or extortion, as well as the supply side of bribery. The law called for criminal statutes to cover corporations, as well as individuals, and made "trading in influence" a crime.

- In February 1999, the first Global Forum on Fighting Corruption and Safeguarding Integrity among Justice and Security Officials was held. Representatives from 92 countries attended the conference united in their belief that corruption was a threat to the economic and social progress of all nations. In a report from this conference, participants declared: "We have considered and shared with one another many practices that help control or punish corruption in public office. . . . We call on our governments to cooperate in appropriate regional and global bodies to rededicate themselves to adopt effective anticorruption principles and practices, and to create ways to assist each other through mutual evaluation."

- In September 1999, prominent Russian politicians, former intelligence chiefs, and lawyers formed a national anticorruption committee in response to the estimated $20 billion annually lost to graft, bribes and kickbacks. The aim of the group was to help Russians acquire legal assistance to expose officials who demand bribes and other favors. This effort marked the first time that the Russian government tried to mobilize a nongovernment attack on graft.

Sources: Michael J. Hershman, "OECD's Convention on Bribery 'Levels the Playing Field'," *Ethikos*, March–April 1999, pp. 1–3, 13; "Global Forum on Fighting Corruption," *EOA News*, Summer–Fall 1999, p. 3; and Guy Chazan, "Corruption Panel Formed in Russia; U.S. Help Sought," *Wall Street Journal*, September 20, 1999, p. A21. Also see Skip Kaltenheuser, "Bribery Is Being Outlawed Virtually Worldwide," *Business Ethics*, May–June 1998, p. 11; and Jon Moran, "Bribery and Corruption: The OECD Convention on Combating the Bribery of Foreign Public Officials in International Business Transactions," *Business Ethics: A European Review*, July 1999, pp. 141–50.

Figure 5-4

International ethics
codes and ethics
issues addressed in
these codes.

Sources: This chart is
adapted from William
C. Frederick, "The Moral
Authority of
Transnational Corporate
Codes," *Journal of
Business Ethics* 10
(1991), pp. 165–77,
particularly table 1,
p. 168; and Kathleen
A. Getz, "International
Codes of Conduct: An
Analysis of Ethical
Reasoning," *Journal of
Business Ethics* 9
(1990), pp. 567–77.

Ethics Issues Addressed	International Ethics Codes*			
	ICC	OECD	ILO	UN/CTC
Economic Development	X	X	X	X
Technology Transfer	X	X	X	X
Regulatory Action	X	X		X
Employment	X	X	X	
Human Rights			X	X
Environmental Protection	X	X		X
Consumer Protection		X		X
Political Action		X		X

*Key for the international codes of conduct:

ICC = International Chamber of Commerce code (1972)
OECD = Organization for Economic Cooperation and Development code (1976)
ILO = International Labor Organization code (1977)
UN/CTC = United Nations Commission on Transnational Corporations code (1984)

have emphasized the need for companies to adhere to universal ethical guidelines when conducting business throughout the world. These codes and the ethical issues they address are shown in Figure 5-4.

More recently, the Reverend Leon Sullivan called on businesses around the world to adopt the Global Sullivan Principles. The objectives of the principles are:

- To support economic, social, and political justice by companies where they do business.

- To support human rights and to encourage equal opportunity at all levels of employment, including racial and gender diversity on decision-making committees and boards.

- To train and advance disadvantaged workers for technical, supervisory, and management opportunities.

- To assist with greater tolerance and understanding among peoples.

- To help improve the quality of life for communities, workers, and children with dignity and equality.

The Global Sullivan Principles embody universal ethical principles of justice, equality, and human dignity and may appeal to business leaders on these grounds. However, the Global Sullivan Principles lack economic incentives to motivate business leaders to incorporate them into their strategic plans or business practices. They do not appear to directly or positively impact the company's profitability in the short term.

For their part, some businesses have initiated efforts to control unethical employee behavior directly. As discussed in the next chapter, corporate codes of ethics have been drafted or recently revised to cover instances of undesirable practices in the global marketplace. International ethical issues, such as bribery and improper payments, conflicts of interest, and receiving gifts, are found in nearly all multinational corporate codes of ethics.

In addition, in 1994 a consortium of European, Asian, and North American business leaders formed the Caux Roundtable. This group drafted the Caux Roundtable Principles for Business, an international standard for ethical conduct emphasizing *kyosei* (i.e., working for the common good) and a respect for human rights.[23]

Some people question the effectiveness of governmental legislation or corporate policies. Rather than establishing rules, some businesses, including Motorola and Reebok, are trying to educate and motivate their employees worldwide to both respect the customs of other nations and adhere to basic ethical principles of fairness, honesty, and respect for human rights.[24] Some who study international business ethics say that such higher standards of ethics already exist. Thomas Donaldson, a leading ethics scholar, has outlined a set of fundamental human rights—including the right to security, to freedom of movement, to subsistence income, and other rights—that should be respected by all multinational corporations. These standards and other ethical values are at the core of the development of transnational codes of conduct promoted by the United Nations and other international organizations.[25]

Ethics, Laws, and Illegal Corporate Behavior

Before discussing specific ways to improve business's ethical performance (in the next chapter), we want to consider the relationship of laws and ethics. Some people have argued that the best way to assure ethical business conduct is to insist that business firms obey society's laws. However, this approach is not as simple as it seems.

Laws and ethics are not quite the same. Laws are similar to ethics because both define proper and improper behavior. In general, laws are a society's attempt to formalize—that is, to reduce to written rules—the general public's ideas about what constitutes right and wrong conduct in various spheres of life. However, it is rarely possible for written laws to capture all of the subtle shadings that people give to ethics. Ethical concepts—like the people who believe in them—are more complex than written rules of law. Ethics deals with human dilemmas that frequently go beyond the formal language of law and the meanings given to legal rules. Sometimes businesses or industries preempt legislation and voluntarily adopt ethically based practices.

> *Such was the case in the mid-1990s when the Interactive Digital Software Association, which represents video game makers, established a five-category system that was voluntarily adopted by the industry to inform consumers of the intended target audience. The video game industry also agreed to provide content warnings, such as mild profanity, and to use warning symbols.*

---

[23] Portions of the Caux Roundtable Principles for Business are presented in Chapter 3.

[24] For a description of Motorola's global ethics program, see R.S. Moorthy, Richard T. DeGeorge, Thomas Donaldson, William J. Ellos, SJ, Robert C. Solomon, and Robert B. Textor, *Uncompromising Integrity: Motorola's Global Challenge* (Schaumburg, IL: Motorola University Press, 1998); see Reebok's company policies on human rights at www.reebok.com/about_reebok/human_rights.

[25] For a complete list of fundamental human rights, see Thomas Donaldson, *The Ethics of International Business* (New York: Oxford University Press, 1989).

*In 2000, the National Football League (NFL) expressed its concern over
online gambling advertisements featured on Yahoo! websites that included
NFL content. NFL spokesperson Brian McCarthy explained, "The NFL has
a long-standing policy against gambling and anything that threatens the
game." While not legally compelled to do so, Yahoo! voluntarily agreed to
block the online gambling advertisements.*[26]

These examples suggest that following laws cannot always define proper action,
that is, what is ethical or unethical. Although laws attempt to codify a society's
notions of right and wrong, they are not always able to do so completely. Obeying
laws is usually one way of acting ethically, and the public generally expects business
to be law-abiding. But at times, the public expects business to recognize that ethical
principles are broader than laws. Because of the imperfect match between laws and
ethics, business managers who try to improve their company's ethical performance
need to do more than comply with laws. Society will generally insist that they heed
ethical principles and laws.

Corporate Lawbreaking and Its Costs

Although estimates vary, lawbreaking in business may cause serious financial losses.
A Department of Justice estimate puts the total annual loss from reported and unreported violations of federal regulations by corporations at $10 to $20 billion. Ten percent of the $1 trillion spent on U.S. health care is believed lost due to fraud every
year. (The problem of Medicare fraud is further discussed in the case study on Colum-
bia/HCA.) The Chamber of Commerce of the United States, a conservative probusiness organization, has estimated that various white-collar crimes cost the public some
$41 billion a year. Others, such as Professor W. Steve Albrecht, inflated that estimate
to as much as $200 billion annually.[27]

One of the most thorough attempts to calculate the financial loss to the country
from corporate crimes was that of a U.S. Senate subcommittee, which put the cost of
corporate crime at between $174 and $231 billion a year. Compared with even the
lesser of these estimates, the $3 to $4 billion annual loss to street crime—robbery,
burglary, assault, and so forth—represents only a small proportion of the economic
cost of crime.

The United States is not the only nation suffering losses from illegal acts. German
officials believed that more than 50 billion marks ($29.07 billion) a year was lost from
the German economy as a result of inflated accounting, tax evasion, and illegal kickbacks.

Beyond these dollar costs of illegal behavior are the physical and social costs. More
than 100,000 deaths each year are attributed to occupational diseases, and many of these
result from violations of health and safety laws. Annually, more than 6,000 workers die
from on-the-job injuries. This amounts to an average of nearly 17 workplace deaths each

---

[26] "Games Industries Introduce Voluntary Ratings System," *Wall Street Journal*, July, 29, 1994, p. B3; and
Mylene Mangalindan, "Yahoo Removes Online Gambling Ads from Web Pages with Content from NFL,"
Wall Street Journal, December 15, 2000, p. B10.

[27] For a discussion of corporate crime, see Kevin Danaher, "Corporate Crime: Three Strikes, You're Out,"
Global Exchange, www.globalexchange.org/corporatecrime.

day. Tragically, many of these deaths might have been avoided if employers and workers were informed about the risks and complied with established safety and health regulations.

Ethics is an inherent part of daily business operations and can be seen in the accounting, finance, marketing, information technology, and other functions of business. What businesses have done to address ethical issues and help employees reach ethical resolutions to knotty business dilemmas is discussed in the next chapter.

Summary Points of This Chapter

- Ethics is a conception of right and wrong behavior, defining for us when our actions are moral and when they are immoral. Business ethics is the application of general ethical ideas to business behavior.
- Ethical business behavior is expected by the public, prevents harm to society, improves profitability, fosters business relations and employee productivity, reduces criminal penalties, protects business against unscrupulous employees and competitors, protects business employees from harmful actions by their employer, and allows people in business to act consistently with their personal ethical beliefs.
- Ethics problems occur in business for many reasons, including the selfishness of a few, competitive pressures on profits, the clash of personal values and business goals, and cross-cultural contradictions in global business operations.
- Similar ethical issues, such as bribery, are evident throughout the world, and many international agencies and national governments are actively attempting to minimize such actions through economic sanctions and international codes.
- Although laws and ethics are closely related, they are not the same; ethical principles tend to be broader than legal principles. Illegal behavior by business and its employees imposes great costs on business and the general public.

Key Terms and Concepts Used in This Chapter

- Ethics
- Ethical principles
- Ethical relativism
- Business ethics
- U.S. Corporate Sentencing Guidelines
- Functional-area ethics
- Ethical egoist
- Bribery
- U.S. Foreign Corrupt Practices Act
- Laws

Internet Resources

- www.dii.org   Defense Industry Initiative on Business Ethics and Conduct
- www.usoge.gov   United States Office of Government Ethics

- www.business-ethics.org   International Business Ethics Institute
- www.business-ethics.com   Business Ethics: Insider's Report on
                                                          Corporate Responsibility
- www.ethicscan.on.ca   EthicScan, Toronto-based ethics
                                                          clearinghouse

---

Discussion Case: *Viagra—Wonder Drug or Ethical Irresponsibility?*

In 1998, Pfizer Inc. announced the availability of a new prescription drug called
Viagra. Initially intended to aid men who had experienced sexual dysfunction or impo-
tency, word of the drug's effectiveness caused healthy men of all ages to seek a
Viagra prescription to enhance their sexual performance. Women, too, were interested
in the drug to increase their sexual satisfaction. Within six months, Pfizer reported
filling over 3 and a half million prescriptions (300,000 prescriptions per week), resulting in over $350 million in sales revenue for the company.

During this same period, critics of the drug emerged, citing concerns over side
effects experienced by some consumers taking it. It was reported that some men with
cardiovascular problems temporarily lost their vision after taking Viagra. The Federal
Aviation Administration advised its pilots to wait at least six hours after using Viagra
before flying. Their concern was the possibility that pilots shortly after taking Viagra
could not distinguish between the colors blue and green, which are used in cockpit
displays and landing guides at airports. The concerns mounted when the Food and
Drug Administration (FDA) received reports that 130 Americans had died after taking
Viagra, mainly from heart attacks, since a side effect of the drug was increased stress
on the heart muscle. Nonetheless, the FDA still considered the drug to be safe since
most of the deaths were among patients who had one or more risk factors. These
included hypertension, obesity, a history of cardiac problems, and cigarette smoking;
thus it was unclear if one of these factors, or the drug itself, was the cause of death.

Pfizer did admit that side effects were observed 3 percent of the time during
Viagra's clinical trials. However, after a storm of negative publicity allegedly linking
Viagra to numerous deaths, the firm agreed to issue new labels that cautioned patients
to use the popular blue pill with care if they had a history of heart disease,
blood-pressure problems, or certain eye disorders. The labels also warned doctors
against prescribing Viagra to men belonging to these high-risk groups.

The company also commissioned a study to investigate the alleged adverse
effects of the drug. Researchers at the University of Pennsylvania reported that the
maximum recommended dosage of Viagra caused no ill effects on the heart for
men with severely clogged arteries. In the study, 14 men with severe coronary
disease—defined as blood vessels more than 70 percent blocked—were given Viagra.
Tests were used to measure blood flow to their heart, and no serious negative effects
were discovered during the study.

The popularity of Viagra and the profits it brought its maker were not missed by
Pfizer's competition. The Icos Company, based in the state of Washington, struck a
lucrative deal with Eli Lilly and Company to develop an impotence drug that appeared
to have fewer side effects than Viagra. The drug, known as IC351, would take three

years to completely develop and reach the market at a cost of $75 million paid up-front by Eli Lilly with "undisclosed milestone payments" to be made during the drug's development. Icos and Eli Lilly would share in the marketing costs and profits once the drug was ready for the marketplace. In June 2000, both Bayer AG and TAP Pharmaceuticals announced plans to develop an impotence pill. Bayer said that its pill would be ready by 2002 and was expected to generate as much as 900 million euros ($838 million) in revenue in the drug's first year on the market.

TAP Pharmaceuticals' announcement of its plans for a Viagra-like drug, called Uprima, was met with consumer protests. In a letter to the director of the FDA, Public Citizen, a Washington, D.C.–based consumer activist group, said that approving Uprima would be a serious mistake, adding to the toll of people injured or killed by drugs that should never have been approved. Public Citizen noted that in preliminary drug trials conducted by TAP Pharmaceuticals, shortly after taking the drug one man crashed his car after losing consciousness and another fell and fractured his skull.

While the initial infatuation with Viagra seemed to calm down two years after its introduction, Pfizer was quite pleased with the overall sales performance of the drug. "There is no reason to be disappointed in the sales," explained Pat Kelly, senior vice president for Worldwide Marketing at Pfizer. "There was a honeymoon effect," but then the company began to see normal usage for the drug. According to one physician, men were realizing that it did not work miracles but was one of several tools for treating impotence. "Older men thought it would make them 20 years old again," said Seth Koppel of the Men's Health Clinics. "But it just doesn't work that way."

Sources: All quotations are from Robert Langreth and Andrea Petersen, "The Morning After: Sales of Viagra Cool Down," *Wall Street Journal,* October 15, 1998, pp. B1, B9. Other information for the case was drawn from Rochelle Sharpe, "Some Viagra Users Temporarily Lost Vision, Reports Says," *Wall Street Journal,* August 12, 1998, p. B6; "Deaths after Taking Viagra Are Confirmed to Total 69 Americans," *Wall Street Journal,* August 26, 1998, p. B11; "FAA Newsletter Says Pilots Taking Viagra Are at Risk," *Wall Street Journal,* October 28, 1998, p. B2; Rochelle Sharpe and Robert Langreth, "Pfizer and FDA Agree to New Warnings on Labels for Viagra, behind 130 Deaths," *Wall Street Journal,* November 25, 1998, p. B7; Ralph T. King, Jr., "Icos Strikes Deal with Eli Lilly to Develop Viagra-Like Drug with Fewer Side Effects," *Wall Street Journal,* October 2, 1998, p. B6; Laura Johannes, "Viagra Found Not to Cause Heart Attacks," *Wall Street Journal,* June 1, 2000, p. B20; "Bayer to Introduce Rival to Viagra in Two Years," *Wall Street Journal,* June 1, 2000, p. B20; and Sarah Lueck, "FDA Is Urged to Reject Rival to Viagra Drug," *Wall Street Journal,* June 6, 2000, p. B5.

Discussion Questions

1. What are the ethical responsibilities for drug manufacturers? Is any drug completely safe, or is the ethical principle "Do no harm" a relative guide?
2. Did Pfizer do enough by pretesting their drug and warning patients of the drug's side effects through product labeling and instructions to physicians? If not, what more could Pfizer have done?
3. Should the FDA require the pharmaceutical industry to conduct more elaborate premarket drug testing or increase their monitoring of customers' use of the drug?
4. Although legal, is it ethical for drug manufacturers to develop and market a drug that promises enhanced sexual performance but could also cause life-threatening side effects?

6

Ethical Reasoning and Corporate Programs

Businesses can take tangible steps to improve their ethical performance. The most important elements of ethical character are managerial values and virtues and the personal character of the employees. Creating or revising various organizational safeguards, such as codes of ethics, ethics committees, and employee ethics training, can improve corporate ethical action. These programs enable employees to improve their ethical reasoning by emphasizing a concern for achieving the greatest good for all those affected by an action while respecting peoples' rights and striving for a just and fair solution.

This chapter focuses on these key questions and objectives:

- What are managers' major goals and values?
- What roles do personal character and spirituality play in business ethics?
- How do a company's culture and work climate influence the ethical views of managers and employees?
- In analyses of ethics issues, how much weight should be given to harms and benefits, to human rights, and to social justice?
- What are the strengths and weaknesses of ethics codes, ethics training programs, ethics hot lines, and similar reform efforts?

G eneral Electric (GE) experienced a dramatic change in 1981 when Jack Welch began his 17-year tenure as the firm's CEO. Contrary to the previous CEO, Reg Jones, who advocated innovation, moral integrity, and loyalty, Jack Welch believed in profits, profits, and profits. This philosophy transformed GE into a model of business success. Under Welch, GE became the world's most profitable and most valuable company, bringing investors 22 consecutive years of dividend increases. Company market share value increased 1,155 percent from 1982 to 1997. By 1997, GE became the first corporation to be valued at over $200 billion, up from $57 billion a decade earlier. By 2000, GE's market value was over $500 billion.

To achieve this success Jack Welch had to administer some harsh directives. More than 300,000 people lost their jobs after Welch took over GE. He closed or sold 98 plants in the United States, 43 percent of the 228 plants GE operated in 1980. As GE chemist Mark Markovitz observed, "All Welch understands is increasing profits. That, and getting rid of people, is what he considers a vision."[1]

Critics challenged Welch's management style after numerous instances of unethical activities within GE. In one of the largest scandals in the 1990s, GE's Kidder, Peabody securities lost $1 billion and the SEC sanctioned three executives for various fraudulent activities. *Dateline NBC,* the premier newsmagazine show in GE's television network, allegedly rigged General Motors pickup trucks with rockets so they would explode on camera. In 1992, managers from GE's aircraft engine division pleaded guilty to stealing $42 million from the United States government and diverting money to an Israeli general to win orders for jet aircraft. The same division paid $7.2 million to the federal government in 1995 to settle a lawsuit brought by a whistle-blower who charged that GE was selling to the U.S. Air Force jet engines that did not comply with the terms of the contract.

Nonetheless, throughout the tumultuous ethics scandals, Welch was praised by the GE board for his financial successes and was handsomely compensated, amassing unexercised options exceeding $100 million by the end of 1996.

Is Jack Welch a model businessperson, proven by his nearly unparalleled financial success, or an unethical businessperson who showed a lack of respect for others and ethical principles, since "winning was everything"? Can an ethical executive also be a financially successful executive, or are ethics and profitability mutually exclusive? If Jack Welch was an unethical executive, how could GE's board prevent this type of leadership?

In this chapter, we examine ways to improve a business's ethical performance. The keys to success are a blend of managers' values and virtues, personal character and spirituality, a company's culture and ethical climate, the tools available for analyzing moral dilemmas, and practical changes in company procedures and structure that permit high ethical performance along with profitable operations.

The Core Elements of Ethical Character

Whether a company improves its ethical performance depends on these core components: the goals, values, and virtues of its managers; the personal character and spirituality of its managers and other employees; and the traditions, attitudes, and business practices built

---

[1] Thomas F. O'Boyle, "Profit at any Cost," *Business Ethics,* March–April 1999, pp. 13–16.

Figure 6-1

Percentage of U.S. managers emphasizing a value focus in 1990 ($N = 413$).

Source: Adapted from James Weber, "Managerial Value Orientations: A Typology and Assessment," *International Journal of Value-Based Management* 3, no. 2 (1990), pp. 37–54, particularly table 5, p. 49. Reprinted by permission of Kluwer Academic Publishers.

Means-Oriented Values	Goal-Oriented Values		
	Self Focus	Other Focus	Totals
Competency focus	53.5%	21.8%	75.3%
Moral focus	18.4	6.3	24.7
Totals	71.9	28.1	

into the company's culture. Good ethical practices not only are possible, but they become normal with the right combination of these components.

Managers' Goals and Values

Managers are one of the keys to whether a company will act ethically or unethically. As major decision makers, they have more opportunities than others to create an ethical tone for their company. The values held by these managers, especially the top-level managers, will serve as models for others who work there.

Figure 6-1 shows that most U.S. managers are focused on themselves and are concerned about being competent. They place importance on values such as having a comfortable and exciting life and being capable, intellectual, and responsible. Researchers also found that new CEOs tend to be more self-interested and short-term focused, possibly in an effort to immediately drive up company profits, rather than valuing long-term investments in research and development or capital expenditures.[2] However, some managers show a strong concern for values that include others, evident in the values of living in a world at peace or seeking equality among people. One out of four managers emphasizes this other set of values—moral values. These managers place greater importance on the value of forgiving others, being helpful, and acting honestly.

In general, American managers' values appear to be relatively stable over time, as discovered in studies looking at managers' values since the 1960s. Yet managers' values may vary across cultures. American managers were found to be more protective of organizational resources and more interested in compliance with rules than Russian managers. German managers were found to be more ethical, although more difficult to work with, than other managers within the European Union. Researchers have found that Chinese were more concerned with profits and more willing to accept bribes than Americans, although Americans were less ethical in their reasoning than subjects from

---

[2] Jeffrey S. Harrison and James O. Fiet, "New CEOs Pursue Their Own Self-Interests by Sacrificing Stakeholder Value," *Journal of Business Ethics* 19 (1999), pp. 301–8.

the developing country of Belize. All in all, values and ethical reasoning appear to differ somewhat across cultures.[3]

> *What about future managers? A survey of over 2,100 graduate business students across the United States found that 79 percent of them felt that a company must weigh its impact on society. This impact could be seen in the company's environmental responsibility, practices of equal opportunity, treatment of workers' families, and other ethical issues. Half of the students surveyed said they would accept lower pay to work for a company that they found "very socially responsible." Nearly half (43 percent) said they would not work for an employer that did not demonstrate ethical responsibility, possibly indicating a shift toward a greater moral value focus.[4]*

Current discussions about effective organizational leadership often center on individuals' values. For example, an **ethical charismatic leader** exhibiting strong moral character is capable of positively influencing an entire department or organization. Although there are risks associated with assuming this higher moral ground, ethical charismatic leaders are seen as other-centered visionaries who bring out the best in their followers. Although varying from the predominant value orientations of American managers in the 1990s, the moral standards of ethical managers may enable business leaders to better address the difficult moral decisions encountered at work.[5] This ethical leadership also may change the negative perception of managers by their employees and the general public. Only 47 percent of employees surveyed in 1999 believed that their senior leaders were people of high integrity. In a *Business Week* poll, businesspersons ranked near the bottom of professions in terms of perceived reputation, along with bankers, journalists, and union leaders.

Virtue Ethics

Some philosophers believe that the ancient Greeks, specifically Aristotle, developed the first ethical theory, which was based on values and personal character. Commonly referred to as **virtue ethics,** it focuses on character traits that a good person should possess, theorizing that these values will direct the person toward good behavior. Virtue ethics is based on a way of being and on what is considered valuable rather than focusing on rules for correct behavior. Moral virtues are habits that enable a person to live according to reason, and this reason helps the person avoid the extremes. Aristotle argued

---

[3] Elizabeth George, Claudio Milman, and Satish P. Deshpande, "A Comparison of Ethical Practices of Russian and American Managers," *International Journal of Value-Based Management* 12 (1999), pp. 129–36; R. J. M. Jeurissen and H. J. L. van Luijk, "The Ethical Reputations of Managers in Nine EU Countries: A Cross-Referential Survey," *Journal of Business* 17 (1998), pp. 995–1005; Laura L. Whitcomb, Carolyn B. Erdener, and Cheng Li, "Business Ethical Values in China and the U.S.," *Journal of Business Ethics* 17 (1998), pp. 839–52; and Richard Priem, Dan Worrell, Bruce Walters, and Terry Coalter, "Moral Judgment and Values in a Developed and a Developing Nation: A Comparative Analysis," *Journal of Business* 17 (1998), pp. 491–501.

[4] Keith Hamkonds, "Bleeding Hearts at B-School?" *Business Week,* April 7, 1997, p. 8.

[5] Jane M. Howell and Bruce J. Avolio, "The Ethics of Charismatic Leadership: Submission or Liberation?" *Academy of Management Executive* 6 (1992), pp. 43–54.

that "moral virtue is a mean between two vices, one of excess and the other of deficiency, and it aims at hitting the mean in feelings, desires, and action."[6]

Moral values acknowledged by Aristotle include courage, temperance, justice, and prudence. St. Thomas Aquinas added the Christian values of faith, hope, and charity to the list of morally desirable virtues. Aquinas believed that these additional values were essential for a person to achieve a union with God, which was a significant purpose in Aquinas's notion of virtue ethics. Additional virtues include honesty, compassion, generosity, fidelity, integrity, and self-control.

Personal Character, Spirituality, and Moral Development

Clarence Walton, a seasoned observer of managerial behavior, says that personal character is one of the keys to higher ethical standards in business. "People of integrity produce organizations with integrity. When they do, they become moral managers—those special people who make organizations and societies better." Others agree, including one longtime business executive who did an in-depth study of 24 business managers noted for high-quality ethical standards in their companies. He emphasizes the close connection between ethical leadership and a person's belief system or values.[7]

Personal Spirituality
Personal spirituality, that is, a personal belief in a supreme being, religious organization, or the power of nature or some other external, life-guiding force, has always been a part of the human makeup. Forty-eight percent of Americans responded that they have had an occasion to talk their about their religious faith in the workplace on a daily basis. And 78 percent admitted that they felt a need in their life for spiritual growth, up from only 20 percent in 1994. Recently, efforts appear to be on the rise to integrate people's work with their spirituality.

> *Companies such as Taco Bell, Pizza Hut, and Wal-Mart hired chaplains to visit employees in the hospital, help with emotional stress, and attempt to prevent suicides. These chaplains also presided at employees' weddings and consoled family members at funerals. Across the country, thousands of top executives began their day at a breakfast prayer meeting. In Minneapolis, 150 business executives gathered for lunch and listened to consultants draw business solutions from the Bible. There were over 10,000 Bible and prayer groups that regularly met in the workplace, according to the Fellowship for Companies for Christ International.[8]*

[6] For discussions of virtue ethics, see Manual G. Velasquez, *Business Ethics: Concepts and Cases,* 4th ed. (Upper Saddle River, NJ: Prentice Hall, 1998), pp. 130–39; Rogene A. Buchholz and Sandra B. Rosenthal, *Business Ethics: The Pragmatic Path beyond Principles to Process* (Upper Saddle River, NJ: Prentice Hall, 1998), pp. 38–42; and Robert C. Solomon, *A Better Way to Think about Business* (New York: Oxford Press, 1999).
[7] Clarence C. Walton, *The Moral Manager* (Cambridge, MA: Ballinger, 1988), p. 33; and James E. Liebig, *Business Ethics: Profiles in Civic Virtue* (Golden, CO: Fulcrum, 1990).
[8] Michelle Conlin, "Religion in the Workplace: The Growing Presence of Spirituality in Corporate America," *Business Week,* November 1, 1999, pp. 151–58.

Research conducted by McKinsey and Company in Australia reported that when companies engaged in spiritual techniques for their employees, productivity improved and turnover was reduced. Employees who worked for organizations they considered to be spiritual were less fearful on the job, less likely to compromise their values and act unethically, and more able to become committed to their work. At Elf Atochem, a subsidiary of the French oil company Elf-Aquitane, teaching people how to be spiritual improved productivity, employee relations, and customer service. The firm reported that it saved as much as $2 million in operating costs by showing its employees how to be more inspired about their work.[9]

However, others disagree with the trend toward a stronger presence of religion in the workplace. They hold the traditional belief that business is a secular, that is, nonspiritual, institution. They believe that business is business and spirituality is best left for the churches, synagogues, and meditation rooms, not the corporate boardrooms or shop floors. This, of course, reflects the separation of church and state in the United States.

Beyond the philosophical opposition toward bringing spirituality into the business environment, there are procedural challenges. Numerous questions arise: Whose spirituality should be promoted, the CEO's? With greater workplace diversity is greater workplace spiritual diversity, so which organized religion's prayers should be cited or ceremony enacted? How should businesses handle employees who are agnostics? Opponents of spirituality at work point to the myriad of implementation issues as grounds for keeping spirituality out of the workplace.

Just as personal values and character are strong influences on employee decision making and behavior in the workplace, personal spirituality and religious values, from all points of the value spectrum, are having an impact on how businesses are operated and where corporate revenues are spent.

Managers' Moral Development

Taken together, personal values, character, and spirituality exert a powerful influence on the way ethical work issues are treated. Since people have different personal histories and have developed their values, character, and spirituality in different ways, they are going to think differently about ethical problems. This is as true of corporate managers as it is of other people. In other words, the managers in a company are liable to be at various **stages of moral development.** Some will reason at a high level, others at a lower level.

A summary of the way people grow and develop morally is diagrammed in Figure 6-2. From childhood to mature adulthood, most people move steadily upward in their moral reasoning capabilities from stage 1. Over time, they become more developed and are capable of more advanced moral reasoning. At first, they are limited to an ego-centered focus (stage 1), fixed on avoiding punishment and obediently following the directions of those in authority. Slowly and sometimes painfully, the child learns that what is considered to be right and wrong is pretty much a matter of reciprocity: "I'll let you play with my toy, if I can play with yours" (stage 2).

[9] See Ian Mitroff and Elizabeth A. Denton, *A Spiritual Audit of Corporate America* (San Francisco: Jossey-Bass, 1999).

Figure 6-2

Stages of moral
development and
ethical reasoning.

Source: Adapted from
Lawrence Kohlberg, *The
Philosophy of Moral
Development* (New
York: Harper & Row,
1981).

Age Group	Development Stage and Major Ethics Referent	Basis of Ethics Reasoning
Mature adulthood	**Stage 6** Universal principles: Justice, fairness, universal human rights	Principle-centered reasoning
Mature adulthood	**Stage 5** Moral beliefs above and beyond specific social custom: Human rights, social contract, broad constitutional principles	Principle-centered reasoning
Adulthood	**Stage 4** Society at large: Customs, traditions, laws	Society- and law-centered reasoning
Early adulthood, adolescence	**Stage 3** Social groups: Friends, school, coworkers, family	Group-centered reasoning
Adolescence, youth	**Stage 2** Reward seeking: Self-interest, own needs, reciprocity	Ego-centered reasoning
Childhood	**Stage 1** Punishment avoidance: Punishment avoidance, obedience to power	Ego-centered reasoning

Direction of Moral Development

In adolescence the individual enters a wider world, learning the give-and-take of group life among small circles of friends, schoolmates, and similar close-knit groups (stage 3). Studies have reported that interaction within groups can provide an environment that improves the level of moral reasoning. This process continues into early adulthood. At this point, pleasing others and being admired by them are important clues to proper behavior. Most people are now capable of focusing on other-directed rather than me-directed perspectives.

On reaching full adulthood—the late teens to early twenties in most modern, industrialized nations—most people are able to focus their reasoning according to society's customs, traditions, and laws as the proper way to define what is right and wrong (stage 4). Stages 5 and 6 lead to a special kind of moral reasoning, because people often can get above and beyond the specific rules, customs, and laws of their own societies. They are capable of basing their ethical reasoning on broad principles and relationships, such as human rights and constitutional guarantees of human dignity, equal treatment, and freedom of expression. In the highest stage of moral development, the meaning of right and wrong is defined by universal principles of justice, fairness, and the common rights of all humanity.[10]

Recently, researchers challenged conventional findings and found that most managers typically rely on criteria associated with reason at stages 2 and 3. Although they may be capable of more advanced moral reasoning that adheres to or goes beyond society's customs or law, managers' ethical horizons most often are defined by their self-interest and immediate work group or family relationships. For managers who reason at stages 2 and 3, their personal rewards, recognition from others, or compliance with the company's rules make up their main ethical compass. While at work, the ethical reference group is relatively narrow. For managers, the right way to do business depends on how it affects themselves (stage 2) and what the boss and their coworkers accept as right and wrong (stage 3 reasoning).[11]

The development of a manager's moral character can be crucial to a company. Some ethics issues require managers to move beyond selfish interest (stages 1 and 2), beyond company interest (stage 3 reasoning), and even beyond sole reliance on society's customs and laws (stage 4 reasoning). Needed is a manager whose personal character is built on a caring attitude toward all affected, recognizing others' rights and their essential humanity (a combination of stage 5 and 6 reasoning). The moral reasoning of upper-level managers, whose decisions affect companywide policies, can have a powerful and far-reaching impact both inside and outside the company.

Corporate Culture and Ethical Climates

Personal values and moral character play key roles in improving a company's ethical performance. However, they do not stand alone, because personal values and character can be affected by a company's culture.

Corporate culture is a blend of ideas, customs, traditional practices, company values, and shared meanings that help define normal behavior for everyone who works in a company. Culture is "the way we do things around here." Two experts testify to its overwhelming influence:

> *Every business—in fact, every organization—has a culture . . . [and it] has a powerful influence throughout an organization; it affects practically everything—from who gets promoted and what decisions are made, to how employees dress and what sports they play. . . . When [new employees] choose a company, they often choose a way of life. The culture shapes their responses in a strong, but subtle way. Culture can make them fast or slow workers, tough or friendly managers, team players or individuals. By*

---

[10] For details and research findings, see Lawrence Kohlberg, *The Philosophy of Moral Development* (San Francisco: Harper & Row, 1981); and Anne Colby and Lawrence Kohlberg, *The Measurement of Moral Judgment, Volume I: Theoretical Foundations and Research Validations* (Cambridge, MA: Cambridge University Press, 1987).

[11] James Weber and Janet Gillespie, "Differences in Ethical Beliefs, Intentions, and Behaviors," *Business & Society* (1998), pp. 447–67.

Figure 6-3

The components of ethical climates.

Source: Adapted from Bart Victor and John B. Cullen, "The Organizational Bases of Ethical Work Climates," *Administrative Science Quarterly* 33 (1988), p. 104.

Ethical Criteria	Focus of Ethical Concern		
	Individual Person	**Company**	**Society**
Egoism (self-centered approach)	Self-interest	Company interest	Economic efficiency
Benevolence (concern-for-others approach)	Friendship	Team interest	Social responsibility
Principle (integrity approach)	Personal morality	Company rules and procedures	Laws and professional codes

the time they've worked for several years, they may be so well conditioned by the culture they may not even recognize it.[12]

Hewlett-Packard, the California-based electronics manufacturer, is well known for a culture that stresses values and ethics. Called the HP Way by employees, the most important values of the culture are confidence in and respect for people, open communication, sharing of benefits and responsibilities, concern for the individual employee, and honesty and integrity. The impact of this ethics-oriented culture is evident to managers and employees alike. A Hewlett-Packard manager commented that "It is not easy to get fired around HP, but you are gone before you know it if it is an ethics issue." Another manager said, "Somehow, the manipulative person, the person who is less open and candid, who shaves the truth or the corners of policies, doesn't last. They either get passed over for promotion or they just don't find this a comfortable environment."

Ethical Climates

In most companies, a moral atmosphere can be detected. People can feel the way the ethical winds are blowing. They pick up subtle hints and clues that tell them what behavior is approved and what is forbidden.

The unspoken understanding among employees of what is and is not acceptable behavior is called an **ethical climate.** It is the part of corporate culture that sets the ethical tone in a company. One way to view ethical climates is diagrammed in Figure 6-3. Three different types of ethical yardsticks are egoism (self-centeredness), benevolence (concern for others), and principle (respect for one's own integrity, for group norms, and for society's laws). These ethical yardsticks can be applied to dilemmas concerning individuals, a company, or society at large.

---

[12] Terrence E. Deal and Allan A. Kennedy, *Corporate Cultures: The Rites and Rituals of Corporate Life* (Reading, MA: Addison-Wesley, 1982), pp. 4, 16.

For example, if a manager approaches ethics issues with benevolence in mind, he or she would stress friendly relations with an employee, emphasize the importance of team play and cooperation for the company's benefit, and recommend socially responsible courses of action. However, a manager using egoism to think about ethical problems would be more likely to think first of self-interest, promoting the company's profit, and striving for efficient operations at all costs.

Researchers have found that multiple climates, or subclimates, may exist within one organization. For example, if employees interacted with the public or government regulators, a society focus coupled with a principle or integrity approach (law and professional code climate) may be found. However, if employees were isolated from these influences and their work was geared toward routine process tasks with a concern toward higher personal pay or company profits, the climate may be self-interest or company interest.[13]

Corporate cultures can also signal to employees that ethical transgressions are acceptable. By signaling what is considered to be right and wrong, corporate cultures and ethical climates can put much pressure on people to channel their actions in certain directions desired by the company. This kind of pressure can work both for and against good ethical practices. In a benevolence ethical climate, the interests of the company's employees and external stakeholders most likely would be given high priority. But in an egoism ethical climate, employees and managers might be encouraged to disregard any interests other than their own. An example is Columbia/HCA, as described in the case study at the end of the book; at this company, the CEO's drive for financial results at any cost may have caused many managers to downplay other stakeholders' interests.

Analyzing Ethical Problems in Business

Business managers and employees need a set of guidelines that will shape their thinking when on-the-job ethics issues occur. The guidelines should help them (1) identify and analyze the nature of an ethical problem and (2) decide which course of action is likely to produce an ethical result. The following three methods of ethical reasoning can be used for these analytical purposes, as summarized in Figure 6-4.

Utility: Comparing Benefits and Costs

One approach to ethics emphasizes the utility, the overall amount of good that can be produced by an action or a decision. This ethical approach is called **utilitarian reasoning.** It is often referred to as cost-benefit analysis because it compares the costs and benefits of a decision, a policy, or an action. These costs and benefits can be economic (expressed in dollar amounts), social (the effect on society at large), or human (usually a psychological or emotional impact). After business managers add up all the costs and benefits and compare them with one another, the net cost or the net benefit should be apparent. If the benefits outweigh the costs, then the action is ethical because it produces the greatest good for the greatest number of people in society. If the net costs are larger

---

[13] James Weber, "Influences upon Organizational Ethical Subclimates: A Multi-Departmental Analysis of a Single Firm," *Organization Science* 6 (1995), pp. 509–23.

Figure 6-4

Three methods of ethical reasoning.

Method	Critical Determining Factor	An Action Is Ethical When . . .	Limitations
Utilitarian	Comparing benefits and costs	Net benefits exceed net costs	Difficult to measure some human and social costs Majority may disregard rights of minority
Rights	Respecting entitlements	Basic human rights are respected	Difficult to balance conflicting rights
Justice	Distributing fair shares	Benefits and costs are fairly distributed	Difficult to measure benefits and costs Lack of agreement on fair shares

than the net benefits, then it is probably unethical because more harm than good is produced.

The main drawback to utilitarian reasoning is the difficulty of accurately measuring both costs and benefits. Some things can be measured in monetary terms—goods produced, sales, payrolls, and profits—but other items are trickier, such as employee morale, psychological satisfactions, and the worth of a human life. Human and social costs are particularly difficult to measure with precision. But unless they can be measured, the cost-benefit calculations will be incomplete, and it will be difficult to know whether the overall result is good or bad, ethical or unethical. Another limitation of utilitarian reasoning is that the majority may override the rights of those in the minority. Since utilitarian reasoning is primarily concerned with the end results of an action, managers using this reasoning process often fail to consider the means taken to reach the end.

In spite of these drawbacks, cost-benefit analysis is widely used in business. Because this method works well when used to measure economic and financial outcomes, business managers sometimes are tempted to rely on it to decide important ethical questions without being fully aware of its limitations or the availability of still other methods that may improve the ethical quality of their decisions.

Example: Is it ethical to close a plant? Using utilitarian reasoning, the decision maker must consider all the benefits (improving the company bottom line, higher return on investment to the investors, etc.) versus the costs (employee layoffs, reduced economic activity to the local community, etc.).

Rights: Determining and Protecting Entitlements

Human rights are another basis for making ethical judgments. A right means that a person or group is entitled to something or is entitled to be treated in a certain way. The most basic human rights are the right to life, safety, free speech, freedom, to be informed, due process, property, and others. Denying those rights or failing to protect them for other persons and groups is normally considered to be unethical. Respecting others, even those with whom we disagree or dislike, is the essence of human rights, provided that others do the same for us. This approach to ethical reasoning holds that individuals are to be treated as valuable ends in themselves just because they are human beings. Using others for your own purposes is unethical if, at the same time, you deny them their goals and purposes.

The main limitation of using rights as a basis of ethical reasoning is the difficulty of balancing conflicting rights. For example, an employee's right to privacy may be at odds with an employer's right to protect the firm's assets by testing the employee's honesty. Rights also clash when U.S. multinational corporations move production to a foreign nation, causing job losses at home but creating new jobs abroad. In such cases, whose job rights should be respected?[14]

In spite of this kind of problem, the protection and promotion of human rights is an important ethical benchmark for judging the behavior of individuals and organizations. Surely most people would agree that it is unethical to deny a person's fundamental right to life, freedom, privacy, growth, and human dignity. By defining the human condition and pointing the way to a realization of human potentialities, such rights become a kind of common denominator of ethical reasoning, setting forth the essential conditions for ethical actions and decisions.

Example: Is it ethical to close a plant? Using human rights reasoning, the decision maker must consider the rights of all affected (the right to a livelihood for the displaced workers or business owners in the local community versus the right of the employees to be informed of the layoffs and plant closing versus the right of the managers to the freedom to make decisions they believe are within their duty to the company, etc.).

Justice: Is It Fair?

A third method of ethical reasoning concerns **justice.** A common question in human affairs is, Is it fair or just? Employees want to know if pay scales are fair. Consumers are interested in fair prices when they shop. When new tax laws are proposed, there is much debate about their fairness—where will the burden fall, and who will escape paying their fair share?

Justice, or fairness, exists when benefits and burdens are distributed equitably and according to some accepted rule. For society as a whole, social justice means that a society's income and wealth are distributed among the people in fair proportions. A fair distribution does not necessarily mean an equal distribution. Most societies try to consider people's needs, abilities, efforts, and the contributions they make to society's welfare. Since these factors are seldom equal, fair shares will vary from person to person and group to group. Justice reasoning is not the same as utilitarian reasoning. A person using utilitarian reasoning adds up costs and benefits to see if one is greater than the other; if

---

[14] For a discussion of ethical rights, see John R. Boatright, *Ethics and the Conduct of Business,* 2d ed. (Upper Saddle River, NJ: Prentice Hall, 1997), pp. 59–65; and Manuel G. Velasquez, *Business Ethics: Concepts and Cases,* 4th ed. (Upper Saddle River, NJ: Prentice Hall, 1998), pp. 85–102.

benefits exceed costs, then the action would probably be considered ethical. A person using justice reasoning considers who pays the costs and who gets the benefits; if the shares seem fair (according to society's rules), then the action is probably just.

Example: Is it ethical to close a plant? Using justice reasoning, a decision maker must consider the distribution of the benefits (to the firm, its investors, etc.) versus the costs (to the displaced employees, local community, etc.). To be just, the firm closing the plant might decide to accept additional costs for job retraining and outplacement services for the benefit of the displaced workers. The firm might also decide to make contributions to the local community over some period of time to benefit the local economy, in effect to balance the scales of justice in this situation.

Applying Ethical Reasoning to Business Activities

Anyone in the business world can use these three methods of ethical reasoning to gain a better understanding of ethical issues that arise at work. More often than not, all three can be applied at the same time. Using only one of the three methods is risky and may lead to an incomplete understanding of all the ethical complexities that may be present. It also may produce a lopsided ethical result that will be unacceptable to others.

Figure 6-5 diagrams the kind of analytical procedure that is useful to employ when one is confronted with an ethical problem or issue. Two general rules can be used in making such an analysis.

The Unanimity Rule

If you want to know whether a decision, a policy, or an activity is ethical or unethical, you first ask the three questions listed in Figure 6-5. As shown in step 2 of the figure, if the answers to all three questions are yes, then the decision or policy or activity is probably ethical. If answers to all three are no, then you probably are looking at an unethical decision, policy, or activity. The reason you cannot be absolutely certain is that different people and groups (1) may honestly and genuinely use different sources of information, (2) may measure costs and benefits differently, (3) may not share the same meaning of justice, or (4) may rank various rights in different ways. Nevertheless, any time an analyst obtains unanimous answers to these three questions—all yeses or all noes—it is an indication that a strong case can be made for either an ethical or an unethical conclusion.

The Priority Rule

What happens when the unanimity rule does not apply? What if there are two yeses and one no, or another combination of the various possibilities? In that case, a choice is necessary. As shown in step 3 of Figure 6-5, a corporate manager or employee then has to assign priorities to the three methods of ethical reasoning. What is most important to the manager, to the employee, or to the organization—utility, rights, or justice? What ranking should they be given? A judgment must be made, and priorities must be determined.

These judgments and priorities will be strongly influenced by a company's culture and ethical climate. A company with a company interest ethical climate would probably assign high value to a utilitarian approach that calculates the costs and benefits to the company. Emphasizing an ethical climate based on a benevolence ethical criterion will

Figure 6-5

An analytical approach to ethical problems.

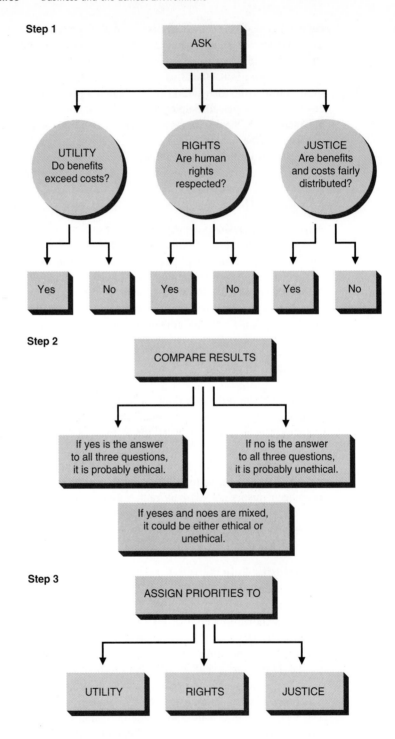

bring forth a greater respect for the rights of employees and the just treatment of all stakeholders. Obeying the law would be a top priority in a law and professional code ethical climate.

The type of ethical reasoning chosen also depends heavily on managers' values, especially those held by top management, and on the personal character of all decision makers in the company. Some will be sensitive to people's needs and rights; others will put themselves or their company ahead of all other considerations.

Making Ethics Work in Corporations

Any business firm that wishes to do so can improve the quality of its ethical performance. Doing so requires a company to build ethical safeguards into its everyday routines. This is sometime called *institutionalizing* ethics. How often organizations adopt these safeguards is shown in Figure 6-6.

Figure 6-6

Organization's ethics safeguards at work.

Ethics Safeguard	1992 Fortune 1000	1999 Fortune 1000	1996 SW PA Organizations	2000 1,500 Employees
Promoted ethics at work	93%		71%	
Developed code of ethics	93	98%	57	79%
Established ethics committee	13		14	
Created ethics office			17	30
Ethics hot line			9	51
Ethics office or hotline		50		
Offered ethics training	25		20	55
Conducted audit/evaluation			11	23

Note: The 1992 and 1999 Fortune 1000 surveys looked at the 500 largest industrial and 500 largest service companies according to the *Fortune* listing. The Southwestern Pennsylvania organizations' survey looked at organizations in that region of all sizes (30 percent of the sampled organizations had less than 50 employees, and 22 percent had more than 1,000 employees) and at multiple industry groups (health care, finance, manufacturing, etc.). The 1,500-employees' survey contacted employees working for companies of all sizes (33 percent of the employees worked in organizations with less than 100 employees, and 36 percent worked in organizations with more than 2,000 employees); 68 percent were for-profit and 31 percent were nonprofit or government organizations.

Sources: 1992 Fortune 1000 = Center for Business Ethics, "Instilling Ethical Values in Large Corporations," *Journal of Business Ethics* 11 (1992), pp. 863–67; 1999 Fortune 1000 = Gary R. Weaver, Linda Klebe Trevino, and Philip L. Cochran, "Corporate Ethics Practices in the Mid-1990s: An Empirical Study of the Fortune 1000," *Journal of Business* 18 (1999), pp. 283–94; 1996 SW Pennsylvania organizations = Beard Center for Leadership in Ethics, *Ethics Initiatives in Southwestern Pennsylvania: A Benchmarking Report* (Pittsburgh, PA: Duquesne University, 1996); and 2000 1,500 employees = Joshua Joseph, *2000 National Business Ethics Survey Volume I: How Employees Perceive Ethics at Work* (Washington, DC: Ethics Resource Center, 2000).

Building Ethical Safeguards into the Company

Managers and employees need guidance on how to handle day-to-day ethical situations; their own personal ethical compass may be working well, but they need to receive directional signals from the company. Several organizational steps can be taken to provide this kind of ethical awareness and direction. Overarching these organizational efforts are two different approaches toward building a program of ethical safeguards, as described in Exhibit 6-A.

Top Management Commitment and Involvement

When senior-level managers signal employees that they believe ethics should receive high priority in all business decisions, a giant step is taken toward improving ethical performance throughout the company. By personal example, through policy statements, and by willingness to back up words with actions, top management can get its message across. The "tone at the top is critical—and it's always monkey see, monkey do," said Martha Clark Goss, vice president and chief financial officer at Booz Allen & Hamilton, a New York consulting firm. Whether the issue is sexual harassment, honest dealing with suppliers, or the reporting of expenses, the commitment (or lack thereof) by senior management and their involvement in ethics as a daily influence on employee behavior are the most essential safeguards for creating an ethical workplace.

Codes of Ethics

As shown in Figure 6-6, nearly all large U.S. corporations and most businesses of any size have **ethics codes.** Their purpose is to provide guidance to managers and employees when they encounter an ethical dilemma. The rationales underlying the ethics codes differ from country to country. In the United States and Latin America, it was found that codes were primarily *instrumental,* that is, provided rules and procedures for employees to follow in order to adhere to company policies or societal laws. In Japan, most codes were found to be a mixture of *legal compliance* and *statements of the company's values and mission.* The values and mission codes also were popular with European and Canadian companies.[15]

Typically, codes of ethics cover issues such as developing guidelines for accepting or refusing gifts from suppliers, avoiding conflicts of interest, maintaining the security of proprietary information, avoiding discriminatory personnel practices, and protecting the environment. The most effective codes are those drawn up with the cooperation and widespread participation of employees. Researchers have found that writing codes of ethics alone was insufficient in promoting ethics at work. Codes of ethics must be frequently and widely distributed among employees and to external stakeholder groups (customers, suppliers, competitors, etc.). The creation of an ethics code must be followed up with employee ethics training to further the influence of the code provisions on day-to-day company activities.[16]

[15] Ronald C. Berenbeim, *Global Corporate Ethics Practices: A Developing Consensus* (New York, Conference Board, 1999).

[16] Betsy Stevens, "Communicating Ethical Values: A Study of Employee Perceptions," *Journal of Business Ethics* 20 (1999), pp. 113–20. For examples of codes, see Patrick E. Murphy, "Corporate Ethics Statements: Current Status and Future Prospects," *Journal of Business Ethics* 14 (1995), pp. 727–40; and Rena A. Gorlin, ed., *Codes of Professional Responsibility: Ethics Standards in Business, Health and Law,* 4th ed. (Washington, DC: The Bureau of National Affairs, 1999).

EXHIBIT 6-A	Two Approaches to Ethics Programs and Their Effectiveness

Lynn Paine, a Harvard Business School professor, described two distinct approaches to ethics programs in a *Harvard Business Review* article in 1994. She identified a *compliance-based* approach and an *integrity-based* approach.

According to Paine, a compliance-based program is rooted in avoiding legal sanctions. Companies pursuing this end will establish for their employees rules and guidelines to follow. This approach emphasizes the threat of detection and punishment in order to channel employee behavior in a lawful direction. Simply stated, "do not break the law, and if you do and you are caught, you will be punished." This lawyer-driven approach assumes that employees are individuals guided by material self-interest, wanting to avoid personal costs while indifferent to the moral legitimacy of their actions.

Unfortunately, compliance programs are challenged by research evidence that showed that employees do care about the moral correctness of their actions. While employees generally want to obey the law, they do so because it is right, not only because if they do not it will hurt them. Therefore, Paine also described an integrity-based approach to ethics programs.

Integrity-based ethics programs combine a concern for the law with an emphasis on employee responsibility for ethical conduct. These programs establish a climate of self-governance for employees based on general principles as guidelines. Often embedded in the company's code of ethics, employees are told to act with integrity and conduct their business dealings in an environment of honesty and fairness. From these values a company will nurture and maintain business relationships and will be profitable. Employees are understood as social beings, concerned for the well-being of others and the organization. Material self-interest and the values and ideals of the organization as espoused by top management influence employees.

In a study published in 1999, researchers found that compliance-based ethics programs fostered lower observed unethical conduct, a willingness to seek ethical advice by employees, and an increase in employee awareness of ethical issues at work. Integrity-based programs also were found to be successful. These programs were associated with greater awareness of ethical issues at work, an increase in a sense of integrity, employees' willingness to seek ethical advice, lower observed unethical conduct, a commitment to the organization, employees' willingness to deliver bad news to supervisors, and the perception that better decisions were made because of the presence of an integrity-based program.

Sources: Lynn Sharp Paine, "Managing for Organizational Integrity," *Harvard Business Review,* March–April 1994, pp. 106–17; and Gary R. Weaver and Linda Klebe Trevino, "Compliance and Values Oriented Ethics Programs: Influences on Employees' Attitudes and Behavior," *Business Ethics Quarterly* 9 (1999), pp. 315–35.

Merck & Company developed a three-step process for drafting its code of ethics. Step 1: Conducting Organizational Analysis. This involved asking a large and representative sample of 10,000 employees from 21 countries the question: "How do we want to be perceived as a company by

*shareholders, customers, suppliers, employees, and the general public?"
Step 2: Drafting the Code. Based on feedback from the employee survey,
focus groups, and interviews, senior management from international
business units drafted the code. The code had five stylistic requirements:
easy to read, practical and relevant, values based, sufficient but not
excessive detail, and graphically appealing. The code was translated into
22 different languages. Step 3: Creating an Awareness of the Code. By
distributing the code and conducting training sessions for its employees,
Merck attempted to increase the awareness of the code. Merck used
outside trainers to conduct the training sessions and the programs were
held in the local language.*[17]

Ethics Committees

About one in six companies surveyed (see Figure 6-6) have created an ethics committee to give guidance on ethics matters. It can be a high-level committee of the board of
directors, usually chaired by an outside board member to create an arm's-length relationship with top management. In other cases, the committee's members are drawn from
the ranks of top management.

*Weyerhaeuser, a forest-products company, put together one of the first
ethics committees in the defense industry in 1977. The committee, consisting of 13 to 19 members, has met regularly ever since to handle many of
the company's 150 ethical issues that arise each year.*

*After Orange and Rockland Utilities, a New York–based power company,
was rocked by charges of embezzlement and making illegal political
contributions, it created an ethics council, along with a code of ethics. The
council included representatives from legal, human resources, and audit—as
expected—but also members from the organization's rank-and-file. Four
union members were selected by management to serve on the council—a
customer service representative, a stock handler, a surveyor, and a secretary.*

Ethics Officers

Continued ethical lapses in large corporations throughout the 1980s and 1990s prompted
many firms to create a new position: the **ethics officer.** "Ten years ago [1986] they were
practically nonexistent," said W. Michael Hoffman, founder and executive director of the
Center for Business Ethics at Bentley College. By 1996, he noted, between 35 and 40
percent of major U.S. companies had an ethics officer.[18]

Many of the earliest companies to establish ethics offices, under the direction of
an ethics officer, were recipients of U.S. government defense contracts, for example,

---

[17] Berenbeim, *Global Corporate Ethics Practices,* p. 23.
[18] Kim Campbell, "Ethics Officers Roam Hall in More U.S. Workplaces," *Christian Science Monitor,* June
21, 1996, p. 8; and Lynette Khalfani, "Business Tries to Keep the Wolves out of the Flock," *Washington
Post,* August 11, 1996, p. H4.

General Dynamics and Martin Marietta. Since 1991, ethics officers have expanded into many industries, particularly heavily regulated enterprises such as telecommunication and utility companies. The Ethics Officers Association claimed over 650 corporate members by 2000. The more developed corporate ethics offices were led by an ethics officer and staff, who utilized many of the ethical safeguards discussed in this chapter to promote ethics at work: codes of ethics, ethics hot lines, ethics training, and ethics audits.[19]

> *When Sprint Corporation was faced with the question—where should the ethics office be housed?—it decided to combine two good answers: law and finance. The law department administered the ethics program on a day-to-day basis, but the chief ethics officer was the company's controller. Top management believed that this arrangement gave the ethics program more credibility and balanced the influence exerted by law and finance.*
>
> *In 1997, the Health Care Compliance Association formed a college for compliance or ethics officers. The college offered three levels of certification: Associate Membership, granted after two years of field experience and 25 hours of compliance training; Fellow Membership, achieved after five years of field experience and 35 hours of training; and Distinguished Fellow, awarded after the individual published an article on compliance, made a substantial contribution to advancing compliance as a profession, served on the College of Compliance Professionals board, and served as a faculty member in the College.[20]*

Ethics Ombudspersons

An ombudsperson is typically seen as part of a company's first line of defense against waste, fraud, abuse, or other unethical actions. This safeguard has gained more popularity among businesses, especially for firms that have experienced lapses in ethical conduct by their managers or employees.

> *Pacific Bell, once part of American Telephone and Telegraph, sailed into rough ethical waters when critics charged the company with using abusive, high-pressure sales tactics, allowing dial-a-porn companies to use its telephone lines, and violating consumers' privacy by selling lists of their names to telemarketers and direct-mail firms. As part of its response, the company established an ombudsman office. Its function was to give a private and confidential hearing to ethics complaints of employees who might be reluctant to report their concerns to their immediate supervisor. The staff then investigated and acted as a go-between. "We're trying to create an environment where employees feel safe raising [ethics] issues, trying to create a support system within the company," said the company's director of external affairs.[21]*

[19] See the Ethics Officers Association website at www.eoa.org.
[20] Andrew W. Singer, "Coming Soon: Certification for Compliance Officers," *Ethikos,* September–October 1998, pp. 12–13.
[21] "Pacific Bell: Dial E for Ethics," *Ethikos,* May–June 1990, p. 5.

Ethics Hot Lines

In some companies, when employees are troubled about some ethical issue but may be reluctant to raise it with their immediate supervisor, they can place a call on the company's **ethics hot line.** These hot lines have become more common, found in half of the businesses surveyed by the Ethics Resource Center in 2000. Their growth may be due to the passage of the U.S. Corporate Sentencing Guidelines in 1991. The Guidelines require a firm to establish an "effective program to detect and deter violations of the law." In many cases, this is interpreted as creating a reporting system that employees can use without fear of retribution.

> When American Electric Power (AEP) in Columbus, Ohio, decided to create an ethics hot line, the firm turned to Pinkerton Services, a well-known investigation services company. AEP felt that staffing the hot line 24 hours a day was a problem for their company. AEP also was worried about trust. Would their employees trust management's promise of confidentiality if they called the hot line? Pinkerton Services answered the calls, wrote down the details of the complaint or question, and assigned the caller a code number. The call was then forwarded to Albert Moeller, AEP's corporate and environmental compliance officer, to determine if an investigation was warranted or what action needed to be taken. In the first two years of operations, the company's hot line received 700 calls. Management believed that the high number of calls was not due to a high level of unethical activity within the company, but due to the commitment toward publicizing the new ethics service.[22]

Daniel Kile, former director of ethics at Bell Helicopter Textron, noted that hot lines typically have three uses. These are (1) to provide interpretations of proper ethical behavior involving conflicts of interest and the appropriateness of gift giving, (2) to create an avenue to make known to the proper authorities allegations of unethical conduct, and (3) to give employees and other corporate stakeholders a way to discover general information about a wide range of work-related topics.[23] An ethics hot line may work with other ethics safeguards, such as at Raytheon where the hot line served as an early warning system for the need to develop a new ethics training program for the firm's supervisors.

Ethics Training Programs

The number of companies offering employee ethics training range from 20 percent for smaller or mid-sized businesses to 55 percent for larger organizations, as shown in Figure 6-6. Training generally was offered annually and held for less than two hours on

---

[22] Andrew W. Singer, "Bracing for Deregulation, AEP Boosts Ethics Training," *Ethikos,* July–August 1997, pp. 1–3, 16.

[23] "Operating an Ethics Hotline: Some Practical Advice," *Ethikos,* March–April 1996, pp. 11–13. Also see Laura Sperry, *Business Conduct and Ethics: How to Set Up a Self-Governance Program* (Chesterland, OH: Business Laws, Inc., 1995).

average. Ethics training was offered to managers, rather than the rank-and-file, and usually involved lectures offered by a company trainer or general group discussions. Ethics training was most often found in larger companies.[24] For example, Union Pacific Railroad, Dun and Bradstreet, Donnelly Corporation, NYNEX, and Levi Strauss all developed extensive training programs in ethics for their employees in the early 1980s. Other firms, such as Honeywell, Northrup, Hughes Aircraft, and Harris Corporation, made significant revisions to update their existing ethics training programs during this time.

> *Lockheed-Martin Corporation in California was known as a technological innovator in the field of ethics compliance. In 1995, the firm was the first to place its code of ethics on the Internet, something commonplace by 2000. A year later, Lockheed-Martin posted its annual compliance training online. By 1999, about 80 percent of the company's compliance training was digitized into CD-ROM training modules, with course topics ranging from export controls, kickbacks and gratuities, to security, military sales, and harassment in the workplace. Employees were required to access the relevant CD-ROM programs for their initial compliance training and then refer to designated programs for their annual refresher courses. Lockheed-Martin cited flexibility, convenience and rapid deployment of information as the key reasons why their ethics training program was on CD-ROMs.[25]*

Ethics Audits

Some firms developed assessments targeting the effectiveness of their ethical safeguards or wanted to document evidence of increased ethical employee behavior. One technique used was an **ethics audit.** Typically, the auditor was required to note any deviations from the company's ethics standards that became evident during the ethics audit and bring them to the attention of the audit supervisor. Often the managers of each operating entity were required to file a report with the auditor on the corrective action they took to deal with any deviations from the standards that emerged in the prior year's audit. Managers also reported on the written procedures they established for informing new employees of the standards and for providing ongoing review of the standards with other employees.

> *Unfortunately, problems with ethics audits emerged in the late 1990s. When it was discovered that Cendant Corporation had claimed $300 million in phony revenues, it was clear that the firm's audit program was not working. A significant contributor to the firm's troubles was the composition of the audit team itself. A chief executive too often picks members "willing to go along with the flow and not rock the boat too much," said Robert "Steve" Miller, chairman of Waste Management. In his view, audit*

---

[24] Beard Center for Leadership in Ethics, *Ethics Initiatives in Southwestern Pennsylvania: A Benchmarking Report* (Pittsburgh, PA: Duquesne University, 1996).
[25] Andrew Singer, "Lockheed-Martin Moves beyond the Internet to Intranet Compliance Training," *Ethikos,* May–June 1999, pp. 5–8.

teams need "several independent directors."[26] *As companies acquire more experience in developing ethics audit, the effectiveness of these ethical safeguards undoubtedly will improve.*

Comprehensive Ethics Programs

The critical component in creating an effective ethics design is the integration of various appropriate ethics safeguards into a comprehensive program. In an Ethics Resource Center survey of U.S. employees, only 33 percent of the employees reported that their employer had developed a comprehensive ethics program, that is, a program integrating a code of ethics, ethics employee training, and an advice line or ethics office. The startling discovery, however, was the dramatic impact a comprehensive ethics program had in creating an ethical work environment for employees. People working at a firm with such a program were more likely to report ethical misconduct in the workplace to the appropriate company authority and be satisfied with the company's investigation of and response to charges of ethical misconduct. In contrast, firms with only a code of ethics were often perceived as less ethically responsible and less able to address ethical misconduct in the workplace than firms without any ethical safeguards.[27] An example of a comprehensive ethics program is described in the discussion case at the end of this chapter.

Corporate Ethics Awards

Firms have been honored for their efforts to create an ethical climate and improve ethical performance. Business Ethics Awards, sponsored by *Business Ethics* magazine, have been awarded since 1989. The criteria for the award include:

- Be a leader in the field, showing the way ethically.
- Have programs or initiatives that demonstrate sincerity and ongoing vibrancy that reaches deep into the company.
- Have a significant national presence whose ethical behavior sends a loud signal.
- Be a standout in at least one area of ethical performance.
- Have recently faced a challenging situation and overcame it with integrity.

Companies recently receiving this award for ethical leadership include SmithKline Beecham, for its path-breaking, $1 billion commitment to eradicating lymphatic filariasis worldwide; BNA, Inc., for over a half century of dedication to employee ownership; Iceland Company, for ethical food retailing that included selling all-organic store-brand vegetables at nonorganic prices in the United Kingdom; and S.C. Johnson, for a 60-year involvement with sustainable community development.[28]

---

[26] Joanne S. Lublin and Elizabeth MacDonald, "Scandals Signal Laxity of Audit Panels," *Wall Street Journal,* July 17, 1998, pp. B1, B9.

[27] See Joshua Joseph, *2000 National Business Ethics Survey, Volume I: How Employees Perceive Ethics at Work* (Washington, DC: Ethics Resource Center, 2000); and *Ethics in American Business: Policies, Programs, and Perceptions* (Washington, DC: Ethics Resource Center, 1994).

[28] "12th Annual Business Ethics Awards," *Business Ethics,* November–December 2000, pp. 10–14.

These and other award-winning firms provide the foundation for a collection of corporate ethics role models. Their commitment to ethical values and efforts to establish effective ethics programs demonstrate that firms can be financially successful and ethically focused.

Summary Points of This Chapter

- Managers' on-the-job values tend to be company oriented, assigning high priority to company goals. Managers often value being competent and place importance on having a comfortable or exciting life, among other values.
- Personal character and spirituality can greatly assist managers when coping with ethical dilemmas. Personal spirituality has emerged as a more common topic for discussion at work and has influenced company-sponsored activities during work hours and after work.
- A company's culture and ethical climate tend to shape the attitudes and actions of all who work there, sometimes resulting in high levels of ethical behavior and at other times contributing to less desirable ethical performance.
- People in business can analyze ethics dilemmas by using three major types of ethical reasoning: utilitarian reasoning, rights reasoning, and justice reasoning.
- Companies can improve their ethical performance by creating a value-based ethics program that relies on top management leadership and organizational safeguards, such as ethics codes, ethics committees, ethics officers, ethics training programs, and ethics audits.

Key Terms and Concepts Used in This Chapter

- Ethical charismatic leader
- Virtue ethics
- Personal spirituality
- Stages of moral development
- Corporate culture
- Ethical climate
- Utilitarian reasoning
- Human rights
- Justice
- Ethics codes
- Ethics officer
- Ethics hot line
- Ethics audit

Internet Resources

- www.ibe.org.uk — The Institute for Business Ethics
- www.inetbureau.com — InterNET Bureau of Business Ethics
- csep.iit.edu/codes — Illinois Institute of Technology, Codes of Ethics Online
- www.eoa.org — Ethics Officers Association

Discussion Case: *PPG's Corporate Ethics Program*

Founded in 1883, PPG Industries was a major global supplier of specialized glass products and industrial and specialty chemicals. In 1999, this Pittsburgh-based multinational operated 120 manufacturing facilities in 23 countries and had sales of $7.8 billion.

In keeping with its reputation as an honest, fair, and capable firm, PPG Industries had developed a multifaceted ethics program. At its core was the *PPG Industries Blueprint,* describing the company's values, statement of mission, and objectives. This document, most recently revised in 1998, identified the company's critical values as dedication to the customer; respect for the dignity, rights, and contributions of employees; recognition of the concerns and needs of society; commitment to integrity and high ethical standards; supplier relationships focusing on continuous improvement and shared responsibility; and responsibility to shareholders.

In order to put these values into practice through policies and programs, PPG management implemented a number of ethical safeguards. For example, PPG's *Business Conduct Policies,* revised in 2000, began with a letter of commitment from PPG Industries' chairman and chief executive officer: "the policies state our highest ethical standards and form the foundation for operating our businesses with uncompromising integrity . . . and in some cases impose regulations on our people and operations that are stricter than the law." The *Business Conduct Policies* defined possible ethical issues encountered by PPG employees, as well as guidelines for handling their ethical challenges. The policy concluded by stating "it is the policy of PPG and its subsidiaries, its agents and employees, to make every effort to operate as good, responsible, and ethical corporate citizens and to comply with all applicable laws of the jurisdiction in which they are present or operating."

Although the *Business Conduct Policies* clearly set the ethical tone for PPG's operations, PPG management felt a need to include an explicit global focus since the firm had acquired several overseas businesses with cultures and histories that differed from PPG's. The Global Ethics Committee was created, with members drawn from PPG operations in Europe, Asia, and South and North America. It was charged with advising top management on ethical issues; making recommendations concerning company policies and codes of conduct; developing an ethics training program; and providing a forum for the review of ethical issues. In addition, it assumed the role of the compliance committee after the passage of the U.S. Federal Sentencing Guidelines in 1991.

One of the most significant actions taken by the Global Ethics Committee was drafting PPG's *Global Code of Ethics.* Specifically, the global code reaffirmed the importance of the company's ethical standards, introduced new and prospective employees to the company's ethical tradition and the high standards to which PPG holds its people, and served as a primary reference document by drawing together main elements of PPG's ethical convictions. The global code covered PPG's relationships with customers, suppliers, and competitors (issues such as gifts, inappropriate entertainment, and product safety) and responsibility to PPG people (such as health and safety and diversity issues). It also discussed protecting corporate assets (such as security of information and intellectual property) and company responsibilities to the public and public officials (ranging from corporate lobbying to environmental responsibility). Finally, the global code addressed differences in local laws and customs and reporting violations or workplace misconduct.

To ensure that any instances of ethical misconduct were reported, PPG instituted the PPG ethics hotline in 1999, a toll-free telephone number maintained by an independent company located in Atlanta, Georgia, which assured callers it would protect their anonymity. Calls from PPG employees ranged from questions about employee relations to reports of fraud, discrimination, conflict of interest, or the release of proprietary information. Based on communications through the ethics hotline, PPG Industries improved communication channels within the firm, changed policies, and prosecuted violators as necessary.

PPG's multifaceted corporate ethics program is one example of a business seeking to maintain an ethical culture while honoring its economic responsibilities. As PPG's current chairman and CEO explained,

> *Let . . . us all work together toward our mutual goals: to furnish goods and services that meet our customers' and society's needs, to provide all employees with a safe, healthy, and fulfilling work environment, to afford our shareholders a superior return on their investment, and to contribute as a good corporate citizen to each nation and each community in which we operate.*

Sources: Quotations are from PPG's *Business Conduct Guidelines* and *Global Code of Ethics.* Additional information taken from the *PPG Industries Blueprint* and interviews with PPG's director of Corporate Security and Compliance, Regis Becker.

Discussion Questions

1. From the ethics cultures defined in this chapter, which ethics culture best describes PPG Industries? Do you think this culture type is the best for promoting ethics in the workplace?
2. How many of the ethical safeguards described in this chapter have PPG Industries adopted in its corporate ethics program?
3. What do you recommend is the next step for PPG Industries' ethics program?

PART FOUR

Business and Government in a Global Society

7

Business and Public Policy

Business decision making and political decision making are closely connected. Business decisions affect politics; political decisions affect business. Government actions are an expression of a nation's public policy and shape the business environment in important ways. Some public policy decisions affect entire industries or specific firms. Managers must understand how the public policy process functions in every nation in which their company operates and be prepared to participate in that process in an ethical and legal manner.

This chapter focuses on these key questions and objectives:

- What are the key elements of the public policy process?
- What major areas of economic policy affect business in every nation?
- How do social welfare policies affect business?
- What are the major forms of government regulation of business?
- What factors drive the growth of regulation? What drives the growth of deregulation?
- Why is international regulation emerging? How does it work?

illiam Clay Ford is the fourth generation of Mr. Fords to hold the top leadership position at the Ford Motor Company. The board of directors of the Ford Motor Co. named him head of the management committee in 1994; by 2000, he had become Ford's chairman. As the twenty-first century begins, "Bill" Ford has critical responsibilities for leading the company his great-grandfather founded in the early 1900s. Like each of the earlier Mr. Fords, he faces great challenges as he tries to improve Ford's position as a world-class automobile company. Not the least of those challenges involves dealing with the changing role of government.

In 1903, when he organized the Ford Motor Co., Henry Ford's relationship with government was relatively simple. There was only one antitrust law on the books, and his business was too small to be bothered by it. There was no federal income tax. Ford faced no serious foreign competition. No unions were permitted in Ford plants, and government regulations about wages, hours, working conditions, and safety and health were unheard of. The government exacted no payments for employee retirement and pension plans because none existed. The company faced no issues of pollution, energy shortages, or consumer complaints about auto safety, all of which in later years would bring the wrath of government down on Ford and the auto industry. Mr. Ford's main worry in those days was a patent infringement suit brought against him by competitors. (He eventually won the lawsuit in the courts.)

When Henry Ford II, the founder's grandson, became chief executive officer in the 1970s, it was a very different world. Government closely observed how Ford and his peers at other auto companies behaved. That single antitrust law known to his grandfather had grown into a tangle of laws and court rulings regulating competition, product pricing, mergers, and acquisitions. Labor laws legalized unions and controlled wages, hours, working conditions, safety and health, and employee discrimination. Federal, state, local, and foreign governments levied taxes on company income, plants and equipment, capital gains, auto and truck sales, and salaries.

Over the course of 100 years, the leaders of Ford have seen government's role in their business become much more extensive and complex. As chairman of the company, Bill Ford knows that Ford Motor Co. faces new challenges in the twenty-first century. Foreign competition has increased in the United States, and the company competes in dozens of countries around the world. In many countries, national governments are partners with Ford's competitors and jointly plan how to compete against it; European and Asian competitors loom large. The company's customers and global workforce include people of many races and nationalities. Technological change is transforming many aspects of the business. Today's Ford Motor Co. is designing automobiles powered by cleaner fuel sources, built of new, safer materials, and controlled by computers with navigation systems that help drivers avoid traffic congestion. Government-set fuel economy, safety, and emissions standards are important factors affecting automobile design. In all of this, government policy—public policy—plays an increasingly important role in the success and operation of the company.

Why are governments involved in such decisions? When, and how, do companies communicate their views on such decisions to officials? What happens when government experts and industry experts disagree about the best way to achieve in the public interest? Such questions are addressed in this chapter, which also relates to topics that are the major ideas in earlier chapters. These include the interactive stakeholder model (Chapter 1); strategic management of public issues (Chapter 2); the relationship of business strategy to social strategy (Chapters 3 and 4); and the influence of public values and ethical expectations on government policies (Chapters 5 and 6).

The Role of Government and Public Policy

Governments create the conditions that make it possible for businesses to compete in the modern economy. They set the rules of the game so that competition in the market can generate benefits for society. In no country in the world do businesses have the absolute right to exist and pursue profits; those rights are always conditioned on compliance with appropriate laws and public policy. Government's role is to create and enforce those laws that *balance* the relationship between business and society. Governments also impose significant costs on businesses through taxes and regulations and hold the power to grant or refuse permission for many types of business activity. Even the largest multinational companies, like Ford Motor Co., which operate in dozens of countries, must obey the laws and public policies of national governments.

The involvement of business with government is one of the main features of the modern global economy. Business firms and governments interact more often and in new ways. Stakeholders often persuade governments to regulate business activities to promote or protect social interests. Public policy is also used to encourage businesses to meet social challenges such as drug use, education, and job creation. Global competition has sharpened the understanding of business and government leaders about alternative ways that they can relate to one another. The relationship between corporations and governments, like that between business and all of society, is a dynamic one.[1]

Government performs a vital role in modern society. Although vigorous debates occur about the proper size of programs government should undertake, there is broad agreement that a society cannot function properly without some government activities. As the world's population increases, individual nations have more citizens whose needs have to be met and whose interests and concerns have to be reconciled into reasonable plans of action. Citizens look to government to meet important basic needs. Foremost among these is security, as in national defense, police departments, and fire departments. These are collective or "public goods," which are most efficiently provided by government for everyone in a community.

In today's world, governments are also expected to provide economic security, essential social services, and to deal with the most pressing social problems that require collective action, or public policy. **Public policy** is a plan of action undertaken by government officials to achieve some broad purpose affecting a substantial segment of a nation's citizens. Or, as former U.S. Senator Patrick Moynihan said, "Public policy is

---

[1] This theme runs throughout American business history. William Clay Ford's leadership of the Ford Motor Co. has drawn many commentaries. See, for example, John Holusha, "Ford Thinks Green for River Rouge Plant," *New York Times,* November 26, 2000, Real Estate, p. 42. A highly readable explanation is Louis Galambos and Joseph Pratt, *The Rise of the Corporate Commonwealth: United States Business and Public Policy in the Twentieth Century* (New York: Basic Books, 1988). See also George Lodge, *Comparative Business-Government Relations* (Englewood Cliffs, NJ: Prentice Hall, 1990).

what a government chooses to do or not to do." In general, these ideas are consistent. Public policy, while differing in each nation, is the basic set of goals, plans, and actions that each national government follows in achieving its purposes. Governments generally do not choose to act unless a substantial segment of the public is affected and some public purpose is to be achieved. This is the essence of the concept of governments acting in the public interest.

Powers of Government

The basic power to make public policy comes from a nation's political system. In democratic societies, citizens elect political leaders who in turn can appoint others to fulfill defined public functions ranging from municipal services (e.g., water supplies, fire protection) to national services, such as public education or national defense. Democratic nations typically spell out the powers of government in the country's constitution (e.g., the U.S. Constitution). Another source of authority is **common law,** or past decisions of the courts, the original basis of the American legal system. In nondemocratic societies, the power of government may derive from a monarchy (e.g., Saudi Arabia), a military dictatorship (Saddam Hussein's Iraq), or religious authority (the mullahs in Iran). These sources of power may interact, creating a mixture of civilian and military authority. The political systems in China, Russia, South Africa, and other nations have undergone profound changes in recent times. And democratic nations can also face the pressures of regions that seek to become independent nations exercising the powers of a sovereign state, as does Canada with Quebec.

Political power and influence shift and change in every nation. In the United States, for example, disagreements about the balance of power between local government and central government prompted the Revolutionary War in the 1700s (colonies versus King George), the Civil War in the 1800s (southern states versus federal government), and major battles in the Congress during the 1990s. The constitutional authority of the U.S. Supreme Court (federal law) versus the Florida Supreme Court (state law) on proper vote-counting standards became a point of dispute in the year 2000 presidential election. Public policy ultimately reflects all of these forces and influences.

Elements of Public Policy

The actions of government in any nation can be understood in terms of several basic elements of public policy. Many factors, or *inputs,* shape a government's policy decisions and strategies to address problems. Economic and foreign policy concerns, domestic political pressure from constituents and interest groups, technical information, and media attention all play a role in shaping national political decisions. The same is true at the state and local level of government.

> *For example, many state and local governments have been asked to ban or regulate the use of cell phones. Some advocates of regulation argue that cell phone users are often inconsiderate of other people and use the phones any time, any place, including restaurants, schools, concerts, and even church services. Cell phone users say this is a case of inconsiderate*

individuals, which cannot be solved by government regulation. Another issue involves public safety issues that arise when people use cell phones while driving. In this case, one group believes that drivers should be prohibited from using cell phones, because their behavior endangers other drivers and pedestrians. These groups have collected accident information and tried to show a linkage between accidents and cell phone use. Government bodies—legislatures, town councils, regulatory agencies—have to consider all of these inputs in deciding whether or not to take action, and if so, what kind of action.

Public policy *goals* can be broad (e.g., full employment) and high-minded (equal opportunity for all) or narrow and self-serving. National values, such as freedom, democracy, and a fair chance for all citizens to share in economic prosperity, have led to the adoption of civil rights laws and economic assistance programs for those in need. Narrow goals that serve special interests are more apparent when nations decide how tax legislation will allocate the burden of taxes among various interests and income groups, or when public resources, such as oil exploration rights or timber-cutting privileges, are given to one group or another. Whether the goals are broad or narrow, for the benefit of some or the benefit of all, most governments have to have a defensible rationale for doing what they do. Thus, it is always important to ask, What public goals are being served by this action?

The rationale for a government decision to regulate cell phone use has to be based on some definition of public interest. The inconvenience of people in restaurants, concerts, or churches may not be enough of an interest to warrant regulating cell phone use. However, the regulation of cell phone use by drivers of trucks and automobiles may have more of a public interest because it will prevent harm to others, including innocent drivers, passengers, and pedestrians. The cost of personal injuries in automobile accidents is high, often amounting to thousands of dollars per victim. Thus, the goals of saving lives, reducing injuries, and eliminating health care costs might justify some form of cell phone regulation. The policy decision would depend, in part, on whether the benefits of the regulation are greater or less than the costs that would be imposed on the public.[2]

Governments use different public policy tools, or *instruments,* to achieve policy goals. In budget negotiations, for example, much discussion is likely to focus on alternative ways to raise revenue—higher tax rates for individuals and businesses, reduced deductions, new sales taxes on selected items (e.g., luxury automobiles, tobacco, gasoline, alcohol). The instruments of public policy involve combinations of incentives and penalties that government uses to prompt citizens, including businesses, to act in ways that achieve policy goals. Governmental regulatory powers are broad and constitute one of the most formidable instruments for accomplishing public purposes.

---

[2] For an assessment of this issue, see Robert W. Hahn, Paul C. Tetlock, and Jason K. Burnett, "Should You Be Allowed to Use Your Cellular Phone while Driving?" *Regulation* 23, no. 3 (2000), pp. 46–55.

If a government (legislature or regulatory body) decided that cell phone use by drivers was a serious risk to public safety, and that action should be taken, the next step would be to select the right policy tool. For example, a local government might issue a ban on cell phone use by drivers of vehicles within the town; violations could be punished with a fine. A state government, however, with its broader jurisdiction, might decide that the best tool would be a regulation requiring cell phone manufacturers (or sellers) to add voice-activated headset equipment to the package, thereby lessening the need for drivers to take their hands off the steering wheel to dial phone numbers.

Public policy actions always have *effects*. Some are intended; others are unintended. Because public policies affect many people, organizations, and other interests, it is almost inevitable that such actions will please some and displease others. Regulations may cause businesses to improve the way toxic substances are used in the workplace, thus reducing health risks to employees. Yet it is possible that other goals may be obstructed as an unintended effect of compliance with such regulations. For example, when health risks to pregnant women were associated with exposure to lead in the workplace, some companies removed women from those jobs. This action was seen as a form of discrimination against women that conflicted with the goal of equal employment opportunity. The unintended effect (discrimination) of one policy action (protecting employees) conflicted head-on with the public policy goal of equal opportunity.

For example, in the mid-1990s the British government decided to turn over the publicly owned and operated railroad system to private businesses in a program called privatization. *It was believed that by running the railroad as a business, improvements in efficiency would be made faster, resulting in improved passenger service at a more reasonable cost. But five years after the privatization, virtually all Britons agree that the results have been disastrous. Safety problems have soared, investments needed to repair trains, stations, and maintenance facilities have not been made, and the system suffers endless delays. Worse, the government still pays more than $2 billion per year in subsidies to the business operators—Railtrack—just to keep the trains running. The effects of privatization may have been worse than the original problems, according to some observers.*[3]

In assessing any type of public policy proposal, then, it is important for managers to develop answers to four questions:

- What inputs will shape and affect the public policy?
- What goals are to be achieved?
- What instruments are being used to achieve goals?
- What effects, intended and unintended, are likely to occur?

Together, these questions provide a framework for understanding how public policy actions will affect the economy and business.

---

[3] Sarah Lyall, "Railroads' Frightful State Is the Talk of Britain," *New York Times,* December 10, 2000, p. 3.

Public Policy and Business

National governments attempt to manage economic growth using fiscal and monetary policy; state governments shape the business environment through a variety of regional economic policies; and local governments affect business through policies that involve operating permits, licenses, and zoning requirements. As illustrated in Figure 7-1, and discussed below, a nation's

Figure 7-1

Public policies affecting business.

National Economic Policy ⟶ Economic Effects	
Policies affecting the macro economy	
Economic growth	Employment/unemployment, welfare assistance
Fiscal policy	Government spending, taxation
Monetary policy	Currency value, interest rates
Policies affecting individual industries or sectors	
Trade policy	Exports/imports (balance of trade), trade barriers (e.g., tariffs)
Industrial policy	Support of priority industries
Social Welfare Policy ⟶ Economic Effects	
Policies affecting the workplace	
Child labor laws	Limited labor pool; labor costs
Minimum wages, maximum hours	Labor costs; safety costs
Safety and health standards	Equipment costs; maintenance
Right-to-know disclosure rules	Release of once-secret information
Policies affecting the marketplace	
Consumer protection safety	Costs of production
Government subsidies to poor, disabled, and needy	Taxation
Policies affecting profitability	
Social Security tax payments	Shared costs to employers and employees
Mandatory retirement benefits	Increased cost of labor; higher costs for older employees
Disability and unemployment compensation rules	Labor costs; dissuades firing employees
Health insurance coverage and benefits	Labor costs; incentive to use managed care plans

economic and social policies affect business by shaping the climate in which companies operate within the nation and across national borders.

National Economic Growth

Government's role as manager of the modern economy is widely accepted today. Political and business leaders in countries around the world recognize that government can create, or destroy, the basic conditions necessary for business to compete and citizens to prosper. This is not a new idea. Historically, European nations during the seventeenth, eighteenth, and nineteenth centuries tried to build strong domestic economies through the colonization of distant lands. Raw materials were brought back, manufactured goods were sold to settlers in the colonies, and the wealth of the colonies became the wealth of the home country.

Today, the role of government in the national economy is executed through macroeconomic policies. Just as the social environment of the colonial era was tied to the underlying economic conditions and the actions of business and government, today's social environment is tied to the effectiveness of government in creating conditions for growth of the modern economy. National governments operate on the assumption that government should create policies that promote economic growth. After World War II, the U.S. Congress passed the Full Employment Act, which established targets for economic growth and unemployment. Congress also adopted policies to encourage investment (e.g., inviting foreign investors to locate facilities in the country); foster technology development (patent protection); provide key services (roads, sanitation, and police protection); and create a capable workforce through education. Each year, dozens of laws are proposed by legislators to improve the nation's business climate and promote economic growth.

> *The United States is the world's largest economy, but it is not among the world's fastest-growing economies. This means that new opportunities are not being created as rapidly in the United States as in other, faster-growing nations. Economists believe that a mature economy like the United States should have about a 3 percent growth rate to meet the needs of population growth. U.S. economic policy is directed toward this goal. Meanwhile, economic growth in other countries may be higher (e.g., People's Republic of China grew at close to 10 percent per year throughout the 1990s) or lower (Russia actually had a negative growth rate in the late 1990s).*

Economic growth affects a nation's capacity to direct resources to social needs and the environment in which businesses operate. High growth means an expanding economy with more opportunities for workers and prosperity for businesses. Low growth can contribute to a nation's social problems, including high unemployment, costly welfare programs, and pressures to raise taxes. Japan and Russia both suffered low economic growth during the past decade, and each has suffered social problems associated with unemployment and a stagnant economy. On balance, political leaders favor economic growth because it creates increased national wealth.

Fiscal policy refers to patterns of government spending and taxation that are intended to stimulate or support the macroeconomy. Governments spend money on many different activities. Local governments employ teachers, trash collectors, police, and firefighters. State governments typically spend large amounts of money on roads, social services, and park lands. National governments spend large sums on military defense, international relationships, and hundreds of public works projects. During the Great Depression of the 1930s, public works projects employed large numbers of people, put money in their hands, and stimulated consumption of goods and services through such "pump priming." Today, fiscal policy remains a basic tool to achieve prosperity. Public works projects (e.g., roads, airports) remain among the most popular means of creating employment while achieving other public goals.

> *The largest public works project in the United States today is the "Big Dig" construction project in Boston, Massachusetts. This project has employed more than 15,000 workers since the early 1990s. The goals are to build a tunnel beneath Boston harbor to connect the city with its airport; tear down an elevated roadway known as the Central Artery through the downtown area; and construct a new underground roadway. This should ease traffic congestion and add acres of usable land for development in Boston's high-priced financial district. These benefits do not come cheaply, however. Cost estimates for the Big Dig project were $2 billion when the project began; by the late 1990s, cost estimates climbed to $7 billion. An audit by the U.S. Department of Transportation in 2000 suggested that the cost would be more than $12 billion by 2002. Some experts believe the total will exceed $14 billion. Costs are being shared by the federal and state governments, and it is expected that user fees and general tax revenues will eventually pay for the project. While no one knows the final cost, it is agreed that at a cost of $2 billion per mile for each of the seven miles of roadway that will be built, the Big Dig will be the most expensive roadway per mile ever built in the United States.*[4]

Taxation Policy

Decisions to raise or reduce taxes on business directly affect how much money government has to spend and how much firms have to invest in new plants, equipment, and people. The same is true of taxes on individuals: After-tax household income affects spending for food, housing, automobiles, and entertainment. Tax rates also affect the money available for savings and reinvestment in the economy. Even minor rules can have large effects: Rules about the tax deductibility of at-home offices, for example, affected more than 20 million at-home businesses in the United States in the late 1990s.

---

[4] As a result of the DOT audit, the senior executive in charge of the project was fired. The DOT called the cost overruns the worst case of mismanagement in the history of federal transportation funding. Extensive reports can be found at www.boston.com, August–December 2000.

Tax policies are often a consequence of other goals that governments seek to achieve. Governments may raise taxes because other needs or commitments are great and the pressures to act exceed the pressures not to raise taxes. When nations are at war, for example, taxes are raised; the collection of taxes becomes more aggressive because of the need to pay the costs of waging war. Peacetime spending priorities also affect tax policies and can be politically possible or impossible depending on the tax consequences.

For example, one of the largest spending plans in decades was President Clinton's proposal to create a national health care system. Designed to provide health care coverage for all Americans, it encountered heavy opposition because of its cost. Estimates of the new taxes needed to finance such a plan ranged from $10 billion to more than $100 billion, and opposition to increased taxes was one of the reasons the proposal was defeated. Although many individuals, companies, and groups agreed on the need to address health care issues, the implications of financing such initiatives undermined support for the plan. In contrast, newly elected President George W. Bush had an easier time creating support for prescription drug coverage in 2001 because the nation had a budget surplus and could act with little increase in taxes.

A nation's **monetary policy** affects the supply, demand, and value of the country's currency. The value of the currency is affected by the strength of the nation's economy relative to the economies of other countries. The amount of money in circulation and the level of demand for loans, credit, and currency influence inflation, deflation, and government objectives.

In the United States, the Federal Reserve Bank, an independent agency whose members are appointed by the president but whose policies are set by the bank's board of governors, plays the role of other countries' central banks. By raising and lowering the interest rates at which private sector banks borrow money from "The Fed," the board of governors is able to influence the size of the nation's money supply and the value of the dollar relative to other national currencies. Managing a nation's monetary policy is exceedingly difficult. A healthy economy requires a supply of money and credit sufficient to enable businesses to maintain economic growth. Too large a money supply may stimulate overbidding for economic resources, that is, *inflation*. Too small a supply of money produces *deflation*, with too few dollars chasing available goods and services.

Asian economies underwent a severe economic crisis in the late 1990s, brought on by monetary policy problems. In 1997, Thailand's government devalued its national currency, the baht, because of inflationary pressures and an overheating of the economy. The decision to devalue the baht was forced on the government by international currency trading, in which experts continuously look for imbalances in the relationship of one nation's currencies to all others. When the traders concluded that Thailand was overvalued, they sold their bahts in favor of other currencies. Thailand's problems were similar to those of Mexico, which was forced to devalue the peso in the mid-1990s, creating a huge loss of assets for people who owned pesos and for businesses that had to repay loans in other curren-cies such as U.S. dollars.[5]

The worth, or worthlessness, of a nation's currency has serious effects on business and society. It affects the buying power of money, the stability and value of savings, and the confidence of citizens and investors about the nation's future. This affects the country's ability to borrow money from other nations and to attract private capital.

Trade Policy

Trade policy refers to those government actions that are taken to encourage or discour-age commerce with other countries. Nations with abundant natural resources such as oil, timber, coal, minerals, and agricultural products favor trade because it creates markets for their goods and helps them promotes economic growth. Nations that are cost-efficient producers of clothing, electronic equipment, computers, and automobiles tend to favor international trade because they can offer better prices to customers than their less effi-cient competitors. But there are social consequences for a nation that opens its borders to trade. Countries without abundant natural resources or efficient manufacturing indus-tries may find trade to be less beneficial for their citizens. Trade may enable wealthy cit-izens to spend money on foreign-produced goods and services, but citizens who are unemployed will not find jobs if local businesses cannot match the cost efficiencies of foreign firms.

Wealthy nations may also find international trade to be a mixed blessing. When the North American Free Trade Agreement (NAFTA) was adopted, U.S. labor leaders feared that jobs would be lost to lower-priced labor in Mexico, creating unemployment and causing social damage to American communities. Environmentalists were concerned that Mexico's more permissive laws would encourage U.S. companies to lower their environmental costs by operating in Mexico rather than the United States. Such consid-erations lead some countries to favor open markets and free trade; others favor protected markets and restricted trade.

Japan illustrates the conflicting goals that nations sometimes have when it comes to trade. Leaders have favored free trade in industries where Japan has a competitive cost advantage or innovative technologies. Japan has lobbied other nations to open their economies to steel, consumer electron-ics, and computers, but it has resisted opening its own economy to trade with nations whose goods and services are less expensive or more advanced. U.S. computer companies, construction firms, and automobile manufacturers had great difficulty getting permission to sell their products in Japan, while producers of fast food, cigarettes, and designer clothing have had a much easier time getting permission to do business in Japan. The most difficult U.S. product to get into Japan was one that affected millions of Japanese farmers: rice. The government refused to permit

---

[5] "Chavalit Decides to Devalue Baht," *Business Day,* July 3, 1997; "Causes of Economic Problems Cited," *Business Day,* July 28, 1997; and "Thanong Shows His Mettle in Effort to Revitalize Economy," *Business Day,* July 30, 1997; all in archives at bday.net.

*imported rice into Japan to protect its farmers. Only an acute shortage of
domestic rice in the mid-1990s, plus pressure from the U.S. government,
created an opportunity for U.S. rice to be imported into Japan.*[6]

Nations often seek to be self-sufficient in some areas of economic activity, such as
farming, to preserve traditions and national values, or in industries that employ many
people and are therefore vital to the social fabric of the economy. For example, France
and Italy have tried to protect traditional family-based farms from foreign competition.
And many nations have sought to protect declining industries that could not meet world-
class efficiencies but employed many thousands of employees. These pressures pressure
governments to create trade barriers by imposing extra charges (tariffs) on imported
goods or strict quality requirements that force the seller to raise the price of the products if they can be sold at all.

Industrial Policy

Many governments have attempted to direct economic resources toward the development
of specific industries. This is known as **industrial policy.** A nation with oil resources
may structure tax and other policies to encourage exploration and production of oil fields.
Many nations have encouraged industries such as steel, automobiles, textiles, and other
large employers through public policy. Governments can also invest in new technologies
(e.g., fiber optics) directly by creating a state-owned enterprise or indirectly by creating
rules and conditions that encourage others to invest in new businesses (e.g., casino gambling). A vigorous debate occurred in the United States during the 1990s as to whether
government should pick winners and losers through industrial policy.[7] U.S. political leaders have generally favored using the power of government to create the *conditions* for
new businesses to grow rather than picking specific industries for growth. Of course,
government spending on aircraft, satellites, hospitals, and countless other products and
services also contributes to the development industries. The Internet, for example, was
the outgrowth of U.S. government investments in packet-switched networking in the
1960s. Funded through the Department of Defense Advanced Research Projects Agency
(ARPA), the goal was to link together a handful of computers that were involved with
defense-related research.[8]

Social Welfare Policies

The last century produced many advances in the well-being of people
across the globe. The advanced industrial nations have developed elaborate systems of social services for their citizens. Developing economies have improved

[6] S. Lenway, K. Rehbein, and L. Starks, "The Impact of Protectionism on Firm Wealth: The Experience of
the Steel Industry," *Southern Economic Journal,* 1990, pp. 1079–93.

[7] This issue was also a prominent argument during the Microsoft antitrust trial. The most important discussion of the industrial policy argument in recent U.S. history is M. Dertouzos, R. Lester, and R. Solow, *Made
in America: Regaining the Productivity Edge, Report of the MIT Commission on Industrial Productivity*
(Cambridge, MA: MIT Press, 1989).

[8] R. Kahn, "The Role of Government in the Evolution of the Internet," *Communications of the ACM* 37,
no. 8 (1994), p. 15. See also, Edward H. Shortliffe, "Networking Health: Learning from Others, Taking the
Lead," *Health Affairs* 19, no. 6 (November–December 2000), pp. 9–22.

key areas of social welfare (e.g., public health) and will continue to do so as their economies grow. International standards and best practices have supported these trends.

Health Policy

Health care is the most essential of social services, in part because public health problems affect a nation's entire population. The United States, Canada, Germany, Japan, and United Kingdom invest heavily in providing health care to their populations. But many diseases begin in one part of the world and travel quickly because of global transportation.

> *When doctors in the Indian City of Surat discovered that they were dealing with an outbreak of pneumonic plague, a deadly communicable disease, the Indian government mobilized its resources to fight the epidemic. More than 40 people died within two weeks, and hundreds, perhaps thousands, of others were infected. The worst problem, however, was the prospect of the epidemic spreading to other cities in India and, potentially, to other countries around the world. The World Health Organization worked with the Indian government to organize public health resources to deal with the plague in Surat, Bombay, and New Delhi, hundreds of miles away. Thousands of health workers—doctors, nurses, and paramedics—were organized to deal with plague victims.[9]*

Advanced industrial societies rely on hospitals, medical technology, and sophisticated pharmaceutical products to improve health. Less wealthy nations also recognize public health as an investment in human resources, as well as a moral obligation. Many nations emphasize meeting basic health care needs through local clinics, community education, and reliance on locally available medicines. Investment in such primary health care tends to produce significant improvement in indicators such as infant mortality, illness rates of small children, and vaccination of the population against disease.

The relationship between health expenditures and benefits has been debated for years in nations around the world. According to a survey of national systems conducted by the World Bank, the United States has a technologically advanced health care system that produces the largest number of sophisticated procedures, such as heart transplants. However, it ranks below other nations in primary health care through programs such as child vaccinations.[10] As shown in Figure 7-2, industrial nations vary in health care expenditures and in the outcomes, or indicators of success, resulting from that spending. The United States, for example, spends more of its gross domestic product on health care than any other nation, yet people in other countries live longer than do Americans. The prevailing attitude among experts is that when a population is viewed as a national *resource,* health expenditures become important *investments* in human capital.

Health policy has become more important as health care costs have grown. In the early 1990s, economic experts said that U.S. health care costs would rise from

---

[9] Laurie Garrett, *Betrayal of Trust: The Collapse of Global Public Health* (New York: Hyperion, 2000).
[10] World Bank, *World Development Report, 1997: The State in a Changing World* (New York: Oxford University Press, 1997). Available at www.worldbank.org/html/extpb/wdr97pa.htm.

Figure 7-2

Comparative health care costs and benefits.

Sources: United Nations, *Human Development Report, 2000* (New York: United Nations Development Program and Oxford University Press, 2000), various tables in Appendix A, "Human Development Indicators." See also, www.undp.org.

Countries in Order of Life Expectancy	Life Expectancy at Birth (average number of years, 1995–2000)	Population (in millions, 1998)	Real GDP (per capita, 1998; amount in U.S. dollars)	Total Expenditures on Health (percent of GDP, 1996–1998)
1. Japan	80.0	126.3	$32,350	5.9%
2. Canada	79.0	30.6	19,170	6.4
3. Sweden	78.6	8.9	25,580	7.2
4. Australia	78.3	18.5	20,690	5.5
5. Greece	78.1	10.6	11,740	5.3
6. France	78.1	58.7	24,900	7.1
7. Spain	78.0	39.6	14,100	5.6
8. Netherlands	77.9	15.7	24,780	6.1
9. Israel	77.8	6.0	16,180	7.0
10. United Kingdom	77.2	58.6	21,410	5.9
11. Germany	77.2	82.1	26,570	8.2
12. United States	76.7	294.0	29,240	6.5
13. Ireland	76.4	3.7	18,910	4.9

approximately 13 percent of GDP to as much as 20 percent by 2010. This sparked fear of runaway costs that would damage the rest of the American economy. Government officials were pressed to control health care costs. This type of pressure eventually led to new legislation to control costs and promoted the rise of health maintenance organizations (HMOs), the merger of hospitals, and growth of private-sector health care companies.

Health issues are entwined with other important areas of public policy. For example, one goal of environmental policy is to protect the health of children and adults from harmful pollutants. This has been influential in the creation of clean water and clean air legislation and in the development of toxic dumping regulations.[11] A study of death rates attributable to pollution showed that developing countries suffered especially heavy loss of life because of pollution-related diseases.

Rising health care costs have spurred a search for innovative ways to make the delivery of health services more efficient and effective. During the 1998–2000 period, for example, dozens of e-commerce businesses were started with an eye toward meeting health care needs in more cost-effective ways. According to one leading scholar

---

[11] Nicholas D. Kristof, "Asian Pollution Is Widening Its Deadly Reach," *New York Times,* November 29, 1997, pp. A1, A7. See discussion of pollution in Chapters 10 and 11.

of e-commerce, there are four distinct types of health e-commerce firms: portals that seek to be the users' first source of information; connectivity firms that link users to specialized data sources (e.g., Healtheon/WebMD); business-to-business (B2B) firms that sell products (e.g., medical equipment) and services to health providers; and business-to-customer (B2C) firms that involve manufacturers and retailers selling directly to consumers (e.g., prescriptions).[12] Governments regulate many of these transactions, such as the sale of prescription pharmaceuticals, and can facilitate or inhibit development through taxation policies. Public policy decisions will directly shape and influence how, and when, Americans will be able to reap the advantages of Internet technology in health care. As such examples suggest, the business community has a large stake in the extent to which public health objectives and costs are imposed on economic activity. While companies in some industries may suffer higher costs, others (e.g., medical equipment and pharmaceutical firms) will benefit from expanded social investment in health.

Social Security

National governments attempt to meet the needs of special segments of their population. Traditionally, orphan children and poor families required assistance; in modern times, children, elderly, disabled, and homeless members of society make up a large and needy population. Many countries have created government-run social security systems that provide guaranteed economic assistance to needy segments of the population.

In the United States, a national commitment has existed since the 1930s, when the Social Security Act was passed (1934). The legislation created a fund into which working Americans paid a small amount of money from each paycheck. The fund grew as worker contributions grew, and the proceeds were used to make monthly Social Security payments to retirees. For decades the system was very successful.

The Social Security system has suffered from two problems. First, the population has aged as baby boomers born in the late 1940s and 1950s have begun to retire in large numbers. People are also living longer and drawing Social Security payments for longer periods of time. Social Security reserves will decline as annual payments to beneficiaries exceed the amounts paid in. Second, the base of younger workers contributing to the Social Security fund is not rising as fast as payments to retirees. Social Security taxes have risen and there are pressures to reduce benefits. Despite several attempts by the U.S. Congress to balance revenues and payments, the system remains in need of long-term solutions. Financial services businesses have lobbied Congress to privatize the system and give individuals options to invest Social Security payments in personal retirement accounts. All of the presidential candidates in the 2000 election proposed ways to save Social Security, but the political outlook for reform seemed cloudy as a new administration took office in 2001. This issue is likely to remain high on the nation's public policy agenda for the next decade.

---

[12] Stephen T. Parente, "Beyond the Hype: A Taxonomy of E-Health Business Models," *Health Affairs* 19, no. 6 (November–December 2000), pp. 89–102. See also, Paul Starr, "Health Care Reform and the New Economy," *Health Affairs* 19, no. 6 (November–December 2000), pp. 23–32.

Entitlements

As nations expand social welfare programs, pressures grow to increase levels of assistance. Once programs are in place, citizens may expect that benefits of such programs will increase. This creates an **entitlement mentality:** people believe they are entitled to, and that the political system (government) will continue to deliver, more assistance.

Entitlements create dilemmas for political leaders. Pressures grow to expand the number of beneficiaries and to ensure that benefits are spread generously among the population. Costs also rise, however, creating a need to balance taxpayer interests against those of recipients. Resentment may occur when the public learns that people or businesses not really in need of benefits are receiving them. The media may portray these as examples of waste, fraud, and abuse.[13] Few nations have developed lasting solutions to the dilemma of providing benefits to the truly needy at a reasonable cost to taxpayers.

Government Regulation of Business

Goals and Objectives

Societies rely on government to establish rules of conduct for citizens and organizations. Because government operates at so many levels (federal, state, local), modern businesses face complex webs of regulations. Companies often require lawyers, public affairs specialists, and experts to monitor and manage the interaction with government (see Chapter 2). Why do societies turn to more regulation as a way to solve problems? There are a variety of reasons.

Economic Objectives

Economic objectives characterize some government regulations, but social goals are paramount in others. One economic argument that supports government regulation is the idea of **market failure:** the marketplace fails to adjust the product price for the true costs of a firm's behavior. For example, there is no market incentive for a company to spend money on pollution control equipment if customers do not demand it. The market fails to incorporate the social cost (the environmental harm) of pollution into the economic equation. Government can use regulation to force all the competitors in the industry to adopt an antipollution standard. The companies will incorporate the extra cost of compliance with the standard into the product price. In this way, the social cost that is imposed on the environment is passed on to the consumers who actually use the environmental resource.

---

[13] See William Julius Wilson, *When Work Disappears: The World of the New Urban Poor* (New York: Random House, 1996; Vintage Books ed., 1997). In 1996, the U.S. Congress passed the Welfare Reform Act. This placed new responsibility with the states to administer welfare programs, including a work-fare requirement. For background, see Mickey Kaus, "The Welfare Mess—How It Got That Way," *Wall Street Journal,* September 12, 1994, p. A16; and "Entitlement Politics, R.I.P.," *Wall Street Journal,* September 28, 1994, p. A18. The cost of entitlements is discussed in Robert Eisner, *The Misunderstood Economy: What Counts and How to Count It* (Boston, MA: Harvard Business School Press, 1994).

Ethical Arguments

There is often an ethical rationale for regulation as well. As discussed in Chapter 6, for example, there is a utilitarian ethical argument in support of safe working conditions: It is costly to train and educate employees only to lose their services because of accidents that are preventable. There are also fairness and justice arguments for government to set standards and develop regulations to protect employees, consumers, and other stakeholders. In debates about regulation, advocates for and against regulatory proposals often use both economic and ethical arguments to support their views.

> *As Internet technology and applications have become more sophisticated, concerns about peoples' privacy have been raised. It is unethical, in the view of critics, for companies to sell private information without customer approval. Faced with public pressure, companies such as Dell Computer, Compaq Computer, Intel, and Motorola working through the Information Technology Industry Council (a trade association) agreed to a set of principles intended to give consumers confidence and trust that privacy rights will be respected when they engage in electronic commerce.*[14] *(See Chapters 12, 13, and 15 for additional information about computer privacy issues.)*

Political Advocacy

Another reason for the expansion of business regulation is the number of advocates who speak for other interests. Environmental groups urge government officials to halt pollution; organizations representing minorities and women seek expansion of equal employment opportunity rules in the workplace; consumer groups advocate government regulations that ensure product quality and safety; and labor unions lobby regulators to set rules that will protect employees from workplace hazards and health risks.

Media Attention

Media attention to disasters and confrontations between business and the public help convince government officials that action is necessary. Throughout history, protests have helped pressure governments into action; in the late twentieth century, as the news media literally connect communities around the globe so that events are seen as they happen, the public and government officials see social needs that should be met. It is hard to resist pressures to act under such conditions (see Chapter 19).

Types of Regulation

Government regulations come in different forms. Some are directly imposed; others are more indirect. Some are aimed at a specific industry (e.g., banking) while others, such as those dealing with job discrimination or pollution, apply to all industries. Some have been in existence for a long time—the Interstate Commerce Commission (ICC) was

---

[14] John Schwartz, "Conference Seeks to Balance Security and Privacy: Microsoft Offers Talking Points and Wares," *New York Times,* December 8, 2000, p. C4.

created in 1887—whereas others, such as those governing state lotteries and other forms of legalized gambling, are of recent vintage in many states.[15] As shown in Exhibit 7-A, regulatory agencies have the challenge of setting rules that are fair and effective in achieving public policy goals.

Industry-Specific Economic Regulations

Our oldest form of regulation by government agency is directed at specific industries such as the railroads, telephone companies, and banks. Regulations of this type are primarily economic in nature and are deliberately intended to modify the normal operation of the free market and the forces of supply and demand. Such modification may come about because the free market is distorted by the size or monopoly power of companies or because the social side effects or consequences of actions in the marketplace are thought to be undesirable. When *market failures* occur, government regulators substitute their judgment for that of the marketplace in such matters as price-setting, capital expansion, quality of services, and the entry of new competitors. For example, railroads were not permitted to raise most rates to shippers without permission from the ICC, nor could they abandon costly service to a community as a free market firm could do. Nor could telephone companies increase their charges to customers, expand into related lines of business, or deny service to customers without first getting the approval of various local, state, and federal agencies.

Many industries have evolved through various stages of government regulation during the past century. Airlines, natural gas, telecommunications, and banking, for example, have gone through periods of rising regulation designed to correct abuses and problems, followed by periods of consolidation and implementation of regulation. When regulatory programs become ineffective, as command-type regulations often do, pressures to deregulate or otherwise reform the industry arise. Views change regarding how much regulation, and of what type, is required. For example, petroleum was regulated during the 1930s to stabilize a volatile oil marketplace that suffered from gluts and excesses of oil. Regulations were followed until the 1970s, when oil prices rose sharply. New regulatory controls were tried, but reformers concluded that oil prices should be deregulated to encourage exploration and development of oil supplies. Regulation always faces problems of staying current with changes that shape the underlying dynamics of an industry.

All-Industry Social Regulations

All-industry social regulations are aimed at such important social goals as protecting consumers and the environment and providing workers with safe and healthy working conditions. Equal employment opportunity, protection of pension benefits, and health care for employees are other important areas of social regulation. Unlike the economic

---

[15] See Richard A. McGowan, *Government and the Transformation of the Gambling Industry* (New York: Edward Elgar, 2001); also, Richard A. McGowan, *Government Regulation of the Alcohol Industry: The Search for Revenue and the Common Good* (Westport, CT: Praeger/Quorum Books, 1997); and Richard McGowan, *State Lotteries and Legalized Gambling: Painless Revenue or Painful Mirage* (Westport, CT: Praeger/Quorum Books, 1994), chap. 6.

EXHIBIT 7-A	Auctioning Off the "Most Precious Natural Resource of the Information Age"

The U.S. government owns one of the most valuable assets in the world—the right to use the nation's airwaves. National governments own the electromagnetic spectrum (air waves) over which messages or data are sent in each country. In the United States, the Federal Communications Commission (FCC) is the agency entrusted with managing proper use of these airwaves.

In 2000, the FCC announced that it would auction off 422 licenses in 195 geographic markets across the United States. The auction will enable private parties (organizations, businesses) to use portions of the electromagnetic spectrum that have been kept out of commercial public use. The decision to license the right to use more of the spectrum, which has been called "the most precious natural resource of the information age," was made by the FCC after extensive debates about whether the public interest would be served by making more frequencies available. So intense was the interest in acquiring these rights that the airwave rights sale was expected to bring in about $15 billion to the U.S. Treasury. But money is not the primary motivation for selling the licenses.

The FCC is responsible for regulating and promoting the communications industries. Companies engaged in wireless communications need electromagnetic frequencies on which they can transmit messages. Many of the bidders for the new licenses were major players in the communications business such as AT&T Wireless, Sprint PCS, and Verizon Wireless. They needed to fill in holes in their networks, enter new cities, increase overall capacity, and gain the national footprint that has eluded them. Other bidders included second-tier firms such as Nextel Communications,

regulations mentioned above, social regulations are not limited to one type of business or industry. Laws concerning pollution, safety and health, and job discrimination apply to all businesses; consumer protection laws apply to all relevant businesses producing and selling consumer goods.

Social regulations typically benefit large segments of society. Critics argue that costs are shared by a narrow segment of society: business and its customers. If the agencies that enforce social regulations do not consider the overall financial impact of their actions, businesses may experience losses and even be forced to close, leaving workers without jobs, communities without tax revenues, and customers without products. This argument does not excuse socially irresponsible conduct. In recent years, more political leaders have recognized that the effect of regulations on an industry's economic health is connected to the public interest.[16]

---

[16] See, for example, the discussion in Murray Weidenbaum, *Business, Government, and the Public,* 3d ed. (Englewood Cliffs, NJ: Prentice Hall, 1997).

Exhibit 7-A continued

VoiceStream Wireless, and Cingular, a joint venture of SBC Communications and Bell South, all of which were looking to expand.

In setting the rules for the auction, the FCC commissioners decided that the public interest required that some of the licenses be reserved for small businesses, minority enterprises, and rural companies. These licenses would enable small niche players to develop services for particular cities or regions. The auction rules therefore set aside some of the licenses for companies with assets less than $500 million and gross revenues of less than $125 million in each of the last two years.

Among the interesting bids received were those from three Alaskan companies owned by 38,000 natives. These companies were working with AT&T Wireless Group. Arctic Slope Regional Corp., Sealaska Corp., and Doyon Ltd., Native-American companies that were created by a special act of Congress in 1970, negotiated a deal with AT&T Wireless wherein cash from the number three wireless-service provider would help them win valuable airwaves in the auction. In return, AT&T had a chance to gain access to some restricted frequencies for less money.

The three Alaska Native Regional corporations, with combined revenue of more than $1 billion from businesses such as oil, mining, and tourism, would follow another native corporation—Cook Inlet Region Inc.—which saw its net income double after joining with VoiceStream Wireless Corp. in 1994 to buy licenses. In 2000, the U.S. wireless market was estimated to be worth about $45 billion.

Sources: Stephen Labaton, "Wireless Licenses Expected to Raise $15 Billion for U.S.," *New York Times,* December 8, 2000, pp. C1, C4. See also, "AT&T, 3 Native Alaska Companies Seek U.S. Airwaves," *Bloomberg News,* December 8, 2000.

Functional Regulations

Certain operations or functions of business have been singled out for special attention by government regulators. Labor practices, for example, are no longer left to the operation of free market forces. Government agencies set minimum wages, regulate overtime pay, establish the rules for labor union campaigns, and mediate serious and troublesome labor–management disputes, including, in recent years, strikes by airline pilots, flight attendants, school teachers, and even professional baseball players. Competition is another business function strongly affected by regulation. Antitrust laws attempt to prevent monopolies, preserve competitive pricing, and protect consumers against unfair practices (see Chapter 9).

Functional regulations, like social regulations, may cut across industry lines and apply generally to all enterprises, as they do in the case of antitrust and labor practices. Or they may, as in the case of regulations governing stock exchanges and the issuance of corporate securities, be confined to specific institutions such as the stock markets or the companies whose stocks are listed on those exchanges. Figure 7-3 depicts these three types of regulation—economic, social, and functional—along with the major regulatory agencies responsible for enforcing the rules at the federal level in the United States. Only

Figure 7-3

Three types of regulation: Industry-specific economic regulation, all-industry social regulation, and functional regulation.

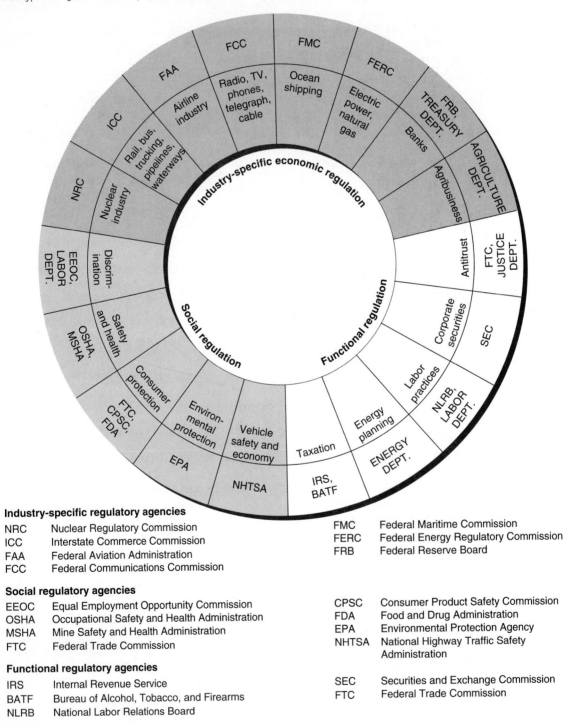

Industry-specific regulatory agencies

NRC	Nuclear Regulatory Commission
ICC	Interstate Commerce Commission
FAA	Federal Aviation Administration
FCC	Federal Communications Commission

FMC	Federal Maritime Commission
FERC	Federal Energy Regulatory Commission
FRB	Federal Reserve Board

Social regulatory agencies

EEOC	Equal Employment Opportunity Commission
OSHA	Occupational Safety and Health Administration
MSHA	Mine Safety and Health Administration
FTC	Federal Trade Commission

CPSC	Consumer Product Safety Commission
FDA	Food and Drug Administration
EPA	Environmental Protection Agency
NHTSA	National Highway Traffic Safety Administration

Functional regulatory agencies

IRS	Internal Revenue Service
BATF	Bureau of Alcohol, Tobacco, and Firearms
NLRB	National Labor Relations Board

SEC	Securities and Exchange Commission
FTC	Federal Trade Commission

the most prominent federal agencies are included in the chart. Individual states, some cities, and other national governments have their own array of agencies to implement regulatory policy.

There is a legitimate need for government regulation in modern economies, but regulation also has problems. Businesses feel these problems firsthand, often because the regulations directly affect the cost of products and the freedom of managers to design their business operations. In the modern economy, there are serious issues of regulatory cost and effectiveness that cannot be overlooked. Each is discussed below.

Costs of Regulation

The call for regulation may seem irresistible to government leaders and officials, but there are always costs to regulation. In recent years, more attention has been given to the costs of government regulation. An old economic adage says, "There is no free lunch." Eventually, someone has to pay for the benefits created. This is the **rule of cost,** and it applies in all socioeconomic systems.

An industrial society such as that of the United States can afford almost anything, including social regulations, if it is willing to pay the price. Sometimes the benefits are worth the costs; sometimes the costs exceed the benefits. The test of **cost-benefit analysis** helps the public understand what is at stake when new regulation is sought. For example, when the U.S. Congress debated the Clinton administration's national health care proposals in the 1990s, opposition increased when it was shown that the plan would impose large regulatory costs. Congress realized that the American public did not want the benefits of a national health care plan at just any cost; they wanted them at little or no cost. On the other hand, when it became known that the National Highway Transportation Safety Agency (NHTSA) had received information about defective Firestone tires more than one year before their recall in August 2000, the public was outraged that NHTSA's budget was not large enough to enable it to analyze the data and protect lives.

Figure 7-4 illustrates the increase in costs of federal regulation in the United States since the 1970s. Economic regulation has existed for many decades, and its cost has grown more slowly than social regulation. This reflects growth in such areas of social regulation as environmental health, occupational safety, and consumer protection. In addition to federal regulatory costs, regulatory expenditures by state and local governments have also risen in this period.

The growth in regulatory programs is not a new phenomenon. As scholars at the Center for the Study of American Business have documented, the growth pattern has been interrupted only briefly during the past three decades. In the early 1980s, President Ronald Reagan led a campaign to cut government regulation. In 1980, 122,000 people staffed federal regulatory agencies; budget cuts reduced the number to 102,000 in 1985. But under President George Bush, staff increases began to push the numbers higher. By

Figure 7-4

Spending on federal regulatory activity. Fiscal years, billions of dollars in obligations.

Source: Center for the Study of American Business.

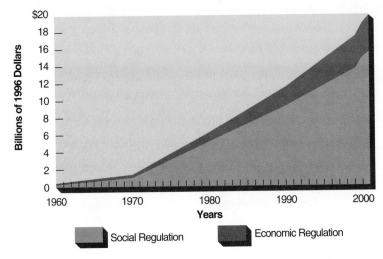

	1960	1970	1980	1990	1999	2000	2001 (est.)
Social	$318	$1,116	$5,303	$9,425	$13,774	$15,004	$15,640
Economic	126	292	996	2,143	3,719	3,916	4,185
Total	$444	$1,408	$6,299	$11,568	$17,493	$18,920	$19,825

Note: These data are in millions; graph is converted to billions.

1992, regulatory personnel equaled the 1980 number. By the year 2000, federal regulatory personnel numbered nearly 130,000 (see Figure 7-5).[17]

Effectiveness of Regulation

The need for regulation must be balanced against both its costs and assessments of whether it will accomplish its intended purpose. The United States has experimented with different forms of government regulation for more than 200 years, and experts have learned that not all government programs are effective in meeting their intended goals. Thus, government is called on from time to time to regulate certain types of business behavior and, at other times, to deregulate that behavior if it is believed that the industry no longer needs that regulation or that other, better, means exist to exercise control (e.g., market pressures from competitors).

Deregulation is the removal or scaling down of regulatory authority and regulatory activities of government. Deregulation is usually a politically popular idea. President Ronald Reagan strongly advocated deregulation in the early 1980s, when he campaigned on the promise to "get government off the back of people." Major deregulatory laws were enacted beginning in 1975 when Gerald Ford was president and continued through

[17] See website at Center for the Study of American Business at Washington University, www.csab.wustl.edu. See also, Melinda Warren, *Federal Regulatory Spending Reaches a New Height: An Analysis of the Budget of the United States Government for the Year 2001,* Regulatory Budget Report 23 (St. Louis: Washington University, Center for the Study of American Business, 2000).

Figure 7-5

Staffing of federal regulatory agencies. Full-time equivalent personnel.

Source: Center for the Study of American Business.

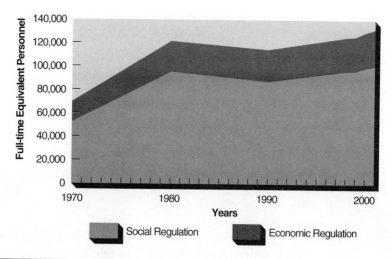

	1970	1980	1990	1998	1999	2000	2001 (est.)
Social	52,693	95,533	87,395	96,136	96,409	99,080	100,583
Economic	17,253	26,258	27,289	28,994	29,318	30,375	31,400
Total	69,946	121,791	114,684	125,130	125,727	129,455	131,983

the administrations of Jimmy Carter, Ronald Reagan, and George Bush. These laws loosened the grip of the federal government on a number of industries and markets:

- Price controls on domestic oil were abolished in 1981.
- The price of natural gas was decontrolled until controls ended in 1987.
- Phased deregulation of commercial airlines removed government-set rates and allowed domestic airlines to compete and more easily make mergers and acquisitions.
- The Civil Aeronautics Board (CAB), the chief airline regulatory agency since the 1930s, was abolished in 1985.
- Intercity trucking companies were permitted to charge lower prices and provide wider services; competitors entered the industry. Railroads, which were tightly regulated for a century, were deregulated and given the freedom to set rates in some parts of their business and to compete in new ways.
- Financial institutions were allowed to be more flexible in setting interest rates on loans and to compete across state lines (interstate banking) in the 1990s.

Deregulation does not always succeed. When gasoline and heating oil prices soared because of rising crude oil prices in 1999 and 2000, the American public complained loudly and demanded that the federal government take action against the oil companies and exporting nations. Similarly, when it became clear that more than 100 deaths were associated with defective Firestone tires, the call for more regulation of auto companies and tire manufacturers was loud and strong. And, as discussed in Exhibit 7-B, the

**EXHIBIT
7-B**

California's Energy Crisis: A Deregulation Failure

In 2001, California consumers faced a major problem: the state's two largest electric utility distributors—Pacific Gas and Electric and Southern California Edison—petitioned the Public Utility Commission (PUC) to raise rates to nearly double their existing levels. This was necessary, the companies said, because the cost of power that had to be purchased from out-of-state suppliers was skyrocketing. The PUC was reluctant to authorize the price increases, but the companies said that if they did not receive more revenue they would be unable to pay their suppliers who, in turn, would stop sending power into California. That would force Southern California Edison and Pacific Gas and Electric to resort to blackouts and other power-saving tactics. As the dispute dragged on, the state and its millions of customers moved toward the brink of crisis.

Electricity production and distribution were a government-run business for much of the twentieth century. Companies such as Southern California Edison and Pacific Gas and Electric grew into giant firms, each with millions of customers, billions of dollars of revenue, and a vast network of power plants, transmission lines, and workforce to install and maintain electric service. Federal agencies such as the Federal Power Commission and the U.S. Energy Department worked with state agencies—such as California's Public Utility Commission—to ensure enough power for all users, and to do so at the lowest possible cost.

By the 1980s, however, many experts believed that the cost of this system was too great and could be reduced by allowing more competition in various segments (production, distribution). A series of laws was passed in the 1990s that deregulated the industry and gave the companies more freedom to find more efficient ways to produce, buy, sell, and distribute energy. In 1994, California's Public Utility Commission envisioned a new, competitive market structure for energy in the state.

Some changes came quickly, as new companies (independent power producers, or IPPs) began producing energy and selling it to the large companies. Southern California Edison and Pacific Gas and Electric needed to buy power from other sources because they did not have enough generating capacity in their own systems. But the price for out-of-state power rose sharply, and the California PUC refused to allow the companies to pass on the cost to their California customers. The result was a squeeze: rising costs, flat revenues, declining profits. During the winter of 2000–2001, the consequences were felt by all Californians. As the crisis continued, and the state's population moved into what was described as a "wartime mood of general mobilization to battle the critical power shortages," everyone wondered whether the old inefficiencies of regulation had been as bad as the problems of current deregulated, competitive markets.

Sources: Rick Lyman, "Cynicism Abounds as Californians Lurch through Energy Shortages," *New York Times,* January 13, 2001, p. A11; Matthew L. Wald, "Negotiators Work on Plan for California Energy Trouble," *New York Times,* January 13, 2001, p. A11; James Sterngold, "California Acting to Relieve Crisis," *New York Times,* January 13, 2001, pp. A1, A11; and Chris Gaither, "The Dog Day in June the Lights Went Out: Silicon Valley's Achilles' Heel Is Exposed," *New York Times,* January 12, 2001, p. C14.

deregulation of California's energy markets produced one of the state's worst crises in decades as power prices soared, blackouts occurred, and two of the state's largest electric companies faced insolvency and bankruptcy.

Proponents of deregulation always contend with the public's desire to see government solve problems. This generates situations in which government is trying to deregulate in some areas while also creating new regulation in others. **Reregulation** is the increase or expansion of government regulation, especially in areas where the regulatory activities had previously been reduced. During the 1990s, the federal government passed laws to toughen worker safety standards, establish new environmental protection standards, set curbs on insider trading of corporate securities, fix requirements for airline collision avoidance equipment, and impose drug testing of train engineers, airline pilots, and others.

Reinventing Government

The trend toward streamlining government, and making its operations more efficient, is called **reinventing government.** This idea derives from the success of businesses in redesigning work to become more efficient and achieve higher quality. It operates on the principle that efficiency can be improved when unnecessary procedures, processes, and people are eliminated. The federal government's efforts to reinvent and modernize government began in the mid-1990s, and federal agencies, including regulatory agencies, undertook hundreds of initiatives to save taxpayers' dollars while better meeting important needs. Annual reports of these efforts are available to citizens.[18]

International Regulation

International commerce unites people and businesses in new and complicated ways. U.S. consumers routinely buy food, automobiles, and clothing from companies located in Europe, Canada, Latin America, Australia, Africa, and Asia. Citizens of other nations do the same. As these patterns of international commerce grow more complicated, governments recognize the need to establish rules that protect the interests of their own citizens. No nation wants to accept dangerous products manufactured elsewhere that will injure its citizens, and no government wants to see its economy damaged by unfair competition from foreign competitors. These concerns provide the rationale for international regulatory agreements and cooperation. Three types of such regulation are discussed below and illustrated in Figure 7-6.

Regulation of Imported Products

Every nation has the power to set standards for products to be sold in the country. When a child in Chicago receives a Christmas toy made in Taiwan, for example, that toy has met the product safety standards set by the U.S. Consumer Product Safety Commission.

---

[18] David Osborne and Peter Plastrik, *Banishing Bureaucracy: The Five Strategies for Reinventing Government* (Reading, MA: Addison-Wesley, 1997). See also, David Osborne and Ted Gaebler, *Reinventing Government: How the Entrepreneurial Spirit Is Transforming the Public Sector* (Reading, MA: Addison-Wesley, 1992). The current status of the National Performance Review initiative is available at www.npr.gov/initiati/index.html. For the original report, see Al Gore, *From Red Tape to Results: Creating a Government That Works Better and Costs Less: Report of the National Performance Review* (Washington, DC: Government Printing Office, 1993).

Figure 7-6

Forms of international
regulation.

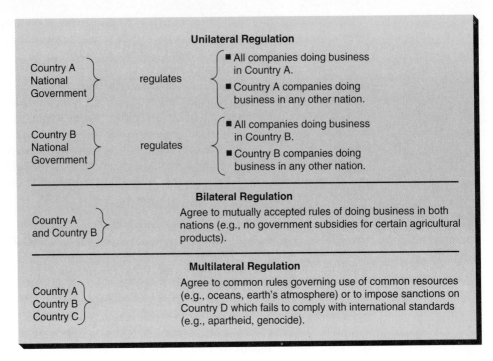

This use of government authority is legitimate, but the standards for foreign products must be the same as for locally produced goods. If the Consumer Product Safety Commission were to set one standard for U.S. companies and a more demanding standard for foreign toy companies, the result would help U.S. companies and hurt foreign competitors. The standard would discriminate against foreign manufacturers, and the practice would likely be deemed a trade barrier in violation of international trade agreements. This could make the United States liable for damages to the foreign toy producers.

Governments, however, are under pressure from other interests, including local companies, labor organizations, and communities, not to open local markets to foreign sellers. These stakeholders may feel threatened by foreign competitors and seek to block them from selling to a "safe" market of customers. The solution lies in cooperative political and economic agreements that favor free trade and discourage protective regulation.

Regulation of Exported Products

Governments have an interest in knowing what products their businesses are exporting to the rest of the world. The federal government is understandably concerned that products that say "Made in America" are of good quality. U.S. companies have sometimes exported products to other nations that were banned from sale at home because of safety concerns. The government is also concerned that U.S. companies not sell military technology to unfriendly nations. In recent years, a number of cases arose in which U.S. businesses illegally sold sophisticated technology with potential military applications to Libya, Iran, and Iraq. These transactions violated U.S. laws that restrict the sale of classified military technology to only those customers approved by the Defense Department.

*For example, EG&G, a manufacturer of specialized electronic equipment
for military use, discovered that some of the triggering devices it manufactured for nuclear weapons were being sold to Iraq. In collaboration with
U.S. officials, a shipment of such devices was traced through a series of
intermediaries to a European customer who was reshipping them to
Baghdad. With the cooperation of foreign officials and EG&G, the illegal
exporters were caught and arrested.*

Regulation of International Business Behavior

Nations have sought to standardize trade practices through various international
organizations. United Nations agencies such as the World Health Organization have
worked with the pharmaceutical industry to create databases on the side effects of
drug products, establish quality standards, and resolve conflicting manufacturing and
marketing practices that might harm the public. Elaborate processes of consultation
between leaders of business, governmental, and nongovernmental organizations (e.g.,
consumer groups) are required to make such changes because of the vast number
of stakeholders involved. The World Health Organization's international marketing
code for infant formula products, for example, required nearly three years of meetings and consultations before a suitable code was ready for adoption by national
governments.[19]

National governments sometimes create special organizations to keep the discussions moving forward. For example, the General Agreement on Tariffs and Trade (GATT)
is a set of international agreements among nations on acceptable trade practices. Periodically, nations agree to another round of negotiations to be hosted in a particular nation.
In recent years, these talks have focused on government subsidies to agriculture that prevent fair competition. Lengthy and complex negotiations eventually produced a new
international body—the **World Trade Organization**—to enforce the new international
trade laws. Still, more than a decade later, in 2002, there is no uniform agreement about
subsidies for many agricultural products.

Nations also cooperate to establish standards for the use of global resources not
owned by any nation. Multilateral international agreements govern ocean fishing, protection of sea mammals such as dolphins and whales, the earth's ozone layer, and dumping of hazardous chemical waste in oceans. In each case, governments acknowledge the
problem cannot be solved through one nation's actions. The result is a framework of
international agreements, standards, and understandings that attempts to harmonize business activity and the public interest.[20]

---

[19] James E. Post, "Codes of Conduct: An Idea Whose Time Has Come," in Oliver Williams, ed., *Global
Codes of Conduct: An Idea Whose Time Has Come?* (South Bend, IN: University of Notre Dame Press,
2000). See also, S. Prakash Sethi, *Multinational Corporations and the Impact of Public Advocacy on
Corporate Strategy* (Hingham, MA: Kluwer, 1994).

[20] Kathleen A. Getz, "International Instruments on Bribery and Corruption," in Oliver Williams, ed., *Global
Codes of Conduct: An Idea Whose Time Has Come?* (South Bend, IN: University of Notre Dame Press,
2000). See also, William C. Frederick, "The Moral Authority of Transnational Corporate Codes," *Journal of
Business Ethics* 10 (1991), pp. 165–77.

The Future

Government interaction with business is a basic feature of all socioeconomic systems. Whether in Europe, Asia, Africa, Latin America, or elsewhere, managers have to deal with government regulations that affect their activities and their businesses.

In the United States, macroeconomic policy has shaped the business environment and government regulation has influenced how companies compete. The pendulum of regulation has swung back and forth for nearly a century, sometimes favoring more control, sometimes less. Pressures to reduce the role of government contend with pressures for more government effort to solve problems in more cost-efficient ways. Every nation faces these choices and seeks ways to create balanced policies that meet the challenge of harmonizing economic growth with the social welfare of citizens. It is for these reasons that the changing role of government is one of the basic driving forces of change in the modern world.

Summary Points of This Chapter

- The key elements of public policy are inputs, goals, instruments to achieve those goals, and effects—both intended and unintended.
- Key national economic policies affecting business in every nation include economic growth, taxation, government spending, the value of money, international trade, and industrial policy.
- Social welfare policies affect business both directly (e.g., workplace rules) and indirectly (government spending) and express the social priorities of a nation. Health care, social security, and education are among a nation's most important social welfare policies.
- Government regulation of business is a mechanism for implementing public choices. Economic, social, and functional regulation of business exists in most countries.
- The role of government regulation has grown because society demands and expects more of government. Public exposure to risk creates powerful pressures on government to regulate business. Deregulation has grown because the public also seeks more efficient use of resources that market pressures typically produce.
- International regulation is emerging because nations recognize their need to cooperate in controlling business activities that cross national borders and affect people in different countries. International regulations focusing on imports, exports, and business practices must be negotiated after countries have reached bilateral or multilateral agreements.

Key Terms and Concepts Used in This Chapter

- Public policy
- Common law
- Fiscal policy
- Monetary policy
- Trade policy
- Industrial policy

- Entitlement mentality
- Market failures
- Rule of cost
- Cost-benefit analysis

- Deregulation
- Reregulation
- Reinventing government
- World Trade Organization (WTO)

Internet Resources

• www.whitehouse.gov	Executive Office of the President of the United States
• www.bea.doc.gov	Bureau of Economic Analysis, U.S. Department of Commerce
• www.census.gov	Bureau of the Census, U.S. Department of Commerce
• www.sec.gov	U.S. Securities and Exchange Commission
• www.npr.gov	National Performance Review ("Reinventing Government: Creating a Government That Works Better and Costs Less")
• www.firstgov.gov	Entry point to all branches of the federal government

Discussion Case: *Protecting Human Food Supplies*

Consumers who are concerned about food safety have had much to worry about in recent years. Episodes of human illness and death traced to contaminated food have challenged the confidence of consumers in the United States, Europe, and other countries. For people who buy billions of dollars of fresh and packaged food in supermarkets, grocery stores, and restaurants each year, food safety has become a serious concern requiring government action.

There are actually several different problems threatening human food supplies. According to food experts, the rate of salmonella illness has doubled over the past 20 years. In the past, cases originated in restaurants or at events where people preparing the food made mistakes. Today, food is often tainted during processing in huge food factories; it may be distributed to millions of people before anyone gets sick. A single day's production at a modern ground beef plant in the United States, for example, can turn out hundreds of thousands of pounds of hamburger, which are then rapidly trucked all over the country. According to the Centers for Disease Control and Prevention, nearly 10,000 people die every year from food poisoning in the United States.

Concerns about the safety of red meat, especially cooked hamburger meat, soared in 1997 when a rash of food-poisoning cases was reported in Denver, Colorado. The illness was traced to the presence of E. coli bacteria in hamburger patties eaten by the victims. All of the meat, investigators found, came from a single processing plant in Nebraska. Investigators identified the likely source of the E. coli bacteria—a human bacteria—that is often introduced into the food supply by workers who may unknowingly spread it to others directly or indirectly. By failing to wash their hands, for example, workers could spread the E. coli bacteria to any food they handled. Thus, it was hypothesized that the contaminated hamburger was infected by an unknown worker at the Nebraska plant.

The U.S. Department of Agriculture regulates meat packing operations and issues inspection permits that allow a packing company to stamp its meat, "USDA Inspected." USDA officials found, however, that they were without authority to close the Nebraska plant. All they could do was threaten the company with loss of permission to use the USDA stamp and publicize the action through the media. Although the company finally agreed to close, the USDA went to the Congress and requested legal authority to close such plants in the future.

Another problem related to red meat arose in Europe when mad cow disease was diagnosed in the United Kingdom in the 1990s. A number of British citizens died from the neurologic condition known as Jakob-Creutzfeld disease. The disease is transmitted when cows eat feed that has been made from animal parts (bones, intestinal parts) from a diseased animal. Animal parts have been fed to cows and other farm animals as a source of protein since World War II. In Britain, it was found that some farmers gave their cattle contaminated feed, resulting in symptoms where the affected cows wandered aimlessly, lost balance, frothed at the mouth, and eventually died. The British government ordered farmers to stop selling meat from such "mad cows," quarantined and tested the herds, and eventually ordered that thousands of cattle be destroyed. Many farmers were put out of business, but the government insisted that action was needed to protect the public from disease. European countries refused to allow British beef to be sold in their countries, despite the European Union's free trade rules that are supposed to create open borders. Pressure from health authorities, the media, and local farmers forced government leaders to ban the British beef. By 2001, incidents of mad cow disease were reported in France, Spain, Ireland, and Germany, and millions of dollars had been spent to identify causes and preventive measures. In the United States, government authorities quarantined a herd of sheep in Vermont that were suspected of carrying the mad cow disease gene. Vermont sheepherders vigorously opposed the government's threat to destroy the entire herd.

Food safety issues are becoming more global as trade and transportation move people and products. Concerns have been rising around the world. Outbreaks of foodborne illnesses have been traced to strawberries, lettuce, alfalfa sprouts, melons, and other kinds of fresh produce, both imported and domestic. When 1,300 cases of cyclospora—a disease that produces severe reactions in humans, including dehydration and diarrhea—were reported to the Centers for Disease Control, the cases were linked to Guatemalan raspberries that had been processed in the United States and distributed to restaurants and stores. The Food and Drug Administration (FDA) banned Guatemalan raspberry exports to the United States for the following year. Bans on products typically remain in effect "until the problem is worked out," said Robert Lake, director of policy for the FDA's Center for Food Safety. "Our objective is not to create trade barriers but make our food safer," said Lake. The Guatemalan government said it was cooperating with U.S. officials.

Consumers have another kind of food safety issue to worry about. In November 2000, Kraft Foods recalled millions of taco shells possibly containing StarLink, a genetically engineered variety of corn that produces the Cry9C protein. This corn has not been approved by government officials (Environmental Protection Agency) for human consumption because of concerns it might trigger allergic reactions among those who consume it. (StarLink corn is approved for animal consumption, however.) Corn processors, such as Kraft and Archer Daniels Midland, have been forced to adopt expensive screening procedures to ensure that the corn they process into flour is free of Cry9C. Inspectors apply a dye to test each batch of corn—if it turns red, it means that Cry9C is present and the entire shipment is rejected. Millions of tons of corn were discarded; farmers and wholesalers were expected to lose billions of dollars because of the tainted corn. Many were asking the federal government for financial assistance.

Sources: David Barboza, "Gene-Altered Corn Changes Dynamics of Grain Industry," *New York Times,* December 12, 2000, pp. A1, A20; Jane E. Brody, "Gene Altered Foods: A Case against Panic," *New York Times,* December 5, 2000, p. D8; "Guatemalan Raspberries Barred from U.S.," *Boston Globe,* December 9, 1997, p. A13; and "Change Cited in Onset of Food-Borne Illnesses," *Boston Globe,* December 10, 1997, p. A20.
Regarding the responses of national governments to mad cow disease, see Sandra Blakeslee, "Stringent Steps Taken by U.S. on Cow Illness," *New York Times,* January 14, 2001, pp. 1, 23; "Irish to Slaughter Cattle," *New York Times,* January 8, 2001, p. A6; Roger Cohen, "Two Named to New German Agency in Shuffle over Beef Disease," *New York Times,* January 11, 2001, p. A10; and Suzanne Daley, "Europe Takes Toughest Steps to Fight Mad Cow Disease," *New York Times,* December 5, 2000, p. A3.

Discussion Questions

1. What public policy issues are raised by these food safety examples? Who are the stakeholders in each of the examples cited in the case?
2. Why should government regulate meat processing?
3. Should Guatemalan raspberries be regulated by the government of the country where they are grown or the country where they are consumed?
4. Should the U.S. food supply quality be the responsibility of the federal government? State government? The food industry through self-regulation? Why do you favor your choice?
5. What can a consumer do to protect herself against mad cow disease? Against an allergic reaction to the Cry9C protein?

8

Managing Business— Government Relations

Businesses face complicated issues in managing their relationships with government. Managers must recognize, and know how to respond to, public issues as they emerge. The dynamics of the public policy process demand that managers understand the political environment and have a strategic view of how stakeholders will behave on specific issues. In most nations, businesses have rights to participate in the political process. Managers need to ensure that their company is seen as a relevant stakeholder when government officials make public policy decisions. Political pressures can also produce ethical dilemmas for managers. The world of politics operates by different rules than the world of business. Sound decisions depend on an understanding of those differences and sound rules of judgment.

This chapter focuses on these key questions and objectives:

- Why do businesses participate in the political process?
- What form does corporate political activity take?
- What role does business play in electoral politics?
- What does strategic management of business–government relations mean?
- Why is it important for business to be involved in public policy decision making?
- How do the problems of the American political system affect business?

he Public Affairs Council (PAC) is a Washington-based group whose 600 members include large manufacturing firms (e.g., Boeing, General Electric, Goodyear, Mead), banks, insurers, and electric power companies, and companies in health services and other industries. PAC members share a common need to manage their relationships with government agencies more effectively. Many of them have business dealings with regulatory agencies and are affected by tax laws and other public policies. The PAC helps its members by providing information and organizing seminars that bring together business and government leaders. This networking is crucial to the process of business–government interaction. One of the PAC's most popular meetings is a briefing that occurs a few days after a national election is held. In 2000, the Public Affairs Council's postelection briefing was held on Wednesday, November 8. However, none of the assembled experts could answer the key question for attendees: Who won the presidential race?

In the weeks that followed, business executives and managers paid close attention to the twists and turns of the contested Florida electoral results. The new president would have a major impact on matters affecting companies of all sizes. For companies that do business around the world, such as Boeing (airplanes) and GE (power systems, medical devices, financial services), it is important to know the new president's priorities for international trade, defense spending, and monetary policy. For companies that operate primarily in the United States, such as Mead (paper products) or Goodyear (tires), it is important to understand the new president's priorities on the environment, health care, taxes, and regulation. And for new companies just starting out as e-commerce or dot-com firms, the new president's priorities on start-up funding for new business, taxation of Internet transactions, and privacy of consumer data could have significant consequences.

Whatever their size, products, or place of business, companies need to understand how the decisions of federal, state, and local government affect them. Most important, managers of these companies must understand how to communicate their views about proposed government actions to elected officials and to those who work in government agencies. Organizations like the Public Affairs Council help managers understand the workings of local, national, and international government bodies.

This chapter focuses on managing government relations and political issues. Businesses do not have an absolute right to exist and pursue profits. The right to conduct commerce and make profits depends on compliance with appropriate laws and public policy. As discussed in Chapter 7, public policy is shaped by many factors. Public issues force companies to monitor public concerns, respond to government proposals, and participate in the political process. This chapter discusses, therefore, how managers and their businesses can meet the challenge of managing business–government relations.

Strategic Management of Government Relations

There is a serious, ongoing debate between those who favor business involvement in government and those who oppose it. This debate involves the question of whether, and to what extent, business should legitimately participate in the political process. As shown in Figure 8-1, some people believe business should stay out of politics, whereas others argue that business must be involved.

Figure 8-1

The case for and against political involvement by business.

Reasons business *should* be involved

- A pluralistic system invites many participants
- Economic stakes are high for firms and industries
- Business counterbalances other social interests
- Business is a vital stakeholder of government

Reasons business *should not* be involved

- Executives are not qualified to engage in political debate
- Business is naive about politics
- Business is too big, too powerful—it is the "500-pound gorilla"
- Business risks its credibility by engaging in partisan politics

Business and politics are increasingly entwined in the modern world in ways that make it impossible for managers to ignore what is going on in political life. Gradually, business leaders have come to recognize that the survival and prosperity of their businesses are connected to political decisions. Although this trend is clear and visible in all nations, critics worry about the amount of influence corporations can wield on specific governmental decisions. The dilemma for managers is quite clear: How can a company participate in the political process on issues that matter to it and to its industry but do so in ways that are consistent with the ethical norms and standards of the society that grants business its legitimacy?

Techniques of Political Action

The techniques used by businesses to participate in governmental politics are similar to those of other interest groups. Three techniques are widely used: direct representation, trade associations, and ad hoc coalitions.

Direct Representation

Many companies assign full-time representatives and staff in Washington, D.C. (or the national capital in countries where they operate) to keep abreast of developments that may affect the company and, when necessary, to communicate with government officials. This presence enables the company's Washington office staff to directly represent the business before the people and agencies involved in determining legislative and regulatory activity. **Lobbying** is the process of communicating with and trying to persuade others to support an organization's interest or stake as they consider a particular law, policy, or regulation. Company lobbyists may be active at the local or state levels, as well as with national government.

Trade Associations

Many companies also join trade associations such as the National Realtors Association (real estate brokers), National Federation of Independent Businesses (small businesses), the National Association of Manufacturers (manufacturers only), or the U.S. Chamber of Commerce (broad, diverse membership), where they count on strength of numbers and a centralized staff to promote their interests with government officials.[1]

> *The U.S. Chamber of Commerce has a membership of more than 200,000 companies. The Chamber has a multimillion-dollar budget, publishes a widely circulated magazine, and operates a satellite television network to broadcast its political messages. The Chamber of Commerce takes positions on a wide range of political, economic, and regulatory questions and actively works to promote its members' views of what conditions are necessary for them to effectively compete in a free marketplace.*

Ad Hoc Coalitions

A third technique that is often used is the creation of ad hoc coalitions. Ad hoc coalitions are used to bring diverse business groups together to lobby for or against particular legislation or regulation. Businesses will sometimes find themselves working with their competitors, companies from other industries, and nonbusiness organizations that share a concern about specific laws, regulations, tax proposals, or other issues. Politics can create unusual alliances and curious conflicts, as the following example illustrates.

> *Several years ago, the U.S. Congress was asked to consider passing a law that would extend daylight saving time. Daylight saving involves setting clocks forward (or backward) in specific areas of the country to lengthen the amount of daylight hours for residents in that area of the country. The original daylight saving time change occurred during World War II as a way of adjusting Americans' daytime activities to the maximum amount of daylight. This helped conserve fuel for winter heating and electricity consumption. Since then, adjustments have been made from time to time by the Congress in response to specific needs. The proposal to lengthen the period of daylight saving came from California, where proponents sought to change the fall-back date from late October to a date in November. Among the proponents were the barbecue grill industry and candy manufacturers, each with a very different view of what should happen. The barbecue industry argued that an extra few weeks of daylight saving would boost the sale of grills, charcoal, and utensils. The candy industry,*

---

[1] The classic discussion of corporate political action is Edwin Epstein, *The Corporation in American Politics* (Englewood Cliffs, NJ: Prentice Hall, 1969). An up-to-date discussion of current trends in American political and civic life is Robert D. Putnam, *Bowling Alone* (New York: Simon and Schuster, 2000), especially chap. 4.

Figure 8-2

Levels of business
political involvement.

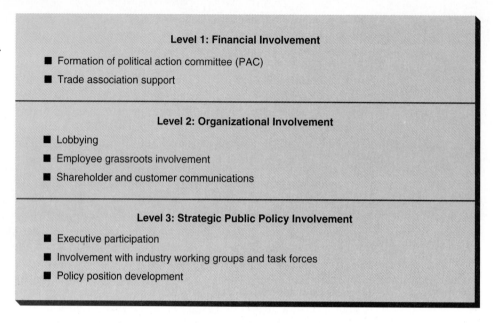

Level 1: Financial Involvement

■ Formation of political action committee (PAC)

■ Trade association support

Level 2: Organizational Involvement

■ Lobbying

■ Employee grassroots involvement

■ Shareholder and customer communications

Level 3: Strategic Public Policy Involvement

■ Executive participation

■ Involvement with industry working groups and task forces

■ Policy position development

however, argued that daylight saving must end before Halloween or candy sales would decline as fewer children went out trick or treating.

The legislative battle eventually drew in police departments, child welfare agencies, television stations, and many other advocates of one or another position. Advocates and opponents of various proposals rearranged themselves many times as different proposals were discussed. In the end, no action was taken because coalitions effectively blocked every proposal.

Political Involvement

Business executives must decide on the appropriate level of political involvement for their company. As shown in Figure 8-2, there are multiple levels of involvement and many ways to participate. To be successful, a business must think strategically about objectives and how specific political issues and opportunities relate to those objectives. This involves the company's stake in the issue and the possible consequences of the proposed action.

A software company that designs and manufacturers products for use in computer systems around the world has a long-term strategic interest in strong copyright laws and other intellectual property protection (IPP) to prevent piracy of ideas and products. The time to start lobbying for such laws is not when the company's hot new product is introduced—that is much too late. Years in advance, the company must be working with others in the political process to secure the intellectual property laws that will protect future generations of ideas and products from piracy. It may need strong laws to protect its domestic (home) market and the commitment of its government to negotiate and enforce IPP agreements with foreign governments.

Strategic interests may be direct or indirect. Many businesses have sought to persuade state, local, and national governments to improve public education. Some do so out of the belief that it is unwise for students to leave schools without the skills needed to get jobs in the modern economy. Others have a longer-term and more self-interested point of view: Future workers who do not have sound education will create a shortage of critical skills and, hence, a problem for the companies that will be seeking to hire skilled employees.

Managing the Political Agenda

Political life reflects larger trends and complexities in society. The political process is an arena in which substance and symbols are often intertwined. Scholars such as E. E. Schattschneider and Murray Edelman view political issues as a dynamic conflict.[2] This view places *conflict* at the center of analysis rather than individuals, leaders, agencies, institutions (e.g., Congress), or political parties. As Roger Cobb and Marc Howard Ross, two of the leading modern advocates of the view, argue,

> *Most of politics revolves around the development and expansion of conflict surrounding evolving political issues. People with grievances need to gain the attention of additional individuals and do this by redefining their most intense concerns to draw others into the battle. A growing maelstrom of concern could catapult an issue to the top of the political heap.[3]*

Cobb and Ross focus on events that are expected to occur, but which do not. Why does this happen? How does it happen? Their analysis concentrates on situations in seven areas, including federal regulatory agencies (e.g., Securities and Exchange Commission, Food and Drug Administration), and public health issues such as national health insurance debates in the 1940s and 1990s. They write,

> *In a variation on Edelman's view that politics is about the distribution of tangible and symbolic benefits, we suggest that agenda conflicts are about both the concrete decision whether government will or will not consider a particular issue and the competing interpretations of political issues to which people attach great emotional significance. Politics, from this point of view, not only determines who gets what, when, and how but also provides a forum for choosing among competing views concerning how we*

---

[2] E. E. Schattschneider, *The Semi-Sovereign People: A Realist's Guide to Democracy in America* (New York: Holt, 1960); and Murray Edelman, *The Symbolic Uses of Politics* (Urbana, IL: University of Illinois Press, 1964). An application of these classic ideas to more recent political life can be found in Michael Lerner, *The Meaning of Ideas* (New York: Free Press, 1997).

[3] Roger Cobb and Marc Howard Ross, eds., *Cultural Strategies of Agenda Denial: Avoidance, Attack, and Redefinition* (Lawrence, KS: University of Kansas Press, 1997), p. ix.

Figure 8-3

The triangle of business–government–society relationships.

Source: John F. Mahon and Richard A. McGowan, *Industry as a Player in The Political and Social Arena* (Westport, CT: Quorum, 1996), p. 29. Used with permission.

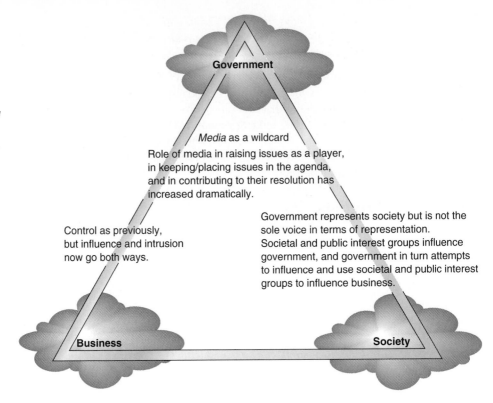

Government

Media as a wildcard
Role of media in raising issues as a player, in keeping/placing issues in the agenda, and in contributing to their resolution has increased dramatically.

Control as previously, but influence and intrusion now go both ways.

Government represents society but is not the sole voice in terms of representation. Societal and public interest groups influence government, and government in turn attempts to influence and use societal and public interest groups to influence business.

Business

Society

should live, what government ought to do, how we relate to the environment, and who the enemies are.[4]

Such ideas are the foundation on which much of the current thinking about corporate political action is based.

Corporate Political Strategy

One of government's roles is to mediate the interests of many diverse people, organizations, and interests in society. John Mahon and Richard McGowan have depicted this relationship as a triangle of interests as shown in Figure 8-3. Business must participate in politics, according to those authors, because there are too many issues of importance to a business upon which government must and will act. Without a corporate political strategy, the company's interests cannot be adequately represented and protected.

What is corporate political strategy? Mahon and McGowan define **corporate political strategy** as "those activities taken by organizations to acquire, develop, and use power to obtain an advantage (a particular allocation of resources or no change in the

---

[4] Cobb and Ross, *Cultural Strategies of Agenda Denial,* p. 29.

Figure 8-4

Motorola's public policy agenda.

Source: Author's archival research and articles published in the *Wall Street Journal, Business Week,* and other business media, 1995–1998.

Level	Example
Product level (Motorola business unit only)	Standards for cellular telephones
Business unit level (Motorola corporate level)	Foreign competitors' dumping practices
Industry level (Motorola and competitors)	Encryption standards/regulations
Multi-industry level (Motorola and noncompetitors)	
■ Specific proposals	U.S. policy on trade sanctions W.T.O. membership for China
■ General proposals	National macroeconomic policies Linking human rights to trade policy

allocation) in a situation of conflict."[5] This definition assumes that the many interests in a society will produce conflict about what to do and how to do it. Whether the issue is as broad as global warming or as specific as the risk posed by dioxin in a particular neighborhood, government is the place where such conflicts are resolved. A corporate political strategy is an approach to such relationships in a way that will enable the company to acquire power, use it, and obtain an advantage from it whenever such conflicts affect the firm or its business activities.

Companies as Stakeholders

The importance of a corporate political strategy can be understood by looking more closely at the public policy agenda of one large and reasonably typical company. The variety of issues around which Motorola, a manufacturer of electronic equipment and related products, has actual or potential conflicts with others in society is shown in Figure 8-4. Notice that the company has a clear and vital business interest in a wide range of political issues. Some are quite specific, involving an individual product (e.g., cellular telephones); others are quite broad, such as the opening of foreign markets to American electronic products. Motorola or companies like it are likely to be engaged in trying to influence what government does in such areas because of their stake in the outcome. They are, in other words, *stakeholders* of the public policy process and the political system.

American Politics in a New Century

Modern business is operating in a political environment whose institutions and processes have been shaped and adjusted over the course of several centuries. The result is a mixture of the old (e.g., antiquated voting systems in the year 2000 presidential election) and the very new (e.g., debates on cyberpolicies).

---

[5] John F. Mahon and Richard A. McGowan, *Corporate Political Strategy: Industry as Players in the Political and Social Arena* (Westport, CT: Quorum Press, 1996), p. 29.

Conflict and Cooperation

In the United States, the relationship between business and government has alternated between conflict and cooperation throughout most of the nation's history. In the colonial era, businesses were oppressed by high taxes and supported independence from England. In the eighteenth and nineteenth centuries, state and national governments often helped new industries get started by granting money, land, or other resources to entrepreneurs who helped build railroads, establish towns, and provide other essential services. But there were also big battles over the stability of money (silver-backed or gold-backed), unfair competition, and outright fraudulent business practices. During the twentieth century, business had periods of intense conflict with government. Since the 1930s, the federal government has actively guided the economy toward growth, full employment, and social well-being. Activist government emerged during the Great Depression, when most people agreed that government should do all that it could to restore economic prosperity. But 50 years of activist government produced a powerful backlash by the 1980s, when President Reagan asserted that "government is the problem, not the solution" to America's needs. During the 1980s and 1990s, some efforts were made to shrink the size of government, narrow its focus, and limit its activities. People have reconsidered how government and business should relate to one another. Business leaders agree that there is a need for strong and effective government to do certain things in a modern society. And government leaders recognize the need for a strong and efficient business sector. Still, as the first presidential campaign of the twenty-first century took place, there was a lively debate between the candidates about precisely where to draw the lines between business and government as we move into a new century.

Political Cynicism

Many Americans believe that the nation's economic and social problems require government to set the economic policy course and create the framework for prosperity. But many others believe that high taxes deprive them of income necessary to make private choices while feeding a big government that is frequently out of touch with its citizens. Presidential campaigns put these debates in clear view for most people.

Political cynicism refers to a social climate of distrust about politics and politicians. America suffered from serious political cynicism in the 1990s. Voters have been upset with a system that seems unable to deliver on its promises. Voter turnout has been low in most elections, and even presidential races have barely drawn 50 percent of registered voters in most states. Candidates for political office often use negative campaigning, in which one candidate attacks the positions and personal qualities (e.g., truthfulness) of his or her opponent. Political advertising has been used to damage the image of opponents because the public responds to such attack ads. Political advertising has become a highly specialized world of polling, focus groups, and segmented audiences. The net result is declining public respect for politicians. The public has come to distrust long-serving incumbents, media-slick new candidates who advocate change, and political campaigns in general. Such negative attitudes ultimately affect how public policy is made and what ideas are turned into legislation and regulation.

There is a continuing debate among political experts about how politics and public policy interrelate. Some believe that those who control the economic system will always find ways to control the political system. Others think that many different interests compete for influence in the political system. A third view holds that the bureaucracy of government itself dominates the political system and that other interests are secondary to the influence of civil servants and career bureaucrats.[6] Finally, there is a "social elite" view, which holds that a relatively small segment of social, business, and political leaders (the elite) makes key decisions without much regard to popular wishes.

The twenty-first century American political scene seems to offer some evidence for each of these views. The United States remains a pluralistic political system in which interest groups abound and have a powerful effect on political life. But because there are so many different interests in modern American society, individual groups rarely have enough power to consistently win on important issues without building consensus. Coalitions have to be formed to advance ideas, specific legislation, or regulations through the complex processes of government. Robert D. Putnam, a sociologist and respected observer of American social and political trends, has noted that "social capital" declines in a society as people fail to collaborate and work together to build what used to be called a *commonwealth*[7] (see discussion in Chapter 16). In today's political environment, amid all the conflict, controversy, and political cynicism, the building of **coalitions** and cooperation among different groups, interests, and stakeholders is an essential aspect of building a successful economy and a successful society.

Coalition Politics

According to some experts, modern political life is such that no special interest is ever powerful enough, by itself, to determine how an issue should be resolved.[8] Other experts argue that coalitions are formed so rapidly and with such resources as to create a type of political gridlock in which action cannot occur. Still others disagree, citing the extent to which a small group of special interests—especially Wall Street and Washington insiders (named the Beltway Bandits because they tend to be located within the road that circles the nation's capital)—must always be included in a winning coalition because they dominate the political agenda or control access to key decision makers.[9]

Political parties have been a vital part of pluralistic society, representing what are sometimes called *grand coalitions* of individuals and interest groups seeking their own welfare through political action. Although political parties are not mentioned in the U.S. Constitution, they have been an important part of the system of representative government. They help the electoral process work by providing a means to develop candidates for public office; they also serve as a rallying point for individuals and groups to work with others who hold similar ideas about how to run the government.

---

[6] Putnam, *Bowling Alone,* see chap. 4.

[7] Putnam, *Bowling Alone.*

[8] Haynes Johnson and David S. Broder, *The System: The American Way of Politics at the Breaking Point* (Boston: Little Brown, 1996).

[9] Johnson and Broder, *The System.* For an historical view of this phenomenon, see Arthur M. Schlesinger, Jr., *The Cycles of American History* (Boston: Houghton Mifflin, 1986).

However, political parties have steadily lost their power to hold together diverse political interests and to keep government running. Party affiliations do not seem as important to citizens today as they did in earlier times. Voters also cross boundaries more often, sometimes voting for Democratic candidates, sometimes for Republicans, and sometimes for independents. Third-party presidential campaigns in 1980 (John Anderson ran against Jimmy Carter and Ronald Reagan), 1992 (Ross Perot ran against George Bush and Bill Clinton), and 2000 (Pat Buchanan and Ralph Nader ran against Al Gore and George W. Bush) symbolize the failing of traditional political parties to represent voters at the national level.

Political parties seem to command more loyalty at the state and local levels, although there is considerable variation, with large numbers of voters registered as independents and more candidates running outside conventional party designations. But the federal Congress has also shown signs of the "party disease." Between 1992 and 1994, when the Democratic party had majority control of the House of Representatives and the Senate, President Bill Clinton failed to achieve his legislative agenda because some Democratic members would not vote with their leaders. Newt Gingrich, who became Republican Speaker of the House of Representatives in 1995, held his party's majority together for a time, but he recognized that the unity would not last. Party solidarity was exhausted during the debates surrounding the impeachment trial of President Clinton, as Democratic and Republican congressional leaders tried to hold their troops in line. In the 2000 elections, the public seemed divided and without much party loyalty.[10]

When the 107th Congress took office in January 2001, it was one of the most divided legislative bodies in American history. Republicans held a slim majority of 12 seats in the House of Representatives, and the U.S. Senate was equally divided, with 50 Republican and 50 Democratic senators. Political observers have speculated that these divisions will affect the ability of the new administration and Congress to make policy. The result will not be known until real issues have to be decided.

Critical Problems

Businesses now operate within a political system that is rife with conflicts, issues, and problems. Political scientists disagree whether the American political system has ever been more embattled; but other nations look to the United States as a democratic model, and pressures are building for major reforms in electoral politics. As a participant in the political process, business has a large stake in ensuring that the system operates in a manner that is consistent with the ideals of democracy. Several of the core problems are discussed below.

Money and Campaign Financing

American politics is very expensive. Candidates for public office at every level of government—from local government officials to the president of the United States—are forced to spend money to get elected. Costs range from a few thousand dollars in local

---

[10] For a useful discussion of the diverse factors that enter into the decision process of elected members of Congress, see David R. Mayhew, *How Congress Acts: Actions in the Public Sphere, James Madison through Newt Gingrich* (New Haven, CT: Yale University Press, 2000).

EXHIBIT 8-A

Money and Politics in Election 2000

Observers expected the 2000 elections to be the most expensive in U.S. political history. But the full dimensions of the spending would not be understood until well after the votes were recorded. According to the Federal Election Commission (FEC), the Republican and Democratic parties raised a total of $1.2 billion in "hard" and "soft" dollars for the 1999–2000 election cycle. This was almost twice the amount raised in the 1998 election and 37 percent more than 1996, the last presidential cycle. (*Note:* this does not include money raised for legal and other expenses associated with the presidential ballot recount in Florida. Federal election law does not require disclosure of money raised for these purposes, and neither the Republican nor Democratic parties voluntarily disclosed the amount of money raised.)

Republicans raised $447.4 million of federal, or hard money. Democrats raised $269.9 million of hard money. These hard money receipts were 10 percent higher for Republicans than in the previous presidential election cycle (1995–96) and 29 percent higher for Democratic committees. The largest percentage increases for both parties occurred in nonfederal, or soft money (funds raised outside the limitations and prohibitions of the Federal Election Campaign Act). Republicans raised $244.4 million, an increase of 73 percent over the 1995–96 period, while Democrats raised $243 million, a 99 percent increase. Soft money represented 35 percent of Republican Party financial activity reported to the FEC and 47 percent of Democratic Party fund-raising.

Congressional campaign spending for the 1999–2000 election cycle grew to more than $858 million, an increase of $240 million, or 39 percent, from 1997–98 levels. (These data are based on FEC reports covering financial activity from January 1, 1999, through November 27, 2000, 20 days after election day.) In addition, at least $9 million was spent by candidates in special elections, and more than $109 million by candidates who lost in primary elections.

Political action committees supported by business, labor, and other special interests accounted for a substantial portion of this fund-raising. (See Figure 8-6, p. 197.) Individual giving to parties and candidates also reflected the interests and concerns of donors.

Source: All data are from Federal Election Commission press releases and reports. See fecweb1.fec.gov/press/011201/partyfunds/html.

elections to tens of millions of dollars for high federal government positions. It is estimated that political spending on federal campaigns alone soared past the $1 billion level in the year 2000 electoral cycle.[11] See Exhibit 8-A for a discussion of money and politics in the 2000 presidential election.

[11] Federal Election Commission, press release, January 12, 2001; see www.fec.gov.

Figure 8-5

Profile of political action committees (PACs), 1974–2000.

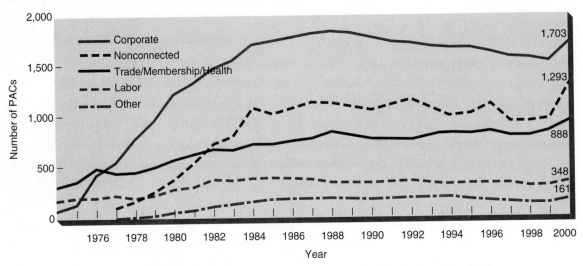

Source: Federal Election Commission. Reported in *Annual Report, 1999* (Washington, DC: Federal Election Commission, 2000).

This dependence on money forces candidates to raise campaign funds from willing donors. Many elected officials, such as members of the House of Representatives, face campaigns every two years. They have to begin raising funds for their next campaign on the day they start their current term. Because they are involved in a **perpetual political campaign,** incumbents and challengers feel the pressure to continuously raise funds. This has an effect on potential donors, such as businesses.

Business is involved in campaign financing in several ways. Direct contributions by corporations to political candidates for national offices are forbidden by federal law; some states, but not all, also place restrictions on corporate contributions to candidates in state elections. Since the mid-1970s, companies have been permitted to spend company funds to organize and administer **political action committees (PACs).** PACs are independently incorporated organizations that can solicit contributions from stockholders and employees and then channel those funds to candidates seeking political office. Companies that have organized PACs are not permitted to donate corporate funds to the PAC or to any political candidate; all donations to company-organized PACs must come from individuals.

As Figure 8-5 shows, PACs have been very popular with business as well as with other groups. Corporate PACs are the most numerous, accounting for over 40 percent of nearly 4,300 PACs, and are among the biggest money raisers and spenders. But as illustrated in Figure 8-6, trade and membership organizations (e.g., National Rifle Association, American Medical Association), labor unions, and nonconnected organizations (e.g., National Association of Realtors) also ranked high in money raised and spent. Labor unions are among the biggest contributors, although as a whole they represent less than 10 percent of all PACs.

Figure 8-6

Financial Activity of Political Action Committees (PACs).

	1999-2000 Number of PACs reporting some activity	Contributions from PACs January 1, 1999 to June 30, 2000 (millions)	Money spent on U.S. Senate races (millions)	Money spent on U.S. House of Rep. Races (millions)	PAC donations to Democratic Senate and House candidates (millions)	PAC donations to Republican Senate and House candidates (millions)
All PACs	4,393	$430.6	$41.6	$122.9	$80.2	$86.3
Corporate PACs	1,703	119.3	18.2	41.0	20.5	40.2
Labor PACs	348	95.7	5.4	28.7	40.2	2.8
Trade/Membership/health organization PACs	888	102.9	10.4	34.7	17.8	27.5
Non-connected PACs	1,293	99.7	6.1	14.8	8.4	12.8
Other	161	12.8	1.3	3.6	2.2	2.8

Notes: (1) Totals may not sum because data have been rounded.
(2) Donations and expenditures do not equal. Donations given in one election cycle may be carried over to another election cycle. There is also a time-lag between the receipt of funds and the use of funds in a campaign cycle.
(3) Political Action Committee donations may have been directed to the campaign committees of certified presidential candidates.
(4) Federal Election Commission has reported these data as of February 2001.

Source: Based on data collected by the Federal Election Commission and reported in various press releases and reports as of February 2001. See www.fec.gov/press/pacsu1800.htm.

Interestingly, the number of PACs seems to have peaked in the late 1980s, although the amount of money raised continues to hit new heights. A chorus of criticism produced congressional investigations of the entire campaign finance system in the late 1990s. Despite the noise, no meaningful campaign finance reform took place in the United States before the 2000 election campaign. The Federal Election Commission has established rules to regulate PAC activities. For example, PACs are not allowed to give more than $5,000 to a single candidate for each election, although the winner of a primary election may be given another $5,000 for the general election. These limits were imposed on all PACs to reduce the role of concentrated wealth in determining the outcome of elections to public office. One consequence is that both candidates and donors keep developing new ways to get around the rules.

The most important problem in campaign financing is **soft money.** Wealthy donors often look for loopholes that will allow them to spend money to support candidates they favor. One popular method has been the payment of soft money. *Soft money* refers to funds donated directly to political parties to finance party-building activities such as televised campaign commercials that do not support a specific candidate, get-out-the-vote drives, and other activities in conjunction with presidential and congressional races. In contrast to the hard money that is closely regulated by FEC rules, contributors are allowed to make donations of unlimited amount to political parties for party-building activities.

In the year 2000 presidential election, both the Democratic and Republican parties paid for advertising that featured their candidates (Al Gore and George W. Bush) and stressed a "vote Democrat" or "vote Republican" theme. These promotions qualified as party-building activities even though they indirectly boosted political candidates. In 2000, the amount of soft money spent in the presidential campaigns soared to an estimated $600 million. This amount was twice the amount of 1996 soft money contributions of $260 million to the two major political parties; the 1996 donations were up from the $86 million raised in the 1992 presidential race.[12]

One consequence of this money game is the candidacy of extremely wealthy individuals (e.g., presidential candidates Steve Forbes and Ross Perot; and John Corzine [New Jersey] and Michael Huffington [California], who each spent tens of millions of dollars from their personal fortunes in bids to become U.S. senators—Corzine won in New Jersey; Huffington lost in California, despite spending an estimated $100 million). Personal fortunes can be used without restriction in support of their political campaigns as long as a candidate refuses to accept public campaign funds.

Lobbying and the Power of Special Interests

For more than 50 years, since the end of World War II, the U.S. federal government has been the focus of both social policy and economic management of the national economy. One consequence is tremendous growth in the number of special interests that are connected to the many decisions made by government. Most important, these interests— groups as diverse as gun owners represented by the National Rifle Association, business interests represented by trade associations such as the National Association of Manufacturers, and poor and needy children represented by the Children's Defense Fund— have learned to use the tools of political influence. They are insiders in the high-stakes game of public policy making.

Business firms and other interests use many tools to directly influence the development of public policy. Most involve efforts to transmit information, express a point of view, or communicate a message to an official or regulator.[13] Lobbying, discussed earlier, involves direct contact with a government official to influence the thinking or actions of that person

---

[12] Federal Election Commission, press release, January 12, 2001. See www.fec.gov.
[13] See Public Affairs Council, *Introduction to Lobbying,* 2000.

on an issue or public policy. It is usually done through face-to-face contact, sometimes in lengthy discussions or in meetings that may last only minutes. **Grassroots programs** are organized efforts to get voters to influence government officials to vote or act in a favorable way. Many companies have asked their shareholders to participate in grassroots efforts to persuade their congressional representatives to reduce capital gains taxes and thereby make stock purchases and other investments more lucrative. These programs send strong messages to elected officials that the desired action is supported by voters.

Another form of mass communication used by business in the public policy arena is **advocacy advertising,** where a company (or trade association) places visible ads describing its view on controversial political issues in prominent newspapers or other media outlets. Mobil (now ExxonMobil) pioneered the use of advocacy advertising in the 1970s on issues such as gasoline price controls and environmental regulations at a time when such a visible "presence" was largely unknown. Managers who sponsor advocacy advertising believe that such ads identify their company as an interested, and active, stakeholder on the particular public policy issue being discussed. In 1999, for example, Mobil ran a series of advertisements that promoted the need for global environmental responsibility, while informing "thought leaders" and the public of its efforts to meet this goal. Today, such ads are commonly found near the editorial page of the leading national newspapers that senior government officials and staffs read (e.g., *Wall Street Journal, Washington Post, New York Times*).

Direct forms of political action also include letter-writing, fax, telegram, telephone, and Internet campaigns to register approval or disapproval of a government official's position on an important issue. Businesses often invite government officials to make visits to local plant facilities, give speeches to employees, attend awards ceremonies, and participate in activities that will improve that official's understanding of management and employee concerns. These activities help to humanize the relationship between government officials and the public, which can otherwise seem distant. Democracy requires citizen access and communication with political leaders. In the United States, with 280 million individuals and millions of businesses, the challenge of maintaining open, balanced communications between officials and the public is complicated and very expensive.

Role of the Media

The 1990s produced an explosion of new media outlets, including television and radio talk shows; public affairs programming (e.g., C-Span), which sometimes presents live coverage of congressional debates; and Internet services. Cable television stations often provide live coverage of hearings, debates, and votes. Critics claim that the growth of these media outlets has resulted in more attention to personalities of government officials than to the content of their ideas. This may be an exaggeration, but there is no doubt that media is very influential in shaping public opinion. Consider, for example, these media stars of the year 2000 presidential campaign.

> *Ted Koppel is the founding host of the popular ABC network late-night program, "Nightline." For 20 years, this program has focused on the major news stories of each day, often bringing together opponents on*

major political issues. Koppel's interviewing is direct and challenging, featuring a sophisticated form of traditional journalism.

Larry King became a media star by broadcasting his talk show from Washington, D.C., five nights a week on Cable News Network (CNN). An aggressive style has won him a loyal following of viewers who expect tough questions and clever talk. Larry King's show has become a "must" stop for national candidates, political figures, and celebrities.

Rush Limbaugh, whose radio and television personality leaves no doubt about his biases, prejudices, and points of view, doesn't try to be balanced in his role as a conservative spokesperson. Limbaugh became one of the most powerful media voices in the new politics of the 1990s. Supporters credit Limbaugh as an influential voice who helped elect Republicans to the House of Representatives and Senate by promoting the "contract with America" theme of Speaker Newt Gingrich during the 1994 elections.

Matt Druge created an Internet service called the Druge Report. It became a familiar and well-known name in January 1998 when it broke the story about President Clinton's alleged involvement with Monica Lewinsky. The website carried the news that Newsweek *magazine had suppressed the story of the alleged affair at the request of independent prosecutor Kenneth Starr. Druge actually made news by "outing" a story that other news organizations were unwilling to publish or broadcast. Once the story was out, however, other news organizations raced to publish their stories.*

People's tastes vary, and different segments of the television viewing audience—that is, the public—favor each of these stars and their programs. These media stars have a powerful effect on how Americans perceive public policy issues facing government and make decisions about whom to believe and whom to trust. Defenders of the media claim this is precisely how the founders envisioned democracy would work: as a contest among a multitude of views and opinions. To these analysts, the solution is to present even more views in more ways. They consider 500-channel cable television stations, interactive media, the Internet, and a public that is more involved in talk-show democracy as positive developments. In California, a Democracy Network was created as a multimedia, online service for voters who wanted to compare the views, finances, and positions of the candidates for governorship.[14] Preliminary data show that the public used all forms of media more frequently during the year 2000 election cycle, and that usage rose rapidly after election day as the uncertainty of the presidential race results continued for many weeks. One very popular website during the election cycle was Voter.com, described in Exhibit 8-B.

---

[14] Virtually every candidate for federal and state elective office had a website in recent campaigns. Most elected officials use their websites for regular updates on pending legislative issues. The Internet is also used by advocacy organizations to communicate with supporters and political officials. See, for example, the websites Grassroots.com and Speakout.com.

EXHIBIT
8-B

VOTER.COM

Justin Dangel was a 26-year-old with a passion for politics, the Internet, and entrepreneurial businesses. These interests came together in the creation of Voter.com, a website that became well known during the 2000 U.S. presidential campaign. By election day—November 7, 2000—the site had attracted more than three million "unique visitors" with a mix of political news, ballot results, and candidate advertising. Dangel thought his brainchild was on the way to lasting success.

The 2000 election was the first in which voters, candidates, and parties relied heavily on the Internet. "We were trying to transform the business of politics itself," said Dangel. The goal was to create new channels of communication between candidates and citizens, lowering the cost of political campaigns and improving citizen access to candidates. "It felt great, like we were in position and were going to do great things. . . . This business, at its core, wasn't just about making money."

Voter.com seemed to have resources for success: money, talent, and endorsements by investors and political experts. Although it faced competitors that also aspired to become "democracy portals," Voter.com earned praise from media such as *Business Week* and *Forbes* for its news features and commentary. Voter.com was bipartisan, with members of both political parties among its senior staff. The company had political expertise and "deep pockets," which allowed it to build identity by running full-page ads in national newspapers. It was highly visible at both the Republican and Democratic national conventions.

Voter.com also confronted serious problems. The company's original focus was on the 500,000 political races taking place at the federal, state, and local levels in 2000. But in reality, only 5,000 races (1 percent) were contested, with well-funded candidates. Thus, revenue from campaign advertising was less than expected. The company's executives concluded that they needed the more lucrative corporate lobbying business to build revenues. Voter.com staff began creating software for web-page creation and online petitions. It sold these programs to companies and organizations such as the NAACP and Common Cause. The company also encountered operational problems of effectively channeling e-mail and political advertising to audiences.

By November 2000, the company had developed a new business model, selling ads in online newsletters. But it was too late. The election was over, the investment climate had turned hostile, and after several more months, Voter.com closed. The message on its website read:

Dear visitors,
Thank you for your loyal readership during the past year and throughout Election 2000. Unfortunately, we are closing down. Quite simply, we were not able to secure sufficient funding to maintain the quality site that you have come to expect and that earned us our reputation as the top political site online. . . . We trust that what we have started will be the basis of a second generation of politics on the Web. It's been our pleasure to serve you in this space. —Voter.com

Source: Ross Kerber, "Out of Office," *Boston Globe*, February 19, 2001, pp. D1, D4. See also www.voter.com.

Critics point to excesses and poor taste as reasons to place restraints or limitations on the way media treat political issues. Many nations limit the media's freedom to report on political issues and the political process. But the U.S. Constitution protects citizens' freedom of speech and freedom of the press. Courts, including the U.S. Supreme Court, have interpreted these constitutional rights in ways that limit what can be done to control the content of media programs, although it is certain that the Constitution's drafters never foresaw television, the Internet, or the information superhighway. Excesses are unlikely to stop unless the public changes its listening and viewing habits.

Transparency of the Political Process

Transparency refers to the degree of openness or visibility of a government's decision-making processes. The openness of America's political system is one of its strengths: It creates opportunities for people to closely observe what decisions are being made and in what way. "Washington is a giant fishbowl," according to one veteran lobbyist, and the result is too much accountability, not too little. As another lobbyist said, "These representatives can't blow their noses without having to answer to someone."[15] Some scholars argue that government officials are agents acting on behalf of people who elected or appointed them (the principals). This view, called **corporate political agency theory,** holds that conditions that enable citizens to observe how elected officials behave will promote action that serves those who put them in office.[16]

Another view is that although elected officials are sent to office to represent their constituents, they are also sent to act in the broad public interest. Sometimes elected officials have to look beyond the interests of voters in their districts and take action—such as approval of new taxes—that will be unpopular but is in the broad public interest. The problem in the current political climate, according to this view, is that officials are unwilling to do so when this occurs in the glaring spotlight of attention to each vote, issue, and constituency. "Vote against your constituents on an important issue," said one 20-year veteran of the House of Representatives, "and you will pay the price of never being able to vote against them again!"[17]

One remedy is to have more closed-door sessions in which votes can be taken without being recorded or reported. However, such a view feeds the mood of public distrust: Legislators might do in private what they dare not do in public. It is doubtful that this approach will solve problems of transparency without adding to public cynicism. When Republicans took power in Congress after the 1994 elections, the new leaders of the Senate and House of Representatives promised to open the process. They soon discovered the need to work behind closed doors to get things done.

Incumbents and Appointed Officials

Public cynicism about political life is fueled by politicians and officials who sometimes act in crude, arrogant, and self-serving ways designed to perpetuate power. This may include doing favors for constituents, directing public works money to local communities,

---

[15] Author's interview; see also, Johnson and Broder, *The System.*

[16] See Barry M. Mitnick, ed., *Corporate Political Agency: The Construction of Competition in Public Affairs* (Newbury Park, CA: Sage, 1993).

[17] Author's interview during 1994 health care debate.

and acting on behalf of local companies caught in regulatory snarls and problems. The greater the seniority of elected officials, the more likely they are to exercise genuine power in government affairs. This makes them targets of political influence, which in turn helps them as fund-raisers and facilitates their reelection and continuation in positions of power.

Experts have offered proposals to minimize abuses of power. One popular idea is **term limits,** which would set a maximum number of years that elected officials could serve. This would weaken the power of long-serving members of Congress, for example, some of whom have served for more than 35 years. It would open committee assignments, create opportunities for new members, and still provide a broad base of experience in the legislature. Opponents argue that term limits would deprive voters and communities of electoral choice and the benefits of experience, including the knowledge, contacts, and credibility that are won with experience.

Although there are signs that voters are dissatisfied with the political system, there are contradictions in public attitudes. Voters often reelect officials for many terms, despite campaigns that focus on the virtues of change. Business faces such dilemmas too. Many business leaders favor term limits in principle, but they then seek the favor of elected officials and provide campaign support to reelection campaigns. Why? The concept of limited terms may seem attractive, but businesses, like other special interests, recognize that incumbents can be very helpful in meeting their needs and solving their problems. This is one reason that PACs and soft money spending so often favors incumbents rather than challengers.

Referendum Politics

The complexity of government decision-making processes can frustrate efforts to transform a popular idea into law. Government committees, procedures, and compromises often stop, delay, or deflect proposals that seem to have broad public support. To counter these bureaucratic obstacles, advocates of change sometimes use a **public referendum,** or popular vote, to force a public ballot on a particular issue.

Many states have adopted laws permitting citizens' initiatives to be placed on the ballot of a general election. The initiative process usually requires that a number of citizens (usually 1 to 5 percent of registered voters) sign a petition asking that the initiative resolution or question be placed on the ballot. If the resolution is adopted by a majority of voters, the legislature is obligated to turn the resolution into law.

California has produced many public referenda, including landmark proposals dealing with taxes, discrimination, affirmative action, and immigration. In 1996, for example, voters adopted Proposition 209, which banned affirmative action in state hiring and public university admissions in California. These proposals often led the way for national political movements. One scholar who studied all of the initiatives placed on California's ballot for more than a decade concluded that it is one of the most important policy arenas in that state.[18]

---

[18] Tom Thomas, "Campaign Spending and Corporate Involvement in the California Initiative Process, 1976–1988," in J. E. Post, ed., *Research in Corporate Social Performance and Policy,* vol. 12 (Greenwich, CT: JAI Press, 1991), pp. 37–61.

The number of referenda questions is rising. In the year 2000 elections, nearly all of the states had ballot questions for voters; some states had more than 10 questions for citizens to vote on. Research shows that the initiatives often propose actions that business interests oppose. A recent California ballot initiative sought to change the pricing of automobile insurance rates. The insurance industry claimed it would be badly hurt by such a law and vigorously opposed the proposition. In Massachusetts, a 1994 ballot proposition launched by a tax reform coalition sought to change the state's 5.95 percent flat tax on earned income into a graduated tax that would set higher rates for higher levels of income. The governor, a former U.S. senator, and business leaders opposed it, saying it was poisonous to impose such taxes on small businesses that are the source of new jobs. In 2000, a ballot proposal to reduce state income taxes from 5.95 percent to 5.00 percent over five years won broad support from business and was passed by Massachusetts voters.[19]

Politics is often said to be "the art of the possible." It involves working together, compromising in order that everyone's interests are taken into account and recognizing that no interest can win, or should win, all the time. Referendum politics appeals to people frustrated at losing in the political process; it is a way of fighting the system. Citizens' initiatives are expensive to launch and sustain, however. Tom Thomas, who studied California's initiative history, concluded that campaign spending affected voting results in the California initiative process, especially in cases where nonbusiness groups sought to impose new regulations or costs on business. By heavily outspending proponents of the initiative, business was often successful in defeating ballot initiatives.

Responsible Business Politics

Political action by business—whether to influence government policy or the outcome of elections—is natural in a democratic, pluralistic society. In the United States, business has a legitimate right to participate in the political process, just as consumers, labor unions, environmentalists, and others do. The rules differ in other nations where culture and legal restrictions may limit business political activities. This presents the problem for companies of managing across borders. See Exhibit 8-C.

Political reform spawns proposals for limitations on lobbying, political spending, and fund-raising by businesses. Some involve a system of public financing (total or matching funds) that would serve to level the campaign playing field. A number of political leaders have offered proposals to require television networks and stations to provide free time for candidates' advertising. As shown in Figure 8-7, other democratic nations utilize a combination of such ideas to reduce the impact of money on electoral politics.

One danger arising from corporate political activity is that corporations may wield too much power. As businesses operate in different communities and countries, it is important that ethical norms and standards guide managers as they deal with political factors. If corporate power tips the scales against other interests in a society, both business and society may lose. This is also true of union power, religious power, consumer power, or any concentrated power that may exist in a democratic society. Whether it is in the

---

[19] "Election Results: Official Tally," *Boston Globe,* November 8, 2000, pp. 1 ff.

EXHIBIT
8-C

Managing across Borders

Political relationships can be difficult to manage in one state or country. When a company operates in many nations, each with states or provinces, the challenge of managing political relationships becomes much more complicated. For many companies, managing across borders requires the highest level of political skill and the involvement of the chief executive officer and senior public affairs manager. The Colonial Mutual Group (CMG), an insurance company, provides an example of how one company strategically manages its government relations in many countries.

Colonial was founded in London in the late 1700s, and now operates in the UK and Australia, where it is one of the country's major insurers. Colonial's business strategy involves taking advantage of market niches in the financial services industry and diversifying the businesses (life insurance, property insurance) in which it operates. The company is also geographically diversified and operates in Australia, New Zealand, and other Asian countries. Colonial tries to focus on business opportunities that will be profitable and those with relatively little competition.

Colonial's public affairs strategy is very focused as well, emphasizing the need to carefully select the issues that matter most to the business and that are winnable. Both the business strategy and the public affairs strategy must be adapted to market conditions. To understand how this approach works, consider the following example. In the late 1990s, Colonial's top management defined its geographic markets as falling into three groups:

- *Mature markets*—Australia, UK, and New Zealand.
- *Existing Asian markets*—Hong Kong, Indonesia, Malaysia, and the Philippines.
- *Potential and new markets*—China, Vietnam, and India.

In the mature markets, Colonial recognized that consumerism, the media, and government regulations create conditions that require major public affairs resources. The public affairs offices in the UK and Australia maintain close cooperation and focus on media, government rule-making, product branding, and communications. The company's Australian public affairs office also serves New Zealand.

The company's approach to Asian markets such as Thailand, Hong Kong, Indonesia, the Philippines, and Malaysia is driven by the characteristics of each market: a less aggressive media, non-English speaking staff, government bureaucracy, and cultural diversity. Colonial's government and media relationships are managed by local employees, language, and culture. There is very little involvement of Colonial's top management in most local public affairs activities.

The company has a somewhat different strategy in China, Vietnam, and India, where it is trying to establish its business. Colonial must negotiate government permission to operate in these countries, which requires high-level government skills, CEO visits, and careful management of relations with government officials, media, and other influential people.

Exhibit 8-C continued

Colonial has learned that if it is to operate in a variety of Asian countries, it must decentralize most government and media relations to local managers. At the same time, the company needs a coordinated approach for dealing with new countries and governments that are sensitive to dealing with the highest rank officials in the company.

Source: Author interviews with executives at CMG, Asia. The assistance of Centre for Corporate Public Affairs in Melbourne, Australia, is gratefully acknowledged.

Figure 8-7

What other countries do to control money in politics.

Source: Michael Oreskes, "The Trouble with Politics: Running versus Governing," *New York Times,* March 21, 1990, pp. A1, A22.

	Public Financing	Limits on Fund Raising or Spending	Television
U.K.	No	Yes	Free time based on party's strength in previous election
France	Reimburse candidates based on votes received	Yes	Free and equal time to candidates
Japan	No	Yes	Candidates given some free time for speeches; no negative advertising
Germany	Reimbursement to parties according to votes received	No	Free time to candidates on public stations

media-rich arena of electoral politics or the corridors of Congress where more traditional lobbying prevails, business leaders must address the issues of how to manage relationships with government and special interests in society in ethically sound ways. Ultimately, business has an important long-term stake in a healthy, honest political system.

Summary Points of This Chapter

- Government makes many decisions that directly and indirectly affect business. It is for this reason that managers and companies feel compelled to participate in the political process.

- Corporate political activity takes two forms: actions focused on influencing governmental policies and decision making, and actions aimed at affecting electoral politics. Political action committees, lobbying, and grassroots programs are among the most popular types of corporate political activities.
- Businesses play a role in electoral politics by providing campaign funds and other forms of support to candidates. Firms take positions on campaign issues, lending support to ideas that support business interests and opposing ideas they believe are harmful.
- Strategic management of government relations involves understanding how a business's long-term economic and social interests are entwined with government policy and then acting to support that relationship.
- Businesses need to be involved in public policy decisions for several reasons: They have a large stake in specific government actions affecting their industry; they also provide a voice that should be heard on many economic and social policy issues.
- Businesses have a stake in the critical issues facing the nation's political system. Campaign financing, the power of special interests, the media's role, incumbency, and referendum politics are among the issues prompting calls for political reform. The way managers conduct their companies' governmental relations will be influenced by changes in these areas.

Key Terms and Concepts Used in This Chapter

- Lobbying
- Corporate political strategy
- Political cynicism
- Coalitions
- Perpetual political campaign
- Political action committees (PACs)
- Soft money

- Grassroots programs
- Advocacy advertising
- Transparency
- Corporate political agency theory
- Term limits
- Public referendum

Internet Resources

- www.fec.gov   Federal Election Commission
- www.allpolitics.com   CNN/Time Allpolitics news service
- www.cq.com   World Wide Washington Congressional Quarterly
- www.citizen.org/congress/reform/   Campaign facts and financial information
  cfr/public_speaking/facts.html
- www.gc.peachnet.edu   Resource links in political science

Discussion Case: *Coca-Cola's Civic Action Network*

Coca-Cola is one of the world's largest beverage companies, with a brand name that is recognized in virtually every corner of the globe. Because the company has a presence in so many countries, and because governments regulate production, marketing, and distribution of Coca-Cola products, the company has developed a large, sophisticated set of government relations resources. One of the company's valuable assets is the Coca-Cola Civic Action Network, known as "Coca-Cola CAN."

The mission of Coca-Cola CAN is to be a nonpartisan, grassroots network of citizens and businesses that have a stake in the success of the Coca-Cola business system. The purpose of Coca-Cola CAN is to educate every member of the Coca-Cola family about national, state, and local issues affecting the soft drink industry. Plus, Coca-Cola CAN provides a system to make sure members' opinions are fairly represented.

Any member of the Coca-Cola family is eligible to enroll in the grassroots network. Among those specifically identified are employees, retirees, customers, suppliers, bottlers, or shareholders. The total number of eligible members is, therefore, in the millions in the United States alone. As the company's invitation states, whatever one's connection to the company, "the threat from governmental regulation and special taxes on soft drinks and juice products is too great for us to ignore."

One of those threats comes in the form of laws that require that consumers pay a refundable deposit on soft drinks, beer, and other carbonated beverages. Nine states require such refundable systems. A tenth state, California, has a related law establishing a redemption value on carbonated-beverage containers. Most of these laws were passed in the 1970s in response to concerns about litter from discarded beverage containers.

State legislatures are the battlegrounds where deposit legislation is often fought. The soft drink industry has developed an industrywide approach to such issues and supports a variety of trade associations that coordinate different facets of the battle. The primary trade association for the soft drink industry is the National Soft Drink Association. NSDA works closely with other associations whose members are stakeholders of the soft drink manufacturers. For example, soft drinks are sold in cans, glass bottles, and plastic containers. The NSDA works closely with the Can Manufacturer's Institute, the Glass Packaging Institute, and the American Plastics Council—all of which are headquartered in Washington, D.C., but also have offices in many state capitols—to organize lobbying campaigns and other forms of political action. The result is that Coca-Cola can draw on its own employees, bottlers, suppliers, customers, shareholders, and industry resources to combat legislative or regulatory proposals that would be costly or damaging to its market position.

Sources: See the Coca-Cola Company website at www.cocacola.com.

Discussion Questions

1. Why did Coca-Cola, a wealthy and well-known company, need to develop the Coca-Cola Civic Action Network?
2. Do you think such a network is worth a budget of $1 million? $5 million? $10 million? What information would you need in order to make a decision about how large Coca-Cola CAN's budget should be?
3. Suppose that the governor of your state suggests that the sales tax on soft drink beverages be raised from 2 percent to 6 percent. What might that do to soft drink sales? What do you think Coca-Cola will do in response to such a proposal?
4. Suppose the governor proposed an increase in taxes on beer and wine but not on soft drink beverages? What do you expect Coca-Cola would do in response to this proposal?

9

Antitrust, Mergers, and Global Competition

All societies face the problem of deciding how much power should be held by leading enterprises. In the United States, antitrust laws have long been used to curb corporate power, to preserve competition, and to protect consumers. The rapid advance of technology and the globalization of the economy, however, have raised new issues concerning business competitiveness. These trends have presented public policymakers and corporate leaders with a need to reconcile corporate power, stakeholder interests, and social responsibility with new realities.

This chapter focuses on these key questions and objectives:

- What dilemma does corporate power present in a democratic society?
- What are the objectives of the antitrust laws, and how are they enforced?
- What are the key issues in contemporary antitrust policy?
- What are the reasons for the recent wave of mergers and acquisitions? How have they affected the relationship between business and its stakeholders?
- How has the rise of new technologies and global competition affected antitrust policy?

he U.S. government's groundbreaking suit against Microsoft Corporation was just one of many antitrust actions at the turn of the century. Consider the following less well-publicized cases.

Seven of the world's largest drug companies—dubbed Vitamins, Inc.—were forced to pay $1.2 billion in 1999 to settle a private antitrust suit brought by some of their biggest corporate customers. The court found that the guilty companies—among them, the European firms Hoffman-LaRoche, BASF, and Rhone-Poulenc, and the Japanese firm Takeda—had conspired for over a decade to fix the prices of raw vitamins they sold to food, beverage, and animal feed companies. As a result, consumers had overpaid for everything from vitamin pills to fortified breakfast cereals. The case showed, said one specialist, that "very large, very serious price-fixing conspiracies can go undetected for a very long time, and they cost consumers millions and millions of dollars a year."[1]

When BP-Amoco announced its intention to acquire rival Arco in 1999 for a record $28 billion, it promised to create the second-largest oil company in the world, after ExxonMobil. But shortly after the announcement, the Federal Trade Commission went to court to block the proposed merger, saying it would produce a near monopoly of Alaskan oil supplies and lead to higher gasoline prices on the West Coast. Federal regulators relented, however, after BP-Amoco agreed to sell Arco's Alaskan properties to another company, and the merger was allowed to go through.[2]

These two examples of competitive conflicts—involving private businesses, the government, and the courts, in both the United States and abroad—illustrate how anticompetitive practices can arise in the free market system. This chapter looks at how the United States and other countries and regions have traditionally sought to preserve and enhance competition through antitrust and related policies. As business becomes increasingly global, and as deregulation and technological change reshape many industries, antitrust and other competition policies are being reexamined.

The Dilemma of Corporate Power

At the heart of antitrust policy, in the United States and in other countries, is the dilemma of **corporate power**—and to what extent it should be checked by government.

Power is often a function of size; and by almost any measure used, the world's largest business enterprises are impressively big, as shown in Figure 9-1. Size can be measured in several ways—by annual sales, profits, and market value—and a company's rank will vary depending on the measurement used. As measured by sales, the big five in 1999–2000 were ExxonMobil (the oil company), General Motors, Ford, and DaimlerChrysler (the big three automakers), and Wal-Mart (a U.S. mass retailer). Among the most profitable were a Hong Kong–based conglomerate (Hutchison Whampoa), a high-technology company (General Electric), a fast-growing bank (Citigroup), and two oil companies (Royal Dutch/Shell and ExxonMobil). High-technology firms General

---

[1] "$1.1 Billion to Settle Suit on Vitamins," *New York Times,* November 4, 1999, p. C1; "Seven Vitamin Makers Settle Antitrust Suit for $1.18 Billion," *Los Angeles Times,* November 4, 1999, p. C1; and "Tearing Down the Façade of Vitamins, Inc.," *New York Times,* October 10, 1999, p. C1.

[2] "FTC Votes to Block Merger of Arco, BP," *Los Angeles Times,* February 3, 2000, p. C1; and "BP Amoco Takeover of Arco Cleared by the FTC," *Financial Times,* April 14, 2000, p. 23.

Figure 9-1

The 10 largest global corporations, 1999–2000.

Source: "The Business Week Global 1,000," *Business Week,* July 10, 2000, pp. 108–44. Used by permission. Copyright © by The McGraw-Hill Companies.

Note: Data for sales and profits are for 1999 fiscal years. Data for market value is as of May 31, 2000.

Rank	By Sales (billions of U.S. $)	By Profits (billions of U.S. $)	By Market Value (billions of U.S. $)
1	ExxonMobil 185.5	Hutchison Whampoa 14.3	General Electric 520.3
2	General Motors 173.2	General Electric 10.7	Intel 416.7
3	Wal-Mart 166.8	Citigroup 10.1	Cisco Systems 395.0
4	Ford Motor 162.6	Royal Dutch/Shell 8.6	Microsoft 322.8
5	DaimlerChrysler 151.0	ExxonMobil 7.9	ExxonMobil 289.9
6	Mitsui 129.8	Bank of America 7.9	Vodafone Airtouch 278.0
7	Mitsubishi 127.1	Microsoft 7.8	Wal-Mart 256.7
8	Toyota Motor 119.7	IBM 7.7	NTT DoCoMo 247.2
9	Itochu 112.8	Philip Morris 7.7	Nokia 242.2
10	General Electric 111.6	Cheung Kong Holdings 7.6	Royal Dutch/Shell 213.5

Electric, Intel, Cisco Systems, and Microsoft topped the world's firms in market value. The largest companies in the world, as measured by sales, are as big as some midsized national economies, as measured by gross domestic product, shown in Figure 9-2. The annual revenues of automaker Toyota, for example, exceed the entire economic output of the country of South Africa. General Motors' revenues are as big as the national economy of Denmark.

These giant enterprises are not completely representative of business in the United States or other nations. The overwhelming majority of business firms are owned by individual proprietors or by small groups of partners. Only one of every five business firms in the United States is a corporation, and many of these corporations are small. The largest firms at the top of the business pyramid are the focus of so much attention because of their size, power, and influence, not because they represent the entire business community.

The companies shown in Figures 9-1 and 9-2 are called **multinational corporations** because they are global in scope, with manufacturing, marketing, and sales that extend into many regions of the world and with employees of many nationalities. If

Figure 9-2

Comparison of multinational corporations' sales and the gross domestic product of selected nations.

Sources: "The Business Week Global 1,000," *Business Week,* July 10, 2000, pp. 108–44; and World Bank, *World Development Report 1999/2000,* table 12, "Structure of Output," pp. 252–53.

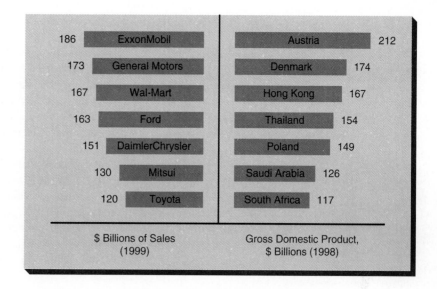

$ Billions of Sales (1999)	Gross Domestic Product, $ Billions (1998)
186 ExxonMobil	Austria 212
173 General Motors	Denmark 174
167 Wal-Mart	Hong Kong 167
163 Ford	Thailand 154
151 DaimlerChrysler	Poland 149
130 Mitsui	Saudi Arabia 126
120 Toyota	South Africa 117

anything, these two figures underestimate the size and influence of these leading multinational corporations. Many of them are linked with one another in worldwide networks of producers, suppliers, distributors, and retailers in a phenomenon sociologist Charles Derber has called *network capitalism.* The growing ease of both communication and transportation across vast distances has meant that businesses can readily coordinate their actions with those of their partners, further leveraging their influence.[3]

The size and global reach of these corporations give them tremendous power. Through their ubiquitous marketing, they influence what people want and how they act around the world. McDonald's, Disney, Microsoft, and Sony products and images are known almost everywhere. These corporations have the resources to make substantial contributions to political campaigns, as discussed in Chapter 8, thus influencing the policies of governments. They dominate not only the traditional domains of product manufacture and service delivery but increasingly reach into such traditionally public sector activities as education, law enforcement, and the provision of social services.

The tremendous power of the world's leading corporations has both positive and negative effects. A big company may have definite advantages over a small one. It can command more resources, produce at a lower cost, plan further into the future, and weather business fluctuations somewhat better. Big companies make tougher competitors against foreign firms. Globalization of markets can bring new products, technologies, and economic opportunities to developing societies. And yet the concentration of corporate power can also harm society. Huge businesses can disproportionately influence politics, shape tastes, and dominate public discourse. They can move production from one site to another, weakening unions and communities. These companies can also use their

---

[3] Charles Derber, *Corporation Nation: How Corporations Are Taking over Our Lives and What We Can Do about It* (New York: St. Martin's Press, 1998).

economic influence to collude to fix prices, divide markets, and quash competition—the direct focus of antitrust policy.

The dilemma of corporate power concerns how business uses its influence, not whether it should have power in the first place. Most people want to know if business power is being used to affirm broad public-purpose goals, values, and principles. If so, then corporate power is considered to be legitimate, and the public accepts large size as just another normal characteristic of modern business. On the other hand, when corporate power is misused—for example, to gain an unfair advantage over competitors, as Microsoft was accused of doing—then public policy may be required to check abuses.[4]

In the United States, antitrust laws, although controversial and far from perfect, stand as a monument to society's efforts to cope with the dilemma of corporate power. For more than a century, since the first federal antitrust law was enacted, U.S. public policy has sought to balance economic power with social control. At the start of the twenty-first century, new realities of global competition and technological change are forcing a reexamination of how power and social control are best balanced. We examine those issues after outlining the goals of antitrust regulation and major U.S. antitrust federal laws.

Antitrust Regulation

Someone once remarked that antitrust is as American as apple pie. Certainly it is an article of faith deeply embedded in the minds of many people. U.S. **antitrust laws** originated in the late nineteenth century in the wake of some spectacular competitive abuses by big business leaders and their companies. An aroused public feared the uncontrolled growth of big business. The first antitrust laws were passed in this climate of fear and mistrust of big business. Since those early years, other antitrust laws have been enacted, and the first laws have been amended. The result is a formidable tangle of laws, regulations, guidelines, and judicial interpretations that present business with a need to carefully manage relationships with competitors and government antitrust officials.

Objectives of Antitrust

Antitrust laws serve multiple goals. Some of these goals—such as preserving competition or protecting consumers against deceptive advertising—are primarily economic in character. As one authoritative source stated, "The U.S. antitrust laws are the legal embodiment of our nation's commitment to a free market economy."[5] Others, though, are more concerned with social and philosophical matters, such as a desire to curb the power of large corporations or even a nostalgic wish to return to the old Jeffersonian ideal of a nation of small-scale farmers and businesses. The result is multiple, overlapping, changing, and sometimes contradictory goals.

---

[4] For two classic analyses of corporate power, see Alfred C. Neal, *Business Power and Public Policy* (New York: Praeger, 1981), p. 126; and Edwin M. Epstein and Dow Votaw, eds., *Rationality, Legitimacy, Responsibility: Search for New Directions in Business and Society* (Santa Monica, CA: Goodyear, 1978). More recent treatments may be found in David C. Korten, *When Corporations Rule the World* (San Francisco: Berrett-Koehler Publishers, 1996); and Carl Boggs, *The End of Politics: Corporate Power and the Decline of the Public Sphere* (New York: Guilford Press, 2000).

[5] Bureau of National Affairs (BNA), *Antitrust and Trade Regulation Report,* vol. 55 (Washington, DC: Bureau of National Affairs, 1988), p. 5–4.

The most important economic objectives of antitrust laws are the following:

First, *the protection and preservation of competition* is the central objective. Antitrust laws do this by outlawing monopolies, prohibiting unfair competition, and eliminating price discrimination and collusion. The reasoning is that customers will be best and most economically served if business firms compete vigorously for consumers' dollars. Prices should fluctuate according to supply and demand, with no collusion between competitors, whether out in the open or behind the scenes, as occurred among the vitamin manufacturers profiled in one of the opening examples of this chapter.

A second objective of antitrust policy is *to protect consumers' welfare by prohibiting deceptive and unfair business practices.* The original antitrust laws were aimed primarily at preserving competition, assuming that consumers would be safeguarded as long as competition was strong. Later, though, policymakers realized that some business methods could be used to exploit or mislead consumers, regardless of the amount of competition. Consider the following hypothetical situations:

> *A company supplying plastic parts for electrical appliances bribed the purchasing agent for the appliance maker to buy the company's parts, even though they were priced higher than those made by a competitor. As a result, the consumer paid more for the appliances. This type of commercial bribery would be forbidden by the antitrust laws because it takes unfair advantage of innocent consumers.*

> *A distributor of compact discs sent purchasing club members more CDs than they had ordered and then demanded payment, substituted one CD for another in some orders, and delayed prepaid orders of some customers for several months. Such practices would be considered to be unfair by antitrust authorities.*

A third objective of antitrust regulation is *to protect small, independent business firms from the economic pressures exerted by big business competition.* Antitrust laws prohibit **predatory pricing**—the practice of selling below a producer's cost in order to drive rivals out of business, as shown in the following example.

> *American Airlines was charged by the U.S. Justice Department in 1999 with slashing fares on some routes in and out of its Dallas, Texas, hub in order to quash competition from low-fare carriers Vanguard, Sun Jet, and Western Pacific. Over a three-year period, the government said, American had lowered prices to below cost to undercut its rivals. Once the smaller carriers had dropped out of the market, American raised its prices again.[6]*

In this instance, although price-cutting by American helped consumers in the short run, it hurt them in the long run, regulators said, by allowing the airline to regain a near monopoly. In recent years, the government has become more aggressive in prosecuting

---

[6] "Antitrust Suit Names American Airlines," *Washington Post,* May 14, 1999, p. Al; and "U.S. Airline Confident It Can Ride out Storm over Washington's Antitrust Suit," *Financial Times,* May 24, 1999, p. 4.

cases of alleged predatory pricing.[7] In other cases, small businesses may be undersold by large ones because manufacturers are willing to give price discounts to large-volume buyers. For example, a tire maker wanted to sell automobile and truck tires to a large retail chain at a lower price than it offered to a small gasoline station. Antitrust laws prohibit giving such discounts exclusively to large buyers unless there is a genuine economic saving in dealing with the larger firm.

In promoting the interests of small business over large business in these ways, antitrust regulations disregard both competition—because big businesses are not permitted to compete freely—and consumer welfare—because big firms could sell at a lower price than small firms. This inconsistency occurs because these laws serve the multiple and sometimes contradictory goals of many different groups. A case that involved possible unfair methods of competition, as well as economic pressure exerted by big business, is profiled in Exhibit 9-A.

A fourth objective of antitrust policy is *to preserve the values and customs of small-town America.* A strong populist philosophy has been part of the antitrust movement from its beginning. Populists favored small-town life, neighborly relations among people, a democratic political system, family-operated farms, and small business firms. They believed that concentrated wealth poses a threat to democracy, that big business would drive small local companies out of business, and that hometown merchants and neighboring farmers might be replaced by large impersonal corporations headquartered in distant cities. Antitrust restrictions on big business, populists believed, might further these social and political goals. One hundred years later, however, these populist goals often conflict with business views of what is required in a world of global competition.[8]

The Major Antitrust Laws

Today's antitrust laws are the outcome of many years of attempting to make American business fit the model of free market competition. Many people have pointed out how unrealistic it is to expect a modern, high-technology, diversified, worldwide corporation to conform to conditions that may have been considered ideal a century ago when both business and society were simpler. The challenge of applying existing antitrust legislation to the technological, financial, political, and social environment of the early twenty-first century begins with an understanding of the major antitrust laws.

Figure 9-3 summarizes the purpose of the four main federal antitrust statutes and the major components of the enforcement process. States also have antitrust laws with similar purposes.

The Sherman Act

Although several states enacted antitrust laws before the federal government did, the Sherman Act of 1890 is considered to be the foundation of antitrust regulation in the United States. This law was the basis for the government's antitrust case against Microsoft Corporation, discussed in a case study at the end of the textbook. The Sherman Act:

---

[7] "Caveat Predator? The Justice Department Is Cracking Down on Predatory Pricing," *Business Week,* May 22, 2000, pp. 116–18.

[8] A lucid historical account may be found in Louis Galambos and Joseph Pratt, *The Rise of the Corporate Commonwealth: Business and Public Policy in the Twentieth Century* (New York: Basic Books, 1988).

**EXHIBIT
9-A**

Chipping away at the Competition

The owner of a small snack-food distribution business in Cleveland's east-side neighborhood was surprised when several mom-and-pop store owners told him they no longer wanted to carry his products. The potato chips, pork rinds, and onion rings the man delivered sold well, and the storeowners had no complaints about his service. "They told me Frito-Lay supervisors had offered them free merchandise, if they stopped carrying my product," the distributor reported. The small businessman consulted an attorney, who told him that Frito-Lay, the country's largest salty-snack corporation and a unit of PepsiCo, might be guilty of antitrust violations. "What is unfair is that they are paying stores not to carry [my client's] product," the attorney said.

After several similar complaints, the Justice Department launched a probe of the snack-food giant, concerned that it might have illegally pressured retailers to squeeze out rival products. But after two and a half years, federal regulators dropped their investigation in 1998 without finding any wrongdoing by Frito-Lay. Commented one industry analyst of the company's behavior, "I'm sure they are very aggressive, but . . . they are also . . . very, very careful." In the aftermath of the failed antitrust probe, many smaller snack-food companies decided to limit themselves to regional, niche markets rather than compete head-to-head with Frito-Lay. "Suicidal is a good definition of trying to go up directly against them," commented the president of Snak King, producer of El Sabroso snacks, aimed at the Latino market in southern California.

Sources: "Chipping away at Competition: Frito Lay Accused of Unfair Tactics against Small Company," *Cleveland Plain Dealer,* March 30, 1997, p. 1B; "Inquiry into Frito-Lay Finds No Wrongdoing in Marketing," *New York Times,* December 23, 1998, p. C2; and "Regional Player Seeks Bite-Size Niches," *Los Angeles Times,* July 6, 1999, p. C1.

- Prohibits contracts, combinations, or conspiracies that restrain trade and commerce (e.g., collusion among a group of producers to fix prices).
- Prohibits monopolies and all attempts to monopolize trade and commerce.
- Provides for enforcement by the Justice Department, and authorizes penalties, including fines and jail terms, for violations.

The Clayton Act

Originally passed in 1914 to clarify some of the ambiguities and uncertainties of the Sherman Act, the Clayton Act, as amended, now:

- Prohibits price discrimination by sellers (as illustrated by the tire maker who was forbidden to sell lower-priced tires to a chain store while selling at a higher price to a smaller independent store).
- Forbids tying contracts that require someone to buy a related and perhaps unwanted product in order to get another one produced by the same company (e.g., it would be illegal for a computer company to force hardware purchasers to accept an unwanted maintenance contract as a condition of sale).

Figure 9-3

Antitrust laws and enforcement at the federal level.

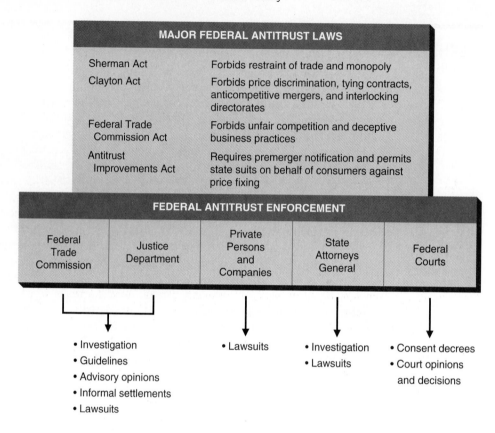

• Prohibits companies from merging through purchase of shares or assets if competition is lessened or a monopoly is created (as illustrated by the FTC's review of the proposed merger between BP-Amoco and Arco).

• Outlaws interlocking directorates in large competing corporations (e.g., Chevron and ExxonMobil would not be permitted to have a single person serve as a member of the board of directors of both companies at the same time).

The Federal Trade Commission Act

This act, too, became law in 1914 during a period when populist sentiment against big business was very strong. In addition to creating the Federal Trade Commission to help enforce the antitrust laws, it prohibited all unfair methods of competition (without defining them in specific terms). In later years, the act was amended to give more protection to consumers by forbidding unfair and deceptive business practices, such as misleading advertising, bait-and-switch merchandising, and other consumer abuses.

The Antitrust Improvements Act

All of the important additions made to the antitrust laws during the 1930s and 1950s were incorporated into the three major laws as summarized above. But in 1976, Congress put a new and separate law on the books. The Antitrust Improvements Act strengthens government's hand in enforcing the other three laws. This law:

- Requires large corporations to notify the Justice Department and the Federal Trade Commission about impending mergers and acquisitions so that the regulators can study any possible violations of the law that may be caused by the merger and order any divestitures necessary to preserve competition (as illustrated by the FTC's order blocking the merger of BP-Amoco and Arco until Arco sold its Alaska oil fields).
- Expands the Justice Department's antitrust investigatory powers.
- Authorizes the attorneys general of all 50 states to bring suits against companies that fix prices and to recover damages for consumers.

Exemptions

Not all organizations are subject to these four antitrust laws. Major league baseball, for example, has been exempt from antitrust regulation since 1922 (although a 1998 law revoked this exemption for labor relations only). This exemption has been criticized for permitting baseball owners to collude to restrict the number of teams, drive up ticket prices, and force concessions from cities eager to attract or keep a major league team.[9] Also not covered by U.S. antitrust laws are labor unions, agricultural cooperatives, insurance companies (which are regulated by state, not federal, laws), and some business transactions related to national defense. The exemption of cooperative research and development efforts is discussed later in this chapter.

Enforcing the Antitrust Laws

The two main antitrust enforcement agencies shown in Figure 9-3 are the Antitrust Division of the U.S. Department of Justice and the Federal Trade Commission. Both agencies may bring suits against companies they believe to be guilty of violating antitrust laws. They also may investigate possible violations, issue guidelines and advisory opinions for firms planning mergers or acquisitions, identify specific practices considered to be illegal, and negotiate informal settlements out of court. During the 1990s, antitrust regulators became more activist, especially in prosecuting price-fixing, blocking anticompetitive mergers, and dealing with foreign companies that had violated U.S. laws on fair competition. At the same time, regulators have tried to be sensitive to the impact of antitrust policy on the competitiveness of U.S. firms internationally, as described in a later section in this chapter.

Antitrust suits also can be initiated by private persons or companies who believe themselves to have been damaged by the anticompetitive actions of a business firm and seek compensation for their losses. Nearly 95 percent of all antitrust enforcement actions

---

[9] For a critique of baseball's antitrust exemption, see Andrew Zimbalist, *Baseball and Billions: A Probing Look Inside the Big Business of Our National Pastime* (New York: Basic Books, 1992); and Frank Dell'Apa, "Do Pro Sports Take Advantage of Their Fans?" *Public Citizen,* May–June 1993.

are initiated by private parties, not government officials, as illustrated by the following example from the world of electronic commerce.

> *In 2000, Bidder's Edge, a small Internet-based company, filed an antitrust lawsuit against eBay, the popular online auction site. Founded in 1997, Bidder's Edge was a so-called auction aggregator. The company did not itself list items for sale online. Rather, it offered its customers tools to search the inventories of various online auction sites—including eBay's— to help them locate items for sale and make informed bids. In 1999, eBay had charged Bidder's Edge with "trespassing" on its site and had acted to block the aggregator's access to its listings. Complained James Carney, CEO of Bidder's Edge, "eBay wants to build a wall around its site." Bidder's Edge responded with an antitrust suit, charging eBay with unfair competition.* [10]

Attorneys general of the various states also may take action against antitrust violators, not only to protect consumers from price-fixing (under the Antitrust Improvements Act) but also to enforce the antitrust laws of their own states. The National Association of Attorneys General has a special section on antitrust laws, and state officials often cooperate in the investigation and prosecution of cases. For example, 19 state attorneys general joined the Justice Department in its suit against Microsoft Corporation.

Finally, the courts usually have the last word in enforcement, and the outcome is never certain. Cases may be tried before a jury, a panel of judges, or a single judge. The Supreme Court is the court of final appeal, and its opinions carry great weight. Antitrust regulators and businesses alike often appeal their cases to this final forum because the stakes are so high and the judicial precedents created by the high court are so important in the long-run development of antitrust regulation.

Key Antitrust Issues

The business community, government policymakers, and the general public have to seek answers to several key issues if the nation's antitrust laws and regulations are to serve both business and society well. Some of the most important ones are briefly discussed.

Monopoly

The key question here is: Is monopoly always bad? Does domination of an industry or a market by one or a few large corporations necessarily violate the antitrust laws? Or, as some ask, should the biggest firms in each industry be broken up? Many major industries and markets are dominated by a handful of mammoth companies; examples include automobiles, tires, computers, computer operating systems, chemicals, insurance, steel, some food and beverage products, and paper. Critics claim that economic concentration eliminates effective price competition, reduces consumer choices, causes firms to grow too large to be efficient, inhibits innovation, and concentrates profits in too few hands.

---

[10] "Bidder's Edge Files Antitrust Counterclaims against eBay," *Business Wire*, February 7, 2000, www. businesswire.com.

The best solution, they say, is to break up the giants into smaller units. Others counter by claiming that big firms have become dominant because they are more efficient. In this view, today's large firms give consumers more, not fewer, choices of goods and services, can finance more innovation than small business, and distribute profits more widely to an increasing number of stockholders. Breaking up large corporations would deprive society of these benefits, say the defenders, and should not be done.

In general, the courts have found that monopoly per se is not illegal. If, however, a firm uses its market dominance to restrain commerce, compete unfairly, or hurt consumers, then it may be found guilty of violating antitrust laws. For example, in the government's suit against Microsoft, the government's argument was not that Microsoft *had* a monopoly but that it *used* its monopoly to hurt its rivals unfairly. Under these circumstances, the law permits the government to break up a monopoly.

Innovation

Another current focus of attention in antitrust policy is innovation. In the early years of antitrust, regulators promoted competition in order to provide consumer choice and keep prices down. This was an appropriate strategy for markets in which technologies were relatively stable. But, in today's fast-paced economy, regulators have increasingly promoted competition in order to foster technological innovation. In other words, the *rationale* for bringing antitrust actions is changing.

> *For example, in 2000 the Justice Department brought suit against Visa and MasterCard. The government's argument was not that these two credit-card giants were artificially propping up prices, but rather that they had colluded to restrain the adoption of innovations like smart cards— ones with embedded chips that could make health and other data available—that might pose a competitive threat.*

The chairman of the Federal Trade Commission commented, "Innovation is more and more the central arena in which competition plays out. [It] is the hot issue for the foreseeable future."[11]

High-Technology Businesses

A related issue is how competition policy should be applied to high-technology businesses. Most antitrust laws were crafted in the late nineteenth and early twentieth centuries—an era when the economy was dominated by extractive, transportation, and manufacturing industries. The economy has now been fundamentally transformed by the rise of the information age, where the primary currency is intellectual property.

Some people argue that the basic principles of antitrust law apply poorly to today's economy. One reason is that monopolies in many high-tech businesses are inherently unstable, because barriers to entry are low, and dynamic technological change constantly changes the basis of competition. For example, Microsoft argued that the rise of information appliances, such as smart phones, undermined its dominance of desktop computing software. The

[11] "Antitrust for the Digital Age," *Business Week,* May 15, 2000, pp. 46–48; and "The Next Big Antitrust Case," *New York Times,* June 15, 2000, p. A26.

EXHIBIT 9-B	Covisint: Collusion among Buyers?

The rise of the Internet has enabled the emergence of purchasing exchanges where businesses can buy and sell with other companies online. One of most important of these was Covisint, a centralized electronic marketplace for the automotive industry that opened in December, 2000. Supported by General Motors, Ford, Daimler-Chrysler, Renault, and Nissan, among others, Covisint promised to be a place where big automakers could interact with tens of thousands of parts suppliers to efficiently transact the many deals necessary to equip new cars and trucks. The business-to-business site held out the potential of cutting costs and streamlining purchasing in a very complex industry. But the initiative raised antitrust concerns. Could a small number of powerful buyers (the automakers), acting in concert, dictate prices and other terms to a large number of weaker suppliers? Usually, in antitrust violations, *sellers* are accused of fixing prices; in this case, it was feared that *buyers* would do so. In late 2000, Covisint was reviewed by antitrust regulators in the United States and Germany and given a green light to proceed. But, warned a report from regulators in the United Kingdom, "Internet technology might seem to offer the ideal microclimate for collusion."

Sources: Richard Meares, "Inside Track: Watchdogs Eye Online Exchanges," *Reuters News Service,* November 2, 2000; "Electronic Commerce: Covisint's Up and Running, but Are Roadblocks Ahead?" *Investor's Business Daily,* November 27, 2000, p. A8; and "Don't Cheat, Children," *Business Week E.Biz,* December 11, 2000, p. 116.

counterargument is that the principles of antitrust law apply perfectly well; in fact, certain characteristics of high-tech industry tend to favor monopoly formation. For example, consumers tend to gravitate toward a standard computer operating system because most software is written for it, creating a kind of natural monopoly. New information technologies also enable some kinds of collaboration that might not have been possible before. For example, some companies have established joint venture Internet sites, sometimes called *e-exchanges,* to sell either to each other or directly to customers.[12] Do these purchasing exchanges violate antitrust laws, or not? One such e-exchange is discussed in Exhibit 9-B.

The courts are struggling to define in what ways high-technology industries are similar to and in what ways they are different from other businesses to which antitrust laws have been applied over the years. The resolution of the Microsoft antitrust case, described in one of the case studies at the end of the book, will be a key milestone in this definition.[13]

One other important issue in antitrust policy, the impact of global competition, is discussed at the end of this chapter.

---

[12] "E-Exchanges May Keep Trustbusters Busy," *Business Week,* May 1, 2000, p. 52.

[13] For further discussion of U.S. regulators' understanding of these issues, see *Anticipating the Twenty-First Century: Competition Policy in the New Hi-Tech Global Marketplace* (Washington, DC: Federal Trade Commission, 1996).

Corporate Mergers

The late 1990s and early 2000s have witnessed a wave of **corporate mergers.** As Figure 9-4 shows, merger and acquisition activity, after falling dramatically in the early 1990s, was up sharply again in the mid-1990s. These new mergers raised, once again, important questions about the social and economic impact of such corporate consolidation. Not surprisingly, antitrust officials were deeply involved in deciding which mergers were acceptable and which were not.

Students of corporate mergers usually distinguish between three different types of business combinations. **Vertical mergers** occur when the combining companies are at different stages of production in the same general line of business. For example, a rubber tire

Figure 9-4

Value of mergers and acquisitions, 1985–1999.

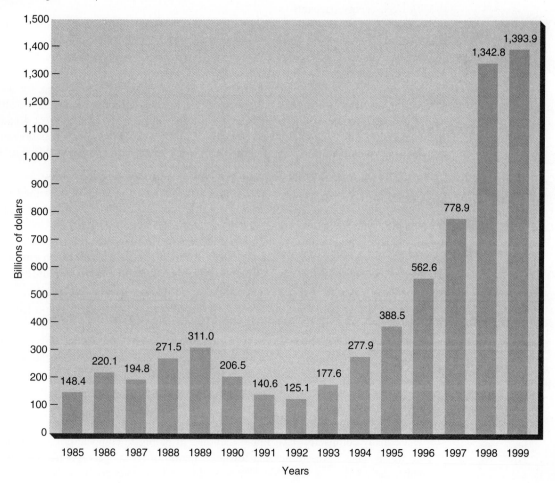

Source: "M&A Profile" published annually by *Mergers & Acquisitions.* Where applicable, the most recently corrected data have been used. Used by permission of *Mergers & Acquisitions.*

manufacturer may combine with a company owning rubber plantations and with a chain of auto parts dealers that sells the tires. Production from the ground up is then brought under a single management umbrella, so it is referred to as a vertical combination.

Horizontal mergers occur when the combining companies are at the same stage or level of production or sales. For example, if two retail grocery chains in an urban market tried to combine, antitrust regulators probably would not permit the merger if the combined firms' resultant market share appeared to lessen competition in that area.

Finally, **conglomerate mergers** occur when firms that are in totally unrelated lines of business are combined. Gulf & Western (G&W), for example, a well-known conglomerate of the 1970s, merged under its corporate umbrella an extraordinary diversity of firms. These included companies that manufactured pipeline equipment, auto and truck parts, cigars, chocolate candy, steel mill equipment, pantyhose, and paperback books; other units ran racetracks, distributed educational films, and staged the Miss Universe and Miss USA beauty pageants.

Corporate mergers seem to occur in waves at different periods of history, each wave with its own distinctive characteristics. The 1950s and 1960s saw many mergers that produced conglomerates. This wave may have been motivated in part by strict antitrust enforcement that made vertical and horizontal mergers more difficult at that time. Most observers seem to agree that one factor stimulating the 1980s surge, by contrast, was the government's general philosophy of deregulation and a more relaxed attitude toward enforcement of the nation's antitrust laws. In this general climate of greater permissiveness, the number of both horizontal and vertical corporate mergers ballooned.

The mergers of the 1990s and early 2000s, for their part, have been driven by several forces.

- *Technological change.* AOL's $165 billion buyout of Time Warner, described in the discussion case at the end of this chapter, was just one of several blockbuster mergers in telecommunications and media, where major companies jockeyed for a favorable position on the emerging information superhighway. The need to keep ahead of advances in biotechnology drove many mergers in the pharmaceutical and chemical industries, such as acquisition of Pharmacia & Upjohn by Monsanto.

- *Changes in the regulatory environment.* Telecommunications deregulation led to a wave of mergers among long-distance phone companies, regional carriers, and cable operators. Several big combinations in health care were spurred by anticipated regulatory changes in the delivery of health care. In financial services, a cluster of mergers followed repeal of a federal law that had prohibited commercial banks, brokerage houses, and insurance companies from operating under the same corporate umbrella.

- *Globalization.* Other deals were prompted by a rapidly globalizing economy in which many companies have found they had to be big to compete effectively on the world stage. "We are moving toward a period of the megacorporate state in which there will be a few global firms within particular economic sectors," commented one investment banker. The acquisition of Chrysler by German automaker Daimler-Benz, for example, gave both companies a wider global reach.

- *Stock price appreciation.* Finally, the long bull market of the late 1990s contributed to the merger wave, as a sharp rise in their market value gave some companies the means to purchase other firms. America Online was able to purchase the much-larger Time Warner, for example, by swapping its highly appreciated stock shares for those of its acquisition target.

Many of the same forces have been echoed in Europe, where a new wave of combinations has swept the continent. Many of these mergers crossed national borders to create new, multinational companies. In just one of many recent transactions, for example, the British cellular firm Vodafone AirTouch acquired the German company Mannesmann in 2000 for $183 billion, creating a telecommunications giant that vaulted from 70 to 6 in that year's rankings of global firms, by market value. The European merger wave was driven, in part, by an effort to remain competitive with U.S.-based firms that had recently grown through their own acquisitions. But it was also driven by the European Union's creation of a common currency, the euro, which reduced foreign exchange risk and made cross-border investments more attractive within the continent. In 1999, for the first time, the number of mergers abroad—most of them in Europe—exceeded the number in the United States.[14]

The Consequences of Corporate Mergers

When the smoke has cleared from the most recent wave of corporate mergers, what will the results be? What stakeholders were helped, and what stakeholders were hurt? No one knows the final story, but some results are already observable.

The megamergers of the 1990s and early 2000s created enormously larger corporations, thus continuing a trend toward bigger and bigger business units. In many cases, this led to greater efficiencies and market clout. When Chemical Banking and Chase Manhattan merged in 1996, for example, the combination of branches and functional areas, like the loan department, led to a leaner and more competitive business. Gillette's purchase of Duracell allowed it to use its global distribution network to sell batteries alongside shaving gear.

Some commentators have expressed concern that mergers may undermine corporate responsibility to various stakeholders. Employees often lose their jobs when companies merge, as duplicate positions are eliminated, and local communities suffer when a large company moves out or shifts its activities to other regions. Following the 1998 merger of Exxon and Mobil, for example, the combined company eliminated no less than 14,000 jobs. Some worried that Ben & Jerry's, known for its charitable contributions, would cut back in the wake of its takeover by the Dutch conglomerate Unilever. The results of mergers are mixed for stockholders. Share values often rise when a merger or acquisition is announced, if shareholders perceive benefits from synergies between the two firms. The share prices of Boeing, Gillette, and Tosco all shot up after they announced merger plans. But shareholders can also be hurt, particularly where an acquisition is overpriced or not well thought out. One study found that about half of large

---

[14] Martin Sikora, "The Panorama of M&A," *Mergers & Acquisitions Journal,* February 1, 2000.

mergers (those valued at over $500 million) had led to at least some decline in share-holder returns.[15]

There will remain a need for economic restructuring in the decades ahead, so mergers and acquisitions will continue. They can serve as a dynamic stimulus, producing gains for shareholders and the entire economy from improved efficiency and market pressure. Experience has shown, however, that when carried to excess such business combinations can be costly in economic and social terms for some stakeholders. Social control, expressed through antitrust policy, will continue to seek the best balance between competition and other social goals.

Global Competition and Antitrust Policy

The first antitrust laws were passed in the United States in the late nineteenth century, when most commerce was regional or national in scope. This is no longer the case. Today, business has greatly expanded its global reach. Foreign sales are a critical part of the revenues of many U.S.-based firms. An increasing proportion of products and services purchased by American consumers are made abroad. Trade barriers are falling, and new regions of the world are rapidly entering the world marketplace.

The rapid globalization of business has created many new challenges for antitrust enforcement. Federal regulators, policymakers, and the courts must now address difficult and complex questions, often not anticipated by the framers of antitrust law, such as the following:

- Should the government permit mergers, joint ventures, or other cooperative arrangements among companies, even if they reduce competition *within* the United States, if they enhance the ability of American businesses to compete internationally?

- Should the government move to break up monopolies *within* the United States if the global marketplace for the products or services offered by these companies is highly competitive? What if these companies help the United States become more competitive internationally?

- Should federal regulators and the courts try to enforce U.S. antitrust laws against foreign companies if these companies operate subsidiaries in the United States? What if these companies simply sell their products or services in the United States?

- What steps can the government take to create a level playing field for U.S. corporations so that U.S. and foreign firms operate under a common set of antitrust rules and regulations?

Interestingly, these issues are faced not only by U.S. regulators but also by government officials in many other countries around the world faced with the challenge of maintaining conditions necessary for fair competition in an increasingly global economy. The following sections will discuss how government, business, and society have tried to answer these questions in recent years.

---

[15] "The Case against Mergers," *Business Week,* October 30, 1995, pp. 122–30.

Antitrust Enforcement and National Competitiveness

Antitrust regulators have become increasingly sensitive to the impact of enforcement on the ability of U.S. firms to compete effectively in the global economy. They have been reluctant to block mergers, break up monopolies, or prevent joint research efforts where these would strengthen the **national competitiveness** of the United States. This sometimes creates dilemmas for regulators, when the goal of a free, competitive market nationally conflicts with the goal of a strong U.S. economy, relative to other countries.

Since the mid-1980s, the government has generally permitted cooperative activities among U.S. firms where appropriate to enhance their competitiveness in the global economy. The National Cooperative Research Act (NCRA), passed in 1984, clarified the application of U.S. antitrust laws to joint research and development (R&D) activities. This law sought to balance the positive effects of cooperative R&D with the preservation of competition by instructing the courts to use a "rule of reason" in assessing individual cases. Companies that wish to form joint R&D activities that may have anticompetitive effects are required to submit notice of their plans to the U.S. attorney general and Federal Trade Commission. If approved, the companies may share information and cooperate in ways that would otherwise violate antitrust standards.

> *An example of an R&D consortium permitted under the NCRA is SEMATECH. Founded in 1987, SEMATECH is a group of 14 semiconductor manufacturers that came together, with support from the Department of Defense, to rebuild the U.S. chip industry in the face of intense Japanese competition. SEMATECH played a significant role in developing several new generations of chip-making technology. By the late 1990s, the U.S. semiconductor industry had achieved a dramatic turnaround in its global market share.*[16]

The U.S. Justice Department has also loosened the rules governing joint production agreements to permit important economies of scale. Joint manufacturing and marketing deals between U.S. and foreign firms are becoming more frequent, often without serious antitrust objections being raised by government. Hewlett-Packard, for example, has formed strategic alliances with Samsung (Korea), Northern Telecom (Canada), and Japanese firms, including Sony, Hitachi, Canon, and Yokogawa. In 1998, the Federal Trade Commission approved a joint venture between Royal Dutch/Shell and Texaco, provided they divested some overlapping operations in Hawaii and California. Such a joint venture might well have drawn antitrust objections on traditional grounds. Noting that the "competitive forces of globalization and technology are driving firms toward complex collaborations," the FTC in 1999 proposed new guidelines on what kinds of joint ventures were permissible under antitrust law.[17]

---

[16] Henry H. Beam, "Technology Fountainheads: The Management Challenge of R&D Consortia," *Academy of Management Executive* 11 (February 1997), pp. 123–24.

[17] "U.S. Proposes Guidelines on Forming Joint Ventures," *New York Times,* October 2, 1999, p. C2; and "When Is Cozy Too Cozy?" *Business Week,* October 25, 1999, pp. 127–30.

Enforcing Antitrust Laws against Foreign Firms

In recent years, the government has become increasingly concerned about possible violations of antitrust law by foreign companies.

In some instances, regulators have moved to prosecute international companies doing business in the U.S. by setting up operations or buying a subsidiary that is believed to have violated antitrust laws. In other cases, U.S. authorities have gone even further, going after foreign companies that violate antitrust law within their own borders. When Swiss drug makers Sandoz and Ciba-Geigy merged, for example, the FTC required the companies to divest some product lines to avoid a monopoly, even though neither company was based in the United States. In the Vitamins, Inc., case mentioned in the opening example of this chapter, the U.S. Justice Department brought its own case for price-fixing against the foreign firms involved, separate from the private court action. "We'll attack these cartels whether the conspirators are in the U.S. or beyond our borders," said one Justice Department official. But some legal observers felt that prosecutors had gone too far. In this view, antitrust laws should not extend to the actions of foreign firms, acting in their own countries.[18]

Harmonizing International Antitrust Policies

Although in many instances antitrust policies in the United States are more stringent than those of its global competitors, other nations have their own versions of antitrust laws, often referred to as *competition policies*. Japan has an antimonopoly law, first implemented during the Allied occupation after World War II, although the Japanese cartels known as *keiretsu* in many cases would probably be illegal under U.S. antitrust laws. The European Union recently adopted a set of competition policies that reflects the newly integrated European economy. In 1994, the European Commission, the EU's executive branch, fined a group of carton-board manufacturers about $165 million for fixing prices—at that time the EU's largest fine ever. U.S. antitrust regulators have worked with officials in developing countries, like Zimbabwe and Kazakhstan, to develop their own domestic antitrust policies.

Some efforts have been made to coordinate antitrust enforcement among nations. Several bilateral (two-country) treaties are in place, and the Organization for Economic Cooperation and Development, a 28-nation group, has worked to coordinate antitrust enforcement. Their goal is to create a level playing field among their members' competing national economies. The issues of antitrust and competition policy have also been taken up in international trade negotiations, such as those over the General Agreement on Tariffs and Trade and ones conducted under the auspices of the World Trade Organization.

But the explosion of international commerce has far outstripped the pace of international negotiations, and global business still lacks a common, enforceable set of competition policies. The lack of common standards poses a problem for businesses engaged in cross-border mergers, which often face conflicting regulatory hurdles in multiple countries. A study published by the Brookings Institution in 2000 recommended a broad

[18] "Tearing Down the Façade of Vitamins, Inc.," *New York Times,* October 10, 1999, sec. 3, p. 1; and "U.S. Trust Busters Increasingly Target International Business," *Wall Street Journal,* February 5, 1997, pp. A1, A10.

multicountry effort to harmonize competition policies. Among other ideas, the study recommended the establishment of regional antitrust authorities in Latin America and Asia and teamwork among regulators of different nations.[19]

Antitrust policymakers are wrestling with the new realities of global business competition. The days of self-contained national economies are gone. Virtually all businesses are touched, directly or indirectly, by the world marketplace. Cooperation among companies of diverse national origins often makes economic sense. But the need for some form of social control on the excesses of anticompetitive business behavior has not disappeared, both in the United States and abroad. The optimal fit between antitrust protection and the global marketplace is not easily achieved.

Summary Points of This Chapter

- The world's largest corporations are capable of wielding much influence because of the central functions they perform in their respective societies and throughout the world. Corporate power is legitimate when used to affirm broad public purposes, but it may also be abused.
- In the United States, antitrust laws have been used to curb the influence of corporations and to protect consumers, small business competitors, and others affected unfairly by noncompetitive practices.
- Courts and regulators have generally maintained in recent years that monopoly does not in itself constitute a violation of antitrust laws. What is important is whether a company has competed unfairly, hurt consumers, or blocked innovation.
- The 1990s and early 2000s witnessed a fresh wave of mergers and acquisitions. The key causes were technological change, globalization, shifts in the regulatory environment, and the booming stock market. Some believed that these mergers were good for stockholders and other stakeholders; others expressed concern about the long-run effects such mergers would have on both business and society.
- The emergence of global competition in many industries has led business and political leaders to adjust antitrust rules to help the United States better compete in the world economy, for example, by permitting joint R&D efforts where appropriate and by blocking anticompetitive practices by foreign firms.

Key Terms and Concepts Used in This Chapter

- Corporate power
- Multinational corporation
- Antitrust laws
- Predatory pricing
- Corporate mergers
- Vertical, horizontal, and conglomerate mergers
- National competitiveness

[19] Simon J. Evenett et al., *Antitrust Goes Global: What the Future Holds for Transatlantic Cooperation* (Washington, DC: Brookings Institution Press, 2000).

Internet Resources

www.usdoj.gov	U.S. Department of Justice
www.ftc.gov	U.S. Federal Trade Commission
www.207.49.1.6/antitrust	American Bar Association, Antitrust Section
www.yahoo.com/Government/Law/Cases	Information on current antitrust cases

Discussion Case: *The AOL–Time Warner Merger*

On January 10, 2000, America Online (AOL), the world's leading provider of Internet access, announced its intention to acquire media giant Time Warner for shares of stock worth around $165 billion. It was the largest corporate merger in history. In combined market value, the two companies—to be called AOL Time Warner after their union—ranked fourth, smaller only than Microsoft, General Electric, and Cisco Systems.

The merger represented a marriage of two of the premier companies from the worlds of new and old media. America Online, led by 41-year-old entrepreneur Stephen M. Case, was the most popular on-ramp to the Internet in the world, with 54 percent of the market in the United States—far and away the largest share. Twenty-two million subscribers logged onto AOL for e-mail, chat, instant messaging, news and information, shopping, and access to the World Wide Web.

For its part, the Time Warner conglomerate included a huge stable of media and entertainment properties. These included television holdings Home Box Office, the WB network, and CNN; the magazines *People, Sports Illustrated,* and *Time;* the record company Time Warner Music; and the film studios Warner Brothers and New Line Cinema. The company's cable affiliates served 20 percent of U.S. market. Road Runner, a subsidiary, was a leading provider of cable-based Internet access.

Robert H. Frank, an economist and coauthor of the book *The Winner-Take-All Society,* praised the merger: "The domain of entertainment and communications . . . has become an environment where success breeds success." Because many costs in the media industry are fixed, he noted, the more customers a company can reach, the more money it makes.

The combination promised important advantages to both companies. For its part, AOL would get content—the magazine articles, television shows, popular songs, movies, and news reports owned by the media giant. "Time Warner has something AOL doesn't have," commented George Bell, president of Excite @ Home. "Great media brands are built up over decades. The time isn't there for Internet companies to build that content."

AOL would also get something else—access to Time Warner's high-capacity fiber-optic cable network. In 2000, most of AOL's customers still logged on using modems and traditional telephone lines. Yet, the company's executives knew that users would increasingly want high-speed Internet access—whether over cable networks or digital subscriber (DSL) lines—to enjoy the full range of media available online. AOL did not have that capability on its own.

For its part, Time Warner gained access to millions of customers, as well as the tantalizing promise of greater global reach as the Internet company expanded into many regions of the world. When people logged on to AOL, their menu of choices would offer Time Warner products, from *People* magazine stories to Tori Amos songs to breaking CNN news coverage.

The merger announcement triggered a review by the Federal Trade Commission. Antitrust regulators could approve the merger, block it, or require one or both companies to divest properties if a monopoly would be created. Many antitrust experts expected the deal to sail through, because most businesses of the two companies did not directly overlap.

Critics, however—including some consumer groups—raised concerns about possible anticompetitive effects of the merger.

Once AOL gained control over a big share of the cable network, what would stop it from monopolizing high-speed Internet access? Perhaps in an effort to head off this criticism, the company pledged—on the day the merger was announced—that it would voluntarily support open access to Time Warner's cable network for all Internet service providers, including its own rivals. Yet, some consumer advocates remained worried. Said Gene Kimmelman, a director of Consumers Union, "[the deal will lead to] tilting the playing field in favor of particular Internet services."

No doubt the merger would increase the concentration of ownership of media, both directly and by accelerating the pace of other telecommunications acquisitions. One danger was that the multiplicity of viewpoints would decline in a world dominated by a few media giants. Others voiced concerns about the growing commercialization of the Internet. "What they [are] really looking forward to [is] creating the biggest shopping mall in the world," warned Ben Bagdikian, an industry critic and author of the book *The Media Monopoly*.

But others felt that technology itself would counteract any threat to competition. "The Internet remains unowned and kind of anarchic," commented David Rubin, dean of the School of Public Communications at Syracuse University. "It really can't be monopolized."

Sources: "Media Megadeal: The Overview," *New York Times*, January 11, 2000, p. A1; "A Merger's Message: Dominate or Die," *New York Times*, January 11, 2000, p. A25; "Brave New Media World," *Christian Science Monitor*, January 14, 2000, p. 11; "Company Town: Media Megamerger Open Access Debate," *Los Angeles Times*, January 12, 2000, p. C4; "Media Megadeal: The Power," *New York Times*, January 13, 2000, p. C1; "Media Megamerger: As the Hopes and Worries Continue," *Los Angeles Times*, January 13, 2000, p. C1; and "Mergers May Shrink Limits of Cyberspace," *Christian Science Monitor*, January 13, 2000, p. 2.

Discussion Questions

1. This chapter discusses four reasons for the current wave of mergers. Which of these reasons, in your opinion, best explains the merger of AOL and Time Warner? Why?

2. This chapter discusses four objectives of antitrust policy. Do you believe the merger of AOL and Time Warner undermines any of these objectives? If so, why?
3. In your opinion, will this merger help or hurt the public interest? Why?
4. If you were an antitrust regulator charged with reviewing this merger for the Federal Trade Commission, would you approve or disapprove this merger? Would you place any conditions on its approval and, if so, what conditions?

PART FIVE

The Corporation and the Natural Environment

10

Ecology, Sustainable Development, and Global Business

The world community faces unprecedented ecological challenges in the twenty-first century. Many political and business leaders have embraced the idea of sustainable development, calling for economic growth without destroying the natural environment or depleting the resources on which future generations depend. Yet the concept has remained controversial, and implementation has been difficult. The task for policymakers and corporate leaders will be to find ways to meet both economic and environmental goals in the coming decades, without sacrificing either.

This chapter focuses on these key questions and objectives:

- What is sustainable development? What are the obstacles to developing the world's economy to meet the needs of the present without hurting future generations?
- What are the major threats to the earth's ecosystem?
- In what ways have population growth, poverty, and industrialization accelerated the world's ecological crisis?
- What environmental issues are shared globally by all nations?
- What steps has the world business community taken to reduce ecological damage and promote sustainable development?

T he Earth Summit was a groundbreaking international conference. Sponsored by the United Nations in 1992, the Conference on Environment and Development, as it was formally known, brought together business and political leaders from around the world. In a series of contentious sessions, the delegates had considered, on one hand, the growing dangers of environmental degradation and, on the other, the urgent need for economic development in poorer nations. Would it be possible, they had asked, to foster economic growth sufficient to lift the majority of the world's people out of poverty, without compromising the ability of future generations to meet their own needs?

In 2000, almost a decade after this important gathering, how far had the world come in achieving these goals? Some evidence did not look encouraging. Consider that at the 1992 gathering:

- Delegates had pledged to attack the problem of global warming, increases in the earth's temperature caused in part by carbon dioxide from the world's factories, utilities, and vehicles. The conference had called on developed countries to cut back to 1990 levels by the year 2000. But only half the developed countries had met this target, and annual emissions of carbon dioxide had reached new highs, threatening disruption of the world's climate.[1]

- Delegates had committed to a framework Convention on Biological Diversity, dedicated to conserving the earth's biological resources, particularly in species-rich tropical forests. But at the turn of the century, the United States had still not signed the treaty, and many species remained endangered. Vast stretches of rain forest had been cut down. In Indonesia, for example, home to large numbers of endangered birds, mammals, and reptiles, tropical forest was being logged for timber and burned to clear land at an astonishing rate, destroying habitat and, not incidentally, causing serious air pollution throughout Southeast Asia.[2]

- Many developed nations had pledged to increase foreign aid to 0.7 percent of their gross national product (GNP) to help poorer countries develop their economies in an environmentally sustainable way. But during the intervening years, aid had actually fallen to just 0.24 percent of GNP, the lowest level since the early 1970s.[3] Now the question was just as urgent as it had been before: Who would pay for the costs of clean development in the poorer countries?

On the other hand, important progress had been made. Although the world population was still growing, the rate of growth had dropped somewhat. The World Bank, an important lender to developing countries, had instituted a strict environmental review process, refusing to fund ecologically destructive projects. Important gains had been made in efforts to restore the health of the ozone layer. And possibly most promisingly, many segments of the global business community had become increasingly active in

[1] The website for the United Nations Framework Convention on Climate Change is available at www.unfcc.de.
[2] The website for the Convention on Biological Diversity is available at www.biodiv.org.
[3] Data on percent of GNP devoted to development assistance are available at the website of the Organization for Economic Cooperation and Development, Development Assistance Committee, at www.oecd.org/dac.

promoting environmentally sound management practices. Could the world's governments, businesses, nongovernmental organizations, and individuals, working together, meet the ecological challenges of the twenty-first century and put the global economy on a more sustainable course?[4]

Ecological Challenges

Humankind is now altering the face of the planet, rivaling the forces of nature—glaciers, volcanoes, asteroids, and earthquakes—in impact. Human beings have rerouted rivers, moved mountains, and burned forests. By the last decade of the twentieth century, human society had transformed about half of the earth's ice-free surface and made a major impact on most of the rest. In many areas, as much land was used by transportation systems as by agriculture. Although significant natural resources—fossil fuels, fresh water, fertile land, and forest—remained, exploding populations and rapid industrialization threatened a day when the demands of human society would exceed the carrying capacity of the earth's ecosystem.[5]

Ecology is the study of how living things—plants and animals—interact with one another in such a unified natural system, or ecosystem. Damage to the ecosystem in one part of the world often affects people in other locations. Depletion of the ozone layer, destruction of the rain forests, and species extinctions have an impact on all of society, not just particular regions or nations.

The Global Commons

Throughout history, communities of people have created *commons*. A commons is a shared resource, such as land, air, or water, that a group of people uses collectively. The paradox of the commons is that if all individuals attempt to maximize their own private advantage in the short term, the commons may be destroyed, and all users—present and future—lose. The only solution is restraint, either voluntary or through mutual agreement.[6] The tragedy of the commons—that freedom in a commons brings ruin to all—is illustrated by the following parable.

> *There was once a village on the shore of a great ocean. Its people made a good living from the rich fishing grounds that lay offshore, the bounty of which seemed inexhaustible. Some of the cleverest fishermen began to experiment with new ways to catch more fish, borrowing money to buy bigger and better equipped boats. Since it was hard to argue with success, others copied their new techniques. Soon fish began to be harder to find, and their average size began to decline. Eventually, the fishery collapsed altogether, bringing economic calamity to the village. A wise elder*

---

[4] Christopher Flavin, "The Legacy of Rio," in Lester R. Brown et al., eds., *State of the World 1997: A Worldwatch Institute Report on Progress toward a Sustainable Society* (New York: W.W. Norton, 1997), pp. 3–22. For current data, including the biannual report *Global Environmental Outlook,* see the website of the United National Environment Programme at www.unep.org.

[5] For a scientific account, see P.M. Vitousek et al., "Human Domination of the Earth's Ecosystems," *Science* 277 (July 1997), pp. 494–99.

[6] Garrett Hardin, "Tragedy of the Commons," *Science* 162 (December 1968), pp. 1243–48.

commented, "You see, the fish were not free after all. It was o
act as if they were."[7]

We live on a **global commons,** in which many natural resourc
grounds in this parable, are used collectively. The image of the e_____
space—a blue and green globe, girdled by white clouds, floating in blackness—shows
that we share a single, unified ecosystem. Preserving the global commons and assuring
its continued use is a new imperative for governments, business, and society. As we move
into the twenty-first century, to quote Maurice Strong, secretary general of the original
Earth Summit, "We now face the ultimate management challenge, that of managing our
own future as a species."

Sustainable Development

The World Commission on Environment and Development, which included leaders from
many industrialized and developing nations, described the need for balance between economic and environmental considerations as **sustainable development.** This term refers
to development that "meets the needs of the present without compromising the ability
of future generations to meet their own needs."[8] The concept includes two core ideas:

- Protecting the environment will require economic development. Poverty is an
  underlying cause of environmental degradation. People who lack food, shelter,
  and basic amenities misuse resources just to survive. For this reason, environmental protection will require providing a decent standard of living for all the
  world's citizens.

- But economic development must be accomplished sustainably, that is, in a way
  that conserves the earth's resources for future generations. Growth cannot occur
  at the expense of degrading the forests, farmland, water, and air that must
  continue to support life on this planet. We must leave the earth in as good
  shape—or better—as we found it.

In short, the idea of sustainable development encompasses a kind of puzzle. It challenges government and business leaders to eradicate poverty and develop the world
economy but to do so in a way that does not degrade the environment or plunder natural resources.

Sustainable development is an appealing idea but also a controversial one. For sustainable development to work, rich nations like the United States and Japan would have
to consume fewer resources and dramatically cut pollution, without simply exporting
environmental stresses to other countries. Some less developed nations, such as China
or Pakistan, for their part, would have to use less destructive agricultural practices, cut

---

[7] Abridgement of "The Story of a Fishing Village," from *1994 Information Please Environmental Almanac.*
Copyright © 1993 by World Resources Institute. Reprinted by permission of Houghton Mifflin Co. All
rights reserved.

[8] World Commission on Environment and Development, *Our Common Future* (Oxford: Oxford University
Press, 1987), p. 8. For an account of the origins of the concept of sustainable development, see W. Adams,
Green Development: Environment and Sustainability in the Third World (London: Routledge, 1990).

**EXHIBIT
10-A**

The Natural Step

The Natural Step (TNS) was founded in 1989 by a prominent Swedish physician, Karl-Henrik Robert. Dr. Robert joined other leading scientists in Sweden to develop a consensus document on how businesses, governments, and individuals could act in a way that was consistent with the principle of sustainable development. Their report was endorsed by the King of Sweden, and a summary was distributed to all households in the country.

The Natural Step encouraged businesses to act voluntarily to cut back on the use of synthetics and nonrenewable resources, minimize their consumption of energy, and preserve natural diversity and ecosystems. Within a decade, over 300 companies and half the cities in Sweden had adopted TNS principles, and the movement was spreading to other countries, including the United States, the Netherlands, and Australia. An example of a company that has followed The Natural Step is IKEA, the Swedish-based global home-furnishings retailer. IKEA signed on, committing itself to the use of materials, technologies, and transportation methods that had the least possible damaging effect on the environment. For example, the company switched from truck to rail shipping where possible to conserve fuel and introduced a new line of furnishings, called the Eco-Line, that used only recycled materials or wood and fibers that had been sustainably harvested. The company said that the initiative not only had enabled it to protect the environment and attract "green" customers, it had actually helped the bottom line by avoiding waste and saving on energy and materials.

Sources: Hilary Bradbury and Judith A. Clair, "Promoting Sustainable Organizations with Sweden's Natural Step," *Academy of Management Executive* 13, no. 4 (November 1999), pp. 63–74; Andrea Larson and Joel E. Reichart, "IKEA and the Natural Step," Darden School of Management, University of Virginia, 1996. Other case studies may be found in Brian Nattrass and Mary Altomare, *The Natural Step for Business: Wealth, Ecology and the Evolutionary Corporation* (Gabriola Island, British Columbia: New Society Publishers, 1999). IKEA's website, including material on the company's environmental policies, is available at www.ikea.com. The website of The Natural Step in the United States is at www.naturalstep.org.

birthrates, and industrialize more cleanly. This would only be possible with the aid of money, technology, and skills from the developed nations.

What would the idea of sustainable development mean for business? One attempt to apply this concept to business operations has been made by an initiative in Sweden called The Natural Step, described in Exhibit 10-A. Other voluntary efforts by the business community to operate with less harm to the environment are addressed in the last section of this chapter and in Chapter 11.

Threats to the Earth's Ecosystem

Sustainable development requires that human society use natural resources at a rate that can be continued over an indefinite period. Human activity affects three major forms of natural resources: water, air, and land. Biologists distinguish between *renewable* resources, such as fresh water or forests, which can be naturally replenished, and *nonrenewable* resources, such as fossil fuels (oil, gas, and coal), which once used are gone forever. Many natural resources, renewable and nonrenewable, are now being depleted or polluted at well above sustainable rates. Consider the following examples.

Water Resources

Only 3 percent of the water on the earth is fresh, and most of this is underground or locked up in ice and snow. Only about one-tenth of 1 percent of the earth's water is in lakes, rivers, and accessible underground supplies and thus available for human use. Water is, of course, renewable: Moisture evaporates from the oceans and returns to earth as freshwater precipitation, replenishing used stocks. But in many areas, humans are using up or polluting water faster than it can be replaced or naturally purified, threatening people and businesses that depend on it.

> *The Ganges River supports more than 400 million Indians, providing water for drinking, irrigation, fishing, transportation, and trade along its 1,500-mile course from high in the Himalayan mountains to the coastal city of Calcutta. Hindus believe the river to be holy, and it is the site of many religious observances. But the Ganges is increasingly polluted, choked with raw sewage, industrial waste, animal carcasses, and even human remains. "Our forefathers worshipped this river; today, it is killing us," said one Indian.*[9]

By one estimate, if society were able to eliminate all pollution, capture all available fresh water, and distribute it equitably—all of which are unlikely—demand would exceed the supply within a hundred years. At the turn of the century, regional shortages had already caused the decline of local economies and in some cases had contributed to regional conflicts. According to a United Nations study, one-third of the world's population lived in countries experiencing moderate to high water stress.[10]

Fossil Fuels

Fossil fuels, unlike water, are nonrenewable. Human society used 60 times as much energy in the late twentieth century as it did in 1860, when industrialization was in its early stages. Most of this came from the burning of fossil fuels; 80 percent of all commercial energy came from the combustion of coal, oil, and natural gas. The amount of fossil fuel burned by the world economy in one year took about a million years to form. No one knows how long present supplies will last, because many reserves remain to be discovered. However, some estimates suggest that oil and gas will begin to run out in about 40 and 60 years, respectively. Coal reserves are more plentiful and could last three to four more centuries, although coal is more polluting than either oil or natural gas. Eventually, however, many fossil fuel reserves will be depleted, and the world economy

---

[9] "Dateline Calcutta: India's Great Ganges Offers a Physical, Mystical Lifeline; Millions Believe in the Ancient Properties of Its Waters, but Pollution Is a Growing Modern Threat," *Atlanta Journal and Constitution,* October 21, 1999, p. 4F; and "New Delhi: A Sewer Runs through It," *Toronto Star,* November 6, 1999.

[10] A report on world water resources may be found at www.wri.org/wri/trends/water.html. See also Sandra Postel, *Pillar of Sand* (New York: W.W. Norton, 1999).

will need to become much more energy efficient and switch to renewable energy sources, such as those based on water, wind, and sunshine.

Arable Land

Arable (fertile) land is necessary to grow crops to feed the world's peoples. Land, if properly cared for, is a renewable resource. Although the productivity of land increased through much of the twentieth century, by the early 2000s much of the world's arable land was threatened with decline. About half of irrigated farmland in developing countries required reclamation because of salinization (excess salt) or poor drainage. In other areas, poor farming practices had caused previously arable land to turn into desert. Other areas had become contaminated by agricultural chemicals or ruined by overly intensive farming practices. In all, nearly 30 percent of the world's vegetated surface had been degraded to some degree by the late 1990s, according to the United Nations.[11]

Forces of Change

Pressure on the earth's resource base is becoming increasingly severe. Three critical factors have combined to accelerate the ecological crisis facing the world community and to make sustainable development more difficult. These are population growth, world poverty, and the rapid industrialization of many developing nations.

The Population Explosion

A major driver of environmental degradation is the exponential growth of the world's population. (A population that doubled every 50 years, for example, would be said to be growing exponentially. Many more people would be added during the second 50 years than during the first, even though the rate of growth would stay the same.) Just 10,000 years ago, the earth was home to no more than 10 million humans, scattered in small settlements. For many thousands of years, population growth was gradual. Around 1950, as shown in Figure 10-1, the world population reached 2.5 billion. World population crossed the 6 billion mark in 1999. The United Nations estimates that the population will eventually level out at a bit under 10 billion around 2150. To gain some perspective on these figures, consider that in the course of a single human lifetime—for example, someone born in 1950 who lived to be 75 years old—the world population will increase by more than 5 billion people.

This growth will not be distributed equally. In the industrialized countries, especially in Europe, population growth has already slowed down. About 95 percent of the world's population growth over the next 30 years is predicted to be in less developed countries, especially in Africa, Latin America, and Asia.

The world's burgeoning population will put increasing strain on the earth's resources. Each additional person uses raw materials and adds pollutants to the land, air, and water. The world's total industrial production would have to quintuple over the next 40 years just to maintain the same standard of living that people have now. Protecting the environment in the face of rapid population growth is very difficult. For example, in

---

[11] "Five Years after Environmental Summit in Rio," *New York Times*, June 17, 1997, p. B14.

Figure 10-1

World population
growth.

Source: United Nations
Population Division,
Long-Range World
Population Projections
(New York: United
Nations, 2000),
table 1, p. 4.

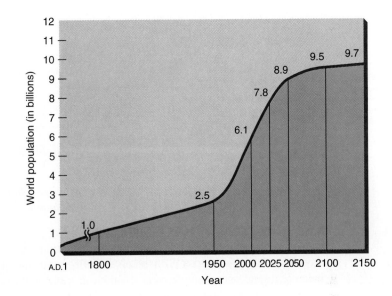

some parts of western Africa, population growth has put great pressure on available farmland, which is not allowed to lie fallow. Because much of the available firewood has
already been cut, people use livestock dung for fuel instead of fertilizer. The result
has been a deepening cycle of poverty, as more and more people try to live off less and
less productive land.

World Poverty

A second important cause of environmental degradation is poverty and the inequality
between rich and poor countries. Although economic development has raised living standards for many, large numbers of the world's people continue to live in severe poverty.
According to 2000 estimates by the United Nations, around 1.2 billion people had
incomes below $1 a day, well below the level needed for a nutritionally adequate diet
and other basic necessities of life. These people—most of them in sub-Saharan Africa,
East and Southeast Asia, on the Indian subcontinent, and in Haiti—lived very near the
margin of subsistence. They had only a tiny fraction of the goods and services enjoyed
by those in the industrialized nations. Almost 800 million suffered from hunger, many
of them malnourished children under the age of five.[12]

> *Some of the most extreme poverty is found on the outskirts of rapidly*
> *growing cities in developing countries. In many parts of the world, people*
> *have moved to urban areas in search of work. Often, they must live*
> *in slums, in makeshift dwellings without sanitation or running water. In*
> *Bangkok, Thailand, a sprawling city of 8 million, 35 percent of the*

---

[12] United Nations Development Programme, *Human Development Report 2000* (New York: Oxford University Press, 2000), p. 8 and table 1, pp. 157–60.

Figure 10-2

Global income
distribution,
1960–1994.

Source: United Nations
Development Program,
*Human Development
Report 1992, 1994, and
1997* (New York: Oxford
University Press).

	Share of Global Income (%)		Ratio of Richest to Poorest
Year	Richest 20 Percent	Poorest 20 Percent	
1960	70.2%	2.3%	30 to 1
1970	73.9	2.3	32 to 1
1980	76.3	1.7	45 to 1
1991	84.7	1.4	61 to 1
1994	85.8	1.1	78 to 1

*population lived in such areas. In Manila in the Philippines, thousands
lived in a garbage dump called Smokey Mountain.*[13]

The world's income is not distributed equally among nations. As Figure 10-2 shows, in 1994 the richest fifth of the world's nations received about 86 percent of all income, while the poorest fifth received little more than 1 percent. Japan's national income, to cite one example, was roughly on a par with that of the entire developing world, which had about 35 times as many people. Inequality is an environmental problem because countries (and people) at either extreme of income tend to behave in more environmentally destructive ways than those in the middle. People in the richest countries consume far more fossil fuels, wood, and meat, for example. People in the poorest countries, for their part, often misuse natural resources just to survive, for example, cutting down trees for fuel to cook food and keep themselves warm.

Industrialization

Parts of the third world are industrializing at a rapid pace. This is positive because it holds out the promise of reducing poverty and slowing population growth. But economic development has also contributed to the growing ecological crisis. Industry requires energy, much of which comes from burning fossil fuels, releasing pollutants of various types. The complex chemical processes of industry produce undesirable by-products and wastes that pollute land, water, and air. Its mechanical processes often create dust, grime, and unsightly refuse. The agricultural "green" revolution—although it has greatly increased crop yields in many parts of the world—has caused contamination from pesticides, herbicides, chemical fertilizers, and refuse from cattle-feeding factories. Industrialization is also often accompanied by rising incomes, bringing higher rates of both consumption and waste.

The Limits to Growth

Some observers believe that the earth's rapid population growth, peoples' rising expectations, and the rapid industrialization of less developed countries are heading for a collision with a fixed barrier: the limited **carrying capacity** of the earth's ecosystem. In this view, the world's resource base—the air, water, soil, minerals, and so forth—is

---

[13] "Warning: All Roads Lead to Asian Cities," *Los Angeles Times,* November 30, 1993, pp. 1, 4. For a traveler's account of environmental devastation in many parts of the world, see Mark Hertsgaard, *Earth Odyssey: Around the World in Search of Our Environmental Future* (New York: Broadway Books, 1998). Chapter 3 discusses Bangkok.

essentially finite, or bounded. If human societies use up resources faster than they can be replenished, and create waste faster than it can be dispersed, environmental devastation will be the inevitable result.[14] According to *Beyond the Limits* by Donella Meadows and her colleagues, human society is already overshooting the carrying capacity of the earth's ecosystem. Just as it is possible to eat or drink too much before your body sends you a signal to stop, so too are people and businesses using up resources and emitting pollution at an unsustainable rate. But because of delays in feedback, society will not understand the consequences of its actions until the damage has been done.

If human society does not change its practices, a collapse may occur, possibly within the lifetimes of many who are alive today. What kind of collapse? Meadows and her colleagues developed several computer models to predict what would happen under different scenarios. If the world continued on its present course, with no major technical or policy changes, they predicted that by the year 2015, food production would begin to fall, as pollution degraded the fertility of the land. Around 2020, nonrenewable resources such as oil would begin to run out, and more and more resources would be needed to find, extract, and refine what remained. By midcentury, industrial production would begin to collapse, pulling down with it the service and agricultural sectors. Life expectancy and population would fall soon after, as death rates were driven up by lack of food and health care.[15]

Critics of the **limits to growth hypothesis** suggest that these doomsday predictions are unnecessarily bleak, because there are important offsets to these limits. Market forces are one such offset. For example, as natural resources such as oil and gas become scarcer, their prices will rise, and people and businesses may be motivated to use natural resources more efficiently or to find substitutes, such as solar power. Another offset is technology. Technological advances may slow environmental degradation by developing more reliable birth control, more productive crops through genetic engineering, or highly efficient, nonpolluting automobiles like the proposed hypercar. The authors of *Beyond the Limits* acknowledge these offsets but stick to their conclusion that if human society does not adopt sustainable development, economic and social catastrophe is just a matter of time.[16]

Global Environmental Issues

Some environmental problems are inherently global in scope and require international cooperation. Typically these are issues pertaining to the global commons, that is, resources shared by all nations. Three global problems that will have major consequences for business and society—all of

---

[14] Herman E. Daly, *Beyond Growth: The Economics of Sustainable Development* (Boston: Beacon Press, 1996); Paul Hawken, Amory Lovins, and L. Hunter Lovins, *Natural Capitalism: Creating the Next Industrial Revolution* (Boston: Little Brown, 1999); and Kenneth Arrow et al., "Economic Growth, Carrying Capacity, and the Environment," *Science* 28 (April 1995).

[15] Donella H. Meadows, Dennis L. Meadows, and Jorgen Randers, *Beyond the Limits: Confronting Global Collapse, Envisioning a Sustainable Future* (Boston: Chelsea Green Publishing Co., 1992).

[16] For a classic critique of an earlier version of the limits to growth hypothesis, see Robert M. Solow, "Is the End of the World at Hand?" *Challenge*, March–April 1973, pp. 39–50. An analysis of the environmental state of the world that comes to a more optimistic conclusion may be found in Gregg Easterbrook, *A Moment on the Earth* (New York: Viking, 1995). Allen Hammond, *Which World? Scenarios for the Twenty-First Century* (Washington, DC: Island Press, 1998), contrasts three possible future environmental scenarios that might arise under differing conditions.

which were extensively discussed at the Earth Summit and various follow-up conferences—are ozone depletion, global warming, and biodiversity.

Ozone Depletion

Ozone is a bluish gas, composed of three bonded oxygen atoms, that floats in a thin layer in the stratosphere between 8 and 25 miles above the planet. Although poisonous to humans in the lower atmosphere, ozone in the stratosphere is critical to life on earth by absorbing dangerous ultraviolet light from the sun. Too much ultraviolet light can cause skin cancer and damage the eyes and immune systems of humans and other species.

In 1974, scientists first hypothesized that chlorofluorocarbons (CFCs)—manufactured chemicals widely used as refrigerants, insulation, solvents, and propellants in spray cans—could react with and destroy ozone. Little evidence existed of actual ozone depletion, however, until 1985, when scientists discovered a thin spot, or hole, in the ozone layer over Antarctica. Studies showed that the hole was indeed the work of CFCs. In the upper atmosphere, intense solar rays had split CFC molecules, releasing chlorine atoms that had reacted with and destroyed ozone. In the early 1990s, scientists for the first time reported evidence of ozone depletion in the northern latitudes over Europe and North America during the summer, when the sun's ultraviolet rays are the strongest and pose the greatest danger.

World political leaders moved quickly in response to scientific evidence that CFCs posed a threat to the earth's protective ozone shield. In 1987, a group of nations negotiated the **Montreal Protocol,** agreeing to cut CFC production and use by 50 percent by 1999. In 1992, the deadline for phasing out manufacture of CFCs completely was moved up to 1996, in view of evidence that the ozone layer was being depleted even faster than feared earlier. Developing countries were given until 2010 to phase out the chemicals completely. As of 2000, 175 countries had signed the original Protocol, and 107 had signed the 1992 amendments.[17]

> By the turn of the century, most businesses in the developed world had completed the transition to CFC substitutes, and many had made money by doing so. Du Pont, Allied Signal, Elf Altochem, and several other chemical companies had developed profitable substitutes for banned ozone-depleting chemicals. All the major appliance manufacturers, such as Electrolux in Sweden and Whirlpool in the United States, had brought out successful new lines of CFC-free refrigerators and freezers, and carmakers had developed air conditioners that operated without the dangerous coolant.

Have the Montreal Protocol and business efforts to respond to it been successful? A study by a commission of world scientists in 1998 found that the concentration of ozone-depleting chemicals in the atmosphere peaked in 1994 and then began a slow decline. The scientists predicted that, because of a lag effect, the highest levels of ozone

---

[17] The text of the Montreal Protocol and its various amendments may be found at www.unep.org/ozone/treaties.htm. A current list of signatories may be found at www.unep.org/ozone/ratif.htm.

Figure 10-3

Global warming.

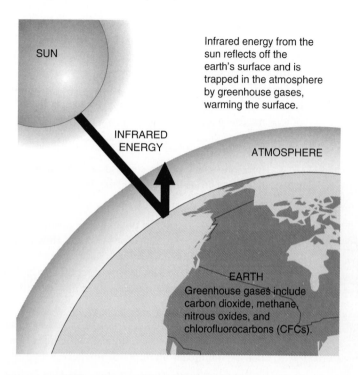

SUN

Infrared energy from the
sun reflects off the
earth's surface and is
trapped in the atmosphere
by greenhouse gases,
warming the surface.

INFRARED
ENERGY

ATMOSPHERE

EARTH
Greenhouse gases include
carbon dioxide, methane,
nitrous oxides, and
chlorofluorocarbons (CFCs).

depletion would occur within the next decade or so. The protective layer would then recover gradually, provided that regulations continued to be effective.[18] The world community still faces the challenge of getting all nations to sign the Montreal Protocol and its amendments and restricting the manufacture of other ozone-depleting substances not yet fully regulated by treaty. But overall—and although ozone depletion will likely get worse before it gets better—this is an example of world governments working together effectively to address a global environmental threat.

Global Warming

Another difficult problem facing the world community is the gradual warming of the earth's atmosphere. Although uncertainty remains about the rate and causes of **global warming,** business and governments have begun to respond to the issue.

The earth's atmosphere contains carbon dioxide and other trace gases that, like the glass panels in a greenhouse, prevent heat reflected from the earth's surface from escaping into space, as illustrated in Figure 10-3. Without this so-called greenhouse effect, the earth would be too cold to support life. Since the Industrial Revolution, which began in

[18] World Meteorological Organization, National Oceanic and Atmospheric Administration, National Aeronautics and Space Administration, European Commission, and United Nations Environment Program, "Scientific Assessment of Ozone Depletion: 1998." An executive summary may be found at www.al.noaa.gov/wwwhd/pubdocs/Assessment98/executive-summary.html#A.

the late 1700s, the amount of greenhouse gases in the atmosphere has increased by as much as 25 percent, largely due to the burning of fossil fuels such as oil and natural gas. According to the 2000 report of the Intergovernmental Panel on Climate Change (IPCC), a group of the world's leading atmospheric scientists, the earth has already warmed by between 0.3 and 0.6 degrees Celsius over the past century (1 degree Celsius equals 1.8 degrees Fahrenheit, the unit commonly used in the United States). If societal emissions of greenhouse gases continue to grow unchecked, the IPCC predicted, the earth could warm by as much as 6 degrees Celsius more in the next century, far more than estimated just five years earlier.[19]

There are many possible causes of global warming. The burning of fossil fuels, which releases carbon dioxide, is the leading contributor. But consider the following additional causes.[20]

- *Deforestation.* Trees and other plants absorb carbon dioxide, removing it from the atmosphere. Deforestation—cutting down and not replacing trees—thus contributes to global warming. Burning forests to clear land for grazing or agriculture also releases carbon directly into the atmosphere as a component of smoke. Large-scale deforestation thus contributes in two ways to global warming.

- *Beef production.* Methane, a potent greenhouse gas, is produced as a by-product of the digestion of some animals, including cows. Large-scale cattle ranching releases significant amounts of methane.

- *Population growth.* Human beings produce carbon dioxide every time they breathe. More people mean more greenhouse gases.

- *CFCs.* In addition to destroying the ozone, these are also greenhouse gases. The Montreal Protocol will have the unintended beneficial consequence of slowing global warming.

If global warming continues, the world may experience extreme heat waves, air pollution crises, damaging wildfires, and even epidemics of tropical diseases in the twenty-first century. The polar ice caps may partially melt, raising sea levels and causing flooding in low-lying coastal areas like Florida, Bangladesh, and the Netherlands. It may become as difficult to grow wheat in Iowa as it is now in arid Utah. Such climate change could devastate many of the world's economies and destroy the habitats of many species.

In 1997, many of the world's nations gathered in Kyoto, Japan, to consider amendments to the Convention on Climate Change, an international treaty on global warming first negotiated at the 1992 Earth Summit. In difficult negotiations, the parties hammered out an agreement that would require industrial countries, such as the United States, to

---

[19] "A Shift in Stance on Global Warming Theory," *New York Times,* October 26, 2000, p. A22. A complete set of materials may be found at IPCC's website at www.ipcc.ch. For a summary of the views of critics of IPCC's conclusions, see "Global Warming: The Contrarian View," *New York Times,* February 29, 2000, p. F1.

[20] For a collection of diverse views on global warming, see Andrew J. Hoffman, ed., *Global Climate Change: A Senior-Level Debate at the Intersection of Economics, Strategy, Technology, Science, Politics, and International Negotiations* (San Francisco: New Lexington Press, 1997).

reduce greenhouse gas emissions more than 5 percent below 1990 levels, over a period of several years. But by 2000, only 13 nations had ratified the Kyoto Protocol, as the agreement was known, and it was doubtful it would ever go into effect. In subsequent negotiations, the group had struggled over controversial proposals that would give each nation allowances for a certain quota of carbon emissions. Countries that reduced their emissions below their quotas would be able to sell allowances to others; those that exceeded their quotas would have to buy allowances on the open market. But different countries were unable to agree how to put such a plan into effect or even if it was a good idea in the first place.

What did world business leaders think about global warming and the proposed solutions, including those debated in Kyoto and in later meetings? Some of the widely divergent perspectives within the business community on this issue are presented in Exhibit 10-B.

Biodiversity

Biodiversity refers to the number and variety of species and the range of their genetic makeup. To date, approximately 1.7 million species of plants and animals have been named and described. Many scientists believe these are but a fraction of the total. The earth contains at least 10 million species and possibly more than 100 million. Scientists estimate that species extinction is now occurring at 100 to 1,000 times the normal, background rate, mainly because of pollution and the destruction of habitat by human society. Biological diversity is now at its lowest level since the disappearance of the dinosaurs some 65 million years ago. The eminent biologist Edward O. Wilson has eloquently stated the costs of this loss:

> *Every species extinction diminishes humanity. Every micro-organism, animal and plant contains on the order of from one million to 10 billion bits of information in its genetic code, hammered into existence by an astronomical number of mutations and episodes of natural selection over the course of thousands or even millions of years of evolution. . . . Species diversity—the world's available gene pool—is one of our planet's most important and irreplaceable resources. . . . As species are exterminated, largely as the result of habitat destruction, the capacity for natural genetic regeneration is greatly reduced. In Norman Myers' phrase, we are causing the death of birth.*[21]

Genetic diversity is vital to each species' ability to adapt and survive and has many benefits for human society as well. By destroying this biological diversity, we are actually undermining our survivability as a species.

Ethicists have recently given greater attention to the responsibilities of humans to conserve the natural environment and to prevent the extinction of other species of plants and animals. This emerging philosophical perspective is profiled in Exhibit 10-C.

---

[21] Edward O. Wilson, "Threats to Biodiversity," in *Managing Planet Earth: Readings from Scientific American Magazine* (New York: W. H. Freeman and Co., 1990), pp. 57–58. This article originally appeared in *Scientific American*, September 1989. Used by permission.

EXHIBIT
10-B

Global Warming: The Many Perspectives of Business

At the turn of the century, different segments of the world business community held widely divergent views on global warming and what, if anything, should be done about it.

On one end of the spectrum stood the Global Climate Coalition (GCC), representing many segments of the oil, coal, chemical, mining, railroad, and auto industries. The GCC downplayed the threat of climate change and argued that any government controls on the emission of greenhouse gases would be costly and premature. Any actions by business, the group maintained, should be entirely voluntary. When asked by a reporter what she hoped would be accomplished at the global climate change talks in Kyoto, Japan, in 1997, the president of the coalition held up her fingers to form a zero.

Although many of the big oil companies subscribed to the GCC's view, a few did not. In 1996, British Petroleum (BP) quit the group, and Royal Dutch/Shell followed shortly thereafter. In 1998, Shell endorsed the Kyoto Protocol and committed to reduce its greenhouse gas emissions even more than the treaty required.

One of the industries most worried about climate change was, perhaps not surprisingly, insurance. In the 1990s, the insurance industry was walloped by a series of huge payouts for major floods, hurricanes, and severe storms. Although no one could pin the blame for sure on global warming, many saw a connection. "There is a significant body of scientific evidence indicating that the [recent] record insured losses from natural catastrophes was not a random occurrence," commented the general manager of Swiss Re, a large European insurer. "Failure to act," he added, "would leave the industry and its policyholders vulnerable to truly disastrous consequences."

A moderate position was staked out by the International Climate Change Partnership (ICCP), representing many big manufacturers and service firms, including AT&T, Du Pont, General Electric, and 3M. This group accepted the evidence for climate change but argued that corporations, not government, should take the lead by identifying profitable opportunities to reduce emissions. AT&T, for example, was interested in promoting telecommuting as an alternative to driving to work.

The electric utility industry seemed unwilling to commit itself unequivocally. While the Edison Electric Institute, a trade group, supported the Global Climate Coalition, not all utilities agreed. The Business Council for Sustainable Energy, representing producers of solar power, wind power, and natural gas—along with some utilities promoting energy conservation—called for stabilization and then reductions of greenhouse gas emissions.

Said one lobbyist for alternative energy producers, "[The oil and coal companies] want you to believe that the science [on global warming] is divided, while business is united. In fact, the reverse is true."

Sources: "Inside the Race to Profit from Global Warming," *Wall Street Journal,* October 19, 1999, pp. B1, B4; David L. Levy and Aundrea Kelley, "The International Climate Change Partnership: An Industry Association Faces the Climate Change Issue," Management Institute for Environment and Business, 1996; Ross Gelbspan, *The Heat Is On: The High Stakes Battle over Earth's Threatened Climate* (Reading, MA: Addison-Wesley, 1997); "Industries Revisit Global Warming: Some Producers Now Support Curbing Greenhouse Gases," *New York Times,* August 5, 1997, pp. A1, A4; and "Green Warrior in Gray Flannel," *Business Week,* May 6, 1996, p. 96. The website of the Global Climate Coalition is at www.globalclimate.org; of the ICCP, at www.iccp.net.

**EXHIBIT
10-C**

The Emergence of Environmental Ethics

Environmental ethics is concerned with the ethical responsibilities of human beings toward the natural environment. In much of Western philosophy, there exists a fundamental dualism, or separation, between humans and nature. Some Western philosophers have believed that the purpose of civilization was to dominate and control the environment (or nature) and other living things. This perspective may be contrasted with an emerging philosophical view that human society is part of an integrated ecosystem and that humans have ethical obligations toward nature. The following quotations are drawn from proponents of the latter view.

A thing is right when it tends to preserve the integrity, stability, and beauty of the biotic community [of living things]. It is wrong when it tends otherwise.

Aldo Leopold

The well-being and flourishing of human and non-human Life on Earth have value in themselves. . . . These values are independent of the usefulness of the non-human world for human purposes.

Arne Naess

What is proposed here is a broadening of value, so that nature will cease to be merely "property" and become a commonwealth. . . . If we now universalize "person," consider how slowly the circle has enlarged . . . to include aliens, strangers, infants, children, Negroes, Jews, slaves, women, Indians, prisoners, the elderly, the insane, the deformed, and even now we ponder the status of fetuses. Ecological ethics queries whether we ought to again universalize, recognizing the intrinsic value of every ecobiotic [living] component.

Holmes Rolston

Sources: The first two quotations are from Susan J. Armstrong and Richard G. Botzler, eds., *Environmental Ethics: Divergence and Convergence* (New York: McGraw-Hill, 1993), pp. 382, 412; the third quotation is from Roderick Nash, *The Rights of Nature* (Madison: University of Wisconsin Press, 1989), pp. 3–4.

A major reason for the decline in the earth's biodiversity is the destruction of rain forests, particularly in the tropics. Rain forests are woodlands that receive at least 100 inches of rain a year. They are the planet's richest areas in terms of biological diversity. Rain forests cover only around 7 percent of the earth's surface but account for somewhere between 50 to 90 percent of the earth's species. Only about half of the original tropical rain forests still stand, and at the rate they are currently being cut, all will be gone or severely depleted within 30 years. The reasons for destruction of rain forests include commercial logging, cattle-ranching, and conversion of forest to plantations to produce cash crops for export. Overpopulation also plays a part, as landless people clear forest to grow crops and cut trees for firewood.

The destruction is ironic, because rain forests may have more economic value standing than cut. Rain forests are the source of many valuable products, including foods, medicines, and fibers. The pharmaceutical industry, for example, each year develops new medicines based on newly discovered plants from tropical areas. The U.S. National Cancer Institute has identified 1,400 tropical forest plants with cancer-fighting properties. As rain forests are destroyed, so too is this potential for new medicines.

> *Madagascar, the fourth-largest island in the world, located off the eastern coast of Africa, is widely regarded as a biological treasure trove. Researchers discovered, for example, that the rosy periwinkle plant, found in the island's tropical rain forest, contained a unique genetic trait that was useful in the treatment of Hodgkin's disease, childhood leukemia, and other cancers. Over 90 percent of Madagascar's rain forest has been cleared, destroying perhaps half of the 200,000 species of plants and animals found there.*[22]

One of the issues discussed at the Earth Summit was the right of nations, such as Madagascar, to a fair share of profits from the commercialization of genetic material for which they are the source. Until a few years ago, drug companies, for example, often collected genetic samples from foreign countries without compensation. In most cases, source countries are now more aware of the commercial value of their biological resources and have required the payment of royalties when genetic material is developed commercially. Partnerships have developed between business firms and source nations that respect the unique contribution of each. For example, Merck Corporation entered into an agreement with Costa Rica's National Biodiversity Institute (INBio). The company received permission to prospect for new medicines from plants and animals in the Costa Rican rain forest, in exchange for $1.1 million and a percentage of any future royalties.[23]

As noted in the introductory section of this chapter, the Earth Summit produced a treaty, the Convention on Biological Diversity, which by 2000 had been ratified by 177 countries. (The United States was not among them.) The treaty commits these countries to draw up national strategies for conservation, protect ecosystems and individual species, and take steps to restore degraded areas. It also allows countries to share in the profits from sales of products derived from their biological resources.

Response of the International Business Community

The international business community has undertaken many initiatives to put the principle of sustainable development into practice.

World Business Council for Sustainable Development

One of the leaders in the global effort to promote sustainable business practices is the World Business Council for Sustainable Development (WBCSD). The Council was formed in 1995 through a merger of the Business Council for Sustainable Development,

---

[22] Jeremy Rifkin, *Biosphere Politics: A New Consciousness for a New Century* (New York: Crown Publishers, 1991), p. 67; and *1994 Information Please Environmental Almanac* (Boston: Houghton Mifflin, 1994), p. 356.

[23] Michele Zebich-Knos, "Preserving Biodiversity in Costa Rica: The Case of the Merck-INBio Agreement," *Journal of Environment and Development,* June 1997, pp. 180–86.

a group of corporate executives who had supported the original Earth Summit, and the World Industry Council for the Environment, a project of the International Chamber of Commerce. In 2000, the Council was made up of about 140 companies, drawn from more than 30 countries and 20 industries. The WBCSD's goals were to encourage high standards of environmental management and to promote closer cooperation among businesses, governments, and other organizations concerned with sustainable development.

The WBCSD called for businesses to manufacture and distribute products more efficiently, consider their lifelong impact, and recycle components. In a series of publications, the group set forth the view that the most eco-efficient companies—those that added the most value with the least use of resources and pollution—were more competitive and more environmentally sound. **Eco-efficiency** was only possible, the Council concluded, in the presence of open, competitive markets in which prices reflected the true cost of environmental and other resources. In the past, environmental costs have not been fully accounted, for example, in calculating measures of production such as the gross domestic product. One study showed, for example, that when the true costs of depletion of timber, oil, and topsoil were included, the economic growth rate of Indonesia from 1971 to 1984 was not 7 percent, as officially calculated, but only 4 percent.[24] The WBCSD recommended revising systems of national accounting to include the costs of environmental damage and pricing products to reflect their full environmental costs.[25]

Several other groups, in addition to the WBCSD, have given serious attention to the idea of sustainable development and its implications for business. Exhibit 10-D profiles the efforts of several important national and international organizations to develop codes of environmental conduct, including the 14000 certification program of the International Organization for Standardization (ISO).

Many individual businesses and industry groups have also undertaken voluntary initiatives to improve their environmental performance. These are the subject of the next section.

Voluntary Business Initiatives

Many firms around the world have tried to determine how sustainable development translates into actual business practice. Some of the more important voluntary initiatives undertaken by businesses include the following:

---

[24] Robert C. Repetto et al., *Wasting Assets: Natural Resources in the National Income Accounts* (Washington, DC: World Resources Institute, 1989).

[25] The WBCSD's publications include two books, Stephan Schmidheiny and Federico J. L. Zorraquin, *Financing Change: The Financial Community, Eco-Efficiency, and Sustainable Development* (Cambridge, MA: MIT Press, 1997); and Stephan Schmidheiny, *Changing Course: A Global Business Perspective on Development and the Environment* (Cambridge, MA: MIT Press, 1992); and several reports on sustainable production and consumption, trade and the environment, environmental impact assessment, and eco-efficiency. See a list of WBCSD's publications at dns.wbcsd.ch/prodoc. Many practical actions that business can take are discussed in Claude Fussler, *Driving Eco-Innovation* (London and New York: Pittman Publishing, 1996).

**EXHIBIT
10-D**

International Codes of Environmental Conduct

A number of national and international business organizations have developed codes of environmental conduct. Among the most important ones are the following.

International Chamber of Commerce (ICC)

The ICC developed the Business Charter for Sustainable Development, 16 principles that identify key elements of environmental leadership and call on companies to recognize environmental management as among their highest corporate priorities.

Global Environmental Management Initiative (GEMI)

A group of over 20 companies dedicated to fostering environmental excellence, GEMI developed several environmental self-assessment programs, including one that helps firms assess their progress in meeting the goals of the Business Charter for Sustainable Development.

Keidanren

This major Japanese industry association has published a Global Environmental Charter that sets out a code of environmental behavior that calls on its members to be "good global corporate citizens."

Chemical Manufacturers Association (CMA)

This U.S.-based industry association developed Responsible Care: A Public Commitment, which commits its member-companies to a code of management practices, focusing on process safety, community awareness, pollution prevention, safe distribution, employee health and safety, and product stewardship. The group is working for the international adoption of these principles.

CERES Principles

These are 10 voluntary principles developed by the Coalition for Environmentally Responsible Economies that commit signatory firms to protection of the biosphere, sustainable use of natural resources, energy conservation, risk reduction, and other environmental goals.

International Organization for Standardization (ISO)

ISO 14000 is a series of voluntary standards introduced in 1996 by the ISO, an international group based in Geneva, Switzerland, that permit companies to be certified as meeting global environmental performance standards.

Sources: For further information on these organizations and their codes, see www.iccwbo.org/charter (International Chamber of Commerce); www.gemi.org (Global Environmental Management Initiative); www.keidanren or jp/english/profile (Keidanren); cmahq.com/rescare.html (Chemical Manufacturers Association); ceres.org (Coalition for Environmentally Responsible Economies); and iso.ch (International Organization for Standardization).

Life-cycle analysis involves collecting information on the lifelong environmental impact of a product, all the way from extraction of raw material to manufacturing to its distribution, use, and ultimate disposal. The aim of life-cycle analysis is to minimize the adverse impact of a particular product at all stages. For example, Dell

Computer has redesigned one of its lines of personal computers with a recyclable chassis and offers incentives to its customers to return their old computers to be taken apart and rebuilt with new internal parts. The redesign greatly reduced waste from discarded PCs.[26]

Industrial ecology refers to designing factories and distribution systems as if they were self-contained ecosystems. For example, businesses can save materials through closed-loop recycling, use wastes from one process as raw material for others, and make use of energy generated as a by-product of production.

An example of industrial ecology may be found in the town of Kalundborg, Denmark, where several companies have formed a cooperative relationship that produces both economic and environmental benefits. The local utility company sells excess process steam, which had previously been released into a local fjord (waterway), to a local pharmaceutical plant and oil refinery. Excess fly ash (fine particles produced when fuel is burned) is sold to nearby businesses for use in cement making and road building. Meanwhile, the oil refinery removes sulfur in the natural gas it produces, to make it cleaner burning, and sells the sulfur to a sulfuric acid plant. Calcium sulfate, produced as a residue of a process to cut smoke emissions, is sold to a gypsum manufacturer for making wallboard. The entire cycle both saves money and reduces pollution.[27]

Design for disassembly means that products are designed so that at the end of their useful life they can be disassembled and recycled. At Volkswagen, the German carmaker, engineers design cars for eventual disassembly and reuse. At the company's specialized auto recycling plant in Leer, built in 1990, old cars can be completely taken apart in just three minutes. Plastics, steel, precious metals, oil, acid, and glass are separated and processed. Many materials are used again in new Volkswagens.

Sustainable development will require **technology cooperation** through long-term partnerships between companies in developed and developing countries to transfer environmental technologies, as shown in the following example.

In 1998, Shell entered a partnership with Eskom, a South African utility company, to provide electricity to 50,000 homes in isolated rural communities not served by the national power grid. The two firms cooperated to set up technologically advanced solar panels and metering units measuring power flow to individual homes. People could pay for the amount of electricity they actually used, without any up-front investment. The cost to customers—averaging about eight dollars a month—was comparable to

---

[26] Matthew B. Arnold and Robert M. Day, *The Next Bottom Line: Making Sustainable Development Tangible* (Washington, DC: World Resources Institute, 1998), p. 31.

[27] Arthur D. Little, *Industrial Ecology: An Environmental Agenda for Industry* (Cambridge, MA: Arthur D. Little, Center for Environmental Assurance, 1991); and "Growth vs. Environment," *Business Week*, May 5, 1992, p. 75. For a full discussion, see R. H. Socolow et al., *Industrial Ecology and Global Change* (New York, NY: Cambridge University Press, 1994).

the amount they had been spending on candles, paraffin, and other less efficient fuels.[28]

Although many companies around the world have undertaken valuable experiments, the idea of sustainable development remains controversial in the business community. Nevertheless, one study showed that nearly 96 percent of corporate executives thought that it was important to do something about sustainable development, and 51 percent thought that their businesses' efficiency would be improved by doing so.[29]

Protecting the environment and the well-being of future generations is, as the founder of the Business Council on Sustainable Development put it, "fast becoming a business necessity and even an opportunity."[30] Environmental regulations are getting tougher, consumers want cleaner products, and employees want to work for environmentally conscious companies. Finding ways to reduce or recycle waste saves money. Many executives are championing the importance of corporations' moral obligations to future generations. The most successful global businesses in coming years may be those, like the ones profiled in this chapter, that recognize the imperative for sustainable development as an opportunity both for competitive advantage and ethical action.

Summary Points of This Chapter

- Many world leaders have supported the idea of sustainable development—economic growth without depleting the resources on which future generations will depend. But achieving sustainable development remains a challenge, and the community of nations has not yet worked out who will pay.
- Major threats to the earth's ecosystem include depletion of nonrenewable resources such as oil and coal, air and water pollution, and the degradation of arable land.
- Population growth, poverty, and rapid industrialization in many parts of the world have contributed to these ecological problems. The limits to growth hypothesis maintains that human society will soon exceed the carrying capacity of the earth's ecosystem, unless changes are made now.
- Three environmental issues—ozone depletion, global warming, and declining biodiversity—are shared by all nations. International agreements have been negotiated addressing all three issues, although more remains to be done.
- Global businesses have begun to put the principles of sustainable development into action through such innovative actions as life-cycle analysis, industrial ecology,

[28] *Building a Better Future: Industry, Technology, and Sustainable Development: A Progress Report* (World Business Council on Sustainable Development, June 2000), p. 19.
[29] Steven Poltorzycki, *Bringing Sustainable Development Down to Earth* (New York: Arthur D. Little, 1998).
[30] Stephan Schmidheiny, "The Business Logic of Sustainable Development," *Columbia Journal of World Business* 27, no. 3–4 (1992), pp. 19–23.

design for disassembly, and technology cooperation. But many believe that voluntary actions by business cannot solve environmental problems without supportive public policies.

Key Terms and Concepts Used in This Chapter

- Ecology
- Global commons
- Sustainable development
- Carrying capacity
- Limits to growth hypothesis
- Ozone
- Montreal Protocol

- Global warming
- Biodiversity
- Eco-efficiency
- Life-cycle analysis
- Industrial ecology
- Design for disassembly
- Technology cooperation

Internet Resources

- www.epa.gov/globalwarming   Environmental Protection Agency global warming site
- www.epa.gov/docs/ozone   Environmental Protection Agency ozone site
- www.unep.org   United National Environmental Program
- dns.wbcsd.ch   World Business Council on Sustainable Development

Discussion Case: *Damming the Yangtze River*

Along the banks of the Yangtze River in central China at the turn of the century, a massive project was underway to construct the largest hydroelectric dam in the world. A visiting journalist described the scene:

> *From horizon to horizon, the ancient landscape here has been sundered, scored, and stripped by the big steel blades of countless front-end loaders. Dust storms rise from monster caravans hauling a million boulders across a riven plain. . . . Mountains are disappearing and a new concrete topography is rising in their place, connected in a manmade design whose foundations are being laid across a dust bowl so broad that it seems almost planetary in scale.*

When completed in 2009, the Three Gorges Dam was expected to be over a mile across and to have the capacity to generate 18,200 megawatts of electricity, 18 times as much as a standard nuclear power plant. This energy would be crucial to the fast-developing Chinese economy, where demand for electricity was projected to double every 15 years. "The dam will make life better for our children," said one construction worker. "They'll have electric lights, TV, be able to study their lessons. With luck they'll go to the university."

The 400-mile-long reservoir and locks that would be created behind the dam would be deep enough to bring oceangoing ships 1,500 miles inland to the city of Chongqing, opening markets in the vast interior of China. The government also hoped that the dam would end the disastrous floods that had inundated the region every five or so years throughout history. In the twentieth century alone, 300,000 lives had been lost and millions of homes destroyed. Most recently, in 1998, a flood on the river had killed 3,656 people and cost the nation $38 billion. The construction effort itself employed 40,000 people and pumped billions of dollars into the local economy.

But the project had its share of critics, both inside and outside China. Before the waters could be unleashed, 1.9 million Chinese, mostly in rural towns and villages along the river, would have to be resettled to higher ground. Homes and jobs would need to be found for them. A quarter-million acres of fertile farmland would be flooded, as would many unexcavated archaeological sites.

The project would inundate the Three Gorges, thought by many to be among the most starkly beautiful scenery in the world. At this point in its course, the Yangtze passes through a narrow passage, with dramatic limestone walls towering as high as 3,000 feet above the river. In addition to destroying this landscape, the dam would radically transform the ecology of the river. Environmentalists pointed out that fish migrations would be blocked and plants and animals adapted to the river habitat would die out.

Moreover, no provisions had been made to treat the billions of tons of industrial and municipal sewage expected to flow into the reservoir. In the past, the fast-moving river had carried untreated waste to the sea. No provisions had been made, either, to relocate existing landfills and dumps, many containing toxic waste, that lay in the area that would be flooded.

But other environmentalists thought that the project had merit. Hydroelectric power, of the sort to be generated by the Three Gorges Dam, was nonpolluting. The main practical alternative to the dam was to build more coal-fired power plants, which in the late-1990s supplied over three-quarters of China's energy. Coal combustion produces sulfur dioxide, a cause of acid rain, and carbon dioxide, a major contributor to global warming. China was already the second-biggest emitter of carbon in the world (after the United States); it was responsible for 13 percent of the world's emissions, even though its economy accounted for only 2 percent of the world's GDP. The air in much of China is fouled by coal dust and smoke, and a quarter of all deaths are caused by lung disease.

Sources: Kari Huus, "The Yangtze's Collision Course," November 22, 1999, www.msnbc.com/news; Arthur Zich, "China's Three Gorges: Before the Flood," *National Geographic* 92, no. 3 (September 1997), pp. 2–33; and "Cracks Show Early in China's Big Dam Project," *New York Times,* January 15, 1996, pp. A1, A4.

Discussion Questions

1. What stakeholders will be helped by the Three Gorges Dam? What stakeholders will be hurt by it?

2. How does construction of a dam on the Yangtze River relate to the issues of global warming, biodiversity, and water pollution discussed in this chapter?

3. Do you agree with the decision of the Chinese government to construct the Three Gorges Dam? Why or why not?

4. What strategies do you believe would best promote economic development in China without destroying the environmental resources on which future generations depend?

11

Managing Environmental Issues

Growing public interest in protecting the environment has prompted political and corporate leaders to become increasingly responsive to environmental issues. In the United States, policymakers have moved toward greater reliance on market-based mechanisms, rather than command and control regulations, to achieve environmental goals. At the same time, many businesses have become increasingly proactive and have pioneered new approaches to effective environmental management.

This chapter focuses on these key questions and objectives:

- What are the main features of U.S. environmental laws, and what are the advantages and disadvantages of different regulatory approaches?
- What are the costs and benefits of environmental regulation?
- What is an ecologically sustainable organization, and through what stages do firms pass as they become more sustainable?
- How can businesses best manage environmental issues?
- Does effective environmental management make firms more competitive?

os Angeles, California, is one of the most smog-ridden cities in the United States. On many days, the city is covered by a dense blanket of orange haze, and residents cannot catch even a glimpse of the lovely San Gabriel mountains just a few miles to the east. In 1994, southern California air-quality regulators, frustrated with old approaches, tried something new—a market-driven plan called RECLAIM. This plan required major overall reductions in smog-producing chemical emissions but permitted individual businesses to buy and sell pollution credits. Hailed by business as a less burdensome and less costly way to reduce urban smog, the RECLAIM program was expected to reduce targeted emissions by 80 percent in its first decade and to enable the region to meet all federal clean air health standards by 2010. By the early 2000s, an active market had emerged, and companies were even trading pollution credits online.[1]

The Environmental Defense Fund (EDF), a leading environmental advocacy organization, believed that its old strategy of suing companies and lobbying legislators was not working well enough. Instead, the group tried a cooperative approach, joining McDonald's Corporation to study the issue of fast-food packaging waste. Over a 10-year period, McDonald's replaced its foam hamburger box with a paper wrapper, got rid of individual condiment packets, recycled tons of cardboard boxes, installed energy-efficient lighting, and made dozens of other changes throughout its thousands of restaurants. Encouraged by this success, EDF initiated a series of partnerships with other major companies, including Johnson & Johnson, Dell Computer, and United Parcel Service. At Starbucks, EDF scientists worked with the gourmet coffee retailer to develop a more environmentally friendly disposable cup.[2]

Dow Chemical Corporation initiated a wide-ranging program called Waste Reduction Always Pays, WRAP for short. The idea was that it would be more efficient, and less expensive, for the company to prevent pollution in the first place than to treat and dispose of pollutants at the "end of the pipe." The company reduced the use of hazardous chemicals in production to cut down on waste. Where this was not possible, the company tried to recycle waste by-products. By the late 1990s, the company reported that WRAP was saving the company over $20 million annually. The company's president concluded that "the most compelling actions industry can take with respect to environmental protection are voluntary."[3]

At the turn of the century, many political leaders, corporate executives, and environmental advocates—like those profiled in these examples—became increasingly concerned that old strategies for promoting environmental protection were failing and new approaches were necessary. In the United States, policymakers moved toward greater reliance on market-based mechanisms, rather than command and control regulations, to achieve environmental goals. Environmentalists engaged in greater dialogue with

---

[1] "This Commodity's Smokin': Companies Trade Smog Credits on Online Exchange," *Los Angeles Times,* April 30, 1997, p. D2. The South Coast Air Quality Management District's description of the program and its results is available at www.aqmd.gov/reclaim/reclaim.html.

[2] "McDonald's Partnership Marks Tenth Anniversary," *EDF Newsletter* 31, no. 1 (April 2000). Information on other environmental alliances in which the Environmental Defense Fund has participated is available at www.environmentaldefense.org.

[3] Information on Dow Chemical Corporation's environmental, health, and safety programs is available at www.dow.com/environment/ehs.html.

industry leaders. Many businesses pioneered new approaches to effective environmental management, such as pollution prevention programs.

The challenge facing government, industry, and environmental advocacy organizations alike, as they tried out new approaches and improved on old ones, was how to further economic growth in an increasingly competitive and integrated world economy while promoting sustainable and ecologically sound business practices.

Role of Government

The U.S. government has been involved in regulating business activities in order to protect the environment at least since the late nineteenth century, when the first federal laws were passed protecting navigable waterways. The government's role in environmental protection began to increase dramatically, however, around 1970, which marks the beginning of the modern environmental era.

Government has a major role to play in environmental regulation. Business firms have few incentives to minimize pollution if their competitors do not. A single firm acting on its own to reduce discharges into a river, for example, would incur extra costs. If its competitors did not do the same, the firm might not be able to compete effectively and could go out of business. Government, by setting a common standard for all firms, can take the cost of pollution control out of competition. It also can provide economic incentives to encourage businesses, communities, and regions to reduce pollution, and it can offer legal and administrative systems for resolving disputes.

Figure 11-1 summarizes the major federal environmental laws enacted by Congress since 1969. In adopting these laws, Congress was responding to strong public concerns and pressures to save the environment from further damage.

The nation's main pollution control agency is the **Environmental Protection Agency (EPA).** It was created in 1970 to coordinate most of the government's efforts to protect the environment. Other government agencies involved in enforcing the nation's environmental laws include the Nuclear Regulatory Commission (NRC), the Occupational Safety and Health Administration (OSHA), and various regional, state, and local agencies.

Major Areas of Environmental Regulation

The federal government regulates in three major areas of environmental protection: air pollution, water pollution, and land pollution (solid and hazardous waste). This section will review the major issues and the laws in each and briefly consider the special problem of cross-media pollution that cuts across all three areas.

Air Pollution

Air pollution occurs when more pollutants are emitted into the atmosphere than can be safely absorbed and diluted by natural processes. Some pollution occurs naturally, such as smoke and ash from volcanoes and forest fires. But most air pollution today results from human activity, especially industrial processes and motor vehicle emissions. Air pollution degrades buildings, reduces crop yields, mars the beauty of natural landscapes, and harms people's health.

The American Lung Association estimated that almost three-quarters of the people in the United States were breathing unsafe air for at least part of each year. According

Figure 11-1

Leading U.S.
environmental
protection laws.

Year	Act	Description
1969	National Environmental Policy Act	Created Council on Environmental Quality to oversee quality of the nation's environment.
1970	Clean Air Act	Established national air quality standards and timetables.
1972	Water Pollution Control Act	Established national goals and timetables for clean waterways.
1972	Pesticide Control Act	Required registration of and restrictions on pesticide use.
1973	Endangered Species Act	Conserved species of animals and plants whose survival was threatened or endangered.
1974 & 1996	Safe Drinking Water Act	Authorized national standards for drinking water.
1974	Hazardous Materials Transport Act	Regulated shipment of hazardous materials.
1976	Resource Conservation and Recovery Act	Regulated hazardous materials from production to disposal.
1976	Toxic Substances Control Act	Established national policy to regulate, restrict, and, if necessary, ban toxic chemicals.
1977	Clean Air Act amendments	Revised air standards.
1980 & 1986	Comprehensive Environmental Response Compensation and Liability Act (Superfund)	Established superfund and procedures to clean up hazardous waste sites.
1987	Clean Water Act amendments	Authorized funds for sewage treatment plants and waterways cleanup.
1990	Clean Air Act amendments	Required cuts in urban smog, acid rain, greenhouse gas emissions; promoted alternative fuels.
1990	Pollution Prevention Act	Provided guidelines, training, and incentives to prevent or reduce pollution at the source.
1990	Oil Pollution Act	Strengthened EPA's ability to prevent and respond to catastrophic oil spills.
1999	Chemical Safety Information, Site Security, and Fuels Regulatory Relief Act	Set standards for the storage of flammable chemicals and fuels.

to one study, air pollution caused by particulate matter, such as soot and dirt from cars, trucks, smokestacks, mining, and construction activity, was responsible for as many as 60,000 premature or unnecessary deaths annually.[4]

The EPA has identified six criteria pollutants, relatively common harmful substances that serve as indicators of overall levels of air pollution. These are lead, carbon monoxide, particulate matter, sulfur dioxide, nitrogen dioxide, and ozone. (Ozone at ground level is a particularly unhealthy component of smog.) In addition, the agency also has identified a list of toxic air pollutants that are considered hazardous even in relatively small concentrations. These include asbestos, benzene, chloroform, dioxin, vinyl chloride, and radioactive materials. Emissions of toxic pollutants are strictly controlled.

> *Failure to comply with clean air laws can be very expensive for business. In 2000, Willamette Industries, a wood products manufacturer, spent over $90 million to settle government charges that it had broken environmental law by discharging toxins into the air from sites in four states. The EPA ordered the company to install $74 million worth of pollution control equipment, pay a $11 million fine, and fund $8 million in environmental projects in communities where its plants were located.[5]*

A special problem of air pollution is **acid rain.** Acid rain is formed when emissions of sulfur dioxide and nitrogen oxides, by-products of the burning of fossil fuels by utilities, manufacturers, and motor vehicles, combine with natural water vapor in the air and fall to earth as rain or snow that is more acidic than normal. Acid rain can damage the ecosystems of lakes and rivers, reduce crop yields, and degrade forests. Structures, such as buildings and monuments, are also harmed. Within North America, acid rain is most prevalent in New England and eastern Canada, regions that are downwind of coal-burning utilities in the midwestern states.[6] Acid rain is especially difficult to regulate, because adverse consequences often occur far—often, hundreds of miles—from the source of the pollution, sometimes across international borders. The major law governing air pollution is the Clean Air Act, first passed in 1970 and most recently amended in 1990. The 1990 Clean Air Act toughened standards in a number of areas, including stricter restrictions on emissions of acid rain–causing chemicals.

The efforts of the U.S. government to reduce acid rain illustrate some of the difficult trade-offs involved in environmental policy. These are described in Exhibit 11-A.

Water Pollution

Water pollution, like air pollution, occurs when more wastes are dumped into waterways than can be naturally diluted and carried away. Water can be polluted by organic wastes (untreated sewage or manure), by the chemical by-products of industrial processes, and

---

[4] American Lung Association, *State of the Air: 2000,* p. 1, available at www.lungusa.org; and "Studies Say Soot Kills up to 60,000 in U.S. Each Year," *New York Times,* July 19, 1993, pp. A1, A16.

[5] "Willamette Industries to Spend More Than $90 Million to Settle Clean Air Act Case," U.S. Environmental Protection Agency Press Release, July 20, 2000.

[6] For summaries of recent scientific data on acid rain, see "Acid Rain: Forgotten, Not Gone," *U.S. News and World Report,* November 1, 1999, p. 70; and "Report on Acid Rain Finds Good News and Bad News," *New York Times,* October 7, 1999, p. A26.

**EXHIBIT
11-A**

Moving Mountains to Fight Acid Rain

As part of its efforts to control acid rain, the U.S. government in 1990 initiated stricter new restrictions on the emission of sulfur dioxide by utilities. Many electric companies complied with the law by switching from high-sulfur coal, which produces more sulfur dioxide when burned, to low-sulfur coal, which produces less. This action had the beneficial effect of reducing acid rain.

But the law had some environmentally destructive results that had been unintended by regulators. Much of the highest-quality low-sulfur coal in the United States is in southern and central West Virginia, in horizontal layers near the tops of rugged mountains. Some coal companies discovered that the most efficient way to extract this coal was through what came to be known as *mountaintop removal.* Explosives were used to blast away up to 500 feet of mountaintop. Massive machines called draglines, 20 stories tall and costing $100 million each, were then used to remove the debris to get at buried seams of coal. In the late 1990s, by some estimates, 15 to 25 percent of the mountains in the affected regions of West Virginia were being leveled.

Although coal operators were required to reclaim the land afterwards—by filling in adjacent valleys with debris and planting grass and shrubs—many environmentalists believed the damage caused by mountaintop removal was severe. Many rivers and creeks were contaminated and habitat destroyed. Aquifers dried up, and the entire region became vulnerable to devastating floods. Many felt it was deeply ironic that a law that had benefited the environment in one way had indirectly harmed it in another.

Source: "Sheer Madness," *U.S. News and World Report,* August 11, 1997, pp. 26 ff. For an account of EPA's acid rain program, see www.epa.gov/acidrain.

by the disposal of nonbiodegradable products (which do not naturally decay). Heavy metals and toxic chemicals, including some used as pesticides and herbicides, can be particularly persistent. Like poor air, poor water quality can decrease crop yields, threaten human health, and degrade the quality of life.

> *In 2000, around 1,000 people in Walkerton, Ontario, a small farming community, became ill with severe diarrhea. About one in ten had to be hospitalized, and at least seven people died. The mass outbreak had been caused by* E. coli *in the municipal water supply. Investigators believed that manure contaminated by the dangerous bacterium had washed into a public well during a heavy rainstorm, and the water company had failed to disinfect the water as required by law.[7]*

[7] "Few Left Untouched after Deadly E. Coli Flows through an Ontario Town's Water," *New York Times,* July 10, 2000, p. A8.

In the United States, regulations address both the pollution of rivers, lakes, and other surface bodies of water and the quality of the drinking water.

The nation's main law governing water pollution is the Water Pollution Control Act, also known as the Clean Water Act. This law aims to restore or maintain the integrity of all surface water in the United States. It requires permits for most *point* sources of pollution, such as industrial emissions, and mandates that local and state governments develop plans for *nonpoint* sources, such as agricultural runoff or urban storm water. The Pesticide Control Act specifically restricts the use of dangerous pesticides, which can pollute groundwater.

The quality of drinking water is regulated by another law, the Safe Drinking Water Act of 1974, most recently amended in 1996. This law sets minimum standards for various contaminants in both public water systems and aquifers that supply drinking wells.

Land Pollution

The third major focus of environmental regulation is the contamination of land by both solid and hazardous waste. The United States produces an astonishing amount of solid waste each year, most of which is disposed of in municipal landfills. About 279 million tons of this waste is considered hazardous and requires special treatment. Improperly disposed waste can leach into groundwater or evaporate into the air, posing a danger to public health. Many businesses and communities have established programs to recycle certain kinds of solid waste. Some of these programs are described in Exhibit 11-B.

Several federal laws address the problem of land contamination. The Toxic Substances Control Act of 1976 requires EPA to inventory the thousands of chemicals in commercial use, identify which are most dangerous, and, if necessary, ban them or restrict their use. For example, polychlorinated biphenyls (PCBs), dangerous chemicals formerly used in electrical transformers, were banned under this law. The Resource Conservation and Recovery Act of 1976 (amended in 1984) regulates hazardous materials from "cradle to grave." Toxic waste generators must have permits, transporters must maintain careful records, and disposal facilities must conform to detailed regulations. All hazardous waste must be treated before disposal in landfills.

Some studies have suggested that hazardous waste sites are most often located near economically disadvantaged African-American and Hispanic communities. Since 1994, EPA has investigated whether state permits for hazardous waste sites violate civil rights laws and has blocked permits that appear to discriminate against minorities. The efforts to prevent inequitable exposure to risk, such as from hazardous waste, is sometimes referred to as the movement for **environmental justice.**[8]

A promising new regulatory approach to waste management, sometimes called source reduction, was taken in the Pollution Prevention Act of 1990. This law aims to reduce pollution at the source, rather than treat and dispose of waste at the end of the pipe. Pollution can be prevented, for example, by using less chemically intensive

---

[8] Christopher H. Foreman, Jr., *The Promise and Perils of Environmental Justice* (Washington, DC: Brookings Institution, 2000); and Bunyan Bryant, ed., *Environmental Justice: Issues, Policies, and Solutions* (Washington, DC: Island Press, 1995).

**EXHIBIT
11-B**

Recycling: How Successful?

Recycling paper, steel and aluminum cans, and plastic and glass containers is becoming increasingly popular. In 1997, more than 7,000 U.S. communities had curbside recycling programs, up from just 1,000 a decade earlier. At many college campuses, businesses, and government offices across the country, people are asked to separate their trash for disposal in brightly marked containers. But what happens to all this carefully sorted trash? Unfortunately, the demand for recycled materials has not kept up with the supply. A 1997 study found that it cost waste management companies— such as industry leaders WMX Technologies Inc. and Browning-Ferris Industries— $142 a ton, on average, to collect and sort recyclables. Prices for recycled materials, however, were wildly volatile. The price of old newspapers, for example, in some years soared to $150 a ton; in other years, it dropped to nothing. As a result, the big waste management companies were losing money on recycling most of the time. Solutions to this problem will involve a combination of new technologies, government incentives, and private initiatives to stabilize prices and develop new markets for used paper, glass, plastic, and metals. A promising development is the Buy Recycled Business Alliance, a group of more than 3,000 companies, including American Airlines, Coca-Cola, and Rubbermaid, that has committed to increasing purchases of recycled materials.

Sources: Frank Ackerman, "Recycling: Looking beyond the Bottom Line," *BioCycle,* May 1997, pp. 67–70; "Recycling: Higher Price, Lower Priority?" *Washington Post,* March 30, 1997, p. A1; "Rethinking Recycling," *Scholastic Update* 29, no. 12 (March 21, 1997), p. 10; and "Recycling Business Stinks," *Arizona Business Gazette,* November 21, 1996, p. 8. For an example of an ambitious state effort to promote business procurement of recycled products, see www.recycleiowa.org.

manufacturing processes, recycling, and better housekeeping and maintenance. **Source reduction** often saves money, protects worker health, and requires less abatement and disposal technology. The law provides guidelines, training, and incentives for companies to reduce waste.

The major U.S. law governing the cleanup of existing hazardous waste sites is the Comprehensive Environmental Response, Compensation, and Liability Act, or **CERCLA,** popularly known as **Superfund,** passed in 1980. This law established a fund, supported primarily by a tax on petroleum and chemical companies that were presumed to have created a disproportionate share of toxic wastes. EPA was charged with establishing a National Priority List of the most dangerous toxic sites. Where the original polluters could be identified, they would be required to pay for the cleanup; where they could not be identified or had gone out of business, the Superfund would pay.

An example of a hazardous waste site on EPA's list is the Brio Superfund site, two former waste disposal plants located near the Southbend subdivision outside Houston, Texas. Local wells have been polluted by dangerous chemicals like xylene, and a black tar-like substance has bubbled into

EXHIBIT
11-C

Superfund: A Small Business View

The owner of a small restaurant in Gettysburg, Pennsylvania, was shocked when she was sued for $76,000 under the Superfund law. The U.S. Environmental Protection Agency had originally sued the owner of a dangerous landfill that had been designated as a Superfund site, to force its cleanup. The landfill owner, in turn, had sued hundreds of small businesses, boroughs, and school districts that had contributed waste to the site over the years. Among them was the restaurant owner, who had hired a commercial waste hauler to carry away her trash, mainly food scraps. "I am here to tell you," the restaurant owner later told a congressional hearing, "that your wonderful idea [the Superfund law] . . . does not work in the real world."

One of the provisions considered as Congress once again debated reauthorization of the law in 2000 would exempt small businesses, such as this restaurant, from liability for Superfund cleanup.

Source: "Superfund and a Tale of a $76,000 Trash Bill," *Christian Science Monitor,* March 12, 1997, p. 3.

driveways and garages. Air pollution is suspected as a possible cause of a rash of birth defects, and children have contracted leukemia and other serious illnesses. The once-thriving community of 2,800 is largely boarded up, and the cleanup has still not been completed.[9]

Remarkably, one in four U.S. residents now lives within four miles of a Superfund site. The 1,200 or so sites originally placed on the National Priority List may be just the tip of the iceberg. Congressional researchers have said that as many as 10,000 other sites may need to be cleaned up.

Although Superfund's goals were laudable, it has been widely regarded as a public policy failure. Although cleanup was well underway at almost all sites by 2000, 213 sites—less than a fifth of the total—had been removed from the list, indicating that no further actions were required to protect human health or the environment. Some analysts estimated that the entire cleanup could cost as much as $1 trillion and take half a century to complete. In a debate on possible Superfund reforms, some policymakers argued that companies should be required to pay only for cleaning up the proportion of a waste site they were actually responsible for, with shares determined by a neutral arbitrator. Others called for clearer priorities for cleanup efforts, focusing attention first on sites posing the greatest risk to public health and those most amenable to remediation, or for lower standards for so-called brownfield sites destined for future industrial use. The opinions of one small business owner about possible reforms of Superfund are described in Exhibit 11-C.

[9] "Brio Superfund Cleanup May Drag on Past 2000," *Chemical Marketing Reporter,* January 15, 1996, p. 7. Data on the current status of the cleanup of Superfund sites may be found at www.epa.gov/superfund.

Cross-Media Pollution

Cross-media pollution refers to pollution that cannot easily be blamed on any specific source, or medium. For example, hazardous wastes disposed in a landfill might leach out, contaminating groundwater, or evaporate, causing air pollution. The migration of pollutants has apparently become more frequent and severe in recent years. Unfortunately, cross-media pollution (also called *multimedia pollution*) is especially difficult to control, because laws and regulatory agencies tend to focus on particular kinds of pollution, such as air or water. Several states have experimented with an integrated approach designed to better control pollution from multiple sources. One place this approach has been tried is the Great Lakes region.

> *Pollution in the Great Lakes comes from many sources, including discharge of waste into the lakes, airborne toxics, pesticide runoff from farmland, and landfill leaching. In the 1990s, regulators experimented with new approaches. For example, agencies responsible for these different pollutants have developed joint remedial plans for several contaminated hot spots.*[10]

New institutional arrangements like these will be needed to achieve integrated regulation of cross-media pollution.

Alternative Policy Approaches

Government can use a variety of policy approaches to control air, water, and land pollution. The most widely used method of regulation historically has been to impose environmental standards. Increasingly, however, government policymakers have relied more on market-based and voluntary approaches, rather than command and control regulations, to achieve environmental goals.

Environmental Standards

The traditional method of pollution control is through **environmental standards.** Standard allowable levels of various pollutants are established by legislation or regulatory action and applied by administrative agencies and courts. This approach is also called **command and control regulation,** because the government commands business firms to comply with certain standards and often directly controls their choice of technology.

One type of standard is an environmental-quality standard. In this approach a given geographical area is permitted to have no more than a certain amount or proportion of a pollutant, such as sulfur dioxide, in the air. Polluters are required to control their emissions to maintain the area's standard of air quality. A second type is an emission standard. For example, the law might specify that manufacturers could release into the air no more than 1 percent of the ash (a pollutant) they generated. Emission standards, with some exceptions, are usually set by state and local regulators who are familiar with local industry and special problems caused by local topography and weather conditions.

---

[10] Barry G. Rabe, "An Empirical Examination of Innovations in Integrated Environmental Management: The Case of the Great Lakes Basin," *Public Administration Review,* July–August 1997, pp. 372–81.

Some people believe that businesses should be given more flexibility in how they meet government environmental standards. A new initiative by EPA to provide greater flexibility, involving one of Intel Corporation's semiconductor plants, is described in the discussion case at the end of this chapter.

Market-Based Mechanisms

In recent years, regulators have begun to move away from command and control regulation, favoring increased use of market-based mechanisms. This approach is based on the idea that the market is a better control than extensive standards that specify precisely what companies must do.

One approach that has become more widely used is to allow businesses to buy and sell the right to pollute, as shown in the opening example of this chapter. The Clean Air Act of 1990 incorporated the concept of **tradable allowances** as a key part of its approach to pollution reduction. The law established emission levels and permitted companies that achieved emissions below the standard to sell their rights to the remaining permissible amount to firms that faced penalties because their emissions were above the standard. Over time, the government would reduce permissible emission levels. The system would therefore gradually reduce overall emissions, even though individual companies might continue to pollute above the standard. Companies could choose whether to reduce their emissions—for example, by installing pollution abatement equipment—or to buy allowances from others. For example, in 1998 the Public Service Company of New Hampshire financed new state-of-the-art pollution equipment by selling 9,000 right-to-pollute credits that it no longer needed.[11] One study showed that the tradable permit program for acid rain may have saved companies as much as $3 billion per year, by allowing them the flexibility to choose the most cost-effective methods of complying with the law.[12]

Another market-based type of pollution control is establishment of emissions charges or fees. Each business is charged for the undesirable waste that it emits, with the fee varying according to the amount of waste released. The result is, "The more you pollute, the more you pay." In recent years, both federal and state governments have experimented with a variety of so-called green taxes or ecotaxes that levy a fee on various kinds of environmentally destructive behavior. In some cases, the revenue from these taxes is specifically earmarked to support environmental improvement efforts. In addition to taxing bad behavior, the government may also offer various types of positive incentives to firms that improve their environmental performance. For example, the government may decide to purchase only from those firms that meet a certain pollution standard, or it may offer aid to those that install pollution control equipment. Tax incentives, such as faster depreciation for pollution control equipment, also may be used.

In short, in the early 2000s the trend was to use more flexible, market-oriented approaches—tradable allowances, pollution fees and taxes, and incentives—to achieve environmental objectives where possible.

---

[11] "Dirty Dealings: The Buying and Selling of Pollution Credits Has Become a Huge Business—and Is Likely to Get Even Bigger," *Wall Street Journal,* September 13, 1999, p. R13.
[12] www.epa.gov/acidrain/overview.

Information Disclosure

Another approach to reducing pollution is popularly known as *regulation by publicity,* or *regulation by embarrassment.* The government encourages companies to pollute less by publishing information about the amount of pollutants individual companies emit each year. In many cases, companies take steps voluntarily to reduce their emissions, to avoid public embarrassment.

The major experiment in regulation by publicity has occurred in the area of toxic emissions to the air and water. The 1986 amendments to the Superfund law, called SARA, included a provision called the Community Right-to-Know Law, which required manufacturing firms to report, for about 300 toxic chemicals, the amount on site, the number of pounds released, and how (if at all) these chemicals were treated or disposed of. EPA makes this information available to the public in the *Toxics Release Inventory,* or *TRI,* published annually and posted on the Internet.

From 1988 to 1998, reporting manufacturers in the United States cut their emissions of these chemicals by 45 percent, according to TRI data. Some of the biggest cuts were made by the worst polluters. These dramatic results were especially surprising to regulators, because many of the hazardous chemicals were not covered under clean air and water regulations at the time. The improvements, in many instances, had been completely voluntary. Apparently, fear of negative publicity had compelled many companies to act. "We knew the numbers were high, and we knew the public wasn't going to like it," one chemical industry executive explained.

The apparent success of this law prompted EPA to expand the toxics release reporting program several times to include utilities, mines, and large recyclers as well as manufacturers and to expand the list of chemicals that must be reported. EPA tried a similar approach in its risk management program rule, requiring many businesses to publish worst case scenarios and their plans to minimize risk. The agency's intention was to use public concern to force businesses to be more proactive in managing environmental risk.[13]

The advantages and disadvantages of alternative policy approaches to reducing pollution are summarized in Figure 11-2.

Civil and Criminal Enforcement

Traditionally, companies that violate environmental laws have been subject to civil penalties and fines. Increasingly, however, regulators have turned to the use of criminal statutes to prosecute companies and their executives who break these laws. Proponents of this approach argue that the threat of prison can be an effective deterrent to corporate outlaws who would otherwise degrade the air, water, or land. Since 1989, about 100 individuals and companies have been found guilty of environmental crimes each year. For example, the owner of a Chicago metal-plating factory was sentenced to 15 months in prison. His crime was ordering a worker to pour 4,000 gallons of cyanide and cadmium waste down a floor drain. The toxic chemicals had killed 20,000 fish in the Chicago River and forced authorities to temporarily shut down a branch of the city sewer system.

The U.S. Sentencing Commission, a government agency responsible for setting uniform penalties for violations of federal law, has established guidelines for sentencing

---

[13] Toxics Release Inventory data may be found at www.rtk.net.

Figure 11-2

Advantages and
disadvantages of
alternative policy
approaches to
reducing pollution.

Policy Approach	Advantages	Disadvantages
Environmental standards	• Enforceable in the courts • Compliance mandatory	• Across-the-board standards not equally relevant to all businesses • Requires large regulatory apparatus • Older, less efficient plants may be forced to close
Market-based mechanisms		
Tradable allowances	• Gives businesses more flexibility • Achieves goals at lower overall cost • Saves jobs by allowing some less efficient plants to stay open • Permits the government and private organizations to buy allowances to take them off the market	• Gives business a license to pollute • Allowances are hard to set • May cause regional imbalances in pollution levels • Enforcement is difficult
Emissions fees and taxes	• Taxes bad behavior (pollution) rather than good behavior (profits)	• Fees are hard to set • Taxes may be too low to curb pollution
Government incentives	• Rewards environmentally responsible behavior • Encourages companies to exceed minimum standards	• Incentives may not be strong enough to curb pollution
Information disclosure	• Government spends little on enforcement • Companies able to reduce pollution in the most cost-effective way	• Does not motivate all companies

environmental wrongdoers. Under these rules, penalties would reflect not only the severity of the offense but also a company's demonstrated environmental commitment. Businesses that have an active compliance program, cooperate with government investigators, and promptly assist any victims would receive lighter sentences than others with no environmental programs or that knowingly violate the law. These guidelines provide an incentive for businesses to develop active compliance programs to protect themselves and their officers from high fines or even prison if a violation should occur.[14]

---

[14] For a discussion of criminal liability in environmental law, and how to avoid it, see Frank B. Friedman, *Practical Guide to Environmental Management,* 8th ed. (Washington, DC: Environmental Law Institute, May 2000), chap. 2.

Figure 11-3

The cost of pollution control in the United States.

Source: EPA, *Environmental Investments: The Cost of a Clean Environment* (Washington, DC: EPA, 1990).

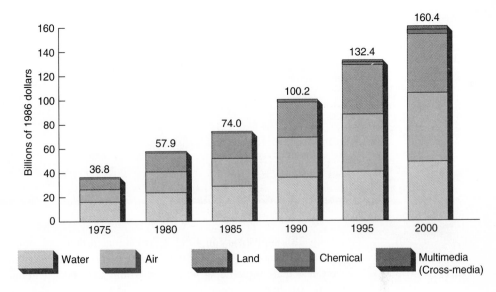

Costs and Benefits of Environmental Regulation

One of the central issues of environmental protection is how costs are balanced by benefits. In the quarter century or so since the modern environmental era began, the nation has spent a great deal to clean up the environment and keep it clean. Some have questioned the value choices underlying these expenditures, suggesting that the costs—lost jobs, reduced capital investment, and lowered productivity—exceeded the benefits. Others, in contrast, point to significant gains in the quality of life and to the economic payoff of a cleaner environment.

As a nation, the United States has invested heavily in environmental cleanup. Figure 11-3 shows U.S. pollution control spending through 2000. According to the EPA, by 1990 environmental spending exceeded $100 billion a year, about 2 percent of the nation's gross national product, and reached around $160 billion annually by 2000. Business spending to comply with environmental regulation has diverted funds that might otherwise have been invested in new plants and equipment or in research and development. Sometimes, strict rules have led to plant shutdowns and loss of jobs. Some regions and industries, in particular, have been hard hit by environmental regulation, especially those with high abatement costs, such as paper and wood products, chemicals, petroleum and coal, and primary metals. Economists often find it difficult, however, to sort out what proportion of job loss in an industry is attributable to environmental regulation and what proportion is attributable to other causes.

The costs of environmental regulation must be balanced against the benefits. In many areas, the United States has made great progress in cleaning up the environment, as these figures show.

- Emissions of nearly all major pollutants in the United States have dropped substantially since 1970, when the Environmental Protection Act was passed. On its

Figure 11-4

Costs and benefits of environmental regulations.

Costs	Benefits
• $160 billion a year spent by business and individuals in the United States by 2000.	• Emissions of nearly all pollutants have dropped since 1970.
• Job loss in some particularly polluting industries.	• Air and water quality improved, some toxic waste sites cleaned; improved health; natural beauty preserved or enhanced.
• Competitiveness of some capital-intensive, "dirty" industries impaired.	• Growth of other industries, such as environmental products and services, tourism, and fishing.

twenty-fifth anniversary in 1995, EPA estimated that total emissions of the criteria air pollutants had declined by 24 percent. Levels of particulates in the air were less than a quarter of what they would have been without controls; lead in the air was just 2 percent of what it would have been. The citizens of Los Angeles experienced one-third fewer days of unhealthy air than they had just a decade earlier, despite huge increases in population and vehicle traffic. These gains in air quality translate into significant reductions in medical costs.

• Water quality had also improved. More than one billion tons of toxic pollutants had been prevented from being discharged into the nation's waterways since the Water Pollution Control Act had gone into effect. Many lakes and riverways had been restored to ecological health. The Cuyahoga River in Ohio, for example, which at one time was badly polluted by industrial waste, had been restored to the point where residents could fish and even swim in the river.

Environmental regulations also stimulate some sectors of the economy. The environmental services and products industry, for example, has grown dramatically since the mid-1980s. While jobs are being lost in industries like forest products and high-sulfur coal mining, others are being created in areas like environmental consulting, asbestos abatement, instrument manufacturing, waste management equipment, and air pollution control. Other jobs are saved or created in industries like fishing and tourism when natural areas are protected or restored. Moreover, environmental regulations can stimulate the economy by compelling businesses to become more efficient by conserving energy, and less money is spent on treating health problems caused by pollution.

Because of the complexity of these issues, economists differ on the net costs and benefits of environmental regulation. In some respects, government controls hurt the economy, and in other ways they help, as summarized in Figure 11-4. An analysis of data from several studies found that, on balance, U.S. environmental regulations did not have a large overall effect on economic competitiveness, because losses in one area tended to balance gains in another.[15] What is clear is that choices in the area of

---

[15] Adam B. Jaffe, Steven R. Peterson, Paul R. Portney, and Robert N. Stavins, "Environmental Regulations and the Competitiveness of U.S. Industry," prepared for the U.S. Department of Commerce, July 1993. For another summary of the evidence that comes to a similar conclusion, see Steven Peterson, Barry Galef, and Kenneth Grant, "Do Environmental Regulations Impair Competitiveness?" prepared for the U.S. EPA, September 1995.

environmental regulation reflect underlying values, expressed in a democratic society through an open political process. Just how much a society is prepared to pay—and how "clean" it wants to be—are political choices, reflecting the give and take of diverse interests in a pluralistic society.

The Greening of Management

Environmental regulations—such as the laws governing clean air, water, and land described in this chapter—establish minimum legal standards that businesses must meet. Most companies try to comply with these regulations, if only to avoid litigation, fines, and, in the most extreme cases, criminal penalties. But many firms are now voluntarily moving beyond compliance to improve their environmental performance in all areas of their operations. Researchers have sometimes referred to the process of moving toward more proactive environmental management as the **greening of management.** This section describes the greening process and discusses what organizational approaches companies have used to manage environmental issues effectively. It also explains why green management can improve a company's strategic competitiveness.

Stages of Corporate Environmental Responsibility

Although environmental issues are forcing all businesses to manage in new ways, not all companies are equally green, meaning proactive in their response to environmental issues. Researchers have identified five stages of environmental responsibility, depicted in Figure 11-5.

According to this model, companies pass through five distinct stages in the development of green management practices. At the *beginner* level, managers ignore potential liability and dismiss the need for specialized environmental programs. Environmental responsibility, if addressed at all, is added onto other programs and positions. Beginners might include older firms established before the modern environmental era, small firms that feel they cannot afford specialized programs, or simply companies in industries where regulatory oversight is perceived to be minimal. *Firefighters,* companies at the next developmental stage, address environmental issues only when they pose an immediate threat, such as when an unexpected accident or spill occurs. Environmental management is seen as an exception to business as usual. Companies as *concerned citizens,* at the third stage, believe environmental protection is worthwhile. They may even have specialized staff; however, they devote few resources and little top management attention to green issues. *Pragmatists* actively manage environmental issues, have well-funded programs, and evaluate risk as well as immediate problems. In addition to having all the programmatic elements of pragmatists, *proactivists*—companies in the final stage of development—also have senior executives who champion environmental responsibility, extensive training, and strong links between environmental staff and other parts of the organization.

> *Environmentally proactive companies often address problems before they are required to do so by government. In 2000, for example, 3M pulled its widely used stain repellent, Scotchguard, off the market after studies found that a key ingredient accumulated in people's blood. Animal studies suggested—although they did not prove—that high doses of this chemical*

Figure 11-5

A five-stage model of corporate environmental responsibility.

Source: Adapted from Christopher B. Hunt and Ellen R. Auster, "Proactive Environmental Management: Avoiding the Toxic Trap," *Sloan Management Review,* Winter 1990, pp. 7–18. Used by permission of the publisher. Copyright 1990 by the Sloan Management Review Association. All rights reserved.

	Commitment of Organization		
Developmental Stage	General Mindset of Corporate Managers	Resource Commitment	Support and Involvement of Top Management
Beginner	Environmental management is unnecessary	Minimal resource commitment	No involvement
Firefighter	Environmental issues should be addressed only as necessary	Budgets for problems as they occur	Piecemeal involvement
Concerned citizen	Environmental management is a worthwhile function	Consistent, yet minimal budget	Commitment in theory
Pragmatist	Environmental management is an important business function	Generally sufficient funding	Aware and moderately involved
Proactivist	Environmental management is a priority item	Open-ended funding	Actively involved

could be harmful. 3M discontinued the popular product even though it was not mandated, and even though the company faced possible losses of $500 million a year in sales. "3M deserves credit for . . . coming forward voluntarily," said the head of the Environmental Protection Agency.[16]

What factors push companies along this continuum from lower to higher levels of corporate environmental responsiveness? One recent study of firms in the United Kingdom and Japan found three main motivations for "going green": the chance to gain a *competitive advantage,* a desire to gain *legitimacy* (approval of the public or regulators), and a moral commitment to *ecological responsibility.*[17] Other research shows that most firms are now in transition from lower to higher stages in the developmental sequence.

The Ecologically Sustainable Organization

An **ecologically sustainable organization (ESO)** is a business that operates in a way that is consistent with the principle of sustainable development, as presented in Chapter 10. In other words, an ESO could continue its activities indefinitely, without altering the carrying capacity of the earth's ecosystem. An ecologically sustainable organization would have moved beyond even the proactivist level in the stage model described earlier. Such

---

[16] "3M's Big Cleanup: Why It Decided to Pull the Plug on Its Best-Selling Stain Repellent," *Business Week,* June 5, 2000, pp. 96–98.

[17] Pratima Bansal and Kendall Roth, "Why Companies Go Green: A Model of Ecological Responsiveness," *Academy of Management Journal,* August 2000, pp. 717–36.

businesses would not use up natural resources any faster than they could be replenished or substitutes found. They would make and transport products efficiently, with minimal use of energy. They would design products that would last a long time and that, when worn out, could be disassembled and recycled. They would not produce waste any faster than natural systems could absorb and disperse it. They would work with other businesses, governments, and organizations to meet these goals.[18]

Of course, no existing business completely fits the definition of an ecologically sustainable organization. The concept is what social scientists call an *ideal type,* that is, a kind of absolute standard against which real organizations can be measured. A few visionary businesses, however, have embraced the concept and begun to try to live up to this ideal.

> *One such business is Interface, a $1 billion company based in Atlanta, Georgia, that makes 40 percent of the world's commercial carpet tiles. In 1994, CEO Ray C. Anderson announced, to many peoples' surprise, that Interface would seek to become "the first sustainable corporation in the world." Anderson and his managers undertook hundreds of initiatives. For example, the company started a program by which customers could* lease, *rather than* purchase, *carpet tile. When tile wore out in high-traffic areas, Interface technicians would replace just the worn units, reducing waste. Old tiles would be recycled, creating a closed loop. In 2000, Interface reported that in six years it had saved $90 million by cutting waste, and revenues and profits had soared. But Anderson said it was "just a start. It's daunting, trying to climb a mountain taller than Everest."[19]*

No companies, including Interface, have yet become truly sustainable businesses, and indeed it will probably be impossible for any single firm to become an ESO in the absence of supportive government policies and a widespread movement among many businesses and other social institutions.

Elements of Effective Environmental Management

Companies that have begun to move toward environmental sustainability have learned that new structures, processes, and incentives are often needed. Some of the organizational elements that many proactive green companies share are the following.[20]

---

[18] Mark Starik and Gordon P. Rands, "Weaving an Integrated Web: Multilevel and Multisystem Perspectives of Ecologically Sustainable Organizations," *Academy of Management Review,* October 1995, pp. 908–35. For a related discussion, see Paul Shrivastava, *Greening Business* (Cincinnati: Thomson Executive Press, 1996), chap. 2, "Sustainable Development and Sustainable Corporations," pp. 21–50.

[19] Interface Corporation, "Sustainability Report 2000"; and Ray C. Anderson, *Mid-Course Correction: Toward a Sustainable Enterprise—The Interface Model* (Atlanta: Peregrinzilla Press, 1998).

[20] Anne T. Lawrence and David Morell, "Leading-Edge Environmental Management: Motivation, Opportunity, Resources, and Processes," *Research in Corporate Social Performance and Policy,* supp. 1 (1995), pp. 99–127; and James Maxwell, Sandra Rothenberg, Forrest Briscoe, and Alfred Marcus, "Green Schemes: Corporate Environmental Strategies and Their Implementation," *California Management Review* 39, no. 3 (March 22, 1997), p. 118 ff.

Top Managers with Environmental Responsibilities

One step many companies have taken is to give environmental managers greater authority and access to top levels of the corporation. Many leading firms now have a vice president for environmental affairs with a direct reporting relationship with the CEO. These individuals often supervise extensive staffs of specialists and coordinate the work of managers in many areas, including research and development, marketing, and operations.

Dialogue with Stakeholders

Environmentally proactive companies also engage in dialogue with external stakeholders, such as environmental organizations. Bristol-Myers Squibb, the pharmaceutical company, for example, has set up an external advisory group—including environmentalists, academics, and key customers—to review its progress toward sustainable development. The company also regularly participates in public meetings in which it discusses with stakeholders its position on various environmental issues it faces.[21]

Line Manager Involvement

Environmental staff experts and specialized departments are most effective when they work closely with the people who carry out the company's daily operations. For this reason, many green companies involve line managers and workers directly in the process of change. At the Park Plaza Hotel in Boston, green teams of employees make suggestions ranging from energy-efficient windows to refillable bottles of soap and shampoo.

Codes of Environmental Conduct

Environmentally proactive companies put their commitment in writing, often in the form of a code of conduct or charter that spells out the firm's environmental goals. A recent study of a group of European companies found, perhaps not surprisingly, that employees at firms with a well-communicated environmental policy were much more likely to come up with creative proposals for helping the environment.[22]

Cross-Functional Teams

Another organizational element is the use of ad hoc, cross-functional teams to solve environmental problems, including individuals from different departments. These teams pull together key players with the skills and resources to get the job done, wherever they are located in the corporate structure. At Lockheed Missiles and Space Corporation's facility in Sunnyvale, California, a Pollution Prevention Committee includes representatives from each of the five major business areas within the company. Each year, the committee selects about a dozen projects from among many proposed from each area. Interdivisional, cross-functional teams are set up to work on approved projects, such as one to recycle wastewater.

---

[21] "Engaging Stakeholders," in Bristol-Myers Squibb, *Report on Environmental Health and Safety Progress,* May 1999. The company's program is also described at www.bms.com/ehs.

[22] Catherine A. Ramus and Ulrich Steger, "The Roles of Supervisory Support Behaviors and Environmental Policy in Employee Ecoinitiatives at Leading European Companies," *Academy of Management Review,* August 2000, pp. 605–26.

Rewards and Incentives

Businesspeople are most likely to consider the environmental impacts of their actions when their organizations acknowledge and reward this behavior. The greenest organizations tie the compensation of their managers, including line managers, to environmental achievement and take steps to recognize these achievements publicly.

Environmental Audits

Green companies closely track their progress toward environmental goals. Some have full-blown environmental audits (comparable to the social audits discussed in Chapter 4) that periodically review environmental initiatives. National Semiconductor Corporation, for example, initiated a new audit protocol that scored company facilities in such areas as air pollution control, water pollution control, hazardous waste management, and groundwater protection. Audits can assess progress and also help spread good ideas across a company. At least two dozen major U.S. firms now publish annual environmental progress reports.

Interorganizational Alliances

Many firms have formed alliances with others to promote mutual environmental goals. For example, the Chemical Manufacturers Association started a program called Responsible Care, committing its member-companies to work together to respond to public concerns about chemicals.[23]

Environmental Partnerships

Another approach, described in one of the examples at the beginning of this chapter, is for businesses to form voluntary, collaborative partnerships with environmental organizations and regulators to achieve specific objectives. These collaborations, called **environmental partnerships,** draw on the unique strengths of the different partners to improve environmental quality or conserve resources.[24]

> *At its vast manufacturing complex in Midland, Michigan, for example, Dow Chemical Corporation cooperated with environmentalists to find ways to slash toxic emissions. Managers and scientists worked together to come up with creative ideas, such as recovering rather than burning dangerous vapors produced in making Saran Wrap. Although the changes cost Dow over $3 million, they were expected to save the company more than $5 million a year, and cut discharges to both air and water by more than 35 percent.*[25]

Many of these programmatic elements represent specific applications of the general model of corporate social responsiveness presented in Chapter 4. This model

---

[23] A recent account may be found in Andrew A. King and Michael J. Lenox, "Industry Regulation without Sanctions: The Chemical Industry's Responsible Care Program," *Academy of Management Journal,* August 2000, pp. 698–716.

[24] Frederick J. Long and Matthew B. Arnold, *The Power of Environmental Partnerships* (Forth Worth, TX: Dryden Press, 1995).

[25] "Chemistry Cleans Up a Factory: Dow and Environmentalists in Rare Accord," *New York Times,* July 18, 1999, p. C1.

describes how companies identify a social problem (in this case, environmental degradation), learn how to tackle it, and finally institutionalize procedures to address the problem on an ongoing, routine basis.

Environmental Management as a Competitive Advantage

Some researchers believe that by moving toward ecological sustainability, business firms gain a competitive advantage. That is, relative to other firms in the same industry, companies that proactively manage environmental issues will tend to be more successful than those that do not. One top business executive who has embraced this view is William Clay Ford, chairman of the Ford Motor Company. Under his leadership, the company undertook development of efficient hybrid gasoline-electric vehicles, set out to remodel its venerable Rouge factory complex as a state-of-the-art environmental facility, and joined a partnership to develop hydrogen fuel cells, a new kind of engine based on a totally renewable energy source. Said Ford, "We can't expand in potentially huge markets such as India and China, and provide a better life for the world's poorest people, unless we can do it in a sustainable way. . . . We look at [sustainability] not just as a requirement, but as an incredible opportunity."[26]

Effective environmental management confers a competitive advantage in four different ways.

Cost Savings

Companies that reduce pollution and hazardous waste, reuse or recycle materials, and operate with greater energy efficiency can reap significant cost savings. An example is Herman Miller, the office furniture company.

> *Herman Miller goes to great lengths to avoid wasting materials. The company sells fabric scraps to the auto industry for use as car linings; leather trim to luggage makers for attaché cases; and vinyl to the supplier to be re-extruded into new edging. Burnable solid waste is used as fuel for a specialized boiler that generates all the heating and cooling for the company's main complex in Zeeland, Michigan. The result is that the company actually makes money from materials that, in the past, it would have had to pay to have hauled away and dumped.*[27]

Product Differentiation

Companies that develop a reputation for environmental excellence and that produce and deliver products and services with concern for their sustainability can attract environmentally aware customers. This approach is sometimes called **green marketing.** The size of the green market was estimated in 2000 to comprise between 10 and 12 percent of consumers.[28] For example, when Home Depot announced it would sell only sustainably harvested wood products, it attracted new customers impressed with its environmental commitment.

---

[26] Speech by Bill Ford, April 14, 2000, available at www.ceres.org/eventsandnews/news/Fordspeech.html.

[27] Herman Miller, "Journey to Sustainability 2000," available at www.hermanmiller.com.

[28] Joel Makower, "Whatever Happened to Green Consumers?" syndicated column, July–August 2000, available at www.igc.org/igc/gateway.

Technological Innovation

Environmentally proactive companies are often technological leaders, as they seek out imaginative new methods for reducing pollution and increasing efficiency. In many cases, they produce innovations that can then be marketed to others, as new regulations spur their adoption in broader markets, as illustrated by the following example.

> *General Electric Power Systems joined with a smaller company, CCS, to develop an innovative catalyst system for gas turbines they called the Xonon. The name was "no NOx" spelled backward, referring to the fact that the product emitted only 1 percent as much nitrous oxide—a contributor to smog—as traditional gas turbines. Utility companies, facing increasingly stringent environmental regulations, eagerly stepped forward to buy the product.*[29]

Strategic Planning

Companies that cultivate a vision of sustainability must adopt sophisticated strategic planning techniques to allow their top managers to assess the full range of the firm's effects on the environment. The complex auditing and forecasting techniques used by these firms help them anticipate a wide range of external influences on the firm, not just ecological influences. Wide-angle planning helps these companies foresee new markets, materials, technologies, and products.

In short, proactive environmental management may help businesses not only promote sustainability but also become more competitive in the global marketplace.[30]

Summary Points of This Chapter

- The United States regulates in three major areas of environmental protection: air pollution, water pollution, and land pollution. Environmental laws have traditionally been of the command and control type, specifying standards and results. New laws have added market incentives to induce environmentally sound behavior and have encouraged companies to reduce pollution at the source.
- Environmental laws have brought many benefits. Air, water, and land pollution levels are in many cases lower than in 1970. But some improvements have come at a high cost. A continuing challenge is to find ways to promote a clean environment and sustainable business practices without impairing the competitiveness of the U.S. economy.

---

[29] "Green Chemistry Proves It Pays," *Fortune,* July 24, 2000, pp. 270 ff.

[30] For a general statement of the argument that environmental management confers a competitive advantage, see Michael E. Porter and Claas van der Linde, "Green and Competitive: Beyond the Stalemate," *Harvard Business Review,* September–October 1995, pp. 120 ff; and Stuart L. Hart, "Beyond Greening: Strategies for a Sustainable World," *Harvard Business Review,* January–February 1997, pp. 66–76. The discussion of the competitive advantages of environmental management is adapted, in part, from Anthony Saponara, "Competitive Advantage in the Environment," *Corporate Environmental Strategy: The Journal of Environmental Leadership* 3, no. 1 (Summer 1995).

- Companies pass through five distinct stages in the development of green management practices. Many businesses are now moving from lower to higher stages. An ecologically sustainable organization is one that operates in a way that is consistent with the principle of sustainable development.
- Effective environmental management requires an integrated approach that involves all parts of the business organization, including top leadership, line managers, and production teams, as well as strong partnerships with stakeholders.
- Many companies have found that proactive environmental management can confer a competitive advantage by saving money, attracting green customers, promoting innovation, and developing skills in strategic planning.

Key Terms and Concepts Used in This Chapter

- Environmental Protection Agency (EPA)
- Acid rain
- Environmental justice
- Source reduction
- Superfund (CERCLA)
- Cross-media pollution
- Environmental standards

- Command and control regulation
- Tradable allowances
- Greening of management
- Ecologically sustainable organization (ESO)
- Environmental partnerships
- Green marketing

Internet Resources

• www.epa.gov	Environmental Protection Agency
• www.envirolink.org	Environmental organizations and news
• GreenBiz.com	Green Business Network
• www.lungusa.org	American Lung Association

Discussion Case: *Common Sense in Arizona*

In 1996, the Environmental Protection Agency signed an historic agreement with Intel Corporation, the nation's largest maker of computer chips. Under the deal, Intel was given almost unlimited flexibility in operating its new factory in Chandler, Arizona, in exchange for reducing pollution even more than the law required. The administrator of the EPA hailed the agreement as a "common sense solution" for both industry and regulators.

"This is an attempt to move away from the regulatory battle and make things performance-related," said an Intel spokesperson. "What we get is flexibility and the ability to run our business as efficiently and effectively as possible, as long as we stay under the limits."

The site of this bold experiment, Intel's $2.5 billion Chandler plant, was the second-largest chip making factory in the world, employing 1,500 workers and with a central clean room spanning a full eight acres.

EPA's deal with Intel was one of the first negotiated under a new federal program called Project XL (for *excellence* and *leadership*). In 1995, the EPA began a major effort, called its *reinvention initiative*. The idea was to create innovative alternatives to current regulatory approaches that would improve environmental quality while making it simpler and less expensive for businesses to comply with environmental rules. Under Project XL, a key part of the initiative, companies could negotiate agreements with EPA to simplify their permitting requirements, as long as they achieved certain overall goals. These agreements would have to be approved not only by EPA but also by affected stakeholders, such as local and state governments, environmentalists, and community organizations.

The agreement with Intel required the company to cap overall air pollution at Chandler at 50 tons a year, below existing EPA limits, and to recycle much of the water used and nonhazardous waste generated at the plant. It also required Intel to monitor its own emissions on an ongoing basis and to report complete and current information on the Internet as well as with the government. In exchange, the company was given a facilitywide permit instead of having to obtain a separate permit for each process.

Intel was pleased, citing the speed with which it could implement changes. "We are the epitome of a quick-to-market company," said the company's government affairs manager for environment, health, and safety. "So we're constantly having to change our processes to keep up with technological progress. . . . Every time we make a change, we have to go back for a permit revision, and by the time we get it, the technology is outdated." Under Project XL, Intel could avoid 30 to 50 extra permit reviews per year.

But some activists criticized the agreement. A group called the Coalition for Responsible Technology (CRT), comprised of over 100 community, environmental, and health and safety organizations, blasted it as a "sweetheart deal" that "turn[ed] back the clock on hard-won laws that protect the environment." The coalition was concerned that the agreement would permit higher emissions of particular toxic chemicals than allowed under existing standards, threatening the health of those working in or living near the factory. CRT was also worried that emissions from the plant would not be routinely monitored by regulators.

A 1999 review of the project by EPA found that Intel had met or exceeded its environmental goals. The company reported that it had saved millions of dollars by avoiding delays in bringing new products to market, and said that its managers had found stakeholder involvement to be valuable. In fact, Intel was so pleased that it had implemented similar programs at two other facilities. In 2000, EPA was in the process of expanding Project XL to include even stronger incentives for going beyond compliance, in an approach the agency called its new *performance track*.

Sources: Further information about Project XL is available at EPA's website at www.epa.gov/ProjectXL. Intel's website is at www.intel.com; that of the Campaign for Responsible Technology is at www.igc.org/svtc/crt.htm.

Discussion Questions

1. Of the alternative policy approaches discussed in this chapter, of which is Project XL an example? If Project XL includes features of more than one regulatory approach, please list these features and state how they have been combined.

2. What are the benefits and costs of the regulatory approach taken by the EPA in this case? Please answer this question from the perspective of the following stakeholders: Intel managers; Intel employees; the Chandler, Arizona, community; environmental organizations; and federal environmental regulators.

3. Do you support Project XL? Why or why not? How might the approach illustrated in this case be modified to address the concerns of various stakeholders in the process?

PART SIX

Business and Technological Change

12

Technology: An Economic–Social Force

Technology is an unmistakable economic and social force in our world. Global communications, business exchanges, particularly through electronic commerce, and the simple tasks that make up our daily lives are all significantly influenced by technology. Whether we are at home, in school, or in the workplace, the emergence of technological innovations has dramatically changed how we live, play, learn, work, and interact with others. These dramatic changes in our global community result in a profound effect on humankind and the world in which we live.

This chapter focuses on these key questions and chapter objectives:

- What are the dominant features of technology, and what fuels technological growth?

- How has e-commerce changed the way businesses operate and how they interact with their stakeholders?

- How has the emergence of technology superpowers affected the global marketplace?

- Are businesses from developing countries participants in or only observers of technological growth?

- How has technology changed our lifestyle at home, our education at school, and our health?

- What factors gave rise to a technological or digital divide, and is this divide widening or narrowing?

he technological revolution is an integral part of the twenty-first century. It affects virtually everything we do—how we live, communicate with others, and learn new things. Yet the degree of technological influence in our lives is still a matter of preference for some people.

Will Clemens was a chief executive for Respond.com, a web-shopping site located in the technologically rich Silicon Valley in northern California. At work, the 29-year-old Clemens was dependent on his personal computer, wireless telephone, and pager. He was immersed in the world of high technology. But at home, Clemens had a very different experience; he was decidedly "unwired." Electricity did not flow throughout his five-bedroom house, a choice he made after heavy rains blew a fuse and the electricity went out. Several long-burning beeswax candles provided light for reading and cooking. There was no television set, no home computer, no telephone service. Clemens's lifestyle reflected the way a few high-tech executives chose to live to escape the overwhelming presence of technology in their lives at work.

At the other extreme of life in a technologically rich world was the DotComGuy. This 26-year-old computer systems manager legally changed his name to reflect his year-long challenge: to live off of e-commerce for one year. He rented a small Dallas town-house with a tiny backyard and did not venture outside for an entire year. He started with a laptop computer and an Internet connection, but the house was far from empty. The DotComGuy purchased all his necessities and luxuries exclusively online. He named his domicile the Dotcompound. It had all the furnishings of a typical bachelor's home—a workout room, postmodern furniture, pets, and gourmet food. The DotComGuy showed the world the advantages of the growing Internet shopping network and the virtually unlimited possibilities afforded by the dot-com world.[1]

While both examples are somewhat extreme, which lifestyle represents the better quality of life? Are people so absorbed in the technological world of business that they need the kind of relief sought by Will Clemens? Or is the world of the DotComGuy the technologically preferred world of the twenty-first century?

The Explosive Force of Technology

Throughout history technology has been an explosive force. It has repeatedly erupted, exerting a tremendous influence on business, humankind, and the world. It appears virtually impossible to stem the advancement of technology. Though the Industrial Revolution created new and serious human problems for some people in society, it was a great advance in the history of civilization. New jobs and skills replaced older ones, living standards were raised, and economic abundance extended life expectancy for millions of people.

Technology continues to grow because of people themselves. Human beings have sampled and embraced the fruits of knowledge. It seems that people have acquired an insatiable desire for it. They forever seek to expand knowledge of their environment, probably because of the excitement of learning and their belief that more knowledge will help them adapt to their environment. As Bill Joy, Sun Microsystems' chief scientist, explained,

---

[1] Pui-Wing Tam, "Taking High Tech Home Is a Bit Much for an Internet Exec," *Wall Street Journal,* June 16, 2000, pp. A1, A8; and Alex Lyda, "Half of the Way Home," *Pittsburgh Post-Gazette,* July 3, 2000, p. A6.

By 2030, we are likely to be able to build machines, in quantity, a million times as powerful as the personal computer of today. . . . As this enormous computing power is combined with the manipulative advances of the physical sciences and the new, deep understanding in genetics, enormous transformative power is being unleashed. These combinations open up the opportunity to completely redesign the world, for better or worse: The replicating and evolving processes that have been confined to the natural world are about to become realms of human endeavor.[2]

Technology Defined

Technology is the application of science, especially in industry or commerce. The dominant feature of technology is change and then more change. Technology forces change on people whether they are prepared for it or not. In modern society it has brought so much change that it creates what is called *future shock,* which means that change comes so fast and furiously that it approaches the limits of human tolerance and people lose their ability to cope with it successfully. Although technology is not the only cause of change, it is the primary cause. It is either directly or indirectly involved in most changes that occur in society.

Some years ago, right after the start of the personal computer revolution, industry experts observed that if automobiles had developed at the same rate as the computer business, a Rolls Royce would cost $2.75 and go 3 million miles on a gallon of gasoline. Today's microcomputers cost less than those of a decade or even a few years ago and offer many times the power and many more times the speed of their predecessors.

Another feature of technology is that its effects are widespread, reaching far beyond the immediate point of technological impact. Technology ripples through society until every community is affected by it. For example, **telecommunications,** the transmission of information over great distances via electromagnetic signals, has played a historically significant and positive role in our society's development. This innovation enhanced international commerce, linked relatives living great distances apart, and enabled us to discover many of the mysteries of outer space. Yet, along with these advances came the potential for a greater invasion of privacy through databases and telemarketing practices. The human touch in our communication with others has been diminished through the convenience of electronic and voice mail.

An additional feature of technology is that it is self-reinforcing. As stated by Alvin Toffler, "Technology feeds on itself. Technology makes more technology possible."[3] This self-reinforcing feature means that technology acts as a multiplier to encourage its own faster development. It acts with other parts of society so that an invention in one place leads to a sequence of inventions in other places. Thus, invention of the microprocessor led rather quickly to successful generations of the modern computer, which led to new banking methods, electronic mail, bar-code systems, and so on.

---

[2] Bill Joy, "Why the Future Doesn't Need Us," *Wired,* April 2000, www.wired.com/wired/archive/8.04/joy.
[3] Alvin Toffler, *Future Shock* (New York: Bantam, 1971), p. 26.

Figure 12-1

Phases in the development of technology.

Technology Level	Phases in the Development of Technology	Approximate Period in the U.S.	Activity	Primary Skill Used
1	Nomadic-agrarian	Until 1650	Harvesting	Manual
2	Agrarian	1650–1900	Planting and harvesting	Manual
3	Industrial	1900–1960	Building material goods	Manual and machine
4	Service	1960–1975	Providing services	Manual and intellectual
5	Information	1975–today	Thinking and designing	Intellectual and electronic

Phases of Technology in Society

Looking in a very general way, we can see that five broad phases of technology have developed, as shown in Figure 12-1. In history, nations have tended to move sequentially through each phase, beginning with the lowest technology and moving higher with each step, so the five phases roughly represent the progress of civilization throughout history.

The current phase of technology is the **information society.** This phase emphasizes the use and transfer of knowledge and information rather than manual skill. It dominates work and employs the largest proportion of the labor force. Work becomes abstract, the electronic manipulation of symbols. Businesses of all sizes, including the smallest firms, are exploring the benefits of the information age. As shown later, the information age affects how we work, learn, and play. It influences our diet and our health.

An information society's technology is primarily electronic in nature and is heavily dependent on the computer and the semiconductor silicon chip. The power of these devices rests on their ability to process, store, and retrieve large amounts of information with great speed. By the beginning of the twenty-first century, the information age had exploded into nearly every aspect of business and society. Civilization had never experienced that much change that fast. These inventions have catapulted societies into **cyberspace,** where information is stored, ideas are described, and communication takes place in and through an electronic network of linked systems. The technology developed in this new age provided the mechanisms for more information to be produced in a decade than in the previous 1,000 years.

Fueling Technological Growth

The dynamic explosion of technological growth is documented in how businesses operate and people live. Underlying this explosive development are two important factors: economic growth and worker productivity, and research and development investment.

Economic Expansion and Worker Productivity

The first factor that fuels technological growth is economic expansion and worker productivity. During the 1990s, U.S. businesses poured more than $2 trillion into computers, software, and other technology products. In 1999 alone, corporate spending on technology grew to $510 billion. This massive spending helped sustain the economic boom that carried the global business community into the twenty-first century. Evidence of a U.S. economic slowdown in 2001, based on weaker company profits and slower consumer spending, led some businesses to adjust their technology spending budgets downward. Spending for computers, communications, and software was predicted to rise just 12 percent, compared with the 22 percent increase in 2000 and 26 percent jump in 1999.[4]

Technology continues to consume a growing share of the global economy. Along with economic growth through technology came increased worker productivity. Productivity, the hourly output of an average worker, is a key to society's quality of life. During the late 1990s, productivity grew at almost twice the rate of the previous two decades. Contrary to prior economic expansions, where productivity declined as companies exhausted their investment ideas and hired less-skilled workers, productivity has increased, since technology is relatively cheap and pervasive. Thus, businesses could afford more technology and workers were more adept in accepting technological improvements. Both conditions led to significant productivity gains during economic expansion.

Research and Development Investment

The second factor fueling technological growth was research and development (R&D). Private R&D budgets steadily declined through 1994 but remarkably rebounded in the late 1990s. Attributed to the fast-growing high-technology industry, by the late 1990s R&D was growing by almost 10 percent a year, a rate four times greater than forecasters had predicted.[5]

> *News Corporation set up a $650 million venture capital fund in 2000 for investing in start-up Internet companies outside the United States. The firm planned to enter into joint ventures with Internet companies from the UK, India, Australia, and New Zealand. This new commitment doubled the amount set aside in 1999 for non-U.S. Internet investments.[6]*

> *Microsoft announced a five-year collaboration with Massachusetts Institute of Technology for the research and development of new technology-based education delivery techniques. Microsoft committed $25 million toward this joint venture. Although only a fraction of the corporation's $400 million annual research budget, this program indicated the first significant entry into high-technology education research by a major high-technology corporation.*

[4] Gary McWilliams, "Corporate Technology Budgets Fall at High Speed," *Wall Street Journal,* December 28, 2000, p. B1.

[5] James P. Miller, "Private R&D Spending Seen Rising 9.3%," *Wall Street Journal,* December 31, 1998, p. A2.

[6] John Lippman, "News Corp. Sets Up $650 Million Fund to Finance Internet Firms Outside U.S.," *Wall Street Journal,* March 13, 2000, p. B16.

Government support of the technology explosion complements private R&D spending. For example, in 1998 the U.S. launched a program of financial assistance for Internet projects in developing countries. While increasing more slowly than industry funding, the U.S. government annually provided over $66 billion to support technology-based research and development. The United States led other industrial nations in technology R&D with 4.6 percent of the nation's gross domestic product in 1999. Sweden was next with 3.5 percent, followed by Britain, Japan, France, and Germany, all which designated more than 2 percent of their GDP to technology. Japanese government officials addressed their relative lack of R&D support by increasing their funding and partnering with Japanese high-tech companies in the quest of surpassing the U.S. high-speed Internet infrastructure by 2005.[7]

The Emergence of High-Technology Business

Technology and business have been intertwined since the Industrial Revolution. The connection between the two became even stronger in the information age, particularly with the advent of electronic business exchanges. Technology influences every aspect of the global marketplace—driving innovation, affecting partnerships, and changing business-stakeholder relationships.

Technology and E-Commerce

During the information age phase of technological development, electronic business exchanges between businesses emerged as a powerful economic and social force. These electronic business exchanges, generally referred to as **e-commerce,** consist of buying and selling goods and services electronically, that is via the Internet. Intel chairman Andrew Grove explains the development of an e-commerce society: "The evolution of e-commerce can be made into, roughly speaking, three stages. One is the electronic-brochure marketing phase. The second one is electronic transactions. The third one, . . . I'll call electronic decisions."[8]

By 2000, many businesses had progressed through the electronic-brochure marketing phase by creating a multitude of web pages. These electronic brochures advertised businesses' products and services over the Internet. As the number of Internet users increased exponentially, the outreach of this type of marketing exceeded all expectations. The second phase emerged as businesses and consumers began to buy and sell over the Internet at an unprecedented pace. In 1999, e-commerce accounted for $52.8 billion in sales for the computer and electronics industry, $14 billion in financial services exchanges, and $12.8 billion of the travel industry sales. Many experts predicted double-digit percentage increases in business-to-business e-commerce for these and other industries by 2003. Overall, companies exchanged $43 billion in business-to-business e-commerce transactions in 1999. Experts estimated that sales would rise to $1.3 trillion

[7] "Tech Torpor Overseas," *Business Week,* December 20, 1999, p. 10; Robert A. Guth, "Japanese Aim to Outspeed U.S. Internet," *Wall Street Journal,* August 31, 2000, p. A17; and Robert A. Guth, "Japan Goes All Out to Catch U.S. in High-Speed Internet Services," *Wall Street Journal,* November 27, 2000, p. B4.
[8] David P. Hamilton, "Inflection Point," *Wall Street Journal,* April 17, 2000, p. R48.

by 2003, accounting for nearly 10 percent of all business-to-business e-commerce sales.[9] E-commerce is a way of life, from large companies and smaller start-up businesses to individuals interested in shopping online.

> *In 2000, the big three U.S. automakers—General Motors, Ford Motor, and DaimlerChrysler—announced a massive dot-com automotive parts exchange program run through the Internet. This combined effort replaced earlier independent efforts launched by each of the automobile manufacturers and was estimated to generate $240 billion in annual purchasing volume with an additional $250 billion from auto suppliers.*
>
> *E-commerce was not reserved for the world's largest companies. Before Michael Furdyk completed the eleventh grade at a Toronto high school he had sold his website for more than $1 million. This sale provided Michael with the venture capital needed to launch Buy-Buddy.com, a web comparison-shopping service. The high school student leased a spacious office suite and supervised 20 employees—including his father, who quit his executive position at NCR Corporation to work for his son. Michael was also in demand as a Microsoft Corporation e-commerce consultant while pursuing his high school diploma.[10]*

The explosion of the Internet led to dramatic changes in how companies conducted business. Long-established companies, such as the 110-year-old Provident American Life & Health Insurance Company in the United States and Japan's 103-year-old Yoneda Silk Parasol, abandoned their brick-and-mortal operations and remade themselves into web-based e-commerce entities. Struggling companies saw e-commerce as a chance to start anew or to beat their rivals. E-commerce offered businesses a way to raise new capital and dramatically reduce their costly overhead.

However, most successful e-businesses kept their feet in both worlds. Internet operations were used to increase customer traffic in their traditional physical stores or to give a boost to a tired product. Sears, Roebuck & Company found that people who bought tools through its Internet site spent up to 27 percent more in its retail stores.

What kinds of businesses moved most quickly into the new economy? Traditional middlemen operations, such as travel and insurance agencies, were attracted to e-commerce because of the ability to exchange information quickly and cheaply over the Internet. Other businesses found the Internet a useful marketplace for discounted or seasonal items, too expensive to sell in a brick-and-mortar store. Specialty items, such as hard-to-find or rare products like used books and collectibles, found their home on the Internet, able to reach millions of potential customers inexpensively and quickly.

---

[9] Robert D. Hof, "A New Era of Bright Hopes and Terrible Fears," *Business Week,* October 4, 1999, pp. 84–98.

[10] Robert L. Simison, Fara Warner, and Gregory L. White, "Big Three Car Makers Plan Net Exchange," *Wall Street Journal,* February 28, 2000, pp. A3, A16; and Rochelle Sharpe, "Teen Moguls," *Business Week,* May 29, 2000, pp. 108–18. Cameron Johnson, Brad Ogden, Paul Dinin, Angelo Sotira, and Rishi Bhat also were high school students who found financial success via e-business ventures and were featured in the May 29, 2000, *Business Week* article.

Some of America's biggest companies resisted moving into e-commerce. They struggled with the changes affecting their salespeople and distributors, many of whom would be circumvented by Internet sales.

> *Hewlett-Packard's medical product unit had an army of 500 sales representatives and dozens of distributors. In 1998, they accounted for more than $1 billion in sales for the company. Hewlett-Packard had prided itself on its reputation of being a people-centered business, conducting business through face-to-face meetings, product demonstrations, and a handshake. These solid customer relations were an integral part of the company and resulted in substantial sale revenues.*
>
> *Managers at Hewlett-Packard decided that e-commerce could not be ignored. They developed an Internet site that enabled their major buyers to place orders over the Internet. Online prices were aligned with prices available through other sales channels, contrary to deep discounts offered by some firms over the Internet. Online orders generated sales commissions for the Hewlett-Packard sales representatives who usually handled those accounts.*[11]

Among its many other marvels, the Internet also revolutionized global financial markets. Using the Internet, investors sharply lowered the cost of saving and borrowing money. It expanded the attractiveness of investing additional capital as more and more people gained access to the financial markets. "The Internet hastens the speed of financial flows and the pace at which the world is getting smaller," explained Jeff Bahrenburg, Merrill Lynch's global investment strategist.

Amazing transformations occurred, as finance became an electronic, Internet world. Markets became more liquid and efficient through the Internet. Movement toward 24-hour investing occurred, as markets remained open all the time. With expanded investment opportunities came worldwide economic growth. More efficient capital markets led to technological innovation and economic expansion, as discussed earlier in this chapter. Customers became increasingly knowledgeable about finance and migrated toward the Internet for a variety of transactions, from mortgages to retirement investments. Online programs provided investors with expert advice and money management guidance. By 2000, 3 million U.S. households had online investing accounts, with $374 million in assets. These numbers were predicted to rise to 9.7 million households and $3 trillion in investments by 2003.[12]

People supported the new electronic economy through their purchase of various consumer products and services. Numerous consumer niches arose online, and consumers were quick to take advantage of these new e-commerce opportunities.

> *Consumers were very interested in searching for and purchasing airline travel tickets online, spending $5 billion in 1999, nearly 7 percent of the*

---

[11] George Anders, "Some Big Companies Long to Embrace Web but Settle for Flirtation," *Wall Street Journal,* November 4, 1998, pp. A1, A14.

[12] Christopher Farrell, "All the World's an Auction Now," *Business Week,* October 4, 1999, pp. 120–28.

industry sales. Numerous sources were available. Expedia.com, Travelocity.com, and Priceline.com were the most used online sites for airline tickets. Yet the major airline carriers exhibited resistance toward entering the world of e-commerce. By mid-1999, the industry's attitude changed regarding e-commerce. Continental Airlines joined with Priceline.com and United Airlines partnered with Buy.com to enable consumers to purchase tickets from the airline carriers. United Airlines reported that in 1999 only 3 percent of its tickets were purchased online but estimated that to increase to 20 percent by 2003. An executive at an Internet research firm commented, "The airlines are not going to reach as many people by sitting back at home and letting people knock on their door. They need to push the inventory out to where the customer wants it."[13]

Other marketing opportunities arose for consumers who were technologically savvy. Whirlpool offered an Internet-ready refrigerator in 2000. Customers could download a recipe from the Internet through a touch screen or order food online from a grocer. Benton Harbor, a Michigan appliance maker, marketed a web-linked oven in Europe, and Merloni Elettrodomestici of Italy introduced an Internet-connected washing machine, providing remote control operation.

Car buying quickly entered the world of e-commerce, as consumers looked for the exact model, price, and special features through the Internet. This Internet service expanded to include signing up owners for personalized web pages and offering financing and insurance online to those purchasing automobiles.

The owner of an Acura dealership in Kansas City, Kansas, puts a picture of the newly purchased automobile with the new owner on the company's website and then e-mails the picture to the new owner. "Hopefully, they are at work and they show their friends." He also sent new owners invitations to barbecues and let them know about service specials. He saw e-commerce as a win-win relationship with his customers.[14]

Businesses' Technological Innovations

Companies welcomed the technologically based e-commerce world by developing innovations that resulted in cost savings, time efficiency, and other advantages in conducting business.

Ford Motor Company created a corporatewide web-portal system to increase the company's ability to reach out to its employees in their homes and save money too. Ford offered to purchase for its employees and install in their homes Hewlett-Packard computers and printers and Internet access through MCI/WorldCom for $5 a month. All 350,000 employees, managers and factory workers alike, were included in this program.[15]

---

[13] Erik Siemers and Edward Harris, "Airlines Begin to Click with Internet-Booking Services," *Wall Street Journal,* August 2, 1999, p. B4.

[14] Fara Warner, "Car Race in Cyberspace," *Wall Street Journal,* February 18, 1999, pp. B1, B12.

[15] Fara Warner, "Ford Planning Corporate Web Portal to Wire All Employees in Their Homes," *Wall Street Journal,* February 4, 2000, p. B4.

A survey conducted by Delphi Group in 2000 found that 55 percent of businesses were actively working on creating company portals for their employees and another 25 percent were planning to launch this type of program within the next two years. Businesses realized that linking employees throughout the organization could lead to better communication flow while cutting the costs.

Technology Superpowers

At the core of high-technology industry are the builders of the information technology system. While the designers of web pages may receive much of the press, the high-technology industry is grounded in the work done by companies that dig the trenches to lay the pipe that contain the fiber-optic cable. In *Business Week*'s Info Tech 100, the top 20 firms included 6 that provide networking and telecommunications to link companies and consumers through the Internet. Other firms on the list included three telecommunication carriers that send information around the world and three that build high-powered servers that keep the Internet running at optimum speed and efficiency. "There are the glamour companies, and then there are the companies that are building the new Net economy," reported Edward J. Zander, president of Sun Microsystems, a maker of computer networks. "We're the lumberyard for the Internet."[16]

By the late 1990s, a small but powerful group of technology superpowers controlled many of the entrance ramps to the Internet. The merger of America Online and Time Warner, described in the discussion case in Chapter 9, created one such company. Then there was Microsoft, with 27.5 million users of its Internet services. Microsoft's effort to ride the "Internet tidal wave"—to use Bill Gates's expression—by bundling its Windows operating system with its browser is presented in a case at the end of the book. Other technology superpowers included Yahoo!, with 27.4 million users; Lycos, with 26.4 million; and Walt Disney Company/Infoseek, with 13.6 million. Exhibit 12-A describes the best-regarded companies according to a recent poll.

Emerging Global Participation

While much of the discussion thus far in this chapter has focused on technological innovation and technology superpowers in the United States, most industrialized countries are formally and aggressively pursuing a strategy to include technology in the lives of its citizens, as shown in Figure 12-2. Global participation in technology is on the rise, as illustrated in the following examples.

> *As Japan entered the twenty-first century, it began its greatest economic and social upheaval since 1868. Massive financial and human resources were amassed to compete with the technological successes shown by the United States. Japan's Softbank, led by its founder Masayoshi Son, allocated $400 million to support new start-up ventures in Japan. In a few years that investment was valued at $50 billion. Yasumitsu Shigeta, founder of a mobile phone retailer, turned Internet investor with $300 million in venture capital, with plans for investing an additional $500*

---

[16] Steve Hamm, Andy Reinhardt, and Peter Burrows, "Builders of the New Economy," *Business Week,* June 21, 1999, pp. 118–22.

EXHIBIT
12-A

Best-Regarded, Digital-Technology Companies

When consumers are asked what companies they most respect in the emerging digital-technology world, their answer may be surprising: ones with tangible products and services.

In a Harris Interactive Inc. and Reputation Institute poll, published in the *Wall Street Journal,* the businesses that received the highest corporate reputation ratings from online consumers were Microsoft, Intel, Sony, Dell Computer, and Lucent Technologies. The only Internet company to crack the top 20 was Yahoo!, at number 18. Microsoft's high ranking was achieved *after* the antitrust case had brought the company substantial negative publicity.

"In the digital survey, reputation was strongly influenced by how well companies support you when something goes wrong with their products and services," explained Joy Sever, senior vice president at Harris Interactive. "Innovation, good service, and product quality are all key to this industry's reputation." The survey included six key factors in reaching the reputation index score: products and services, workplace environment, financial performance, emotional appeal, social responsibility, and vision and leadership.

Source: Ronald Alsop, "The Best Reputations in High Tech," *Wall Street Journal,* November 18, 1999, pp. B1, B6.

million. Numerous other venture capital efforts launched two Japanese Internet incubators, Neoteny and Netage.[17]

Similar potential for technological growth was seen in China. "China probably represents the largest wireless market worldwide," said Lucent Technologies Asian vice president Scott Erickson. This wireless market was attractive to many non-Chinese investors since 43 million Chinese had cellular telephones but few were connected to the Internet. Motorola was the first company to develop a completely Chinese-made, handheld combination mobile phone, computer, and wireless Internet device. In 2000, 60 percent of the 45 million Koreans had mobile phones, but less than half were connected to the Internet. With billions of dollars of direct foreign investment in high-tech companies, Korea was on the verge of entering the global digital community.

Brazil provided an interesting global test case for technological development over the question of free or fee Internet access. Brazil's Universo Online (UOL) and Terra Networks, part of a Spanish telecommunications company, offered free Internet access to all interested Brazilians. This strategy directly conflicted with America Online Latin America's approach of offering Internet subscription service for a fee. AOL Latin America

[17] Irene Kunii, "The Web Spinners," *Business Week,* March 13, 2000, pp. 81–88.

Figure 12-2

Technology is everywhere.

Source: Data taken from *Computer Industry Almanac,* reported in "The Global Battle: Innovation and Technology," *Wall Street Journal,* September 26, 2000, p. R6.

Computers (in millions)

Region	1993	2005 (estimate)
North America	77	230
European Union	44	250
Asia-Pacific	25	257
Latin America	3	44
Worldwide	149	781

	Percent of Phone Lines Linked to Digital Exchanges in 1999	Cell Phone Subscribers in 1990 (in millions)	Cell Phone Subscribers in 1999 (in millions)
United States	89%	5.3	86.0
Finland	100	0.2	3.4
Germany	100	0.3	23.5
France	98	0.3	21.4
China	100	>0.1	43.2
India	99	>0.1	1.2
Japan	100	0.9	56.8

reported having 65,000 subscribers before the free Internet option was offered, accounting for less than 3 percent of all Brazilians. Shortly after the competition began, Brazil's UOL added 800,000 participants of the 1 million new subscribers to Internet service. The long-term viability of offering free Internet service by relying primarily on advertisement revenues remained to be seen.

European businesses entered the telecommunications field in a big way in 2000. While the use of cellular telephones was higher in Europe than the United States, Internet use lagged significantly behind. This changed as Europeans discovered the speed of the Internet and the vast opportunities afforded by this technology. Companies, such as KLM Airlines and BP-Amoco, changed their business practices and began to link with suppliers and customers via the Internet. E-business transactions in Europe were expected to jump from $15 billion in 1999 to $178 billion by 2001.[18]

Developed and developing countries in Asia, South America, and Europe joined North America in efforts to increase access to technology for businesses and individuals.

[18] Stephen Baker and William Echikson, "Europe's Internet Bash," *Business Week E.Biz,* February 7, 2000, pp. EB40–44.

A globally connected world emerged that changed how businesses operate, how people communicate, and the quality of our lives.

Technology in Our Daily Lives

People around the world are acquiring access to more technological innovations than ever before. Although some argue that the increased access is available to only some people (as discussed in the special issue section on the digital divide later in this chapter), residents of developing countries increasingly enjoy energy-powered appliances, entertainment devices, and communications equipment. Individuals and businesses in developed countries in North America, Europe, and portions of Asia are depending more than ever on electronic communication devices, thus increasing access to information needed for decision making and conducting business transactions. New technologies also are an important part of individuals' work. By 1999, four out of five managers used desktop computers in the United States, with fax machines, answering machines, voice mail, and cellular telephones used by more than half of all American managers.

Individuals and businesses are going online, that is using the Internet. Certainly one of the most visible and widely used technological innovations of recent years has been the Internet, or the World Wide Web. The **Internet** is a global electronic communications network linking individuals and organizations. It enables its users to send and receive electronic mail (e-mail) and access information from virtually any library. Springing to life in 1994, this conduit of information revolutionized how business was conducted, students learned, and households operated.

Nearly 375 million people around the world were wired into the Internet by 2000, with new websites increasing at a rate of 10,000 per day. The Computer Industry Alliance predicted that by 2005, 10 percent of the world's population, or 600 million people, will have Internet access. Predictions of accelerated Internet use were fueled by continued innovations like WebTV networks, new devices that enabled users Internet access via their television sets, and technology that allows people to connect to the Internet via mobile cellular telephones and portable personal data assistant devices. By 2000, nearly 9 million Japanese and Europeans exchanged e-mail and surfed the Internet from their mobile telephones. The global market for mobile digital devices—cellular telephones and pocket computers—rocketed past the demand for personal computers by 2000 and was predicted to top 1 billion users worldwide by 2003.[19]

Europe and Asia fully embraced the cell phone craze. **M-commerce,** *commerce conducted via mobile or cell telephones, provided consumers with an electronic wallet when using their cellular telephone. People traded stocks or made consumer purchases of everything from hot dogs to*

---

[19] For additional information regarding the pervasive use of technology at home and work, see Steve Hamm, Andy Reinhardt, and Peter Burrows, "Builders of the New Economy," *Business Week,* June 21, 1999, pp. 119–22; "A Wide Net," *Wall Street Journal,* December 6, 1999, p. R6; Keith H. Hammonds, "Americans Are Getting Hooked on the Home PC," *Business Week,* March 23, 1998, p. 32; and Amanda Mujica, Edward Petry, and Dianne Vickery, "A Future for Technology and Ethics," *Business and Society Review,* 1999, pp. 279–90.

Figure 12-3

Significant developments and predictions in the evolution of the computer.

Source: See William M. Bulkeley, "The Course of Change," *Wall Street Journal,* November 16, 1998, p. R4, for his sources in compiling a table adapted for this figure.

1977	Apple II is introduced to consumers.
1981	IBM PC is introduced to consumers.
1984	Apple Macintosh introduces consumers to the mouse and graphical user interface.
1994	Commercial users go online, and the World Wide Web is born.
2001	Satellite network revolutionizes high-speed data communications around the world.
2003	Voice recognition is incorporated into hand-held personal computer technology.
2005	Access to the Internet is available to all in developed countries.
2007	Internet sales account for all business-to-business transactions and 25 percent of all retail sales.
2007	Top-ranked universities offer degrees online, driving 33 percent of all colleges out of business.
2008	Telephones provide translations, making cross-language communication easier.
2008	Electronic cash arrives, making hand-held currency obsolete.
2010	Supercomputers perform as many calculations (20 million billion per second) as the human brain.

washing machines and countless other products. France Telecom marketed a cell phone with a built-in credit-card slot for easy wireless payments. "M-commerce is the next wave of growth," said Ron Sommer, chief executive officer of Deutsche Telekom AG. Sommer's German telephone company had 14.4 million wireless subscribes by August 2000, with the untapped U.S. market targeted for 2002.[20]

People also were more dependent on their computers, with a computer in nearly half of all U.S. households by 2000. Whether a desktop, laptop, or networked to a mainframe, computers provided educational and entertainment opportunities for children, personal financial management advice, and access to the Internet from home, work, or while traveling. Major developments in the evolution of the computer are identified in Figure 12-3.

New technological devices for faster and easier communication are being developed at an increasingly rapid pace. A March 2000 *Business Week* article, "Welcome to 2010," described a number of cutting-edge innovations envisioned by technologists. For example, there was the "ear ring," a lightweight, ear-mounted telephone equipped with a single "follow you anywhere" phone number and connected to the Internet via a personal data assistant. The "e-quill" was described as a writing device that could capture handwritten messages and send them to a personal data assistant or some other graphic display. Technologists predicted that thumbprints would replace credit-card numbers, identification numbers, and a stream of forgettable passwords by 2010, making conducting business on the Internet easier and faster.

The technological invasion also targeted the schools. Spending on technology in U.S. public schools, grades kindergarten through 12, doubled in six years in the 1990s. Fees levied on business telephone service bills directed $2.25 billion over five years to subsidize access to the Internet for schools and libraries in the United States. When

---

[20] Gautam Naik and Almar Latour, "M-Commerce: Mobile and Multiplying," *Wall Street Journal,* August 18, 2000, pp. B1, B4.

children in America entered their classrooms for the 2000 school year, 90 percent of them entered buildings with at least one connection to the Internet, compared to 35 percent in 1994. More than half of all classrooms had Internet connections.

Technology democratized education by enabling some students in the poorest and most remote communities to access the world's best libraries, instructors, and courses available through the Internet. A digital learning environment provided students with skills to rapidly discover and assess information needed to solve complex problems.[21]

The new technological revolution in education for the 2000s was online education. A spokesperson for International Data Corporation predicted that the number of students taking undergraduate and graduate courses online would increase from 710,000 in 1999 to 2.23 million by 2002. This would account for 15 percent of all higher-education students. Educational institutions, such as Oxford University in the United Kingdom and LifeLongLearning and the University of Phoenix in the United States, pioneered online learning.[22] Businesses have sprung up to profit from this trend, such as BigChalk.com, Unext.com, and Xanedu.com. Online education is a major business opportunity, as well as enabling nontraditional students access to educational opportunities previously unavailable since they were unable to attend traditional, daytime courses offered on campus.

Seemingly everywhere we turn—whether in our homes or in school or in the workplace—the technology invasion is all around us, and its influences and opportunities seem inescapable.

Medical Information via the Internet

The explosion of medical information on the Internet has dramatically affected people's lives. How people are examined, diagnosed, and treated; how health-related information is collected and stored; and the time and costs associated with health care have all been changed by technological innovations within the past decade.

> *On February 25, 1999, drugstore.com opened its virtual doors on the Internet and began to fill orders for nearly 19,000 medical-related items and drug prescriptions. From toothpaste to Valium, individuals could electronically acquire what they needed to feel better, minimize illness, or generally improve their quality of life. Other medical-oriented Internet companies also began at this time. PlanetRx, Soma.com, and Rx.com launched their enterprises to try to crack the $155 billion industry dominated by a few drugstore chains—Walgreens, Rite Aid, and Drug Emporium. But even these mega-drugstores had their own websites by 2000. The trip to the local drugstore was now only a click away on the computer.[23]*

---

[21] William C. Symonds, "Wired Schools," *Business Week,* September 25, 2000, pp. 116–28.

[22] See Joseph Weber, "School Is Never Out," *Business Week,* October 4, 1999, pp. 164–68; and Robert Cwiklik, "Online Courses Reach Students beyond a University's Walls," *Wall Street Journal,* October 29, 1998, p. B9.

[23] Janet Rae-Dupree, "A Real Shot in the Arm for a Virtual Pharmacy," *Business Week,* March 8, 1999, p. 40.

Besides access to pharmaceuticals and health items, the Internet also provided medical information. An estimated 52 million Americans used the Internet to gain knowledge about diseases and treatment, investigate how to participate in clinical studies, and find low-fat recipes. This type of Internet surfing among Americans was more common than looking for sports scores, stock quotes, or online shopping.[24]

In cyberspace the doctor is always in. Individuals can search for an insomnia treatment at 3:00 in the morning and ask as many questions as they want. They can even search for information anonymously, maintaining privacy, no matter how embarrassing their questions. While the Internet provides a wealth of medical information, the quality or reliability of this information can sometimes be suspect. Some protections to aid individuals using the Internet for medical information came into existence. For example, two medical search engines were created to screen medical information for accuracy and timeliness: Medical World Search (www.mwsearch.com) and Mental Health Net (www.cmhc. com). In addition, the Health on the Net Foundation (www.hon.ch), a nonprofit organization based in Geneva, Switzerland, offered a seal of approval for medical Internet sites. To earn this approval, a website had to follow the organization's guidelines, which included the prominent identification of the web sponsor and keeping information up-to-date.[25]

Special Issue: The Digital Divide

Some people were concerned that the phenomenal development and use of technology was greater in developed than developing countries or among some segments of the population than others in developed countries. This gap between those who have technology and those who do not was called the **digital divide.** While some debated the severity of the phenomenon, most agreed that it existed.

There were alarming statistics proving that the digital divide existed in America. In 1999, about 28 percent of Caucasian households had Internet access, compared to 9 percent of Black and Hispanic households. A year later it was reported that Internet access differed significantly according to household income—only 10 percent of low-income households had Internet access, compared to 75 percent of all households with incomes over $75,000. Education was also a factor—about 17 percent of high school graduates had Internet access, whereas nearly half of all individuals with a college degree or more were connected to the Internet.[26]

In May 2000, researchers at BellSouth and Emory University reported that although "often the digital-divide issue is framed as urban versus rural . . . our study suggests that education and age are more important." In a study of Oregon senior centers, 70 percent of the centers were found to lack Internet access and less than half of the centers even had computers for the senior citizens to use. Oregon senator Ron Wyden said, "We've got a long way to go to make sure that vulnerable elderly folks are in a position to get

---

[24] "Web Users Search for Medical Advice Most Often," *Wall Street Journal,* November 27, 2000, p. B14.
[25] Rebecca Quick, "CybeRx: Getting Medical Advice and Moral Support on the Web," *Wall Street Journal,* April 30, 1998, p. B10.
[26] See Marcia Stepanek, "A Small Town Reveals America's Digital Divide," *Business Week,* October 4, 1999, pp. 188–98; and the Digital Divide Network at www.digitaldividenetwork.org.

access to information that can improve the quality and affordability of health care—and in many instances provide the absolutely key link to the community."[27]

It appears that the digital divide did exist within the United States, influenced by race, income, education, and age. Further investigations revealed that the digital divide was not restricted to the United States. For example, Central and Eastern European countries experienced the digital divide primarily due to their lack of an Internet infrastructure. Since most people and nongovernmental organizations were dependent on telephone dial-up connections to the Internet, access to information was slow and often disrupted by telephone line breakdowns. In addition, Internet use was charged on a per-minute rate per local telephone call, too expensive for most individuals or smaller businesses in these countries. A global digital divide was recognized in the late 1990s at a United Nations conference.

> *We are profoundly concerned at the deepening maldistribution of access, resources, and opportunities in the information and communication field. The information and technology gap and related inequities between industrialized and developing nations are widening: a new type of poverty— information poverty—looms.*[28]

As stated at the beginning of this section, most people would not argue that the digital divide did not exist; yet many saw the divide or gap narrowing. In a study conducted by the Forrester Research Group, researchers found that the number of African-American households online grew in 2000. Thirty-three percent were now online, compared to 43 percent of white households. Ekaterina Walsh, author of the study, explained, "Now it's getting easier and it costs much less to be online . . . and that's why we are seeing a surge in online penetration across all ethnic groups, including those that are less wealthy."[29]

> *PowerUp, a nonprofit organization supported by many businesses and community development organizations, was launched in 1999. Led by Steve Case, then chairman and CEO of America Online, along with a $10 million contribution from the Case Foundation, established by Case and his wife, Jean, PowerUp was committed to use technology to help children develop character and competence while addressing the critical digital divide that existed in the United States. The AOL Foundation donated 100,000 AOL accounts and support resources to develop PowerUp Online, a portal that linked inner-city youths to a number of children's websites. AmeriCorps, a U.S. government-sponsored program that recruits volunteers to work in impoverished areas, provided more than 400 young people to oversee the PowerUp program in schools, boys and girls clubs, and inner-city community centers.*[30]

---

[27] Jan Kornblum, "Digital Divide Leaves Country and City Behind," www.digitaldividenetwork.org.

[28] United Nations' Statement on Universal Access to Basic Communication and Information Services, www.itu.int/acc/rtc/acc-rep.htm.

[29] John Cochran, "The Digital Divide Narrows," ABCNews.com, www.abcnews.go.com.

[30] Margaret Johnston, "Tech Companies Team to Shrink Digital Divide," e-Business World @ IDG.net, November 8, 1999, www.idg.net.

In addition, many companies recognized the digital divide as a business opportunity and launched new programs not only to narrow the gap between those who had technology access and those who did not, but also to capitalize on an emerging consumer base and market. Hewlett-Packard announced its "World e-Inclusion" program through which the firm expected to sell, lease, or donate $1 billion in Hewlett-Packard products and services in developing countries in 2001. Rob Glaser, chairman and CEO of Real-Networks, created the RealNetworks Foundation through which the company provided 5 percent of each quarter's profits to foster the "progressive social impact of digital technologies." Numerous other business commitments were announced and opportunities were discussed at a conference held in October 2000 attended by many of the top executives of the world's leading technology firms. The central question posed at this conference was: Is the global digital divide a problem or business opportunity?[31]

It is clear that high-technology businesses, along with governments and community groups, must address the evidence that the digital divide does exist so that access to technology becomes more easily available to all people regardless of their race, income, education, age, or residence.

The unmistakable economic and social force of technology is evident in every part of the world, in every industry, and in every aspect of our lives. The technologically driven information age has changed how businesses operate and the quality of our lives, regardless of where we live or what we do. These profound changes give rise to important, and possibly perplexing, questions about whether technology should be controlled or who should manage technology and its growth. These issues are discussed in the following chapter.

Summary Points of This Chapter

- Technological change, which tends to be self-reinforcing, has widespread effects throughout business and society. Some of these effects are beneficial, and some are not. Technological growth is fueled by economic expansion, worker productivity, and research and development investment.
- E-commerce, or online business, has changed how businesses offer, sell, and account for their goods and services and interactions with their stakeholders. Individuals are investing and buying goods and services online at an astonishing rate.
- Technology superpowers have built an infrastructure for the information society, enabling people and businesses around the world to communicate and conduct business with each other, spawning the system of e-commerce.
- Businesses from developing countries are quickly becoming active participants in the telecommunications revolution, spurred by government support and direct foreign investments.

---

[31] For a thorough presentation of the conference discussions see "A New Business Frontier," *Business Week,* December 18, 2000, special advertising section.

- The current phase of technology—the information society—has changed our lifestyle, education, and health by providing more information with easier access at a quicker pace.
- Differences in education, income, and age appear to contribute most to creating a digital divide. With improved technology infrastructure in developing countries and business ventures addressing Internet access, it appears that the digital divide is narrowing.

Key Terms and Concepts Used in This Chapter

- Technology
- Telecommunications
- Information society
- Cyberspace

- E-commerce
- Internet
- M-commerce
- Digital divide

Internet Resources

- www.sirc.org
- www.allec.com
- www.ecrc.ctc.com
- www.digitaldividenetwork.org

Social Issues Research Center
All E-Commerce
Electronic Commerce Resource Center
Digital Divide Network

Discussion Case: *Ethical Principles for E-Commerce*

E-commerce clearly has had, and will continue to have, a major impact on global business. Technology is changing the way individuals conduct business. There are benefits, such as the convenience of shopping at home via the Internet, but there are also aspects of e-commerce that have less desirable consequences: the reduction of individual privacy and the decrease of trust in the business environment.

A noted scholar in the information technology field argued that two forces threaten an individual's privacy: the enhanced capabilities of information technology to gather, store, combine, and disseminate information, and the increasing value of information. In addition, e-commerce reduces the sensory exposure to the product and the salesperson and fewer attributes are verifiable, thus the level of trust is lessened. For two partners to reach an agreement that each will fulfill, there must be a level of transaction trust.

Managers encountering these and other issues in e-commerce are further confounded by the lack of ethical principles to guide their decisions and behavior. In 2000, a group of scholars proposed the following set of principles as a framework for the discussion and development of ethical guidelines for e-commerce. Their ultimate goal was the creation of a list of principles that could be adopted by organizations.

Ethical Principles for E-Commerce

Organizations of all sizes and industry membership are encouraged to adopt and practice these principles in their e-commerce operations. As an organization endorsing Ethical Principles for E-commerce, we are committed to:

1. Publicly announcing our support of these principles in organizational publications, particularly our annual report (if a publicly traded firm), and through the Internet.
2. Developing and implementing organizational policies and procedures to ensure compliance with Ethical Principles for E-commerce.
3. Provide training for our employees to ensure that they adhere to the organizational policies and procedures created to ensure compliance with Ethical Principles for E-commerce. In addition, we are committed to providing continuing support, such as help lines, to assist our employees to act in compliance with the organization's policies and procedures.
4. Taking all appropriate disciplinary action against any employee discovered to have violated organizational policies or procedures created in the spirit of Ethical Principles for E-commerce.
5. Consistently abide by clearly stated record-keeping procedures and database controls, as well as make available these data to parties with legitimate claims to the information.
6. Create an internal audit system to ensure that we maintain organizational compliance with our procedures and controls and to detect any breaches of these systems within our organization.
7. Report, on an annual basis, a statement of our e-commerce operations, with respect to the ethical issues described in Ethical Principles for E-commerce, as well as our efforts to create organizational compliance mechanisms to foster an ethical climate in the emarketplace.
8. Be open to an annual audit by a certified audit specialist, such as Account-Ability, an organization committed to assist organizations with the goal of socially and ethically responsible management.

Source: Based on A. Graham Peace, James Weber, Kathleen Hartzel, and Jennifer Nightingale, "Ethical Issues in eBusiness: A Proposal for Creating the eBusiness Principles," working paper, Duquesne University, 2000.

In proposing these principles, the scholars noted, "The pace of change in the technology field is astounding. We believe that the adoption of Ethical Principles for E-commerce will significantly minimize the potential for these society-threatening ethical breaches. Technology, e-commerce and the lucrative world of the e-marketplace are seductive and the benefits appear to be unlimited. However, ethical care must be taken to ensure that the convenience and economic gains for e-commerce are not outweighed by the ethical problems that they might create."

Discussion Questions

1. As an employee, consumer, or member of society, do you believe businesses engaged in e-commerce should adopt these ethical principles of e-commerce? Why or why not?

2. As an owner or manager of a business engaged in e-commerce, would you adopt these ethical principles? Why or why not?

3. Is compliance to these principles enforceable by government? An industry group? An independent organization, such as AccountAbility?

13

Managing Technological Challenges

Technology fosters change and more change. Technological change has raised ethical and social questions of privacy, security, ownership, and health and safety. What are the implications of this fast-paced change on our society and those who live in it? Moreover, who is responsible for determining how much technological change should occur or how fast things should change? Should technology be controlled, and if so, who should be in charge of managing technology and the challenges it poses for humans and cultures in our global community? Bill Joy, Sun Microsystems' chief scientist, warned of the dangers of rapid advances in technology:

> The experiences of the atomic scientists clearly show the need to take personal responsibility, the danger that things will move too fast, and the way in which a process can take on a life of its own. We can, as they did, create insurmountable problems in almost no time flat. We must do more thinking up front if we are not to be similarly surprised and shocked by the consequences of our inventions.[1]

[1] Bill Joy, "Why the Future Doesn't Need Us," *Wired*, April 2000, www.wired.com/wired/archive/8.04/joy.

This chapter focuses on these key questions and objectives:

- What initiatives have businesses voluntarily taken to protect the privacy of their stakeholders?
- How secure is information in a free access, information society?
- Should businesses manage technological change, and if so, how?
- Is businesses' control of intellectual property threatened in an information society?
- What ethical and social challenges arise due to technological breakthroughs in science and medicine?

echnology is taking on a life of its own, as shown by the increasing number of uncontrolled situations involving the use of information on the Internet.

A hacker accessed the records of more than 5,000 patients at the University of Washington's Medical Center in 1999. The hacker, identified only as a 25-year-old Dutch man named Kane, reportedly broke into the database to publicize the vulnerability of medical data rather than to use it maliciously. The databases were used for patient follow-up for research and quality-assessment purposes. While detailed patient records were stored in separate systems, the records assessed by the hacker included the patients' names, Social Security numbers, and medical conditions. Edwin Gould, a 65-year-old retired Seattle engineer and heart patient whose name was in the database, found the incident troubling. Given the university's large computer-sciences program, "I would think they'd be a little more sophisticated than that," said Gould.

A different challenge in controlling information arose in 2000, when a press release apparently generated by Emulex Corporation, a California maker of fiber-channel adapters, caused the company's stock price to plummet. The press release warned Internet investors of an earnings restatement, an executive resignation, and an investigation of the firm by the Securities and Exchange Commission. None of these reports were true. The reports were bogus, posted by Mark Jacob, a 23-year-old man who liked to "play the market" and had recently suffered significant financial losses. Nonetheless, the message took on a life of its own and caused widespread fear and panic selling of the company's stock. By the time the hoax had been discovered and stock trading was halted, the stock plunged 60 percent and the company's market value dropped from $2.45 billion to $1.62 billion.[2]

It appears that the warnings voiced by Bill Joy are relevant today, as well as for the future. Businesses and individuals are mesmerized by the lure of technology, especially the Internet. How well guarded are important pieces of information, such as medical records? Should anyone be allowed to report anything about a firm on the Internet, even if the information is false? Who should set the limits on how technology is used and who should manage technology?

Although it may not be clear who is in the best position to set limits on how technology is used or who should manage it, there are numerous emerging challenges that technology poses for society. These include issues of privacy, security, ownership, and health and safety.

Businesses Protecting Privacy

The presence of technology and information at work is obvious. As shown in Figure 13-1, the average American worker sent or received over 200 messages a day in 1999. Nearly half of the people

---

[2] Ann Carrns, "Hacker's Break-In at University Hospital Heats Up Debate on Security Standards," *Wall Street Journal,* December 11, 2000, p. B4; and Terzah Ewing, Peter Waldman, and Matthew Rose, "Bogus Report Sends Emulex on a Wild Ride," *Wall Street Journal,* August 28, 2000, pp. C1, C6.

Figure 13-1

Workers keeping in touch.

Source: Adapted from Don Clark, "Managing the Mountain," *Wall Street Journal,* June 21, 1999, p. R4.

The daily number of messages sent and received daily by an average American office worker:

Telephone	51	Post-it messages	13
E-mail	37	Telephone message slips	9
Voice mail	22	Pager	8
Postal mail	19	Cell phone	5
Interoffice mail	18	Overnight couriers	3
Fax	14	Express mail	2

Total messages sent and received daily = 201

surveyed reported that they had difficulty with the work generated by this high volume of messages. The temptation for employees to use the Internet for nonwork-related activities also has become a crisis at many firms. Vault.com surveyed 1,244 employees and found that over 90 percent admitted to surfing nonwork-related websites while on the job. They characterized this phenomenon as "the millennium cigarette break." As discussed in Chapter 17, businesses' desire to monitor information accessed by their employees raises important privacy issues.

> Using software developed by Content Advisor, Inc., firms monitored or blocked employees' access to material categorized under topics such as dating, sports, and personal finance. Farm Bureau Insurance used the software to block pornographic sites on its company's computers. Farm Bureau was concerned that accessing pornographic websites would be construed as a "hostile work environment" and support claims of sexual harassment at work.

In response to employees' challenges that these practices were invasions of their privacy, many businesses developed a **privacy policy,** which explains what use of the company's technology is permissible and how the business will monitor employee activities. Columbia/HCA Healthcare issued an "electronic communication policy" to its employees warning them that it might be necessary for authorized personnel to access and monitor the contents of their computer's hard drive. The issue of employee monitoring is further explored in Chapter 17.

Issues of privacy also spilled over to the business-consumer relationship. In 1998, the Federal Trade Commission found that only 14 percent of all commercial websites operated by businesses informed consumers of how they used personal data and gave consumers a chance to withhold information. A year later, a majority of all websites offered consumers a choice regarding how their information would be used.[3] An example of an Internet site's privacy policy is shown in Exhibit 13-A.

Additional efforts by businesses to manage stakeholder privacy emerged in 2000 with the Platform for Privacy Preference Project (P3P). This program provided users with

---

[3] John Simons, "New Internet Privacy Law Appears Less Likely with Release of New Survey," *Wall Street Journal,* May 13, 1999, p. B9.

EXHIBIT
13-A

Amazon.com Privacy Notice

Amazon.com knows that you care how information about you is used and shared, and we appreciate your trust that we will do so carefully and sensibly. This notice describes our privacy policy. By visiting Amazon.com, you are accepting the practices described in this Privacy Notice.

The information we learn from customers helps us personalize and continually improve your shopping experience at Amazon.com. Here are the types of information we gather.

What Personal Information about Customers Does Amazon.com Gather?

- Information You Give Us. . . . We use the information that you provide for such purposes as responding to your requests, customizing future shopping for you, improving our stores, and communicating with you.
- Automatic Information. . . . [L]ike many websites, we use "cookies," and we obtain certain types of information when your web browser accesses Amazon.com.
- Information from Other Sources. . . . [W]e sometimes receive updated delivery and address information from our shippers or other sources so we can correct our records and deliver your next purchase or communicate more easily.

Does Amazon.com Share the Information It Receives?

Information about our customers is an important part of our business, and we are not in the business of selling it to others. We share customer information only with the subsidiaries Amazon.com, Inc., controls and as described below.

- Affiliated Businesses We Do Not Control. . . . [A]n example of which is drugstore.com, our health and beauty merchant . . .
- Agents. . . . Examples include fulfilling orders, delivering packages, sending postal mail and e-mail, . . . and providing customer service. . . .
- Protection of Amazon.com and Others. We release account and other personal information when we believe release is appropriate to comply with law, . . . protect rights, property or safety of Amazon.com, our users, or others.
- With Your Consent. . . . [Y]ou will receive notice when information about you might go to third parties and you will have an opportunity to choose not to share the information.

The policy also covers questions involving "How Secure Is Information about Me?" "What Information Can I Access?" "What Choices Do I Have" and "Children."

Source: For a complete version of the policy see www.amazon.com/exec/obidos/subst/mics/policy/privacy.

software that enabled them to define which pieces of personal information they were willing to divulge on the Internet. The software also alerted the consumers if additional information was requested by businesses and what the businesses planned to do with the information. P3P was added to some Internet browsers at no additional cost or was available to be downloaded free off the Internet.[4] (Chapter 15 provides additional discussion of consumer Internet privacy.)

Industry and Government Efforts to Manage Privacy

In addition to the various responses undertaken by businesses to protect individuals' privacy, businesses banned together to support industry self-regulation to combat technological abuses that invaded one's privacy. In 1998, eight leading Internet companies, including America Online, Microsoft, and Netspace, joined TRUSTe, an industry organization, in announcing an online privacy awareness campaign. The companies pledged to set aside a portion of their websites for banner ads promoting Privacy Partnership, a program aimed at informing consumers about their online privacy rights. Two years later, 18 Internet health sites joined TRUSTe's efforts by creating Hi-Ethics, Inc., and developed privacy standards governing personal information submitted to health-related websites.[5] (Additional industry efforts are described in Chapter 15.)

Although companies appeared to be willing to address the issue of Internet privacy, some skeptics believed that there was a need for international supervision of the Internet. However, international management of technology would not be easy to achieve.

> U.S. and European officials took a positive step in the direction of international privacy protection in 2000. U.S. companies had been seeking a way to conduct business in Europe without risking lawsuits and prosecution for violating Europeans' privacy. The European Commission agreed that personal data could be collected and used by U.S. Internet companies only if the subject unambiguously had given consent, the data were needed to complete a contract (such as for billing), the data were required by law or needed to protect the company's vital interests, or the data were needed for law-enforcement purposes.[6]

Nevertheless, it will be difficult to achieve international government control of privacy, especially as it pertains to the Internet. The management of privacy may need to come from the Internet companies themselves. As stated in a *Business Week* article, "to develop into the world's largest marketplace, the Net must provide the same guarantees as any marketplace. . . . In short, before societies en masse start buying cars and taking out mortgages online, they'll need to ensure customers that their transactions are secure and legally binding."[7]

---

[4] Heather Green, "Privacy: Don't Ask Technology to Do the Job," *Business Week,* June 26, 2000, p. 52.

[5] Rebecca Quick, "Internet Giants Plan Campaign to Teach Consumers Their Online Privacy Rights," *Wall Street Journal,* October 7, 1998, p. B9; and "Health Web Sites Will Form Privacy, Accuracy Policies," *Wall Street Journal,* December 13, 2000, p. A4.

[6] Brandon Mitchener and David Wessel, "U.S. in Tentative Pact Protecting Europeans' Privacy," *Wall Street Journal,* February 20, 2000, p. B6.

[7] Stephen Baker, "Taming the Wild, Wild Web," *Business Week,* October 4, 1999, pp. 154–60.

The Management of Information Security

Businesses were acutely aware of the importance of maintaining information in a secure location and guarding this valuable resource. How best to manage information security was a major challenge for businesses.

> *The phrase "I love you" assumed an entirely new meaning on May 4, 2000, when it was the teaser for an e-mail message. As users opened the e-mail in Asia, Europe, and North America, the devastatingly destructive power of this e-mail message became clear. Before the day was over, Ford Motor, Microsoft, Estée Lauder, and the U.S. Army and Navy operations were shut down due to infected files caused by the e-mail. When a person opened the e-mail, messages were automatically sent to everyone in the victim's e-mail address book.*
>
> *Simultaneously, a virus began to delete artwork files and alter music files, making them inaccessible on the victim's hard drive. The virus also directed the victim's Internet-browser software to visit four websites in the Philippines where another malicious software was downloaded. That software searched for passwords on the hard drive and sent them to an Internet account in the Philippines. What the "I love you" virus demonstrated was the lack of control over the management of information stored on computers and the ease in which someone could access this information.*[8]

Other acts of sabotage were directed toward specific Internet companies. On February 7, 2000, Yahoo!, one of the world's most popular web portals, was shut down for three hours after an attack on its system. The attack was generated by more than 50 different Internet addresses and created such a demand in a short period of time that Yahoo! could not serve all the web pages that were requested. The next day, Buy.com and eBay were temporarily shut down. "We were hit with a coordinated denial-of-service attack that appears to be very similar to what happened to Yahoo!," explained Buy.com chief executive Gregory J. Hawkins.[9]

Computer security breaches took on many forms, as shown in Figure 13-2, and they are on the rise. In 1996, only 40 percent of managers reported having a breach in their information security, but more than 60 percent noted that they had this type of problem just two years later. The losses began to pile up with businesses reporting nearly $100 million in lost services and goods in 1997 and more than $120 million annually in 1998 and 1999.

The corporate nemesis is called a computer hacker. **Computer hackers** are individuals often with advanced technology training who, for thrill or profit, breach a business's information security system. The most popular route taken by hackers was the Internet, due to its free access and difficulty in tracing who initiated the attack. The business community's fear of being vulnerable to hackers increased when Scholastic, Inc.,

---

[8] Ted Bridis, "Virus Gives 'Love' a Bad Name," *Wall Street Journal,* May 5, 2000, pp. B1, B4.

[9] Khanh T. L. Tran, "Yahoo! Portal Is Shut Down by Web Attack," *Wall Street Journal,* February 8, 2000, p. B6; and Khanh T. L. Tran and Rhonda L. Rundle, "Hackers Attack Major Internet Sites, Temporarily Shutting Buy.com, eBay," *Wall Street Journal,* February 9, 2000, pp. A3, A10.

Figure 13-2

Types of security
breaches.

Source: Patrick
Casabona and Songmei
Yu, "Computer Fraud:
Financial and Ethical
Implications," *Review
of Business*, Fall 1998,
pp. 22–25.

> 44% Computer frauds involving theft of money
> 18% Illegal trespasses, theft of services
> 16% Damage to software
> 12% Alterations to data
> 10% Theft of information

released the results of its poll taken in 2000. It revealed that 48 percent of the elementary and middle school students surveyed did not consider hacking a crime.[10] Businesses hoped that the detection and prosecution of hackers would deter their behavior.

> *Calvin Cantrell pleaded guilty to the most extensive illegal breach of the nation's telecommunications infrastructure to date. Calvin and other hackers gained access to the network of telephone companies, including AT&T, GTE, MCI, and Sprint. They broke into credit-reporting databases belonging to Equifax and TRW. At various times, Calvin and his friends in crime—nicknamed the "Phonemasters" by the FBI—eavesdropped on telephone calls, compromised secure databases, and redirected communications at will. They had access to the nation's power grid, air traffic control systems, and unpublished telephone numbers at the White House. According to FBI estimates, this group of hackers accounted for about $2 million in business losses.*[11]

Businesses' Responses to Invasions of Information Security

As the number, severity, and ease of hacker attacks on businesses soared in the late 1990s, businesses began to see the necessity of investing more and more resources into protecting their information. Executives from every major Internet provider met with President Clinton in 2000 to brainstorm over Internet security. While suggested approaches varied, there was widespread agreement that actions were needed.

> *In 2000, PricewaterhouseCoopers launched a new subsidiary to provide storage for digital certificates for companies fearful of breaches of information security. Digital certificates are encrypted computer files that can serve as both identification cards and signatures online. The subsidiary, called beTrusted, relied on a 950-person network of computer security consultants already employed at PricewaterhouseCoopers. Other companies turned to intrusion-detection systems, or IDS, to beef up their information security. An IDS acts like a motion detector, monitoring a network or server for certain actions. Specific "attack signatures" can be detected,*

[10] See Cybercitizen Partnership website at www.cybercitizenpartners.org.
[11] John Simons, "How a Cyber Sleuth, Using a 'Data Tap,' Busted a Hacker Ring," *Wall Street Journal*, October 1, 1999, pp. A1, A6.

such as opening or changing names of critical files, downloading large amounts of data from key documents, or sending classified information out as e-mail attachments.

When a group of suspected hackers broke into a U.S.-based computer system in 2000, they thought they had successfully penetrated the security system guarding an important website. Rather, they had technologically walked into a *honeypot,* a system used by security professionals to lure hackers to a fabricated website and track their every move. For the next month, every keystroke made and cybermovement taken by the hackers was recorded. Lance Spitzner, creator of numerous honeypot traps, posted his findings of hacker activities on the Internet for the security community to see and learn from these discoveries.[12]

The Chief Information Officer

If the responsibility of managing technology with its many privacy and security issues fell to business organizations themselves, much of this responsibility was entrusted to the **chief information officer (CIO).** Many firms elevated the role of their data-processing managers by giving them the title of chief information officer. Additional business responsibilities accompanied this new title. The corporate CIO must successfully manage the increasing number of computers and software packages necessary for business as well as develop long-term information strategies. "It's the sharp edge of the business, a tool for revenue generation," explained William E. Kelvie, former CIO of Fannie Mae. "Every business needs an executive who can harness the latest technology to reach out to customers and suppliers with seamless, up-to-the-minute data communications."[13]

The benefits of having an innovative CIO were clear to most businesses. Peter Solvik, CIO at Cisco Systems, was credited with slashing $1.5 billion in costs by using Internet technologies for everything from human resources to manufacturing. At General Electric, CIO Gary Reiner was responsible for moving $5 billion in goods and services through the Internet, which helped improve the company's operating margins. Dawn Lepore, CIO at Charles Schwab, discovered that online trading cost only 20 percent as much as conventional trading and helped boost the firm's gross operating margin. The job of implementing these fundamental changes in business operations increasingly was entrusted to the company's CIO, whose duties now involved much more than keeping the computers properly functioning.

CIOs increasingly must see the big corporate picture. The CIO must set, align, and integrate an information technology vision with the company's overall business objectives. The CIO serves as the "coach" in guiding the information technology resources of the firm toward the long-term business goals.

[12] Keith Johnson, "Around the World, Hackers Get Stuck in 'Honeypots,' " *Wall Street Journal,* December 19, 2000, p. A18; and see Spitzner's website at project.honeynet.org.
[13] Andy Reinhardt, "From Gearhead to Grand High Pooh-Bah," *Business Week,* August 28, 2000, pp. 129–30.

Government Efforts to Protect Information Security

President Clinton created the Cyber-National Information Center (Cyber-NIC) in 2000, as a response to businesses' request for government assistance. The Cyber-NIC established a place where companies could work together to address cybersecurity problems and crises. In addition, a think tank comprised of individuals from the private and public sectors regularly met to consider cybersecurity issues. Among the companies involved were Microsoft, IBM, America Online, Yahoo!, Electronic Data Systems, Lucent Technologies, eBay, Nortel Networks, Iridium, and AT&T. The U.S. government also committed funding for computer-security research and college scholarships for students who agreed to work for the government as computer-security specialists. As President Clinton explained, "Today, our critical systems, from power structures to air-traffic control, are connected and run by computers. We must make those systems more secure so that Americans can be more secure."[14]

The Management of Adult-Oriented Information

Many believe that the Internet pornography industry is the most active and lucrative area of e-commerce. While most corporate home pages received thousands of hits per month, the top adult websites averaged more than 1 million viewers per day. One anonymous operator of an adult website believed that 80 to 90 percent of all e-commerce on the Internet was conducted at adult sites. A senior researcher for Forrester Research, a company that specialized in the entertainment business, estimated that adult websites grossed $700 million to $1 billion in 1999.[15]

The popularity of adult-oriented websites was seen when Victoria's Secret, a maker of women's lingerie, launched a fashion show on the Internet. The company reported that 1.5 million viewers logged on to see its merchandise. Or, consider that the hottest name on the Internet, based on the number of pages using a person's name, was Pamela Lee, former star of the television series *Baywatch*. Some calculated that Ms. Lee's name was cited on over 150,000 web pages, most trying to capitalize on her name recognition to sell products or services.

Some countries aggressively monitored and tried to control activities associated with these websites for objectionable adult-oriented materials. Yahoo! Japan, Japan's most popular website, had its Tokyo offices raided by police investigating the possible sale of illegal pornographic material on its auction site. This raid followed action taken against the parent company, U.S.-based Yahoo!, Inc., which was ordered by the French government to block French users from accessing Nazi memorabilia on its U.S. servers.[16]

Because of the right to free speech, the U.S. government has not banned access to adult-oriented material on the Internet. Yet, there were a few efforts seeking to control underage access to these sites. While many adult sites asked users to verify that they were of legal age, this "control" was easily circumvented.

---

[14] "Clinton Seeks Extra Funds to Fight Cyber-Terrorism," *Wall Street Journal,* January 10, 2000, p. B12.

[15] Leslie Miller and Bruce Schwartz, "SEX on the Internet," *USA Today,* January 29, 1999, p. 1A.

[16] Mylene Mangalindan and Kevin Delaney, "Yahoo! Ordered to Bar the French from Nazi Items," *Wall Street Journal,* November 21, 2000, pp. B1, B4; and "Police Raid Yahoo Japan Office in Pornography Probe," *Wall Street Journal,* November 28, 2000, p. A23.

In response to parents' interest in preventing their children from accessing adult-oriented sites, a number of new businesses emerged. For example, several major Internet companies launched a site called GetNetWise. It provided parents with information on adult-oriented websites, including reading material and downloadable software that could safeguard their children when they were online. Supported by America Online, AT&T, Walt Disney, Microsoft, Excite@Home, Lycos, and Yahoo!, GetNetWise was organized into four sections: online safety guide, special browsers and other tools for families, areas where you can report trouble, and websites appropriate for children. In the family tools area, parents could find filtering programs, such as SurfWatch, Cyber Patrol, and Net Nanny. These programs worked with their Internet browser to block out violent, politically incorrect, or X-rated web pages.[17]

> *AT&T launched another initiative aimed at protecting children from adult-oriented material on the Internet when it formed a partnership with Tim Robertson, son of evangelist Pat Robertson. FamilyClick.com included an Internet service provider that acted as a gateway to the Internet in exchange for a monthly fee. The service automatically barred access to specific sites and electronic mail that parents found objectionable for their children. AT&T committed $20 million to the project. Explained Leo Hindrey, chief executive officer of AT&T's Broadband & Internet Services Group, "This is about thoughtful control over content that might be offensive to families."[18]*

In 1998, President Clinton signed into law the Child Online Protection Act. Advocates of protecting children from adult-oriented material applauded the government's action. The law required adult sites to collect and verify proof of age before allowing Internet visitors to gain access to material that was deemed "harmful to minors." The penalty for sites that did not comply with the law was a $50,000 fine or six months in prison for the website operator. Yet four months later, a federal judge ruled that the law would result in self-censorship. The judge cited his "personal regret" that this decision would "delay once again the careful protection of our children." But, he added, "we do more harm in this country if the First Amendment protections were chipped away in the name of protecting children."[19] (Similarly, the U.S. government initially passed the Communications Decency Act in 1996; but this law was struck down by the courts as unconstitutional and in violation of the First Amendment. Many thought that the Child Online Protection Act was a softer and more acceptable effort to protect children from adult-oriented material available on the Internet.)

Protecting Intellectual Property

With advances in technology, protecting the ownership of property became more challenging than ever. The ideas, concepts, and other symbolic creations of the human mind are often referred to as

[17] Edward C. Baig, "Shielding Children from Cyber Perils," *Business Week*, August 16, 1999, p. 117.
[18] Leslie Cauley, "AT&T Plans Internet Venture with Son of Evangelist to Block Data for Children," *Wall Street Journal*, July 19, 1999, p. B6.
[19] Pamela Mendels, "Setback for a Law Shielding Minors from Adult Web Sites," *New York Times*, February 2, 1999, p. 12.

Figure 13-3

Software piracy around the world.

Source: Data from Business Software Alliance, www.bsa.org.

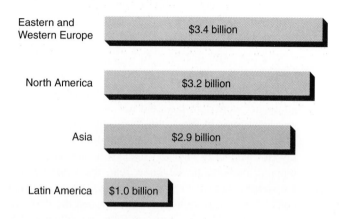

Annual Loss of Sales in U.S. Dollars

Eastern and Western Europe $3.4 billion

North America $3.2 billion

Asia $2.9 billion

Latin America $1.0 billion

intellectual property. In the United States, intellectual property is protected through a number of special laws and public policies, including copyrights, patents, and trademark laws. Not all nations have policies similar to those in the United States. With the ease of accessing information through technology, especially the Internet, came serious questions regarding protecting intellectual property. From software and video-game piracy to downloading copyrighted music for free, many new means for using others' intellectual property unlawfully emerged. What steps did businesses take to protect their property?

Software Piracy and Business Responses

The illegal copying of copyrighted software, or **software piracy,** is a global problem, as shown in Figure 13-3. This activity was most noticeable in Eastern and Western Europe, where some experts estimated that $3.4 billion in lost sales occurred in 1998 due to software piracy. These losses compared to the $3.2 billion lost in North America and $2.9 billion in Asia. But this problem spread to other parts of the world. Investigators found nearly $1 billion in lost sales due to software piracy in Latin America, with Brazil, Mexico, and Argentina the most affected countries. More than 6 out of every 10 software applications in that region were illegal copies.[20]

> *One of the companies most injured by the increase in software piracy was Microsoft, which launched an aggressive campaign to attack software pirates. In 2000, the company announced action against 7,500 Internet listings for allegedly pirating their products to 33 countries. "What we are seeing is that counterfeiters are more effective in distributing their software globally and anonymously using the Internet," said Microsoft attorney Tim Cranton. In Asia, Europe, and the Middle East, Microsoft identified 2,274 instances of suspected piracy and sent notices to the*

[20] Stephen Baker and Inka Resch, "Piracy!" *Business Week,* July 26, 1999, pp. 90–94; and "TechNotes: Pirate's Booty," *BusIndustry,* September 1998, p. 83.

*website owners to remove the illegal products listed for sale. In addition,
the company participated with local government and police in raiding
various locations suspected of housing pirated software and filed lawsuits
seeking damages.*[21]

Companies have sought assistance on the issue of software piracy from governmental agencies and the courts both inside and outside the United States. For example, in 1998, the Argentinean Supreme Court upheld a lower court ruling that the country's antiquated copyright laws did not cover software, thus denying software manufacturers any legal basis to attack those with pirated materials in Argentina. However, the outcry from U.S. software makers and vendors was so strong that within months the Argentinean Chamber of Deputies made software piracy a crime punishable by fines or imprisonment, or both. In the same year, the United States passed the **Digital Millennium Copyright Act,** making it a crime to circumvent antipiracy measures built into most commercial software agreements between the manufacturers and their users.[22]

Since 1988, the Business Software Alliance (BSA) has been an international representative for the world's leading software companies before governments and consumers. BSA sought to educate computer users on software copyright laws, lobby for public policy that would foster innovation and expand software companies' trade opportunities, and aggressively fight against software piracy. Its members included Apple Computers, Corel, Macromedia (Asia), Microsoft, Symantec, and many other influential businesses in the software industry.

A call to the Business Software Alliance hot line resulted in Budget Rent-a-Car Corporation agreeing to a $403,000 settlement for using unlicensed software at some of its rental offices. The Budget Rent-a-Car case represented only one instance in a string of companies caught by the Business Software Alliance and its hot line. Companies were found using more copies of a software package than they paid for, often believing they could copy from a purchased software package without legal violation or believing that they would not be caught if they did.

*Other firms attacked those who sold or distributed pirated software. Sega
of America Inc. shut down 185 websites, including auctions on eBay and
Amazon.com, which allegedly sold pirated game software. Citing the Digital Millennium Copyright Act of 1998, Sega said it was protected against
software pirates and that the individuals selling or distributing pirated
software were liable under civil and criminal prosecution. "We're using
this act to send a clear message [to the websites and other companies],"
said a Sega spokesperson. "They are liable for the content that is on their
service." Amazon.com reported that on the day it received Sega's letter*

---

[21] Rebecca Buckman, "Microsoft Steps Up Software-Piracy War," *Wall Street Journal,* August 2, 2000, p. B6.

[22] Jonathan Friedland, "Software Makers Assail Argentine Piracy Ruling," *Wall Street Journal,* February 6, 1998, p. A17; "Argentina Gets Tough on Software Pirates," *South America Report,* December 1, 1998; and John Simons, "Congress Passes Copyright Law for Internet Items," *Wall Street Journal,* October 13, 1998, p. B14.

they removed the single questionable item and barred the seller from its auction service. In addition, eBay said it worked with Sega to remove the questionable items once they were notified of the problem.[23]

Pirating Copyrighted Music and Business Responses

By the late 1990s, technology enabled individuals to download music from the Internet at a faster pace than ever before and store the music for repeated listening. Individuals downloaded millions of songs onto their computers, burned them onto CDs, and had their favorite collections of songs available for their listening pleasure whenever they wanted—all without the cost of purchasing the music. Of course, this process denied legitimate compensation to the artists who created the music or to the companies that manufactured or distributed these artists' CDs.

The Recording Industry Association of America (RIAA) sued Diamond Multimedia Systems in 1998 for selling a hand-held device known as the Rio. The Rio could store and play back music transferred to the device from a personal computer. Individuals were no longer tied to the computer to listen to their favorite downloaded songs, since the Rio enabled people to take the music wherever they wanted to go. The RIAA argued that the Rio supported piracy from the Internet and was an illegal recording device in violation of the 1992 Audio Home Recording Act. This act outlawed devices that allowed recordings of copyrighted digital music without either a means of copyright protection or nominal royalty for the artists. In response to the lawsuit, Diamond Multimedia Systems adopted a technology for protecting copyrights on its Rio music player. By incorporating copyright-detection software technology into future generations of Rio devices, it was easier for music publishers to get paid for selling music on the Internet.[24]

Another approach businesses used to protect music copyrights involved **streaming.** Streaming referred to a customized, on-demand radio service. These were harder to pirate, because copies of the music were not downloaded and stored on users' hard drives, creating virtual libraries. Streaming provided music distributors with new revenues from selling subscriptions to the music for which they held the copyright. The benefits of this proposal were seen almost immediately. When a court ordered San Diego–based MP3.com to pay $10 million for creating a database of more than 45,000 CDs without copyright permission, the company agreed to a licensing fee. MP3.com agreed to pay 1.5 cents each time it copied a track of music and about 0.3 cents when a customer downloaded the song.[25]

---

[23] "Sega Closes 185 Web Sites to Fight Software Piracy," *Wall Street Journal,* July 21, 2000, p. B5.

[24] Dean Takahashi, "Firm Is Sued in Dispute on Distribution of Recorded Music over the Internet," *Wall Street Journal,* October 12, 1998, p. B6; and Don Clark, "Diamond Multimedia Adopts a Method to Guard Copyrights on Its Rio Player," *Wall Street Journal,* April 23, 1999, p. B2.

[25] Steven V. Brull, "If You Can't Lick 'Em, License 'Em," *Business Week,* June 26, 2000, p. 46.

The legal, ethical, and economic issues emerging from the technological advances in recording and distributing music are further explored at the end of this chapter in the discussion case on Napster.

Managing Scientific Breakthroughs

Dramatic advances in the biological sciences also propelled the impact of technology on our lives and business practices. Scientific breakthroughs began to shake societal norms in the late 1990s and promised to continue to provide amazing discoveries in the twenty-first century. These unprecedented innovations brought new, improved methods of health care and agricultural progress as well as numerous ethical challenges regarding the quality and safety of life.

> *As Bill Joy of Sun Microsystems warns, "The twenty-first century technologies . . . are so powerful that they can spawn whole new classes of accidents and abuses. Most dangerously, for the first time, these accidents and abuses are widely within the reach of individuals or small groups. They will not require large facilities or rare raw materials. Knowledge alone will enable the use of them."*[26]

Human Genome

Hailed as the most significant scientific breakthrough since landing a man on the moon, Celera Genomics Group announced in 2000 that they had finished the first sequencing of a **human genome.** To explain, strands of human deoxyribonucleic acid, or DNA, spread across 23 chromosomes in the nucleus of every human cell in a unique pattern for every human. These strands comprise four chemical units, or letters, used over and over in varying chemical sequences. These replicated letters total 3 billion and form the words, or genes—our unique human signature, so to speak—that instruct cells to manufacture the proteins that carry out all of the functions of human life.

By completing the first sequencing of a human DNA makeup, the identification of tens of thousands of human genes will be significantly faster. The identification of human genes is critical to the early diagnosis of life-threatening diseases, new ways to prevent illnesses, and the development of drug therapies to treat a person's unique genetic profile. A new era of medicine, as well as great opportunity for biotechnology companies, appeared to be born with the decoding of the human genome.

While advances in understanding human DNA were exalted as one of the human race's greatest achievements, ethical challenges emerged in private and public research focusing on genetics.

> *For example, the economic underdevelopment of parts of China made this country an intriguing laboratory for scientists seeking to understand genetics. Many rural families lived in isolation for generations, making it easier for genetic researchers to trace illnesses, such as hypertension or asthma, through relatives. With the growing wealth and mobility within China,*

---

[26] Joy, "Why the Future Doesn't Need Us."

genetic scientists were under increasing time pressure to acquire data from the Chinese people before these conditions disappeared. Yet along with this unique opportunity for scientific discovery were the social and ethical challenges of using human beings as test subjects, when they might not fully understand the risks or possibilities for exploitation.[27]

Similar ethical questions emerged within the United States as scientists conducted a growing number of experiments on humans having various genetic conditions. One family, who possessed Brugada syndrome in their genes, wondered how their neighbors might react if they learned of the family's genetic condition. Would employers want to hire someone who might die prematurely or require an expensive implantable defibrillator? Would they be eligible for individual health care coverage or be able to afford life insurance if their condition was known? The underlying fear for this family and others with genetic conditions was whether they would be treated fairly if their genetic fingerprints became public.

The debate over whether advances in human genome sequencing and genetic research outweigh the risks or harms will continue for years to come. What is clear is that our scientific understanding of the human body and its makeup has changed and significant technological innovations are on the horizon. What is not clear is who, if anyone, can manage these changes to better ensure the improvement of the quality of our lives and society.

Biotechnology

Complementing the discovery of DNA sequencing were numerous medical breakthroughs in the area of regenerative medicine. **Tissue engineering** offered the promise that failing human organs and aging cells could be rejuvenated or replaced with healthy cells or tissues grown anew. "The current chemical era of medicine may, in retrospect, appear to be a clumsy effort to patch rather than permanently repair our broken bodies," said William A. Haseltine, a leading genetic scientist. "Cellular replacement may keep us young and healthy forever."[28] While the promise of immortality may be overstated, regenerative medicine provided a revolutionary technological breakthrough for the field of medicine.

Hundreds of biotechnology companies and university laboratories answered the call and began to develop new ways to replace or regenerate failed body parts. Research included efforts to insert bone-growth factors or stem cells into a porous material cut to a specific shape, creating new jaws or limbs. Genetically engineered proteins were successfully used to regrow blood vessels that might repair or replace heart valves, arteries, and veins. The process to regrow cartilage was used to grow a new chest for a boy, and a human ear was grown on a mouse. Doctors at Children's Hospital in Boston grew bladders from skin cells and implanted them in sheep. Enamel matrix proteins were used to fill tooth cavities in dogs. Human trials were planned once animal testing proved successful.

---

[27] Leslie Chang and Laura Johannes, "Geneticists Focus on a Controversial Treasure: All the DNA in China," *Wall Street Journal,* September 13, 2000, pp. B1, B4.

[28] Catherine Arnst and John Carey, "Biotech Bodies," *Business Week,* July 27, 1998, pp. 56–63.

Cloning

In 1986, a Danish scientist announced the first successful cloning of a sheep. Shortly thereafter, a University of Wisconsin scientist succeeded with cows. Ten years later, in 1996, the Roslin Institute in Scotland announced that it had cloned healthy calves from fetal cells. Another significant breakthrough occurred in 1997, when Ian Wilmut of the Roslin Institute unveiled Dolly, the first mammal to be cloned from adult cells. A year later, scientists from the University of Massachusetts reported that they had discovered a method of cloning cows with a process that was simpler and more efficient than Wilmut's method. Another major advancement in the evolution of cloning occurred in South Korea in late 1998 when researchers cloned an embryo from the cell of a 30-year-old woman. This experiment brought us even closer to the real possibility of human cloning.

These breakthroughs brought a wide array of opinions and responses from businesses, governments, medical groups, and the public. A sampling of the variety of views can be seen in the differing religions' positions on cloning, as shown in Exhibit 13-B.

EXHIBIT 13-B

Where Religions Stand on Human Cloning

The religious groups most strenuously opposed to human cloning were Roman Catholics and the Southern Baptists. The Catholic Church condemned cloning in the late 1980s, well before the possibility seemed real to scientists. The Catholic Church saw cloning as an affront to human dignity. While the Church supported scientific progress, it taught that anything that separated sexual intercourse from procreation was wrong. The Southern Baptists similarly condemned human cloning, but rather on the grounds that cloning was an assault on the family and an inappropriate "overreaching" of man in the modern age.

The Islamic stance on cloning was closely aligned with the Catholics' and Southern Baptists' views. Islam was concerned with the paternal lineage of a child; thus, this religion opposed children cloned from women. Islam was also a community-oriented religion; therefore, individuals should remain connected with their circle of blood relatives. Islamic law, for example, forbade adoption to prevent the contamination of a lineage, encouraging members to provide humanitarian help to orphaned children.

Moderately opposed to cloning were most other Protestant faiths and most Jews. These groups generally believed that scientists should proceed but with caution, emphasizing individual choice. These religions condoned cloning under certain circumstances, such as for an infertile couple with no other way to conceive, but would probably resist it for purely narcissistic or cosmetic reasons.

Generally approving of cloning were Hindus and Buddhists. These religions were more open to cloning because they believed in reincarnation and did not distinguish between sexual and asexual reproduction. Cloning was creating life, which was welcomed as a reincarnation birth.

Source: Hanna Rosin, "Thou Shalt Not Clone?" *Pittsburgh Post-Gazette,* July 26, 2000, p. A3.

Fears arose as soon as the first successful cloning experiment was announced to the public. Whether it was a vision of Jurassic Park dinosaurs running loose in a metropolitan downtown area or the eerie absurdity of cloning multiple Adolph Hitlers in the film *The Boys of Brazil,* fears of cloning living tissue invaded our lives. In 1997, when Dolly appeared on the cloning scene, there were no laws on record that prevented scientists from attempting human cloning. Experts recognized that the technique used in Scotland to clone a sheep was so simple and required so little high-tech equipment that most biology laboratories with a budget of a few hundred thousand dollars could attempt it. The ease with which this experiment could be attempted using human DNA cells and the lack of governmental control quickly brought the public and the scientific community's fears over cloning to an unprecedented level.

In June 1997, the U.S. National Bioethics Advisory Commission proposed that scientists be barred from implanting a cloned embryo into a woman's uterus. However, this proposal did not ban scientists from cloning embryos used for research but not implanted into a woman. The group of scientists, lawyers, and ethicists based much of their opposition on concerns for a fetus's safety and urged that the ban be respected at least through the year 2002.[29] This debate inevitably will continue for years to come.

Genetically Engineered Foods

The biotechnological revolution targeting human regeneration of body parts was also adapted for use by the agricultural industry. Technological advances in genetics and biology led to an unprecedented number of innovations. **Genetic engineering,** altering the natural makeup of a living organism, allowed scientists to insert virtually any gene into a plant and create a new crop, or an entire new species. The economic force of this technological revolution was immediately apparent. Venture capitalists injected $750 million into the agricultural industry, an area generally ignored by venture capitalists throughout the 1980s.

Schools of salmon and trout were engineered to grow twice as fast as before. Soybeans, cotton, corn, and other crops were genetically engineered to resist pests or to be impervious to herbicides used to control weeds. Some were altered to yield a higher nutritional value. Cows, sheep, and goats were treated to produce drugs in their milk. "We are starting the century of biology," announced J. Craig Venter, president of the Institute for Genomic Research. The payoff potential was huge.[30]

A severe backlash to biotechnological innovations was seen regarding **genetically modified foods,** or GM foods, that is, food processed from genetically engineered crops. In Europe, protesters called GM food "Frankenstein foods." Public skepticism grew when a study reported that rats fed with genetically modified potatoes suffered immune-system damage. Many schools and food suppliers in England, France, and other North European countries banned genetically modified foods. Several cities in France declared themselves "GM-free." Heinz Corporation, a U.S.-based food producer, announced that it no longer would sell GM foods in Europe. Other firms found the initial excitement of GM foods short-lived.

---

[29] Laurie McGinley, "U.S. Bioethics Panel to Recommend Ban on Cloning to Produce a Human Being," *Wall Street Journal,* June 9, 1997, p. B3.

[30] John Carey, "We Are Now Starting the Century of Biology," *Business Week,* August 31, 1998, pp. 86–87.

In 1998, Monsanto Company announced that it was the first company to genetically engineer corn to resist rootworm, an insect that caused $1 billion in damages annually to the United States' largest crop. The company reported that farmers would no longer have to spend $150 million annually on chemicals to control rootworm, which infested about 15 million acres. Yet less than a year later, Monsanto was "Public Enemy No. 1," according a comment made by Norman Baker in the British House of Commons. Anti-Monsanto sentiments echoed across England. Prince Charles vowed that Monsanto's biotech food would never pass his royal lips. British newspapers called Monsanto the "Frankenstein food giant," and some referred to the company as "MonSatan." "Many people here really hate Monsanto," said Isabelle Gineste, a member of the English Townswomen's Guilds, a civic group. "The rest of us are just scared."[31]

What had happened to Monsanto and the emerging bioengineered food industry? Why had public opinion turned negative? Consumers in Europe were the first to sound the alarm over genetically modified food. Australia, Japan, and South Korea soon followed Europe's lead.

Soon American consumer and environmental groups challenged the safety of genetically altered foods. Late in 1999, antibiotechnology activists disrupted the World Trade Organization meeting in Seattle. Greenpeace protesters showed up at Kellogg's headquarters in Battle Creek, Michigan, demanding that the cereal manufacturer only use natural grain in its products. Numerous lawsuits were filed against the U.S. government and biotechnology companies demanding that engineered foods be studied more carefully, labeled, and in some cases pulled off the market.

Biotech companies were quick to resist the movement toward labeling their products. "If you label, you're telling consumers that there is something wrong with this product," argued Gene Grabowski, vice president for communications at the Grocery Manufacturers of America. "In Britain, they put mandatory labels on and they've killed biotechnology."[32] Companies, however, pointed to studies showing that GM foods were indistinguishable from their non-GM counterparts. The U.S. government apparently agreed, because the Food and Drug Administration declined to restrict the use of most genetically engineered foods or to require labels.

Although opposition to bioengineered food was seen in many countries, in other countries genetically modified food was welcomed. Russia and Argentina embraced this new technology, as did China.

After losing the battle to insects and finding that pesticides often were ineffective on the North China Plain, where cotton was the primary crop, cotton growing began to flourish again. "I was the first one in the village to plant these new [bioengineered] cotton seeds, but when everyone saw

---

[31] Scott Kilman, "Monsanto Says Its Corn Resists the Rootworm," *Wall Street Journal,* August 21, 1998, p. A2; and Scott Kilman and Helene Cooper, "Monsanto Falls Flat Trying to Sell Europe on Bioengineered Food," *Wall Street Journal,* May 11, 1999, pp. A1, A10.

[32] Margaret Kriz, "Global Food Fight," *National Journal,* March 4, 2000, pp. 688–93.

how great the results were, they started growing again, too," said An
Deyin, a Chinese farmer.

China's leaders made genetic research a top scientific priority, funneling billions
of government dollars into research on modifying the genes of crops and vegetables.
Government leaders saw genetic crop production as a source of stable food supplies and
the path to a national presence in the agricultural import-export arena.[33] By March 2000,
1.2 to 2.4 million acres of biotech crops had been planted in China. Professor Zhangliang
Chen estimated that within 5 to 10 years, half of the country's fields would be planted
with GM rice, potatoes, and other crops.

Despite legislation seeking to control the distribution of genetically modified food
in Australia, 61 percent of Australians said that they were willing to try genetically modified food, but 89 percent wanted the food products labeled.

In the United States, support for genetically modified foods was mixed. In a study
released in April 2000, the U.S. Department of Agriculture reported that American farmers were cutting back on genetically modified products. Corn production using genetic
seeds, for example, dropped 24 percent. Farmers reported that social and market factors
were influencing their decisions on whether to use genetically modified seeds. Yet other
American food producers were convinced that GM foods were the way of the future.

Luman Foods, a closely held maker of vegetarian snacks, said that it
would advertise the fact that it used genetically modified soybeans in its
meatless jerkies. "They have it all wrong," said Greg Caton, president of
Luman Foods. As argued in the company's website, the company was not
reluctant to boast about its use of genetic foods. "It's publicity and it's the
right side of the issue," proclaimed the firm's president.[34]

The controversies over genetic engineering, cloning, and genetically modified food
production raised serious ethical and social issues embedded in these technological
advancements. The question over the role of businesses, social activist groups, or governments in overseeing these developments also was raised and must be addressed, as
new technological innovations appear on the horizon.

Summary Points of This Chapter

- Businesses have addressed many privacy issues at work and in e-commerce by
developing privacy policies and becoming involved in voluntary industry initiatives
such as TRUSTe.
- Acts of sabotage by computer hackers threaten companies' control of information,
causing businesses to develop numerous information security measures.

[33] Karby Leggett and Ian Johnson, "China Bets Farm on Promise (and Glory) of Genetic Engineering," *Wall
Street Journal,* March 29, 2000, p. A17.
[34] "Jerky with a Message?" *Wall Street Journal,* February 24, 2000, p. A1.

- Businesses have entrusted the management of technology to their chief information officers. For issues that go beyond the business organization and affect society in general, it is unclear whether businesses, social groups, or governments—or some combination of these groups—should manage technology and its change.
- Threats of software and music piracy challenge businesses' ownership of their property, calling for industry and governmental responses to these ethical violations.
- Fears associated with human genetic research, human cloning, and genetically modified foods have raised objections from social and religious groups. Businesses have attempted to address these fears and dispel false concerns, while seeking the benefits of scientific technological breakthroughs.

Key Terms and Concepts Used in This Chapter

- Privacy policy
- Computer hackers
- Chief Information Officer (CIO)
- Intellectual property
- Software piracy
- Digital Millennium Copyright Act

- Streaming
- Human genome
- Tissue engineering
- Genetic engineering
- Genetically modified foods

Internet Resources

- www.privacyalliance.com   Online Privacy Alliance
- www.truste.org   TRUSTe
- www.bsa.org   Business Software Alliance
- www.foe.co.uk   Friends of the Earth
- www.nhgri.nih.gov   National Human Genome Research
                                                      Institute

Discussion Case: *Napster—Free Access or Musical Piracy?*

Little did Shawn Fanning know that when he dropped out of Northeastern University at age 17 to finish writing a software program in 1999 that he would be instrumental in creating a landmark judicial ruling on the use of information found on the Internet.

Napster, the free software that Fanning created, enabled Internet users to download, listen to, record, and swap music stored on their personal or institutional computers. Most of these songs were pirated versions of copyrighted music. The idea caught on like wildfire, particularly among college students. By 2000, a tracking service found that nearly 23 million people a month were visiting Napster and similar sites. "If I need a single song, I just use Napster—it's faster," explained Jeffrey, a 14-year-old interviewed in a *Business Week* feature on Napster.

With the widespread use of Napster and the creation of new Napster-like sites on the Internet, the legal response from musicians and record companies alike was strong. In April 2000, the rock group Metallica sued Napster, along with three schools that allowed students to download the group's music via Napster, for copyright infringement.

Two months later, the Recording Industry Association of America (RIAA) filed a motion for a preliminary injunction to block all major-label content from being traded through Napster. The RIAA accompanied its lawsuit with a full-scale media blitz, dispatched staffers to speak on college campuses, and provided executives to testify before government hearings. Recognizing the ethical questions raised by students using Napster and the fears of becoming targets for lawsuits, many universities banned or restricted the use of Napster-like services on campus. More than 300 schools joined the RIAA's "Soundbyting" antipiracy initiative, which included a 50-minute lesson plan and its own website with a "Copyright 101" section.

Napster executives quickly responded to the protests. After the Metallica lawsuit was filed, the company booted more than 300,000 members from its service for downloading Metallica songs. Yet Napster executives soon realized that they also had to develop a strong legal defense. They made three main arguments.

First, they said, Napster was a mere conduit of information, like a telephone network or an Internet service. Thus, they were exempt from federal law for being held responsible for the copyrighted material they might transmit, as long as they took reasonable steps to keep it off their systems. RIAA responded that Napster must accept their responsibility for facilitating the piracy of the RIAA's material and not pass it off to those downloading the music.

Second, Napster argued that its operations functioned as an Internet search engine, a category protected by the 1998 Digital Millennium Copyright Act. However, the RIAA countered with the argument that Napster had not taken the necessary legal steps required of search engines in dealing with copyright violations. Napster's vendors had been found openly selling bootlegged compact discs, that is, pirated music.

Third, Napster argued, "We are like a VCR." In an earlier decision, the Supreme Court had ruled VCRs could be used without infringing copyright, for example, when a person recorded a television show for later viewing at home. Experts for the recording industry countered that this court decision applied to personal use, not sharing music files with hundreds or even thousands of strangers via the Internet, and covered only digital audio and videotapes, not computers or the Internet.

In 2001 a three-judge appellate panel upheld an earlier ruling by a Federal judge ordering Napster to dramatically curb its music-exchange service. The judges said that downloading music via Napster was not like video recording since Napster directly profited from the illegal activity. According to the judicial ruling, Napster "knowingly encourages and assists in the infringement of copyrights." The most significant legal blow to Napster was the ruling that the company was liable for copyright infringement by its 50 million users, making Napster vulnerable to billions of dollars in damages in civil suits from music publishing and recording companies.

Sources: Richard Siklos and Steven V. Brull, "Download This!" *Business Week,* May 29, 2000, p. 127; Lee Gomes and Anna Wilde Mathews, "Napster Suffers a Rout in Appeals Court," *Wall Street Journal,* February 13, 2001, pp. A3, A16; Lee Gomes and Martin Peers, "Napster Loses Round in Suit to Shutter It," *Wall Street Journal,* May 9, 2000, p. B25; Anna Wilde Mathews, "Industry's Public-Relations Blitz," *Wall Street Journal,* June 20, 2000, pp. B1, B4; Lee Gomes, "Napster Stakes Out 'Fair Use' Defense of Music Sharing," *Wall Street Journal,* July 5, 2000, p. B2; and Spencer E. Ante, "Inside Napster," *Business Week,* August 14, 2000, pp. 112–21.

Discussion Questions

1. Do you agree with the judges' ruling in this case? Why or why not?

2. Should music be freely available to Internet users (Napster's view), or did Napster foster infringement of copyright violations (the view voiced by some musicians and the RIAA)?

3. Where do you draw the line when information is freely available via the Internet, yet try to respect the artists' intellectual property and rights to royalties from their creations?

PART SEVEN

Responding to Stakeholders

327

14

Stockholders and Corporate Governance

Stockholders occupy a position of central importance in the corporation because they are the company's legal owners and they expect high levels of economic performance. But the corporation is not always run solely for their benefit, so they contend with management and the board of directors for control of company policies. Recent changes in corporate governance have strengthened the influence of stockholders and increased the attention given to this stakeholder group by managers and boards of directors.

This chapter focuses on these key questions and objectives:

- Who are stockholders, and what are their goals and legal rights?

- Who controls the corporation, and how has the power of stockholders, relative to that of boards of directors and managers, shifted in recent years?

- What have social activist investors done to change corporate policies?

- What are the pros and cons of employee ownership of corporations?

- Are top corporate executives paid too much?

- How are stockholders affected by insider trading, and how does the government protect against stock market abuses?

I n 2000, Durk Jager stepped down as chairman and CEO of Procter & Gamble at the request of his board of directors. During Jager's brief year and a half at the helm, the company's share price had been driven down 50 percent by investors disappointed by unexpectedly low earnings. The board clearly felt it had to take decisive action to turn performance around. "Boards are moving very quickly," commented one owner of Procter & Gamble stock. "It's 'off with their heads.'" But other investors expressed disappointment. "There's no patience," said a representative of Ohio's public pension system. "It's discouraging."[1]

The Province of St. Joseph Capuchin, a small Catholic religious order based in Milwaukee, placed a resolution on the 2000 shareholder ballot of Merck, calling on the company to price their pharmaceutical drugs "at reasonable levels" to ease the burden on the elderly and the uninsured. The company opposed the proposal, citing the high cost and risk of research and development for new medicines. Despite support from 15 other institutional investors, the Catholic brothers' proposal received less than 10 percent of the vote. But the company agreed to advocate prescription drug coverage for recipients of Medicare, Medicaid, and other public health insurance programs.[2]

Telecom Italia, the Italian phone company, angered some of its foreign investors in 1999 when it proposed to spin off its Internet and wireless operations. TIAA-CREF, a large U.S. pension fund that had significant holdings in the company, protested loudly that the move would unfairly benefit the Telecom Italia's majority shareholder, Olivetti. "We communicated our views to the Italian government that an action that disadvantages minority shareholders will cause doubt as to the credibility of the Italian marketplace," said the pension fund's investment counsel. After a campaign organized by TIAA-CREF, Telecom Italia backed down. This incident was part of what many observers saw as a spread of shareholder activism from the United States to other countries, following the growing globalization of stock trading.[3]

Why have boards of directors, like Procter & Gamble's, become so involved in day-to-day decision making? Should managers of big firms like Merck pay attention to the wishes of stockholders such as the Province of St. Joseph Capuchin? Why do institutional investors, such as public pension funds, carefully track management decisions in firms in which they own stock? How have foreign companies, like Telecom Italia, responded to challenges from stockholders from both the United States and other countries?

Each of these examples and the questions they raise involve the complex relationship between the corporation and its legal owners, the stockholders. Management and boards of directors face very difficult issues in responding to corporate owners and balancing their demands with other company goals. This chapter addresses this important set of issues and relationships.

---

[1] "Procter & Gamble Ousts CEO Jager," *Bloomberg News,* June 8, 2000, www.bloomberg.com.
[2] "Clerics Take on Drug Companies," *Boston Herald,* October 10, 1999, p. 1. Copies of the shareholder proposal and the company's response are available at www.thecorporatelibrary.com/resolutions. The Interfaith Center on Corporate Responsibility (info@iccr.org) publishes an annual report on proxy resolutions submitted by social activist shareholders, such as this one.
[3] "Hark! The Shareholders Are Restless in Europe," *New York Times,* December 12, 1999, p. C4. The spread of shareholder activism abroad has been supported by the International Corporate Governance Network, an alliance of institutional investors, including the TIAA-CREF. Its website may be found at www.icgn.org.

Stockholders

Stockholders—or shareholders, as they also are called—are the legal owners of business corporations. By purchasing a *share* of the company's stock, they become part owners of the company. For this reason, stockholder-owners have a big stake in how well their company performs. The firm's managers must pay close attention to their needs and assign a high priority to their interests in the company.[4]

Who Are Stockholders?

Two types of stockholders own shares of stock in U.S. corporations: individual and institutional.

Individuals may own stock directly, by purchasing shares in companies, usually through a stockbroker. Or they may own shares indirectly, for example, by purchasing shares of a mutual fund, buying an insurance policy, or participating in a pension fund or supplemental retirement account, such as an IRA or a 401(k) plan. Since the 1960s, growth in the numbers of such **institutional investors** has been phenomenal. Studies by the securities industry showed that in 1999, institutions accounted for 58 percent of the value of all equities (stocks) owned in the United States, worth a total of $10.9 *trillion*— more than five times the value of institutional holdings a decade earlier.[5]

Almost half—49 percent—of all U.S. adults own shares of stock, either directly as individuals or indirectly through an institution. Stockholders are a diverse group. People from practically every occupational group own stock: professionals, managers, clerks, craft workers, farmers, retired persons, and homemakers. Although older people are more likely to own stock, young people (aged 21 to 34) make up about a quarter of all share-owners. Not all shareholders are wealthy; the median family income of owners of stock is $50,000; and the median value of their portfolios is $15,500.[6]

Figure 14-1 shows the relative stock holdings of individual and institutional investors from the 1960s through the end of the century. It shows the growing influence of the institutional sector of the market over the past four decades.

Objectives of Stock Ownership

Individuals and institutions own corporate stock for a number of reasons.

Economic Objective

Foremost among these reasons is the goal of receiving an economic gain, or return on investment. People could place such money in a bank and earn interest with relatively little risk; however, many people choose stocks because they believe such investments will produce a greater gain. Different types of corporate ownership produce varying levels of return through dividends and an increase in stock price. A company that pays

---

[4] The following discussion refers to publicly held corporations, that is, ones whose shares of stock are owned by the public and traded on the various stock exchanges. U.S. laws permit a number of other ownership forms, including sole proprietorships, partnerships, and mutual companies.

[5] Securities Industry Association, "Holdings of U.S. Equities Outstanding," 2000. These data are based on analysis of the Federal Reserve Bank's flow of funds accounts.

[6] "This Time It's Different," *Time,* January 8, 2001, pp. 18–22; New York Stock Exchange, "Shareowner-ship, 1998"; and Peter D. Hart Research Associates, *A National Survey among Stock Investors* (New York: *Nasdaq,* February 1997).

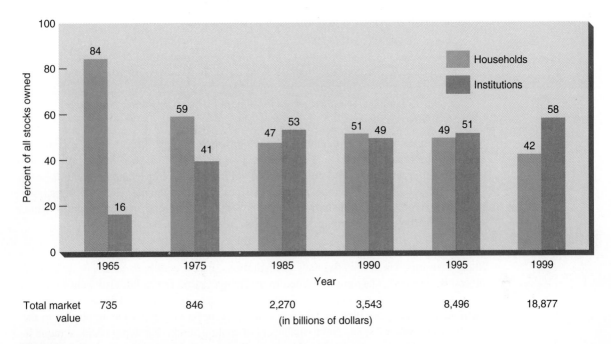

Figure 14-1

Individual household versus institutional ownership of stock in the United States, 1965–1999.

Source: Securities Industry Association, *Securities Industry Factbook* (New York: Securities Industry Association, 2000). Based on Federal Reserve flow of funds accounts (revised). Used by permission.

a relatively high dividend (6 to 7 percent) is not likely to have rapid price appreciation. Conversely, a company with good growth prospects and whose stock is likely to appreciate in price can choose to pay a lower dividend, if any at all, and still attract investors. Investors may pursue current income through high dividends or future income through capital appreciation, depending on their personal goals and willingness to assume risk.

Social Objective

Some investors use stock ownership to achieve social or ethical objectives. A growing number of mutual funds and pension funds use *social screens* to select companies in which they invest, weeding out ones that pollute the environment, discriminate against their employees, make dangerous products like tobacco or weapons, or do business in countries with poor human right records. In 1999, according to the Social Investment Forum, $2.16 trillion in the United States was invested in mutual funds or pensions using social responsibility as an investment criterion, up from $1.19 trillion in 1997, accounting for about one in every eight investment dollars. During this period, socially responsible investment grew at about twice the rate as all assets under professional management.[7]

[7] Social Investment Forum, "1999 Report on Socially Responsible Investing Trends in the United States," available at www.socialinvest.org/areas/research/trends.

In recent years, socially responsible investing has spread from the United States to Europe and beyond. In the United Kingdom, for example, the market for stock funds using social screens grew more than 60 percent, from $2.6 to $4.2 billion, from 1998 to 2000. In 2000, the British government passed new rules requiring pension funds to disclose the extent to which they had used social, environmental, or ethical criteria in selecting investments.[8]

Most evidence shows that socially screened portfolios provide returns that are competitive with the broad market.[9]

Social criteria may also be used when selling stocks. For example, some have at various times called for *divestment* (sale of stock) from companies that had operations in China, where some products were made by forced labor, and in Nigeria and Burma, where repressive military regimes had been accused of human rights abuses.

Mixed Objectives

Many investors, whether individuals or institutions, invest with both economic and social objectives in mind. They are interested in receiving a good return but also want to invest in socially responsible companies. Such investors require their stockbrokers or investment advisers to apply both social and economic criteria they regard as important to the purchase and sale of stock. Some managers of mutual funds that apply social screens in selecting stocks have argued that this approach may increase economic returns. Recent research suggests a long-term positive relationship between social responsibility and financial performance.[10]

Corporate Control

There are other reasons for investing in corporate stock. Some investors are interested in gaining control of the corporation. This may be for the purpose of improving efficiency by cutting costs and implementing new strategies, merging the firm with another business, or selling its assets to buyers who will pay more for the parts than for the whole company. Such investments also may have a long-term economic purpose, but the immediate objective is to take control of the company and its assets. One group of investors, sometimes called *corporate raiders,* may try to take control of a corporation against the will of top management in a *hostile takeover.* Other investors may purchase stock simply in order to influence management strategy, perhaps by gaining a seat on the board of directors. One variant of this, called *relationship investing,* is discussed later in this chapter.

---

[8] "Ethical Investment Practices Expand in U.K. in Response to New Legislation," *Wall Street Journal,* June 19, 2000, p. B19A.

[9] "A Conscience Doesn't Have to Make You Poor," *Business Week,* May 1, 2000, pp. 204–08. For an academic study of this subject, see John B. Guerard, Jr., "Is There a Cost to Being a Socially Responsible Investor?" *Journal of Investing* 6 (Summer 1997), pp. 11–18.

[10] Sandra Waddock and Samuel B. Graves, "The Corporate Social Performance-Financial Performance Link," *Strategic Management Journal* 18, no. 4 (1997), pp. 303–19; and Sandra Waddock and Samuel B. Graves, "Quality of Management and Quality of Stakeholder Relations: Are They Synonymous?" *Business and Society* 36 (September 1997), pp. 250–79.

Stockholders' Legal Rights and Safeguards

To protect their financial stake in the companies whose stocks they hold, stockholders have several legal safeguards. Specific rights of stockholders are established by law. Stockholders have the following legal rights, and these vary somewhat among states: They have the right to share in the profits of the enterprise if directors declare dividends. They have the right to receive annual reports of company earnings and company activities, and they have the right to inspect the corporate books, provided they have a legitimate business purpose for doing so and that it will not be disruptive of business operations. They have the right to elect directors and to hold those directors and the officers of the corporation responsible for their acts, by lawsuit if they want to go that far. Furthermore, they usually have the right to vote on mergers, some acquisitions, and changes in the charter and bylaws and to bring other business-related proposals before the stockholders. And finally, they have the right to sell their stock. Figure 14-2 summarizes the major legal rights of stockholders.

Many of these rights are exercised at the annual stockholders' meeting, where directors and managers present an annual report and shareholders have an opportunity to approve or disapprove of management's plans. Approval is generally expressed by reelecting incumbent directors, and disapproval may be shown by attempting to replace them with new ones. Because most corporations today are large, typically only a small portion of stockholders attend to vote in person. Those not attending are given an opportunity to vote by absentee ballot, called a **proxy.** The use of proxy elections by stockholders to influence corporate policy is discussed later in this chapter.

Stockholder Lawsuits

If stockholders think that they or their company have been damaged by actions of company officers or directors, they have the right to bring lawsuits in the courts. Lawsuits may be brought either by individual shareholders or by a group of individuals in a class action. **Shareholder lawsuits** may be initiated to check many abuses, including insider trading, an inadequate price obtained for the company's stock in a buyout (or a good price rejected), lush executive pension benefits, or fraud committed by company officials. For

Figure 14-2

Major legal rights of stockholders.

- To receive dividends, if declared
- To vote on
    Members of board of directors
    Major mergers and acquisitions
    Charter and bylaw changes
    Proposals by stockholders
- To receive annual reports on the company's financial condition
- To bring shareholder suits against the company and officers
- To sell their own shares of stock to others

example, shareholders of health care insurer Aetna sued after the board rejected a buyout offer at $70 a share, when the stock was selling in the low 40s.[11]

In the 1990s, many companies, especially in high-technology industries, complained that they were targets of frivolous shareholder lawsuits. In 1995, in response to these concerns, Congress passed legislation that made it harder for investors to sue companies for fraud. But some executives felt that the legislation had not gone far enough, because many shareholder suits disallowed under federal law could still be filed in state courts, and they called on Congress for a uniform national standard for securities lawsuits. Some investor groups, consumer activists, and trial lawyers opposed such a move. A citizens' initiative in California called Proposition 211, that would have made it *easier* for investors to sue companies for fraud, was defeated after many businesses rallied against it.

Corporate Disclosures

Giving stockholders more and better company information is one of the best ways to safeguard their interests. The theory behind the move for greater disclosure of company information is that the stockholder, as an investor, should be as fully informed as possible in order to make sound investments. By law, stockholders have a right to know about the affairs of the corporations in which they hold ownership shares. Those who attend annual meetings learn about past performance and future goals through speeches made by corporate officers and documents such as the company's annual report. Those who do not attend meetings must depend primarily on annual reports issued by the company and the opinions of independent financial analysts.

In recent years, management has tended to disclose more information than ever before to stockholders and other interested people. Prompted by the Securities and Exchange Commission, professional accounting groups, and individual investors, companies now disclose a great deal about their financial affairs, with much information readily available on investor relations sections of company web pages. Stockholders can learn about sales and earnings, assets, capital expenditures and depreciation by line of business, details of foreign operations, and many other financial matters. Corporations also are required to disclose detailed information about directors and top executives and their compensation. In addition, many companies have begun reporting detailed information about their social and environmental, as well as financial, performance. These trends toward greater corporate disclosure are further discussed in Chapters 4 and 20.

Corporate Governance

The term **corporate governance** refers to the overall control of a company's actions. Several key stakeholder groups are involved in governing the corporation.

- *Managers* occupy a strategic position because of their knowledge and day-to-day decision making.
- The *board of directors* exercises formal legal authority over company policy.
- *Stockholders,* whether individuals or institutions, have a vital stake in the company.

---

[11] "The Right Doctor for Aetna?" *Business Week,* May 1, 2000, p. 172.

- *Employees,* particularly those represented by unions or who own stock in the company, can affect some policies.
- *Government* is involved through its laws and regulations.
- *Creditors* who hold corporate debt may also influence a company's policies.

The following discussion concentrates on the roles of three groups that traditionally govern the corporation in addition to stockholders: the board of directors, top management, and creditors.

The Board of Directors

The board of directors is a central factor in corporate governance because corporation laws place legal responsibility for the affairs of a company on the directors. The board of directors is legally responsible for establishing corporate objectives, developing broad policies, and selecting top-level personnel to carry out these objectives and policies. The board also reviews management's performance to be sure that the company is well run and stockholders' interests are protected.[12]

Corporate boards are legally permitted to vary in size, composition, and structure to best serve the interests of the corporation and the shareholders. A number of patterns do exist, however. Corporate boards average 11 members, with the largest boards in banks and defense contractors, and the smallest in small and midsized firms, especially in high-tech industries. Of these members, it is likely that about 80 percent will be *outside* directors (not managers of the company). These may include chief executives of other companies, retired executives of other firms, major shareholders, bankers, former government officials, academics, and representatives of the community. Almost three-quarters of all companies have at least one woman on the board, and 60 percent have at least one member who is a member of an ethnic minority.

Most corporate boards perform their work through committees. The executive committee (present in 60 percent of corporate boards) works closely with top managers on important business matters. The audit committee (present in virtually all boards) is normally composed entirely of outside directors; it reviews the company's financial reports, recommends the appointment of outside auditors, and oversees the integrity of internal financial controls. The compensation committee (99 percent), also normally staffed by outside directors, administers and approves salaries and other benefits of high-level managers in the company. The nominating committee (74 percent) is charged with finding and recommending candidates for officers and directors, especially those to be elected at the annual stockholders' meeting. A significant number of corporations (19 percent) now have a special committee devoted to issues of corporate responsibility. Compensation for board members averages almost $40,000 a year. Many directors receive company stock in addition to these fees.[13]

---

[12] For an overview of the role and functions of the board of directors, see Marianne Jennings, *The Board of Directors: 25 Keys to Corporate Governance* (New York: Lebhar-Friedman Books, 2000).

[13] The figures in the preceding two paragraphs are based on data presented in Korn/Ferry International, 26th Annual *Board of Directors Study, 1999.* All data are for 1998.

Figure 14-3

The best boards of directors.

Source: "The Best and Worst Boards: Our New Report Card on Corporate Governance," *Business Week,* November 25, 1996, p. 86. Based on a survey of large pension fund and money managers and experts in corporate governance. Used by permission. Copyright © by the McGraw-Hill Companies.

The best boards:

- Evaluate performance of the CEO annually in meetings of independent directors.
- Link the CEO's pay to specific performance goals.
- Review and approve long-range strategy and one-year operating plans.
- Have a governance committee that regularly assesses the performance of the board and individual directors.
- Pay retainer fees to directors in company stock.
- Require each director to own a significant amount of company stock.
- Have no more than two or three inside directors.
- Require directors to retire at 70 years of age.
- Place the entire board up for election every year.
- Place limits on the number of other boards on which its directors can serve.
- Ensure that the audit, compensation, and nominating committees are composed entirely of independent directors.
- Ban directors who directly or indirectly draw consulting, legal, or other fees from the company.
- Ban interlocking directorships: "I'm on your board, you're on mine."

Board committees, which may meet several times each year, give active directors very important powers in controlling the company's affairs. In addition, when the entire board meets, it hears directly from top-level managers and has an opportunity to influence their decisions and policies.

What kind of boards work the best? A survey by *Business Week* identified the characteristics of the most effective boards of directors of U.S. companies, as shown in Figure 14-3. Although most big companies have adopted the corporate governance practices shown in this figure, many small companies have not.

> A recent study of dot-com firms showed that their boards tended to be small and to have few outside members. Timothy Koogle, CEO of the web portal Yahoo!, defended these practices, saying that in the world of Internet business "speed is everything. Keeping the board small and concentrated really helps." But the study's author disagreed, noting that small boards dominated by insiders run "counter to the principles of good corporate governance put forth by most of today's governance experts."[14]

Top Management

Professional managers generally take the leading role in large corporations. These managers might have backgrounds in marketing and sales, in engineering design and production, or in various aspects of financial analysis. The expanding scale and complexity of national

---

[14] "Dot Com Boards Are Flouting the Rules," *Business Week,* December 20, 1999, p. 130; and "Study Finds Dot-Com Boards Are Less Independent, in Conflict with Governance Principles," www.irrc.org/presss_releases/01102000dotcom.html.

and international business call for management specialists to guide the affairs of most big companies. The source of their power is a combination of their managerial expertise and simply being given organizational responsibility for carrying out the needed work.

Managers increasingly tend to consider their responsibilities as being primarily to the company rather than just to the stockholders. They perceive themselves to be responsible for (1) the economic survival of the firm; (2) extending its life into the future through product innovation, management development, market expansion, and other means; and (3) balancing the demands of all groups in such a way that the company can achieve its objectives. This viewpoint considers shareholders to be just one of several stakeholder groups that must be given attention. Concerning their specific responsibilities to owners, managers today often express the belief that "what is good for the company in the long run is good for the stockholder." Some observers believe that the power of top managers has declined somewhat in recent years, as boards of directors, institutional stockholders, and other stakeholders have grown more assertive.

Many top managers have an equity stake in the companies they lead, often because they are compensated in part by grants of stock or stock options. This may create a conflict of interest, to the extent that the interests of a company and its stockholders diverge. For example, managers with significant stock holdings may take actions to push up the value of the stock in the short term rather than ones that would benefit the long-term health of the company.

Creditors

Since the 1980s, creditors have become a powerful influence in the governance of corporations. Traditionally, creditors have lent money to businesses to help them finance the purchase of new buildings, equipment, or the expansion of a business into new areas of activity. In the 1980s, a number of financiers persuaded corporate executives that issuing high-risk, high-yield bonds, known as *junk bonds,* could enable them to acquire other firms, reorganize them, sell off unwanted portions, and both meet the debt payments and improve total corporate financial performance.

The idea was appealing, and dozens of companies used such financing to build larger and larger corporate empires. The threat of unwanted takeover bids became so serious that many managers sought to find ways of making their companies "private"— that is, eliminating the public stockholders. This led, in turn, to further use of debt in a series of **leveraged buyouts (LBOs).** An LBO uses debt financing (bonds or borrowed money) to purchase the outstanding shares of stock from public shareholders. For management, this arrangement replaces impatient shareholders, who are ready to sell their stock to the highest bidder, with a creditor whose view is longer-term. As long as the company can continue to pay the high yield on the bonds, management is relatively well protected from hostile takeover action. During the recession of the early 1990s, however, many users of debt financing found that revenues were insufficient to pay bond interest. The result was often bankruptcy or even complete dissolution of the company. This course of action was forced by the creditors, who wanted some return—even if less than full value—on the money they had loaned. Dealing with creditors has therefore become a major corporate governance issue for companies.[15]

[15] Michael C. Jensen, "Eclipse of the Public Corporation," *Harvard Business Review,* September–October 1989, pp. 61–74.

The Process of Corporate Governance

Who will govern the corporation internally is a central issue facing business. There is no easy answer to the question, Who's in charge? The current system of corporate governance is the product of a long historical process, dating back to the emergence of the modern, publicly held corporation in the late 1800s. This section presents two contrasting models of corporate governance, against which recent developments may be compared.

According to the traditional, legal model of corporate governance, stockholders hold the ultimate authority in the firm. In this view, stockholders exercise control through their legal right to elect the board of directors. The directors, in turn, hire top management, set overall strategy, and are responsible for making sure stockholders earn a fair return from a well-managed operation. These principles of governance are embodied in corporate law and in the legal rights stockholders enjoy, as shown in Figure 14-2. In the traditional model, stockholders are the group at the top of the chain of command within the firm.

Many analysts of the modern corporation, however, have long maintained that the traditional model is not a very realistic picture of how companies really work. In this revisionist view, several forces counteract the legal power of stockholders. Most shareholders in the United States historically have been individuals who owned a small number of shares. Typically, shareholders as a group were (and still are) geographically dispersed, and government rules made it difficult for them to contact each other or to organize on behalf of their collective interests. Most owners of stock who disapproved of management were more likely to do the "Wall Street walk"—simply selling their shares and walking away—than they were likely to try to change corporate policy.

By the same token, boards of directors—rather than controlling managers, as the traditional model suggested—were more likely to be controlled by them. Members of the board, in practice, were (and still are in many companies) nominated by top managers and served at their pleasure. Contested elections for board seats were rare. Board members, who usually served on a part-time basis, often lacked the information or expertise to challenge full-time managers and were likely to rubber-stamp decisions placed before them. In the revisionist view, then, corporate governance was turned on its head, with top managers having the ultimate authority—and with stockholders at the bottom.[16] The traditional and revisionist models are contrasted in Figure 14-4.

Recent trends in corporate governance suggest that neither model may any longer be an accurate description of how corporations are run. The power of external stakeholder

---

[16] A discussion of the legal basis for the roles of stockholders, boards, and managers in the modern corporation may be found in *Principles of Corporate Governance* (Philadelphia: American Law Institute, 1994). Early statements of the revisionist argument appear in Robert A. Gordon, *Business Leadership in the Large Corporation* (Berkeley: University of California Press, 1948); and Myles Mace, *Directors: Myth and Reality* (Boston: Harvard Business School Press, 1971). For more recent discussions of corporate governance, see *Harvard Business Review on Corporate Governance* (Boston: Harvard Business School Press, 2000); Margaret M. Blair, *Ownership and Control: Rethinking Corporate Governance for the Twenty-First Century* (Washington, DC: Brookings Institution, 1995); and Carolyn Kay Brancato, *Institutional Investors and Corporate Governance: Best Practices for Increasing Corporate Value* (Burr Ridge, IL: Irwin Professional, 1996).

Figure 14-4

Traditional and revisionist models of corporate governance.

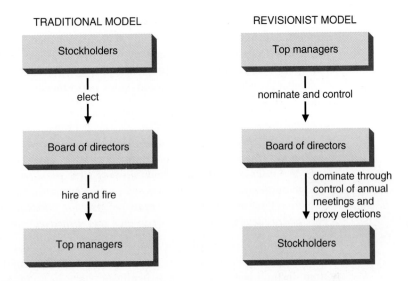

groups has increased, as discussed in Chapter 1. Within the firm, the relative power of various groups active in corporate governance has changed significantly, both in the United States and in other countries. Stockholders, particularly large institutions, and boards of directors have both become more assertive relative to top management. Social activist shareholders have exerted influence through the proxy (absentee ballot) election process, and in some cases workers have exercised control through new forms of stock ownership. These important developments are profiled in the next section.

Current Trends in Corporate Governance

The Rise of Institutional Investors

As shown earlier, institutional investors—pensions, mutual funds, endowment funds, and the like—have enlarged their stockholdings significantly over the past two decades and have become more assertive in promoting the interests of their members. This trend has had important implications for corporate governance.

One reason institutions have become more active is that it is more difficult for them to sell their holdings if they become dissatisfied with management performance. Large institutions have less flexibility than individual shareholders, because selling a large block of stock could seriously depress its price and therefore the value of the institution's holdings. Accordingly, institutional investors have a strong incentive to hold their shares and organize to change management policy. One example of such activism by institutional investors, at Archer Daniels Midland, is presented in the discussion case at the end of this chapter.

In 1985, the Council of Institutional Investors was formed. Since then, the Council has grown to more than 100 members and represents institutions and pension funds with investments exceeding $1 trillion. The Council developed a "Shareholder Bill of

Rights" and urged its members to view their proxies as assets, voting them on behalf of shareholders rather than automatically with management. The activism of institutional shareholders often improved company performance. One study showed that in the five years before and after a major pension fund became actively involved in the governance of companies whose shares it owned, stock performance improved dramatically relative to the overall market.[17]

> *Institutional owners have also influenced change by seeking out companies that practice good corporate governance. A survey of 200 such investors in the United States, Europe, Asia, and Latin America conducted by McKinsey & Company found that they were prepared to pay a premium of more than 20 percent for the shares of a company that hired outside directors, were responsive to investor requests for information, evaluated their board members, and followed other established governance practices.*[18]

Relationship investing occurs when large shareholders—pensions, mutual funds, or a group of private investors—form a long-term, committed link with a company. Often, institutional owners buy a significant stake in a company and acquire a seat on the board, or at least meet frequently with management. The benefits of relationship investing are that companies gain a long-term commitment from key shareholders, who in turn get more say in management. At Sears, for example, a leading advocate of relationship investing, Robert A. G. Monks, bought a major share in the company and then convinced managers to spin off its financial units and make other major changes. In a book describing his approach, Monks stated that "greater accountability to long-term owners is the most efficient, beneficial, and . . . natural way to order the elements of our current corporate governance system."[19] Some observers maintained that the movement for shareholder rights had matured, as many corporations increasingly accepted an enlarged role in corporate governance for institutional owners.[20]

The activism of institutional investors has begun to spread to other countries. In many cases, U.S.-based pension and mutual funds that have acquired large stakes in foreign companies have spearheaded these efforts. By 2000, about one in every eight dollars controlled by American pension funds and endowments was invested in overseas stocks or bonds.[21] To protect their globalized investments, fund managers have become active in proxy battles in Japan, Britain, Hong Kong, and many other countries. Although

---

[17] Council of Institutional Investors, "Does Shareholder Activism Make a Difference?" available at www.cii.org/mono.htm.

[18] "Good Corporate Governance Will Spur Investor Premiums, According to Survey," *Wall Street Journal,* June 19, 2000, p. B6.

[19] Robert A. G. Monks, *The Emperor's Nightingale: Restoring the Integrity of the Corporation in the Age of Shareholder Activism* (Reading, MA: Addison-Wesley, 1998), p. xxiii. See also, Robert A. G. Monks and Nell Minow, *Watching the Watchers: Corporate Governance for the 21st Century* (Oxford: Blackwell Publishers, 1996).

[20] Analysis of the growing importance of institutional shareholder activism may be found in Michael J. Rubach, *Institutional Shareholder Activism: The Changing Face of Corporate Ownership* (New York: Garland Publishers, 1999), and Michael Useem, *Investor Capitalism: How Money Managers Are Changing the Face of Corporate America* (New York: Basic Books, 1996).

[21] *U.S. Investment Management Report 1999* (Greenwich, CT: Greenwich Associates, 2000), p. 3.

these efforts have usually been unsuccessful, in the long run they may influence corporate governance abroad, as the following example shows.

> *In Germany, a representative of CalPERS, the California state employees' pension fund, stood up at the annual meeting of a major utility company and denounced shareholder voting restrictions, calling them "an embarrassing anachronism which pulls Germany out of step with international norms." The restrictions were not changed, but the German press gave the incident wide coverage, calling the confrontation "unprecedented."*

A study conducted by the Conference Board in 2000 found increasing ownership of foreign stock by U.S. institutional investors, giving them "increasing economic clout in international markets."[22]

Movements for shareholder rights often confront formidable obstacles abroad, where stock markets may be smaller and corporate governance is often dominated by networks of allied businesses, creditors, and managers—to the exclusion of stockholders. Many countries do not share the U.S. principle of "one share, one vote" or traditions of open debate at shareholder meetings. Even so, stockholders have successfully ousted top executives in Britain, organized for higher dividends in Japan, and blocked antitakeover provisions in the Netherlands. In 1999, the Organization for Economic Cooperation and Development (OECD) adopted a set of *Principles of Corporate Governance,* and that organization and the World Bank launched a series of roundtables in Asia, Latin America, and Russia to promote discussion of the topic.[23] The movement for the rights of shareholders, like the investments they hold, is becoming increasingly globalized.

Changing Role of the Board of Directors

Like institutional investors, some boards of directors have also become more assertive. At both ailing and healthy companies, boards have stopped rubber-stamping management policies and have begun thinking more independently. As the Procter & Gamble example that opens this chapter illustrates, some boards have fired their chief executives. Others have redirected, reorganized, and generally rethought their companies. One CEO commented, "[boards] are thinking through the whole process of corporate governance—what they're responsible for—and going into more detail about it."

The new assertiveness of some boards has several sources. Directors have found themselves pressured by institutional investors anxious to protect their shareholders' interests. Another factor has been an increase in lawsuits against board members. A number of court decisions have held directors personally liable for poor management decisions, making them more sensitive to their responsibilities to stockholders. Organizational reforms of the board have also led to increased independence from management. Growing representation by outside directors is one such trend; outsiders now make up

---

[22] The Conference Board, Global Corporate Governance Research Center, "Institutional Investor Five-Country Study," May 31, 2000; summary available at www.conference-board.org.
[23] See www.oecd.org/daf/corporate-affairs/governance.

over 80 percent of board members, on average. Another such reform is separation of the duties of the chief executive and the board chairman, rather than combining the two in one person as is done in many corporations. With this split in responsibilities, a board has an improved chance of receiving completely candid reports about a company's affairs. Many of these changes in the role and organization of the board of directors have now become common in Europe, as well as in the United States.[24]

Social Responsibility Shareholder Resolutions

Another important current trend in corporate governance is the rise of **social responsibility shareholder resolutions,** such as the resolution offered by the Province of St. Joseph Capuchin, illustrated in one of the opening examples of this chapter.[25]

The Securities and Exchange Commission allows stockholders to place resolutions concerning appropriate social issues, such as environmental responsibility or alcohol and tobacco advertising, in proxy statements sent out by companies. These SEC rules reflect a belief that stockholders should be allowed to vote on social as well as economic questions that are related to the business of the corporation. The SEC has tried to minimize harassment by requiring a resolution to receive minimum support in order to be resubmitted— 3 percent of votes cast the first time, 6 percent the second time, and 10 percent the third time it is submitted within a five-year period. Resolutions cannot deal with a company's "ordinary business," such as employee wages or the content of advertising, since that would constitute unjustified interference with management's decisions in running the company.[26]

In recent years, the number and variety of social responsibility shareholder resolutions have continued to increase. Shareholder activists in 2000 sponsored 145 resolutions dealing with major social issues at meetings of more than 100 corporations. More than 100 church groups were joined by individual shareholders, unions, environmental groups, and a growing number of pension funds. Many of these groups were members of a coalition, the Interfaith Center on Corporate Responsibility (ICCR), which coordinated the activities of the social responsibility shareholder movement. Some of the key issues raised in these resolutions included executive compensation, environmental responsibility, alcohol and tobacco advertising, equal employment opportunity, and investments in countries with human rights problems.

Since shareholder resolutions opposed by management rarely garner enough votes to be adopted, what is their point? There are several answers. The annual meetings provide a forum for debating social issues. Stockholders have a legal right to raise such issues and to ask questions about how their company is responding. In some cases, activists' main motivation in filing resolutions is simply to engage top managers in a dialogue about controversial issues and to force them to explain or justify their policies in a public forum.

---

[24] For an account of recent changes in the practices of boards of directors in Europe, see L. Van Den Berghe and Liesbeth De Ridder, *International Standardisation of Good Corporate Governance: Best Practices for the Board of Directors* (Dordrect, the Netherlands: Kluwer Academic Publishers, 1999).

[25] For general historical background on the rise of investor social activism, see Lauren Talner, *The Origins of Shareholder Activism* (Washington, DC: Investor Responsibility Research Center, 1983); and David Vogel, *Lobbying the Corporation: Citizen Challenges to Business Authority* (New York: Basic Books, 1978).

[26] Current SEC rules on shareholder proposals may be found at www.sec.gov/rules/final.

To avoid the glare of publicity, an increasing number of corporations have met with dissident groups prior to the annual meeting and have agreed to take action on an issue voluntarily. For example, in 2000 Ford Motor Company agreed to endorse the CERES Principles, a code of environmental conduct, after three years of discussion between the company and shareholders who had backed resolutions in support of the code.[27]

Employee Stock Ownership

A final trend, one that affects a small but growing number of U.S. corporations, is the form of stock ownership known as an **employee stock ownership plan (ESOP).** An ESOP is a kind of benefit plan in which a company purchases shares of its own stock and places them in trust for its employees. The idea is to give employees direct profit-sharing interest in addition to their wage and salary income. ESOP advocates claim that this kind of share ownership benefits the company by increasing worker productivity, reducing job absenteeism, and drawing management and employees closer together into a common effort to make the company a success. Not only do ESOP participants receive regular dividends on the stock they own, but workers who quit or retire can either take their stock from the fund or sell their shares back to the company. A major financial benefit to an ESOP company is that its contributions to the plan are tax deductible.

Beginning in the mid-1970s, ESOPs grew at an explosive pace, mainly because of new federal and state laws that encouraged their formation. From less than 500 in 1975, ESOPs grew to about 11,500 by 2000, covering over 8.5 million employees and controlling over $400 billion in corporate stock. Most ESOPs are in private companies, but they have become more popular in public firms as well.[28]

> *An example of an employee-owned company is United Airlines. In 1994, the airline set up an ESOP, and employees traded a 15 percent cut in pay for 55 percent of the stock. United workers not only owned a majority of the airline, but they also participated in management directly—from brainstorming teams at the lowest levels up to the board of directors, where they held 3 out of 12 seats. Five years later, the stock price had tripled, and revenues and profits were at record levels. The presence of an ESOP did not inoculate the company against labor strife, however, as conflict between the airline and its pilots and mechanics in 2000 demonstrated.*[29]

Studies have shown that where employee ownership is linked with participative management practices, as at United, companies experience significant gains in performance.[30]

---

[27] The text of the speech by Bill Ford announcing his endorsement of the CERES Principles is available at www.ceres.org/eventsandnews/news/Fordspeech.html.

[28] National Center for Employee Ownership, "Statistical Profile of Employee Ownership," available at www.nceo.org/library/eo_stat.html.

[29] "Departing Chairman Says United Is Worth Copying," *Washington Post,* July 7, 1999, p. E1; and "From Milestone to Millstone?" *Business Week,* March 20, 2000, p. 120.

[30] A summary of the literature on the link between employee ownership and performance may be found at www.nceo.org/library/corpperf.html.

In sum, the past decade has been a period of fluidity and flux in corporate governance. The answer to the question, Who governs the corporation? is becoming: Many people and groups. The authority of top managers has been increasingly checked by powerful groups of institutional investors, newly assertive boards of directors, and in a smaller number of cases, by activist shareholders and worker owners. It is clear that the process of corporate governance is undergoing significant change, much of it leading to a greater dispersion of power within the firm and a greater emphasis on enhancing shareholder value.

Special Issue: Executive Compensation

An issue of increasing controversy is **executive compensation.** Even as the authority of top managers has diminished, in some respects, their salaries have soared. Are top managers paid too much, or are their high salaries and bonuses a well-deserved reward for their contributions to the companies they lead? This debate has been the focus of much recent attention by boards of directors, shareholders, and government regulators seeking to increase the accountability of top managers.

Executive compensation in the United States, by international standards, is very high. In 1999, the chief executives of the largest corporations in the United States earned, on average, $12.4 million, including salaries, bonuses, and the present value of retirement benefits, incentive plans, and stock options, according to *Business Week* magazine. It had been a good decade for CEOs; this figure was more than six times their compensation in 1990.[31] By contrast, top managers in other countries earned much less. Although the pay of top executives in Europe was catching up, it was still generally well below what comparable managers in the United States earned. This caused friction in some international mergers. When Daimler acquired Chrysler, for instance, its managers were distressed by the pay disparity between the two firms; the CEO of the U.S. company, to cite just one example, made 11 times as much as his German counterpart.[32]

Another way to look at executive compensation is to compare the pay of top managers with that of average employees. In the United States, CEOs in 1999 made about 475 times what the average worker did.

Why are American executives paid so much? Corporate politics play an important role. Graef S. Crystal, a compensation expert and critic of inflated executive pay, argued in his book *In Search of Excess* that one reason salaries are so high is that they are set by compensation committees of boards of directors. These committees are usually made up of individuals handpicked by the CEO; often, they are CEOs themselves and sensitive to the indirect impact of their decisions on their own salaries. Moreover, compensation committees rely heavily on the advice of consultants who conduct surveys of salaries in similar firms. Crystal argued that since boards usually want to pay their own executives above the median for comparable firms, "it doesn't take a Ph.D. in statistics to figure out that under those circumstances, the median is going to keep going up."[33]

---

[31] "Special Report: Executive Pay," *Business Week,* April 17, 2000, pp. 100–42.
[32] "Chrysler Pay Draws Fire Overseas," *Wall Street Journal,* May 26, 1998, pp. B1, B12.
[33] Graef S. Crystal, *In Search of Excess: The Overcompensation of American Executives* (New York: W.W. Norton, 1991). A more recent treatment by the same author may be found in Graef S. Crystal, Ira T. Kay, and Frederic W. Cook, *CEO Pay: A Comprehensive Look* (New York: American Compensation Association, 1997).

Some observers say that the comparatively high compensation of top U.S. executives is justified. In this view, well-paid managers are simply being rewarded for outstanding performance. For example, Louis Gerstner earned $560 million during his first seven years at the helm of IBM. During this period, the stock price rose 828 percent. To at least some shareholders, his eye-popping pay was clearly worth it. A major share of the increase in executive compensation in the 1990s can be accounted for by the exercise of stock options (a benefit whose value typically rises with stock prices), reflecting the bull market during much of that decade—a development that benefited shareholders as well as executives. This was particularly true in the high-tech sector, where chief executives of the top firms made a well-above average $27 million in 1999, mostly from the exercise of stock options.[34]

Supporters also argue that high salaries provide an incentive for innovation and risk taking. In an era of intense global competition, restructuring, and downsizing, the job of CEO of large U.S. corporations has never been more challenging, and the tenure in the top job has become shorter. Another argument for high compensation is a shortage of labor. In this view, not many individuals are capable of running today's large, complex organizations, so the few that have the necessary skills and experience can command a premium. Today's high salaries are necessary for companies to attract or retain top talent, especially in competition with dot-com start-ups offering big stock option packages. Why shouldn't the most successful business executives make as much as top athletes and entertainers?[35]

On the other hand, critics argue that inflated executive pay hurts the ability of U.S. firms to compete with foreign rivals. High executive compensation diverts financial resources that could be used to invest in the business, increase stockholder dividends, or pay average workers more. Multimillion dollar salaries cause resentment and sap the commitment—and sometimes lead to the exodus of—hardworking lower and midlevel employees who feel they are not receiving their fair share.[36] As for the performance issue, critics suggest that as many extravagantly compensated executives preside over failure as they do over success. A study published in the *Harvard Business Review* concluded that "in most publicly held companies, the compensation of top executives is virtually independent of performance."[37]

Some shareholders activists have tried to rein in excessive executive compensation. For example, CalPERS, the big institutional investor, opposed reelection of members of Bank of America's compensation committee after they had raised their CEO's

---

[34] "Report on Executive Pay: In the Options Age, Rising Pay (and Risk)," *New York Times,* April 2, 2000, p. C1. A critique of high executive pay may be found in Sarah Anderson and Ralph Estes, "The Decade of Executive Excess: The 1990s" (Washington, DC: Institute for Policy Studies, September 1999).

[35] A defense of high executive pay may be found in Andrew Brownstein and Morris J. Panner, "Who Should Set CEO Pay? The Press? Congress? Shareholders?" *Harvard Business Review,* May–June 1992, pp. 28–38.

[36] "Look Out Below: Does a Big Pay Gap between the Top Executive and the New Tier Feed Turnover?" *Wall Street Journal,* April 6, 2000, p. R3.

[37] Michael C. Jensen and Kevin J. Murphy, "CEO Incentives—It's Not How Much You Pay, but How," *Harvard Business Review,* May–June 1990, pp. 138–49.

pay to $76 million a year, despite an earnings shortfall.[38] Executive compensation has also been the subject of government regulations. Under SEC rules, companies must clearly disclose what their five top executives are paid and lay out a rationale for their compensation. A separate chart must report the company's stock and dividend performance. These rules expand stockholders' rights by making it easier for them to determine a manager's total compensation and whether it is justified by the firm's record. The SEC also allows nonbinding shareholder votes on executive and director compensation. A 1993 law prohibits companies from taking a tax deduction on executive salaries in excess of $1 million annually, although most compensation experts say it has not made much difference in compensation practices.

Some companies have responded to these stakeholder pressures by changing the process by which they set executive pay. Most firms now staff their compensation committees exclusively with outside directors and permit them to hire their own consultants. At American Exploration Co., an oil and gas company, the board voted against extra compensation for top executives after an independent consultant told them it was not necessary to remain competitive. Other companies have sought to restructure compensation to tie top executives' pay more closely to performance. A few top managers have even taken pay cuts or refused compensation altogether—like Netscape's CEO James Barksdale, who accepted no salary or bonus in 1997 after his company's stock price plummeted. Some firms, including Du Pont and Tandem Computers, have made stock options available to all employees, giving everyone—not just the top executives—a stake in the company's performance. A tiny handful of companies have ruled that top executives cannot earn more than a certain multiple of others' pay.

The active debate over excessive executive compensation was part of the larger issue of the relative power within the corporation of managers, directors, and stockholders and of the regulation of their roles by government.

Government Protection of Stockholder Interests

Securities and Exchange Commission

The major government agency protecting stockholders' interests is the Securities and Exchange Commission. Established in 1934 in the wake of the stock market crash and the Great Depression, its mission is to protect stockholders' rights by making sure that stock markets are run fairly and that investment information is fully disclosed. The agency, unlike most in government, generates revenue to pay for its own operations.

Government regulation is needed because stockholders can be damaged at times by abusive practices. One area calling for special efforts to protect and promote stockholder interests is insider trading.

Insider Trading

Insider trading occurs when a person gains access to confidential information about a company's financial condition and then uses that information, before it becomes public knowledge, to buy or sell the company's stock. Since others do not know what an inside

[38] "CalPERS Protests BofA Chief's Huge Pay," *San Francisco Chronicle,* April 12, 2000, p. A1.

trader knows, it is possible for the insider to make advantageous investments or sell stock well in advance of other stockholders.

Insider trading is illegal under the Securities and Exchange Act of 1934, which outlaws "any manipulative or deceptive device." The courts have generally interpreted this to mean that it is against the law to:

- Misappropriate (steal) nonpublic information and use it to trade a stock.

- Trade a stock based on a tip from someone who had an obligation to keep quiet; for example, a man would be guilty of insider trading if he bought stock after his sister, who was on the board of directors, told him of a pending offer to buy the company.

- Pass information to others with an expectation of direct or indirect gain, even if the individual did not trade the stock for his or her own account.

In an important 1997 case, *U.S.* v. *O'Hagen,* the Supreme Court clarified insider trading law. The court ruled that someone who traded on the basis of inside information when he or she *knew* the information was supposed to remain confidential was guilty of misappropriation, whether or not the trader was directly connected to the company whose shares were purchased. In the 1997 case, the court upheld the conviction of a Minneapolis lawyer who had made millions trading stock options after he learned of a pending takeover involving a client of his firm. Under the new court interpretation, insider trading rules would cover a wide range of people—from lawyers, to secretaries, to printers—who learned of and traded on information they knew was confidential. They would not, however, cover people who came across information by chance, for example, by overhearing a conversation in a bar. In this situation, the trader would not necessarily know the information was confidential.[39]

The best known kind of insider trading occurs when people improperly acquire confidential information about forthcoming mergers of large corporations, in order to buy and sell stocks before the mergers are announced to the public. The well-known insider trading scandals of the 1980s were of this type. More recently, another kind of insider trading, called *front-running,* has become more common. Front-runners place buy and sell orders for stock in advance of the moves of big institutional investors, such as mutual funds, based on tips from informants. This form of insider trading is often harder for regulators to detect and prosecute.[40]

The number of insider trading cases brought by the SEC in the late 1990s was well ahead of earlier years. Many of these cases involved not big-time investment bankers, as in the 1980s, but lower-level corporate employees and their friends and family members.[41]

Many instances of insider trading have emerged in the former communist countries of Eastern Europe. The transition there to a market economy was generally not accompanied by adoption of the same kinds of government controls that exist in the United States. The result was, in many instances, stock price manipulation and insider trading. The president of one mutual fund with investments in Eastern Europe, speaking of the Czech Republic,

---

[39] "Supreme Court Upholds S.E.C.'s Theory of Insider Trading," *New York Times,* June 26, 1997, pp. C1, C23.
[40] "The New, Improved Game of Insider Trading," *Fortune,* June 7, 1999, pp. 115–21.
[41] "The Boeskys of Main Street: Suspect Trading Rises, with New Kinds of Insiders Seen," *New York Times,* April 16, 1997, p. D1.

complained, "Like most post-communist countries, there was an ingrained system—never tell the truth and always help your buddies."[42]

Insider trading, whether in new market economies or established ones, is contrary to the logic underlying the stock markets: all stockholders ought to have access to the same information about companies. None should have special privileges or gain unfair advantages over others. Only in that way can investors have full confidence in the fairness of the stock markets. If they think that some investors can use inside knowledge for their own personal gain while others are excluded from such information, the system of stock buying might break down because of lack of trust.

Stockholders and the Corporation

Stockholders have become an increasingly powerful and vocal stakeholder group in corporations. Management dominance of boards of directors has weakened, and shareholders, especially institutional investors, are pressing directors and management more forcefully to serve stockholder interests. Institutional investors also have acquired new power as creditors, using their purchases of corporate bonds as an additional form of leverage on corporate management. Shareholder activists and worker-owners have also changed the contours of corporate governance.

Clearly, stockholders are a critically important stakeholder group. By providing capital, monitoring corporate performance, assuring the effective operation of stock markets, and bringing new issues to the attention of management, stockholders play a very important role in making the business system work. A major theme of this book is that the relationship between the modern corporation and *all* stakeholders is changing. Corporate leaders have an obligation to manage their companies in ways that attempt to align stockholder interests with those of employees, customers, communities, and others. Balancing these various interests is a prime requirement of modern management. Although stockholders are no longer considered the only important stakeholder group, their interests and needs remain central to the successful operation of corporate business.

Summary Points of This Chapter

- Individuals and institutions own shares of corporations as a means of economic gain. Social purposes sometimes guide investors, as when certain businesses are avoided because of their negative social impacts. Shareholders are entitled to vote, receive information, select directors, and attempt to shape corporate policies and action.
- The corporate governance system is the relationship among directors, managers, shareholders, and sometimes creditors. It determines who has legitimate power and how this power can be exercised. Corporate governance has changed in recent years. Newly assertive institutional investors and boards of directors have challenged the authority of top management.

---

[42] "A U.S. Fund Manager in Prague Has Found Privatization Corrupt," *New York Times,* December 3, 1997, p. D8.

- Activists have influenced corporate actions in some cases through social responsibility shareholder proposals, although such proposals rarely gain enough votes to pass.
- Employee stock ownership programs (ESOPs) give employees a stake in the financial success of a company and may enhance worker commitment and productivity.
- Some observers argue that the compensation of top U.S. executives is justified by performance and that high salaries provide a necessary incentive for innovation and risk taking in a demanding position. Critics, however, believe that executive compensation is too high. In this view, high pay hurts firm competitiveness and undermines employee commitment.
- Insider trading is illegal and unethical. It benefits those with illicitly acquired information at the expense of those who do not have it. Ultimately, it undermines fairness in the marketplace.

Key Terms and Concepts Used in This Chapter

- Stockholders
- Institutional investors
- Proxy
- Shareholders' lawsuits
- Corporate governance
- Leveraged buyouts (LBO)
- Relationship investing

- Social responsibility shareholder resolutions
- Employee stock ownership plan (ESOP)
- Executive compensation
- Insider trading

Internet Resources

- www.nyse.com   New York Stock Exchange
- www.irrc.org   Investor Responsibility Research Center
- www.cii.com   Council of Institutional Investors
- www.socialinvest.org Social Investment Forum
- www.thecorporatelibrary.com The Corporate Library (Governance)

Discussion Case: *Shareholders Demand Reforms at Archer Daniels Midland*

In 1996, a group of irate institutional investors converged on the annual stockholders meeting of Archer Daniels Midlands (ADM) demanding reform. The Decatur, Illinois–based company, which called itself the "supermarket to the world," was a global producer of agricultural goods such as corn syrup, vegetable oil, and ethanol. Since 1970, the company, under the leadership of CEO Dwayne Andreas, had seen its market value soar from $78 million to almost $12 billion.

The agribusiness giant was reeling from bad news. Just days earlier, the company had pled guilty to federal charges that it had conspired to fix the prices of lysine and citric acid, two widely used ingredients in food products. It had agreed to pay a $100 million criminal fine, the largest in the history of antitrust enforcement. ADM's first quarter fiscal year profits, $174 million, were more than wiped out by the cost of the fines and $90 million in related civil settlements.

Many institutional shareholders blamed the company's troubles, in part, on the unusually cozy relationship between ADM's management and its board of directors. The *New York Times* called ADM "a virtual family fief under Mr. Andreas's iron-fisted control." Of the 17-person board of directors, 10 were current or former executives or relatives of Andreas; several others were considered personally loyal to him. Some shareholders believed that, because of its lack of independence, the board had failed to exercise strict oversight over the company's operations.

"The $100 million fine is shareholder assets that are being squandered to pay for criminal activity that never should have occurred," said a representative of CalPERS, the California public pension fund. "Where was the board of directors?"

One group of institutional investors, led by the California and Florida pensions, proposed that a majority of the board be comprised of outsiders. Another proposal, by the pension fund for New York City firefighters, called for secret shareholder voting. These proposals received 42 and 46 percent of the votes cast, unusually high for ones opposed by an incumbent board. Some investors also called for Andreas's resignation.

Although the shareholder proposals failed, the company took steps voluntarily to reform its governance process. Four managers, all with close ties to Andreas, stepped down from the board, and several other members were replaced. Two executives implicated in the price-fixing scandal, including Andreas's son and heir apparent, left the company. And the board approved a new governance structure, in which Andreas would share power as part of a four-person executive committee.

But big shareholders were not mollified. "We do support companies that distribute power when there are signs of trouble," said a representative of the Council of Institutional Investors in 1996. "But this is shocking . . . instead of bring[ing] in a new CEO, they do this." In 1997, Dwayne Andreas finally retired as CEO at the age of 79, although he remained chairman of the board. He was succeeded by G. Allen Andreas, Dwayne's nephew and former head of the company's European operations.

In 2000, the composition of ADM's 13-person board remained virtually unchanged from four years earlier; only 5 members were outsiders. The firm's stock price was down 25 percent, coming off a drop of 30 percent the previous year. In naming the company to its "worst board of directors" list that year, *Fortune* magazine noted, "Think of ADM's board as the Albania of corporate America: It goes its own bizarre way, the results are terrible, and it doesn't really care what you think."

Sources: "America's Worst Boards: These Six Aren't Just Bad, They're Horrible," *Fortune,* April 17, 2000, p. 241; "The Best and Worst Boards," *Business Week,* January 24, 2000, p. 142; "The Tale of the Secret Tapes," *New York Times,* November 16, 1997, pp. B1, B10; "ADM's New CEO: Allen Andreas," *Chicago Tribune,* April 18, 1997, Business Section p. 1; "It Isn't Dwayne's World Anymore," *Business Week,* November 18, 1996, p. 82; "Andreas Creates Executive Team," *Washington Post,* November 1, 1996, p. F3; "Archer Daniels Midland Agrees to Big Fine for Price Fixing," *New York Times,* October 15, 1996, A1, C3; "ADM Governance Committee Urges Broad Changes in Board Makeup," *Milling and Baking News,* January 23, 1996, p. 10; and additional news reports appearing in the *New York Times, Chicago Tribune, Washington Post,* and *Wall Street Journal.* Archer Daniels Midland's website may be found at www.admworld.com.

Discussion Questions

1. Why were some institutional investors dissatisfied with actions of Archer Daniels Midland's management and board of directors?
2. Do you believe that the composition of the board of directors was a factor in the company's involvement in the price-fixing scandal? Why or why not?
3. As an individual shareholder of Archer Daniels Midland, would you have been satisfied with the company's managers and board of directors? With the subsequent actions of the institutional investors? If not, what could you do about it?
4. Do you believe that the actions of top management, the board of directors, and shareholders in this case are consistent with the trends in corporate governance discussed in this chapter? Why or why not?

15

Consumer Protection

Safeguarding consumers while continuing to supply them with the goods and services they want, at the prices they want, is a prime social responsibility of business. Many companies recognize that providing customers with excellent service and product quality is an effective, as well as ethical, business strategy. Consumers, for their part, have become increasingly aware of their rights to safety, to be informed, to choose, and to be heard—and, increasingly, of their right to privacy. Government agencies serve as watchdogs for consumers, supplementing the actions taken by consumers to protect themselves and the actions of socially responsible corporations.

This chapter focuses on these key questions and objectives:

- Why did a consumer movement develop in the United States?

- What are the major rights of consumers?

- In what ways do government regulatory agencies protect consumers? To what extent *should* government protect consumers?

- How can consumer privacy online best be protected?

- Is there a product liability crisis, and what reforms, if any, should be made?

- How have socially responsible corporations responded to consumer needs?

State Farm was shocked in 1999 when an Illinois court ordered the firm to pay $1.2 billion in damages to its policyholders. The judge found that the insurance company, well known for its "like a good neighbor" slogan, had defrauded its customers by using shoddy generic parts to fix wrecked autos. State Farm vigorously defended itself, saying it steered clear of more expensive brand-name replacement parts to keep policy costs down. In the early 2000s, the price of car insurance policies issued by State Farm and many other companies rose sharply. An industry economist said the main reason was that after the State Farm lawsuit, many insurers had quit using generic parts.[1]

DoubleClick, a leading Internet advertising company, ran into trouble in 2000 when it decided to collect and sell information about people who viewed ads it placed online. The company planned to link users' names, addresses, and credit history with information about their web-surfing behavior to create a database of personal profiles that would be a gold mine for marketers. But the company backed off after a storm of criticism from consumer privacy advocates, saying it would wait for an agreement between government and industry on privacy standards. Said DoubleClick's chief executive, "I made a mistake."[2]

In 1999, food manufacturers Gerber and Heinz both announced that they would no longer produce baby food containing genetically modified corn and soybeans. These so-called GM crops had been "bio-engineered" to be resistant to some pests and commonly used weed-killers, making them cheaper and easier for farmers to grow. Extensive testing by the Food and Drug Administration and others showed that GM foods were "as safe as other foods in the grocery store," and the agency had approved their use without special labeling. But many customers, especially in Europe, were concerned that GM foods might carry unknown dangers. Said a top executive of Novartis, Gerber's parent company: "I have got to listen to my customers. So, if there is an issue, or even an inkling of an issue, I am going to make amends."[3]

These three episodes demonstrate some of the complexities of serving consumers today. Companies face challenging, and often conflicting, demands to produce high-quality products or services, keep prices down, and meet the changing expectations of their diverse customers around the world. This chapter examines these issues and the various ways that consumers and their advocates, government regulators, the courts, and proactive business firms have dealt with them.

Pressures to Promote Consumer Interests

As long as business has existed—since the ancient beginnings of commerce and trade—consumers have tried to protect their interests when they go to the marketplace to buy goods and services. They have haggled over prices, taken a careful look at the goods

---

[1] "State Farm: What's Happening to the Good Neighbor?" *Business Week,* November 8, 1999, pp. 138–46; and "Cost of Insurance for Cars Is Rising across the Nation," *New York Times,* May 27, 2000.

[2] "DoubleClick Backs off on Net Data," *Boston Globe,* March 3, 2000, p. C1; and Jeffrey Rosen, "The Eroded Self," *New York Times Magazine,* April 30, 2000, pp. 46ff.

[3] "Gerber Baby Food, Grilled by Greenpeace, Plans Swift Overhaul," *Wall Street Journal,* July 30, 1999, pp. A1, A6; and "Frankenstein Foods?" *Newsweek,* September 13, 1999, pp. 33–35.

they were buying, compared the quality and prices of products offered by other sellers, and complained loudly when they felt cheated by shoddy products. So consumer self-reliance—best summed up by the Latin phrase, *caveat emptor,* meaning "let the buyer beware"—has always been one form of consumer protection and is still practiced today.

However, the increasing complexity of economic life, especially in the more advanced industrial nations, has led to organized, collective efforts to safeguard consumers. These organized activities are usually called consumerism, or the **consumer movement.** In the United States, the consumer movement first emerged in the Progressive Era of the 1910s; later waves of consumerism occurred in the 1930s during the New Deal and in the 1960s as part of the broader movement for social change at that time (discussed in Chapter 3).

The Anatomy of Consumerism

At the heart of consumerism in the United States is an attempt to expand the rights and powers of consumers. The goal of the consumer movement is to make consumer power an effective counterbalance to the rights and powers of business firms that sell goods and services.

As business firms grow in size and market power, they increasingly acquire the ability to dominate marketplace transactions with their customers. Frequently, they can dictate prices. Typically, their advertisements sway consumers to buy one product or service rather than another. If large enough, they may share the market with only a few other large companies, thereby weakening some of the competitive protections enjoyed by consumers where business firms are smaller and more numerous. The economic influence and power of business firms may therefore become a problem for consumers unless ways can be found to promote an equal amount of consumer power.

Most consumers would feel well protected if their fundamental rights to fair play in the marketplace could be guaranteed. In a well-known speech delivered in the early 1960s, President John F. Kennedy told Congress that consumers were entitled to four different kinds of protections:

1. *The right to safety*—to be protected against the marketing of goods that are hazardous to health or life.

2. *The right to be informed*—to be protected against fraudulent, deceitful, or grossly misleading information, advertising, labeling, or other practices, and to be given the facts to make an informed choice.

3. *The right to choose*—to be assured, wherever possible, access to a variety of products and services at competitive prices; and in those industries in which competition is not workable and government regulation is substituted, to be assured of satisfactory quality and service at fair prices.

4. *The right to be heard*—to be assured that consumer interests will receive full and sympathetic consideration in the formulation of government policy and fair and expeditious treatment in its administrative tribunals.

The **consumer bill of rights,** as it was called, became the guiding philosophy of the consumer movement. If those rights could be guaranteed, consumers would feel more confident in dealing with well-organized and influential corporations in the marketplace. In recent years, some activists and government regulators have begun to call for laws protecting a fifth consumer right, the *right to privacy*. This issue is discussed further in the section in this chapter on consumer privacy in the Internet age.

Reasons for the Consumer Movement

This consumer movement exists because consumers want to be treated fairly and honestly in the marketplace. Some business practices do not meet this standard. Consumers may be harmed by abuses such as unfairly high prices, unreliable and unsafe products, excessive or deceptive advertising claims, and the promotion of some products (such as cigarettes or farm products contaminated with pesticides) known to be harmful to human health.

Additional reasons for the existence of the consumer movement are the following:

- *Complex products have enormously complicated the choices consumers need to make when they go shopping.* For this reason, consumers today are more dependent on business for product quality than ever before. Because many products are so complex—a personal computer or an automobile, for example—most consumers have no way to judge at the time of purchase whether their quality is satisfactory. Many of the component parts of such products are not visible to consumers, who therefore cannot inspect them even if they have the technical competence to do so. Consumers find that they are almost entirely dependent on business to deliver the quality promised. In these circumstances, unscrupulous business firms can take advantage of uninformed consumers.

- *Services, as well as products, have become more specialized and difficult to judge.* When choosing lawyers, dentists, colleges, or hospitals, most consumers do not have adequate guides for evaluating whether they are good or bad. They can rely on word-of-mouth experiences of others, but this information may not be entirely reliable. Or when purchasing expensive items such as refrigerators, householders have not only to judge how well the items will perform but also to know what to do when they break down. The consumer faces a two-tier judgment problem in making purchases: First, is the product a good one? Then, what will good service cost? The uninformed or badly informed consumer is frequently no match for the seller who is in the superior position.

- *When business tries to sell both products and services through advertising, claims may be inflated or they may appeal to emotions having little to do with how the product is expected to perform.* Abercrombie & Fitch, the fashion retailer, for example, has been criticized for promoting its clothing to teens in magazine-style catalogs that are packed with sexual imagery, like scantily clad young men playing with water hoses.[4] The inappropriate use of sexual references or images in advertising is further discussed in Chapter 19.

---

[4] "Fashion's Frat Boy," *Newsweek,* September 13, 1999, p. 40.

- *Product safety has often been ignored.* Ever since Ralph Nader's well-publicized charges in the early 1970s about the hazards of driving the Corvair,[5] automobile safety has increasingly become a matter of public concern. As interest in health and nutrition grew, many consumers worried about food additives, preservatives, pesticide residues, and the potential hazards of genetically modified crops. If the public could not count on business to screen out these possible dangers to consumers, to whom could they turn for help? Consumer concerns led eventually to corrective actions by consumer advocacy groups, government regulators, the courts, and businesses themselves.

Consumer Advocacy Groups

One of the impressive features of the consumer movement in the United States is the many organized groups that actively promote and speak for the interests of millions of consumers. One organization alone, the Consumer Federation of America, brings together over 260 nonprofit groups to espouse the consumer viewpoint; it represents more than 50 million Americans. A nonprofit organization, Consumers Union, conducts extensive tests on selected consumer products and services and publishes the results, with ratings on a brand-name basis, online and in *Consumer Reports* magazine. Consumer cooperatives, credit unions, websites catering to consumers, and consumer education programs in schools and universities and on television and radio round out an extensive network of activities aimed at promoting consumer interests.

The most-publicized consumer advocate is Ralph Nader, who with his associates formed a network of affiliated organizations. Public Citizen, founded in 1971, became the umbrella organization for specialized units, the main fund-raising organization, and a publishing arm for consumer publications. The Health Research Group has taken the lead in urging the government to require warning labels on dangerous products, set exposure limits on hazardous substances, and alert the public to possibly dangerous medical products on the market, such as silicone breast implants. Other organizations under the Public Citizen umbrella include the Litigation Group, which gives legal assistance to people who have difficulty in gaining adequate access to the court system; Congress Watch, which monitors Congress; and Global Trade Watch, which educates consumers about the impact of economic globalization. Nader's organization is also allied with a network of state and local activist groups.[6]

How Government Protects Consumers

The federal government's involvement in protecting consumers' interests is extensive. During the 1960s and 1970s, Congress passed important laws to protect consumers, created new regulatory agencies, and strengthened older consumer protection agencies. These developments meant that consumers, rather than relying solely on free market competition to safeguard their interests, could also turn to government for protection. During

---

[5] Ralph Nader, *Unsafe at Any Speed: The Designed-in Dangers of the American Automobile* (New York: Grossman, 1972).
[6] Further information about Public Citizen is available at www.citizen.org.

most of the 1980s, a deregulatory attitude by the federal government tended to blunt federal initiatives on behalf of consumers. However, state governments became more active, particularly regarding price-fixing, car insurance rates, and corporate takeovers that threatened jobs and consumer incomes. The mid-1990s to early 2000s witnessed a revival of regulatory activism in some areas of consumer protection, such as the government's effort to regulate nicotine as a drug. Some speculated that the Republican administration that took office in 2001 would scale back enforcement of antitrust and other consumer protection laws, tipping the balance in favor of business interests.

> *One area of consumer protection likely to receive legislative action in the early 2000s is health care. Both major political parties in the United States have voiced support for some kind of* patients' bill of rights *that would protect consumers of medical services. Such a bill might, for example, require health plans to guarantee access to emergency and specialty care, ban contract clauses that prevent doctors from informing their patients about all treatment options, or permit patients to sue their health plans for harm caused by the denial of covered benefits.*

Goals of Consumer Laws

Figure 15-1 lists some of the safeguards provided by **consumer protection laws.** Taken together, these safeguards reflect the five goals of government policymakers and regulators outlined at the beginning of this chapter.

First, some laws are intended to provide consumers with better information when making purchases. Consumers can make more rational choices when they have accurate information about the product, thereby making comparison with competing products easier. For example, the Truth in Lending Act requires lenders to inform borrowers of the annual rate of interest to be charged, plus related fees and service charges. The laws requiring health warnings on cigarettes and alcoholic beverages broaden the information consumers have about these items. Knowing the relative energy efficiency of household appliances, which must be posted by retailers, permits improved choices. Manufacturers, retailers, and importers must specify whether warranties (a guarantee or assurance by the seller) are full or limited, must spell them out in clear language, and must give consumers the right to sue if warranties are not honored.

Deceptive advertising is illegal. Manufacturers may not make false or misleading claims about their own products or competitors' products. For example, in 1999 Stanley Works settled charges brought by the Federal Trade Commission that it had deceptively advertised its Husky and other brands of household tools as "made in America" when, in fact, they had significant foreign content. This was in violation of FTC rules.[7]

Federal law also requires food manufacturers to adopt a uniform nutrition label, specifying the amount of calories, fat, salt, and other nutrients contained in packaged, canned, and bottled foods. The same kind of information about fresh fruits and

---

[7] "Stanley Works, Five Other Companies, Settle FTC Made-in-America Charges," *Wall Street Journal,* January 20, 1999, p. A4.

Figure 15-1

Major consumer
protections specified
by consumer laws.

Information protections

Hazardous home appliances must carry a warning label.

Home products must carry a label detailing contents.

Automobiles must carry a label showing detailed breakdown of price and all related costs.

Credit loans require lender to disclose all relevant credit information about rate of interest, penalties, and so forth.

Tobacco advertisements and products must carry a health warning label.

Alcoholic beverages must carry a health warning label.

All costs related to real estate transactions must be disclosed.

Warranties must specify the terms of the guarantee and the buyer's rights.

False and deceptive advertising can be prohibited.

Food and beverage labels must show complete information.

Food advertising must not make false claims about nutrition.

Direct hazard protections

Hazardous toys and games for children are banned from sale.

Safety standards for motor vehicles are required.

National and state speed limits are specified.

Hazardous, defective, and ineffective products can be recalled under pressure from EPA, CPSC, NHTSA, and FDA.

Pesticide residue in food is allowed only if it poses a negligible risk.

Pricing protections

Unfair pricing, monopolistic practices, and noncompetitive acts are regulated by FTC and Justice Department and by states.

Liability protections

When injured by a product, consumers can seek legal redress.

Privacy protections

Limited collection of information online from and about children is allowed.

Other protections

No discrimination in the extension of credit is allowed.

vegetables, as well as fish, must be posted in supermarkets. Strict new rules define what can properly be labeled "organic."

A second aim of consumer legislation is to protect consumers against possible hazards from products they may purchase. Required warnings about possible side effects of pharmaceutical drugs, limits placed on flammable fabrics, the banning of lead-based paints, and inspections to eliminate contaminated or spoiled meats are examples of these safeguards. In 1998, following several outbreaks of bacterial poisoning, the government required most fresh fruit and vegetable juice producers to implement good manufacturing practices to ensure safety and mandated that all unpasteurized juice carry a warning label. One incident of bacterial contamination in food that occurred before these rules were implemented, involving fresh fruit juice made by Odwalla, Inc., is described in a case study at the end of the textbook. The role of the government in protecting consumers from unsafe food is also addressed in the discussion case at the end of Chapter 7.

Congress has also recently addressed the problem of pesticide and herbicide residues left on farm products. Some of these chemicals cause nerve damage if consumed in large quantities; others have produced cancers in test animals. Children are thought to be especially at risk. In 1996, Congress repealed the 1958 Delaney Clause, which had banned all food additives known to cause cancer, and replaced it with a single standard for fresh and processed food. The new standard allowed pesticide residue in food only if it posed a negligible risk, except for some stronger provisions designed to protect children. The goal of the new law was to protect the public's health without causing unnecessary harm to agricultural producers.

The third and fourth goals of consumer laws are to promote competitive pricing and consumer choice. When competitors secretly agree to divide up markets among themselves, or when a single company dominates a market, this artificially raises prices and limits consumer choice. Both federal and state antitrust laws forbid these practices, as discussed in Chapter 9. Competitive pricing also was promoted by the deregulation of the railroad, airline, trucking, telecommunications, banking, and other industries in the 1970s and 1980s. Prior to deregulation, government agencies frequently held prices artificially high and, by limiting the number of new competitors, shielded existing businesses from competition.

A fifth and final goal of consumer laws is to protect privacy. This issue has just recently begun to receive regulatory attention, as discussed later in this chapter. The Children's Online Privacy Protection Act, which went into effect in 2000, limits the collection of information online from and about children under the age of 13.

Major Consumer Protection Agencies

Figure 15-2 depicts the principal consumer protection agencies that operate at the federal level, along with their major areas of responsibility. The oldest of the six is the Department of Justice, whose Antitrust Division dates back to the end of the nineteenth century. Its functions are described further in Chapter 9. The Food and Drug Administration was founded in the first decade of the twentieth century. The Federal Trade Commission was established in 1914 and has been given additional powers to protect consumers over the years, including in the area of online privacy. Three of the agencies—the Consumer Product Safety Commission, the National Highway Traffic Safety Administration, and the National Transportation Safety Board—were created during the great wave of consumer regulations in the 1960s and early 1970s. Not pictured in Figure 15-2 are the Department of Agriculture, which has specific responsibility for the inspection of meat and poultry, and the Environmental Protection Agency, which has authority over genetically modified food and some chemicals that may affect consumers.

The Civil Rights Division of the Department of Justice enforces the provisions of the Civil Rights Act that prohibit discrimination against consumers. A recent case brought by this division is described in Exhibit 15-A.

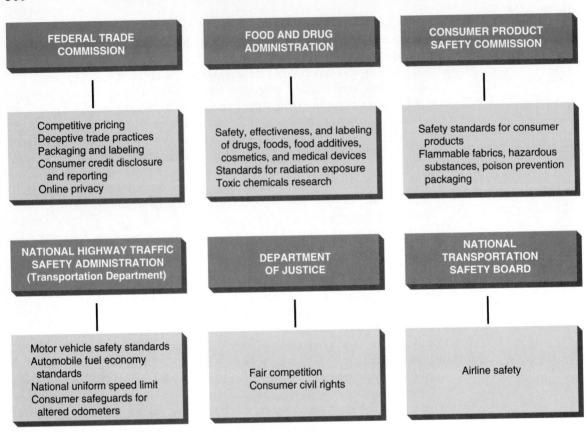

Figure 15-2

Major federal consumer protection agencies and their main responsibilities.

The National Highway Traffic Safety Administration affects many consumers directly through its authority over automobile safety. For example, the agency develops regulations for car air bags, devices that work by inflating rapidly during a collision, preventing the occupant from moving forward and striking the steering wheel or dashboard. Since 1998, driver and passenger-side air bags have been required as standard equipment on most cars. After concern emerged about possible hazards of the air bags themselves to children and small adults, the agency modified its rule to permit consumers to disable passenger-side airbags, if they could demonstrate a good reason, such as the need to place a small child in the front seat. The agency also said that automakers could offer less powerful bags as an option. Eventually, the NHTSA said it would require so-called smart air bags that would adjust the force of deployment according to the weight of the occupant.[8] The agency also has authority over the safety of automobile tires, the focus of the recent Firestone tire recall, discussed in Chapters 2 and 19.

One consumer protection agency with particularly significant impact on the business community is the Food and Drug Administration (FDA). The FDA's mission is to assure

---

[8] The most recent rules concerning air bags are available at www.nhtsa.dot.gov/airbags.

**EXHIBIT
15-A**

Welcome to Hotel Discrimination

In March 2000, Adam's Mark settled a class-action lawsuit, brought by the U.S. Justice Department, charging that the upscale hotel chain had systematically discriminated against African-American customers. Although admitting no wrongdoing, Adam's Mark agreed to pay $8 million. Some of this amount would go to guests who had been subjected to bias, and some would fund scholarships and internships in hospitality management at historically black colleges. The hotel also agreed to bring in an outside monitor to make sure it complied with a nondiscrimination plan.

The lawsuit arose from an incident that occurred at the chain's Daytona Beach, Florida, hotel the previous spring, during an event called Black College Reunion. According to the plaintiffs, African-American guests, unlike others, were made to wear orange wristbands to get into the hotel. Rooms they checked into had had furniture, including couches, chairs, and lamps, removed. Participants in the event had to pay cash for room service and at the hotel restaurant instead of charging to their rooms as was normally permitted.

One of the guests who originally brought the suit, a 27-year old African-American insurance adjuster who had come to the reunion, said, "I work as hard for my dollar as anyone else. If I want to spend that dollar for a hotel room, I deserve the same treatment as anyone else. That made me upset, and I was ready to go forward and do whatever it took to get things changed at Adam's Mark."

Many observers said that the bias shown by the Adam's Mark was not unusual. In a national Gallup poll, half of blacks surveyed said that within the past month they had personally been treated unfairly because of race in situations such as shopping, dining out, or using public transportation. Some called this phenomenon *retail racism*.

Sources: "Hotel Settles Black Discrimination Suits," *Atlanta Journal and Constitution,* March 22, 2000, p. 3A; "Hotel Chain Settles Federal Race Bias Case," *Washington Post,* March 22, 2000, p. A1; "A Weapon for Consumers; the Boycott Returns," *New York Times,* March 26, 2000, p. D4; and "New Face of Racism in America," *Christian Science Monitor,* January 14, 2000, p. 1.

the safety and effectiveness of a wide range of consumer products, including pharmaceutical drugs, medical devices, foods, and cosmetics. The agency has authority over one *trillion* dollars' worth of products, about a quarter of all consumer dollars spent each year.

One of the FDA's main jobs is to review many new products prior to their introduction. This job requires regulators to walk a thin line as they attempt to protect consumers. On one hand, the agency must not approve products that are ineffective or harmful. One the other hand, the agency must also not delay beneficial new products unnecessarily. The FDA can also pull existing products off the market if they are found to harm consumers. For example, in 1997 the agency ordered the diet drug fenfluramine—part of a popular combination treatment called *fen-phen*—withdrawn after it was linked to serious heart problems in some users. Historically, the FDA has had a reputation as a cautious agency that has advocated tough and thorough review prior to approval. This policy has stood in contrast to those of its counterparts in Europe and some other nations, which have tended to favor quick approval followed by careful field monitoring to spot problems. In recent years, the FDA has been under pressure from some business groups to adopt a more European-like approach, speeding up the review and approval process for new drugs and devices.

All six government regulatory agencies shown in Figure 15-2 are authorized by law to intervene directly into the very center of free market activities, if that is considered necessary to protect consumers. In other words, consumer protection laws and agencies substitute government-mandated standards and the decisions of government officials for decision making by private buyers and sellers.

The debate over whether government should become involved in protecting consumer privacy is discussed in the next section of this chapter.

Consumer Privacy in the Internet Age

In the early twenty-first century, rapidly evolving information technologies have given new urgency to the broad issue of **consumer privacy.** Shoppers have always been concerned that information they reveal in the course of a sales transaction—for example, their credit-card or driver's license numbers—might be misused. But in recent years, new technologies have increasingly enabled businesses to collect and use vast amount of personal data about their customers and potential customers, especially those who shop online. The danger is not only that this information might rarely be used fraudulently but also that its collection represents an unwarranted incursion into personal privacy. Consider the following hypothetical case:

> *Sandra, a college student, used her personal computer to surf the web. She established accounts at several online shopping sites to buy books, clothing, and CDs, and she downloaded some music and video files onto her hard drive using free software a friend recommended. She also established a free e-mail account at a popular portal and set her browser to open to its page. Soon, Sandra began receiving online ads for products similar to ones she had bought earlier, as well as for credit cards, an auto loan, and even a travel package for spring break. Sandra did not realize that several of the websites she had visited had tracked her online activity and had used this information to develop a profile of her that they had sold to Internet advertisers.*

Behind Sandra's experience was a technology somewhat whimsically called a *cookie,* an identifying marker placed on a user's computer hard drive during visits to some websites. The cookie is used to identify the user during each subsequent visit to the site that placed the cookie. Internet businesses can use this information to build profiles of users' online surfing and shopping behavior over time. If sold to advertisers, this information can be used to target online solicitations.

Many e-businesses have welcomed this technology as an efficient way to learn about the characteristics and preferences of their customers. For example, a cruise line operator might find out that a visitor to its site was a scuba enthusiast, prompting it to deliver information on tours to prime dive sites. The danger, however, is that detailed

---

EXHIBIT
15-B

Toysmart.com

Toysmart.com enjoyed a brief, glorious run as an online retailer of children's toys before falling on hard times and filing for bankruptcy in the dot-com shakeout of 2000. Under the guidance of the bankruptcy court, the company began selling its assets to pay off its debts. The company entered into an agreement with Walt Disney Co., which was also the largest investor in toysmart.com, to sell the Internet retailer's 250,000 customer files to Disney. Customer data are normally considered a business asset.

The Federal Trade Commission strongly objected and filed suit to block the sale, saying it would violate toysmart.com's promise to shoppers that it would never sell their personal information. Several members of Congress and privacy advocates also criticized the deal. Their concern was that former toysmart.com shoppers would be exposed to unwanted promotions from Disney or any other company with which Disney shared the information.

After several weeks of negotiations, the FTC reached an agreement with toysmart.com under which the retailer could sell its database only to a family-oriented company that would buy the entire website and agree to adhere to its privacy policy. Toysmart.com also agreed to delete the 2,000 records that the FTC claimed had been collected in violation of the Children's Online Privacy Act.

This did not satisfy everyone, however. Shortly after, the attorneys general of 38 states joined together to oppose this agreement. Said Massachusetts attorney general Thomas F. Reilly, "Toysmart had an explicit promise to consumers that their privacy would be protected and their information would not be shared with a third party. . . . I see the sale not only as a threat to consumers but also to the Internet."

In a hearing on the case, federal judge Carol Kenner opined that she had "fundamental problems" with the FTC settlement allowing the web retailer to sell its database. Faced with opposition by the judge, toysmart.com withdrew the controversial database from the market before the hearing could be completed, making the issue moot. But some privacy advocates worried that the wave of dot-com failures would lead to more pressure to sell customer information in the future.

Source: "States Weigh In on Toysmart Privacy Case," *Boston Globe,* July 26, 2000, p. C1.

---

personal information, possibly of a sensitive nature, could fall into the wrong hands. Research shows that consumers are increasingly concerned about the potential threat to their privacy. A poll conducted in 2000 for *Business Week* magazine, for example, found that fully 90 percent of Internet users expressed discomfort about websites creating personal profiles that linked their real names with their browsing habits and shopping patterns.[9] A recent controversy surrounding a retailer that tried to sell data on its customers is profiled in Exhibit 15-B.

[9] "It's Time for Rules in Wonderland," *Business Week,* March 20, 2000, pp. 83–96.

The dilemma of how best to protect consumer privacy, while still fostering legitimate Internet commerce, has generated a wide-ranging debate. Three major solutions have been proposed: consumer self-help, industry self-regulation, and privacy legislation.

- *Consumer self-help.* In this view, the best solution is for Internet users to use technologies that enable them to protect their own privacy. For example, special software can help manage cookies, encryption can protect messages, and surfing through intermediary sites can provide user anonymity. "We have to develop mechanisms that allow consumers to control information about themselves," commented a representative of the Center for Democracy and Technology, a civil liberties group.[10] Critics of this approach, however, argue that many unsophisticated web surfers, like Sandra, are unaware of these technologies, or even of the need for them. Moreover, tools for protecting privacy can always be defeated by even more powerful technologies.

- *Industry self-regulation.* Many Internet-related businesses have argued that they should be allowed to regulate themselves. One group of companies, including many in the computer industry, have backed a voluntary privacy scheme called an Open Profiling Standard (OPS). Under this system, information about users would be stored in a protected file on their own hard drive. When users visited a participating website, they would be able to control what information, if any, that site could access. Another group of companies, called the Online Privacy Alliance, advocated adoption of voluntary policies for protecting the privacy of individuals' information disclosed during electronic transactions.[11] One advantage of the self-regulation approach is that companies, presumably sophisticated about their own technology, might do the best job of defining technical standards. Critics of this approach feel, however, that industry rules would inevitably be too weak and would never be adopted by all businesses. By 2000, 62 percent of electronic businesses had some kind of voluntary privacy policy, according to the Federal Trade Commission.

- *Privacy legislation.* Finally, some favor new government regulations protecting consumer privacy online. The Federal Trade Commission in 2000 announced its support for new laws that would establish "basic standards of practice for the collection of information online."[12] Such laws would require businesses, for example, to notify consumers whenever information was collected, ask them to *opt on* (or allow them to *opt out*), and give them access to their files and a means of correcting errors. Some electronic businesses object to online privacy laws, saying they would limit their ability to serve customers. Others, however, think they would benefit business by allaying the public's worries about shopping on the Internet. Consumer privacy rules have already been adopted by the European Union, where information collected for one purpose cannot be sold for another purpose without the individual's consent.

---

[10] More information about privacy protection for consumers is available at www.cdt.org (Center for Democracy and Technology), epic.org/privacy (Electronic Privacy Information Center), and www.crypto.org (Internet Privacy Coalition).

[11] Available at www.privacyalliance.org. For another industry group, see www.ecommercegroup.org.

[12] A full copy of the 2000 report of the Federal Trade Commission, "Privacy Online: Fair Information Practices in the Electronic Marketplace," is available at www.ftc.gov/reports/privacy2000.

Any approach to online privacy would face the challenge of how best to balance the legitimate interests of consumers—to protect their privacy—and of business—to deliver increasingly customized products and services in the Internet age.

Special Issue: Product Liability

In today's economy, consumers' relationships with products they use and their relationships with producers of those products are complicated and abstract. The burden of responsibility for product performance has been shifted to the producer, under the legal doctrine of **product liability.** Although many businesses have offered money-back guarantees and other similar policies, consumers have demanded that businesses assume a larger burden of responsibility for the safety of their products. The result has been a strengthening of product liability laws and more favorable court attitudes toward consumer claims. Walls protecting producers from consumer lawsuits have crumbled, and there has been a dramatic increase in product liability suits. These trends have led many business groups to call for reforms of the nation's product liability laws.

Strict Liability

Over the years, courts have increasingly taken the position that manufacturers are responsible for injuries resulting from use of their products. Under prevailing court interpretations, it is not necessary for consumers to prove either negligence or breach of warranty by the producer. Nor is the consumer's own negligence necessarily an acceptable defense by the manufacturer. If a product is judged to be inherently dangerous, manufacturers can be held liable for injuries caused by its use. This doctrine, known as **strict liability,** extends to all who were involved in the final product—suppliers, sellers, contractors, assemblers, and manufacturers of component parts. The following well-publicized case illustrates the extent to which businesses can be held liable, under this strict standard.

> *In 1994, an 81-year-old woman was awarded $2.9 million by a jury in Albuquerque, New Mexico, for burns suffered when she spilled a cup of hot coffee in her lap. The woman, who had purchased the coffee at a McDonald's drive-through window, was burned when she tried to open the lid as she sat in her car. In court, McDonald's argued that customers like their coffee steaming, that their cups warned drinkers that the contents are hot, and that the woman was to blame for spilling the coffee herself. But jurors disagreed, apparently swayed by arguments that the woman's burns were severe—requiring skin grafts and a seven-day hospital stay—and by evidence that McDonald's had not cooled down its coffee even after receiving many earlier complaints. McDonald's appealed the jury's verdict and later settled the case with the elderly woman for an undisclosed amount.*[13]

---

[13] "How a Jury Decided that a Coffee Spill Is Worth $2.9 Million," *Wall Street Journal,* September 1, 1994, pp. A1, A5; and "McDonald's Settles Lawsuit over Burn from Coffee," *Wall Street Journal,* December 2, 1994, p. A14.

In this case, McDonald's was held liable for damages even though it provided a warning, and the customer's actions contributed to her burns.

Huge product liability settlements, like the McDonald's case, are well publicized, but they remain the exception. In the late 1990s, one in five noncriminal cases was a tort (liability) case; plaintiffs won only 29 percent of product liability cases filed. The average settlement in all tort cases was $141,000, although a few settlements were much higher.[14]

> *Laws enabling consumer suits are stronger in the United States than in many other industrial countries. Japan, for example, did not pass a product liability law until 1995, and such cases are still extremely difficult for consumers to win in court. In the Japanese law's first five years, plaintiffs won only 6 out of 37 judgments, and in no case did the company's liability exceed $50,000. "[Japan] is a place where companies can get away with actions that would never be tolerated in the U.S. or Europe," commented one attorney.*[15]

Business Efforts to Reform the Product Liability Laws

Many businesses have argued that the evolution of strict liability has unfairly burdened them with excess costs. Liability insurance rates have gone up significantly, especially for small businesses, as have the costs of defending against liability lawsuits and paying large settlements to injured parties. Moreover, businesses argue that it is unfair to hold them financially responsible in situations where they were not negligent.

Businesses have also argued that concerns about liability exposure sometimes slow research and innovation. For example, many pharmaceutical companies halted work on new contraceptive methods because of the risk of being sued. Despite the need for new contraceptives that would be more effective and also provide protection against viral diseases, such as herpes and AIDS, research had virtually come to a halt by the late 1990s, according to some public health groups.[16]

Faced with many liability suits and the costs of insuring against them, business has lobbied for changes in the law. Over the past two decades, several bills have been introduced in Congress that would establish the following principles in product liability suits:

- *Set up uniform federal standards for determining liability.* Companies would not have to go through repeated trials on the same charges in many different states, which would lower legal costs for companies and help them develop a uniform legal strategy for confronting liability charges in court.

- *Shift the burden of proving liability to consumers.* Consumers would have to prove that a manufacturer knew or should have known that a product design was defective before it began producing the item. Under present law and judicial

---

[14] U.S. Department of Justice, Office of Justice Programs, Bureau of Justice Statistics, "Federal Tort Trials and Verdicts," February 1999, available at ojp.usdoj.gov/bjs/pub.

[15] "Can Japanese Consumers Stand Up and Fight?" *Business Week,* September 11, 2000, p. 54.

[16] "Birth Control: Scared to a Standstill," *Business Week,* June 16, 1997, pp. 142–44; and "Fears, Suits, and Regulations Stall Contraceptive Advances," *New York Times,* December 27, 1995, pp. A1, A9.

interpretations, a company is considered to be at fault if a product injures the user, whether or not the company was negligent.

- *Eliminate some bases for liability claims.* Products not measuring up to a manufacturer's own specifications—for example, poorly made tires that blow out at normal speeds—could be the basis for a liability claim, but the vast majority of liability cases go further and blame poorly designed products or a failure of the manufacturer to warn of dangers.

- *Require the loser to pay the legal costs of the winner.* If a plaintiff (consumer) refused an out-of-court settlement offer from the company and then received less in trial, he or she would have to pay the company's legal fees—up to the amount of his or her own fees. This would discourage many plaintiffs from proceeding to trial.

- *Limit punitive damages.* Punitive damages punish the manufacturer for wrongdoing rather than compensate the victim for actual losses. Although many punitive damage awards are small, some awards in recent years—like those in some tobacco lawsuits described in the case at the end of the textbook—have been in the multimillions of dollars.[17] One proposal would limit punitive damages to $250,000 or three times compensatory damages, whichever was greater.

Although product liability reform proposals such as these have been supported by many business groups, including the Business Roundtable and the National Association of Manufacturers, they have faced vigorous opposition from consumers' organizations and from the American Trial Lawyers Association, representing plaintiffs' attorneys. These groups have defended the existing product liability system, saying that it puts needed pressure on companies to make and keep products safe. As of 2000, tort reform had been passed in several state legislatures but not in the U.S. Congress.

One alternative to product liability lawsuits, called **alternative dispute resolution,** is described in Exhibit 15-C.

Positive Business Responses to Consumerism

The consumer movement has demonstrated to business that it is expected to perform at high levels of efficiency, reliability, and fairness in order to satisfy the consuming public. Because business has not always responded quickly or fully enough, consumer advocates and their organizations have turned to government for protection. On the other hand, much effort has been devoted by individual business firms and by entire industries to encourage voluntary responses to consumer demands. Some of the more prominent positive responses are discussed next.

Total Quality Management

In recent years, many businesses have adopted a philosophy of management known as **total quality management (TQM).** This approach, which borrows from Japanese management techniques, emphasizes achieving high quality and customer satisfaction through teamwork and continuous improvement of a company's product or service. TQM businesses seek to "delight the customer," as shown in the following example.

[17] "Product Suits Yield Few Punitive Awards," *Wall Street Journal,* January 6, 1992, p. B1.

**EXHIBIT
15-C**

An Alternative to Product Liability Lawsuits

Product liability lawsuits cost businesses and consumers a lot of money, and many cases are held up for years in backlogged courts. Often, large proportions of any settlement go to attorneys rather than to the people who were injured by defective products. Businesses are unable to predict the extent of their liability exposure. Is there a better way to resolve disputes between businesses and consumers?

Some people think that alternative dispute resolution (ADR) may be an answer. In ADR, a professional mediator works with both sides to negotiate a settlement outside the traditional court system. Generally, if the negotiation fails, the parties can still proceed to trial. The nonprofit American Arbitration Association has developed a panel of experts skilled in resolving liability claims. Several for-profit organizations, such as JAMS/Endispute of Irvine, California, also provide ADR services.

Supporters of ADR say that it saves money that would be spent on lawyers' fees, so that more can go to plaintiffs in a settlement. Cases can be resolved quickly, rather than waiting for an opening on a busy judge's calendar. Critics, however, worry that ADR deprives plaintiffs of their day in court, and injured consumers may get less than if their cases were heard before a jury.

Eventually, ADR may be widely used to settle individual complaints brought under mass torts, such as those involving injuries from asbestos, tobacco, or defective medical devices. In this situation, a court would set up a procedure and a set of rules by which individuals could negotiate a settlement tailored to the facts of their own case. Some businesses feel that such a process would enable them to better predict, and budget for, future liabilities.

Source: John Gibeaut, "At the Crossroads," *American Bar Association Journal,* March 1998.

At the Saturn plant in Spring Hill, Tennessee, TQM methods have been used to produce a car of superior quality. Joint labor-management teams designed the car from the start to compete head-on with popular Japanese imports. Workers can stop the assembly line if they see a defect. Saturn keeps in close contact with car buyers, so it can correct any problems that crop up. The result has been a vehicle that has been extremely popular with customers. Saturn has consistently ranked at or near the top of all cars, foreign and domestic, in the J. D. Power surveys of customer satisfaction.[18]

Total quality management is a response to pressure from consumer activists and an attempt by business to address its customers' needs. It is an example of the interactive

[18] "Cadillac, Saturn Rank among Top Automakers in Three-Year Owner Survey," *Detroit News,* August 31, 1999, p. 1C; and Barry Bluestone and Irving Bluestone, "Reviving American Industry: A Labor-Management Partnership," *Current,* May 1993, pp. 10–16.

strategy discussed in Chapter 2, where companies try to anticipate and respond to emerging stakeholder expectations. One of the primary changes created by the TQM movement has been for companies to focus on the customer. This occurs in many different ways.

Voluntary Industry Codes of Conduct

In some cases, businesses in an industry have banded together to agree on voluntary codes of conduct, spelling out how they will treat their customers. Often, this action is taken to forestall even stricter regulation by the government. One such voluntary code is described in the following example.

> *The Air Transport Association, an industry group, adopted a "customer service commitment" in 1999. The airlines promised to notify passengers when flights were canceled, feed and assist stranded passengers, pay more for lost luggage, and quote the lowest available fare over the phone. The industry's action stemmed from an incident the year before, when hundreds of passengers had been stuck for hours on the runway in planes unable to take off during a Detroit snowstorm. In the ensuring furor, Congress threatened to pass a passenger bill of rights. "We have felt the whip," said UAL's chairman, explaining the companies' voluntary action.[19]*

Consumer Affairs Departments

Many large corporations operate consumer affairs departments, often placing a vice president in charge. These centralized departments normally handle consumer inquiries and complaints about a company's products and services, particularly in cases where a customer has not been able to resolve differences with local retailers. Some companies have installed **consumer hot lines** for dissatisfied customers to place telephone calls directly to the manufacturer.

> *One of the largest hot lines, General Electric's Answer Center, fields three and a half million questions a year on thousands of products. One technician diagnosed a mysterious refrigerator noise by asking the customer to hold the phone up to the appliance. Another advised a frantic caller on how to extract a pet iguana from the dishwasher. "This isn't a job for the faint of heart," said one consultant who works with company consumer hot lines.[20]*

Many companies now communicate with their customers and other interested persons through websites on the Internet. Some sites are interactive, allowing customers to post comments or questions that are answered by e-mail by customer relations staff.

Experienced companies are aware that consumer complaints and concerns can be handled more quickly, at lower cost, and with less risk of losing goodwill by a consumer

---

[19] "Airlines Promise Measure to Boost Customer Service," *Wall Street Journal,* June 18, 1999, p. A6; and "Airlines, Being Pressed, Offer Modest Reforms to Customers," *New York Times,* June 18, 1999, p. A32.
[20] "What's This? Confused or Curious, Consumers Know Where to Call," *Newsday,* October 18, 1995, p. B37.

affairs department than if customers take a legal route or if their complaints receive widespread media publicity.

Product Recalls

Companies also deal with consumer dissatisfaction by recalling faulty products. A **product recall** occurs when a company, either voluntarily or under an agreement with a government agency, takes back all items found to be dangerously defective, as Ford and Firestone did following a series of accidents caused by tire tread separation on Explorers in 2000. Sometimes these products are in the hands of consumers; at other times they may be in the factory, in wholesale warehouses, or on the shelves of retail stores. Wherever they are in the chain of distribution or use, the manufacturer tries to notify consumers or potential users about the defect so that they will return the items. A recalled product may be repaired, replaced, or destroyed, depending on the problem, as the following example illustrates.

> *In 2000, By Us International Co., Ltd., of Taiwan, in cooperation with the Consumer Product Safety Commission, announced it would voluntarily recall front suspension forks installed on some Brunswick brand mountain bikes, after it had received numerous complaints that the forks had broken, injuring riders. The company offered to have all defective forks replaced, for free.*[21]

In other cases, companies may simply stop shipping products whose safety is questionable. In 1999, for example, Mattel voluntarily decided to quit making toys made with plasticizers, chemicals designed to soften products like teething rings. Although regulators had not banned plasticizers, some preliminary studies suggested they might pose a hazard.[22]

The four major government agencies responsible for most mandatory recalls are the Food and Drug Administration, the National Highway Traffic Safety Administration, the Environmental Protection Agency (which can recall polluting motor vehicles), and the Consumer Product Safety Commission.

Consumerism's Achievements

After nearly 40 years of the consumer movement, its leaders can point to some important gains for U.S. consumers. Consumers today are better informed about the goods and services they purchase, are more aware of their rights when something goes wrong, and are better protected against inflated advertising claims, hazardous or ineffective products, and unfair pricing. Several consumer organizations serve as watchdogs of buyers' interests, and a network of federal and state regulatory agencies acts for the consuming public.

Some businesses, too, have heard the consumer message and have reacted positively. They have learned to assign high priority to the things consumers expect—high-quality goods and services, reliable and effective products, safety in the items they buy, fair prices, and marketing practices that do not threaten important human and social values.

---

[21] Information on this and other recalls is available at www.cpsc.com and at www.safetyalerts.com.
[22] "Mattel Plans to Use Organic-Based Plastic for Toy Production," *Wall Street Journal,* December 8, 1999, p. B2.

All of these achievements, in spite of negative episodes that occasionally occur, bring the consuming public closer to realizing the key consumer rights: to be safe, to be informed, to have choices, and to be heard, as well as the newer right to privacy.

Summary Points of This Chapter

- The U.S. consumer movement represents an attempt to promote the interests of consumers by balancing the amount of market power held by sellers and buyers.
- The four key consumer rights are the rights to safety, to be informed, to choose, and to be heard. Recent discussion has focused on consumers' right to privacy.
- Consumer protection laws and regulatory agencies attempt to assure that consumers are treated fairly, receive adequate information, are protected against potential hazards, have free choices in the market, and have legal recourse when problems develop. They also protect children's privacy online.
- Rapidly evolving information technologies have given new urgency to the issue of consumer privacy. Three approaches to safeguarding online privacy are consumer self-help, industry self-regulation, and protective legislation.
- Business has complained about the number of product liability lawsuits and the high cost of insuring against them. But efforts to reform product liability laws have been opposed by consumer groups and lawyers representing victims of dangerous or defective products.
- Socially responsible companies have responded to the consumer movement by giving serious consideration to consumer problems, increasing channels of communication with customers, instituting arbitration procedures to resolve complaints, and recalling defective products. They have also pursued voluntary codes of conduct and total quality management in an effort to meet, and even anticipate, consumers' needs.

Key Terms and Concepts Used in This Chapter

- Consumer movement
- Consumer bill of rights
- Consumer protection laws
- Deceptive advertising
- Consumer privacy
- Product liability

- Strict liability
- Alternative dispute resolution
- Total quality management (TQM)
- Consumer hot lines
- Product recalls

Internet Resources

- www.cpsc.gov   U.S. Consumer Product Safety
                                                      Commission
- www.ftc.gov   U.S. Federal Trade Commission
- www.igc.apc.org:80/cbbb   Better Business Bureau
- www.consumerfed.org   Consumer Federation of America

Discussion Case: *Smith & Wesson's Gun Deal*

In March 2000, Smith & Wesson, one of the oldest and best-known gun manufacturers in the United States, struck an unusual deal. The company accepted a wide range of restrictions on how it made, sold, and distributed handguns in exchange for settlement of lawsuits brought against it by a group of U.S. cities and counties. In the deal, brokered by the U.S. Secretary of Housing and Urban Development, the gun maker paid no money but agreed to:

- Put a trigger lock on all guns it made, and within three years to develop new "safe" guns that could be fired only by their owners.
- Keep a record of the digital "fingerprints" of casings fired from all guns it made, so that police could more easily trace guns used to commit crimes.
- Put hidden serial numbers on all guns that criminals would be less likely to scratch off.
- Require its dealers to sell no more than one handgun at a time without a 14-day waiting period, and to certify that customers had passed a gun safety course.
- Require gun show dealers to run a background check on all buyers.

The government had been able to force these concessions from Smith & Wesson because the company faced possible financial ruin in court. In the late 1990s, more than 20 cities and counties had brought suit against the firearms industry, demanding compensation for the medical and law enforcement costs of dealing with the aftermath of gun violence.

Two hundred million guns are in circulation in the United States, and a third of all households own at least one. Every year, 150,000 Americans are injured and 34,000 die from gun violence; and gunfire is predicted to surpass cars as the leading cause of non-natural death by 2003. The cost of medical care for gunshot victims is $2.3 billion a year. Much of the cost of gun violence is borne by local governments, which fund police departments, courts, and public hospitals.

The governments bringing suit argued that gun manufacturers were liable for these costs because they had failed to apply commonsense consumer product safety standards to firearms. So-called Saturday night specials—cheap, easily hidden handguns—for example, lacked locks or other protective devices and sometimes misfired, causing unintentional injury. Some guns, like automatic assault rifles, seemed to have been customized for killing. Moreover, gun makers knowingly made large shipments to regions that had lax gun laws, looking the other way while weapons fell into the hands of criminals.

Most manufacturers, however, disputed these arguments. They pointed out that guns are legal; in fact, they are the only consumer products that the U.S. Constitution (in the Second Amendment) guarantees the right to own. No one, least of all gun manufacturers, has ever claimed that guns do not kill. Guns have a legitimate, even beneficial, purpose in hunting, self-defense, and law enforcement. Deaths and injuries from firearms are the responsibility of the people wielding them, not their manufacturers.

In the midst of this litigation, Smith & Wesson's go-it-alone settlement—which went well beyond existing gun control laws—appeared to other gun makers as nothing short of treasonous. "I think that a fair number of Smith & Wesson customers will no longer want to purchase their products because of this agreement, and they will lose market share," said a representative of rival Beretta U.S.A. The powerful National Rifle Association denounced Smith & Wesson for running up "the white flag of surrender." Dealers were especially miffed, and some said they would no longer carry the company's products.

The Smith & Wesson settlement was the first time a gun maker had voluntarily agreed to safety rules. Although various gun control provisions regulate firearm sale and ownership, the National Rifle Association and the gun lobby have for years effectively blocked the government from regulating guns as a consumer product. Smith & Wesson's CEO, Ed Shultz, was under no obligation to make concessions on safety. But clearly, he felt he had a gun to his head. "At some point," he told a reporter, "the company has to save itself."

Sources: "Gun Makers See Betrayal in Decision by Smith & Wesson," *New York Times,* March 18, 2000, p. A8; "The Gun Deal Is Half-Cocked," *Business Week,* April 3, 2000, p. 39; "High Noon in Gun Valley," *Newsweek,* March 27, 2000, pp. 26–29; "Gun Maker Agrees to Accept Curbs," *New York Times,* March 18, 2000, p. A1; and "Cost of Treating Gun Victims Put at $2.3 Billion," *Buffalo News,* August 4, 1999, p. 14A.

Discussion Questions

1. Do you think that Smith & Wesson acted responsibly in negotiating a deal to settle lawsuits against it? Why or why not? Say how different stakeholders would respond to this question.

2. In what ways, in your view, are guns similar to or different from other consumer products, such as pharmaceutical drugs, cars, and food, discussed in this chapter? Do you think the government ought to have the authority to regulate gun safety or not?

3. In your opinion, should gun makers be held liable for the costs to local governments of gun violence? Do you think the principle of strict liability should apply in this case or not?

4. What do you think is the best way to reduce deaths and injuries from guns: stricter government regulation of gun safety, voluntary actions by gun makers, more responsible firearm use by individuals, tougher crime enforcement, or liability lawsuits against manufacturers? Why do you think so?

16

The Community and the Corporation

When a business has a good relationship with its community, it can make an important difference in the quality of that community's life and in the successful operation of the company. Communities look to businesses for help in coping with local problems and for civic leadership; firms expect to be treated in fair and supportive ways by the local community. This idea operates for companies of all sizes. As companies expand their operations, they develop a wider set of community relationships. Whether local, regional, or global, corporate citizenship reflects a company's business and social values.

This chapter focuses on these key questions and objectives:

- What interdependencies exist between companies and communities in which they operate?
- Why do businesses respond to community problems and needs?
- How is social capital created when businesses become involved in addressing community problems?
- How does volunteerism contribute to building strong relationships between businesses and communities?
- What is the role of philanthropy in community life, and how does strategic philanthropy relate to this trend?
- How are social partnerships between businesses and the communities used to address today's pressing social problems?

W hen America Online and Time Warner merged in 2001, most of the newspaper and media stories focused on the business issues: product lines, markets, and audiences. But each of the companies also had impressive records of community involvement and deserved reputations as good corporate citizens. As their leaders—Steve Case (AOL) and Gerald Levin (Time Warner)—assumed their new roles in the merged company, questions arose about what focus the new company would bring to its community relationships. Steve Case had been a pioneer in Internet corporate citizenship, leading AOL to create many innovative ways to support community and public causes through the powerful AOL portal. Gerald Levin had supported Time Warner's development as a more traditional corporate citizen, with heavy sponsorship of artistic, cultural, and educational causes. In the words of one senior executive at the new company, "we need to understand our citizenship strategy as clearly as we understand our business strategy."[1]

A few months earlier, IBM's chairman and chief executive officer, Louis V. Gerstner, Jr., gave a speech to a large group of California business and political leaders in which he said, "the issue of public education's bearing on a healthy society and a competitive economy has been my passion for close to 30 years." He described the central problem this way: "Our generation has witnessed the wasting decline of the one institution that has to be good enough, and strong enough to carry our country forward into this new century. . . . I believe that in this networked world the single greatest factor separating winners and losers in all industries and in fact, in all societies, will be the ability to use information and build a culture based on knowledge and the ability to learn." As the leader of a great company, Gerstner has urged IBM managers and employees in every office, plant, and facility around the world to find creative ways to improve and encourage better education for everyone.[2]

Every community faces the need for reliable blood supplies, especially during the months when donations drop. Hospitals work closely with the American Red Cross and other organizations to assure a steady supply, but there are times when crises produce intense pressures on community resources. Employees at Ford Motor Company facilities in southeastern Michigan lined up to help restock the storm-battered southeastern Michigan blood supplies during the winter of 2001. "We're at a critical level, with less than a day's supplies of most blood types," said Mary Anne Stella, chief operating officer for the regional Red Cross, which declared a blood emergency as snow and cold weather severely curtailed the usual blood drives at local schools, churches, and community centers. December and January—with the holidays, bad weather, and illness—are typically the worst time for donations, which must tally 700 to 1,000 pints every day to adequately supply medical facilities in southeastern Michigan. Blood drives are increasingly productive at Ford, which prides itself on its corporate citizenship. Total donations by local hourly and salaried Ford employees grew from 7,400 units in 1998 to more than 13,000 in 1999, and Stella said the Dearborn-based automaker remains the top corporate donor in southeastern Michigan. Ford president and CEO Jacques Nasser said that donating blood "is safe, fast, and easy, and it saves lives. Each donation can

---

[1] Author's interview, January 2001.

[2] Louis V. Gerstner, Jr., "Status Report: Public Education in America," address to Commonwealth Club of California, October 12, 2000, reprinted in *Vital Speeches of the Day,* December 15, 2000, pp. 134–37.

Figure 16-1

The firm and its
communities.

Source: Based in part
on a discussion in
Edmund M. Burke,
*Corporate Community
Relations: The Principle
of the Neighbor of
Choice* (Westport, CT:
Praeger, 1999),
chap. 6.

Community	Stakeholder Interest
■ Site community	■ Geographical location of a company's operations, offices, or assets
■ Fence-line community	■ Immediate neighbors receiving the positive and negative effects of business activities
■ Impact communities	■ Affected by externalities from facility (e.g., pollution, traffic)
■ Cyber communities	■ All parties that use the Internet to learn about the company
■ Communities of interest	■ Stakeholders that have a real interest in the company
■ Communities of practice	■ Those who engage in similar activities or practices (IT experts, ethics officers, community experts)
■ Employee community	■ Those who work or live near facility

save the lives of as many as four people—people with leukemia, cancer, anemia, severe burns, or those undergoing surgery for illness or injury. Giving blood is a gift of life and it meets one of our community's most basic needs, both to deal with medical emergencies and to support ongoing medical treatment. And it's one of the easiest ways for any of us to give just a little, and make a big difference."[3]

Why do companies like America Online, Time Warner, IBM, and Ford invest in community organizations, activities, and projects? What benefits do companies gain from such activities? What would happen if business did not participate in community activities? The examples illustrate the relationship between corporations and the communities in which they operate, and this chapter focuses on why many companies believe that being a good neighbor and an involved citizen is part of their basic business mission. The chapter also looks at how companies participate in community life and how they build partnerships with other business, government, and community organizations. The core question that we consider throughout this chapter is: What does it mean to be a good corporate citizen in the twenty-first century?

Community Relations

The **community** discussed in this chapter involves a company's area of local business influence. As shown in Figure 16-1, an organization interacts with a variety of communities, each with a different type of stake (benefit or risk) or interest in the company's activities. The communities discussed in this chapter consist of individuals and organizations, residing in a specific geographic area or political jurisdiction, affected by the firm's economic and social involvement. A bank in a large metropolitan area, for example, has numerous stakeholders (see the stakeholder model in Chapter 1)

---

[3] Press releases supplied by Ford Motor Company and American Red Cross Southeastern Michigan Blood Services Region, January 2001. See www.ford.com/community.

and may define its community as the central city and the towns and suburbs in which it does business. A local merchant's community relationships may involve the cities or towns surrounding its business, while a large multinational firm (e.g., ExxonMobil, General Motors, or IBM) has relationships with the many separate communities in local areas where it operates around the world. In all cases, both company and community have a mutual dependence that is significant in both economic and social terms.

The involvement of business with the community is called **community relations.** Community relations today are quite different from those of 50 or 100 years ago. Advances in technology, especially information technology, population shifts in the United States and much of the industrialized world, and the global redesign of business operations are putting great pressures on the traditional business–community relationship. Community relationships are also entwined with cultural norms. Business decisions have become more complex, and the impact of those decisions has loomed larger in the life of communities. Keeping community ties alive and healthy is a major task for today's businesses.

Social Capital and Civic Engagement

Social capital is a phrase that describes the degree of "connectedness," willingness to help, friendliness, and goodwill among any group of people in an organization or community. Many experts believe that the level of social capital—which is hard to measure precisely but clear when it is either present or absent—is an excellent indicator of members' quality of life. According to American sociologist Robert D. Putnam, managers and administrators have recognized the importance of social capital for nearly 100 years. In 1916, for example, the school superintendent of West Virginia wrote that the promotion of interaction among individuals and families would benefit the schools and students: "The community as a whole will benefit by the cooperation of all its parts, while the individual will find, in his associations the advantages of the help, the sympathy, and the fellowship of his neighbors."[4]

The idea of social capital is at the heart of the corporation–community relationship in the twenty-first century. Healthy communities require cooperation, a willingness to work with others, and a spirit of voluntarism from individuals and organizations. Social capital has both a private face and a public face; it is simultaneously a "private good" and a "public good" (see Chapter 7). Some benefits of an investment in social capital go to the community, some to the individual. Most important, networks of community members—individuals and organizations—foster a collective commitment to making communities better for all. This is the basic idea of **civic engagement.** Higher levels of civic engagement by individuals and organizations promote problem solving and an improvement in the quality of community life. When companies like Ford and IBM, described at the beginning of the chapter, work to address community problems such as blood shortages and education, their civic engagement is designed to build a better community. In management terms, civic engagement and the development of

---

[4] L. J. Hanifan, school superintendent of West Virginia, 1916, quoted in Robert D. Putnam, *Bowling Alone: The Collapse and Revival of American Community* (New York: Simon and Schuster, 2000), p. 19.

social capital produces an ideal type win-win outcome because it enables everyone to be better off.

Many corporations have established special coordinators (community relations managers) to interact with local citizens, develop local programs, manage donations of goods and services, work with local governments, and encourage employee volunteerism in nonprofit and civic groups.[5] These actions are, in effect, business investments intended to produce more social capital in the community. Companies are involved with local communities on many diverse issues, including education reform, fighting crime, environmental risk management, local taxes, and improving the lives of the homeless. Their aims are to improve local conditions that produce or attract a workforce qualified to meet the company's needs and to build a positive relationship between the firm and important local groups. Community relations managers work closely with other corporate offices that link the corporation to the external world, such as the employee relations, public relations, and public affairs offices (see Chapter 2). All of these links form important bridges between the corporation and community groups.[6]

Limited Resources Face Unlimited Community Needs

Every community has social needs requiring far more resources than are normally available. Choices must be made and priorities established. In some instances, the community decides the priorities, but in other instances, business influences community priorities directly. Further, in all cases, once management has decided to help serve a need, it still must decide how its resources can best be applied to that need. This means that any action management takes will result in some dissatisfaction from those who get no help and from those who do not get as much help as they want.

Figure 16-2 illustrates the variety of expectations that communities have of business. Each year, companies receive requests for artistic, educational, and charitable assistance serving both special groups and the community as a whole. A business may agree to support some, but not all, of these requests, and its work with these groups will consume hundreds of days of employee time and thousands of dollars of company resources. Meanwhile, the company must still meet its business objective of serving customers competitively throughout the nation.

Community Involvement and Firm Size

Community involvement has become part of the corporate lifestyle for employees in many organizations. Studies show that both large and small businesses, whether they are local firms or branches of national firms, tend to be active in community affairs.[7]

---

[5] See James E. Post and Jennifer J. Griffin, *The State of Corporate Public Affairs* (Washington, DC: Foundation for Public Affairs, 1996).
[6] Boston College Center for Corporate Community Relations, "Profile of the Community Relations Profession," regularly updated in *Community Relations Profile*. See www.bcccr.org.
[7] Center for Corporate Public Involvement, *Helping Families, Strengthening Communities: The Life and Health Insurance Industry Annual Report on Community Involvement* (Washington, DC: American Council of Life Insurance and Health Insurance Association of America, 1995). See also, www.ccpi.org for additional information.

Figure 16-2

What the community and business want from each other.

Business Participation Desired by Community	Community Services Desired by Business
■ Support for art and cultural activities ■ Support for traffic management ■ Participation in urban planning and community development ■ Support of local health care programs ■ Support of hospitals and health care clinics ■ Support of schools ■ United Way campaign support—both leadership and funding ■ Assistance for less advantaged people ■ Support for pollution control ■ Participation in emergency planning ■ Support of local recycling programs	■ Education and cultural resources that appeal to employees ■ Family recreation facilities ■ Public services—e.g., police and fire protection; sewer, water, and electric services ■ Taxes that are equitable and do not discourage business operations ■ Business participation in community life and decision making ■ Adequate transportation system— roads, rail, airport, harbor ■ Public officials who operate honestly and with integrity ■ Cooperative problem-solving approach

Business leaders bring knowledge and ability to civic and community matters. Much of this activity involves participation in local and regional groups (e.g., business councils, associations, and roundtables); leadership on civic task forces; and personal involvement of executives as directors, trustees, or advisers to schools, community groups, and collaborations. Through such activities executives become familiar with local needs and issues and involved in finding ways for businesses and communities to cooperate.

Large companies usually have more public visibility in community affairs than smaller companies (see Chapter 4). These firms are larger, more established, and help to characterize their surrounding towns (e.g., "Chicago is the home of . . ."). Executives often serve as board members or advisers to community organizations and participate in philanthropy, volunteerism, and resolution of public issues when the headquarters is located in the community.

When a company has many branch offices and facilities, community involvement extends into those cities and towns and corporate policy has to be implemented in local settings. An effective policy has to recognize the unique needs of each community in which the firm is involved. This makes it desirable for corporate headquarters to give local managers broad leeway to make community-related decisions.

> *Target Stores is a retailer with more than 600 stores throughout the United States. Community involvement—which Target calls its Good Neighbor program—is a basic part of every store's business strategy. Local store managers are expected to develop innovative community outreach programs to reinforce the message that Target is a good neighbor whose deeds make the community a better place for all to live. Target is not alone in assigning community relations responsibility to local managers. Research studies have found that nearly 60 percent of firms have delegated local community relations responsibilities, including*

corporate contributions, to managers in local plants, branch offices, and service branches.[8]

Foreign-owned companies also participate in community affairs, at home and abroad. The profile of activities in which such companies participate is often similar to that of domestic companies. As illustrated in Exhibit 16-A, the community-based activities of the NBS financial services company in South Africa are similar to the activities of financial services companies in the United States. This pattern exists in many countries and suggests that businesses and communities everywhere develop local norms and expectations of what companies should do to be good corporate citizens. When a new company enters a community and begins to engage with local stakeholders, it will quickly learn how it is expected to assume the role and responsibilities of a corporate citizen in the new community. (Global corporate citizenship is discussed in Chapter 20.)

Small business participation in community activities is just as important as large business involvement. Small business representatives, such as automobile dealers, restaurants, real estate brokers, supermarkets, and other retail merchants, significantly influence the quality of community life. They tend to be personally and professionally involved in community affairs, often expressing a deep commitment to the community based on many years of residence. In large urban areas, different ethnic neighborhoods may exist, often with family-operated stores, restaurants, and services. Cultural norms may affect the willingness of such business owners to participate in community development activities. In many cities, community development corporations (CDCs) exist to help bring together and focus the energy of local residents and businesses to improve neighborhood life for all.

Local businesses are often members of the local community's civic organizations, such as the chamber of commerce and Kiwanis and Rotary clubs. These organizations work on community issues such as parking and traffic, business development, and cooperation with local schools. In one community, for example, a real estate brokerage donated the time of its employees to several local middle schools that needed adult assistance to run a weekly bottle and can recycling collection. Every Friday morning, teams of real estate brokers worked with students at each middle school to receive the bottles and cans dropped off by residents during the morning commuting hours.

Community Acceptance and Support of Business

The relationship of business and community is one of mutual interdependence. Each has responsibilities to the other because each has social power to affect the other. This *power-responsibility* equation applies to both parties and underscores a key point: Success is a matter of mutual support rather than opposition.

Communities do not have to accept or endorse the presence of a business. Communities frequently object to the presence of companies that will create too much traffic, pollute water supplies, or engage in activities that are offensive, hazardous, or inappropriate. The company must earn its informal **license to operate**—or right to do business—from the community. In communities where democratic principles apply, citizens have the right to exercise their voice in determining whether a business will or will

---

[8] Data provided by company. The program is discussed in Molly McKaughan, *Corporate Volunteerism: How Families Make a Difference* (New York: The Conference Board, 1997).

EXHIBIT
16-A

NBS: Community Banking in South Africa

NBS, a division of BoE, is one of South Africa's leading financial institutions. BoE is the fifth largest banking and investment organization in South Africa, listed on the Johannesburg Stock Exchange, with assets of more than $15 billion (U.S.). Once a "building and loan society" (similar to a savings and loan institution in the United States), NBS is a modern financial institution specializing in community-based savings and home loan programs. It has 149 branches in South Africa and employs 2,200 people. As an up-to-date provider of financial services, NBS has also developed telephone and Internet banking services.

Corporate social investment is part of NBS's business plan. The company's financial success depends on the strength of the communities where it does business and the country as a whole. For this reason, NBS invests in social projects that will build stronger communities. The NBS Corporate Social Investment (CSI) program operates through three mechanisms:

1. Through its NBS Centenary Foundation, established in 1982, NBS has sponsored the development of 34 preschools that benefit 3,000 children in various communities. It is known that the first seven years are most important to the development of a child, but South Africa's government provides no direct funding for preschool education at this time. To fill this need, the NBS Foundation works with education and child care organizations to provide teacher training and on-site support to urban and rural preschools. Communities contribute 10 percent of the cost of a preschool.

2. Through its General Development Fund, NBS makes annual donations and maintains corporate memberships that support charities and nongovernmental organizations engaged in business development and skills training, arts and cultural activities, health and welfare, conservation and environmental projects, and education partnerships. NBS has a particular interest in developing financial literacy and helping build a national culture of savings. A partnership with SMILE (St. Mary's Interactive Learning Experience) has resulted in the "Money" program for primary school learners. The focus is on developing life skills around the theme of money, saving, banking and entrepreneurship while developing English language, literacy, and communication skills. NBS has an "open door" policy which encourages schools and educators to visit branches. Many of the children visit a bank for the first time.

3. Through its Staff Participation Campaign, NBS supports the personal involvement of its employees in community projects. Employee fund-raising for community activities is matched by contributions from the company, through its public affairs division, thereby doubling the amount of resources available to the community. This aspect of the CSI program is described as a "cornerstone," because it links the interests of three critical NBS stakeholders: employees, customers, and the community.

Sources: Lora Rossler, vice president of Public Affairs, NBS, presentation at annual meeting of Business for Social Responsibility, November 2000, author interview; company publications; www.nbs.co.za, www.boe.co.za.

Figure 16-3
Business and the
community need
support from each
other.

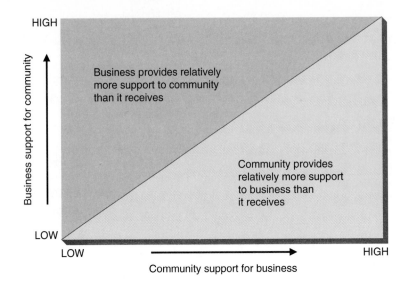

HIGH

Business support for community

Business provides relatively
more support to community
than it receives

Community provides
relatively more support
to business than
it receives

LOW

LOW   HIGH

Community support for business

not be welcome. When permits are being debated, both the community and the company have an opportunity to explain to one another what is expected and what is needed for a successful operation to begin.

The concept of a social contract is fundamental to the relationship between business and the community. Businesses normally expect various types of support from the local communities in which they operate. As previously shown in Figure 16-2, businesses expect fair treatment, and they expect to be accepted as a participant in community affairs because they are an important part of the community. They also expect community services such as a dependable water supply and police protection. Companies are encouraged to remain in the community and grow if there are appropriate cultural, educational, and recreational facilities for their employees and, of course, if taxes remain reasonable. Businesses also have come to recognize that they rely heavily on the public school system and other local services to run their businesses efficiently.

This combination of business–community mutual support is illustrated in Figure 16-3. The diagonal line in the diagram illustrates the situation when a business receives support from the community that is equal to that which it provides to the community. Sometimes, a business will invest more in the community than the community seems to provide in return; this is the area above the diagonal. Conversely, a community sometimes provides much more support to a business than the firm contributes to the community; this is the area below the diagonal. Ideally, the business and community provide relatively equal amounts of support to each other and, more important, their interaction moves from the lower left end of the box to the upper right. This signifies a high degree of interaction and relatively equal amounts of support for one another. As a company grows, it provides more jobs, tax revenues, volunteers for community projects, support to local charities, and so forth. But positive relationships between a company and a community are sometimes difficult to develop.

Figure 16-4

Meeting community needs—percentage of life insurance companies involved in community projects.

Source: Data collected by the American Council of Life Insurers.

Type of Project	Percentage of Reporting Companies Involved (1999)
Education	88%
Youth	83
Art and culture	81
Local health	76
Neighborhood improvement	63
Housing	60
Homeless	50
Hunger	48
Minority programs	43
AIDS education/treatment	42
Senior citizen/retiree	39
Low-income/minorities health	39
Disaster relief	39
Drug and alcohol abuse	38
Crime prevention	35
Day care	31
Prenatal and well-baby health	30
Safety	24
Hard to employ	24
Environment	23
Other	17

Wal-Mart has encountered serious local objection to its plans to build superstores and distribution centers in a number of local communities. Wal-Mart's founder, Sam Walton, now deceased, was fond of saying that he would never try to force a community to accept a Wal-Mart store. "Better to go where we are wanted," he is reported to have said. In recent years, however, that view is less often endorsed by Wal-Mart management. In a series of high-profile local conflicts, Wal-Mart sparked intense local opposition from several communities that were worried about traffic patterns, safety, and negative effects on local small businesses from the opening of giant Wal-Mart facilities. The problem seems likely to grow more complex for Wal-Mart as it continues its expansion into international markets.[9]

Strengthening the Community

Business initiatives have helped improve the quality of life in communities in many ways, some of which are listed in Figure 16-4. Although not exhaustive, the list suggests the range of community needs that a corporation's executives are asked to address. These community concerns challenge managers to apply talent, imagination, and resources to develop creative ways to strengthen the community while still managing their businesses as profitable enterprises.

[9] Wal-Mart's problems with local communities are extensively documented. For the company's perspective on its community relationships, see www.walmart.com.

Improving Economic Development

Business leaders and their companies are frequently involved in local or regional economic development, which is intended to bring new businesses into an area or to otherwise improve local conditions. Central business districts, unlike older and often neglected poorer residential areas, have benefited from businesses during recent decades. Business has helped transform these business areas in major U.S. cities into a collection of shining office buildings, entertainment facilities, fashionable shopping malls, conference centers, and similar urban amenities. In spite of these developments, many urban areas have become forbidding and inhospitable places, fraught with drugs, violence, and frighteningly high crime rates. The commitment of more than 60 companies and other organizations to the Minnesota HEALS program, described in Chapter 4, illustrates how communities are fighting these conditions. A group of concerned companies, including Honeywell, General Mills, and Allina Health Systems worked closely with police and civic groups to form Minnesota HEALS (hope, education, law, and safety). This cross-sector initiative was designed to address public safety issues through development and community improvement. In so doing, the companies also addressed employee recruitment and retention concerns.[10]

Through extensive cooperative efforts, planners are trying to control development so that the central business districts will again become attractive to all citizens. Some of the ingredients needed are police protection that ensures safety, open spaces devoted to fountains, green grass, and trees, outdoor sitting areas, arcades, a variety of attractive stores, outdoor cafes, theaters, and interesting people.

The rush of business development can present problems, as well as opportunities, for a community.

> *When Toyota announced that it would build an automobile plant in Georgetown, Kentucky, residents were both pleased and anxious. The plant was expected to add as many as 3,500 jobs, but local people worried about how the community would be able to absorb the influx of outsiders and how their tightly knit community would be affected. Acknowledging its responsibility for the expected changes, Toyota gave Georgetown $1 million to build a community center. By working closely with local government officials, acknowledging their responsibility, and communicating openly about expected problems, Toyota helped the community become a more dynamic place to live while expanding its business presence. The company later announced another expansion of its facility, adding more than 1,000 jobs to the payroll. Toyota executives cited the positive relationship with the community as a contributing factor in the expansion decision.*[11]

---

[10] See Chapter 4, p. 83. The experience has been extensively studied by Dr. Barbara W. Altman, "Minnesota HEALS: Next Steps in Corporate/Community Partnerships for Crime Reduction," private correspondence. See also, Bradley K. Googins and Steven A. Rochlin, "Creating the Partnership Society: Understanding the Rhetoric and Reality of Cross-Sector Partnerships," *Business and Society* 105, no. 1 (Winter 2000), pp. 127–44.

[11] The community involvement of foreign companies in the United States is discussed in David Logan et al., *Global Corporate Citizenship—Rationale and Strategies* (Washington, DC: Hitachi Foundation, 1997).

The problems that accompany metropolitan growth (e.g., congestion) are not limited to large cities. Office building has mushroomed in many suburban areas; almost two-thirds of new office space built in the 1990s was in the suburbs, creating in many metropolitan areas what is called *urban sprawl.* Technological changes permit many business operations to be located away from central headquarters, and suburban building and rental costs are usually much less than those of center-city locations. In the San Francisco suburb of Walnut Creek, for example, local citizens voted to bar large-scale office buildings and retail projects until traffic congestion was relieved. One of the most celebrated cases of a major company failing to get its license to operate may have been the failed effort of the Disney Company to build a history theme park near Civil War battle sites in Virginia. Residents were concerned about traffic from the park, but they were also worried about the long-term impact of office and residential construction on their communities. Despite the benefits that would flow from new jobs and tax revenues, fierce opposition eventually forced Disney to cancel its plans.[12]

Housing

Suburban areas appeal to businesses because of generally less crowded conditions. Many people choose to live in suburban communities, which usually feature more open space and some sense of the small-town atmosphere that is rooted in American culture. Many suburban communities have grown during periods of prosperity, as families sought to move from apartments to houses or from smaller homes to more spacious dwellings. When communities have endured layoffs and plant closings, they are often pleased to have any new businesses open. But rarely will communities ignore public concerns about the types of growth and businesses that locate there. To avoid community backlash and an antigrowth attitude, business leaders need to work with community groups in balancing business growth with respect for community values. Community planning efforts by municipal governments, done in cooperation with private industry, represent one of the steps that businesses can take to achieve this balance.

Life and health insurance companies have taken the lead in programs to revitalize neighborhood housing through organizations such as Neighborhood Housing Services (NHS) of America. NHS, which is locally controlled, locally funded, nonprofit, and tax-exempt, offers housing rehabilitation and financial services to neighborhood residents. Similar efforts are being made to house the homeless. The New York City Coalition for the Homeless includes corporate, nonprofit, and community members. In Los Angeles, Transamerica Life Companies, a founding partner of the Greater Los Angeles Partnership for the Homeless, has provided money and sent trained people to assist the partnership's efforts. Banks are also involved in meeting the housing needs of low-income residents. And, as illustrated in Exhibit 16-B, corporations often work with nongovernmental organizations (NGOs) such as Habitat for Humanity to build or repair housing.

---

[12] See the discussion case at the end of this chapter. Disney's effort to acquire nearly 3,000 acres for Disney's America began in the late 1980s. Several years of intense controversy followed before Disney stopped the project. Proponents tried to resurrect it, but opposition has remained strong. In 2001, Disney said it had no plans to continue incurring costs to create Disney's America.

EXHIBIT 16-B

Abbott Laboratories Helps Habitat for Humanity

Habitat for Humanity is a worldwide organization that builds homes and sells them to low-income families on a no-profit, no-interest basis. Habitat was founded in 1976 and has built more than 30,000 homes throughout the world. It has more than 1,000 affiliates in its worldwide network. Among its affiliates are people employed by companies such as Abbott Laboratories, a pharmaceutical and health care products manufacturer that employs more than 50,000 people. About 15,000 Abbott employees and retirees live in Lake County, Illinois, where Abbott's world headquarters is located. Employees of Abbott Laboratories are involved in many types of volunteer activity in their local communities, so it was no surprise when a group decided to form the Abbott Chapter of Habitat for Humanity. The Abbott Chapter has worked closely with Lake County's Habitat organization to identify needs and plan a construction project. Local government officials have also been instrumental in identifying sites for Habitat projects and for obtaining needed permits. Since its formation, the Abbott Chapter has helped renovate several buildings in North Chicago and Waukegan, Illinois.

Robin Coleman and her four children learned that they had been selected as the family to work with the Abbott Chapter in building a new house in North Chicago. Habitat families are selected on the basis of need, ability to make a low mortgage payment, and a willingness to help construct the homes of others as well as their own. With the help of more than 200 Abbott employee volunteers, a $38,000 grant for materials from the Abbott Laboratories Fund, and more than 500 hours of sweat equity by the Coleman family, Habitat volunteers built the house in less than one year. Cheers and tears of joy were abundant when Coleman and her family received the keys to their new home.

A dedication ceremony was held at the new Coleman family home. Abbott officials, the mayor of North Chicago, Habitat for Humanity officials, and many of the volunteers attended. Jim Donovan, an R&D quality manager in Abbott's diagnostic division and president of the Abbott Chapter of Habitat, said, "All the people involved in this project have felt a great sense of pride in contributing to the future of the Coleman family as well as to the community."

Sources: Information provided by the corporate communications department, Abbott Laboratories, Abbott Park, Illinois. See also, Abbott Laboratories website, www.ABBOTT.com/community/community_relations.html.

Under the federal **Community Reinvestment Act (CRA),** banks are required to demonstrate their commitment to local communities through low-income lending programs and to provide annual reports to the public. This has led many banks to begin viewing the inner city as a new opportunity for business development. Many banks have even created special subsidiaries that have as their mission the development of new lending and development in needy urban neighborhoods.

Education Reform

The aging of the post–World War II baby boom generation and the subsequent decline in the number of entry-level workers have forced businesses to pay attention to the quality of the workforce. In assessing how the available workforce can be improved, many businesses have recognized that local public schools are a critical resource. Amid severe criticism of America's public schools, which began in the 1980s with the publication of a report entitled *A Nation at Risk,*[13] businesses have become deeply involved in education reform.

Thousands of local partnerships have been formed between schools and businesses. Many of these collaborations, or *adopt-a-school partnerships,* brought companies into contact with schools and teachers, many for the first time. Business leaders now participate on school boards and as advisers to schools and government officials who need business-specific training. The National Alliance of Business (NAB), for example, developed a social compact project in which local businesses pledged their assistance and support to local schools. Demonstration projects in 12 cities led to an improved understanding of the factors required for successful business–education collaboration.

According to one leading research organization, business involvement in education has passed through four stages, or waves. Beyond business support for programs (first wave) and the application of management principles to school administration (second wave), business has become increasingly committed to public policy initiatives (third wave) and collaboration with all of education's stakeholders to reform of the entire system (fourth wave). Louis Gerstner's comments at the beginning of this chapter illustrate the view held by many business leaders: Education is critical to success in a knowledge economy, and schools must be improved so that they are equal to the task. Otherwise, people and nations will fall behind in this worldwide competition. In states such as California, where Gerstner delivered his speech, support for changing traditional education has produced a variety of new ideas: adding an extra 30–40 days to the school year; Saturday classes; more after-school academic programs; tutoring; use of computers and the Internet to support traditional classroom education.[14]

The need for improvement in worker skills also draws businesses into the world of worker training and retraining, especially efforts to train the disadvantaged. Much of this participation has come about as a result of federal job legislation, which requires that public sector job-training programs be supervised by private sector managers through private initiative councils (PICs) in every community where federal funds are used. Businesses have generally welcomed this chance to participate as a way to better match school and community efforts with business workforce opportunities and needs. Moreover, in the late 1990s, as employment surged and companies were unable to find enough skilled workers, many businesses turned to improving the job skills of existing employees.

---

[13] National Commission on Excellence in Education, *A Nation at Risk: The Imperative for Educational Reform* (Washington, DC: U.S. Government Printing Office, 1983).

[14] Jodi Wilgoren, "Calls for Change in the Scheduling of the School Day: Adding Hours, Months," *New York Times,* January 10, 2001, pp. A1, A18.

Jobs, Training, and Welfare Reform

Government leaders have called on American businesses to help address one of the most vexing and costly social problems—welfare reform. Welfare is a form of public assistance to those who are unable to work and live an independent and self-sufficient life. Most societies have some basic form of public assistance to the needy, and some countries (Germany, France, and the United States) are known for their relatively generous assistance programs. As the costs of such programs have risen, however, many citizens have pressured their governments to curb the cost of welfare-assistance programs.

In the United States, the movement to reform welfare programs included tightening eligibility for assistance, limiting the length of time one can claim welfare benefits, and most important in the view of many experts, requiring welfare recipients to earn their eligibility by working in an approved public job. These programs—known as *workfare* in many states—depend heavily on businesses to provide job opportunities. When he signed the Welfare Reform Act in 1994, President Clinton called on American businesses to come forward with innovative job-training opportunities to help move people from welfare to workfare. In time, a number of companies, including Marriott (see Chapter 17) and Pennsylvania Blue Shield, responded by creating new job and training programs. Although the challenges were great, and progress slow, some of these programs did prove successful. George Grode, senior vice president of Pennsylvania Blue Shield, discussed the factors that made his company's program successful:

> *Training, realistic goal-setting, and steady, constructive feedback are three key elements of any successful program intended to promote movement from the world of welfare to the world of work. Collaboration between the private sector employers and public sector support agencies is also essential. The rewards can be high for the employer, the employee, and all taxpayers, as is shown by our experience. Over a three-year period, 208 former welfare workers were trained, hired, and retained as productive members of our workforce. The government saved 2.4 million (dollars) in welfare benefits, and collected 1.3 million (dollars) in payroll taxes.*[15]

Technical Assistance to Government

In many cities, businesses have been actively involved in programs to upgrade the quality of local government. They provide special advice and technical expertise on budgeting, financial controls, and other management techniques. Many of the techniques of total quality management pioneered in the private sector are now being adapted to the analysis and improvement of government programs. Business know-how in these matters can inject vitality and efficiency into government systems that are often overburdened, obsolete, and underfinanced.

---

[15] Felice Davidson Perlmutter, *From Welfare to Work* (New York: Oxford University Press, 1997). Also, John C. Winfrey, *Social Issues: The Ethics and Economics of Taxes and Public Programs* (New York: Oxford University Press, 1998).

Aid to Minority Enterprise

In addition to programs to hire and train urban minorities for jobs in industry, private enterprise has extended assistance to minority-owned small businesses that must struggle for existence in the inner cities. These businesses are often at a great economic disadvantage: They do business in economic locations where high crime rates, congestion, poor transportation, low-quality public services, and a low-income clientele combine to produce a high rate of business failure. Large corporations, sometimes in cooperation with universities, have provided financial and technical advice to minority entrepreneurs and have helped launch programs to teach managerial, marketing, and financial skills. They also have financed the building of minority-managed inner-city plants and sponsored special programs to purchase services and supplies from minority firms. Still, in the view of many, there is the need, and opportunity, for businesses to do much more.

> *In January 1998, Reverend Jesse Jackson announced a new campaign by his Rainbow/PUSH coalition to get Wall Street firms and the nation's largest companies to expand diversity programs and extend more economic opportunity to people of color. The campaign is called the "Wall Street Project." Reverend Jackson put the issue in these terms: "We'll pay for not investing; we're in one big tent." The view was endorsed by U.S. Treasury Secretary Robert Rubin, a former Wall Street banker himself, who said, "Our economy is going to fall short of its potential unless it is for all of us. . . . Inclusion is critical to the bottom line."*
>
> *Jackson continued, "Riker's Island [a New York prison] is a more expensive university than NYU [New York University]," referring to the high cost per year of caring for prisoners who do not contribute to the nation's well-being. "What's missing in this dialogue has been corporate America. They must lead the way on making the case, as educators and in skills and training. There is this wealth gap here, the biggest since 1929."[16]*

Reverend Jackson's initiative has produced results in New York and been expanded to other financial centers. It has also been adapted to include a focus on Silicon Valley in California (with an emphasis on high-tech jobs) as well as Wall Street.

Environmental Programs

The positive impacts of business on the community are balanced by a number of negative effects, including environmental problems. As local landfills near capacity, for example, communities have become concerned about the disposal of solid wastes. Citizen groups using slogans like NIMBY ("not in my back yard") or GOOMBY ("get out of my back yard") have resisted development of additional landfills to handle solid-waste disposal, to which businesses contribute in great quantities. So high was public concern about solid-waste disposal in Seattle, for example, that Procter & Gamble began a pilot project there to collect and recycle disposable diapers. Seattle's families provided an

---

[16] Quoted in Peter Truell, "On Wall Street, Fervent Pleas for Minorities," *New York Times*, January 16, 1998, p. C4. Updated at www.rainbowpush.org/wallstreet.

enthusiastic test case for P&G's experiment in recycling, and the company learned important lessons about public perceptions of the environmental impact of its products.

Community perceptions of environmental risk can have a powerful effect on the ability of companies to operate existing facilities and to expand their businesses. Chemical companies are among the industrial manufacturers facing such problems. They have created **community advisory panels (CAPs)** to bridge communications between managers of their facilities and residents of local communities. These advisory panels have a continuing dialogue with plant managers and bring issues of public concern to the meetings. The chemical industry formally adopted this approach as part of the Responsible Care Program commitments all its members make to the communities in which they operate. And, as shown in Exhibit 16-C, in communities where basic public

---

**EXHIBIT
16-C**

Business Meets the Maquiladoras*

The south Texas border with Mexico is not the usual hotbed of corporate community affairs. It is, however, a hotbed of commercial activity as companies from around the world establish manufacturing and assembly operations called *maquiladoras*. Inexpensive Mexican labor and easy access to American markets make the maquiladoras the vehicle for boomtown development.

The boomtowns are growing in areas where social problems—including no schools, no housing, and no social infrastructure to hold together the community—abound. In El Paso, for example, low wages and the prestige of a "Made in the USA" label have helped keep employment high, with more than 20,000 jobs added to the apparel industry in one year alone. More than 100 million pairs of jeans are made in El Paso each year. But the stiff competition also helps keep El Paso as the poorest metropolitan region in the United States, with personal incomes only 59 percent of the national average. Patricia Fogerty, a former NYNEX community affairs officer who lives in McAllen, Texas, says, "Some [companies] are finding they have to develop the entire social infrastructure in the towns."

A model for doing so is being developed by the El Paso Community Foundation. It organizes Hispanic wives of workers to do community work and serves as a bridge between employers and social problems in the border communities. Among the leadership companies that have partnered with community groups are Levi Strauss, General Electric, Sierra West, and Alcoa. Yet the maquiladora conditions are so bad that many church groups in the United States are campaigning to press companies to do much more in dealing with these poor and needy communities on both sides of the border.

---

*There are two accepted spellings for this word. We have chosen to use *maquiladora* rather than *machiladora*, which also appears in published materials.
Sources: Allen R. Myerson, "Jeans Makers Flourish on Border," *New York Times*, September 29, 1994, pp. D1, D9; and "Machiladora Blues," in Craig Smith, ed., *Corporate Philanthropy Report* 5, no. 1 (August–September 1989), p. 12.

services (e.g., sanitation) are lacking, companies often find themselves leading the effort to create better living conditions for local citizens.

Disaster Relief

One common form of corporate involvement in the community is disaster relief. Throughout the world, companies, like individuals, provide assistance to local citizens and communities when disaster strikes. When major floods occurred in the midwestern United States in 1994, for example, assistance worth millions of dollars poured into affected communities from companies across the country and overseas. And when eastern Canada, including Montreal and much of the province of Quebec, was devastated by ice storms, assistance poured in from Canadian and U.S. companies. Hundreds of volunteers from electric companies in the United States rushed to help restore electric power to more than 3 million Canadian residents.

> *The willingness of companies to provide emergency assistance is an international phenomenon. When an earthquake seriously damaged the Japanese port city of Kobe in 1995, individuals and businesses from all over the world sought to provide assistance. Abbott Laboratories, a health care products company headquartered near Chicago, Illinois, joined dozens of other companies to provide needed medical products for Kobe's survivors. Abbott contributed 1,600 cases of sterile water, intravenous solutions, antibiotics, and medicine to a coordinated relief effort organized by AmeriCares, a private international relief organization based in New Canaan, Connecticut. A shipment of more than 200,000 pounds of materials was airlifted to Japan where another organization, the Japan International Rescue Action Committee, distributed the products to earthquake victims in Kobe.*

Networks of nonprofit agencies, such as the American Red Cross and AmeriCares, are instrumental in aligning resources with needs in such instances. International relief efforts are becoming more important, as communications improve and people around the world are able to witness the horror of disasters. The deadly earthquakes that occurred in El Salvador and India in 2001 produced global relief efforts in which businesses, nonprofit organizations, and individual volunteers worked together to support the thousands of homeless and injured people. Corporate involvement in such efforts, then, is an extension of the natural tendency of people to help one another when tragedy strikes.

Corporate Giving

America is a generous society. According to information collected by the Internal Revenue Service, individuals and organizations give more than $150 billion each year to churches, charities, and other nonprofit organizations. American businesses are a small, but important, part of this broad cultural tradition of giving. One of the most visible ways in which businesses help communities is through gifts of money, property, and employee service. This **corporate philanthropy,** or **corporate giving,** demonstrates the commitment of businesses to assist the communities by supporting such nonprofit organizations as United Way, Community Chest, and individual hospitals,

Figure 16-5

Corporate
contributions as a
percentage of pretax
net income.

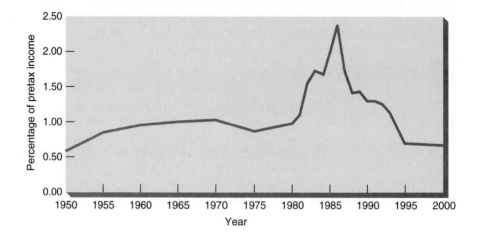

schools, homeless shelters, and other providers of important community services (see discussion in Chapter 3).

The federal government has encouraged corporate giving for educational, charitable, scientific, and religious purposes since 1936.[17] The current IRS rule permits corporations to deduct from their taxable income all such gifts that do not exceed 10 percent of the company's before-tax income. In other words, a company with a before-tax income of $1 million might contribute up to $100,000 to nonprofit community organizations devoted to education, charity, science, or religion. The $100,000 in contributions would then reduce the income to be taxed from $1 million to $900,000, thus saving the company money on its tax bill while providing a source of income to community agencies. Of course, there is nothing to prevent a corporation from giving more than 10 percent of its income for philanthropic purposes, but it would not be given a tax break above the 10 percent level.

As shown in Figure 16-5, average corporate giving in the United States is far below the 10 percent deduction now permitted. Though it varies from year to year, corporate giving has been closer to 1 percent of pretax income since the early 1960s, with a rise that reached a peak in 1986. Although a few corporations, including a cluster headquartered in the Minneapolis–St. Paul metropolitan area, have pledged 5 percent of their pretax income, most companies average between 1 and 2 percent of pretax income.[18] Even at the national average of 1 percent giving, substantial amounts of money are channeled to education, the arts, and other community organizations. Corporate giving totaled more than $11 billion in 1999, including more than $3.5 billion for education.

Some critics have argued that corporate managers have no right to give away company money that does not belong to them. According to this line of reasoning, any

---

[17] The evolution of corporate philanthropy is summarized in Mark Sharfman, "Changing Institutional Rules: The Evolution of Corporate Philanthropy, 1883–1953," *Business and Society* 33, no. 3 (December 1994), pp. 236–69; and "Charities Tap Generous Spirit of Hong Kong," *Wall Street Journal,* November 3, 1994, pp. B1, B8.
[18] Audis Tillman, *Corporate Contributions in 1999* (New York: The Conference Board, 2000).

income earned by the company should be either reinvested in the firm or distributed to the stockholders who are the legal owners. The courts have ruled, however, that charitable contributions fall within the legal and fiduciary powers of the corporation's policymakers. Corporate contributions are one additional way in which companies link themselves to the broader interests of the community, thereby advancing and strengthening the company rather than weakening it.

Companies also help local communities through the substantial number of business donations that are not recorded as philanthropy because they are not pure giving. Routine gifts of products and services for local use are often recorded as advertising expenses. Gifts of employee time for charity drives and similar purposes usually are not recorded, and the costs of soliciting and processing employee gifts, such as payroll deductions for the United Way, usually are not recorded as corporate contributions. Still, they add value to the local community of which the company is a part.

Many large U.S. corporations have established nonprofit **corporate foundations** to handle their charitable programs. This permits them to administer contributions programs more uniformly and provides a central group of professionals that handles all grant requests. Foreign-owned corporations use foundations less frequently, although firms such as Matsushita (Panasonic) and Hitachi use sophisticated corporate foundations to conduct their charitable activities in the United States. As corporations expand to more foreign locations, pressures will grow to expand international corporate giving. Foundations, with their defined mission to benefit the community, can be a useful mechanism to help companies implement philanthropic programs that meet this corporate social responsibility.

Corporate Giving in a Strategic Context

One way to stretch the corporate contributions dollar is to make sure that it is being used strategically to meet the needs of both the recipient and the donor. Creating a strategy of mutual benefits for business and society is one of the major themes of this book, and this type of strategic philanthropy is a means of achieving such win-win outcomes. As shown in Figure 16-6, **strategic philanthropy** blends traditional corporate philanthropy with giving programs that are directly or indirectly linked to business goals and objectives. In the 1990s many companies had transformed their corporate philanthropic giving to this strategic focus, and this transformation is continuing in the early 2000s.

One traditional way of linking business goals to charitable giving is **cause-related marketing.** Originally pioneered by American Express as a way to promote wider use of its credit card, many companies have now created formulas for making contributions to nonprofit organizations based on how many of the particular nonprofit organization's members use the company's credit card or purchase its products. Johnson & Johnson broke new ground when it introduced Arthritis Foundation pain-relief medicine in the mid-1990s. The company agreed to make a contribution to the Arthritis Foundation, based on a percentage of new revenue from each package of pain reliever sold under the AF name. Such activities increase corporate giving while enhancing the revenues of the donors.

Some experts note that strategic philanthropy actually occurs in two forms. One, called *strategic process giving,* applies a professional business approach to determine the

Figure 16-6

Strategic
philanthropy produces
business and
community benefits.

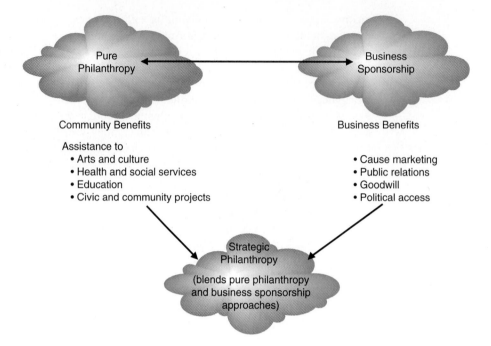

Pure
Philanthropy

Business
Sponsorship

Community Benefits

Assistance to
• Arts and culture
• Health and social services
• Education
• Civic and community projects

Business Benefits

• Cause marketing
• Public relations
• Goodwill
• Political access

Strategic
Philanthropy

(blends pure philanthropy
and business sponsorship
approaches)

goals, budgets, and criteria for specific grants. The second approach, called *strategic out-come giving,* emphasizes the links between corporate contributions and business-oriented goals such as introducing a new product, providing needed services to employees (e.g., child care centers), or maintaining positive contacts with external stakeholder groups (e.g., Asian-Americans). Pressures to justify the use of every corporate dollar are leading managers to develop new ways to tie charitable contributions and high-profile community concerns to business goals. This, it is asserted, helps produce more win-win outcomes for the business and the community.

Priorities in Corporate Giving

The distribution of corporate contributions reflects how the businesses view overall community needs. As shown in Figure 16-7, from the early 1980s to the present, the corporate giving pie has been divided in approximately the same way. These percentages are not identical among different companies and industries, however; some companies tend to favor support for education, whereas others give relatively greater amounts to cultural organizations or community groups.

The actual contributions of an individual company will depend on company goals and priorities. Corporate giving is often justified as a social investment that benefits business in the long run by improving the community, its labor force, the climate for business, or other conditions affecting business. An alternative view is that routine local gifts are a normal expense of operating a business in the community and should be treated like other public relations expenses. Another view holds that the corporation is a citizen

Figure 16-7

Distribution of
corporate
contributions.

Source: Composite
based on data reported
in reports prepared by
the Conference Board.

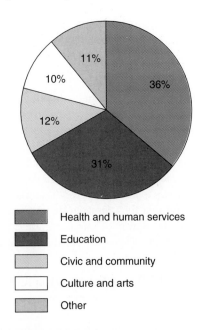

- Health and human services
- Education
- Civic and community
- Culture and arts
- Other

and, as such, has a citizenship responsibility to give without regard to self-interest. Some believe that giving should be linked to business purposes as exemplified in the cause-related marketing pioneered by American Express. The customer gets the product or service, the charity receives a contribution, and company sales grow.

Another point of view is that some corporate gifts take on the characteristics of taxes. Since it is widely believed that corporations should be good citizens, helpful neighbors, and human institutions, the community's expectations come close to imposing some types of gift giving on the corporation as a form of *unofficial tax*. The gifts are given to retain public approval.

The newest development in this field is the emergence of an approach called **venture philanthropy.** According to one group of experts, venture philanthropy is a style of charitable giving in which donors invest major funding, and their own time, talents, and expertise, in philanthropic projects that are issue-oriented rather than institution-oriented.[19] They are entrepreneurial, innovative, and strategically significant; they promise to "make a difference" and can be evaluated by reference to readily observable, concrete, and quantifiable results. This style of giving is becoming popular among new donors whose fortunes have been made in the new economy.

> *For example, in early 2001 the Ellis L. Phillips Foundation began an organized campaign to encourage more new donors to participate in "making a difference" through a unique venture philanthropy approach modeled on venture capital as found in new businesses. They invited prospective business donors to a meeting. The invitation read: "We here*

---

[19] *The Catalogue of Philanthropy* (Boston, MA: Ellis Phillips Foundation, 2001), p. 51.

*invite anyone interested in becoming a 'donor-investor' to participate in a
'venture-capital' type meeting where a select number of 'cutting-edge'
programs will make presentations about their work in the community and
their need for 'venture-capital funds.' "*

Regardless of whether gifts are considered to be an investment, an expense, philanthropy, or a tax, most of their costs are ultimately passed on to consumers, making corporate giving in the long run a cost of doing business. Businesses are, then, acting partly as agents and trustees for the community, receiving funds and distributing them according to perceived and expressed community needs. In the trusteeship role, businesses respond to various stakeholder claims in the community, and one of these responses is support to those whose claims are perceived as being either legitimate or so powerful that they threaten the business if not satisfied. Thus, both the legitimacy of claim and the power of claimants are considered when making a decision concerning corporate giving. (See also our discussion in Chapter 4.)

The Role of Volunteerism

Volunteerism involves the efforts of people to assist others in the community through unpaid work. The United States has a long and distinguished tradition of volunteerism, with many examples dating back to the founding of communities as the population moved west across the continent (see discussion in Chapter 3). In the 1980s, this spirit of volunteerism was invoked by U.S. presidents Ronald Reagan and George Bush as a way to address community problems without further growth in government programs. For its part, the business community formed the Council on Private Sector Initiatives as a means to encourage voluntary business–community activities; many business leaders agreed to promote voluntary action in their own communities.

Volunteerism received a much-publicized boost when the first President Bush launched his 1,000 Points of Light campaign to celebrate 1,000 voluntary efforts by individuals and organizations to solve problems in American communities. In the 1990s, volunteerism was spurred by the work of the Points of Light Foundation, a catalyst for stimulating voluntary action programs in local communities.[20] Volunteerism received another push in 1997 when former presidents Jimmy Carter, Gerald Ford, and George Bush and then-president Bill Clinton supported an initiative led by General Colin Powell to address the problems of America's youth, including education and community involvement, in a bipartisan call for broad voluntary action. The campaign was high profile, with extensive media coverage of events and General Powell's personal involvement.[21] In 2001, President George W. Bush promised to extend the spirit of volunteerism by enlisting churches and other faith-based organizations in a sweeping set of commitments to improve the lives of needy citizens.[22]

[20] For a report on current activities, see Points of Light Foundation at www.pointsoflight.org.
[21] Colin Powell, *My American Journey* (New York: Random House, 1995). In 2001, General Powell was named U.S. secretary of state by president-elect George W. Bush.
[22] Frank Bruni and Laurie Goodstein, "New Bush Office Seeks Closer Ties to Church Groups," *New York Times,* January 29, 2001, pp. A1, A18. President Bush signed two executive orders to implement this initiative. One order created the White House Office of Faith-Based and Community Initiatives. The second order established offices within five federal departments—Justice, HUD, HHS, Labor, and Education—to ensure greater cooperation between government and the independent sector. See President Bush's statement in the *New York Times,* January 30, 2001, p. A18.

Businesses, large and small, are often enlisted as allies in efforts to improve communities. Managers are asked to announce, publicize, and promote community events, fund-raisers, and so on among staff members, employees, and associates. Some companies provide money, supplies, T-shirts, transportation, or other resources to these community efforts. Corporate community relations managers are often asked to coordinate these efforts.

Large sporting events provide opportunities for communities to join in a massive volunteer effort. When the 2000 Summer Olympic Games were held in Sydney, Australia, for example, many Australian companies provided volunteers, refreshments, souvenirs, and other assistance to the Games. Similarly, Coca-Cola, Bell South, and other leading companies from Atlanta became leaders of that city's campaign to host the 1996 Summer Olympic Games. In both instances, corporate volunteer commitments were an important element of the winning city's bid to host the event. By the time the Olympic Games were held, dozens of companies in each city had coordinated tens of thousands of days of volunteer work in support of the Olympics.

Although most companies and communities are involved in activities that are less visible than the Olympic Games, nearly every city and local community has a variety of needs that require the helping hands of volunteers. Mayors and other local government officials depend on the goodwill and cooperative spirit of businesses and citizens to do the work of community building. This means that in addition to providing jobs, paying taxes, and directing charitable contributions dollars to worthy causes, there is a role for companies as catalysts in encouraging volunteerism that helps build local communities. This is part of the process of developing the social capital, or "social glue," that holds communities together.

The Need for Partnerships

The need for **public–private partnerships** between business and government is apparent when dealing with community problems. The idea of such partnering is not new. As one group of business executives wrote 20 years ago:

Whether growing or contracting, young or old, large or small, in the Frost Belt or Sun Belt, America's urban communities possess the resources of an advanced and affluent society: highly educated and skilled individuals, productive social and economic institutions, sophisticated technology, physical infrastructure, transportation and communications networks, and access to capital. Developing this potential will require cooperation. . . . Public–private partnerships are a source of energy and vitality for America's urban communities.[23]

The truth of that statement remains valid in the twenty-first century. The advent of a new administration and national leaders who appear committed to principles of local community leadership, voluntary activity, and a stated faith in the power of communities to shape

---

[23] Committee for Economic Development, *Public–Private Partnership: An Opportunity for Urban Communities* (New York: Committee for Economic Development, 1982), p. 1.

their futures suggests there will be new initiatives that will require business engagement in community affairs.

Corporate restructuring and downsizing has underscored the importance of this effort. Many community problems are people problems involving hopes, attitudes, sentiments, and expectations for better human conditions. Neither government nor business can simply impose solutions or be expected to find quick and easy answers to problems so long in the making and so vast in their complications. Moreover, neither government nor business has the financial resources to solve these issues. Grassroots involvement is needed, where people are willing and able to confront their own needs, imagine solutions, and work to fulfill them through cooperative efforts and intelligent planning. In that community-oriented effort, government, nonprofit organizations, and businesses can be partners, contributing aid and assistance where feasible and being socially responsive to legitimately expressed human needs.

A study by the Conference Board and the Urban Institute identified three distinct strategies that corporations can use to become effective partners with urban communities.[24] One is to become *directly involved* in addressing specific problems in specific neighborhoods or communities. A second approach is to *develop partnerships* with the community wherein the community's needs and priorities guide the form and type of corporate activity. The third strategy is for the corporation to be involved in the community through *intermediary organizations*, such as a citywide umbrella organization that helps to coordinate the efforts of many local businesses and nonprofits. More recently, Googins and Rochlin identified comparable factors that account for the success of community-based partnerships.[25]

Communities need jobs, specialized skills, executive talents, and other resources that business can provide. Business needs cooperative attitudes in local government, basic public services, and a feeling that it is a welcome member of the community. Under these circumstances much can be accomplished to upgrade the quality of community life. The range of business–community collaborations is extensive, giving businesses many opportunities to be socially responsible. Corporate restructuring, erratic growth patterns, and an explosion of community needs challenge the communities we live in every day. Still, by using management skills, corporate philanthropy, employee volunteerism, and other creative means, companies can work with nonprofit organizations and government to make a positive impact on the quality of community life.

Summary Points of This Chapter

- Businesses and communities have a mutual dependence that is both economically and socially significant. Many of a company's stakeholders—employees, suppliers, customers—may reside in the community and be affected by its problems and

---

[24] Googins and Rochlin, "Creating the Partnership Society"; and George Petersen and Dana Sundblad, *Corporations as Partners in Strengthening Urban Communities*, Research Report 1079–94 (New York: The Conference Board, 1994).
[25] Googins and Rochlin, "Creating the Partnership Society."

benefits. Thus, many businesses participate in community affairs and support community interests as well as their own.

- Many corporations have established a community relations office that connects their activities to local needs and community groups and develops strategies for creating win-win approaches to solving community problems.

- Corporate community involvement with educational, charitable, scientific, and community programs helps to build social capital and sustain vital community institutions. This involvement also benefits the business in a variety of ways, including its reputation as a good place to work and a committed citizen.

- Corporate volunteerism involves encouraging employees to participate in projects that address a wide range of community needs. Some companies have made volunteerism an explicit way to connect their business and citizenship strategy.

- Corporate philanthropy is one way for businesses to support community groups with direct financial support. Strategic philanthropy represents a way of linking corporate giving and business goals. Successful strategies for coping with community problems often involve a mixture of philanthropy and other forms of cooperation among businesses, government, volunteers, labor unions, and community organizations.

- The development of public–private partnerships has proven to be effective in tackling some problems in education, economic development, and social service needs. Partnerships and volunteerism provide models of a shared responsibility in which business and communities address social problems. Many businesses and communities are creating new strategies based on these models.

Key Terms and Concepts Used in This Chapter

- Community
- Community relations
- Social capital
- Civic engagement
- License to operate
- Community Reinvestment Act (CRA)
- Community advisory panels (CAPs)
- Corporate philanthropy (corporate giving)
- Corporate foundations
- Strategic philanthropy
- Cause-related marketing
- Venture philanthropy
- Volunteerism
- Public–private partnerships

Internet Resources

- www.disney.com   Walt Disney Company
- www.fdncenter.org   The Foundation Center
- www.cof.org   Council on Foundations
- www.bc.edu/cccr   Boston College Center for Corporate Community Relations

- www.pointsoflight.org   Points of Light Foundation
- helping.org   A "giving" portal
- wfaa.com   Companies Who Care

Discussion Case: *Walt Disney and the License to Operate*

Walt Disney Company is one of America's leading entertainment corporations, and is well known for its animated movies (*Fantasia, The Little Mermaid,* and *The Lion King*), characters (Mickey Mouse and Donald Duck), and theme parks (Disneyland, Disney World, Euro Disney). Public support for cartoon characters and enjoyable entertainment is a valuable asset for the company, but it has not been enough to overcome hostility to some of Disney's expansion plans.

The company encountered fierce opposition to its plans to build an American history theme park called Disney's America on a 3,000-acre tract of land in Haymarket, Virginia. The site is located about 35 miles southwest of Washington, DC, near the Manassas National Battlefield Park, site of the battles of Bull Run, two of the Civil War's bloodiest battles. Plans called for building a theme park, with as many as 2,281 homes, 1,340 hotel rooms, and about 1.96 million square feet of retail and commercial space.

Critics immediately argued that the thousands of visitors expected at such a theme park would overwhelm the ability of local communities to absorb and manage side effects. An opposition group, calling itself Protecting Prince William County, was quickly formed to challenge the Disney plan. But local and county officials, after working with Disney's staff, concluded that the negative effects were exaggerated and would, in any event, be outweighed by benefits the region would reap. These benefits included 19,000 jobs and nearly $50 million in new tax revenues. Both the jobs and the tax revenues were seen as vital to the long-term welfare of the county's communities and residents.

A group of historians, including several famous Civil War experts, campaigned against the Disney project through an organization called Project Historic America. They argued that the virtual reality battles would trivialize and sanitize the true battles that had been fought at the site. The Piedmont Environmental Council, a coalition of 70 groups and more than 5,000 families, took a different approach: They sued Disney, alleging violations of state and federal environmental laws.

The battle raged for years, and the opposition proved so strong that Disney was forced to drop the project. Recognizing that his community would get neither jobs nor new tax revenues, Mayor Jack Kapp of Haymarket, Virginia, spoke more directly: "People around here are devastated. It's an economic blow to Prince William County. I feel like I've been to a funeral today."

Sources: Based on articles in the *New York Times* and the *Wall Street Journal* appearing in 1993–98. See especially Sallie Hofmeister, "Disney Vows to Seek Another Park Site," *New York Times,* September 30, 1994, p. A12; and Michael Janofsky, "Town 'Devastated' by Loss of Project," *New York Times,* September 30, 1994, p. A12.

Discussion Questions

1. What was Disney's motivation to locate in Haymarket, Virginia? What special features did the location have that were important to the project's success?

2. What do you believe the Disney's America project meant to the long-term relationship between the company and Virginia? What did it mean to the company? Who gets the greatest benefit? Who suffers the biggest loss? (Use Figure 16-3 to discuss.)

3. Why did Disney fail to gain a license to operate from the Virginia communities? What could it have done differently?

4. What are the elements of community partnership that are essential to the success of a development effort such as Disney's America?

17

Employees and the Corporation

Employees and employers are engaged in a critical relationship affecting the corporation's performance. There is a basic economic aspect to this relationship. Employees provide labor for the firm; employers compensate workers for their contribution of skill or productivity. Yet, also present in the employee–employer exchange are numerous social, ethical, legal, and public policy issues. Attention to the multiple aspects of this association can benefit the firm, its workers, and society.

This chapter focuses on these key questions and objectives:

- What rights do workers have to organize and bargain collectively?

- As government regulation of employee safety and health issues increases, what are the obligations of business to protect workers?

- Do employers have a duty to provide job security to their workers?

- To what extent do employees have a right to privacy? Can businesses legitimately monitor employee communications, police romance in the office, test for drugs or alcohol, or subject employees to honesty tests?

- Do employees have a duty to blow the whistle on corporate misconduct, or should employees always be loyal to their employer?

- What are the special obligations of multinational corporations to their employees around the world?

A computer programmer for Timekeeping Systems, a manufacturer of bar-code readers in Cleveland, Ohio, was fired after he circulated e-mail to his coworkers. In his electronic memo, written on his office computer, the programmer had criticized the company for unilaterally changing its vacation policy. Timekeeping Systems' vice president, charging that the e-mail was "inappropriate and intentionally provocative," demanded a written apology. When the programmer refused, he was immediately discharged.[1]

Should employees, like this programmer, have a right to criticize their employers using a company e-mail system? Does the programmer enjoy a right to free speech in this instance? Does Timekeeping Systems have a right to prohibit use of its property to organize opposition to its policies?

A former Teacher of the Year in Chatham County, Georgia, was fired after authorities found a partially smoked marijuana cigarette in her unlocked car. As part of a "drug-free schools" program, the school board had sponsored searches of the school parking lot with drug-sniffing dogs. When confronted, the popular teacher initially refused to take a drug test, saying she wanted to talk with her lawyer. A urinalysis taken the next day showed no trace of illegal substances. The teacher sued, demanding her job back.[2]

Was this employer justified in using dogs to search employees' cars for drugs, and in firing this teacher? Was this employee justified in refusing to take a drug test right away? Who do you think was right in this case, the school board or the teacher?

Nike Corporation, the maker of athletic shoes and apparel, was criticized by student activists and others for low wages in plants that made their products in Vietnam and elsewhere in Asia. Young women who cut, sewed, and glued sneakers for a Nike subcontractor outside Ho Chi Minh City, for example, earned on average about $550 *a year*, including overtime pay. Although very low by U.S. standards, this wage was well above the Vietnamese average, and there was no shortage of job applicants.[3]

What is a fair wage in this case? Should multinational companies pay their overseas workers enough to enjoy a decent family standard of living, even if this is well above the legally mandated wage or above wages common in the area for similar kinds of work?

All three of these difficult questions will be addressed later in this chapter. As the situations giving rise to them suggest, the rights and duties of employers and employees in the modern workplace are incredibly complex—and have become more so, as business has become increasingly global.

The Employment Relationship

As noted in Chapter 1, employees are a primary stakeholder of business—and a critically important one. Businesses cannot operate without employees to make products, provide services, market to customers, run the organization internally, and plan for the future. At the same time,

[1] "Your Manager's Policy on Employees' E-Mail May Have a Weak Spot," *Wall Street Journal,* April 25, 2000, pp. A1, A10.
[2] "Supreme Court Asked to Review Teacher Firing for Drug Test Refusal," *Workplace Substance Abuse Advisor,* March 23, 2000.
[3] B. Baum, "Study Concludes that Nike Workers Can More than Make Ends Meet," *Athenaeum,* August 27, 1999. For more detail, including additional references, see the case study "Nike's Dispute with the University of Oregon" at the end of the book.

Figure 17-1

Rights and duties of
employees and
employers.

Employee Rights/Employer Duties	Employee Duties/Employer Rights
• Right to organize and bargain	• No drug or alcohol abuse
• Safe and healthy workplace	• No actions that would endanger others
• Privacy	• To treat others with respect and without harassment of any kind
• Discipline fairly and justly applied	• Honesty; appropriate disclosure
• To blow the whistle	• Loyalty and commitment
• Equal employment opportunity	• Respect for employer's property and intellectual capital
• To be treated with respect for fundamental human rights	

employees are dependent on their employers for their livelihood and often much more, including friendship networks, recreational opportunities, health care, retirement savings, even their very sense of self. Because of the importance of the relationship to both parties, it must be carefully managed, with consideration for both legal and ethical obligations.

The employment relationship confers rights and duties on both sides. (A *right* means someone is entitled to be treated a certain way; rights often confer *duties* on others.) Some of these responsibilities are legal or contractual; others are social or ethical in nature. For their part, employers have an obligation to provide some measure of job security, a safe and healthy workplace, and equal opportunity for all. They are obliged to pay a decent wage and to respect workers' rights to organize and bargain collectively, as guaranteed by U.S. law and the laws of many other nations. Employers must also respect employees' rights to privacy and, to some extent at least, their rights to free speech and to do what they want outside the workplace.

But employees also have a duty to behave in acceptable ways. For example, most would agree that employees should not abuse drugs or alcohol in a way that impairs their work performance, use company e-mail to send offensive messages, or take the employer's property for their own personal use. Employees should deal with customers and coworkers in an honest, fair, and nondiscriminatory way. They should not reveal proprietary information to others outside the company, unless there is compelling reason to do so, such as an imminent threat to the public's safety. Some of the main rights and duties of employers and employees are summarized in Figure 17-1. How to balance these sometimes-conflicting obligations poses an ongoing and frequently perplexing challenge to business.

This chapter considers the rights and duties, both legal and ethical, of the two parties in the employment relationship. The following chapter explores the related issue of workforce diversity and discusses the specific legal and ethical obligations of employers with respect to equal employment opportunity.

Workplace Rights

Employees in the United States enjoy several important legal guarantees. They have the right to *organize and bargain collectively,* to have a *safe and healthy workplace,* and, to some degree, to *job security.* This section will explore these three rights, emphasizing U.S. laws and regulation, but with comparative references to policies in other nations.

The Right to Organize and Bargain Collectively

In the United States, and in most other nations, employees have a fundamental legal right to organize **labor unions** and to bargain collectively with their employers. The exceptions are some communist countries (such as China, Vietnam, Cuba, and North Korea) and some military dictatorships (such as Myanmar, also known as Burma), where workers are not permitted to form independent unions. Labor unions are organizations, such as the Service Employees International Union or the Teamsters, that represent workers on the job. Under U.S. laws, most private and public workers have the right to hold an election to choose what union they want to represent them, if any. Unions negotiate with employers over wages, working conditions, and other terms of employment. Employers are not required by law to agree to the union's demands, but they are required to bargain in good faith. Sometimes, if the two sides cannot reach agreement, a strike occurs, or employees apply pressure in other ways, such as refusing to work overtime.

The influence of labor unions in the United States has waxed and waned over the years. During the New Deal period in the 1930s, many workers, particularly in manufacturing industries such as automobiles and steel, joined unions, and the ranks of organized labor grew rapidly. Unions negotiated with employers for better wages, benefits such as pensions and health insurance, and improved job safety—significantly improving the lot of many workers. Since the mid-1950s, however, the proportion of American workers represented by unions has declined. In 1999, only about 14 percent of all employees were union members. (The percentage was higher—37 percent—in government employment.)

Some observers believe, however, that unions in the United States may be poised for recovery. The AFL-CIO, the major federation of labor unions, elected new leaders in 1995 who vowed to devote more resources to organizing new members. In 1999, for the second consecutive year, the number of workers who were union members in the United States actually rose, although the proportion unionized remained steady.[4]

A possible indicator of labor's resurgence was the successful 2000 strike by two unions against Verizon, the telecommunications giant formed just months earlier by a merger of Bell Atlantic, GTE, and Vodafone. The Communications Workers of America and the International Brotherhood of Electrical Workers made important gains, including wage improvements, limits on mandatory overtime, and a simplified procedure for signing up union members in the company's fast-growing wireless division. According

---

[4] "Labor Union Membership Increases Second Year in Row to 16.48 Million," *Wall Street Journal,* January 20, 2000, pp. A2, A4.

to one commentator, the Verizon strike demonstrated that unions had gained "a surprising foothold into the Information Economy."[5]

Labor union power was evident in other ways in the early 2000s. Unions organized in the political arena, using political action committees and other methods (discussed in Chapter 8); attended shareholder meetings of companies where they represented workers; and voted shares of stock in which their pension funds were invested (discussed in Chapter 14) to pursue their institutional objectives.

Some labor unions departed from their traditional adversarial approach to work cooperatively with employers for their mutual benefit. At Saturn, AT&T, and Kaiser Permanente (a large health maintenance organization), for example, management and unions forged new partnerships aimed both at giving workers a greater say in the business and improving quality and productivity. However, in some industries, old-line labor–management conflict predominated. Airline schedules were snarled in 2000 when pilots refused to work overtime because of disagreements over their union contract. Organized labor was dealt a blow when Wal-Mart decided no longer to cut its own meat, after butchers at several of its big superstores began to unionize. The move effectively halted the first successful union organizing drive at the nation's largest nongovernment employer.[6] And in the new economy sector, Amazon.com used its internal website to distribute antiunion materials to its managers in an effort to block organizing efforts among its employees.[7]

The Right to a Safe and Healthy Workplace

Many jobs are potentially hazardous to workers' safety and health. In some industries, the use of high-speed and noisy machinery, high-voltage electricity, high temperatures, or sophisticated chemical compounds poses risks. Some occupations, such as construction, underground and undersea tunneling, drilling, and mining, are particularly dangerous. Extensive training and careful precautions are necessary to avoid accidents, injuries, and illnesses.

In 1999, a worker at Rocky Mountain Steel in Pueblo, Colorado lost both of his arms after he touched a live wire and was jolted with 34,500 volts of electricity. The man was a laborer who normally did another job but had been ordered to clean some insulators. "They [the laborers] had no electrical knowledge and no training," charged a union official at the plant.[8]

Over the past few decades, new categories of accidents or illnesses have emerged, including the fast-growing job safety problem of repetitive motion disorders, such as the wrist pain sometimes experienced by supermarket checkers, meatcutters, or keyboard

---

[5] Robert Kuttner, "Verizon's Crash Course in High-Tech Unionism," *Business Week,* September 11, 2000, p. 28. See also, "Labor Makes Its Call to the Future," *Washington Post,* September 3, 2000, p. B1.

[6] "Pro-Union Butchers at Wal-Mart Win a Battle, Lose War," *Wall Street Journal,* April 11, 2000, pp. A1, A4.

[7] "Amazon.com Is Using the Web to Block Unions' Efforts to Organize," *New York Times,* November 29, 2000, p. C1.

[8] "Steel Mill Deaths Prompt In-Depth OSHA Probe," *Denver Post,* April 18, 2000, p. C1.

operators. The number of health problems attributed to the use of video display terminals and computer keyboards has increased tenfold in the past decade. In response, many businesses have given greater attention to **ergonomics,** adapting the job to the worker rather than forcing the worker to adapt to the job. For example, ergonomically designed office chairs that conform to the shape of the worker's spine may help prevent low productivity and lost time due to back injuries.[9]

Annually, nearly 6 million workers in private industry are injured or become ill while on the job, according to the U.S. Department of Labor. This amounts to about 7 hurt or sick workers out of every 100. Some of the highest rates are found in the primary and fabricated metals, transportation equipment, food processing, rubber, and air transportation industries. In general, manufacturing jobs are more risky than service sector jobs.[10] Older workers are at greater risk; they are nearly four times as likely as younger ones to die from job-related injuries.[11]

Workplace violence—a particular threat to employee safety—is profiled in Exhibit 17-A.

In the United States, the Occupational Safety and Health Act, passed in 1970 during the great wave of social legislation discussed in Chapter 7, gives workers the right to a job "free from recognized hazards that are causing or likely to cause death or serious physical harm." This law is administered by the **Occupational Safety and Health Administration (OSHA).** Congress gave OSHA important powers to set and enforce safety and health standards. Employers found in violation can be fined and, in the case of willful violation causing the death of an employee, jailed as well. In the example of the laborer mentioned above, OSHA fined Rocky Mountain Steel $32,500 for violations contributing to the accident.

OSHA has had considerable success in improving worker safety and health. Since 1970, when the agency was created, the overall workplace death rate has been halved. Very serious occupational illnesses, such as brown lung (caused when textile workers inhale cotton dust) and black lung (caused when coal miners inhale coal dust), have been significantly reduced. The rate of lead poisoning—suffered by workers in smelters and battery plants, among other workplaces—has been cut by two-thirds. Deaths from trench cave-ins have been reduced by 35 percent, to cite several examples. Although many businesses have credited OSHA with helping reduce lost workdays and worker compensation costs, others have criticized the agency's rules as being too costly to implement and administer. For example, in 1999 OSHA proposed new rules that would require many employers to devise ergonomics programs. Many employers immediately attacked the proposal, charging that the $4 billion a year it would cost was excessive.[12]

In part in response to employer criticisms, OSHA has entered into cooperative partnerships with employers, aimed at improving occupational safety and health for the benefit of both companies and their workers.

---

[9] "New Ergonomic Chairs Battle to Save the Backs of Workers, for Big Bucks," *Wall Street Journal,* June 8, 1999, p. B11A.

[10] Available at stats.bls.gov.

[11] "For Older Employees, on-the-Job Injuries Are More Often Deadly," *Wall Street Journal,* June 17, 1997, pp. A1, A10.

[12] "Employers Criticize New Ergonomic Standards," *Wall Street Journal,* November 23, 1999, pp. A3, A8.

**EXHIBIT
17-A**

Violence in the Workplace

Stories of angry or distraught employees, ex-employees, or associates of employees attacking workers, coworkers, or superiors at work have become more frequent. For example, there is a growing trend for workers who have lost their jobs—or who face some other financial threat—to seek vengeance, often in calculated and cold-blooded fashion. In a particularly shocking incident, a software tester for a technology firm in Wakefield, Massachusetts, who apparently thought his wages were going to be garnished and his car repossessed, shot and killed seven coworkers in a bloody rampage the day after Christmas, 2000.

Homicide is the second-leading cause of death on the job (only vehicle accidents kill more). Every year, close to 1,000 workers are murdered and another one and a half million are assaulted at work in the United States. Police officers, security guards, taxi drivers, prison guards, bartenders, mental health workers, and gas station attendants are most at risk. Although workplace violence is often considered an American problem, a survey by the International Labor Organization found that workplace assaults were actually more common in several other industrial nations—including France, England, and Argentina—than in the United States.

OSHA has developed recommendations to help employers reduce the risk of violence. Employers should try to reduce high-risk situations, for example, by installing alarm systems, convex mirrors, and pass-through windows. They should train employees in what to do in an emergency situation. Unfortunately, many companies are poorly prepared to deal with these situations. Only 24 percent of employers offer any type of formal training to their employees in coping with workplace violence.

Sources: "Massacre at the Office," *Newsweek,* January 8, 2001, p. 27; "Going Postal Hits the Private Sector," *Washington Post,* November 7, 1999, p. A3. The homicide and assault statistics are based on the Bureau of Labor Statistics Census of Fatal Occupational Injuries, available at the OSHA website at www.osha.gov/oshainfo/priorities/violence.html. See also "Job Violence: A Global Survey," *Business Week,* August 17, 1998, p. 22.

For example, OSHA's office in Atlanta partnered with a private insurance company to provide safety seminars and on-site risk assessments to local businesses. One result was that Horizon Steel Erectors, a construction contractor, established a program to protect its workers from falls. Horizon reported a 96 percent reduction in accident costs per man-hour as a result of the program.[13] In another example, in 2000 OSHA partnered with Ford Motor Company and its union, the United Automobile Workers, to track health and safety incidents, file reports, and hold an annual review aimed at improving health and safety conditions in Ford's plants.[14]

---

[13] Described on OSHA's website at www.osha.gov/oshinfo/success.html.

[14] "OSHA, Ford, and UAW Form Worker Safety Partnership," press release by Ford Motor Company, December 5, 2000, available at www.prnewswire.com.

Some businesses have developed their own systems to reduce the threats of workplace injuries. One of the more popular and widespread methods is workplace safety teams. Safety teams are generally made up of equal numbers of workers and managers. In operation, these teams not only reduce employee accidents but also lower workers' compensation costs. The effect is particularly dramatic at small companies that typically do not have the financial or human resources to develop the more elaborate and costly safety programs and committees found in large corporations.

The special problem of smoking in the workplace—a safety and health threat both to smokers and nonsmokers—is addressed in the discussion case at the end of this chapter.

The Right to a Secure Job

Do employers have an obligation to provide their workers with job security? Once someone is hired, under what circumstances is it legal, or fair, to let him or her go? In recent years, the expectations underlying this most basic aspect of the employment relationship have changed, both in the United States and in other countries around the globe.

In the United States, since the late 1800s, the legal basis for the employment relationship has been **employment-at-will.** Employment-at-will is a legal doctrine that means that employees are hired and retain their jobs "at the will of"—that is, at the sole discretion of—the employer. However, over time, this doctrine has been eroded by a number of laws and court decisions that have dramatically curtailed U.S. employers' freedom to terminate workers. Some of the restrictions on employers include the following:

- An employer may not fire a worker because of race, gender, religion, national origin, age, or disability. The equal employment and other laws that prevent such discriminatory terminations are further described in Chapter 18.

- An employer may not fire a worker if that act would constitute a violation of public policy, as determined by the courts. For example, if a company fired an employee just because he or she cooperated with authorities in the investigation of a crime, this would be illegal.

- An employer may not fire a worker if, in doing so, it would violate the Worker Adjustment Retraining Notification Act (WARN). This law, passed in 1988, requires most big employers to provide a 60-day advance notice whenever they lay off a third or more (or 500 or more, whichever is less) of their workers at a work site.

- An employer may not fire a worker simply because the individual was involved in a union organizing drive or other union activity.

- An employer may not fire a worker if that act would violate an implied contract, such as a verbal promise, or basic rules of "fair dealing." For example, an employer could not legally fire a salesperson just because he or she had earned a bigger bonus under an incentive program than the employer wanted to pay.

Of course, if workers are covered by a collective bargaining agreement, it may impose additional restrictions on an employer's right to terminate. Many union contracts say that employees can be fired only "for just cause," and workers have a right to appeal the employer's decision through the union grievance procedure. Many European countries and Japan have laws that extend "just cause" protections to all workers, whether or not they are covered by a union contract.

The commitments that employers and employees make to each other go beyond mere legal obligations, however. Cultural values, traditions, and norms of behavior also play important roles. Some have used the term **social contract** to refer to the *implied understanding* (not a legal contract, but rather a set of shared expectations) between an organization and its stakeholders. This concept includes, perhaps most significantly, the understanding between businesses and their employees.

Research suggests that the social contract governing the employment relationship has varied across cultures and also across time. For example, in Europe employers have historically given workers and their unions a greater role in determining company policy than do most U.S. employers. Employee representatives are often included on boards of directors, in a practice sometimes called *codetermination.* For many years, big Japanese companies offered a core group of senior workers lifelong employment; in exchange, these workers felt great loyalty to the company. This practice became less widespread in the 1990s, as the Japanese economy contracted. In the former Soviet Union, many enterprises felt an obligation to provide social benefits, such as housing and child care, to their workers. These benefits declined with the advent of privatization in these formerly state-run economies.

Beginning in the late 1980s and continuing into the 1990s, fierce global competition and greater attention to improving the bottom line resulted in significant corporate restructuring and downsizing (termination) of employees in many countries. With this trend came a new way of thinking about the employee–employer relationship, which some researchers called a *new social contract.* Bonds between employers and employees weakened. Companies aimed to attract and retain employees not by offering long-term job security but rather by emphasizing interesting and challenging work, performance-based compensation, and ongoing professional training. For their part, employees were expected to contribute by making a strong commitment to the job task and work team and to assume a share of responsibility for the company's success. But they could not count on a guaranteed job. The new message to employees was: You are responsible for your lifetime employment. It is not the responsibility of the employer.[15]

In the boom economy at the turn of the century, however, many labor markets tightened, and downsizing slowed or stopped in some parts of the economy. In some instances, employers seemed more willing to offer long-term commitments to workers, if it would help them retain valued talent.[16] Pressure from employees who wanted greater job security and benefits also played a role, as illustrated in Exhibit 17-B. In any case, finding the right balance in the employment relationship between commitment and

[15] James E. Post, "The New Social Contract," in Oliver Williams and John Houck, eds., *The Global Challenge to Corporate Social Responsibility* (New York: Oxford University Press, 1995); and Barbara W. Altman and James E. Post, "Challenges in Balancing Corporate Economic and Social Responsibilities," working paper, Boston University, Boston, 1994.
[16] "We Want You to Stay, Really," *Business Week,* June 22, 1998, pp. 67–72.

EXHIBIT 17-B

Contingent Workers in the New Economy

Should companies have strong or weak bonds with their employees? When businesses invest in their employees—by providing a well-structured career, benefits, and job security—they reap the rewards of enhanced loyalty, productivity, and commitment. But such investments are expensive, and long-term commitments make it hard for companies to adjust to the ups and downs of the business cycle. Some firms resolve this dilemma by employing two classes of employees: permanent workers, who enjoy stable employment and full benefits, and temporary workers, who do not. The U.S. Labor Department estimates that over 10 million Americans on the job—about 1 in every 14—are temporary, or *contingent,* workers. On university campuses, to cite one example, many faculty members are part-timers who are not on a tenure (career) track and are often paid much less per course and receive fewer, if any, benefits. But at some companies, contingent workers have fought to upgrade their status. At Microsoft, temporary workers sued the company, charging that they had been wrongly denied benefits paid to permanent employees doing similar work. In 2000, Microsoft settled the suit, offering to pay $97 million to some 8,000 contingent employees. The company also upgraded many temporary employees to "blue badge," or permanent, status.

Source: "Microsoft to Pay $97 Million to End Temp Worker Suit," *Los Angeles Times,* December 13, 2000, p. C1.

flexibility—within a basic context of fair dealing—remains a challenge to socially responsible businesses.

Privacy in the Workplace

An important right, in the workplace as elsewhere, is privacy. **Privacy** can be most simply understood as the right to be left alone. In the business context, privacy rights refer primarily to protecting an individual's personal life from unwarranted intrusion by the employer. Many people believe, for example, that their religious and political views, their health conditions, their credit history, and what they do and say off the job are private matters and should be safe from snooping by the boss. Exceptions are permissible only when the employer's interests are clearly affected. For example, it may be appropriate for the boss to know that an employee is discussing with a competitor, through e-mail messages, the specifications of a newly developed product not yet on the market.

But other areas are not so clear-cut. For example, should a job applicant who is experiencing severe financial problems be denied employment out of fear that he may be more inclined to steal from the company? Should an employee be terminated after the firm discovers that she has a serious medical problem, although it does not affect her job performance, since the company's health insurance premiums may dramatically increase? At what point do company interests weigh more heavily than an employee's right to privacy? This section will address several key workplace issues where these privacy dilemmas often emerge: electronic monitoring, office romance, drug and alcohol abuse, and honesty testing.

Electronic Monitoring

As discussed in Chapters 12 and 13, changing technologies have brought many ethical issues to the forefront. One such issue is employee **electronic monitoring.** New technologies—among them, e-mail, voice mail, Internet browsing, and digitally stored video—enable companies to gather, store, and monitor information about employees' activities. A company's need for information, particularly about its workers, may be at odds with an employee's right to privacy. Consider the following example:

> *In 2000, two dozen employees at the* New York Times' *business office in Norfolk, Virginia, were fired after it was learned they had used the e-mail system at work to pass around dirty jokes and sexual images. Managers told the employees that their behavior was unprofessional and left the firm vulnerable to liability in harassment lawsuits.*[17]

Employee monitoring has exploded in recent years, reflecting technological advances that make surveillance of employees easier and more affordable. A 2000 survey found that nearly three-quarters of U.S. firms recorded and reviewed their employees' communications on the job, a proportion that had doubled during the previous three years.[18] Most of the monitoring was electronic; it included reviewing e-mail messages, computer files, and patterns of Internet use. Special software permitted employers to automatically scan messages or files for key words or to flag a supervisor when a particular website was accessed or phone number dialed.

Management justifies the increase in employee monitoring for a number of reasons. Employers have an interest in efficiency. When employees log onto the Internet at work to trade stocks, plan their vacations, or chat with friends by e-mail, this is not a productive use of their time. Employers also fear lawsuits if employees act in inappropriate ways. An employee who views pornographic pictures on a computer at work, for example, might leave the boss open to a charge of sexual harassment—if other workers observed this behavior and were offended by it. (Sexual harassment is further discussed in the following chapter.) The employer also needs to make sure that employees do not disclose confidential information to competitors or make statements that would publicly embarrass the company or its officers.

Is electronic monitoring by employers legal? For the most part, yes. The Electronic Communications Privacy Act (1986) exempts employers. In general, the courts have found that privacy rights apply to personal, but not business, information and that employers have a right to monitor job-related communication. In an important 1996 case, an employee sued his employer after he was fired for deriding the sales team

---

[17] "Those Bawdy E-Mails Were Good for a Laugh, until the Ax Fell," *Wall Street Journal,* February 4, 2000, p. A1.

[18] American Management Association, "American Companies Increase Use of Electronic Monitoring," April 12, 2000, available online at www.amanet.org.

in an internal e-mail, referring to them as "back-stabbing bastards." The court sided with the company, saying it owned the e-mail system and had a right to examine its contents. Yet some have criticized recent court decisions like this one, saying that public policy should do a better job of protecting employees from unwarranted secret surveillance.[19]

In seeking to balance their employees' concerns about privacy with their own concerns about productivity, liability, and security, businesses face a difficult challenge. One approach is to monitor employee communication only when there is a specific reason to do so, such as poor productivity or suspicion of theft. For example, the chipmaker Intel Corporation chose not to check its employees' e-mail routinely, feeling this would undermine trust.[20] Most management experts recommend that employers, at the very least, clearly define their monitoring policies, let employees know what behavior is expected, and apply any sanctions in a fair and even-handed way.

Romance in the Workplace

Another issue that requires careful balancing between legitimate employer concerns and employee privacy is romance in the workplace. People have always dated others at work. In fact, one study showed that one-third of all long-term relationships began on the job, and 30 percent of all managers said they had had one or more romantic relationships at work during their careers.[21] Yet office romance poses problems for employers. If the relationship goes sour, one of the people may sue, charging sexual harassment—that is, that he or she was coerced into the relationship. When one person in a relationship is in a position of authority, he or she may be biased in the evaluation of the other's work, or others may perceive it to be so.

For many years, most businesses had a strict policy of forbidding relationships in the workplace, especially those between managers and those reporting to them. They assumed that if romance blossomed, one person—usually the subordinate—would have to find another job. Recently, however, business practices have begun to change. Explained one legal expert, "You just can't control human nature, and you're not going to fire well-trained people simply because they're having a relationship. There's more of a practical view—to manage the relationship rather than ban it."[22] Many companies now allow managers to get involved with subordinates, so long as they do not supervise them directly. If a relationship develops, it is up to the people involved to come forward and to change assignments if necessary. A few companies require their managers to sign a document, sometimes called a *consensual relationship agreement,* stipulating that an office relationship is welcome and voluntary, to protect against possible harassment lawsuits if the people involved later break up.

---

[19] For example, see the position of the American Civil Liberties Union, available at www.aclu.org.
[20] "More Companies Monitor Employees' E-Mail," *Wall Street Journal,* December 2, 1999, p. B8.
[21] Dennis M. Powers, *The Office Romance* (New York: Amacom Books, 1998); and "Quietly, Dot-Coms Rewrite the Rules on Office Romance," *New York Times,* December 26, 1999, sect. 3, p. 8.
[22] "The One Clear Line in Interoffice Romance Has Become Blurred," *Wall Street Journal,* February 4, 1998, pp. A1, A8.

Employee Drug Use and Testing

Abuse of drugs, particularly hard drugs such as heroin and cocaine, can be a serious problem for employers. Only a small fraction of employees use illegal drugs. But those that do can cause serious harm. They are much more likely than others to produce poor quality work, have accidents that hurt themselves and others, and steal from their employers. Some break the law by selling drugs at work to support their habits. Drug abuse costs the U.S. industry and taxpayers an estimated $110 billion a year. This figure includes lost productivity, medical claims, rehabilitation services, and accidents caused by drugs.[23]

One way business has protected itself from these risks is through **drug testing.** Two-thirds of companies test employees or job applicants for drugs, according to a study reported in 2000.[24] Significant drug testing first began in the United States following passage of the Drug-Free Workplace Act of 1988, which required federal contractors to establish and maintain a workplace free of drugs. At that time, many companies and public agencies initiated drug testing in order to comply with government rules. Commercial clinical laboratories that conduct workplace drug tests for employers reported a steady decline in positive tests over the 1990s and into the early 2000s; between 4 and 6 percent of employees tested positive in the most recently reported results.[25]

Typically, drug testing is used on three different occasions.

- *Pre-employment screening.* Some companies test all job applicants or selected applicants before hiring, usually as part of a physical examination, often informing the applicant ahead of time that there will be a drug screening.

- *Random testing of employees.* This type of screening may occur at various times throughout the year. In many companies, workers in particular job categories (e.g., operators of heavy machinery) or levels (e.g., supervisors) are eligible for screening at any time.

- *Testing for cause.* This test occurs when an employee is believed to be impaired by drugs and unfit for work. It is commonly used after an accident or some observable change in behavior.

Employee drug testing is controversial. Although businesses have an interest in not hiring, or getting rid of, people who abuse drugs, many job applicants and employees who have never used drugs feel that testing is unnecessary and violates their privacy and due process rights. The debate over employee drug testing is summarized in Figure 17-2. In general, proponents of testing emphasize the need to reduce potential harm to other people and the cost to business and society of drug use on the job. Opponents challenge the benefits of drug testing and emphasize its intrusion on individual privacy.

---

[23] National Institute of Health statistics, available at www.silk.nih.gov/silk/niaaa1/database/cost7.txt.

[24] American Management Association data, available at www.amanet.org.

[25] "Decline Continues in Workplace Drug Use," *Workplace Substance Abuse Advisor,* July 17, 2000. SmithKline Beecham's testing data are reported at www.ncadd.org.

Figure 17-2

Pros and cons of employee drug testing.

Arguments favoring employee drug testing
- Business cooperation with U.S. "War on Drugs" campaign
- Improves employee productivity
- Promotes safety in the workplace
- Decreases employee theft and absenteeism
- Reduces health insurance costs

Arguments opposing employee drug testing
- Invades an employee's privacy
- Violates an employee's right to due process
- May be unrelated to job performance
- May be used as a method of employee discrimination
- Lowers employee morale
- Conflicts with company values of honesty and trust
- May yield unreliable test results
- Ignores effects of prescription drugs, alcohol, and over-the-counter drugs
- Drug use an insignificant problem for some companies

Alcohol Abuse at Work

Another form of employee substance abuse—which causes twice the problems of all illegal drugs combined—is alcohol use and addiction. About 7 percent of full-time employees are "heavy" drinkers—that is, they had five or more drinks on five or more occasions in the past month. Like drug abusers, they can be dangerous to themselves and others. Studies show that up to 40 percent of all industrial fatalities, and 47 percent of industrial injuries, are linked to alcohol. The problem is not just hard-core alcoholics, however. Most alcohol-related problems in the workplace, one study found, were caused by people who occasionally drank too much after work and came in the next day with a hangover or those who went out for a drink on their lunch break. U.S. businesses lose an estimated $67 billion per year in reduced productivity directly related to alcohol abuse.[26]

Company programs for drug abusers and alcohol abusers are often combined. Since the 1980s, an increasing number of firms have recognized that they have a role to play in helping alcoholic employees. As with drug rehabilitation programs, most alcoholism programs work through employee assistance programs (EAPs) that offer counseling and follow-up. Roughly 90 percent of Fortune 500 companies provide EAPs for alcohol and drug abusers. (The figure is much lower for small companies, though, only 1 in 10 of

---

[26] "Hangovers Cause U.S. Billions," *Workplace Substance Abuse Reporter,* June 29, 2000. The statistics reported in this paragraph are available online at the website of the National Council on Alcohol and Drug Dependencies at www.ncadd.org.

which have such programs.) In general, EAPs have been very cost effective. General Motors, for example, estimated that it had saved $3,700 for each of the employees enrolled in its EAP.

Employee Theft and Honesty Testing

Employees can irresponsibly damage themselves, their coworkers, and their employer by stealing from the company. Employee theft has emerged as a significant economic, social, and ethical problem in the workplace. It accounts for an estimated 60 percent of all retail losses, and employee-related thefts occur 15 times more often than shoplifting. The U.S. Department of Commerce estimates that employee theft of cash, merchandise, and property costs businesses $40 to $50 billion a year. Employee theft accounts for 20 percent of the nation's business failures. In Canada, employee theft costs firms $20 billion a year.[27]

Many companies in the past used polygraph testing (lie detectors) as a preemployment screening procedure or on discovery of employee theft. In 1988, the Employee Polygraph Protection Act became law. This law severely limited polygraph testing by employers and prohibited approximately 85 percent of all such tests previously administered in the United States. In response to the federal ban on polygraphs, many corporations have switched to written psychological tests, or **honesty tests,** that seek to predict employee honesty on the job. These pen-and-paper tests rely on answers to a series of questions that are designed to identify undesirable qualities in the test taker. When a British chain of home improvement centers used such tests to screen more than 4,000 applicants, theft dropped from 4 percent to 2.5 percent, and actual losses from theft were reduced from 3.75 million pounds to 2.62 million pounds.

The use of honesty tests, however, like polygraphs, is controversial. The American Psychological Association noted that there is a significant potential for these tests to generate false positives, indicating that the employee probably would or did steal from the company even though this is not true. After extensively studying the validity of honesty tests and the behavior they try to predict, two academic researchers concluded that the tests were, at best, accurate only 14 percent of the time. Critics also argue that the tests intrude on a person's privacy and discriminate disproportionately against minorities.[28]

In all these areas—monitoring employees electronically, policing office romance, testing for drugs, and conducting psychological tests—businesses must balance their needs to operate safely, ethically, and efficiently with their employees' right to privacy.

Whistle-Blowing and Free Speech in the Workplace

Another area where employer and employee rights and duties frequently conflict involves free speech. Do employees have the right openly to express their opinions about their company and its actions? If so, under what conditions do they have this right?

---

[27] "A Critical Look at Loss Prevention and Employee Theft," *Vito's Private Investigation Newsletter,* www.americasbright.com/employer/vito/new961101.html, November 1–15, 1996.

[28] Dan R. Dalton and Michael B. Metzger, "'Integrity Testing' for Personnel Selection: An Unsparing Perspective," *Journal of Business Ethics,* February 1993, pp. 147–56.

The U.S. Constitution protects the right to free speech. What this means is that the *government* cannot take away this right. For example, the legislature cannot shut down a newspaper that editorializes against its actions or those of its members. However, the Constitution does not explicitly protect freedom of expression *in the workplace.* Generally, employees are *not* free to speak out against their employers, because companies have a legitimate interest in operating without harassment from insiders. Company information is generally considered to be proprietary and private. If employees were freely allowed to expose issues to the public and allege misconduct, on the basis of their personal points of view, a company might be thrown into turmoil and be unable to operate effectively.

On the other hand, there may be situations in which society's interests override those of the company, so an employee may feel an obligation to speak out. When an employee believes his or her employer has done something wrong or harmful to the public and reports the alleged organizational misconduct to the media, government, or high-level company officials, **whistle-blowing** has occurred.

> *One of the most publicized whistle-blowers of recent years was Dr. Jeffrey Wigand, whose dramatic story was later portrayed in the movie* The Insider. *Dr. Wigand, a scientist and chief of research for cigarette maker Brown & Williamson, came forward with inside information that his employer had known that nicotine was addictive and had actively manipulated its level in cigarettes. His allegations, made under oath, made an important contribution to the success of litigation against the tobacco industry.*[29]

Another case, in which whistle-blowers at Cendant Corporation revealed a shocking pattern of accounting fraud, is illustrated in Exhibit 17-C.

Speaking out against an employer can be risky; many whistle-blowers find their charges ignored or, worse, find themselves ostracized, demoted, or even fired for daring to go public with their criticisms. Whistle-blowers in the United States have some legal protection against retaliation by their employers, though. As noted earlier in this chapter, most workers are employed *at will,* meaning they can be fired for any reason. However, most states now recognize a public policy exception to this rule. Employees who are discharged in retaliation for blowing the whistle, in a situation that affects public welfare, may sue for reinstatement and in some cases may even be entitled to punitive damages. Federal law also provides some protection for employees who blow the whistle on government contractors, and in 2000, an executive order extended this protection to airline employees who report safety violations.

Moreover, whistle-blowers sometimes benefit from their actions. The U.S. False Claims Act, as amended in 1986, allows individuals who sue federal contractors for fraud to receive up to 30 percent of any amount recovered by the government. In the 1990s, the number of whistle-blower lawsuits—perhaps spurred by this incentive—increased significantly, exposing fraud in the country's defense, municipal bond, and pharmaceutical industries. Whistle-blower suits against one health care firm, Columbia/HCA, are described in a case study at the end of this book.

---

[29] Dr. Wigand's story is told in Philip J. Hilts, *Smoke Screen: The Truth behind the Tobacco Industry Cover-Up* (Reading, MA: Addison-Wesley, 1996). For more on the public and private suits against the tobacco industry, see "The Tobacco Deal" case study at the end of the textbook.

**EXHIBIT
17-C**

Accountants Blow the Whistle at Cendant Corporation

In 1998, Cendant Corporation, a conglomerate formed through a merger of HFS Inc. and CUC International, was rocked by a scandal touched off by whistle-blowers. Two employees—both CUC accounting managers who had stayed on after the merger—came forward to the chief financial officer with a shocking allegation.

The accounting managers reported that CUC, over a period of several years, had systematically "cooked the books," fraudulently deferring expenses and inflating revenue by hundreds of millions of dollars. As a result, CUC had looked much more attractive as an acquisition target than it actually was. A later investigation by the Securities and Exchange Commission confirmed that CUC had simply entered completely fictional numbers into its financial reports and then shifted accounts to mislead the company's auditors.

A week later, Cendant announced publicly that it would have to restate its prior years' earnings. The company's stock plummeted, wiping out $19 billion in market value. Over the next two years, Cendant struggled to recover. CEO Henry Silverman restructured the board, sold off many noncore assets, repurchased stock, and paid out almost $3 billion to settle lawsuits brought by outraged shareholders. But the company's stock remained depressed, and some analysts thought Cendant was vulnerable to takeover.

What happened to the whistle-blowers? In 2000, the two managers who had come forward with the bad news settled various charges in connection with the case in federal court. One agreed not to become an officer of a public company but was not required to pay a fine; the other paid a civil penalty of $25,000. Things looked much worse for other executives involved in the fraud, however. Although their cases had not yet been settled, several faced possible fines in the millions of dollars.

Sources: "Whistle-Blowers Set Off Cendant Probe," *Wall Street Journal,* August 13, 1998, pp. A1, A8; "Henry Silverman's Long Road Back," *Business Week,* February 28, 2000, pp. 126ff; and "Asleep at the Books: A Fraud That Went On and On and On," *New York Times,* June 16, 2000, p. C1. Cendant's SEC filings regarding the fraud are available in the investor relations section of the company's website at www.cendant.com.

Whistle-blowing has both defenders and detractors. Those defending whistle-blowing point to the successful detection and prosecution of fraudulent activities that result. Under the False Claims Act, more than three billion dollars has been returned to the federal government that would otherwise have been lost to fraud.[30] Situations dangerous to the public or the environment have been exposed and corrected because insiders have spoken out. Yet opponents cite hundreds of unsubstantiated cases, often involving disgruntled workers seeking to blackmail or discredit their employers.[31]

[30] "Government's False Claim Recoveries Rise," *Associated Press,* February 24, 2000, www.aol.com.
[31] Catherine Yang and Mike France, "Whistle-Blowers on Trial," *Business Week,* March 24, 1997, pp. 172–74, 178.

When is it morally justified for an employee to blow the whistle on his or her employer? According to one expert, three main conditions must be satisfied to justify informing the media or government officials about a corporation's actions. These are

- The unreported act would do serious and considerable harm to the public.
- Once such an act has been identified, the employee has reported it to his or her immediate supervisor and has made his or her moral concern known.
- If the immediate supervisor does nothing, the employee has tried other internal pathways for reporting the problem.[32]

Only after each of these conditions has been met should the whistle-blower go public.

Working Conditions around the World

Much of this chapter has focused on the employment relationship, and the legal and ethical norms governing it, in the United States. Yet workplace institutions differ dramatically around the world. Laws and practices that establish fair wages, acceptable working conditions, and employee rights vary greatly from region to region. As illustrated by the opening example of this chapter that described Nike's subcontractors in Vietnam, these differences pose a challenge to multinational corporations. By whose standards should these companies operate?

Recent headlines have turned the public's attention to the problem of **sweatshops**, factories at which employees, sometimes including children, are forced to work long hours at low wages, often under unsafe working conditions. Several well-known companies in addition to Nike—including Wal-Mart, Liz Claiborne, and Disney—were criticized for tolerating abhorrent working conditions in their overseas factories or those of their contractors. McDonald's ran into a firestorm of controversy when it was revealed that 14-year-olds were working in a subcontractor's factory in China making Winnie the Pooh, Hello Kitty, and other plastic toys to be packaged with children's meals. The fast-food retailer quickly investigated and told the subcontractor it would not tolerate child labor, which was against the company's policy.[33] In recent years, student groups have put pressure on companies by rallying to prevent their colleges and universities from buying school-logo athletic gear, clothing, and other products made under sweatshop conditions. The issue has been raised in trade negotiations and at meetings of international bodies such as the World Trade Organization.

Fair Labor Standards

The term *labor standards* refers to the conditions under which a company's employees—or the employees of its suppliers, subcontractors, or others in its commercial chain—work. Some believe that labor standards should be universal; that is, companies should conform to common norms across all their operations worldwide. Such universal rules

---

[32]Richard DeGeorge, *Business Ethics*, 4th ed. (Englewood Cliffs, NJ: Prentice Hall, 1995), pp. 231–38.
[33] "McDonald's Vows to Probe Report about Toy Factory," *Wall Street Journal*, August 28, 2000, p. B10. An investigative report on sweatshops in Europe may be found in "Workers in Bondage," *Business Week*, November 27, 2000, pp. 146–62.

are sometimes called **fair labor standards.** For example, such standards might include a ban on all child labor, establishment of maximum work hours per week, or a commitment to pay a wage above a certain level. Others think that what is fair varies across cultures and economies, and it is often difficult to set standards that are workable in all settings. For example, in some cultures child labor is more acceptable, or economically necessary, than in others. A wage that would be utterly inadequate in one economic setting might seem princely in another.

In the face of growing concerns over working conditions overseas, a debate has developed over how best to establish fair labor standards for multinational corporations. Several approaches have emerged.

Corporate Codes of Conduct

In this approach, companies voluntarily adopt a set of standards that they expect their own plants and those of their contractors to follow. One of the first companies to adopt such a code was Levi Strauss, a U.S. apparel maker. After the company was accused of using an unethical contractor in Saipan, the company reviewed its procedures and adopted a wide-ranging set of guidelines for its overseas manufacturing. Reebok, Boeing, DaimlerChrysler, and other companies have followed suit.

NGO Codes of Conduct

Nongovernmental organizations (NGOs) have also attempted to develop fair labor standards. For example, the Council on Economic Priorities has developed a set of workplace rules called Social Accountability 8000, or SA 8000. Modeled after the quality initiative of the International Organization for Standardization, ISO 9000, SA 8000 establishes criteria for companies to meet in order to receive a "good working condition" certification. Other groups, including the International Labour Organization and the Caux Roundtable, have also worked to define common standards to which companies can voluntarily subscribe. In 2000, the United Nations sponsored the Global Compact, a set of labor, human rights, and environmental standards, and invited corporations to endorse them.[34]

Industrywide Codes

Yet a third approach is for groups of companies, sometimes with participation of government officials, NGOs, and worker and consumer representatives, to define industrywide standards that they can all agree to. In 1996, for instance, the Apparel Industry Partnership was formed to develop a set of rules for the clothing and footwear industries. In 1998, this group formed the Fair Labor Association (FLA), which established a workplace code of conduct and a system for monitoring overseas factories. Companies that agreed to participate could put a "service mark," a kind of seal-of-approval, on their products. This would help consumers avoid products made under substandard conditions. (The FLA is further described in the case study on Nike, at the end of the book.)

Whatever the approach, certain common questions emerge in any attempt to define and enforce fair labor standards. These include the following.

---

[34] "Companies, U.N. Agree to Rights Compact; Environmental, Labor Criteria Set," *Washington Post,* July 27, 2000, p. A6.

- *What wage level is fair?* Some argue that market forces should set wages, so long as they do not fall below the level established by local minimum wage laws. Others argue that multinational corporations have a moral obligation to pay workers enough to achieve a decent family standard of living; still others feel that they should pay workers a fair share of the sale price of the product or of the company's profit.

- *Should standards apply just to the firm's employees or to all employees in its commercial chain?* Some say that while the responsibility of a firm to its own employees is clear, its responsibility to the employees of its subcontractors is indirect and therefore of lower importance.

- *How should fair labor standards best be enforced?* Adherence with fair labor standards—unlike national labor laws, for example—is strictly voluntary. Companies can adopt their own codes or agree to one of the NGO or industry codes.

EXHIBIT 17-D

Monitoring Compliance at Mattel, Inc.

Mattel, Inc., the maker of Barbie dolls, Fisher-Price toys, Hot Wheels cars, and many other children's playthings, is the world's largest toy company. Many of its products are manufactured in overseas factories, mostly in Asia. In 1998, Mattel developed a detailed code of conduct, called its Global Manufacturing Principles. Covering both Mattel's factories and those of its subcontractors and suppliers, the principles addressed a wide range of labor issues. These included wages (at least minimum wage or local industry standard, whichever was higher), child labor (workers had to be at least 16 years old or the local minimum, whichever was higher), and health and safety (compliant with the standards of the American Conference of Government Industrial Hygienists).

Mattel also considered how it could best enforce its code and convince its customers it was serious about doing so. In an innovative move, the company created an independent auditing organization, the Mattel Independent Monitoring Council (MIMCO). Chaired by three outside experts, MIMCO was given a generous budget and access to all facilities and records of Mattel and its subcontractors and was charged with carrying out regular inspections and making their results public.

MIMCO released it first audit in late 1999. A review of eight factories in China, Indonesia, Malaysia, and Thailand—which among them handled 70 percent of the toy maker's production—found that the company generally complied with its own code. However, the monitors found some problems, particularly at several factories in China where workers complained of exhaustion, inadequate dormitory space, and a lack of on-site medical facilities. The company vowed to look into and correct any incidents of noncompliance.

Sources: "Asian Mattel Plants Found to Meet Standards," *Los Angeles Times,* November 19, 1999, p. C2; "Business Ethics: Sweatshop Wars," *The Economist,* February 27, 1999, p. 62; and "Policing Global Labor Practices," *Christian Science Monitor,* May 18, 2000, p. 9. MIMCO's audits are available at Mattel's website at www.mattel.com/corporate/company/responsibility.

But who is to say that they, and their contractors, are actually living up to these rules? In response to this concern, a debate has emerged over how best to monitor and enforce fair labor standards. Some have advocated hiring outside accounting firms, academic experts, or advocacy organizations to conduct independent audits to determine if a code's standards are being met. The efforts of one company, Mattel, to devise a verifiable procedure for monitoring its code of conduct in overseas factories is profiled in Exhibit 17-D.

As businesses have become more and more global, companies have faced the challenge of operating simultaneously in many countries that differ widely in their working conditions. For these companies, abiding by government regulations and local cultural traditions in their overseas manufacturing may not be enough. Many business leaders have realized that subscribing to fair labor standards that commit to common norms of fairness, respect, and dignity for all their workers is an effective strategy for enhancing their corporate reputations, as well as meeting the complex global challenges of corporate social responsibility.

Employees as Corporate Stakeholders

The issues discussed in this chapter illustrate forcefully that today's business corporation is open to a wide range of social forces. Its borders are very porous, letting in a constant flow of external influences. Many are brought inside by employees, whose personal values, lifestyles, and social attitudes become a vital part of the workplace.

Managers and other business professionals need to be aware of these employee-imported features of today's workforce. The employment relationship is central to getting a corporation's work done and to helping satisfy the wishes of those who contribute their skills and talents to the company. The task of a corporate manager is to reconcile potential clashes between employees' human needs and legal rights and the requirements of corporate economic production.

Summary Points of This Chapter

- U.S. labor laws give most workers the right to organize unions and to bargain collectively with their employers. Some believe that unions are poised for resurgence after many years of decline.
- Job safety and health concerns have increased as a result of rapidly changing technology in the workplace. Employers must comply with expanding OSHA regulations and respond to the growing trend toward violence at work.
- Employers' right to discharge at will has been limited, and employees now have a number of bases for suing for wrongful discharge. The expectations of both sides in the employment relationship have been altered over time by globalization, business cycles, and other factors.
- Employees' privacy rights are frequently challenged by employers' needs to have information about their health, their work activities, and even their off-the-job

lifestyles. When these issues arise, management has a responsibility to act ethically toward employees while continuing to work for a high level of economic performance.

• Blowing the whistle on one's employer is often a last resort to protest company actions considered harmful to others. It can usually be avoided if corporate managers encourage open communication and show a willingness to listen to their employees.

• The growing globalization of business has challenged companies to adopt fair labor standards to ensure that their products are not manufactured under substandard, sweatshop conditions.

Key Terms and Concepts Used in This Chapter

• Labor union
• Ergonomics
• Occupational Safety and Health Administration (OSHA)
• Employment-at-will
• Social contract
• Privacy

• Electronic monitoring
• Drug testing
• Honesty tests
• Whistle-blowing
• Sweatshops
• Fair labor standards

Internet Resources

• www.drugfreeworkplace.org
• www.osha.gov

• www.whistleblowers.org
• www.aclu.org
• www.afl-cio.org

Institute for a Drug-Free Workplace
Occupational Safety and Health Administration
National Whistleblower Center
American Civil Liberties Union
American Federation of Labor–Congress of Industrial Organizations

Discussion Case: *Smoking in the Workplace*

In the early 2000s, the debate over smoking in the workplace heated up. Many employers—some acting voluntarily and some because they were forced to by local and state antismoking laws—banned smoking on the job or restricted it to a few separate areas. Some policies were particularly strict. At Kimball Plastics, an electronics manufacturer, for example, workers were subject to discipline if even a whiff of tobacco smoke was detected on their breath, hair, or clothes. A few firms even adopted the extreme policy of refusing to hire smokers at all, even if they limited their tobacco use to off-work hours.

Employers cited several reasons for adopting antismoking rules. Secondhand smoke—smoke emitted from a lit cigarette, cigar, or pipe or exhaled by a smoker—causes nearly 50,000 nonsmoker deaths in the United States each year, according to medical research. Nonsmoking employees could be sickened, or even killed, by exposure to others' tobacco smoke at work. In the 1990s, a group of nonsmoking flight attendants successfully sued the tobacco companies, claiming that their health had been injured by their exposure to smoke in enclosed aircraft cabins before smoking was banned on airplanes in the United States. Secondhand smoke can be a particular problem for employees in workplaces where smoking is common, such as bars and restaurants.

Moreover, smoking employees cost money. Studies have shown that over $47 million is lost annually due to productivity loss and disability time related to smoking. Smokers, on average, cost the firm $753 annually in medical expenses and miss two more workdays per year than nonsmokers do. Many firms offer their employees smoking-cessation programs, which cost about $165 per person.

For their part, employees who smoke have been divided in their reaction to tobacco restrictions or bans at work. Some smokers have welcomed the opportunity to quit, and many have taken advantage of company-paid cessation programs. A study by researchers at the University of California found that employees who were covered by strong workplace smoking policies were more likely to quit the habit than other smokers, perhaps motivated by their inability to light up on the job. Other smokers, however, were incensed at what they perceived as a violation of personal rights and freedoms. They resented having to go outside to smoke, particularly in bad weather. Some even argued that smoking was, in effect, an addiction to nicotine, and so their right to smoke should be protected under the Americans with Disabilities Act (further described in the following chapter).

Lawmakers weighed in on both sides of the issue. Many towns and cities, and some states, passed antismoking ordinances or laws. To cite one example, California's Smoke-Free Workplace Act, passed in 1995, prohibited smoking in most indoor job settings. But many states, sometimes the same ones, also passed laws making job discrimination against smokers illegal. Although these laws did not affect smoking bans or restrictions in the workplace, they did prohibit companies from refusing to hire smokers and from firing employees who continued to smoke.

Many other countries have historically been more tolerant of smoking, both in the workplace and elsewhere, than the United States. At the turn of the century, however, this was beginning to change. Finland, for example, in 2000 became the first European country to classify tobacco smoke as a carcinogen (cancer-causing substance) and to require employers to protect their workers from exposure, and the British government debated similar measures.

Sources: "UC Study Says Workplace Smoking Ordinances Help Employees Quit," *Cal-OSHA Reporter,* May 5, 2000; "Finland No Longer Passive about Secondhand Smoke," *Los Angeles Times,* July 25, 2000, p. A1; and "Employers Face New Curbs on Smoking at Work," *Financial Times,* September 6, 2000, p. 6.

Discussion Questions

1. Should employers have the right to ban or restrict smoking by their employees at the workplace? Why do you think so?
2. Should employers have the right to ban or restrict smoking by the employees off the job, for example, in their own homes or cars? Why do you think so?
3. Should the government regulate smoking at work? If so, what would be the best public policy? Why do you think so?
4. Should multinational firms have a single corporate policy on smoking in the workplace, or should they vary their policies depending on local laws and norms of behavior in various countries where they do business?

PART EIGHT

Social Issues

18

Managing a Diverse Workforce

The workforce in the United States is more diverse than it has ever been, reflecting the entry of women into the workforce, immigration from other countries, the aging of the population, and shifting patterns of work and retirement. Equal opportunity laws and changing societal expectations have challenged corporations to manage workforce diversity effectively. Full workplace parity for women and persons of color has not yet been reached. However, businesses have made great strides in reforming policies and practices in order to draw on the skills and contributions of their increasingly varied employees.

This chapter focuses on these key questions and objectives:

- Who are employees today in the United States? In what ways is the workforce diverse, and how can it be expected to change over time?

- Where do women and persons of color work, and what are they paid? What roles do they play as managers and business owners?

- What role does the government play in securing equal employment opportunity for historically disadvantaged groups? Is affirmative action an effective strategy for promoting equal opportunity, or not?

- In what ways does diversity confer a competitive advantage?

- How can companies best manage workforce diversity, making the workplace welcoming, fair, and accommodating to all employees?

- What policies and practices are most effective in helping today's employees manage the complex, multiple demands of work and family obligations?

Marriott International, the large hotel chain, employs 135,000 workers in 54 countries, doing jobs ranging from managing vacation resorts, to flipping burgers, to cleaning bathrooms and changing sheets. Their employees speak 30 different languages and represent 50 or so distinct cultures. Many of Marriott's employees in the United States are immigrants, some are in welfare-to-work programs, and many are single parents. A large proportion work nights or odd hours. "They have very complex lives," said the company's director of work/life programs. In an effort to address its employees' needs, Marriott established a toll-free phone line, where social workers provided consultations on a wide range of personal issues in many languages. In Atlanta, it built a state-of-the-art child care center that operated around the clock. In Boston, the company sponsored a series of fatherhood seminars to provide support to working dads. Marriott credited its innovative programs with helping it attract and retain committed employees from many backgrounds.[1]

The example of Marriott Corporation demonstrates both the promise and the perils of a workforce that encompasses tremendous diversity on every imaginable dimension. Having many different kinds of workers can be a great benefit to businesses, as it gives them a wider pool from which to recruit talent, many points of view and experiences, and an ability to reach out effectively to a diverse, global customer base. Yet it also poses great challenges, as business must meet the mandates of equal employment laws and help people who differ greatly in their backgrounds, values, and expectations get along, and succeed, in the workplace.

The Changing Face of the Workforce

Human beings differ from each other in many ways. Each person is unique, as is each employee within an organization. Individuals are also similar in many ways, some of which are more readily visible than others. The term **diversity** refers to variation in the important human characteristics that distinguish people from one another. The *primary* dimensions of diversity are age, ethnicity, gender, mental or physical abilities, race, and sexual orientation. The *secondary* dimensions of diversity are many; they include such characteristics as communication style, family status, and first language.[2] Individuals' distinguishing characteristics clearly impact their values, opportunities, and perceptions of themselves and others at work. **Workforce diversity**—diversity among employees—thus represents both a challenge and an opportunity for businesses.

At the beginning of the twenty-first century, the U.S. workforce is as diverse as it has ever been, and it is becoming even more so. Consider the following major trends:[3]

---

[1] "Fathers, with Their Companies in Tow, Make a Move toward the Homestead," *Boston Globe,* August 8, 1999, p. F1; and "Marriott's Bid to Patch the Child Care Gap Gets a Reality Check," *Wall Street Journal,* February 2, 2000, p. B1. Marriott's website is at www.marriott.com.

[2] This definition is based on Marilyn Loden, *Implementing Diversity* (New York: McGraw-Hill, 1995), chap. 2, "Defining Diversity."

[3] The figures in the following paragraphs are drawn from Anita U. Hattiangadi, *The Changing Face of the Twenty-First Century Workforce: Trends in Ethnicity, Race, Age, and Gender* (Washington, DC: Employment Policy Foundation, 1998).

- *More women are working than ever before.* Married women, those with young children, and older women, in particular, have greatly increased their participation in the workforce. By 2020, the Bureau of Labor Statistics estimates that half of all workers will be women, about equal to their share of the population. One effect of this trend is that more employed men have wives who also work—changing the nature of their responsibilities within the family.

- *Immigration has profoundly reshaped the workplace.* The foreign-born share of the population has more than doubled since 1970, with the largest numbers of immigrants coming to the United States from Asia and Latin America. The leading countries of origin are now Mexico, the Philippines, China, Cuba, and India. Legal immigrants accounted for fully half of the increase in the workforce in the 1990s. Moreover, as many as 5 million undocumented (illegal) immigrants are believed to be living in the United States, and many of them are employed. These trends mean more linguistic and cultural diversity in many workplaces.

- *Ethnic and racial diversity is increasing.* Hispanics (defined by the Census as persons of Spanish or Latin American ancestry), now about 10 percent of U.S. workers, are expected to comprise 14 percent by 2020. Asians and Pacific Islanders are predicted to increase their workforce share from 4 to 6 percent during this same period. The proportion of African-Americans is expected to hold steady at around 11 percent. In some regions, these trends will be much more pronounced. For example, in California, by 2020, white non-Hispanics are expected to constitute only a third of the population.

- *The workforce will continue to get older.* As the baby boom generation matures, birthrates drop, and people live longer and healthier lives, the population will age. Many of these older people will continue to work, whether out of necessity or choice. As one expert put it, "The American labor force will become somewhat more brown and black in the next 20 years, but its most pervasive new tint will be gray."[4] Employers will have to find new ways to accommodate retirement-aged workers.

Workforce diversity creates many new employee issues and problems. This chapter will consider the changing face of today's workplace and its implications for business management. Laws and regulations clearly require that businesses provide equal opportunity and avoid discrimination and harassment. How to meet, and exceed, these mandates presents an ongoing challenge to businesses seeking to reap the benefits of a well-integrated yet culturally diverse work population. We turn first to two important dimensions of workplace diversity: gender and race.

Gender and Race in the Workplace

Gender and race are both important primary dimensions of workforce diversity. Women and persons of color have always worked, contributing both paid and unpaid labor to the economy.

[4] Richard W. Judy and Carol D'Amico, *Workforce 2020: Work and Workers in the Twenty-First Century* (Indianapolis: Hudson Institute, 1999), p. 122.

Figure 18-1

Proportion of women
in the labor force,
1950–2000.

Source: U.S. Bureau of
Labor Statistics.

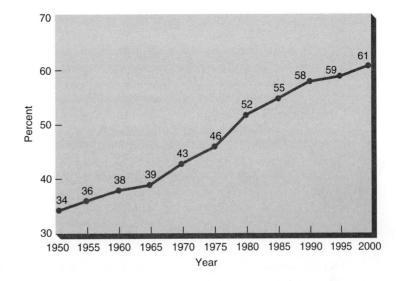

Yet the nature of their participation in the labor force has changed, posing new challenges
to business.

Women and Minorities at Work

One of the most significant changes in the past half-century has been the growing labor
force participation of women. During the period following World War II, the proportion
of women working outside the home rose dramatically, as shown in Figure 18-1. In 1950,
about a third of adult women were employed. This proportion has risen almost steadily
since, standing at 61 percent in 2000. Participation rates (the proportion of women in
the workforce) have risen for all groups of women, but the most dramatic increases have
been among married women, mothers of young children, and middle-class women, those
who had earlier been most likely to stay at home. Men's participation rates declined
somewhat during this period; by the year 2005, the proportions of adult women and men
at work are projected to be within 7 percentage points of each other (66 percent and
73 percent, respectively).

Women have entered the workforce for many of the same reasons men do. They
need income to support themselves and their families. Having a job with pay also gives
a woman psychological independence and security. The high cost of living puts financial pressure on families, frequently pushing women into the labor force just to sustain
an accustomed standard of living or to put children through college or care for aging
parents. The inadequacies and uncertainties of retirement plans and health care programs
frequently mean that women, as well as men, need to save, invest, and plan for the future.
When women divorce, they often can no longer rely on a partner's earnings for support.

The rapid rise of female labor force participation in the postwar years also reflects
the expansion of segments of the economy that were major employers of women. In

1940, about one-third of all U.S. jobs were white-collar (not requiring manual labor); by 1980, over half were white-collar. Professional, technical, and service jobs also grew relative to the economy. The creation of many new positions in fields traditionally staffed by women produced what economists call a demand-side pull of women into the labor force. More "women's jobs" meant more women working.

Labor force participation rates for minorities, unlike those of women, have always been high. For example, in 1970 about 62 percent of all African-Americans (men and women combined) worked; the figure is about 65 percent today. Participation rates have also been consistently high for most other minority groups. The key change here has been the move of persons of color, in recent decades, into a wider range of jobs as barriers of discrimination and segregation have fallen; minorities have become better represented in the ranks of managers, professionals, and the skilled trades. These trends will be further discussed later in this chapter.

The Gender and Racial Pay Gap

One persistent feature of the working world is that women and persons of color on average receive lower pay than white men do. This disparity, called the **pay gap,** narrowed somewhat during the 1980s and the 1990s for some groups, as Figure 18-2 shows. But at the turn of the century, black men and white women still earned only about three-quarters of white men's pay; and black women earned even less, relative to white men. The pay gap for Hispanics, already large, actually grew slightly during the past 15 years. (These data are based on full-time workers only.) In 2000, a congressional hearing taking a fresh look at the pay gap between women and men revealed stark disagreements about its cause. Some thought that the continuing gender disparity in pay was evidence of sex discrimination by employers and called on legislators to strengthen equal pay laws. Others, however, thought that the gap reflected women's choices to pursue lower paying jobs or slower advancement because of time off for child rearing.[5]

Many observers believe that the pay gap persists, in part, because of what is called **occupational segregation.** This term refers to the inequitable concentration of a group, such a minorities or women, in particular job categories. The large pay gap for Hispanic workers, for example, partly reflects their concentration in several low-paid occupations. Forty-five percent of farm workers and 37 percent of private household cleaners and servants are of Hispanic origin, according to the Census Bureau, although Hispanics make up only 10 percent of the workforce as a whole. Although women, for their part, have made great strides in entering occupations in which they were formerly underrepresented, many remain concentrated in a few sex-typed jobs that some have called the "pink-collar ghetto." Women still make up 98 percent of preschool and kindergarten teachers, 91 percent of bookkeepers, 96 percent of nurses, and 99 percent of secretaries, for example. Eliminating the pay gap will require, therefore, business programs and government policies that create opportunity

---

[5] "Panel Asks Why Women Still Earn Less; New Legislation Urged to Close Gender Pay Gap," *Washington Post,* June 9, 2000, p. E3.

Figure 18-2

The pay gap, 1985–2000 median weekly earnings of full-time workers, as a percentage of those of white men.

Source: U.S. Census Bureau, *Statistical Abstract of the United States 2000,* Table 696, p. 437. Data for Hispanic men and Hispanic women for 1985 are not available.

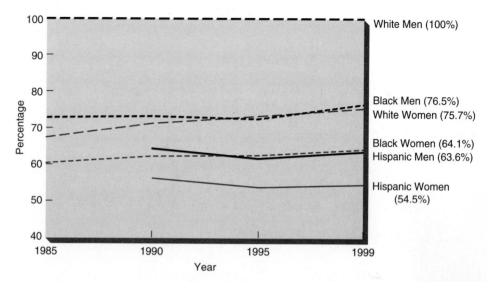

for women and people of color to move out of more segregated jobs into ones where the pay and chances for upward mobility are greater.[6]

The most prestigious and highest-paying jobs in a corporation are in top management. Because most corporations are organized hierarchically, management jobs—particularly those at the top—are few. For that reason, only a small fraction of workers, of whatever gender or race, can hope to reach the upper levels in the business world. White men have traditionally filled most of these desirable spots. The mandate for business now is to broaden these high-level leadership opportunities for women and persons of color, a topic to which we turn next.

Where Women and Persons of Color Manage

Over 8 million U.S. women were managers by late 1990s, doubling their numbers in one decade. In 1998, as Figure 18-3 reveals, more than 4 out of every 10 managers—and a majority of managers in some categories—were women. Clearly, women have broken into management ranks. Women are more likely to be managers, though, in occupational areas where women are more numerous at lower levels, including health care, personnel management, and education. They also are concentrated in service industries and in finance, insurance, real estate, and retail businesses. Women managers have also made gains in newer industries, such as biotechnology, where growth has created opportunity.

Where do persons of color manage? As is also shown in Figure 18-3, both African-Americans and Hispanics are underrepresented in management ranks in the United States; making up just 7.6 and 5.6 percent of managers, respectively. But they

[6] The data in this paragraph are drawn from table 669, "Employed Civilians by Occupation, Sex, Race, and Hispanic Origin," pp. 416–18ff. In the U.S. Census Bureau, *Statistical Abstract of the United States 2000.*

Figure 18-3

Where women and minorities manage.

Source: U.S. Census Bureau, *Statistical Abstract of the United States, 2000,* table 669, pp. 416–18.

	Percentage of Total, 1999		
	Female	**Black**	**Hispanic**
All occupations	46.5%	11.3%	10.3%
Managerial and professional	49.5	8.0	5.0
Executive, administrative, and managerial	45.1	7.6	5.6
Public officials and administrators	51.1	14.0	4.9
Financial managers	51.1	7.0	5.4
Personnel and labor relations managers	60.4	10.9	6.3
Purchasing managers	47.4	8.9	5.6
Marketing, advertising, and public relations managers	37.6	4.8	2.7
Educational administrators	62.5	15.0	4.8
Health care managers	77.4	8.9	6.6
Property and real estate managers	49.4	6.6	8.9
Management–related occupations*	57.8	9.8	5.3

* Includes accountants and auditors.

have approached parity in a few areas. Blacks make up 14 percent of all public sector managers (more than their 11 percent of the workforce), reflecting less discrimination and more opportunity in organizations like public schools, the post office, and government agencies. Hispanics are best represented in property management and real estate. Figure 18-3 shows the continuing underrepresentation of blacks and Hispanics in other management categories.

Breaking the Glass Ceiling

A few exceptional women and persons of color have reached the pinnacles of power in corporate America. Carleton Fiorina, for example, became the first woman ever to head a Dow 30 company when she was appointed CEO of Hewlett-Packard in 1999.[7] When Lloyd Ward, an African-American, became chief executive of appliance-maker Maytag that same year, it capped an extraordinary career rise from an impoverished childhood in a rural town west of Detroit.[8]

[7] "The Boss," *Business Week,* August 2, 1999, p. 76; and "These Women Rule," *Fortune,* October 25, 1999, p. 94.
[8] "The Saga of Lloyd Ward," *Business Week,* August 9, 1999, p. 58.

These high-achievers remain unusual, however. Although women and minorities are as competent as white men in managing people and organizations, they rarely attain the highest positions in corporations. Their ascent seems to be blocked by an invisible barrier, sometimes called a **glass ceiling.** According to Catalyst, in 1999 only 12 percent of the officers of leading corporations were women, and only a quarter of these were in positions with responsibility for profit and loss.[9] Women are also scarce on corporate boards; only 11 percent of board members of Fortune 500 firms were women in 1999. Although over half of the boards of large U.S. companies include at least one ethnic minority, their overall representation among directors remains low. African-Americans, for example, make up only 3 percent of board members at major U.S. companies.[10]

Failure to attain the topmost jobs in some cases is due to lack of experience or inadequate education. Because gender and racial bias have kept women and minorities out of management until recent years, few have had time to acquire the years of experience that are typical of most high-ranking executives. Also, in earlier years women and minorities were discouraged from entering graduate schools of engineering, science, business, and law, the traditional pathways to top corporate management. Even as those barriers have been lowered, though, these groups remain underrepresented at executive levels.

What continues to hold women and minorities back? Recent studies by the U.S. Department of Labor and others have identified several reasons for the persistence of the glass ceiling. One barrier is **glass walls:** fewer opportunities to move sideways into jobs that lead to the top. Female and minority managers are often found in staff positions, such as public relations or human resources, rather than in line positions in such core areas as marketing, sales, or production where they can acquire the broad management skills necessary for promotion. Some disadvantaged workers also experience what one sociologist called the "sticky floor," meaning they do not advance because they are concentrated in low-level jobs that do not lead to well-defined career paths.[11]

Another problem is that in filling top positions, recruiters rely on word-of-mouth—the old boys' network from which women and persons of color are often excluded. Other causes include a company's lack of commitment to diversity and too little accountability at the top management level for equal employment opportunity.[12]

Women and Minority Business Ownership

Some women and minorities have evaded the glass ceiling and risen to the top by founding or taking over their own businesses.

By 1999, more than 9 million businesses—almost two-fifths of all those in the United States—were owned or controlled by women, according to the National Foundation for Women Business Owners. Of these, one in eight was owned by a woman

---

[9] "The CEO Still Wears Wingtips," *Business Week,* November 22, 1999, p. 85.

[10] "Has the Glass Ceiling Really Been Shattered?" *Black Enterprise,* February 2000, p. 146.

[11] Karen Engberg, *It's Not the Glass Ceiling, It's the Sticky Floor* (Amherst, NY: Prometheus Books, 1999).

[12] Ann M. Morrison, Randall P. White, and Ellen Van Velsor, *Breaking the Glass Ceiling: Can Women Reach the Top of America's Largest Corporations?* Updated ed. (Cambridge, MA: Perseus Press, 1994); and U.S. Department of Labor, "Good for Business: Making Full Use of the Nation's Human Capital: A Fact Finding Report of the Federal Glass Ceiling Commission," March 1995.

of color. In recent years, women have formed new businesses at roughly twice the rate of men. Although most female-headed firms are small, collectively they employ more than 27 million people in the United States, more than the Fortune 500 firms do worldwide.[13]

> *An example of a successful female entrepreneur is Catherine Hughes, founder and chairperson of Radio One, a company that owns more than 50 radio stations, mainly in urban markets. Hughes, who is black, started the business in 1980, when she was general manager at Howard University's FM station, by buying a defunct R&B station. For several years, Hughes slept in the station, ran her own morning talk show, and pounded the pavement in the afternoon looking for advertisers. By the mid-1980s, the station was turning a healthy profit, and Hughes began acquiring other stations. The company went public in 1998, and by 2000 Hughes's net worth was estimated at more than $60 million. "I was determined to make this work," Hughes said.*[14]

Contrary to popular belief, female entrepreneurs are just as successful as men, according to a study of more than 400 midwestern small firms. The researchers reported that "the determinants of survival and success operated in much the same way for men and women. . . . Despite the widely shared assumption that women are less apt than men to innovate, for example, we found no evidence of women's being less likely to do this in their businesses. Moreover, we found no evidence that men were more confident of their business abilities."[15]

Minorities have also used business ownership as a path to success. According to the Small Business Administration, there were more than 3 million minority-owned businesses in the United States by 1997. Within this group, Hispanic-owned businesses were the most numerous, followed by those owned by Asians and African-Americans. Immigrants were responsible for a good share of the entrepreneurial spirit in the minority community; nearly half of Hispanic business owners and more than two-thirds of Asian business owners were born outside of the United States.[16]

Government's Role in Securing Equal Employment Opportunity

Eliminating workplace discrimination and ensuring equal job opportunity has been a major goal of public policy in the United States for four decades. This section reviews the major laws that govern business practices with respect to equal opportunity, affirmative action, and sexual and racial harassment.

---

[13] For current statistics, see the website of the National Foundation for Women Business Owners at www.nfwbo.org.

[14] "Top Ten Black Female Entrepreneurs," *Essence,* October 1999, p. 104; and *Investor's Business Daily,* August 21, 2000, p. A4.

[15] Arne L. Kalleberg and Kevin T. Leicht, "Gender and Organizational Performance: Determinants of Small Business Survival and Success," *Academy of Management Journal,* March 1991, pp. 157–58.

[16] "Minorities in Business" (Washington, DC: U.S. Small Business Administration, 1999).

Equal Employment Opportunity

Beginning on a major scale in the 1960s, U.S. presidents issued executive orders and Congress enacted laws intended to promote equal treatment of employees, that is, **equal employment opportunity.** These government rules apply to most businesses in the following ways:

- Discrimination based on race, color, religion, sex, national origin, physical or mental disability, or age is prohibited in all employment practices. This includes hiring, promotion, job classification and assignment, compensation, and other conditions of work.

- Government contractors must have written affirmative action plans detailing how they are working positively to overcome past and present effects of discrimination in their workforce. However, affirmative action plans must be temporary and flexible, designed to correct past discrimination, and cannot result in reverse discrimination against whites or men.

- Women and men must receive equal pay for performing equal work, and employers may not discriminate on the basis of pregnancy.

Figure 18-4 outlines the major laws and one executive order that are intended to promote equal opportunity in the workplace. The provisions of the most recent equal employment opportunity law, the Americans with Disabilities Act, are further described

Figure 18-4

Major federal laws and executive orders prohibiting job discrimination.

Equal Pay Act (1963)—Mandates equal pay for substantially equal work by men and women.

Civil Rights Act (1964; amended 1972, 1991)—Prohibits discrimination in employment based on race, color, religion, sex, or national origin.

Executive Order 11246 (1965)—Mandates affirmative action for all federal contractors and subcontractors.

Age Discrimination in Employment Act (1967)—Protects individuals who are 40 years of age or older.

Equal Employment Opportunity Act (1972)—Increases power of the Equal Employment Opportunity Commission to combat discrimination.

Pregnancy Discrimination Act (1978)—Forbids employers to discharge, fail to hire, or otherwise discriminate against pregnant women.

Americans with Disabilities Act (1990)—Prohibits discrimination against individuals with disabilities.

Family and Medical Leave Act (1993)—Requires companies with 50 or more employees to provide up to 12 weeks unpaid leave for illness, care of a sick family member, or the birth or adoption of a child.

EXHIBIT 18-A

Accommodating Persons with Disabilities

The Americans with Disabilities Act (ADA) of 1990 requires employers to make accommodations for disabled workers and job applicants and prohibits employers from discriminating on the basis of a person's disability. A disabled worker is defined by the law as one who can perform the essential functions of a job, with or without reasonable accommodations. The law prohibits employers from asking in a job interview, for example, about a person's medical history or past treatment for mental illness or alcoholism. And it requires employers to make reasonable accommodations, for example, by modifying work equipment, adjusting work schedules, or making facilities accessible. The courts have interpreted the ADA to cover persons with acquired immunodeficiency syndrome (AIDS). This means that discrimination against persons with AIDS, or who are infected with HIV (the virus that causes AIDS) is prohibited, so long as the person can perform the essential elements of the job.

The ADA has proved to be controversial. Disability advocates have argued that the law has been weakly enforced by the government; they point out that even after more than a decade since the ADA was passed, only about one-third of disabled Americans are employed. But many businesses have complained about the law, citing its vagueness, the high cost of compliance, and the expense of defending against lawsuits. The vice president of human resources policy for the National Association of Manufacturers called the law "a constant nuisance" and said it was the source of "an awful lot of mischief."

Sources: "Collecting on a Promise: Disabled Say They Are Still Fighting for Rights 10 Years after Disabilities Act," *San Francisco Chronicle,* July 26, 2000, p. A1. Information about the law is available online at www.eeoc.gov.

in Exhibit 18-A. The major agency charged with enforcing equal employment opportunity laws and executive orders in the United States is the **Equal Employment Opportunity Commission (EEOC).** The EEOC was created in 1964 and given added enforcement powers in 1972 and 1990.

Companies that fail to follow the laws shown in Figure 18-4 often find themselves facing expensive lawsuits. One of the more sensational examples of a suit against racial discrimination in the workplace in recent years involved Texaco.

A number of African-American employees sued the big oil company, charging discrimination. In the course of investigating the case, these employees' attorneys obtained a copy of a tape recording, apparently of top Texaco executives at a meeting to discuss how to respond to the lawsuit. The tape seemed to contain offensive racial epithets as well as discussion of destroying evidence that would be harmful to Texaco's position. When a transcript of the tape was published, it was very embarrassing for the company. Texaco settled the lawsuit out of court, *agreeing to pay $176.1 million over five years, then the largest settlement in the history of racial discrimination suits in the United States. The company also created organizational programs promoting racial sensitivity at work.*[17]

Another recent case involving a company that was alleged to have discriminated against its African-American employees is described in the discussion case at the end of this chapter. Potentially costly lawsuits can involve other forms of discrimination as well, such as those based on age, gender, or disability.

Affirmative Action

One way to promote equal opportunity and remedy past discrimination is through **affirmative action.** Since the mid-1960s, major government contractors have been required by presidential executive order to adopt written affirmative action plans specifying goals, actions, and timetables for promoting greater on-the-job equality. Their purpose is to reduce job discrimination by encouraging companies to take positive (that is, affirmative) steps to overcome past employment practices and traditions that may have been discriminatory.

Affirmative action became increasingly controversial in the late 1990s and early 2000s. In some states, new laws (such as Proposition 209 in California) were passed banning or limiting affirmative action programs in public hiring and university admissions, and the issue was debated in Congress and in the courts. Backers of affirmative action argued that these programs provided an important tool for achieving equal opportunity. Roger Wilkins, a well-known African-American historian, supported this view. "We believe," he wrote, "that minorities and women are still disadvantaged in our highly competitive society and that affirmative action is absolutely necessary to level the playing field."[18] Some large corporations backed affirmative action programs, finding them helpful in monitoring their progress in providing equal job opportunity. General Electric, AT&T, and IBM, for example, have said that they would continue to use affirmative action goals and timetables even if they were not required by law.

Critics, however, argued that affirmative action was inconsistent with the principles of fairness and equality. Some pointed to instances of so-called **reverse discrimination,** which occurs when one group is unintentionally discriminated against in an effort to help another group. For example, if a more qualified white man were passed over for a job as a firefighter in favor of a less qualified Hispanic man to remedy past discrimination in a fire department, this might be unfair to the white candidate. Critics of affirmative action also argued that these programs could actually stigmatize or demoralize the very groups they were designed to help. For example, if a woman were hired for a top management post, other people might think she got the job just because of affirmative action preferences, even if she were truly the best qualified. This might undermine

---

[17] "Texaco to Pay $176.1 Million in Bias Suit," *Wall Street Journal,* November 18, 1996, pp. A3, A6.

[18] Roger Wilkins, "The Case for Affirmative Action; Racism Has Its Privileges," *The Nation,* March 27, 1995, pp. 409–16.

her effectiveness on the job or even cause her to question her own abilities. For this reason, some women and persons of color called for *less* emphasis on affirmative action, preferring to achieve personal success without preferential treatment.[19]

In 1995, the Supreme Court ruled in an important decision that affirmative action plans were legal but only if they were temporary and flexible, designed to correct past discrimination, and did not result in reverse discrimination. Under this ruling, quotas (for example, a hard-and-fast rule that 50 percent of all new positions would go to women, say, or African-Americans) would no longer be permitted in most situations. Clearly, affirmative action is an issue that will continue to be debated, not just in the courts but in business, society, and government generally.

Sexual and Racial Harassment

Government regulations ban both sexual and racial harassment. Of the two kinds, sexual harassment cases are more prevalent, and the law covering them is better defined. But racial harassment cases are growing in frequency and as a concern to employers.

Sexual harassment at work occurs when any employee, woman or man, experiences repeated, unwanted sexual attention or when on-the-job conditions are hostile or threatening in a sexual way. It includes both physical conduct—for example, suggestive touching—as well as verbal harassment, such as sexual innuendoes, jokes, or propositions. Sexual harassment is not limited to overt acts of individual coworkers or supervisors; it can also occur if a company's work climate is blatantly and offensively sexual or intimidating to employees. Women are the targets of most sexual harassment. Sexual harassment is illegal, and the U.S. Equal Employment Opportunity Commission is empowered to sue on behalf of victims. Such suits can be very costly to employers who tolerate a hostile work environment, as the following example shows.

> *In 1998, Mitsubishi Motor Manufacturing of America, Inc. (MMMA) paid $34 million to settle the largest sexual harassment case in U.S. history. In its suit against the company, the EEOC alleged that several hundred female employees at the company's assembly plant in Normal, Illinois, had been subject to "gross discrimination." The EEOC claimed that male managers and workers had propositioned women, grabbed their breasts and genitals, and called them* bitches *and* whores. *"It's very much a hostile environment," said one woman who had filed a complaint.*[20]

Harassment can occur whether or not the targeted employee cooperates. It need not result in the victim's firing or cause severe psychological distress. The presence of

---

[19] See, for example, Ward Connerly, *Creating Equal: My Fight against Race Preferences* (San Francisco, CA: Encounter Books, 2000); and Shelby Steele, *The Content of Our Character* (New York: Harper Perennial Library, 1991). A discussion of the effects of ending affirmative action may be found in "The End of Affirmative Action," *New York Times Magazine,* May 2, 1999, p. 44.

[20] "Mitsubishi Will Pay $34 Million in Sexual Harassment Suit," *Wall Street Journal,* June 12, 1998, p. B4; and "EEOC Sues Mitsubishi Unit for Harassment," *Wall Street Journal,* April 10, 1996, pp. B1, B8.

a hostile or abusive workplace can itself be the basis for a successful suit. In an important legal case decided by the Supreme Court in 1993, a woman manager at a truck-leasing firm was subjected to repeated offensive comments by the company president. For example, he asked her in front of other employees if she used sex to get a particular account and suggested that the two of them "go to the Holiday Inn to negotiate [her] raise." The manager quit her job and sued. The Supreme Court upheld her charges, saying that the president's behavior would reasonably be perceived as hostile or abusive, even though it had not caused "severe psychological injury" or caused the woman to be unable to do her job.[21] The court also ruled, in another case, that a company could be found guilty as a result of actions by a supervisor, even if the incident was never reported to top management.

Women employees regularly report that sexual harassment is common. From 38 to 60 percent of working women have told researchers that they have been sexually harassed on the job. Managers and supervisors are the most frequent offenders, and female office workers and clerical workers are the main targets. As many as 90 percent of incidents of harassment are never reported. This kind of conduct is most likely to occur where jobs and occupations are sex-segregated and where most supervisors and managers are men.

Racial harassment is also illegal, under Title VII of the Civil Rights Act. Under EEOC guidelines, ethnic slurs, derogatory comments, or other verbal or physical harassment based on race are against the law, if they create an intimidating, hostile, or offensive working environment or interfere with an individual's work performance. Although fewer racial than sexual harassment charges are filed, their numbers doubled during the 1990s, and employers have been liable for expensive settlements.[22] For example, American Eagle was sued by an African-American mechanic who charged the commuter airline with tolerating a racially hostile atmosphere—including racist graffiti in the men's bathroom and offensive cartoons on the bulletin board—in its Miami, Florida, maintenance hangar. The man was awarded close to a million dollars.[23]

What can companies do to combat sexual and racial harassment—and protect themselves from expensive lawsuits? In two important court cases in 1998, the Supreme Court helped clarify this question. The court said that companies could deflect lawsuits by taking two steps. First, they should develop a zero-tolerance policy on harassment and communicate it clearly to employees. Then, they should establish a complaint procedure—including ways to report incidents without retaliation—and act quickly to resolve any problems. Companies that took such steps, the court said, would be protected from suits by employees who claimed harassment but had failed to use the complaint procedure.[24]

---

[21] "Court, 9-0, Makes Sex Harassment Easier to Prove," *New York Times,* November 10, 1993, pp. A1, A15.

[22] "Employers Face Greater Liability in Race Cases," *Wall Street Journal,* July 1, 1999, pp. B1, B2. Information on the latest government policies on racial and sexual harassment may be found at the website of the Equal Employment Opportunity Commission at www.eeoc.gov.

[23] "Mechanic Wins $950,000," *Wall Street Journal,* October 13, 1999, p. C3; and "What Some Call Racist at American Eagle, Others Say Was in Jest," *Wall Street Journal,* April 20, 1999, pp. A1, A8.

[24] "Finally, a Corporate Tip Sheet on Sexual Harassment," *Business Week,* July 13, 1998, p. 39; and "Justices' Ruling Further Defines Sex Harassment," *Wall Street Journal,* March 5, 1998, pp. B1, B2.

Developing mechanisms for preventing sexual and racial harassment is just one important action companies can take. Others positive steps by businesses are discussed in the following section.

What Businesses Can Do: Diversity Policies and Practices

All businesses, of course, are required to obey the laws mandating equal employment opportunity and prohibiting sexual and racial harassment; those that fail to do so risk expensive lawsuits and public disapproval. But it is not enough simply to follow the law. The best-managed companies go beyond compliance to implement a range of policies and practices that make the workplace welcoming, fair, and accommodating to all employees. It is to these voluntary policies that we turn next.

Businesses that manage diversity effectively enjoy a strategic advantage. While fundamental ethical principles, discussed in Chapter 6, dictate that all employees should be treated fairly and with respect for their basic human rights, there are also bottom-line benefits to doing so.

- Companies that promote equal employment opportunity generally do better at attracting and retaining workers from all backgrounds. This is increasingly important as the pool of skilled labor grows more diverse.

- Businesses with employees from varied backgrounds can often more effectively serve customers who are themselves diverse.

- The global marketplace demands a workforce with language skills, cultural sensitivity, and awareness of national and other differences across markets. For example, Maria Elena Lagomasino, senior managing director of Chase Manhattan's Global Private Banking Group, credited her Cuban heritage with helping her do her job more effectively. "When I got into private banking with Latin American customers," she commented, "I found my ability to understand their reality a great advantage."[25]

- Finally, companies with effective diversity programs can avoid costly lawsuits and damage to their corporate reputations from charges of discrimination or cultural insensitivity.

Companies that manage diversity effectively take a number of related actions, in addition to obeying all relevant laws. Research shows that these actions include the following.

Articulate a clear diversity mission, set objectives, and hold managers accountable.

An example of a company that has done so is mortgage lender Fannie Mae. The company's overall mission is to increase the availability and affordability of housing for low-, moderate-, and middle-income Americans. This means, of course, that the company works with a diverse group of customers. Fannie Mae recognizes that one way to do this well, in the words of one of its written core commitments, is "to foster a diverse workforce and recognize

---

[25] "Chasing a Global Edge," *Fortune*, July 19, 1999.

and value every individual's unique skills and perspectives." The company's Office of Diversity develops goals, conducts training, administers a mentoring program, and monitors compliance at all levels.[26]

Three-quarters of Fortune 500 companies have diversity programs, mostly training designed to promote sensitivity and awareness. At United Parcel Service, senior-level managers are required to attend a one-month diversity and leadership course. Another important step is to reward managers. At Monsanto, for example, a portion of all bonuses paid to "people managers" is based on how well their departments meet various diversity goals.[27]

Spread a wide net in recruitment, to find the most diverse possible pool of qualified candidates. Those in charge of both hiring and promotion need to seek all workers who may be qualified, both inside and outside the company. This often involves moving beyond word-of-mouth networks, which may produce a pool of applicants who are similar to people already working for the company or in particular jobs. One company's successful effort to promote diversity in its hiring and promotion practices is described in the following example.

> *As part of an agreement to settle a sex-discrimination class action lawsuit, Home Depot, Inc., introduced an innovation: a computerized hiring and promotion system called Job Preference Program, or JPP for short. The company installed computer kiosks in every store, where job applicants could take basic skills tests and fill out questionnaires about their experience and career goals. Existing employees were encouraged to register their long-term aspirations. The JPP computer then made suggestions about needed skills, forwarded resumes to managers seeking to fill positions, and told applicants about jobs they might not have thought about that matched their ambitions. In the first year after the system was introduced in 1999, the number of female managers at Home Depot increased by 30 percent, and the number of minority managers by 28 percent.*[28]

Identify promising women and persons of color, and provide them with mentors and other kinds of support. What techniques work to shatter the glass ceiling? One study of a group of highly successful women executives found that most had been helped by top-level supporters and by multiple chances to gain critical skills. Some companies have promoted mobility by assigning mentors—more-senior counselors—to promising female and minority managers and by providing opportunities that include wide-ranging line management experience. In 1989, for example, Motorola revamped its career planning process to identify high-potential women and give them the opportunities they needed to merit promotion. By 1997, Motorola had 38 female vice presidents, up from

[26] "Diversity Works at Fannie Mae," available at www.fanniemae.com.

[27] "Diversity Training Programs Help Reduce Risk of Bias Suits," *Business Insurance,* July 12, 1999, p. 1. For a guide to diversity training, see William Sonnenschein, *The Diversity Toolkit* (Chicago: Contemporary Books, 1997).

[28] "To Hire a Lumber Expert, Click Here," *Fortune,* April 3, 2000, p. 267.

just 2 when the program started. Bell Atlantic's Leadership for the Millenium program develops promising middle level managers; 35 percent of participants are minorities.[29]

Set up diversity councils to monitor the company's goals and progress toward them. A **diversity council** is a group of managers and employees responsible for developing and implementing specific action plans to meet an organization's diversity goals. Sometimes, a diversity council will be established for a corporation as a whole; sometimes, it will be established within particular business units. An example of a company that has used diversity councils effectively is Pitney Bowes, a maker of business communication machines. In 1992 and again in 1997, the company adopted a diversity strategic plan, with specific objectives for the next five-year period. Diversity councils were set up in each business unit to implement programs to meet these objectives. Each year, progress toward the company's objectives was assessed. Minorities now make up 41 percent of Pitney Bowes' employees, and women make up 39 percent; the company has repeatedly been named to lists of the best employers of women and persons of color.[30]

Another important step businesses can take to manage diversity effectively is to accommodate the wide range of family and other obligations employees have in their lives outside work. This subject is discussed in the next section.

Balancing Work and Life

The nature of families and family life has changed, both in the United States and in many other countries. The primary groups in which people live are just as diverse as the workforce itself. One of the most prominent of these changes is that dual-income families have become much more common. According to U.S. Census data released in 2000, in more than half of all married couples with children, both parents worked at least part-time. This was up from just a third of such families in 1976. Families have adopted a wide range of strategies for combining full- and part-time work with the care of children, elderly relatives, and other dependents. Commented the president of the Work and Family Institute, speaking of dual-career families: "It's time to move beyond, is it good, is it bad, and get to: how do we make it work?"[31] How to help "make it work" for employees trying to balance the complex, multiple demands of work and family life has became a major challenge for business.

Child Care and Elder Care

One critical issue for business is supporting workers with responsibilities for children and elderly relatives.

The demand for **child care** is enormous and growing. Millions of children need daily care, especially the nearly 7 out of every 10 children whose mothers hold jobs. A major source of workplace stress for working parents is concern about their children;

[29] "The Diversity Elite," *Fortune,* July 19, 1999, pp. 8–25; Lisa A. Mainiero, "Getting Anointed for Advancement: The Case of Executive Women," *Academy of Management Executive,* May 1994, pp. 53–63; and "Breaking Through," *Business Week,* February 17, 1997, p. 64.

[30] Information about Pitney Bowes' diversity programs is available at www.pb.com.

[31] "Dual Income Families Now Most Common," *San Francisco Chronicle,* October 24, 2000.

and problems with child care are a leading cause of absenteeism. Businesses lose an estimated $3 billion a year because of child-related absences.[32]

Business has found that child care programs, in addition to reducing absenteeism and tardiness, also improve productivity and aid recruiting by improving the company's image and helping to retain talented employees. In 2000, 90 percent of large U.S. companies provided some type of child care assistance, including referral services, parent education, dependent-care accounts, and vouchers. One in 10 large companies provided on-site child care services. An example is Johnson Wax, a consumer products firm that cares for 400 children in a state-of-the-art center at its Racine, Wisconsin, headquarters. "This isn't a benefit," explained a company spokesperson. "It's a good business decision because we want to attract the best."[33]

In addition to their responsibilities for children, many of today's families must find ways to care for aging parents and other older relatives. This issue will become increasingly important to businesses in the coming decade as baby boomers pass through their 40s and 50s, the prime years for caring for elderly parents. More than one in four households now care for an older person, and nearly two-thirds of Americans under the age of 60 think they will have **elder care** duties within the next decade. According to the Conference Board, by 2005, 37 percent of workers will be more concerned with caring for a parent than for a child, a major shift.[34]

Many businesses have adopted programs to support workers caring for older relatives. Almost half of the large corporations surveyed by Hewitt Associates, a benefits company, offer some such assistance. The most common kind is providing information and referrals to services for the elderly. "It was great to have someone to talk to, someone who cared," said a customer service representative for AT&T who used the company's referral program to find help for her mother, who had Alzheimer's and lived with her. Also available at many firms are dependent-care accounts, long-term care insurance, and emergency backup care. One of the best steps companies can take is to give people the time off they need to deal with the often unpredictable crises that occur in families caring for the elderly. In addition to its referral services, AT&T, for example, also has a policy that permits employees to take up to 12 months of unpaid leave in any 24-month period to care for an older relative.[35]

When a mother or father is granted time off when children are born or adopted and during the important early months of a child's development, it is called a **parental leave;** when the care of elderly relatives is involved, it is called a **family leave.** Under the Family and Medical Leave Act (FMLA), passed in 1993, companies that employ 50 or more people must grant unpaid, job-protected leaves of up to 12 weeks to employees faced with serious family needs, including the birth or adoption of a baby. Smaller companies, not covered by the FMLA, usually do less for expectant and new parents and for those with ill family members.

---

[32] "INFObrief: Childcare" (New York: Catalyst, 1994).

[33] Data are from Hewitt Associates, "More Employers Offer Work/Life Benefits to Gain Edge in Tight Labor Market," press release issued May 4, 2000, available at www.hewitt.com.

[34] "Who Needs You Most," *Business Week,* June 22, 1998, p. 8; and "New Work Issue: Elder Care," *Seattle Times,* February 29, 2000, p. A1.

[35] "Employers Stepping Up in Elder Care," *USA Today,* August 3, 2000, p. 3B.

Work Flexibility

Companies have also accommodated the changing roles of women and men by offering workers more flexibility through such options as flextime, part-time employment, job sharing, and working from home (sometimes called *telecommuting* because the employee keeps in touch with coworkers, customers, and others by phone or over the Internet).

Aetna Life & Casualty, one of America's biggest insurance companies, demonstrates the benefits of the many kinds of work flexibility for both company and employees.

> *In some departments at Aetna, as many as 40 percent of employees work flextime schedules, beginning and quitting at different times of the day. Others share jobs, with each working half a week. Many jobs are held on a part-time basis, leaving the worker time to be at home with children or elderly parents. Several hundred Aetna employees telecommute from their homes. The company has a Work/Life Strategies unit to assist employees in using these programs to meet family needs without seriously disrupting company routines. Aetna estimates it saves $1 million a year by not having to train new workers.*[36]

Aetna is not the only corporation using these practices. A 2000 survey of large companies revealed that 74 percent offered some kind of flexible work schedules, up from 66 percent in 1994. Forty-seven percent offered part-time work, 28 percent permitted job sharing, and 28 percent allowed employees to work from home.[37]

However, many observers believe that most careers are still structured for people who are prepared to put in 40 hours a week at the office—or 50 or 60—giving their full and undivided commitment to the organization. Many women and men have been reluctant to take advantage of various flexible work options, fearing that this would put them on a slower track, sometimes disparagingly called the *mommy track* or *daddy track*. In this view, businesses will need to undergo a cultural shift, to value the contributions of people who are prepared to make a serious, but less than full-time, commitment to their careers.

What would such a cultural shift look like? Some have used the term **family-friendly corporation** to describe firms that would fully support both men and women in their efforts to balance work and family responsibilities. Job advantages would not be granted or denied on the basis of gender. People would be hired, paid, evaluated, promoted, and extended benefits on the basis of their qualifications and ability to do the tasks assigned. The route to the top, or to satisfaction in any occupational category, would be open to anyone with the talent to take it. The company's stakeholders, regardless of their gender, would be treated in a bias-free manner. All laws forbidding sex discrimination would be fully obeyed. Programs to provide leaves or financial support for child care, elder care, and other family responsibilities would support both men and women

---

[36] "As Aetna Adds Flextime, Bosses Learn to Cope," *Wall Street Journal,* June 18, 1990, pp. B1, B5; "Work and Family," *Business Week,* June 28, 1993, p. 83; and "The Childless Feel Left Out When Parents Get a Lift," *New York Times,* December 1, 1996, p. C12.

[37] Hewitt Associates, "More Employers Offer Work/Life Benefits."

EXHIBIT 18-B	A Family-Friendly Company

A Family-Friendly Company

The most family-friendly company in the United States, according to a survey conducted for *Business Week* by the Center on Work and Family, is First Tennessee National Corp., a midsize regional bank based in Memphis, Tennessee. First Tennessee runs a Family Matters program that integrates family considerations into every aspect of the bank's operations. Some of the program's innovations include:

- On-site child care, or vouchers for employees who prefer to use other providers.
- Flexible scheduling, including condensed workweeks, job sharing, and telecommuting.
- Fitness centers.
- Jobs designed to accommodate family needs.
- A classroom visitation program that allows parents time off to participate in school activities.

The Family Matters program, managers believe, has had important bottom-line benefits. An internal study showed that employees were less likely to leave the bank, and so were customers. First Tennessee's customer retention rate was 95 percent, well above the industry average. During the program's first three years, profits at the bank were up 55 percent.

"We flip-flopped our entire corporate philosophy," said First Tennessee's CEO Ralph Horn. "Here it's employees first versus putting the shareholders first like at other financial institutions. The philosophy is that profit begins with satisfied employees."

Sources: "Family Values: Corporations Find Family Programs Increase Employee Motivation as Well as the Bottom Line," *Incentive*, December 1996, pp. 23–27; and "Balancing Work and Family," *Business Week*, September 16, 1996, p. 74.

employees and help promote an equitable division of domestic work. And persons could seek, and achieve, career advancement without committing to a full-time schedule, year after year.[38] An example of a family-friendly company is given in Exhibit 18-B.

An important step businesses can take is to recognize, and provide benefits to, non-traditional families. Some firms now offer domestic partner benefits to their gay and lesbian employees, extending health insurance and other benefits to the same-sex partners of employees. Although U.S. law does not explicitly bar discrimination based on sexual orientation, some local laws do; and many firms have found that extending health insurance and other benefits to the same-sex partners of employees is an effective strategy

---

[38] *Working Women* magazine publishes an annual list of the "100 Best Companies for Working Mothers." The current year's list may be viewed at www.wwn.com.

EXHIBIT
18-C

Domestic Partner Benefits

Corporations in the United States have slowly begun to acknowledge differences in employee sexual orientation and lifestyles. Gay and lesbian employees have become a vocal minority, winning important victories in the courts. Faced by this pressure, some firms have adopted new policies. By 2000, 93 of the Fortune 500 companies provided benefits, such as health insurance, to the domestic partners of gay and lesbian employees. Lotus Development was the first major employer to offer spousal benefits to same-sex partners; it was followed by many others, including AT&T, Chase Manhattan, Microsoft, United Airlines, and the Big Three automakers. Other steps companies have taken to support their homosexual employees have included written antidiscrimination policies, management training on sexual diversity issues, and visible gay and lesbian advertising.

Sources: "Numbers," *Time*, June 19, 2000, p. 33. An organization called glvReports.com publishes on its website an annual ranking of major companies, based on their policies as employers of gays and lesbians.

for recruiting and retaining valuable contributors. Domestic partner benefits are further described in Exhibit 18-C.

No other area of business illustrates the basic theme of this book better than the close connection between work and life. Our basic theme is that business and society are closely and unavoidably intertwined, so that what affects one also has an impact on the other. As the workforce has become more diverse, business has been challenged to accommodate their employees' differences. When people go to work, they do not shed their identities at the office or factory door. When employees come from families where there are young children at home, or where elderly parents require care, companies must learn to support these roles. Businesses that help their employees achieve a balance between work and life and meet their obligations to their families and communities often reap rewards in greater productivity, loyalty, and commitment.

Summary Points of This Chapter

- The U.S. workforce is as diverse as it has ever been and is becoming more so. More women are working than ever before, many immigrants have entered the labor force, ethnic and racial diversity is increasing, and the workforce is aging.
- Women and persons of color have made great strides in entering all occupations, but they continue to be underrepresented in many business management roles, especially at top levels. Both groups face a continuing pay gap. The number of women-owned businesses has increased sharply, and many minorities, especially immigrants, also own their own businesses.

- Under U.S. law, businesses are required to provide equal opportunity to all, without regard to race, color, religion, sex, national origin, disability, or age. Sexual and racial harassment are illegal. Affirmative action plans remain legal, but only if they are temporary and flexible, designed to correct past discrimination, and do not result in reverse discrimination.
- Companies that manage diversity effectively have a strategic advantage because they are able to attract and retain talented workers from all backgrounds, serve a diverse customer base, and avoid expensive lawsuits and public embarrassment.
- Successful diversity management includes articulating a mission, recruiting widely, mentoring promising women and persons of color, and establishing mechanisms for assessing progress.
- Many businesses have helped employees balance the complex demands of work and family obligations by providing support programs such as child, elder care, flexible work schedules, domestic partner benefits, and telecommuting options.

Key Terms and Concepts Used in This Chapter

- Diversity
- Workforce diversity
- Pay gap
- Occupational segregation
- Glass ceiling
- Glass walls
- Equal employment opportunity
- Equal Employment Opportunity Commission (EEOC)
- Affirmative action

- Reverse discrimination
- Sexual harassment
- Racial harassment
- Diversity council
- Child care
- Elder care
- Parental leave
- Family leave
- Family-friendly corporation

Internet Resources

- www.eeoc.gov U.S. Equal Employment Opportunity Commission
- www.workfamily.com Work and Family Connection
- www.wfd.com Work/Family Directions, Inc.
- www.sba.gov U.S. Small Business Administration

Discussion Case: *Coca-Cola Faces Charges of Racial Discrimination*

On June 15, 2000, lawyers in Atlanta, Georgia, announced that they had reached a settlement in a far-reaching racial discrimination lawsuit against Coca-Cola. Negotiations had gone down to the wire. That day was the deadline for filing the papers necessary to have the case certified as a class action; if this had happened, the plaintiffs would have turned over to the court 30 boxes of documents, expected to be highly damaging to Coke's corporate reputation.

The terms of the settlement were not revealed. But plaintiffs were expected to receive a significant amount of money, and Coca-Cola was expected to agree to big steps to improve its management of diversity.

The case had begun just over a year earlier, when eight employees had sued Coca-Cola, charging the company with discrimination against African-American employees in pay, promotions, and performance evaluations. If the case had become a class action, as many as 1,500 additional salaried black employees could have joined the lawsuit.

Some saw irony in the charges against the world's biggest soft drink company. Coca-Cola was headquartered in Atlanta, Georgia, a city known for its racially progressive policies and whose slogan was "too busy to hate." The company espoused a commitment to diversity and had a long record of support for historically black colleges and nonprofit organizations. Coke was one of the best-known and most widely consumed products in the world—enjoyed by people of all nationalities and ethnic backgrounds.

But on closer inspection, Coke's track record proved tattered. In the lawsuit, the black plaintiffs charged that they were paid "dramatically" less than their white counterparts. For example, in 1998, according to the suit, the median salary for African-Americans working at corporate headquarters was $36,000, compared with $55,000 for whites. The plaintiffs also charged that few minority executives advanced to top positions, and that many were trapped behind "glass walls . . . [that] virtually segregate[d] the company into divisions where African-American leadership [was] acceptable, and divisions where it [was] not."

Evidence also emerged that Coke management had known for some time that a problem was simmering, and it had failed to take decisive action. In 1995, the company had requested an internal report on its management of diversity. The project was headed by Carl Ware, then president of Coke's Africa division and the company's top-ranking black executive. Ware's report found that some minority employees felt "humiliated, ignored, overlooked or unacknowledged." It recommended a mentoring program, specific diversity goals, and executive accountability for results, among other actions.

In 1997, the U.S. Department of Labor Office of Federal Contract Compliance conducted an audit of Coca-Cola and found pay inequities based on race and gender; in response, the company signed a conciliation agreement in which it agreed to provide more opportunities for women and minorities.

A month after the lawsuit was filed, Coke chairman M. Douglas Ivester, saying that there "will be no room for discrimination in any form," appointed a diversity council, jointly chaired by Ware and by Jack Stahl, president of the North America division (who was white). As the year progressed, however, things did not go well for Coke or for Ivester, and diversity issues seemed to be put on the back burner. In the face of declining earnings, a falling stock price, and a product recall in Europe, Ivester reshuffled his management team. Ware, alienated by the reorganization, retired from the company in November.

In December, the board forced out Ivester and replaced him with Douglas Daft. One of Daft's first moves was to rehire Ware as the company's executive vice president for corporate affairs. He also created a new position of vice president of diversity strategies, promoted several key African-American executives, and declared that compensation for all top executives would be tied to meeting diversity goals.

In May 2000, Coca-Cola announced plans to invest $1 billion in Africa over three years to build bottling and canning plants and to launch new brands. It also committed another $1 billion to purchasing supplies from minority- and women-owned businesses and to provide scholarships, internships, and charitable contributions aimed at minority communities. Commented the plaintiffs' lawyer, "External investment is long overdue. However, the internal issues remain for African-American employees who have suffered a discriminatory regime for years."

Sources: "Coca-Cola Reaches Settlement with Some Workers in Bias Suit," *New York Times,* June 15, 2000, p. C1; "Coke CEO to Tie Pay to Diversity Goals," *Wall Street Journal,* March 10, 2000, p. B7; "Coke Talks Were Intense, Mediator Says," *Atlanta Journal and Constitution,* June 18, 2000, p. 1G; "Suit Is Filed against Coke by Current, Past Employees Who Allege Racial Bias," *Wall Street Journal,* April 26, 1999, p. B4; "Coke Aims $1 Billion at Diversity," *Atlanta Journal and Constitution,* May 16, 2000, p. 1A; "Federal Investigation into Coca-Cola Shifts to Pay-Bias Concerns," *Wall Street Journal,* June 16, 2000, p. B8; and "Coke Was Told in '95 of Need for Diversity," *Wall Street Journal,* May 20, 1999, pp. A3, A4.

Discussion Questions

1. From the evidence presented in the case, do you think that Coca-Cola violated any U.S. equal employment opportunity laws? If so, which ones, and why?
2. Assess the steps taken by the company prior to the lawsuit to manage workforce diversity. Do you think these steps were sufficient? Why or why not?
3. If you were a Coca-Cola executive, what actions would you take in the wake of the settlement to promote equal opportunity for all employees? How would you communicate your diversity program to your employees and to the public?

19

Business and the Media

Media communications—the World Wide Web, televisions, DVDs, CDs, radios, newspapers, movies, and books—have an enormously important effect on the relationship between business and the general public. Some argue that the recent growth and concentration of media businesses in the United States have increased the power of that industry over society to an unsettling level. This increase in media's influence draws attention to critical media issues and the importance of media businesses' social responsibilities.

This chapter focuses on these key questions and objectives:

- How has the media industry increased its influence on business and the general public?

- What are the major issues at the core of the media's ethical and social responsibilities?

- How have governments around the world regulated the use of the media for business, especially the tobacco industry?

- How can businesses influence their image in the media?

H undreds of people in Belgium and France, including teenagers and schoolchildren, reported symptoms of nausea and dizziness after drinking Coca-Cola products in the summer of 1999. After weeks of denying that the problem was due to the company's lack of quality control in the production process, Coke admitted that defective carbon dioxide and contamination from a fungicide were to blame for the incidents. As a result of the reported illnesses, the firm launched the largest product recall in its history. Even so, the European Union's executive commission publicly criticized Coca-Cola's slow response and hesitation in accepting responsibility for the illnesses caused by the company's quality control failures.

When Julia Roberts starred in the movie *Erin Brockovich,* based on the real life experience of a courageous legal assistant who took on a utility giant, Pacific Gas & Electric (PG&E), the firm was forced to relive its media nightmare. The film focused on a lawsuit accusing the utility company of air and water contamination affecting the residents of Hinkley, a small town in southern California. It was rumored that the executives at PG&E were so concerned over the making of the movie that they reportedly planted spies on the set to keep track of what was being said about the firm. The firm denied this allegation, but admitted "PG&E did not respond to the groundwater problem as openly, quickly or thoroughly as it should have." The renewed publicity over the event was the last thing the utility firm wanted to see.

When Carnival Cruise Lines teamed up with Visa, the credit-card company, the partnership resulted in a memorable commercial. The message was: Use your Visa card when making reservations on Carnival Cruise ships because "we don't take American Express." American Express executives pointed out that the cruise line accepted their credit card until the partnership with Visa. More important, just after reaping the benefits of the commercial exposure with Visa, Carnival Cruise quietly returned to the policy of accepting American Express credit cards.[1]

The challenges confronting businesses when interacting with the media often are complex and filled with ethical and social issues. Did Coca-Cola respond too slowly and defensively to the allegations of consumer illnesses caused by drinking its product? Is it fair for Pacific Gas & Electric to be subjected again to negative publicity through the release of a movie based on its earlier irresponsibility? Was it ethically responsible for Carnival Cruise Lines to refuse American Express credit cards only to gain publicity through Visa commercials and then to revert back to its original policy once the Visa, commercial aired? This chapter will explore these and other issues involving businesses' relationships with society as manifested through the media.

The Media Industry

The **media** is defined as a means of communication that widely reaches or influences people. The media industry includes *broadcast technology* (the sending and receiving of messages/images via transmission equipment, cable lines, wireless devices, and receivers), *broadcasting business* (news entertainment, movies, etc.)

---

[1] Brandon Mitchener and Betsy McKay, "EU Panel Criticizes Coke's Explanation in Drinks Scare," *Wall Street Journal,* August 17, 1999, pp. A12, A14; David Lazarus, "PG&E Case as Villain in New 'True-Story' Movie," *San Francisco Chronicle,* March 16, 2000, pp. A1, A17; and Paul Beckett, "'And It Doesn't Take American Express'—For the Time Being," *Wall Street Journal,* April 12, 1999, pp. A1, A14.

and *service delivery* (cable companies, theaters, video stores, and so on that interface with the consuming public). This industry has long been an important factor in how information is delivered to people. Whether it was through a newspaper, radio, phonograph, or television, the public learned about major events or was entertained by their favorite actors, musicians, or sports teams. Recently, with the advent of age-of-information technology, the delivery of information by the media has changed in many ways. Internet service, digital cable, and wireless communications are challenging standard telephone lines, radio airwaves, and access to libraries as convenient channels of communication.

The extensive merger activity in the United States, discussed in Chapter 9, spilled over into the media industry. At the core of this merger activity was the consolidation of old and new media communication industries. For example, the America Online (AOL) merger with Time Warner, featured in Chapter 9's discussion case, brought together Time Warner's print, television, music, and movie media companies with AOL's Internet and high-capacity, fiber-optic cable businesses.

> *In a three-year period between 1998 and 2000, AT&T, a telephone communications company, spent more than $110 billion to transform itself into a major media player by buying cable and Internet companies. AT&T persuaded Comcast to withdraw its offer to purchase MediaOne, enabling the nation's largest telephone company to be in a position to become the nation's biggest cable company. To get Comcast to withdraw its bid for MediaOne, AT&T agreed to offer telephone service to all Comcast subscribers, extending AT&T's access via cable to 62 million U.S. households. AT&T's efforts resulted in a massive base for selling local, long-distance, wireless, video, and Internet communications. AT&T's new media businesses were so large that the company split these activities into four business lines.*[2]

The media industry in the United States became a collection of integrated media companies, with more and more power becoming concentrated in fewer and fewer businesses as the possibilities for electronic communication increased at an unprecedented pace. The trend toward media mergers spread to other countries as well. Television Azteca, Mexico's second-largest television broadcast company, acquired Unefon, a Mexican telephone company. Microsoft expanded into the German television market. MCI/World-Com spent $1 billion providing Europe with fiber-optic cable. Olivetti's hostile takeover of rival Telecom Italia further consolidated the communications industry in Italy. The Luxembourg-based CLT-UFA merger with Pearson TV created a $3.6 billion company controlling many of Europe's television and radio stations.[3] Most experts predicted that merger activity among media companies around the world would intensify as the ability to reach more and more customers through electronic communications increased.

---

[2] David Bank, "As Worlds Collide, AT&T Grabs a Power Seat," *Wall Street Journal,* May 6, 1999, pp. B1, B11; and Leslie Cauley and Rebecca Blumenstein, "Suddenly, AT&T's Strategy to Dominate Cable Industry Looks Difficult to Achieve," *Wall Street Journal,* January 11, 2000, p. 13.

[3] "The Race to Wire Europe," *Business Week,* June 7, 1999, pp. 48–50; and "A Media Star Is Born," *Business Week,* April 24, 2000, pp. 136–37.

Media's Ethical and Social Responsibilities

The nature of the media industry created a number of important and highly controversial issues inherent to the business media-public relationship. With the dramatic increase in the size and influence of the media industry, these issues are even more important than in the past. All of these issues raised questions about businesses' ethical and social responsibilities. As discussed earlier, the media themselves are businesses, and they are expected to adhere to the same ethical and social responsibility principles that apply to all other businesses. Some media executives and businesses have welcomed their responsibilities; others appear slow in acknowledging that their increased power requires greater attention to their impact on society.

The Image Issue

One important issue that arises when discussing media's ethical and social responsibilities is the **image issue.** How does the media portray various groups in society? Are ethnic groups cast as second-class citizens, or are women only portrayed in a subservient role by the media? The portrayal of women and men in the media is discussed in Exhibit 19-A.

EXHIBIT 19-A

Gender Bias in the Media

A Canadian media watchdog organization, Child & Family Canada, looked at how men were portrayed in video games, a $15-billion-a-year industry. They found that "Video games more than any other medium, promote male dominator, racist behavior as glamorous and erotic, the only possible response and the essential requirement for winning."

Child & Family Canada also looked at gender portrayal on television, particularly in commercials. They reported that commercial television suggested that the women in this society were almost always young, white, large-breasted, and mainly preoccupied with how they looked and what they wore. They were dependent on men for approval and protection; they were largely seen as caregivers and nurturers, rarely as initiators and leaders. They also tended to be helpless victims of violence, which often was sexual in nature.

On the other hand, men were rarely vulnerable and seldom showed their feelings. They were usually in control, preoccupied with fast cars, prone to drinking beer with their buddies, and used weapons. They most often were the "voice of authority," selling products or providing information.

The stereotyping of genders in the media extended to children as well. Girls were shown as passive; they were preoccupied with their appearance and played with dolls rather than computers or video games. Boys were more active, frequently aggressive, cared more about sports and war games, and had only male friends.

Source: Meg Hogarth, "We Are What We Watch: Challenging Sexism and Violence in the Media," Child & Family Canada, www.cfc-efc.ca/docs.

Although the United States is a multicultural and ethnically diverse country, film and television images tell a different story. In a 1997 study, ethnic minority groups were found to make up 15.7 percent of prime-time drama casts, but they represented 25.4 percent of the population. Only 26 percent of major characters in movies were women, although they comprised 51 percent of the population. People 65 years and older were less than 2 percent of characters portrayed during prime-time television, but they represented 12.7 percent of the U.S. population. An American Psychological Association task force concluded that minorities were not only underrepresented on television but were "segregated in specific types of content, and rarely engage in cross-ethnic interactions."[4]

Children Now, a U.S. children's advocacy organization, reported similar results. Only 2 out of 10 Latino and Asian children and 4 out of 10 African-American children said they saw people of their race "very often" on television compared to 7 out of 10 Caucasian children. According to Children Now president, Lois Salisbury, "These findings show that kids of all races are aware of media's stereotypes starting at a young age and understand their power to share opinions." This study also concluded that children were more likely to associate positive characteristics with Caucasian characters on television and negative characteristics with minority characters.[5]

> *Many people were offended when a Virginia police officers' association ran an advertisement promoting its annual dinner-dance in a local newspaper. The drawing used in the ad appeared to portray a Caucasian couple dancing, an African-American bellhop, and a dark-skinned waiter. An organization of African-American police officers demanded an apology, saying that the ads depicted African-Americans in stereotyped, demeaning roles. "It really was offensive as soon as I saw the faces," commented one African-American captain in the department. The police chief apologized and said "In today's society, we need to be more aware of issues like this that can be perceived as insensitive."*[6]

NAACP President Kweisi Mfume noted that none of the new shows for the 1999 television season had minorities in starring or leading roles. "This glaring omission is an outrage and a shameful display by network executives who are either clueless, careless, or both. We intend to make it clear that the frontier of television must reflect the multiethnic landscape of today's modern society."[7]

It appears that some executives have become more sensitive toward how underrepresented minority groups were in the media industry. In 2000, the cable network Showtime created an hour-long series entitled "Resurrection Blvd." The show not only featured a predominantly Latino family as its cast but also employed mostly Latinos in the crew. NBC mandated that producers hire minority writers and provided additional

---

[4] See *Mediascope: Diversity in Film and Television,* www.mediascope.org/fdivers.

[5] "New Study Finds Children See Inequities in Media's Race and Class Portrayals," Children Now, May 6, 1998, www.childrennow.org/media/race.

[6] "Blacks' Portrayal in Police Union Ad Draws Complaints," *Washington Post,* February 27, 1996, p. B1.

[7] "NAACP Mulls Action against TV Networks over Minority Roles," *Wall Street Journal,* July 13, 1999, p. B8.

funding to hire a minority writer for each of the network's second-year television shows. These efforts began to address the poor image and underrepresentation of racial groups in the media industry, although additional measures were certain warranted.

The Values Issue

The **values issue** focuses on the power of the media to shape social attitudes and values. The values issue goes beyond the image issue because values are one of the basic determinants of human behavior and social attitudes. Most of us acquire our values from early life experiences, from our families or observing others and their behavior. The media has ascended to a predominant role of shaping values early in our lives, particularly with the increased frequency of media inputs from television, music, the Internet, and other means.

Children in the United States watch an average of three to four hours of television a day. By the time they graduate from high school, they have spent more time watching television than they have in the classroom.[8] This gives the media an importance that goes far beyond its ability to inform, to entertain, and to promote the sale of goods and services. As a values source, the electronic media tends to act as parent, school, church, peer, and counselor all rolled into one.

The presence and impact of violence on television and in the movies has been debated for decades. Recently, the boom in video games seemingly has increased the presence of violence in society.

> *The Center for Media and Public Affairs reported that the 50 top grossing movies in 1998 contained 2,319 violent scenes, and 1,377 were categorized as "serious violence." CBS was found to be the most violent television network, with an average of 10 serious acts of violence per episode. Cable television's USA came in second, with an average of eight violent acts per episode. Researcher Tracy Dietz examined 33 popular video games and found that nearly 80 percent of the games included aggression or violence as part of the strategy or object.*[9]

The Federal Trade Commission released a report in 2000 that criticized the film, recording, and video game industries for marketing violence. The FTC concluded, "despite voluntary rating and labeling systems adopted by the industries over the past few years, all three industries have used marketing strategies to entice young consumers to buy products that the industries themselves deemed inappropriate."[10] Of the 44 teen-oriented films rated R for violence, the FTC found that 80 percent were aimed at youths under the age of 17.

The industry executives were mixed in their responses to the FTC study. One marketing executive testified before Congress admitting that the company strategy was to

[8] The Albany Clinic, "Children and Watching TV," www.mhcnca.org.
[9] Christopher Stern, "Violence Sells Tickets, Report Says," *Lycos Entertainment*, September 22, 1999, news.lycos.com/stories/Entertainment/Business; and Tracy L. Dietz, "An Examination of Violence and Gender Role Portrayals in Video Games," *Sex Roles,* March 1998, pp. 425–42.
[10] Kevin Sack, "FTC to Say Violence Marketed to Young," *Pittsburgh Post-Gazette,* September 10, 2000, p. A20.

find the elusive teen target audience and make sure everyone between the ages of 12 and 18 was exposed to their R-rated films. However, Jack Valenti, president of the Motion Picture Association of America, provided a different view of the situation. He questioned the FTC's definition of terms, such as teen and violent. He cited industry market research that showed that 81 percent of adults with young children were satisfied with the existing voluntary ratings system. "The FTC ought to say thank goodness for the movie industry. We don't deserve this kind of savagery from the FTC or any other part of the American government," said Valenti.[11]

> *One example of the media demonstrating its responsiveness to controlling violence on television was seen during the 2000 Olympic games. Nike ran an ad during the 2000 Olympic games that featured track star Suzy Hamilton. The ad showed Hamilton chased by a masked man with a chainsaw, a parody of the horror film,* Friday the 13th. *Hamilton escaped from the danger "thanks to her Nikes." After more than 2,000 viewers called NBC to complain of the violent nature of the commercial, the network dropped the ad. "We accepted the ad subject to audience complaint, and it was pulled [the next morning]."*[12]

The media industry launched a series of 13 public-service announcements in 2000, soon after the release of the negative FTC study. These announcements featured television stars urging children to not be bullies, parents to lock up their guns, and everyone to watch their language so as to not encourage hostile outbursts. The ads provided the National Campaign against Youth Violence's toll-free telephone number.

Does the increase of violence in the media really have an impact in our society? A *Frontline* episode on PBS looked at the influence of television violence on viewers' behavior. Researcher Leonard Eron found that the more violent the programs that children watched at home, the more aggressive they were in school. Similarly, David Phillipps, a scientist at the University of California at San Diego, studied the aftermath of heavily publicized heavyweight prizefights and found that the murder rate in the U.S. increased for several days after the fights. Professor John D. Murray at Kansas State University reviewed studies investigating the impact of televised violence on viewers' behavior from the 1950s to the present. He concluded that nearly all of the reports confirmed the harmful effects of media violence on the behavior of children, teens, and adults who viewed such programming.[13]

When protesters of violence in the media turned toward the government for help, Representative Henry Hyde proposed a bill that would have outlawed the sale of extremely violent movies, video games, and books to minors, specifically material that featured flagellation, torture, or rape. He wanted to establish a standard of violent obscenity similar to the one that prohibits the sale of pornography to minors. The bill failed by a 282–146 vote

[11] Glenn R. Simpson and John Lippman, "Violence, Sex Marketed in Ads Targeting an Underage Audience, FTC Study Says," *Wall Street Journal*, September 11, 2000, p. A16.
[12] Joe Flint and Suzanne Vranica, "NBC Axes Nike Ad for Olympics as Viewers Decry Violent Theme," *Wall Street Journal*, September 19, 2000, p. B8.
[13] See John D. Murray, "Impact of Televised Violence," www.ksu.edu/humec.

on the strength of lobbying from the media industry and civil rights groups. But some believed that efforts toward controlling violence in the media would be more successful if their backers emphasized the economic costs of violence.

> *Researchers found that television viewers were less likely to remember a commercial message if they saw it in the middle of a violence-ridden program. The study suggested that brutal action scenes made television viewers angry, interfering with their ability to take in a sales pitch. People who watched commercials during violent programming had a harder time recalling the name of the product advertised. Moreover, people who watched ads during violent programs remembered fewer details from the ads and had a harder time picking out the brands advertised later when shown a variety of similar products. The researchers concluded: Violence on television may be harmful to advertisers!*[14]

Whether it is violence or the familiar idea that "sex sells," challenges have been raised by society against using these strategies in the media. Marketers found that advertising a message to the global community was often a difficult and challenging task, as shown in this example.

> *Leo Burnett Worldwide, a global advertising firm, developed an advertisement for breast-cancer awareness in 2000. The ad showed an attractive woman in a sundress drawing stares from men on the sidewalk. The announcer said, "If only women paid as much attention to their breasts as men do." The company reported that viewers in Japan saw the ad as a humorous way to draw attention to an important health issue. The ad was a great success until it was shown in France. Despite the fact that sex was more widely discussed in France than Japan, the French people were offended by using humor to talk about a serious disease.*[15]

Violence and sex are just two of the many values that the media industry is accused of promoting to their viewers, and many believe that these themes could have a serious impact on what happens in society. The ethical and social responsibilities of the media industry to carefully monitor the instances of violence and sex and the impact that these themes may have in society are paramount.

The Fairness and Balance Issue

The **fairness and balance issue** is about how the media reports business activities. Since the 1970s, probusiness organizations have claimed that the coverage of business activities generally has been unfair to business. In addition, business leaders believe that the media does not provide viewers with enough information to make rational decisions about controversial issues, such as the transportation of toxic wastes or the need for product

[14] Sally Beatty, "Madison Avenue Should Rethink Television Violence, Study Finds," *Wall Street Journal*, December 1, 1998, p. B8.
[15] Sarah Ellison, "Sex-Themed Ads Often Don't Travel Well," *Wall Street Journal*, March 31, 2000, p. B7.

recalls. There are many reasons given for this tension. One reason for inadequate media business reports is that few reporters are well trained in financial and business matters, a reality that many media people acknowledge. Another reason sometimes given is that most journalists tend to be leaning toward the left in their social and political outlook, although some television shows featuring controversial topics ensure that both liberal and conservative viewpoints are presented.

From 1949 to 1987, the Federal Communications Commission (FCC) was entrusted with enforcing the **Fairness Doctrine.** It required television and radio broadcasters to cover both sides of important or controversial issues and to give the opportunity for contrasting viewpoints to be aired. The Fairness Doctrine gave the FCC authority to rule on the fairness of broadcasts. This law was repealed in 1987, but an FCC ruling in 2000 opened the door for the regulatory agency to revisit the necessity of such a law. The question of whether the media fairly portrays businesses and executives was the focus of a study undertaken by Pinnacle Worldwide.

> *Pinnacle Worldwide, an independent public relations firm headquartered in Minneapolis, reported differences in opinions between business and media executives. The firm discovered that business executives rated their ethical behavior as an 80 on a 100-point scale, while media leaders gave business executives an ethics rating of 30 points. Other sharp discrepancies were found in the study. For example, the study asked: To what degree do you believe that ethical issues always are part of the final decision-making process in multinational companies? Business executives gave the question an average of 80 points (with 100 points being "always"), while media leaders rated business executives at 30 points on this question. Respondents were also asked: Given more stringent securities laws, are business-people more candid and forthright than they used to be? Business executives gave this question an average of 60 points; media leaders rated business executives at 42 points.*

Pinnacle Worldwide advised businesses to seek out or generate opportunities to communicate their values and principles through the news media. "Too many businesses appear to be taking an ostrich position," said Jerry Klein, president of Pinnacle Worldwide. "By burying their heads in the sand, they leave the rest of their operations vulnerable to misunderstanding and misinformation. The new media plays a vital role in communicating information."[16]

The Free Speech Issue

The **free speech issue** is about how to find a balance between the media's constitutional right to free expression and business's desire to be fairly and accurately depicted in media presentations, as well as to present its views on controversial public issues. While free speech affects many groups and organizations in society, our discussion focuses on business.

The legal precedent of free speech in the United States can be seen as far back as the original Constitution. The First Amendment of the U.S. Constitution says, in part,

---

[16] "'Yes, We Are' . . . 'No, You're Not' Survey Shows Corporate Executives, Media Differ Markedly on Opinions of Ethical Behavior in Business," Pinnacle Worldwide news release, December 1998, www.pinnacleww.com/survey-ethics.

"Congress shall make no law . . . abridging the freedom of speech, or of the press." State governments also are prohibited, under the due process clause of the Fourteenth Amendment, from passing laws that impair free speech or interfere with a free press. Although these constitutional provisions are subject to continual interpretation and reinterpretation by government regulators, by the courts, and by general public opinion, their fundamental meaning does not change through time. Constitutional guarantees of free press mean that the privately owned, profit-seeking media are free to print, broadcast, and distribute messages to the general public without getting authorization from government officials.

Another aspect of free speech in the media involves the trustworthiness of what is said in the media by businesses or other organizations. While people in the United States have the right to speak freely, they are not allowed to speak lies or mislead the public. What is the truth? and Where does marketing hype cross the line becoming lying or false impression? are highly controversial questions. An example from the 2000 U.S. presidential campaign is shown in Exhibit 19-B.

Other instances of questionable marketing messages have been identified, further raising challenges to the conflict between free speech and honesty.

EXHIBIT 19-B

Did the Republican Party Use a Subliminal Ad in the 2000 Campaign?

Questions of fair play in advertising were raised after leaders of Al Gore's Democratic presidential campaign in 2000 claimed that a Republican National Party ad had flashed the word "rats" across the screen when showing the vice president's face. The Republicans developed the controversial 30-second ad as an attack on Vice President Gore's prescription drug position. They claimed that the brief appearance of the word was inadvertent, resulting from the use of a blown-up version of the word *bureaucrats*.

The ad fueled a new debate over the use of **subliminal advertisements,** an advertising ploy that directs a message to our subconscious rather than conscious mind. The word or figure is flashed so quickly across the screen that some people believe that the view can only register the message subliminally. The use of subliminal ads was first discussed in the 1950s, spurred by Vance Packard's book *The Hidden Persuaders*. Media experts claimed that no serious professional subscribes to the belief that subliminal ads influence viewers. "It simply does not exist and is not taken seriously," claimed one advertising executive.

Yet in 1974, the Federal Communications Commission thought the use of subliminal ads was serious enough to rule them "contrary to the public interest." Twenty years later a survey by the *Journal of Advertising Research* showed that 62 percent of the people believe advertisers were using subliminal ads.

Regarding the Republicans' political campaign ad in 2000, FCC chairman William Kennard said "the use of such ads violates FCC policy and [the] agency could launch a full investigation if a complaint was filed by the Democratic Party."

Source: Kathy Chen and Glenn Simpson, "GOP Commercial Resurrects Debate on Subliminal Ads," *Wall Street Journal,* September 3, 2000, p. B10.

U.S. aspirin makers came under pressure from the Food and Drug Administration to stop promoting aspirin as reducing the risk of a first heart attack. Their claims were based on a scientific study that said taking an aspirin every day had lowered the risk of heart attacks in middle-aged men. The FDA said that the study's findings were preliminary, were restricted to the test group, and could not be recommended for the general population. After meeting with FDA officials, the companies voluntarily stopped their initial advertising claims and ran ads that encouraged people to have an aspirin on hand to take in case they experienced apparent heart attack symptoms.

Advertisers have been accused of being insensitive in their marketing of adult-oriented products to minors, such as alcohol. Brown-Forman Corporation, maker of Jack Daniel's whiskey and Southern Comfort liquor, hired Internet ad company DoubleClick to place banner ads on websites in an effort to reach a broader consumer market. Websites such as Food Network and getmusic.com were selected. But the alcohol ad banners also ran on United Media's Comics.com site, the home page for the cartoon comic strips of Ziggy and Garfield. DoubleClick admitted its mistake but not until thousands of web surfers, many of them children, saw the ads. Another DoubleClick customer, Finlandia Vodka, encountered the same problem. Its ads ended up on the Comics.com site, which angered Finlandia executives, a company owned by the Finnish government. "We wouldn't be that stupid to advertise to kids," said a Finlandia spokesperson.[17]

Unfortunately not all ethically questionable advertisements of adult-oriented products are mistakes.

According to a report released by the Center for Media Education, alcohol marketers explicitly targeted underage consumers mostly through websites that featured entertaining music. At Absolutvodka.com, web surfers were greeted by a drum-beating rhythm. At Malibu-rum.com, visitors entered the "Malibu Sound Studio" to experiment with playing new sounds or entering an online music contest. The Budweiser.com website featured the familiar voices of the television lizards, Louis and Frank. According to the Center for Media Education, "Beer and liquor companies not only appeal to youth, but target and aggressively market to them." Less than half of the sites analyzed by the Center's researchers made attempts to block underage visitors, and the barriers the companies did create were easily circumvented.[18]

Controversy was created when designer Calvin Klein used sexual images of young people in his company's ads, as discussed in Exhibit 19-C.

Businesses have a constitutionally protected right to freely speak through the media, but they must be balance this right with a caution against harming others,

---

[17] Kathryn Kranhold, "To Dismay of All Involved, Liquor Ads Pop Up on Web Sites for Kids," *Wall Street Journal,* May 8, 2000, pp. B1, B4.

[18] Sally Beatty, "Alcohol Firms Boost Online Ads to Youth," *Wall Street Journal,* December 17, 1998, p. B10.

**EXHIBIT
19-C**

Calvin Klein's "Pornographic" Ads

During the summer of 1995, Calvin Klein, the clothing designer, unveiled a new advertising campaign for CK jeans. A series of print advertisements, bus posters, billboards, and TV spots featured adolescent-looking models in a variety of provocative poses, many with their underwear casually exposed. In one of the most notorious television spots, a young man was shown leaning against a dingy paneled wall, as an off-camera male voice talked to him. "You got a real nice look," the gravelly voice said. "How old are you? Are you strong? You think you could rip that shirt off you? That's a real nice body. You work out? I can tell."

The ad campaign generated a storm of protests. Commentators denounced the ads as just one step short of child pornography. The conservative American Family Association threatened a boycott of stores selling the jeans and called for a government investigation. Some magazines, including *Seventeen*, refused to carry the ads. At the end of August, after the campaign had run for only a few weeks, Klein withdrew the ads voluntarily. He refused to apologize, however, defending the ads as a tribute to the "spirit, independence, and inner worth of today's young people."

The brief ad campaign and flurry of negative publicity that followed had the combined effect of powerfully boosting sales of CK jeans to young people. In September, the editor of *Fashion Network Report* noted that the jeans were "flying out of the stores" and called Klein a "marketing genius" who had cleverly timed the controversy to coincide with the back-to-school buying period. In response to public protest, the Justice Department launched an investigation. Two months later, however, government regulators backed off after determining that the company had not used underage models or in any way violated child pornography laws.

In 1997, Calvin Klein changed course, introducing a new ad campaign for perfume showing a wholesome family relaxing at the beach. The company's ad agency described the spots as showing "the eternal love between parents and child." The very conservatism of the new campaign, ironically, prompted some to attack the company for "hypocrisy." Once again, Calvin Klein ads had generated their own publicity.

Sources: "Calvin Klein Finds Family Values," *Boston Globe,* February 28, 1997, p. C2; "Calvin Klein Ads Cleared," *Washington Post,* November 16, 1995, p. D7; and "Where Calvin Crossed the Line," *Time,* September 1, 1995, p. 64.

especially the powerless youth in our society. The three examples discussed above—using subliminal advertisements, placing alcohol ads on websites designed for children, and creating a controversial ad using adolescent-looking actors in provocative poses—sharply pose the question: Where does one draw the line regarding what is acceptable? Government regulators, media and business executives, and the general public will debate the answer to this difficult question for many years.

Special Issue: Government Regulation of Tobacco Advertising

The role of the government in regulating the media industry and businesses' use of the media to market their products and services has been discussed earlier in this chapter. The FTC's report on the increasing presence of violence on television and in films, the possible resurrection of the Fairness Doctrine by the FCC, and the FDA's monitoring of aspirin advertisements are all examples of government regulators' desire to protect the public from the media and business advertisements in the media.

Various stakeholder groups challenged the advertisement of tobacco products. Some felt that children were unfairly targeted as a vulnerable consumer group, citing the use of cartoon characters such as Joe Camel. Others believed that the health care costs for smokers incurred by society were unfair and escalating due to tobacco advertisements. The tobacco industry countered with the argument that the firms were marketing a legal product to adults and should not be restricted by laws or regulation. Most tobacco executives publicly agreed that selling to children was wrong and the use of advertisements targeting youth sales should be stopped.

In 1998, the National Association of Attorneys General (NAAG), a national organization of the 50 states' chief lawyers, and the tobacco industry's largest companies reached a settlement that resulted in the most significant restriction of an industry's use of the media to market products. The landmark agreement called for firms in the tobacco industry

- To prohibit all targeting of youth in their advertisements, promotions, and marketing of tobacco products.

- To ban all use of cartoons in their advertising, promoting, packaging, or labeling of tobacco products.

- To prohibit advertising tobacco brand names at all concerts, youth sporting events, or any athletic event between opposing teams in any football, basketball, baseball, soccer, or hockey league.

- To eliminate all outdoor advertisement and transit advertisement of tobacco products.

- To prohibit payments for the use, display, reference to, or use as a prop of any tobacco product in any motion picture, television show, theatrical production, or other live performance, live or recorded performance of music, commercial film, or video or video game.

- To ban the tobacco industry from marketing, distributing, offering, selling, or licensing of any apparel or other merchandise whose sole function is to advertise a tobacco product.

- To stop the distribution of free samples of tobacco products except in adult-only facilities.

- To halt gifts to underage persons based on the exchange of a tobacco product's proof of purchase.

- To prevent the use of a tobacco brand name on any nationally recognized or nationally established brand name of a nontobacco product.

- To require tobacco companies to affirm their commitment to comply with this agreement, to designate an executive-level manager to identify methods to reduce youth access to and the incidence of youth consumption of tobacco products, and to encourage their employees to become involved in efforts toward reducing youth consumption of tobacco products.[19]

The fallout from this agreement was felt across the media industry. Many media institutions suffered significant losses in revenue as tobacco companies were forced to pull their advertisements from vehicles that targeted a youth audience. Philip Morris, the nation's largest tobacco company, spent $214.8 million in magazines alone to advertise its tobacco products in 1999. More than one-third of Time's *Sports Illustrated* advertisement revenue came from Philip Morris. Yet Philip Morris, in compliance with the NAAG agreement, pulled its advertisements from 42 magazines that reported a teen readership of more than 15 percent.[20] Promoters of concerts and sporting events were required to find new sponsors. The impact was felt as far as the apparel industry, which counted on marketing products with a tobacco brand name or logo.

Government efforts against the tobacco industry can be found in many countries. For example, advertisements of tobacco products were controlled or banned in Japan, Poland, Hong Kong, and Nepal. The European Union required tobacco manufacturers to increase the size of the health warnings on cigarette packs, banned the use of terms such as *mild* and *light* since consumers believed that these cigarettes were less harmful, and created stricter limits on tar and nicotine content. EU officials cited an estimated 500,000 smoking-related deaths in the EU as motivation for their actions. However, in June 2000, a senior advisor to the EU's highest court recommended that the EU not go as far as the United States in banning all tobacco advertisement.[21]

Canada banned all print advertisements of tobacco products and had the world's biggest and bluntest warnings about the harms of cigarette smoking, such as "Smoking can kill you." The Canadian Health Ministry considered bolder warning labels, including one that showed a healthy and a diseased lung. Other proposals included a warning label with teeth rotting from mouth cancer or a gangrenous foot due to poor circulation attributed to smoking. The Canadian government was committed to increasing the shock value of cigarette warning labels.[22]

How Businesses Influence Their Public Image

With the growing power of the media to affect society, businesses must be more attentive to the various ways the media can influence their images. How a business is portrayed in the media, how it handles a crisis covered by the media, and how it trains its employees to interact with the media are all critical elements of the business–society relationship.

[19] Master Settlement Agreement, National Association of Attorneys General, www.naag.org/tobac.

[20] "Magazines Brace for Cigarette Ad Pullout," *Wall Street Journal,* June 7, 2000, p. B5.

[21] Thanassis Cambanis, "EU Backs Tough Cigarette Rules to Curb Smoking-Related Deaths," *Wall Street Journal,* June 30, 2000, p. 12; and Brandon Mitchener, "High Court Adviser Urges EU to Scrap Ban on Tobacco Ads and Sponsorship," *Wall Street Journal,* June 16, 2000, p. B8.

[22] Julian Beltrame, "Warning: These Cigarette Labels Could Really Gross You Out," *Wall Street Journal,* June 7, 1999, p. B1.

Public Relations Society of America

The **Public Relations Society of America** (PRSA) is a professional association of public relations officers. In its own words, the organization is committed to "the fundamental values of individual dignity and free exercise of human rights" and believes that "the freedom of speech, assembly, and the press are essential to the practice of public relations." In serving its clients' interests, the PRSA is dedicated to "the goals of better communication, understanding, and cooperation among diverse individuals, groups, and institutions of society."[23] To this end, the PRSA adopted a Member Code of Ethics in 2000, replacing previous standards and codes for the industry in place since 1950. The new code presented six professional core values for its members and the public relations profession. These core values were

- *Advocacy.* We serve the public interest by acting as responsible advocates for those we represent. We provide a voice in the marketplace . . . to aid informed public debate.

- *Honesty.* We adhere to the highest standards of accuracy and truth in advancing the interests of those we represent and in communicating with the public.

- *Expertise.* We acquire and responsibly use specialized knowledge and experience. We advance the profession through continued professional development, research, and education. We build mutual understanding, credibility, and relationships among a wide array of institutions and audiences.

- *Independence.* We provide objective counsel to those we represent. We are accountable for our actions.

- *Loyalty.* We are faithful to those we represent, while honoring our obligation to serve the public interest.

- *Fairness.* We deal fairly with clients, employers, competitors, peers, vendors, the media, and the general public. We respect all opinions and support the right of free expression.[24]

Public Relations, Public Affairs

The most fundamental media strategy for any organization is to design and manage an effective public relations and public affairs program. Chapter 2 in this book describes the major features of a socially responsive business, which include a strong public affairs function. A good public affairs program sends a constant stream of information from the company to stakeholders and keeps its doors open for dialogue with stakeholders whose lives are affected by company operations. Public affairs should be proactive, not reactive. Channels of communication with the media should be established on a continuing basis, not just after a problem has arisen. Once this step has been taken, a company can view the media as a positive force that can help the

---

[23] Public Relations Society of America website, www.prsawest.org.

[24] Excerpts from the PRSA code reprinted with permission from the Public Relations Society of America. For the full text of the Member Code of Ethics 2000, see www.prsawest.org/codeofethics.

company communicate with the public. Some companies have learned this lesson the hard way.

> *The Walt Disney Company experienced a media embarrassment when it reported that an image of a topless woman appeared in their 1999 re-release of an animated children's video,* The Rescuers. *The company recall of the 3.4 million copies of the video was voluntary, since Disney did not receive any complaints from the viewers of the video. The image appeared on just 2 of the 110,000 frames in the film—appearing for only one-fifteenth of a second, too fast to be seen without freezing these frames of the film. According to the company, the error was due to an apparent prank that had been embedded in the film's master negative since its original release in 1977. "We caught it too late," explained Disney video chief Michael O. Johnson. "We're not happy with the situation and we are doing everything we can to fix it."[25]*

A business's positive, prosocial actions can improve its media image, as shown in the following example.

> *Venezuelan media and communications companies responded to the need for emergency efforts in their country, offering them an opportunity for positive media coverage. Just before Christmas in 1999, large portions of the country were ravaged by floods and landslides, which resulted in the deaths of as many as 25,000 people and caused the evacuation of more than 100,000 residents. The nation's two leading newspapers collected, organized, and distributed information about lost relatives, emergency aid, and homeless shelters online. At one point, the Venezuelan Civil Defense ministry had the names of 1,400 flood refugees, while the newspapers had several thousand names and status reports on these people located on the newspaper's websites.[26]*

Crisis Management

Media relations are a vital part of **crisis management.** Crisis management is the process companies use to respond to unexpected and high consequential shocks, such as accidents, disasters, catastrophes, and injuries. A specially chosen crisis management task force devotes full time to coping with the problem and trying to find solutions. In many companies, a media-contact person is a key member of this group, and contingency plans are made beforehand on how media relations are to be handled during any emergency period. In highly visible emergencies, an outside public relations firm may be called in to develop an ongoing plan for dealing with the media and assuring that the company's point of view is included in media presentations. The uniqueness of the crisis is the challenge for a crisis management team. "It is true that every corporate crisis is unique; that is to say, the underlying circumstances are unique, the individuals who are involved

---

[25] Bruce Orwall, "Disney Recalls 'The Rescuers' Video Containing Image of a Topless Woman," *Wall Street Journal,* January 11, 1999, p. A27.

[26] Thomas T. Vogel, Jr., "Venezuelan Telecoms and Media Firms Assume Lead Role in Disaster Efforts," *Wall Street Journal,* December 21, 1999, p. A16.

are unique to that company or to that organization, the facts, the timing, and anything else going on in the marketplace is unique. Therefore, every situation has to be managed on its own terms."[27]

What is a crisis? Although every crisis is unique, there are certain characteristics that emerge time and again to define a crisis:

- *Surprise.* The organization is not ready for the event, it happens without warning, and managers are left trying to react to events beyond their control.

- *Lack of information.* Even though managers often operate in an information-rich environment, when a crisis strikes they may be forced to act quickly without full and complete information.

- *Escalating pace of events.* Once a crisis begins, it often sets in motion a chain of events that increases in number and complexity for the company.

- *Intense scrutiny.* During a crisis, every single decision made by executives is closely scrutinized and subject to immediate assessment by the media, government officials, and many other external stakeholders. Crisis management is management in a fishbowl. Feedback comes quickly, whether it is praise, criticism, or condemnation.

Organizations can learn from their handling of crises over time. One researcher, Debra A. Kernisky, reported that Dow Chemical Company changed its crisis management approach as the company responded to the issues related to Agent Orange, a chemical used by the U.S. military during the Vietnam War that allegedly exposed countless U.S. soldiers to serious adverse health problems.

> In the early 1980s, during the height of criticism from the media and social groups, Dow Chemical's press releases had an antagonistic tone and were filled with technological language. By the late 1980s, the tone of the bulletins had softened and focused broadly on technological and health issues. Kernisky found "Dow moved beyond simple 'public relations' activities, and thrust the company more proactively into the range of voices responding to significant issues of importance within society."[28]

Many experts believe that James E. Burke wrote the book on crisis management when, as chairman of Johnson & Johnson, he dealt with the Tylenol crisis. During this crisis, eight people died and many were taken ill due to what was believed to be a nonproduction-related tampering of Tylenol capsules. Burke's strategy was: Be visible, be sympathetic, and be responsive.

> In 2000, Coca-Cola's management team faced a crisis. The crisis, described at the beginning of this chapter, resulted in hundreds of children in Europe becoming nauseated and dizzy after drinking a Coke product. Belgium, Luxembourg, France, Spain, and the Netherlands all banned Coke products for a time. These circumstances created a serious situation for Coca-Cola. Their response to this crisis and negative media coverage seemed to follow the

---

[27] Ray O'Rourke, "Managing in Times of Crisis," *Corporate Reputation Review* 1 (1997), pp. 120–25.
[28] Debra A. Kernisky, "Proactive Crisis Management and Ethical Discourse: Dow Chemical's Issues Management Bulletins 1979–1990," *Journal of Business Ethics* 16 (1997), pp. 843–53.

Figure 19-1

Crisis management model.

Source: Adapted from Ian I. Mitroff, Paul Shrivastava, and Firdaus E. Udwadia, "Effective Crisis Management," *Academy of Management Executive* 1, no. 3 (1987), ex. 1, p. 284.

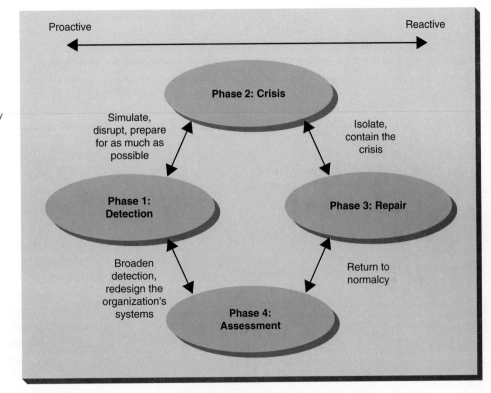

"Burke strategy" as a responsive company. Coca-Cola's CEO flew to Belgium to investigate the situation and published an apology in Belgian newspapers. Coca-Cola set up a special consumer hotline to field concerns over the safety of Coke products, and the company offered to pay all medical bills associated with the illnesses caused by the contaminated Coke products.[29]

Crisis management around the world is a concern for all executives. A recent report in *Asian Business* found that corporate communications in Asia, particularly related to crisis management, had matured over the past 20 years. Senior executives and their financial and legal advisers were more inclined to involve corporate communications consultants and public relations officers in the early stages of a crisis.[30]

So what should a manager do when confronted with a crisis? Numerous models and guidelines have been developed. An adaptation of one such model developed by three crisis management scholars is shown in Figure 19-1. This model describes four phases of effective crisis management: detection, crisis, repair, and assessment. *Detection* emphasizes attention to the organization's early warning systems—monitoring techniques, environmental scanning, and control systems—designed to inform management when a crisis is more likely to occur. Next is the *crisis* phase. At this phase the crisis has occurred and management is challenged to identify the nature and degree of the

[29] "Coke's Hard Lesson in Crisis Management," *Business Week,* July 5, 1999, p. 102.
[30] Bob Fienberg, "Communicating in a Crisis," *Asian Business,* May 1999, pp. 70–71.

crisis. Then comes the *repair* phase, where emergency plans are implemented and public relations responses are given. Finally in the *assessment* phase, the organization must ask itself, What have we learned from this experience and what can be changed to prevent or minimize the occurrence of a similar crisis in the future?

As indicated in the crisis management model, organizations are encouraged to be proactive in the detection phase, yet are generally reactive in the repair phase since the crisis is upon the organization and the crisis management team must respond. Implicit in the model is the following guideline: The more proactive an organization is in preparing for a crisis, the better it will be in its response when the crisis occurs.

A company that many feel handled a crisis well, Odwalla, is profiled in a case at the end of this book. A critique of two different crisis management strategies is presented at the end of this chapter in the discussion case.

Media Training of Employees

Another media strategy businesses can follow is to give **media training** to executives and employees who are likely to have contact with the media. Media training is necessary because communicating with the media is not the same as talking with friends or coworkers.

As a company representative, an employee is normally assumed to be speaking for the company or is expected to have special knowledge of company activities. Under these circumstances, the words one speaks take on a special, official meaning. In addition, news reporters sometimes challenge an executive, asking penetrating or potentially embarrassing questions and expecting instant answers. Even in more deliberate news interviews, the time available for responding to questions is limited to a few seconds. Moreover, facial expressions, the tone of one's voice, and body language can convey both positive and negative impressions.

Many large businesses routinely send a broad range of their employees to specific courses to improve their media skills. Media communication experts generally give their clients the following advice.

- Resist the temptation to see reporters and journalists as the enemy. Business media representatives should build bridges with the media. Employees should resist avoiding the media and not withdraw into a shell of silence, which tends to generate suspicion that the company has something to hide.

- Employees should be instructed to keep the long-term reputation of the company in mind.

- Being open and honest is a successful media strategy. Honesty is the best policy, especially since media personnel will investigate to confirm all information a business provides and the truth will be uncovered.

- Businesses should make communications a priority and the training of the company spokesperson a critical and ongoing program.[31]

---

[31] These guidelines and other suggestions are discussed in Mike Haggerty and Wallace Rasmussen, *The Headlines vs. the Bottom Line: Mutual Distrust between Business and the News Media* (Arlington, VA: The Freedom Forum First Amendment Center, 1994), pp. 89–92.

The importance of developing a solid media relations program cannot be emphasized enough, as businesses that have experienced media crises can attest to. The problem is that the need for a media response to a crisis cannot be anticipated, so a business must be always ready and trained for any possible problem. This is a daunting task for businesses and their managers; but it is a critical challenge as businesses seek to deal with their ethical and social responsibilities to the public.

Summary Points of This Chapter

- The influence of the media industry has significantly increased through the merger of old media industries—radio, television, books, and newspapers—with new media industries—the Internet, cable, and wireless communication.
- The major issues that provide focus for the media's ethical and social responsibilities are the image issue, the values issue, the fairness and balance issue, and the free speech issue.
- Many governments, especially the United States, have regulated the tobacco industry's use of print, radio, and television ads. The U.S. government also has banned distribution of merchandise with a tobacco company's logo, advertisement at concerts or sporting events, and other media activity.
- There are many ways businesses can improve their media image. Effective media strategies include a public relations program, crisis management, and media training for key employees. Crisis management guidelines include defining the problem, setting goals, managing information, planning for the worst case, and not giving up.

Key Terms and Concepts Used in This Chapter

- Media
- Image issue
- Values issue
- Fairness and balance issue
- Fairness Doctrine

- Free speech issue
- Subliminal advertisements
- Public Relations Society of America
- Crisis management
- Media training

Internet Resources

- www.mediascope.org   Mediascope
- www.cfc-efc.ca   Child & Family Canada
- www.prsawest.org   Public Relations Society of America
- www.prwatch.org   Center for Media and Democracy
- www.ftc.gov/bcp/menu-ads   U.S. Federal Trade Commission,
                                 Consumer Protection/Advertising

Discussion Case: *Same Crisis, Two Different Responses—Bridgestone/Firestone and Ford*

In August 2000, Bridgestone/Firestone, the nation's second-largest tire manufacturer, announced a recall of 6.5 million ATX, ATXII, and Wilderness AT tires mainly used on Ford Explorer sport-utility vehicles. The recall was a result of 118 U.S. deaths allegedly due to tire tread separation leading to accidents, as well as more than 40 deaths abroad. (The reported number of deaths allegedly due to faulty Firestone tires rose to 172 by February 2001.) Retail sales of Firestone-brand tires plunged 40 percent in the United States two months after the recall. When it is all over Bridgestone/Firestone estimated that the recall would cost the company $450 million. The cause of the problem that led to the fatalities was still not known for sure months after the recall, although studies were underway investigating the weight of the Ford Explorer, Ford Motor Company's tire inflation advice, Firestone's tire assembly procedures and materials, and Firestone's quality control measures.

While facing a similar management crisis, the two companies involved, Bridgestone/Firestone and the Ford Motor Company, adopted very different media responses.

Bridgestone/Firestone announced the tire recall on August 9 as the crisis hit full stride. Consumers rushed to the tire dealerships for tire replacements. Unfortunately, the dealerships did not have sufficient stock to handle the massive demand, and many consumers were confused whether they needed to have their tires replaced. Firestone reacted with a full-page advertisement in business newspapers on August 16 providing a detailed, three-step procedure to determine if the consumer's vehicle had the tires that were being recalled and giving an 800-number to call to locate the nearest Firestone Tire and Service Center.

Ten days after the recall announcement, John Lampe, president of Bridgestone/Firestone Tire Sales, published an open letter to Firestone recall customers confirming that the recall was taking place, informing them that the replacements were free of charge, and seeking the "understanding, cooperation, and loyalty" of its customers. Lampe's letter emphasized that his company was "committed to your safety." Five days after Lampe's letter, similar ads featuring Masatoshi Ono, chief executive of Bridgestone/Firestone, appeared in major business newspapers. During this period, the tire company hired an outside public relations firm, Ketchum, to improve its tarnished image and in 2001 launched a major advertising campaign to win back sales. Firestone offered prospective customers a "30-day test drive" of Firestone replacement tires with an unconditional money-back guarantee.

The media strategy adopted by Bridgestone/Firestone was tempered by the Japanese culture, since the Japanese-based Bridgestone Corporation owned the company. Bridgestone's president and CEO Yoichiro Kaizaki historically had been silent when it came to public relations matters. For example, a few years earlier, after a disgruntled employee committed suicide after complaining of his demotion to Kaizaki, the executive had remained silent for four months and then had spoken out defiantly against the employee. Similarly, Kaizaki maintained a stoic silence during the recall until a month later. Finally, on September 11, Kaizaki spoke at a press conference and expressed regret over the controversy but deflected all attempts by Ford to place the blame on his firm. This defensive tone also was seen in a September 20 letter from

Masatoshi Ono to Ford Motor. The letter stated: "Immediately prior to the recall, we had asked you to test the Explorer to determine whether an inflation pressure higher than 26 psi would be acceptable for the Explorer. . . . [W]e urge you to inform all Explorer owners that the proper inflation pressure . . . on the Explorer is 30 psi . . . [This] provides the consumer with an additional four pounds of safety margin." (On October 10, Lampe replaced Ono as chief executive of Bridgestone/Firestone in the United States, and Yoichiro Kaizaki resigned as Bridgestone Japan's president and CEO on January 21, 2001.)

The slowness in responding to public outcry and the resistance to accepting any blame for the tragedy was characteristic of the Bridgestone/Firestone media strategy. For example, in mid-October when pressures mounted again from consumer activist groups to learn more about the tire recall and safety issue, the firm reacted four days later by publicizing "progress reports" through full-page ads in business newspapers. These reports emphasized how Firestone was meeting the proposed tire recall timetable and defended the firm's tires and safety record. In December 2000, Firestone announced that it was in the final stages of the recall, an accomplishment that a government regulatory agency described as "a phenomenal effort," according to Firestone's press release.

Ford Motor Company was intimately involved in the product recall and safety issue as well. Ford had selected the Firestone tires for its vehicles; the tires were the only major equipment used by the automobile manufacturer that had their own warranty. The media strategy employed by Ford was more proactive and extensive than that deployed by Firestone during this crisis.

Days before Firestone's first full-page ads appeared in business newspapers, Ford ran its own full-page ads with the headline "The Firestone tire recall: Does it affect your Ford Motor Company vehicle?" By August 14, Ford had stepped up the recall of Firestone tires, exceeding Firestone's efforts, by directing Ford dealerships to replace Firestone tires. Ford also shut down several of its assembly lines to immediately divert more tires to its dealerships for tire replacement.

Ford's public relations campaign hit full stride by the end of August. In contrast to the silence and defensive tone of the Japanese-owned Bridgestone, Ford took a more personal and direct approach. Ford's chairman William Clay Ford, Jr., announced, "Anything that affects the reputation of the Ford Motor Company is of vital interest to me." During the months following the announced recall, Ford's CEO Jacques Nasser became a familiar face to many Americans by appearing in television commercials during prime viewing time—a Monday night National Football League preseason game, Fox network's *Ally McBeal,* and the "Battle at Bighorn" golf match between Tiger Woods and Sergio Garcia. In these ads, Nasser pledged Ford's commitment to its customers by informing them that more than 1 million tires had been replaced and giving his "personal guarantee that no one at Ford will rest until every recalled tire is replaced." Ford followed up with regularly appearing full-page ads in business newspapers almost every week during September and October.

Sources: Ford Motor advertisement, *Wall Street Journal,* August 11, 2000, p. B5; Robert L. Simison, "Ford Steps Up Recall without Firestone," *Wall Street Journal,* August 14, 2000, pp. A3, A6; Firestone advertisement, *Wall Street Journal,* August 16, 2000, p. B7; Firestone's "Open Letter," *Wall Street Journal,* August 21, 2000, p. A17; Anne Marie Chaker, "Corporate Crisis Ads Draw Chilly Reviews," *Wall Street Journal,*

August 31, 2000, p. B2; Jeffrey Ball and Joseph B. White, "Ford's Chairman Speaks Out about Firestone Crisis," *Wall Street Journal,* September 15, 2000, pp. B1, B4; "Firestone Breaks with Ford over Tire Pressure," *Wall Street Journal,* September 22, 2000, pp. A3, A10; "Sales of Firestone-Brand Tires Plummet," *Wall Street Journal,* November 13, 2000, pp. A3, A10; and Phred Dvorak and Michael Williams, "Embattled CEO of Japan's Bridgestone Resigns," *Wall Street Journal,* January 21, 2001, p. A6.

Discussion Questions

1. Using the crisis management model, Figure 19-1, trace the facts from this case through the four phases in the model and assess the firm's crisis management actions at each phase.

2. As a consumer, do you prefer Bridgestone/Firestone's or Ford's media strategy? Why? What elements of the media strategy do you find most important or preferred?

3. Does the fact that a Japanese company, Bridgestone, owns Firestone justify the type of media strategy employed by that firm? Should the Japanese company have been more responsive to the American public? If so, how?

4. Was the media fair in its coverage of this issue? Was it accurate? Timely? Balanced?

20

Global Social Issues
for a New Century

The desire for economic growth and profitability is leading many companies to do business in countries other than their home nation. Whether a company buys resources, manufactures products, or sells goods and services in foreign markets, doing business across borders inevitably draws a company into a web of global social, economic, and political issues. Some issues are specific to the company, while others involve the entire global business system. Understanding what these issues are, why they exist, and how to manage them is vital to managers and companies. This chapter addresses some of the emerging social issues arising in the global economy of the twenty-first century.

This chapter focuses on these key questions and objectives:

- Why do businesses decide to operate in international locations, and what goals and objectives do they have when pursuing an international business strategy?

- What social issues challenge a company's international supply and operations strategies?

- What social issues challenge a company's international marketing strategies?

- How do companies manage social and political issues involving conflicts between two or more countries in which they do business?

- What global corporate citizenship strategies do companies follow in the countries where they operate? What makes a global corporate citizenship strategy different than a domestic corporate citizenship strategy?

e live in a world that seems increasingly small, more connected, and highly inter-dependent. It is a world in which business strategy is often entwined with public policy and ethical issues, as these examples illustrate.

- The newspaper headline carried a clear, but chilling, business message: "Citing European Banana Quotas, Chiquita Says Bankruptcy Looms." Chiquita Brands International, the world's largest producer of bananas, and a household name in the United States, announced that it was unable to pay its debts and was being forced to file for bankruptcy protection. The underlying cause, according to the company, is the U.S. government's inability to force the European Union to trade freely and fairly. Chiquita contends that European quotas on bananas grown in Latin America, as Chiquita's are, have cost the company more than $200 million a year since 1992 and pushed it to the edge of ruin. Chiquita has been in operation for more than 130 years.[1]

- De Beers, the South African diamond mining giant that has made its name an "international emblem of elegance and extravagance," announced that it was joining forces with LVMH-Moet Hennessy Louis Vuiton, the French luxury retailer that has harnessed the brand-name power of some of the world's finest goods. The two companies agreed to create a new company that would open stores in the world's most fashionable cities to sell diamond jewelry branded with the De Beers name. In so doing, De Beers is entering the lucrative retail portion of the global market for diamonds that is estimated to have grown to more than $50 billion, in large measure because of De Beers's worldwide advertising themes (e.g., "A diamond is forever"). De Beers has traditionally received all of its revenue from selling diamonds to dealers and retailers, not to retail customers. The venture with LVMH would enable De Beers to capture some of the profits from retail diamond sales. De Beers's strategy may have been influenced by two factors: Its control over diamond markets has weak-ened as nations such as Canada, Russia, and Australia began competing for a slice of the market, and various organizations have highlighted the role that diamonds (and, implicitly, De Beers) play in financing conflict and violence in Africa.[2]

- Motorola, one of the world's largest manufacturers and sellers of cell phones, announced that it was closing its U.S. cell phone manufacturing facility (in Harvard, Illinois), thereby laying off 2,500 employees. The closing would com-plete the company's move to shift all of its cell phone production to facilities outside the United States, including China, Brazil, and Scotland. This news came days after the company published financial results for 2000 that showed it had lost global market share and profitability on its cell phone business. By lowering labor costs and shifting its manufacturing outside the United States, Motorola

---

[1] See Anthony DePalma, "Citing European Banana Quotas, Chiquita Says Bankruptcy Looms," *New York Times,* January 17, 2001, pp. A1, C15.
[2] Henri E. Cauvin, "De Beers and LVMH Linking Up in Retail Venture," *New York Times,* January 17, 2001, p. W1.

said it would become more competitive and profitable. However, financial analysts were unsure whether Motorola's plan would succeed because the global economy was slowing down in 2001. The company issued a statement acknowledging that the outlook for its business would largely be determined by tighter financing conditions and regulatory decisions, like lower taxes and tariffs, worldwide. The company's chief executive officer, Christopher B. Galvin, said: "We are still in the early phase of this change in [the] economic cycle. Therefore, its pace and direction are not firmly predictable. Motorola has managed successfully through economic cycles in every decade since its founding in 1928."[3]

What do Chiquita Brands, De Beers, and Motorola have in common? What opportunities and threats do their managers see in the global business environment? How should they respond to these issues? Who are their global stakeholders, and how are these stakeholders affected—positively and negatively—by the companies' actions? These questions suggest a few of the ways that corporate business strategies are tied to social issues in the global economy of the twenty-first century. In this chapter, we examine the new and emerging relationships between global business and global social issues. As companies grow, they are likely to carry on business activities across national borders. But each move into a new country introduces the firm into a new social and political environment that requires managers who understand local culture, politics, and the relationship between business and society.

Global Commerce Today

Global commerce has taken place for hundreds of years, dating back in some form to the colonial era (1492 to the early 1900s). But during the last 50 years, since the end of World War II, global commerce has transformed the world's economy. **Globalization,** or the process of integrating the world through commerce, technology, culture, and politics, has been a powerful influence on business for many years. Powerful trends have accelerated the globalization process in recent times.

Dominant Trends

International trade—exports and imports—and communications technology have powered the globalization process in the past decade, with governments, businesses, and international institutions such as the World Bank and International Monetary Fund (IMF) all playing important roles in creating the framework of ideas and policies that support globalization. Many factors have contributed to this process and are discussed in other chapters of this book. Shifts in government policy, for example, have opened markets to international goods and services from countries around the world (see Chapter 1). As discussed in Chapter 7, when countries resist free trade, as the European Union (EU) members have done in their decision to control the import of bananas, serious economic harm can be done to companies that compete against rivals in global markets. The EU decision to impose tariffs on bananas occurred in 1992, when it decided to favor imports

---

[3] Simon Romero, "Motorola Profit Fell in Fourth Quarter," *New York Times,* January 11, 2001, p. C6.

from Europe's banana-growing former colonies in Africa and the Caribbean. This cut deeply into the market share controlled by Chiquita and other companies that grow bananas in Central and South America. Despite the protests of Chiquita and other importers of bananas from Central and South America, and the political efforts of the U.S. government to negotiate a more level playing field, the EU persisted in its banana tariff policy. The cumulative effect on Chiquita Brands was the loss of nearly $2 billion of revenue over the course of the decade.

Another powerful trend has been the movement of capital and jobs to those countries and locations where companies can produce the best return on their investment and economic efficiencies produced. For Motorola, the decision to close its last U.S. cell phone manufacturing facility was the end of a long process of shifting production to more cost-effective locations, such as China. The international financial system is the powerful fuel for these processes. Experts estimate that one to three trillion dollars change hands in the international currency market every day. These transactions take many forms, but they are all directed toward one goal: putting money in places (countries, industries, companies) where it has a good chance to earn a return on investment for its owner. As long as investment funds flow freely (most is done electronically), even slight changes in the business environment of a country can quickly attract, or drive away, international investors.

Motorola's experience in China illustrates how the process works. The company started manufacturing in China during the late 1980s, and throughout the 1990s it was the single largest U.S. investor in China. In 1997, while celebrating the tenth anniversary of the company's partnership with the government and local businesses, Motorola's chief executive referred to China as the company's "second home." Today, many companies have "second homes" in Asia, Europe, and Latin America. While some areas have not yet absorbed foreign business operations on the scale of China, there are many reasons to believe economic development will eventually reach these countries. Favorable economic and regulatory policies, and the presence of workforce populations that are educated and trained to work in modern facilities (see Chapter 17), are good predictors of countries where future growth will occur. The development of major production and research and development facilities in countries around the world has been a feature of global businesses for many years, and the trend seems likely to accelerate in the next decade.

Scope and Scale

According to United Nations estimates, there are more than 37,000 multinational companies operating in the modern global economy. Many estimates suggest there are more than 50,000 multinational companies, and a few believe that there may actually be close to 100,000 companies doing business across international borders. A precise number is probably impossible to define, in part because there is no common method for counting subsidiaries, joint ventures, or those companies that use the Internet to easily conduct some aspects of commerce across borders. It seems clear, however, that global business transactions now account for a significant percentage of all global economic activity.

Global Business Models

There are many ways for firms to enter and compete in the global marketplace. Many companies build a successful business in their home country, then export their products or services to buyers in another country. In other words, they develop international or **global market channels** for their products. Chiquita bananas are easily found in many countries because the company has developed market channels over the course of its 100-year history. Other firms begin in their home country but realize that they can make more money by using **global locations** for some part of their operations. This decision leads to establishing plants or other operations in the foreign country. Many drug companies, for example, have established manufacturing facilities in Ireland because of favorable tax treatment by the government and an educated workforce.

A third strategy involves purchasing components or other supplies from sellers in other countries. In other words, they develop international or **global supply chains.** Companies in the clothing and apparel business, such as Nike, Reebok, Patagonia, or Timberland, have extensive systems of suppliers outside the United States and have invested heavily in responding to labor and human rights issues. Today, many companies have all three elements of global business—market channels, foreign locations, and international supply chains. Moreover, even small companies can launch their businesses into the global market from the start, purchasing supplies or selling products to international partners and clients from the outset. The Internet makes such new global business models possible (see Chapters 12 and 13).

Whether the underlying business model involves an international location, market channel, or supply chain, two factors will affect the number of social issues the firm must manage and how they must do so. One factor is the competitive pressure to continuously improve products, services, and efficiency. *Speed-to-market* is a synonym for an unrelenting pace of change that creates expectations among customers, investors, and employees that new products—with improved features and better performance—will be brought into the market as fast as possible. For many years, new automobiles were announced at the beginning of a "model year." Today, that idea has given way in many industries—especially consumer products such as cell phones—to the notion of continuous brand improvement. One result is that only the newest products, not yet imitated or matched by competitors, can command a premium price in the market. As soon as a competitor can match the product's features, price competition will take place and erode the profitability of the original product. As Motorola learned in its cell phone business, even a leading company's market share can quickly be lost under such competitive conditions. (In 1997, Motorola was the world's leading manufacturer of cell phones with a 30 percent share of market; by 2000, it had fallen well behind Nokia, and had only 13 percent market share. Nokia reportedly held a 33 percent share at the end of 2000.)

The second factor affecting all global businesses is that communication crosses national borders at cyberspeed. This means that the company must assume that its actions will be visible to competitors, suppliers, government officials, and nongovernmental organizations, or NGOs (see below). The company must assume it is operating in a world of openness, or *transparency* (defined in Chapter 8). This may be less important to small

Figure 20-1

Globalization: pros
and cons.

Sources: Based on
arguments in Thomas L.
Friedman, *The Lexus
and the Olive Tree* (New
York: Anchor Books,
2000); David Korten,
*When Corporations
Ruled the World* (San
Francisco: Berrett-
Kohler, 1998); and
Business Week, special
issue on globalization,
April 24, 2000.

Pros	**Cons**
■ Productivity grows more quickly when countries produce goods and services in which they have a comparative advantage; raises per capita GDP and standard of living.	■ Jobs in the domestic economy are lost as imports replace homemade goods and services.
■ Global competition creates price competition and minimizes inflation.	■ Companies operate in fear of foreign competition and keep wages as low as possible.
■ An open economy spurs innovation and improves the flow of new ideas.	■ Employers force employees to take wage cuts and require them to share health care costs.
■ Export jobs often pay better than other jobs.	■ Employers threaten to close local operations and move jobs out of the country.
■ Unfettered capital flows give the country access to foreign investment funds; this helps to keep interest rates low.	

companies, whose actions draw very little public attention. But for large companies, such as De Beers, Chiquita, or Motorola, size means that the world is watching.

Global Social Issues

Pros and Cons of Globalization

A force that has changed the world in the ways that globalization has worked in recent time is not without problems and negative consequences. In this section, we discuss some of the major factors and issues involved in this important debate. As shown in Figure 20-1, there are nearly as many cons as pros associated with globalization. But it is not just a matter of numbers: There are major differences of opinion as to whether globalization is a good thing for the world's population, environment, and social order. As Figure 20-1 suggests, pain is always associated with the change that globalization produces. People do lose jobs, companies do fail, and some stakeholders are certain to bear costs of change while some others benefit. This pain fuels the debate. Thomas Friedman, a reporter for the *New York Times* and author of the best-selling book *The Lexus and the Olive Tree,* describes globalization in these terms:

> [G]lobalization is not simply a trend or a fad but is, rather, an interna-
> tional system. It is the system that has now replaced the old Cold War
> system, and, like that Cold War system, globalization has its own rules and
> logic that today directly or indirectly influence the politics, environment,
> geopolitics and economics of virtually every country in the world.[4]

---

[4] Thomas L. Friedman, *The Lexus and the Olive Tree* (New York: Anchor Books, 2000), p. ix.

The activities of international lending institutions such as the World Bank and International Monetary Fund have promoted global economic thinking among political leaders around the world. Both of these organizations use funds provided by wealthy nations such as the United States, Japan, Germany, and others to assist countries that are in dire economic straits. The World Bank makes grants and loans to build roads, dams, airports, and other infrastructure projects that enable a nation to develop its resources and become able to participate in international commerce. The IMF makes loans to the national governments of countries that are suffering severe economic trouble. IMF loans require that the borrowing government institutes a plan that forces its leaders to manage the nation's economy in a fiscally sound manner. IMF loan agreements are often called "bitter medicine" because they require political leaders to impose hardship on their country's citizens.[5]

Nongovernmental Organizations

Globalization has also spurred the creation and growth of a large number of **nongovernmental organizations (NGOs)** concerned with such issues as environmental risk, labor practices, worker rights, community development, and human rights. According to the Worldwatch Institute, a research center that tracks global environmental issues, the number of NGOs has soared in recent years. In 1909, there were approximately 176 international NGOs (groups with offices and constituencies in several nations); in 1996, according to the *Yearbook of International Organizations,* there were more than 20,000 NGOs. National NGO groups have also grown in number and activity: In 1960, the average country had 122 NGOs; by 1988, that number had grown to 485. In the United States, the number of NGOs is estimated to be more than 2 million, 70 percent of which are less than 30 years old. A similar pattern exists in Europe, where half of all NGOs were founded in the last decade.[6]

Experts attribute the growth of NGOs to several factors, including the new architecture of global economic and political relationships. As the Cold War has ended, with democratic governments replacing dictatorships, an openness has occurred in many societies. More people, with more views, are free to express their happiness or anger with government, business, or one another. Forming around specific issues and broad concerns (environment, human rights), NGOs have become voices that must be considered in the public policy debates that occur. Jessica Matthews, president of the Carnegie Endowment for International Peace, explains the rise and power of NGOs in these terms:

> *The most powerful engine of change in the . . . rise of nonstate actors is the computer and telecommunications revolution. . . . In every sphere of activity, instantaneous access to information and the ability to put it to use multiplies the number of players who matter and reduces the number who command great authority.*[7]

---

[5] "Does Anybody Love the IMF or World Bank?" *Business Week,* April 24, 2000, pp. 46–48.

[6] Curtis Runyan, "Action on the Front Lines," *World-Watch,* November–December 1999, pp. 12–22. Statistics are cited on page 14.

[7] Quoted in Runyan, "Action on the Front Lines," p. 15. Matthews's quotation is taken from her 1997 article in *Foreign Affairs.*

For businesses and managers, it is clear that the opportunities that globalization provides will come at a cost. That cost will take the form of a more open, active engagement with stakeholders to define acceptable practices and to create a common interest. It will also require a deeper understanding of why social issues are so directly connected to the process of globalization.

Cultural Distance

When a company crosses borders to do business, it is crossing not only geographic boundaries but cultural, political, and social boundaries as well. Managers must recognize and understand that each culture has its values, beliefs, and symbols. Of course, language differences are often the most obvious indicator of these differences—the ability or inability to communicate freely, with common understanding, poses one of the greatest barriers to the genuine understanding of another culture. The difference between societies is referred to as **cultural distance.**

As shown in Chapter 1, and throughout this book, even businesses operating in one community or one nation cannot function successfully without taking into account a wide variety of stakeholder needs and interests. When companies do business in several countries, the number of stakeholders to be considered in decision making increases dramatically. And companies such as Coca-Cola, McDonald's, and Microsoft, which operate in nearly all of the 200 sovereign nations that exist today, have had no choice but to address this great diversity in building their organizations.

Historically, companies that operated internationally often had an **ethnocentric perspective.** This perspective views the home nation as the major source of the company's capital, revenue, and human resources. The home country's laws are viewed as dominant, and the company flies the flag of its home nation. Today's businesses have discovered that they must consider the world, not just one nation, as their home. Companies that have such a **geocentric perspective** adapt their policies and practices to different cultures and environments while maintaining their worldwide identity and business mission. Examples of geocentric firms include well-known companies such as Shell, ExxonMobil, and BP-Amoco in the petroleum industry; Nestlé, Procter and Gamble, and Unilever in food products; General Motors, DaimlerChrysler, Toyota, and Ford in automobiles; and Novartis, Johnson & Johnson, Merck, Pfizer, Glaxo, and SmithKlineBeecham in the pharmaceutical and health care products industry.

Companies such as IBM, General Electric, and Shell have long histories of bringing their managers from around the world to meetings and workshops for the purpose of expanding everyone's understanding of the world in which their company operates. At Dow Chemical, technical specialists from plants around the world are connected by information technology and physically meet several times each year to discuss advances in science and technology. European firms, including Nestlé (Switzerland), ABB (Asea Brown, Boveri, a Swedish-Swiss firm), and Unilever (United Kingdom–Netherlands) have led the way toward internationally diverse corporate board membership.

Small companies also develop a geocentric perspective when they do business across borders and in different cultures. Managers throughout the southwestern United States, for example, speak Spanish, understand Mexican culture, and engage in cross-border commerce. Citizens of Maine, New York, Michigan, and Washington State know the importance of trade with Canadians and are likely to have a keen sense of such issues as Quebec's movement for independence from Canada. It is not the size of the business that accounts for a company's geocentric outlook. Geographic location and awareness of the social and cultural features of the firm's stakeholders reinforce the importance of an open approach to cultural differences. To be a global company in the modern economy is to build a geocentric perspective into every aspect of the business organization.

Business operates in a world of diversity (see discussion in Chapter 18). Business opportunities depend greatly on the size and wealth of a population. The population is growing around the world, but at quite different rates. Birthrates in Africa, Latin America, and South Asia, for example, are two or three times greater than in Europe and North America. Companies that sell consumer products such as packaged food, clothing, and even automobiles need to go where people are located. Eventually, fast-food restaurants, entertainment, telecommunications, and other consumer products will flow to population centers around the world. To do business in world markets, a company must design a business plan that fits with the cultural, competitive, and political realities of diverse societies defined by features such as language, religion, and traditions.[8]

Anti-Americanism

There are problems, of course, and communities do not always welcome new commercial ventures with open arms. For example, when Starbucks opened one of its coffee shops near the Forbidden City in Beijing, strong objections arose from Chinese residents who complained that they were being "Americanized" in one of China's most revered cultural places.[9] Similar problems have challenged McDonald's as it has spread its fast-food culture to thousands of locations around the globe. Their arrival has not been welcome in some places: In France, for example, an irate sheep farmer, Jose Bove, caused severe damage to a McDonald's restaurant in the town of Millau. Although the French court found the farmer guilty, he was treated as a national hero by fellow citizens for trying to protect French culture from invasion.[10]

The problems of anti-Americanism extend beyond coffee and hamburgers to all aspects of culture. Critics sometimes complain that American business—and global companies in particular—are engaged in cultural imperialism that overruns local cultures and traditions. Because music, art, and other forms of entertainment help transmit cultural

---

[8] See Lee A. Tavis, *Power and Responsibility: Multinational Managers and Developing Country Concerns* (South Bend, IN: University of Notre Dame Press, 1997).

[9] Craig S. Smith, "Globalization Puts a Starbucks into the Forbidden City in Beijing," *New York Times,* November 25, 2000, p. C1. See also, Martin Fackler, "Starbucks in the Forbidden City Has Some Chinese Aghast," *Los Angeles Times,* November 29, 2000, p. 3.

[10] See "The Making of a McMartyr," *Financial Times,* September 14, 2000, p. 16.

values and beliefs, these are often the battleground in the so-called culture wars (see Chapter 19).

Culture is inevitably exported through the marketing of products, services, and the media messages used to advertise them. These values and beliefs are not always welcome. As Western commercialism becomes the dominant culture around the world, the result is what experts call **monoculturalism.** In Canada, for example, a number of national magazines pressed the government to ban distribution of *Time* and *People* magazines from the United States because they fail to present news and events affecting the lives of Canadian citizens. This influx of U.S. magazines and media undermines the viability of local media to showcase Canadian culture, politics, and events. A common refrain is that Canada is not the fifty-first state in the United States and that the country needs a media that builds pride in Canada. (The role and importance of media in modern society is discussed in Chapter 19.)

American political values, such as democracy and free speech, also draw criticism in some countries. In 2000, for example, Chinese authorities issued a one-year ban on TNT's Cartoon Network. The action against TNT, owned by AOL Time Warner, was interpreted as a warning to the company that the Communist Party would not tolerate open Internet access using the AOL portal. Chinese bureaucrats have long insisted that America Online should not allow unapproved content to circulate via its Internet portal. Chinese authorities seek to block certain types of communication and censor information believed to be threatening to the government.[11] Other countries have taken similar positions.

> *Singapore, for example, took steps in 1996 to hold the country's three Internet service providers (ISPs), which provide users with an Internet link, responsible for removing "objectionable material" from Internet public forums (chat rooms, message boards). Unregulated information could, says George Yeo, Singapore's information minister, "undermine our values and traditions."[12]*

These barriers are sometimes understandable, even if impractical. For example, the French government attempted to regulate Yahoo! because it violated French law and offended the "collective memory" of the country, an allusion to the Holocaust years, by allowing online auctions of Nazi paraphernalia on its English-language auction site (see Exhibit 20-A).[13]

"Affluenza"

The economic prosperity and high standard of living enjoyed by many Americans is often the target of criticism by others in the world community. Although many people seek to emulate the culture and economic style of American life—including the abundance of

[11] Steven Roback, "Daffy Duck No Laughing Matter to China," *San Francisco Chronicle,* April 16, 2000, magazine section, p. 7.

[12] George Cole, "Censorship in Cyberspace," *Financial Times,* March 21, 1996, p. 20.

[13] John Tagliabue, "French Uphold Ruling against Yahoo on Nazi Sites," *New York Times,* November 20, 2000, p. C8.

EXHIBIT 20-A

Yahoo! in France

In January 2001, a French judge ordered Yahoo Inc. to prevent users of its portal from accessing pro-Nazi websites on the Internet or from purchasing Nazi memorabilia through its online auction site. The French court was enforcing French law, even though Yahoo! is an American company, because its site could be viewed on a computer in France.

Memories of the Nazi occupation remain vivid in France, and French laws prevent glorification or promotion of Nazi views. The memorabilia offered for sale on the Yahoo! auction site included Nazi flags, medals with insignias, and other items. These products cannot be legally sold in France through any sales channels. Thus, the court reasoned, Yahoo! has to block the sale of these items on its website.

The company's problem with French authorities is symptomatic of broader issues involving the Internet and ideas that are deemed dangerous to society. In the United States, the constitutional doctrine of free speech protects virtually any kind of language or idea, however offensive it might be to large portions of the population. The same rights do not exist in many other nations. For example, the German and French governments have sought to ban Nazi propaganda and vehicles, such as websites and books, used to promote them. In the United States, great pressure has grown to ban or limit the distribution of violent or hate materials, but citizens still retain some rights to hold and express such views.

Source: John Tagliabue, "French Uphold Ruling against Yahoo on Nazi Sites," *New York Times,* November 20, 2000, p. C8.

goods and services—there are concerns that some nations suffer from too much prosperity and too little emphasis on human values. This "disease" is sometimes called **affluenza,** a combination of two words, *affluence* and *influenza.* In other words, a society has affluenza when it becomes "sick" through overconsumption. Criticism of conspicuous consumption is not new; excessive materialism and the gap between rich and poor have drawn protests and social criticism for centuries. In the twenty-first century, the criticism emphasizes that rich nations consume more resources per person than do poor nations. This consumption contributes to greater destruction of the world's nonrenewable resources. As discussed in Chapters 10 and 11, the ecological consequences of these patterns—for example, energy consumption, pollution of air and water, and environmental degradation—are great and cannot be sustained into the foreseeable future.

Beyond the problems associated with excessive materialism, business must be concerned with other societal issues that are connected to chronic poverty. As discussed in Chapter 11, the problems of global poverty are deep-seated. The world's business and political leaders must work together to create the type of win-win economic growth strategies that will help people move out of poverty, while also being ecologically and socially sustainable.

Political Issues

International Cooperation

In the twenty-first century, it seems clear that business, government, and society must cooperate with one another to create economic and political conditions that will facilitate economic growth and social development. The role of government is critical, because it has the sovereign power and responsibility to shape opportunities for markets, and businesses, to efficiently allocate resources for economic growth. International agencies such as the World Bank and International Monetary Fund play extremely important roles as coordinators of financial resources, knowledge, and technical assistance to nations in need. And NGOs are critical to shaping the policy choices and options in each country as well as being on the front lines of change in each location.

One of the unintended consequences of past international assistance efforts has been the persistent poverty and inability of some nations to pay off past debts. Some people believe that a country that borrows money from the international community (through one of the international agencies), should be required to pay the interest and principal on that debt before receiving more assistance. However, there are countries so destitute and lacking in economic resources as to make it impossible to repay old debts. The international community has agreed on the importance of implementing various **debt relief,** or debt forgiveness, policies that would enable debtor nations to stop paying interest and principal payments in exchange for commitment to an internationally approved strategy to improve the economy through adoption of sound social and political policies.

> *In December 2000, for example, international debt relief in the amount of $34 billion was extended to 22 countries, including Rwanda (71 percent reduction), Mozambique (72 percent), Bolivia (49 percent), Nicaragua (72 percent), Tanzania (53 percent), and other heavily indebted poor countries whose per capita gross domestic product placed them near the bottom of all nations and whose international debt was so great as to make repayment a near impossibility. These countries entered into agreements with international agencies that will reduce or eliminate portions of their debt obligations, thereby freeing them to invest in growth-oriented practices and policies. The conditions for such relief packages are that the government use the money saved to assist their citizens through education, health, and other basic services.*[14]

Repressive Political Regimes

One of the most challenging issues facing multinational companies is how to deal with governments that engage in antidemocratic and outright repressive behavior toward their own citizens. One example of the dilemma presented to companies is illustrated in the

---

[14] "Debt Relief for the Poorest Countries: Milestone Achieved," a joint statement by Horst Kohler (IMF) and James Wolfensohn (World Bank), December 22, 2000. World Bank website, www.worldbank.org. The United States' position favoring this action is described by Samuel R. Berger, "A Global Gap That Open Markets Can't Close," *New York Times,* January 20, 2001, p. A19. Berger was President Clinton's national security adviser at the time this action was taken.

case of Shell in Nigeria, presented at the end of this book. Many companies believe that it is important not to interfere in the domestic political practices of a host nation's government. In the case of a government that acts in the interest of its people, and does not engage in repressive actions, companies have relatively clear guidelines about how to behave.

> *For example, if Citibank, which is headquartered in the United States, conducts business in Japan, it is likely to avoid most political activity in that country. If Japan's government adopts a monetary policy that will damage the investment of American investors in Japan, however, Citibank officials may feel obligated to communicate those views to the government's representatives.*

A more difficult problem exists, however, when the government of the host country engages in repressive or antidemocratic actions against its own citizens. This may occur as the government seeks to preserve its own political power or, as has sometimes happened, to help companies with which it has close economic relationships. In South Africa, for example, during the 1970s, the government enforced a policy of apartheid, or racial separation, that discriminated against the black majority of the population in favor of the white minority population. Companies were not permitted to hire blacks for skilled positions, at higher pay, if any white employees were available to do the work. And separate facilities such as cafeterias and rest rooms had to be maintained—one set for white employees, another for blacks. American companies were pressured by their U.S. investors, employees, and government officials to stop following the South African law and to ignore or violate apartheid laws. Many companies were reluctant to do so, however, since it meant breaking South Africa's laws and facing legal liability and penalties. Companies such as Johnson & Johnson, Pepsi, Motorola, and others decided that the best course of action was to withdraw from South Africa rather than continue to face sanctions from various stakeholders.

Nations that violate international standards of law and political freedom may become the focus of international political and economic **sanctions.** Such sanctions affect business in several ways: Nations may refuse to trade with that nation, pressure the government to step down, or order their companies not to carry on business with any company from the target country because of the repressive actions.

> *For example, Burma has been ruled by a military regime for many years, and political freedoms have been seriously limited during this period. The international community agreed to impose sanctions on the country, which is heavily dependent on oil revenues. Unocal, an American multinational firm, is one of the few U.S. companies to remain in Burma. The company manages an oil pipeline and facility that is an important source of revenue to the government. Despite strong pressure from U.S. investors, churches, and human rights activists, Unocal has refused to withdraw from the country.*[15]

---

[15] The authors are grateful to Lisa Wimberly Allen for her firsthand account of conditions in Burma.

Sanctions must be used with care. For example, in 1989 Chinese authorities moved against demonstrators who had occupied Tiananmen Square in Beijing. After weeks of protests, military power was used to forcibly remove the protestors. The naked use of military power, followed by the deaths and arrests of many Chinese youth, created outrage and anger in many countries, including the United States. Great pressure was put on the U.S. Congress to retaliate by imposing trade sanctions that would ban companies from doing business with China. President George H. W. Bush, who had served as U.S. ambassador to China, issued a strong condemnation of the massacre but not formal sanctions. This allowed U.S. companies to continue doing business in China. Over the course of the 1990s, economic and political relations improved as the American government pursued a foreign policy of "constructive engagement" that business leaders supported. But relations deteriorated in 2001 when China detained a U.S. surveillance plane and its 24 crew members after a midair collision with a Chinese fighter jet. The incident set back political relations and threatened economic relations.

Global Standards

As discussed in earlier chapters, many international and industry groups have created global standards and codes of conduct. These codes and statements aspire to state the world's expectations for how companies behave in dealing with issues such as environmental risks, labor rights, and community impacts (see Chapters 6, 10, 11, and 17). An important aspect of these codes is the commitment companies make to public reporting of information about their practices. Public disclosure of business practices regarding labor conditions, environmental risks, and human rights is based on the assumption stated many years ago by former U.S. Supreme Court justice Louis Brandeis: "Sunlight is the best disinfectant."

Global Corporate Citizenship

As companies expand their sphere of commercial activity around the world, expectations grow that they will behave in ways that enhance the benefits and minimize the risk to various stakeholders. This is the essence of legitimacy in a global economy. As discussed in Chapter 16, a company must earn, and maintain, its "license to operate" in every country in which it does business through its efforts to meet stakeholder expectations.

Three ideas guide much of modern understanding about a corporation's private and public roles and responsibilities, whether at home or abroad. First, it is generally accepted that a company is responsible for the direct consequences that flow from its business activities. Thus, a chemical firm is accountable for its discharges into local rivers, for the quality for the products it sells, and for the safety of its operations.

Second, a company's responsibilities are not unlimited. The chemicals discharged by a local plant, for example, cannot be distinguished from those discharged by dozens of other facilities. At that point, government is required to correct the collective problem and allocate the costs among all businesses. When dealing with air pollution in Mexico City, for example, there are so many contributors to the pollution that government must find a fair way to set standards and allocate costs.

Third, businesses should reconcile and integrate their private, profit-seeking activities with their public responsibilities. No society holds the view that human beings are accountable only for themselves. Societies cannot function when such ideas prevail. Thus, when a corporation or a business enterprise is part of a community, the leaders of that business are expected to assume responsibility for the community's welfare. Managers must find ways to harmonize the drive for profits with its public responsibilities. We call this *corporate citizenship* (see Chapters 4 and 16).

When a company is doing business across borders in more than one country, the idea of citizenship must be translated into the concept of **global corporate citizenship.** A research report from one of the leading academic centers defines the concept in these terms:

> *Global corporate citizenship is the process of identifying, analyzing, and responding to the company's social, political, and economic responsibilities as defined through law and public policy, stakeholder expectations, and voluntary acts flowing from corporate values and business strategies. Corporate citizenship involves actual results (what corporations DO) and the processes through which they are achieved (HOW they do it).*[16]

This definition underscores several major themes discussed throughout this book:

- Managers and companies have responsibilities to all of their stakeholders.
- Corporate responsibility involves more than just meeting legal requirements.
- Corporate responsibility requires that a company focus on, and respond to, stakeholder expectations and undertake those voluntary acts that are consistent with its values and business mission.
- Corporate citizenship involves both what the corporation does and the processes through which it engages stakeholders and makes decisions.

The following section illustrates some of the ways companies translate these ideas into everyday business practices.

Citizenship Strategies and Business Strategies

What is required to be a good global corporate citizen? How do companies actually link a global corporate citizenship strategy to a global business strategy? Businesses tend to develop community relations and citizenship strategies on the basis of characteristics in their industry. Companies in the mining and natural resources industries, for example, invest substantial resources in developing livable communities for employees in the remote areas where exploration and extraction often occurs. In Western Australia, mining companies still operate "company towns," which are almost totally dependent on the companies for schools, public services, and safety.[17]

Companies that manufacture products also face community issues similar to the natural resources firms. Dependencies are high; local residents and neighborhoods are concerned about the adverse effects of pollution, traffic, and other risks. Global retail businesses tend to develop citizenship programs that emphasize contact with consumers and communities. Entertainment and the sale of consumer products are often associated

---

[16] James E. Post, *Managing the Challenge of Global Corporate Citizenship,* Policy Paper Series (Chestnut Hill, MA: Boston College Center for Corporate Community Relations, 1999), p. 8. The document is available through the Center website, www.bc.edu/cccr.

[17] See examples of global community service cited in Noel M. Tichy, Andy R. McGill, and Linda St. Clair, *Global Corporate Citizenship: Doing Business in the Public Eye* (San Francisco: New Lexington Press, 1997).

Figure 20-2

Business models and citizenship models— a comparison.

Source: James E. Post, *Meeting the Challenge of Global Corporate Citizenship* (Chestnut Hill, MA: Boston College Center for Corporate Community Relations, 2000), p. 35.

	Business Model	**Citizenship Model**
Key question	*How do we make money?*	*How do we become effective citizens?*
Elements	• Product • Market/customer • Technology • Manage assets wisely	• Minimize risk to others • Build stakeholder trust • Cultivate relationships • Assist community groups
Results	• Revenues • Profits • Goodwill • Reputation	• Revenues • Cost control • Stakeholder trust • Reputation

with public events, ranging from rallies to concerts and festivals. Commercial sponsorship and community involvement go together for companies with highly visible brand names, such as Coca-Cola, Levi Strauss, and Wal-Mart. Internet and e-commerce firms are also developing distinctive citizenship patterns, with companies as AOL Time Warner, IBM, Cisco Systems, and Lucent providing interesting global models of citizenship and business strategy. A company's business model and its citizenship model address different questions, but each adds to the organization's success by developing positive relationships with key stakeholders (see Figure 20-2).

For many companies engaged in global business activities, global citizenship practices are an important part of the company's identity. Lucent Technologies provides an instructive example of how global citizenship fits with global business.

> *In 1996, Lucent Technologies held its first Global Days of Caring, now an annual volunteerism event that celebrates the vast amount of time and effort that employees donate to community projects worldwide. For a company that has nearly 150,000 employees worldwide, with operations in more than 90 nations, Global Days of Caring are a time for recognition, appreciation, and support to do more. During its 2000 Global Days of Caring, some 17,000 volunteers supported more than 500 projects, donating more than one million hours of service worldwide. While the traditions of volunteerism are not as deep in some nations as in the United States, Lucent had more than 4,300 volunteers engaged in more than 40 projects in 26 countries outside the United States.*[18]

Global corporate citizenship often involves a variety of local, regional, and global programs. One consortium of companies, known as the London Benchmarking Group, has created the framework illustrated in Figure 20-3.

---

[18] Tichy, McGill, and St. Clair, *Global Corporate Citizenship*, p. 22. Also see the Lucent website under the "community involvement" heading, www.lucent.com.

Figure 20-3

The pyramid of global citizenship activities.

Source: London Benchmarking Group Model, described in James E. Post, *Meeting the Challenge of Global Corporate Citizenship* (Chestnut Hill, MA: Boston College Center for Corporate Community Relations, 2000).

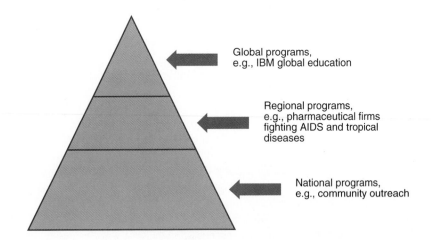

Global programs, e.g., IBM global education

Regional programs, e.g., pharmaceutical firms fighting AIDS and tropical diseases

National programs, e.g., community outreach

Global citizenship also includes the activities of those companies in other countries that are pioneering new approaches to doing business. One such example is O Boticario, a Brazilian cosmetics firm that has developed innovative ways of working to save Brazil's natural resources (see Exhibit 20-B). The company has recognized the link

---

EXHIBIT 20-B

O Boticario Invests in Nature and Community

O Boticario is a Brazilian cosmetics company that started in 1977 as a small pharmacy. The company developed a direct distribution system that enlisted hundreds of small- and medium-sized entrepreneurs in the distribution of its products. This franchise network now includes more than 1,700 points-of-sale and 10,000 employees. Each new link creates a network of relationships with local suppliers and other businesses. As a result, O Boticario's name and products are familiar throughout Brazil.

O Boticario's business is successful, in part, because it is also active in promoting quality-of-life standards. In the 1999 annual report, Miguel Krigsner, the firm's president, writes: "It is not just a matter of producing and generating wealth. Brazil is a country characterized by widespread dearth and contrast that strike one's eye. We should be on the watch for the needs to transform such a reality." He continues, "True change will only occur when a coherent participation of the entrepreneurial class will lead to proposals and solutions being submitted with an aim at promoting human values in a society and the strengthening of citizenship."

O Boticario put these words into action when it created the O Boticario Nature Protection Foundation in 1990 to mobilize action in the environmental area. One of the foundation's most notable projects has been the support of photographer Orlando Azevedo, whose "Heart of Brazil—500 Years" project is building awareness of Brazil's natural treasures.

Exhibit 20-B continued

Brazil is Latin America's largest country in terms of geography and population. Its cities teem with millions of people, and its natural resources have made its mining, extraction, and forestry industries among the world's richest. The Amazon is the world's largest rain forest, but it is shrinking as people cut trees to develop farms, cattle ranches, and open-pit mining operations. Environmental groups in Brazil and other countries are trying to preserve the rain forest, but it is a difficult challenge. As long as economic incentives to exploit the rain forest exceed the incentives to conserve it, there is no doubt that the forest will continue to be destroyed. One of the irreplaceable aspects of the rain forest is its biological diversity. Millions of plants and trees makes it a rich source of herbs, roots, and berries from which cosmetics, creams, and other beauty products can be made. The world's cosmetic and pharmaceutical companies are actively studying the properties of these plants to find new substances for their products.

Between 1991 and 1999, the O Boticario Foundation—a nonprofit organization—became known for its capacity to achieve protection and conservation of threatened animal species and natural assets. In 1999 alone, the foundation sponsored 34 technical and scientific events and 115 other projects, delivered 12 training courses, and promoted 44 exhibits. Many activities were performed in partnership with official institutions and nongovernmental organizations. The foundation's projects involved saving endangered species and rare plants, and O Boticario was recognized for this work by Brazil's Ministry of Environment.

The O Boticario Foundation is now extending its work into the communities located near the ecological resources it is working to save. Education and community development projects are being implemented with the same type of imagination and leadership the company brought to the cosmetics business and to environmental issues. As Miguel Krigsner said, "To say that the O Boticario is engaged in social responsibility process is [to go] back to its origins." From its start, this has been a company committed to customers, employees, and community.

Sources: Maria de Lourdes Nunes, president of O Boticario Foundation, presentation at annual meeting of Business for Social Responsibility, November 2000; and author interview. Company documents: O Boticario, *Social and Environmental 1999 Year-End Balance Sheet,* www.boticario.com.br.

between preservation of Brazil's unique natural resources and the cosmetics industry's dependence on forests for new products derived from native flora and fauna. The company has also recognized that local communities must be improved if local citizens are to be active in protecting the forest. In this way, both the business and community programs are developed together.

New Tools for a New Century

Managers continuously create and use new tools and techniques to improve their work in every area of a business. Information technology speeds modern accounting and financial analysis; sophisticated computer programs enable products to be manufactured with greater precision, quality, and lower cost; the Internet helps companies better communicate with customers, providing useful information more quickly; human resources managers develop new combinations of full-time, part-time, and independent contractors to meet their companies' demands for talent and skills.

The process of innovation to become more productive also applies to challenges of managing stakeholder relationships and social and political issues. This section discusses several of the new tools being used by leading firms to more effectively manage their business–society relationships. These new tools include

- Reputation management.
- The development of "triple bottom line" accounting techniques.
- The use of the Internet for improved communication with stakeholders.

All of these tools are used in support of a redefinition of organizational wealth that emphasizes positive stakeholder relationships as the ultimate source of wealth. Sustainability—a concept that integrates economic, ecological, and social objectives—is the ultimate goal.

Reputation Management

Companies that are operating in a global economy have to provide consumers and users with good reasons to purchase their product or service. Rarely, if ever, is one company the only provider of a product or service. As price competition grows and product performance differences diminish, consumers look for the something extra that distinguishes one company from another. Corporate reputation is one of those considerations.

Consumers generally like the idea of doing business with a "good company," one with a positive reputation for the way it treats employees, customers, and communities. Companies that demonstrate respect for the environment and commitment to human rights around the world have developed loyal customers. In this way, corporate reputation is one of the **intangible assets** that adds to the organization's wealth (see Figure 20-4). While it is impossible to see or feel an organization's reputation for integrity or fair dealing, knowledgeable customers, investors, and members of the community recognize the value of dealing with a company whose reputation is positive. *Fortune,* a leading business magazine, has created a sophisticated corporate reputation ranking system and publishes an annual list of "America's Best Companies."[19] Public relations advisers have recognized the importance of this area and developed a professional organization, The Reputation Institute, to advance the field of reputation management.[20]

Reputation is not the only intangible asset of the company. Intellectual property (IP), including ideas and knowledge in the memory of employees, is a valuable asset of the firm. Some forms of intellectual property can be legally protected by patent, trademark, or copyright. Other forms of IP may reside in the knowledge of individual employees (e.g., customer lists or passwords), and the company may ask its employees to sign agreements not to compete with the firm for a specified period of time after they leave (see Chapter 17).

---

[19] See *Fortune,* special corporate reputation issue, April 2001.

[20] See Charles Fombrun, *Reputation* (Boston: Harvard Business School Press, 1996). See also, www.reputationinstitute.org and articles in the *Corporate Reputation Review.*

Figure 20-4

The new wealth:
stakeholder
relationships.

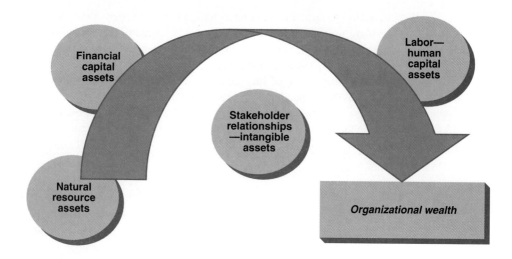

Reputation and the trust that exists between the stakeholder and the company are very important forms of **relational capital**—the relationships existing between the company and its stakeholders that are of value to the firm. Relational capital usually does not appear on a firm's accounting statements, except as a "residual" (e.g., goodwill) number. The importance of stakeholder relationships may not receive a financial estimation until the company is sold or acquired, at which time the premium that must be paid for the firm's stock is treated as a payment for accumulated goodwill (see Chapter 13).

New developments in the accounting profession are creating more sophisticated ways for management to account, and report, the true value of a firm's intangible assets. More stakeholders are also demanding more information about corporate practices. This disclosure reveals more information to the public about environmental costs, for example, or about the firm's use of suppliers or subcontractors in developing nations where labor safety standards may be of concern. As discussed in earlier chapters (Chapters 3, 4, 7, 8, 10, and 11), disclosure provides greater corporate accountability for policies and practices.

Triple Bottom Line

One of the most interesting, and potentially important, accounting developments is the creation of the so-called **triple bottom line** method of accounting. The traditional single bottom line consists solely of the financial results of the company's economic activity, derived from basic economic concepts of revenues and costs. The double bottom line estimates and incorporates the costs of externalities, such as environmental damage and nonrenewable resource use, into the firm's profit (bottom line) calculation. Some companies (e.g., Skandia) have developed techniques for measuring the positive benefits of employee education on a firm's human capital or the value of volunteer services to local communities. In a reaction to the narrow focus on short-term financial performance, accountants and management experts have tried to develop broader measures of how well a firm is doing today and how well prepared it is for tomorrow. The idea of a **balanced scorecard** approach has pushed the frontiers of accounting by emphasizing the importance of long-term as well as short-term performance results.[21] This approach has been enthusiastically embraced by thousands of companies and managers in the U.S. and internationally.

The triple bottom line builds on these ideas and is the most elaborate system of accounting for social and ecological consequences developed to date. According to John Elkington, a British business consultant and creator of the triple bottom line concept,

> *[The] three lines [of the triple bottom line] represent society, the economy and the environment. Society depends on the economy—and the economy depends on the global ecosystem, whose health represents the ultimate bottom line. The three lines are not stable; they are in constant flux, due to social, political, economic and environmental pressures, cycle and conflicts. . . . Unfortunately, these new forms of accountability have taken most parts of the accountancy world by surprise, with most accountants ill-prepared for the challenge.*[22]

According to Elkington, the triple bottom line approach goes beyond the balanced scorecard in several important ways. The balanced scorecard aims to capture how companies create value through investments in customers, suppliers, employees, processes, technology, and innovation. The four main dimensions of performance are financial, customer, internal/business process, and learning and growth. But there is nothing of the environment or social capital. Indeed, in their book *The Balanced Scorecard*, Kaplan and Norton acknowledge the problem when they describe their meeting with the senior management of a chemical company: "They felt that they needed to move beyond compliance . . . [and] insisted that outstanding environmental and community performance was a central part of the company's strategy and had to be an integral part of its scorecard."[23] To address such needs at Shell, the global energy firm, Elkington and his associates developed operational measures for many of Shell's environmental and social impacts, both positive and negative. As illustrated in Figure 20-5, the core idea is to identify and measure a company's impact on the environment and society at every stage of the business value-creation process, or **value chain.** Although triple bottom line accounting is still in its early stages, executives at companies such as Shell recognize that such methods are the new generation of management tools they must create if the public is to understand the total economic, ecological, and social impact of global corporations.

Stakeholder Communication

The Internet has enabled companies to develop sophisticated methods of communicating with their stakeholders. Messages can be sent to employees, customers, suppliers, and other stakeholders in an instant, seeking information, assistance, or action. What

---

[21] Robert Kaplan and David Norton, *The Balanced Scorecard* (Boston: Harvard Business School Press, 1996).

[22] John Elkington, *Cannibals with Forks: The Triple Bottom Line of Twenty-First Century Business* (London: Thompson, 1997); see www.sustainability.co.uk/philosophy/triple-bottom. Elkington's views are also included in an important commentary in *The Shell Report, 1998*, which can be accessed at www.shell.com.

[23] Kaplan and Norton, *The Balanced Scorecard*, p. 35.

Environmental impacts (negative)

- Direct air/water pollution
- Resource damage
- Use of nonrenewable resources

- Air and water pollutants
- Use of toxics
- Waste streams
- Noise, radiation

- Excessive packaging
- Open-system waste streams

Environmental impacts (positive)

- Offset damage to conservation land
- Improvements
- Upgraded usage

- Emergency risk management
- Continuous reduction of toxics
- Recycled materials

- Reduced packaging (volume)
- Less toxic packages
- Public service messages

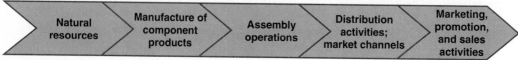

Business Value Chain

Social impacts (negative)

- Industry dependence
- Company towns

- Worker rights
- Labor safety
- Human rights

- Trade practices
- Transport safety

- Competition
- Local retailers
- Service needs

- Advertising messages
- Media images
- Overpromotion

Social impacts (positive)

- Jobs
- Education
- Infrastructure

- Community involvement
- Contributions/giving
- Volunteerism

- Less expensive products
- Innovation

- Cause marketing
- New knowledge

Figure 20-5

The business value chain and triple bottom line impacts.

once took days or weeks to effect, can now be done in days or hours. (For information as to how companies are using the Internet in managing political issues, see the discussion in Chapter 8.) Information about corporate financial information is now readily available to investors, professors, and business students on various websites. The same is true with social and environmental information at leading companies. Readers are encouraged to look at the websites identified at the end of this chapter to understand the range of relevant business–society information available to the public.

The Quest for Sustainability

The long-term future of businesses and communities depends on an identical requirement—the support and contribution of diverse stakeholders. For a business, the support of stakeholders such as employees, customers, suppliers, investors, and business partners is vital to continued prosperity. Likewise, the support of individual citizens, voluntary organizations, businesses, and government are necessary for a healthy, sustainable community. Companies and communities succeed or fail as a result of, in large measure, the quality of the relationships they create and maintain. **Sustainability,** then, is the idea that a business must pursue economic results, plus sound environmental results, plus social well-being for its stakeholders.

Businesses in the twenty-first century face challenges on many fronts: intense competition, little customer loyalty, changing technology, and employees who are looking for compensation, career development, and quality of life. It is a long and challenging list of issues for the modern manager, whether that individual works in a local restaurant, automobile dealer, financial service office, or e-commerce firm. The sustainable organization, like the sustainable community, requires cooperation, commitment, and courageous leadership. When he was inaugurated as forty-third president of the United States, George W. Bush urged the nation to seek a "common good" and "affirm a new commitment to live out our nation's promise through civility, courage, compassion, and character." "Civility," he went on to say, "is not a tactic or a sentiment. It is the determined choice of trust over cynicism, of community over chaos. And this commitment, if we keep it, is a way to shared accomplishment."[24]

These themes are not foreign to the study of business in the twenty-first century. Organizations, no less than individuals, need the trust of their stakeholders and their commitment to shared visions and principles. The role of business in society is not static; it is always changing. The drivers of change in the modern world—global competition, technology, ethics and values, respect for the environment, the changing role of government—guarantee that business will continue to be a dynamic, vital aspect of life for people around the world. That is a great challenge to future managers and entrepreneurs, and it also a great opportunity to create a world in which each person is respected for who they are, encouraged to develop their full potential, and engaged in creating communities that function to make every person's life more fulfilling.

Summary Points of This Chapter

- The globalization of business is driven by many factors. The demand for many goods and services is global, and modern transportation and communication systems enable companies to meet consumer demand around the world. The decline of trade barriers, opening of markets in economies that were once closed to trade, and dynamic growth in developing nations all contribute to worldwide economic activity.
- When companies operate plants, or have suppliers in other countries, they must understand the conditions in which those operations and business partners function. The company must oversee the standards that are applied to all of their stakeholders. Labor conditions are a particularly important source of global social issues today.
- When a company puts a product or service into the stream of commerce, it has a responsibility to any person who purchases or uses it. When markets are global, companies have more difficulty knowing who is using the product, and how.
- Companies sometimes discover that they are doing business in two or more countries that are in conflict over economic or political issues. Each country may exert pressure on companies to stop doing business with their enemy.

[24] George W. Bush, Presidential Inaugural Address, January 20, 2001.

- Global citizenship begins with perspective, respect, and commitment to work within the framework of a nation's values and ethics. Global companies develop an ethnocentric perspective that recognizes the uniqueness of each nation's social, political, and cultural characteristics. Corporate citizens work to support, not change, each host nation's institutions and culture. Through a partnership strategy, global companies work with local organizations to identify and support causes that link the company's business strategy to its community involvement.

Key Terms and Concepts Used in This Chapter

- Globalization
- Global market channels
- Global locations
- Global supply chains
- Nongovernmental organizations (NGOs)
- Cultural distance
- Ethnocentric perspective
- Geocentric perspective
- Monoculturalism

- Affluenza
- Debt relief
- Sanctions
- Global corporate citizenship
- Intangible assets
- Relational capital
- Triple bottom line
- Balanced scorecard
- Value chain
- Sustainability

Internet Resources

- www.e-civicus.org — A global network of nongovernmental organizations
- www.worldbank.org — The World Bank
- www.weforum.org — World Economic Forum
- www.bsr.org — Businesses for Social Responsibility
- www.sustainability.co.uk — The company that developed the triple bottom line methodology
- www.wto.org — World Trade Organization
- www.wtowatch.org — Nongovernmental oversight group

Discussion Case: *The Battle of Seattle*

World economic leaders met in Seattle, Washington, in December 1999 to discuss global economic conditions and policy priorities. Officially, this was a meeting of the World Trade Organization (WTO). Unofficially, it was the battleground that drew worldwide media attention to social issues that the delegates did not intend to discuss: environmental damage, job losses, and unacceptable social conditions attributable to the global economic system. Outside the convention center, large crowds protested about the dark side of international trade: concern about environmental degradation, unemployment, wages in developing nations, social and economic justice, genetically modified organisms, and other issues. By protesting the WTO meeting, and by doing so in visible ways, the demonstrations provoked a police response that captured media attention and became known as "the Battle in Seattle."

In the aftermath of the confrontations, political leaders and WTO participants were chastened by the violence; many said they had not appreciated the deep antagonism to trade liberalization. The Seattle police department was criticized for its tactics, although its defenders pointed to the provocative behavior and property damage caused by demonstrators. Protest organizers acknowledged that the parade had been infiltrated by members of groups that favored the use of violence as a means of protest.

Several weeks later, a convention of biotechnology experts and industry representatives was held in Boston. Massive precautions were taken to separate protestors from the convention meetings. Antibiotech rallies were held, but only minor confrontations took place and police made few arrests. Boston police commissioner Paul Evans complimented the department members on having learned important crowd-management lessons from the Battle of Seattle.

During the summer of 2000, world economic leaders convened in Washington, DC, for a meeting of the International Monetary Fund and in Prague, Czech Republic, for a World Bank meeting. Major street protests took place in both cities, and delegates were forced to stay within fortress-like hotel compounds. A few months later, in November 2000, the World Economic Forum held a regional meeting in Melbourne, Australia. Once again, protesters were in evidence. Conflict had become part of the international trade agenda.

At the inauguration of U.S. President George W. Bush, in January 2001, an estimated 250,000 protestors gathered, bringing media attention to such issues as animal rights, genetically modified foods, environmental damage, and labor rights issues associated with international trade practices. Less than week later, World Economic Forum leaders gathered in Davos, Switzerland, for discussions about promoting economic growth and political reform. Protestors were present. The U.S. State Department issued an official warning to citizens traveling to Europe that possible "disorderly and violent" demonstrations could occur during the meeting of political, business, and cultural leaders in Davos.

The Davos meeting was organized into a series of panels to address key issues. Sharply different opinions about globalization were immediately evident. Warren Staley, chief executive officer of Cargill, USA, argued the benefits of the free trade system and urged support for a global food system in which each country produced whatever gives them a competitive advantage. His view found favor with many business leaders, who argued what is referred to as the TINA principle: "there is no alternative." But Vandana Shiva, director of the Research Foundation for Science, Technology, and Ecology in India, strongly disagreed. She said, "For every dollar traded, 10 dollars worth of poverty is created. Farmers' incomes in India have crashed to a mere 20 percent of what they were, and more and more people are unable to buy food." There *must* be an alternative.

United Nations secretary general Kofi Annan appealed to the entire global business community to support the UN Global Compact, which stresses the importance of sustainable economic, environmental, and social strategies. He said

If we cannot make globalization work for all, in the end it will work for none. The unequal distribution of benefits and the imbalances of rule making, which characterize globalization today, inevitably will produce backlash and protectionism. And that, in turn, threatens to undermine and ultimately unravel the open world economy that has been so painstakingly constructed over the course of the past half-century.

The idea of a backlash was clearly expressed by a panel dealing with the role of nongovernmental organizations. Lori Wallach, director of Global Trade Watch, a U.S.-based NGO that studies trade issues, rejected the notion that globalization, in its current form, holds the key to alleviating poverty and underdevelopment. She cited World Bank statistics that show per capita GDP in many emerging economic regions (Latin America and Africa) rose more quickly between 1960 and 1980—before the trade liberalization of the Uruguay Round—than in the last two decades. The existing multilateral rules "are not working, are not accountable, and are not TINA [there is no alternative]. And people finally are beginning to get that." She added that the protest movement has won a moral victory of sorts by forcing its opponents to adopt stringent security measures at their international meetings. "Turning Davos into something close to a near police state creates a wonderful press opportunity for us," she said. "It demonstrates the lack of legitimacy of the global elite."

As business, government, and NGO leaders look ahead, there is uncertainty about globalization and its effects. The benefits of trade seem real, but they are not shared equally among countries or by populations within nations. The side effects of trade—environmental, labor, and human rights issues—are sometimes greater than the benefits. Although there are many theories about what should happen, it is difficult to manage the many practical steps needed for progress to occur. Indeed, the World Trade Organization, seeking to convince another country to host the next round of high-level trade talks, was having trouble finding a host city for its follow-up to the Seattle meeting. Only two countries, Chile and the Persian Gulf state of Qatar, offered to host the next meeting because of expected violence and protests.

When the WTO's 140 member-nations selected Doha, the capital of Qatar, NGOs were critical of the choice because Qatar is an authoritarian regime with alleged human rights violations. Qatar officials pledged to allow unfettered access to the country during the conference and to permit demonstrations—a rare sight in the conservative country—as long as they are peaceful. The NGOs that were accredited to attend the Seattle meeting will also be accredited to go to Doha, according to the director general of the WTO. But as one NGO member said, "It will be very hard to organize 'Son of Seattle' in the Persian Gulf. But we will find a way to be there . . . to let them know we are watching and that they cannot impose trade tyranny on the world."

Sources: "U.S. Advises Its Citizens of Economic Protests," *Boston Globe,* January 21, 2001, p. A16; Elizabeth Olson, "With Seattle a Vivid Memory, WTO Seeks a New Host City," *New York Times,* January 22, 2001, p. W1; and Elizabeth Olson, "WTO Picks Qatar Capital as Meeting Site," *New York Times,* January 31, 2001, p. W1. See also, official session summaries from World Economic Forum, 2001, at www.worldeconomicforum.org.

Discussion Questions

1. What factors led to the Battle of Seattle? What do protestors really want? Do street protests actually affect what happens in the global economy?
2. What is the role of international organizations such as the World Bank and International Monetary Fund in maintaining the global trade system that some favor and others despise?
3. Do you agree or disagree with UN secretary general Kofi Annan's assessment of the need to correct the unequal distribution of benefits and imbalances in power?
4. What tools and resources will NGO organizations have available to them at the next WTO meeting in Qatar? How might they use these tools to achieve their goals?

Case Studies
in
Corporate Social Policy

ODWALLA, INC., AND THE E. COLI OUTBREAK

October 30, 1996, was a cool, fall day in Half Moon Bay, California, a coastal town an hour's drive south of San Francisco. At the headquarters of Odwalla, Inc., a modest, two-story wooden structure just blocks from the beach, company founder and chairman Greg Steltenpohl was attending a marketing meeting. Odwalla, the largest producer of fresh fruit and vegetable-based beverages in the western United States, had just completed its best-ever fiscal year, with sales of $59 million, up 40 percent over the past 12 months.

The company's CEO, Stephen Williamson, urgently knocked on the glass door and motioned Steltenpohl into the hall. Williamson, 38, a graduate of the University of California at Berkeley and a former investment banker, had served as president of Odwalla from 1992 to 1995, when he became CEO.

It was unlike him to interrupt a meeting, and he looked worried. "I just got a call from the King County Department of Health," Williamson reported. "They've got a dozen cases of E. coli poisoning up there in the Seattle area. A number of the families told health officials they had drunk Odwalla apple juice." E. coli O157:H7 was a virulent bacterium that had been responsible for several earlier outbreaks of food poisoning, including one traced to undercooked Jack-in-the-Box hamburgers in 1993.

Steltenpohl was puzzled. "What do they know for sure?"

"Right now, not a whole lot. It's just epidemiology," Williamson replied. "They don't have any bacteriological match-ups yet. They said it might be a while before they would know anything definitive."

"We'd better see what else we can find out."

Steltenpohl and Williamson returned to their offices, where they began placing calls to food safety experts, scientists at the Food and Drug Administration and the Centers for Disease Control, and the company's lawyers. A while later, Steltenpohl came out to speak to his next appointment, who had been waiting in the lobby for over an hour. "I'm awfully sorry," the chairman said apologetically. "I'm not going to be able to see you today. Something important's happening that I've got to deal with right away."

History of Odwalla, Inc.
Odwalla, Inc., was founded in 1980 by Steltenpohl, his wife Bonnie Bassett, and their friend Gerry Percy. Steltenpohl, then 25, was a jazz musician and Stanford graduate with a degree in environmental science. The group purchased a used hand juicer for $200 and began producing fresh-squeezed orange juice in a backyard shed in Santa Cruz, California. They delivered the juice to local

By Anne T. Lawrence. This is an abridged version of a full-length case, "Odwalla, Inc., and the E. Coli Outbreak (A), (B), (C)," *Case Research Journal* 19, no. 1, Winter, 1999. Abridged and reprinted by permission of the *Case Research Journal.* This case was written with the cooperation of management, solely for the purpose of stimulating student discussion. Sources include articles appearing in the *Natural Foods Merchandiser, Nation's Business, San Jose Mercury News, Rocky Mountain News, San Francisco Chronicle, Seattle Times, Fresno Bee, New York Times, Wall Street Journal,* and *Squeeze* (Odwalla's in-house newsletter); press releases issued by Odwalla and by the American Fresh Juice Council; and Odwalla's annual reports and prospectus. Odwalla's website may be found at www.odwallazone.com. Copyright © Anne T. Lawrence and the North American Case Research Association. All rights reserved.

restaurants in a Volkswagen van. Steltenpohl later said that he had gotten the idea from a book, *100 Businesses You Can Start for Under $100*. His motivation, he reported, was simply to make enough money to support his fledgling career as a musician and producer of educational media presentations. The company's name came from a jazz composition by the Art Ensemble of Chicago, in which Odwalla was a mythical figure who led the "people of the sun" out of the "gray haze," which the friends chose to interpret as a reference to overly processed food.

During the 1980s, Odwalla prospered, gradually extending its market reach by expanding its own distribution and production capabilities and by acquiring other juice companies. In 1983, the company moved into a larger production facility and added carrot juice to its product line. In 1985—the same year Odwalla incorporated—the company purchased a small local apple juice company, Live Juice. With apple added to the line, the company expanded its distribution efforts, moving into San Francisco and further north into Marin County. In 1986, Odwalla purchased Dancing Bear Juice Company in Sacramento and assimilated that company's juice products and distribution network in central California.

The company financed its rapid growth in its early years through bank loans and private stock offerings in 1991, 1992, and 1993. In December 1993, the company went public, offering for sale one million shares of common stock at an initial price of $6.375 a share. The proceeds of the initial public offering were used in part to construct a 65,000 square foot state-of-the-art production facility in Dinuba, in California's agricultural Central Valley.

The company also made additional acquisitions. In June 1994, the company acquired Dharma Juice Company of Bellingham, Washington, to distribute its products in the Pacific Northwest. In January 1995, Odwalla purchased J.S. Grant's, Inc., the maker of Just Squeezed Juices, which became the distributor for Odwalla products in the Colorado market. The strategy appeared to be successful. By 1996, Odwalla, which already controlled more than half the market for fresh juice in northern California, had made significant inroads in the Pacific Northwest and Colorado and was poised to extend its market dominance into New Mexico, Texas, and southern California.

Product Line   The company considered its market niche to be "fresh, minimally processed juices and juice-based beverages."

The company produced a range of products from fresh juice, some single strength and some blended. Odwalla chose fun, clever names, such as Strawberry C-Monster (a vitamin C-fortified fruit smoothie), Femme Vitale (a product formulated to meet women's special nutritional needs), and Guava Have It (a tropical fruit blend). Packaging graphics were brightly colored and whimsical. Pricing was at the premium level; a half gallon of fresh-squeezed orange juice retailed for around $5.00; a 16-oz. blended smoothie for $2.00 or more.

Odwalla was committed to making a totally fresh product. In the company's 1995 annual report, for example, the letter to shareholders stated:

> Our juice is FRESH! We believe that fruits, vegetables and other botanical nutrients must be treated with respect. As a result, we do not heat-treat our juice, like the heavily processed products made by most other beverage companies.

The company's products were made without preservatives or any artificial ingredients, and the juice was not pasteurized (heat treated to kill microorganisms and to extend shelf life). Unpasteurized juice, the company believed, retained more vitamins, enzymes, and what Steltenpohl referred to as the "flavor notes" of fresh fruits and vegetables.

Although Odwalla did not pasteurize its juice, it took many steps in the manufacturing process to assure the quality and purity of its product. To avoid possible contamination, the company did not accept ground apples, only those picked from the tree. Inspectors checked field bins to see if there was any dirt, grass, or debris; and bins with evidence of ground contact were rejected. The company's manufacturing facility in Dinuba was considered the most advanced in the industry. The plant operated under a strict code of Good Manufacturing Practices. At Dinuba, apples were thoroughly washed with a sanitizing solution of phosphoric acid and scrubbed with whirling brushes. All juice was produced under extremely strict hygienic standards.

Marketing

Odwalla marketed its products through supermarkets, warehouse outlets, specialty stores, natural food stores, and institutions such as restaurants and colleges. Slightly over a quarter of all sales were with two accounts—Safeway, a major grocery chain, and Price/Costco, a discount warehouse.

A distinctive feature of Odwalla's strategy was the company's direct store distribution, or DSD, system. Most sites, from supermarkets to small retailers, were provided with their own stand-alone refrigerated cooler, brightly decorated with Odwalla graphics. Accounts were serviced by route salespeople (RSPs), who were responsible for stocking the coolers and removing unsold juice that had passed its "enjoy by" date. RSPs kept careful records of what products were selling well, enabling them to adjust stock to meet local tastes. As an incentive, salespeople received bonuses based on their routes' sales, in addition to their salaries.

Although the DSD system was more expensive than using independent distributors, it allowed the company to maintain tight control over product mix and quality. Moreover, because the company assumed responsibility for ordering, stocking, and merchandising its own products within the store, Odwalla in most cases did not pay "slotting" and other handling fees to the retailer.

Corporate Culture

The fresh juice company was always, as Steltenpohl put it, "values driven." In 1992, around 80 Odwalla employees participated in a nine-month process that led to the creation of the company's vision, mission, and core values statements. These focused on nourishment, ecological sustainability, innovation, and continuous learning.

Concerned that rapid growth might erode common commitment to these values, in 1995 the company initiated annual three-day training sessions, held on site at multiple locations, known as Living Vision Conferences, for employees to talk about the application of the vision to everyday operating issues. An internal process the company called Vision Link sought to link each individual's job to the Odwalla vision. Managers were expected to model the company's values. The company called its values a "touchstone [for employees] in assessing their conduct and in making business decisions."

In addition, Odwalla instituted a "strategic dialogue" process. A group of 30 people, with some fixed seats for top executives and some rotating seats for a wide cross-section of other employees, met quarterly in San Francisco for broad discussions of the company's values and strategic direction.

Social responsibility and environmental awareness were critical to Odwalla's mission. Community service efforts included aid to farm families in the Central Valley, scholarships to study nutrition, and gifts of cash and juice to many local community organizations. The company instituted a recycling program for its plastic bottles. It attempted to divert all organic waste away from landfills—for example, by selling pulp for livestock feed and citrus peel for use in teas and condiments and past-code juice for biofuels. In the mid-1990s, the company began the process of converting its vehicle fleet to alternative fuels. Odwalla's corporate responsibility extended to its employees, who received innovative benefits that included stock options, extensive wellness programs, and an allowance for fresh juice. The company won numerous awards for its environmental practices, and in 1993, *Inc.* magazine honored Odwalla as Employer of the Year.

During these years, the Odwalla brand name became widely identified with a healthful lifestyle, as well as with California's entrepreneurial business climate. In an oft-repeated story, Steve Jobs, founder of Apple Computer, was said to have ordered unlimited quantities of Odwalla juice for all employees working on the original development of the Macintosh Computer.

The E. Coli Bacterium

The virulent strain of bacteria that threatened to bring down this fast-growing company was commonly known in scientific circles as Escherichia coli, or E. coli for short.

The broad class of E. coli bacteria, microscopic rod-shaped organisms, are common in the human intestinal tract, and few pose a danger to health. In fact, most E. coli play a beneficial role by suppressing harmful bacteria and synthesizing vitamins. A small minority of E. coli strains, however, cause illness. One of the most dangerous of these is E. coli O157:H7. In the intestine, this strain produces a potent toxin that attacks the lining of the gut. Symptoms of infection include abdominal pain and cramps, diarrhea, fever, and bloody stools. Most cases are self-limiting, but approximately 6 percent are complicated with hemolytic uremic syndrome, a dangerous condition that can lead to kidney and heart failure. Young children, the elderly, and those with weakened immune systems are most susceptible.

E. coli O157:H7 (or 157) lives in the intestines of cows, sheep, deer, and other animals. The meat of infected animals may carry the infection. E. coli is also spread to humans through fecal contamination of food. For example, apples may be contaminated when they fall to the ground and come in contact with cow or deer manure. Secondary infection may also occur, for example, when food is handled by infected persons who have failed to wash their hands after using the toilet. Unfortunately, only a small amount of 157—as few as 500 bacteria—is required to cause illness. As one epidemiologist noted, "It does not take a massive contamination or a major breakdown in the system to spread it."

E. coli O157:H7 is known as an emergent pathogen, meaning that its appearance in certain environments is viewed by researchers as a new phenomenon. The organism was first identified in 1982, when it was involved in a several outbreaks involving under-cooked meat. Since then, poisoning incidents had increased dramatically. By the mid-1990s, about 20,000 cases of E. coli poisoning occurred every year in the United States; about 250 people died. Most cases were believed to be caused by undercooked meat. Although a serious threat, E. coli is not the most common food-borne illness. In the United States, five million cases of food poisoning are reported annually, with 4,000 of these resulting in death. Most cases are caused by mistakes in food preparation and handling, not by mistakes in food processing or packaging.

E. Coli in Fresh Juice

It was widely believed in the juice industry that pathogens like E. coli could not survive in an acidic environment, such as citrus and apple juice. Odwalla apple juice had a pH (acidity) level of 4.3. (On the pH scale, 7 is neutral, and levels below 7 are increasingly acidic.) Odwalla did conduct spot testing of other, more pH-neutral products. The Food and Drug Administration, although it did not have specific guidelines for fresh juice production, indicated in its Retail Food Store Sanitation Code that foods with a pH lower than 4.6 were not potentially hazardous.

In the early 1990s, however, scattered scientific evidence emerged that E. coli O157:H7 might have undergone a critical mutation that rendered it more acid-tolerant. In 1991, an outbreak of E. coli poisoning sickened 23 people in Massachusetts who had consumed fresh, unpasteurized apple cider purchased at a roadside stand. A second, similar incident occurred in Connecticut around the same time. In a study of the Massachusetts outbreak published in 1993, the *Journal of the American Medical Association* reported that E. coli O157:H7, apparently introduced by fecal contamination of fresh apples, had unexpectedly survived in acidic cider. The journal concluded that E. coli O157:H7 could survive at a pH below 4.0 at the temperature of refrigerated juice. The journal recommended strict procedures for sanitizing apples used to make fresh juice, all of which Odwalla already followed.

Although the FDA investigated both instances in New England, it did not issue any new regulations requiring pasteurization of fresh juice, nor did it issue any advisories to industry. At the time of the Odwalla outbreak, neither the FDA nor state regulators in California had rules requiring pasteurization of fresh apple juice.

Considering the Options

In the company's second-floor conference room, later in the day on October 30, Steltenpohl and Williamson gathered the company's senior executives to review the situation.

King County officials had identified about a dozen cases of E. coli infection associated with Odwalla apple juice products. But, as Steltenpohl later described the situation, "It was all based on interviews. They didn't yet have bacteriological proof." Washington health officials had not yet made a public announcement, nor had they ordered or even recommended a product recall.

Conversations with federal disease control and food safety specialists throughout the day had turned up troubling information. From them, Odwalla executives had learned of the two earlier outbreaks of E. coli illness associated with unpasteurized cider in New England. And they had been told that 157 could cause illness in very minute amounts, below levels that would reliably show up in tests. The FDA had indicated that it planned to launch an investigation of the incident but did not suggest that Odwalla had broken any rules.

Management understood that they had no *legal* obligation to order an immediate recall, although this was clearly an option. Another possibility was a nonpublic recall. In this approach, the company would quietly pull the suspect product off the shelves and conduct its own investigation. If a problem were found, the company could then choose to go public with the information.

The company carried general liability insurance totaling $27 million. It had little debt and about $12 million in cash on hand. The cost of various options, however, was hard to pin down. No one could be sure precisely how much a full or partial product recall would cost, if they chose that option, or the extent of the company's liability exposure.

Ordering a Recall

At 3 P.M., Steltenpohl and Williamson, about four hours after they had received the first phone call, issued a public statement.

> Odwalla, Inc., the California-based fresh beverage company, issued today a national product recall of fresh apple juice and all products containing fresh apple juice as an ingredient. . . . Our first concern is for the health and safety of those affected. We are working in full cooperation with the FDA and the Seattle/King County Department of Public Health.

The recall involved 13 products, all containing unpasteurized apple juice. At the time, these 13 products accounted for about 70 percent of Odwalla's sales. The company did not recall its citrus juices or geothermal spring water products.

"Stephen and I never batted an eyelash," Steltenpohl later remembered. "We both have kids. What if it had turned out that something was in the juice, and we left it on the shelf an extra two weeks, or week, or even two days, and some little kid gets sick? What are we doing? Why are we in business? We have a corporate culture based on values. Our mission is nourishment. We really never considered *not* recalling the product. Looking back, I suppose the recall was the biggest decision we made. At the time, it seemed the only possible choice."

Once the decision to recall the product had been made, the company mobilized all its resources. On Thursday morning, October 31, 200 empty Odwalla delivery trucks rolled out from distribution centers in seven states and British Columbia with a single mission: to get the possibly tainted product off the shelves as quickly as possible. Organizing the recall was simplified by the facts that Odwalla operated its own fleet of delivery vehicles and that, in most cases, the product was displayed in the company's own coolers. The delivery drivers simply went directly to their own accounts and removed the recalled juices. In cases where the product was shelved with other products, Odwalla worked with retailers to find and remove it.

A group of employees in San Francisco, one of the company's major distribution centers, later recounted the first day of the recall:

> Every single person who is or was an RSP, express driver, or merchandiser, worked that first full day and the next.

What was amazing was there were a lot of people who we didn't even have to call to come in. It might have been their day off, but they'd call to ask, "What can I do?"

Right. They'd ask, "When should I come in? Where do you need me to be?" . . . It was an amazing effort. . . . We were able to make it to every single account on that first Thursday. That's a thousand accounts.

Within 48 hours, the recall was complete. Odwalla had removed the product from 4,600 retail establishments in seven states and British Columbia. "This is probably as speedy as a product recall gets," a stock analyst commented. "They probably accomplished it in world-record time."

On October 31, as it was launching its recall, the company also took several additional steps.

- The company announced that it would pay all medical expenses for E. coli victims, if it could be demonstrated that Odwalla products had caused their illness.

- The company offered to refund the purchase price of any of the company's products, even those that had not been recalled.

- The company established a crisis communications center at its headquarters and hired a PR firm, Edelman Public Relations Worldwide, to help it handle the crush of media attention. It also set up a website and an 800 hot line to keep the public and the media apprised of the most recent developments in the case. Twice-daily media updates were scheduled.

- The company decided to extend the recall to include three products made with carrot juice. Although these products did not contain apple juice, carrot juice was produced on the same line. Until the company had determined the cause of the outbreak it felt it could not guarantee the safety of the carrot juice products.

On October 31, as the company's route salespeople were fanning out to retrieve the juice, Odwalla's stock price was plummeting. The company's stock lost 34 percent of its value in one day, falling from 18⅜ to 12⅛ on the NASDAQ exchange. Trading volume was 20 times normal, as 1.36 million shares changed hands.

Tracking the Outbreak

Over the next few days, the full extent of the outbreak became clearer. In addition to the cases in Washington, new clusters of E. coli poisoning were reported by health authorities in California and Colorado. As the company received reports about individual cases, Steltenpohl and Williamson attempted to telephone families personally to express their concern. They were able to reach many of them.

On November 8, a 16-month-old toddler from a town near Denver, Colorado, who had developed hemolytic uremic syndrome, died following multiple organ failure. Tests later showed antibodies to O157:H7 in the girl's blood. It was the first, and only, death associated with the E. coli outbreak. Steltenpohl immediately issued a statement that read:

On behalf of myself and the people at Odwalla, I want to say how deeply sad-
dened and sorry we are to learn of the loss of this child. Our hearts go out to
the family, and our primary concern at this moment is to see that we are doing
everything we can to help them.

Steltenpohl, who had spoken with the girl's parents several times during her hospitalization, flew to Denver, with the family's permission, to attend the child's funeral. The girl's
father later told the press, "We don't blame the Odwalla company at all. They had no bad
intentions throughout all this, and they even offered to pay all of [our child's] hospital
bills. I told them yesterday that we don't blame them, and we're not going to sue."

By the time the outbreak had run its course, 61 people, most of them children, had
become ill in Colorado, California, Washington, and British Columbia. Except for the
Colorado youngster, all those who had become ill, including several children who had
been hospitalized in critical condition, eventually recovered.

Investigation of the Outbreak

As the outbreak itself was running its course, the investigation by both the company and federal and state health
authorities proceeded. On November 4, the FDA reported that it had found E. coli
O157:H7 in a bottle of unopened Odwalla apple juice taken from a distribution center in
Washington State. As it turned out, this was the only positive identification of the pathogen
in any Odwalla product. Eventually, 15 of the 61 reported cases (5 in Colorado and 10
in Washington) were linked by molecular fingerprinting to E. coli found in the Odwalla
juice sample. The origin of contamination in the other 46 cases remained unknown.

Meanwhile, federal and state investigators converged on Odwalla's Dinuba manufacturing plant, inspecting it from top to bottom, in an attempt to find the source of the
pathogen. On November 18, the FDA announced that it had completed its review of the
Dinuba facility and had found no evidence of E. coli O157:H7 anywhere in the plant.
The investigators then turned their attention to the growers and packers who supplied
apples to the Dinuba plant, on the theory that the company might have processed a batch
of juice containing some ground apples contaminated by cow or deer feces. In their
interim report, the FDA noted that although no E. coli was found at Dinuba, "microbial
monitoring of finished product and raw materials used in processing [was] inadequate."
Odwalla sharply challenged this conclusion, noting that the FDA did not have any
requirements for microbiological testing.

Searching for a Solution

The recall placed enormous financial pressure on the company, and
challenged its executives to decide how and when to reintroduce
its products to the market.

As a short-term measure, Odwalla announced on November 7 that it would immediately reintroduce three of its recalled products, all juice blends, that had been refor-
mulated without apple juice. These products would continue to be produced at Dinuba,
but not on the apple processing line. In announcing the reformulation, Steltenpohl told
the press, "Until we are assured of a completely safe and reliable method of producing
apple juice, we will not include it in our juices."

But the reformulation of a few blended juice smoothies was hardly a long-term solution, since apple juice was a core ingredient in many of the company's top-selling products. Odwalla urgently needed to find a way to get apple juice safely back on the market. How to do so, however, was not obvious.

To assist it in finding a solution to the problem, Odwalla assembled a panel of experts, dubbed the Odwalla Nourishment and Food Safety Advisory Council, to recommend ways to improve product safety. In late November, with the help of these experts, Odwalla executives conducted detailed scenario planning, in which they reviewed a series of possible options. Among those they considered were the following:

- **Discontinue all apple juice products.** In this scenario, the company would eliminate all apple juice and blended juice products until it could be fully assured of their safety.

- **Improve manufacturing processes.** In this scenario, the company would take a number of steps to improve hazard control at various points in the production process, for example, through modified product handling procedures, multiple antiseptic washes, routine sample testing, and stricter controls on suppliers.

- **Modify labeling.** Another option was to disclose risk to the consumer through product labeling. For example, an unpasteurized product could be sold with a disclaimer that it was not suitable for consumption by infants, the elderly, or those with compromised immune systems, because of the very rare but still possible chance of bacterial contamination.

- **Use standard pasteurization.** Standard pasteurization involved slowly heating the juice to a point just below boiling and holding it at that temperature for several minutes. The heat killed dangerous microorganisms and also had a side benefit of extending the shelf life of the product. Standard pasteurization, however, also destroyed many of the nutritional benefits of raw juice.

- **Use modified pasteurization.** Modified pasteurization, also known as flash pasteurization, involved quickly heating the juice to a somewhat lower temperature, 160 degrees F., and holding it very briefly at that temperature to kill any harmful bacteria. In tests of this procedure, Odwalla technicians found that it yielded an apple juice that had a "lighter" taste than unpasteurized juice, but with a more "natural" taste than standard pasteurized apple juice. The process destroyed some nutrients, but fewer than standard pasteurization. Flash pasteurization did not, however, extend the shelf life of the product.

- **Use alternative (non–heat-based) technologies for removing pathogens.** The company also examined a number of alternative methods of killing pathogens. These included a high-pressure process in which pressure was used to explode the cell walls of bacteria; a process in which light waves were directed at the juice to destroy pathogens; the use of electricity to disrupt bacteria; and the use of herbal antiseptic products.

A key factor in the decision, of course, was what customers wanted. The company commissioned some market research to gauge consumer sentiment; it also carefully monitored public opinion as revealed in calls and letters to the company and discussions on public electronic bulletin boards, such as America Online.

The company also had to consider its financial situation. Remarkably, despite the recall, sales for the quarter ending November 30, 1996, were actually 14 percent ahead of the same period for 1995 because of excellent sales prior to the outbreak. The E. coli incident, however, had caused significant operating losses. By the end of November, the recall had cost the company about $5 million. Expenses had included the cost of retrieving and destroying product, legal and professional fees, and increased marketing costs. At the end of the fiscal quarter, Odwalla had a cash position of about $9 million, down from $12 million at the time of the outbreak.

On December 5, Odwalla announced that it had decided to flash pasteurize its apple juice. In a statement to the press, Williamson stated:

> Odwalla's first priority is safety. After much consideration and research, we chose the flash pasteurization process as a method to produce apple juice. It is safe, yet largely preserves the great taste and nutritional value allowing Odwalla to remain true to its vision of optimal nourishment. Importantly, we will continue to aggressively pursue the research and development of alternative methods to bring our customers safe, unpasteurized apple juice.

The following day, all apple juice and blended juice products were reintroduced to the market with flash pasteurized juice. The label had been redesigned to indicate that the product had been flash pasteurized, and Odwalla coolers prominently displayed signs so advising customers.

At the same time, the company moved forward with its expert panel to develop a comprehensive Hazard Analysis Critical Control Points (HACCP) (pronounced hassip) plan for fresh juice production. HACCP was not a single step, but a comprehensive safety plan that involved pathogen control at multiple points in the juice production process, including sanitation of the fruit, testing for bacteria, and quality audits at several points in the process. The company also continued to monitor new, alternative technologies for controlling bacterial contamination.

Regulating the Fresh Fruit Juice Industry

In the wake of the E. coli outbreak, public concern about food safety mounted, and federal and state regulators began considering stricter regulation of the fresh fruit juice industry. On December 16, the FDA sponsored a public advisory hearing in Washington, DC, to review current science and to consider strategies for improving the safety of fresh juice. Debate at the two-day hearings was wide-ranging.

Steltenpohl and Williamson represented Odwalla at the hearing. In their testimony, the Odwalla executives reported that they had decided to adopt flash pasteurization but argued *against* government rules requiring all juice to be heat-treated. "Mandatory pasteurization would be a premature and unnecessary step in light of the vast new technologies emerging," Steltenpohl told the hearing. He warned the panel that mandates could "lead to widespread public fears about fresh food and beverages."

Steltenpohl and Williamson called on the FDA to continue to explore different methods for producing fresh juice safely. In addition, they called for industry self-regulation aimed at adoption of voluntary standards for safe manufacturing practices and hazard control programs. The Odwalla executives reported that they viewed flash pasteurization as the last line of defense in a comprehensive program to eliminate pathogens.

Some other juice makers and scientists supported Odwalla's position. Several small growers vigorously opposed mandatory pasteurization, saying they could not afford the expensive equipment required. A representative of Orchid Island Juice Company of Florida asked, "What level of safety are you trying to achieve? We don't ban raw oysters and steak tartare, although the risks are much higher. Nor do we mandate that they be cooked, because it changes the flavor." A number of food safety experts testified about emerging technologies able to kill pathogens without heat treatment.

Some scientists and industry representatives, however, were on the other side. Two major firms, Cargill and Nestlé, both major producers of heat-treated juice products, argued vigorously for a government mandate, saying that "other technologies just won't do the job." Dr. Patricia Griffin of the Centers for Disease Control and Prevention noted that "current production practices do not guarantee the safety of apple cider, apple juice, and orange juice." She called for pasteurization of apple juice and cider, as well as product labels warning customers of potential risk. A representative of the Center for Science in the Public Interest called for a label warning the elderly, infants, and persons with suppressed immune systems to avoid fresh, unpasteurized juice.

Several days after the hearing, the advisory panel recommended against mandatory pasteurization, for the moment at least, calling instead for "good hazard control" at juice manufacturing plants and in the orchards that supplied them. However, an FDA spokesman added, "we can never say that forced pasteurization is completely off the boards." The agency indicated that it would continue to study a number of alternative approaches to improving juice safety, including mandatory pasteurization.

Looking to the Future   In May 1997, Steltenpohl reflected on the challenges facing Odwalla:

> Our task now is to rebuild a brand and a name. How you rebuild . . . these are important decisions. You can make what might be good short-term business decisions, but they wouldn't be the right thing. The decisions we make now become building blocks for the [company's] culture. We have to look at what's right and wrong. We need a clear moral direction.

Discussion Questions

1. What factors contributed to the outbreak of E. coli poisoning described in this case? Do you believe that Odwalla was responsible, wholly or in part, for the outbreak? Why or why not?
2. What do you believe Odwalla should have done as of October 30, 1996? As of November 11, 1996? In each instance, please list at least three options and state the arguments for and against each.
3. What steps, if any, should Odwalla take as of the point the case ends?
4. Do you consider Odwalla's voluntary recall decision to be an act of corporate social responsibility? Why or why not?
5. What is the appropriate role for public policy in the area of food safety? Assess the role of government authorities in this case. In your view, did they act properly?

On June 16, 1995, the International Olympic Committee (IOC) announced the selection of Salt Lake City, Utah, as the site for the 2002 Olympic Winter Games. Salt Lake City had been campaigning for the right to host an Olympics for more than 30 years. On November 23, 1998, scandal erupted as the first suggestions of bribery and corruption connected to the Salt Lake Organizing Committee's (SLOC) bid campaign were leaked to the press. KTVX-TV, a Salt Lake City television station, suggested that the SLOC had made payments for tuition to Sonia Essomba, daughter of the late Rene Essomba, an IOC member from Cameroon. Soon after the news broke, SLOC officials investigated the allegation and acknowledged that a Salt Lake City scholarship and international assistance program had made payments of approximately $400,000 to 13 foreign students, some of whom were relatives of IOC members. Marc Hodler, a senior IOC member from Switzerland, called the payments a "bribe" and alleged that at least three other recent Olympic elections had been corrupted. He also charged that four agents, one an IOC member, had "made a living" selling votes of IOC members.

In the months that followed, further allegations began to be made public. The SLOC was accused of trying to influence votes by providing free plastic surgery, health care, shopping sprees, ski weekends, first-class air travel, luxury accommodations, fur coats, and other expensive gifts to IOC members and their families. These gifts included $10,000 worth of guns and rifles made by Browning, a Utah-based firearms maker. Browning reported that it had shipped a shotgun and rifle, valued at about $1,000, to the office of the IOC president just one month before Salt Lake City was awarded the 2002 bid. The shipment had been made at the request of the SLOC.

As the charges mounted, the scope of the allegations began to widen. Rumors surfaced about escort services and prostitution, allegedly paid for by members of the SLOC. It was discovered that a relative of an IOC member had been employed by a company whose chairman was an SLOC member, while others had been employed by the Salt Lake City government and even by the SLOC itself. Further questions arose as it was determined that one IOC member had made a $60,000 profit on a Utah land deal shortly after Salt Lake City won the bid. And details were uncovered regarding cash payments that had allegedly been made to various organizations affiliated with IOC members and to IOC members directly. Members of the SLOC were accused of improper conduct in their bid campaign, while members of the IOC were under attack for both encouraging and accepting gifts and favors from the SLOC that were in direct violation of IOC rules.

This case was written by Julie E. Seger, MBA, Graduate School of Business, Duquesne University (May 1999), under the supervision of James Weber. Used by permission. This case was prepared from publicly available materials, including news stories appearing in the *Wall Street Journal, Maclean's, Newsweek, USA Today, Pittsburgh Post-Gazette, Time,* and *Sports Illustrated.* Online sources included ABCnews.com (ABC News) and CNNSI.com (CNN Sports). Additional information was obtained from the following websites: www.olympic.org (IOC), www.sls2002.org (SLOC), and www.olympic-usa.org (USOC).

Within four months of the initial allegations, 30 IOC members had been implicated in the scandal, and the value of alleged gifts, travel, scholarships, medical care, and cash payments had reached more than $1 million. The details of the activities of members of the IOC and members of the SLOC shocked the public. The allegations placed a great strain on the reputation of the Olympics—an athletic competition that had always represented the highest standards of behavior and ethical conduct.

Had the members of the SLOC acted unethically for the right to host the 2002 Olympic Games? Had the activities of the IOC members been appropriate? How had the bid process, its foundation embedded in the history and culture of the Olympic movement, gone awry?

The International Olympic Committee

The IOC was a private organization headquartered in Lausanne, Switzerland, whose mission was to lead the Olympic movement in accordance with the Olympic charter. The Olympic movement was based on a philosophy of life called *Olympism,* which, according to the Olympic charter, "seeks to create a way of life based on the joy found in effort, the educational value of good example and respect for universal fundamental ethical principles." IOC members represented each of the 115 countries that participated in the Olympic Games. They were expected to exemplify the high standards of behavior that the Olympic movement represented. They pledged, through the Olympic oath, to keep themselves "free from any political or commercial influence."

Since 1980, the IOC had been headed by Juan Antonio Samaranch. Samaranch, a Spanish marquis, had been a member of the IOC since 1966 when he worked as a leading sports official in Francisco Franco's fascist administration. He later became Spain's first ambassador to Moscow. As IOC president, Samaranch's lifestyle was likened to that of a head of state. His expenses, paid by the IOC or bid cities, included commutes by helicopter, first-class air travel, and luxury accommodations. Many have suggested that his lifestyle may have set a poor example for the other members of the IOC.

Referred to as "your Excellency," Samaranch had been described as an autocratic leader who tried to avoid conflict and encouraged harmony and unity within the Olympic family. His primary goal was to expand the Olympics and make the Games more profitable. During his presidency, he brought more countries (many of which were Third World countries), more women, and more former athletes into the IOC. He was also widely credited for building the Olympics into a multimillion dollar empire. His understanding of the commercial potential of the Olympic Games was evident as early as 1981, when he initiated an international marketing campaign that helped to transform the Games from a worldwide sporting event into a big business.

Responsibility for selecting the sites for future Olympic Games fell to the full IOC, under the direction of the president. The selection process began with interested national Olympic committees (NOCs) selecting a site from their country and presenting their selection to the IOC. IOC members routinely traveled to the nominated cities to tour facilities and evaluate the sites. While some cities had existing facilities, many only had plans for proposed structures that would be built if their city were chosen. These plans, as well as existing structures, all required the final approval of the International

Federations, so it was not critical that IOC members approve the actual event facilities of the proposed site. As a result, candidate cities focused their efforts on impressing IOC members with their hospitality and friendliness. As part of this effort, it had been customary for bid committees to give gifts to IOC members who were visiting their city.

Traditionally, the Olympics was not a large revenue generator. As a result, there was not a lot of competition to host the event. The 1976 Montreal Games had lost millions of dollars, and the 1980 Moscow Games had not been profitable either. Los Angeles was selected as the host for the 1984 Olympics after competing with only one other city. The 1984 Olympics, however, proved to be a turning point in the history of the event. Peter Ueborroth headed the Los Angeles Organizing Committee and was determined to create an Olympic sensation. By the time closing ceremonies had ended, the 1984 Olympic Games had netted $225 million in profits.

Suddenly, the campaign to be selected as host of the Olympic Games became highly competitive. In 1985, 12 cities began bids for the 1992 Winter Games. It soon became clear that candidate cities were willing to invest large sums of money in their campaigns. That same year, one candidate city hired caterers and flew in lobster and kiwi fruit for an IOC meeting, at a cost of $1.9 million. As the competition increased, bid cities committed up to $50 million to their campaigns. By some estimates, each set of Summer and Winter Games could be worth as much as $10 billion due to corporate sponsorships, broadcast rights, and increased economic activity in the host city. The economic impact of the Games in Salt Lake City was estimated to include $2.8 billion in sales, 23,000 job-years of employment, and $80 million to $140 million in state and local government revenue, after costs. Corporate sponsors were expected to contribute $859 million.

The Hodler Rules

In May 1987, the IOC approved guidelines to help control the spending excesses of campaign cities. Swiss IOC member Marc Hodler announced that visits to bid cities by IOC members could not exceed three days, and gifts had to be restricted to information and documentation or, at most, "souvenirs." These guidelines, commonly known as the Hodler rules, also prohibited IOC officials from accepting gifts valued at more than $150 from bidding cities. The IOC believed that these regulations would help to minimize the costs to candidate cities and, at the same time, set standards for giving and receiving gifts.

While the Hodler rules provided some guidance to IOC members and bid cities, they did not cover many of the perks enjoyed by IOC members. For example, they did not address the issue of transportation and accommodations. Members were still allowed to accept first-class plane tickets, accommodations in five-star hotels, and lavish dinners; the rules limited the number of trips they could make, not how they got there or where they stayed. According to Robert Helmick, a former IOC member and former USOC president, first-class airfare for each member and a guest was "the minimum that's expected [from a bid city] before they get to the gifts." In fact, first-class airfare, luxury accommodations, expensive dinners, transportation, and entertainment were all standard for IOC members visiting bid cities. This expectation may have developed as a result of the background of many IOC members. The IOC had traditionally included members of the world's royal families as well as other elites who were used to luxury and special privileges.

In 1991, officials from one bid committee formally complained to the IOC that "many IOC members expected to receive gifts above and beyond what anyone would judge to be courteous and gracious" and estimated that abuse of travel privileges by IOC delegates had cost the committee in excess of $700,000. During the 1998 Winter Olympic Games in Nagano, Japan, Samaranch's hotel bill alone was about $80,000, and Salt Lake City had budgeted $42,200 for his suite during the 2002 Olympic Games. Although Samaranch was exempt from the restrictions on gift giving because he had no vote on the committee, IOC vice president Dick Pound indicated that Samaranch possessed "the loudest nonvote anyone can imagine."

The Salt Lake City Campaign

The Salt Lake Organizing Committee was well aware of the rules and expectations established by the IOC. By the time the city had been awarded the right to host the 2002 Games, the SLOC had engaged in five bid campaigns spanning a period of 30 years. Salt Lake City was considered the cultural and political center of Utah, with a population of one million residents, many of whom were of the Mormon faith. With the majority of its population believing in "being honest, true, chaste, benevolent, virtuous, and in doing good to all men," it seemed to be the perfect site for an event that embodied sportsmanship and honor.

The SLOC, chaired by Thomas Welch, was formed in 1986 to help strengthen Salt Lake City's efforts to woo the Olympics. In the campaign for the 1998 Winter Olympic Games, the city had competed vigorously with Nagano. While Nagano had a proposal based mostly on sketches of proposed facilities, Salt Lake City already had world-class facilities in place. They were very confident that they would win the bid. But in 1991 Nagano won the right to host the 1998 Olympics by only four votes. Later, Nolan Karras, a board member for the SLOC, acknowledged that "the rumor among delegates was that Nagano bought it."

As the scandal surrounding Salt Lake City's bid campaign grew, additional allegations about Nagano and other earlier bid campaigns began to surface. A member of another U.S. city's bid committee, Rick Nerland, said that he was approached twice by agents asking for cash payment for a bloc of IOC votes during the bid for the 1992 Olympic Games. Questions arose in connection with the Nagano bid for the 1998 Olympic Games when Japanese Olympic officials confirmed that they had contracted an agent to help with their campaign. A senior bid committee member acknowledged that campaign expense books, previously reported as lost, had instead been intentionally burned. It was also revealed that one-third of the cost of the construction of an Olympic Museum in Lausanne was paid for by Japanese donors at the time of Nagano's bid. In addition, Bruce Baird, a member of the bid committee for Sydney, indicated that one IOC member and an intermediary had approached him with a request for cash in exchange for votes during the bid for the 2000 Olympic Games.

Although detailed information regarding Nagano's bid campaign would not be made public until much later, Salt Lake City organizers had heard rumors that Nagano had presented expensive video cameras to each IOC member prior to the vote for the 1998 Olympic Games. It was not difficult to determine that the SLOC had missed the mark with its gift of disposable cameras. According to Kim Warren, international relations coordinator for the committee in 1991 and 1992, "we just knew Nagano wasn't playing straight. You can't believe the crap they were pulling. We were giving out salt-water taffy and cowboy hats; they were giving out computers."

Following the loss to Nagano, Salt Lake City's campaign to win the 2002 games intensified. In 1989, the SLOC began to collect information regarding the likes and dislikes of IOC members. This was considered standard practice for bid cities and enabled them to determine which members were agreeable to accepting gifts and what gifts were most appropriate. SLOC vice president Dave Johnson was responsible for gathering this information and for keeping track of which members were going to vote for Salt Lake City, which were not, and which were undecided. The committee's mission for international relations, presented in 1991, was to "plan and implement a strategy to secure the winning number of IOC member votes for Salt Lake City." Their goals included establishing and maintaining "long-term, vote-influencing relationships with IOC members" and "long-term relationships with other key people of the Olympic Family . . . who would influence an IOC member's vote." The committee's annual budget grew from $540,000 for the 1992 fiscal year to over $3.7 million for the 1995 fiscal year.

On June 16, 1995, Salt Lake City needed 45 IOC votes to secure its place in Olympic history. It received 54 of the valid 89 votes while the closest competitors received only 14 votes each. A little over three years later, as allegations of bribery and corruption were erupting, many Olympic insiders would comment on the irony that surrounded that overwhelming margin of victory. Salt Lake City had not had any real competition for the 2002 Games.

IOC Members Defend Their Actions

As the scandal broke, many individual members of the IOC vigorously defended themselves against charges of corruption. Some denied that payments made to them were intended for their personal benefit. In the Olympic community, providing assistance to NOCs, especially in developing countries, was strongly encouraged and considered by many to be a contribution to "Olympic solidarity." Jean-Claude Ganga, an IOC member from Congo, said that the $70,000 he had accepted was for children's charities and had been distributed to the NOCs of Central Africa, Congo, and Niger. He also indicated that his frequent visits to Salt Lake City had been health-related and that his offer to pay for medical care had been refused. Anton Geesink, an IOC member from the Netherlands, indicated that the $5,000 he had accepted had gone directly to the Anton Geesink Foundation, a non-profit foundation that supported Olympic educational programs. Charles Nderitu Mukora, an IOC member from Kenya, explained that payments totaling $34,650 were accepted by the Charles Mukora Sports Foundation to support sports development in Kenya and world youth sporting activities.

Other members considered payments to be personal donations from individuals who also happened to be associated with the SLOC. Louis Guirandou-N'Diaye, an IOC member from the Ivory Coast, considered a $5,000 donation to the NOC of Côte d'Ivoire to be a personal donation, as did Sergio Santander, an IOC member from Chile, who received $20,050 from Thomas Welch to help finance Santander's reelection campaign for mayor of the capital of Chile.

Other IOC members defended educational assistance and employment assistance for relatives by saying that they were not responsible for the activities of other individuals. Some IOC members denied that they had any knowledge that the SLOC had incurred additional expenses on their behalf. These members indicated that they believed the additional courtesies were donated by contributors. Some claimed that expenses linked to them were inflated and may have included the additional cost for SLOC members and their guests who participated in the visits.

While their responses to allegations varied, the IOC members all denied that the payments in any way influenced their vote in the bid for the 2002 Olympic Games. Ganga indicated, "I have done nothing wrong. I will not become rich because I voted for Salt Lake City." He contended that Salt Lake City did not win the right to host the Olympic Games by bribery, but "because they were the best."

The IOC Investigation

On December 11, 1998, the IOC established an ad hoc commission to investigate the facts relating to allegations of improper conduct by its members in connection with the Salt Lake City bid campaign.

In its conclusions, presented to the IOC executive board on March 11, 1999, the commission acknowledged that some members had violated the Olympic charter by engaging in conduct "incompatible with the status of an IOC member," while others had acted in a way that created "the appearance of improper conduct." The commission noted, however, that in many parts of the world, business dealings were expected to include a certain amount of gift giving, and many IOC members lived in societies that operated this way.

> When passing judgment on what has been characterized as "improper gift giving," one cannot overlook the fact that gifts viewed as "improper" in some parts of the world are looked upon with a totally different perception in many other areas. Thus, for some highly respected, totally honest and incorruptible members, any ongoing relationship, including with members of all bid committees, is by definition based on very personal friendship. This naturally and openly implies exchanges of gifts, visits and other personal attentions.

The commission argued, moreover, that the problem lay in part with bid cities that had exceeded the Hodler limits, putting IOC members in a difficult position.

> It is clear that many candidate cities have not respected their limit with regard to the value of gifts. The Hodler rules contain no specific sanctions should the value of such gifts exceed the stipulated amount. The IOC members do not request that they receive gifts. If gifts are received, IOC members are in somewhat of an awkward position. It is difficult to refuse or return a gift without risking that the donor will be insulted. Nor is it polite, having received an unsolicited gift, to ask how much it may have cost. The same may not be true with respect to individualized gifts, but the normal protocol gifts have become routine (whatever their cost) and have no possible effect on the outcome of any candidate cities' efforts to attract the Games.

The commission indicated that it relied on the United States Organizing Committee (USOC) and other NOCs to assist in "upholding the principles underlying the Olympic movement." It believed that the USOC should have been "more active in discharging its responsibilities, including the bringing of any violation of the rules to the attention of the IOC."

The IOC acknowledged that difficulties might have emerged when, over the course of years of association in a tight-knit Olympic community, business relationships evolved into personal friendships. Although the IOC did not believe that those relationships were necessarily unethical, it agreed that accepting direct payments from the SLOC for personal benefit would be considered unacceptable. According to the IOC, members engaging in this conduct would have "been unworthy of and jeopardized the interests of the IOC in a manner incompatible with the duties and obligations pertaining to" their membership. It concluded, however, that no criminal actions had occurred, and that in any case, the gifts had had no effect on the outcome of the selection process.

The SLOC and USOC Investigations

The Salt Lake Organizing Committee, and its U.S. parent organization, also undertook to investigate the allegations of scandal. The SLOC first conducted an informal review of its financial records and then established a board of ethics to formally investigate the committee's activities.

In its subsequent report, the SLOC board of ethics criticized the IOC for not providing "clear and explicit guidelines" for bid cities to follow and "mechanisms" to ensure that the guidelines were enforced. They also criticized the IOC's support of NOC assistance programs because of the "inherent conflict of interest" that occurs when financial assistance is provided to a voting member's country.

The SLOC also denied that payments were in any way related to the bid or that they had received any promised votes in exchange for the payments. Thomas Welch said: "Never, not once in all that time, seven years, did an IOC member offer a vote for money. I never offered anything to get anyone to vote for us . . . If you measure our conduct the way people in this city do business, it's no different. You support your friends and their causes, and that's what we tried to do." IOC vice president Richard Pound agreed, saying that nothing "amounted to a quid pro quo, the purchase and sale of a vote. It was a willingness to please."

SLOC vice president Dave Johnson placed some of the blame on the IOC. He said that the IOC did "nothing to protect bidding cities" from the pressures exhibited by certain IOC members. In fact, the SLOC had written a letter to Samaranch in 1991 complaining about the activities of one of the agents. No action was ever taken.

Although the SLOC denied that any criminal activity had taken place, some members privately expressed regret about what had happened. Ken Bullock, an SLOC trustee said, "obviously, we did break the rules. If you want something bad enough, you stretch the boundaries." He also passed some of the blame on to the IOC saying, "The IOC allowed this sucking up." Robert Garff, another SLOC member, agreed: "I can't say our hands are clean, but the system has been flawed for years. So in some sense, we're the victims."

For its part, the USOC set up a Special Bid Oversight Commission to address the issue of bid city campaigning. The commission concluded that most of the blame for the scandal belonged with the IOC. According to the head of the commission, former Senate majority leader George Mitchell, "What the Salt Lake City people did was wrong. But they did not invent the culture. It was in existence and attributable in part to the closed processes and unaccountability at the international level." The report indicated that that the conduct tolerated by the IOC was "potentially illegal and inevitably corruptive" and that the IOC had ignored conduct that was "flourishing."

Repercussions

In the midst of all the controversy surrounding the Salt Lake City bid scandal, the SLOC and the USOC were continuing to try to prepare for the upcoming Olympic Games. To add to their troubles, the USOC still needed to raise an additional $250 million from sponsors to help pay for the Games in Salt Lake City. While the IOC and the USOC had assured sponsors that quick, decisive action would be taken, corporate sponsors were concerned about the extent to which the scandal had tarnished the image associated with the Olympic rings. The influence and impact of these sponsors on the Olympic community's ability to carry out the Olympic Games was immense. In addition to hundreds of minor sponsors, the Olympic movement had 11 major sponsors that contributed $50 million each for the right to use the Olympic rings in their corporate promotions for a four-year period. Nine of these sponsors had U.S. operations, and only two of them had signed up beyond the 2000 Summer Olympic Games in Sydney. In addition to the corporate sponsors, the IOC was concerned with placating NBC, which had paid $3.5 billion to broadcast all of the Olympic Games from the year 2000 until the year 2008.

Many of the major Olympic sponsors spoke out about the scandal in Salt Lake City. A spokesman from Coca-Cola's Olympic Marketing Department said "anything that tarnishes the Olympic movement will have a negative impact on the image of the Games to consumers all around the world. That's very important to us." According to a spokeswoman from the United Parcel Service of America, Inc., "ethics and integrity are everything to us. For the protection of the Olympic brand, this is a critical issue." David D'Allesandro, president of John Hancock Mutual Life Insurance, called for the IOC to investigate and take action throughout the Olympic structure. He said

> If they fail to do that and something else comes up, the rings won't be tarnished; they'll be broken. If they simply line up 12 IOC members and shoot them and think they can go back to Switzerland, they're wrong. They can't come back a year from now and say, "Oops, here's another one; there was a leak and we happened to hear about it." Boardrooms will shake if this is mishandled. That includes NBC's.

When one corporate sponsor, US West, delayed a $5 million sponsorship payment in response to the scandal, many people began to wonder what would happen if the SLOC could not raise the remaining $250 million it needed. Utah officials had signed a contract with the IOC in 1991 indicating that the state, and its taxpayers, would take responsibility for any deficit that Salt Lake City could not cover. The SLOC remained confident that the sponsors would contribute and suggested that the Games could be scaled back if the money were not raised. The IOC indicated that the Games could be canceled or moved to another city if Salt Lake City was unable to meet its financial obligations.

Discussion Questions

1. Who, or what, was responsible for the Olympics bribery scandal, in your opinion? In your answer, please evaluate the degree of responsibility of the International Olympic Committee, the U.S. Organizing Committee, the Salt Lake Organizing Committee, individual members of these groups, and the cultures within which these groups were operating.
2. Drawing on the methods of ethical analysis presented in Chapter 5, do you think that the IOC and the SLOC did anything wrong? Why, or why not?
3. What would you do, as of the point at which the case ends, if you were a member of the SLOC? Of the IOC? If you were a business that had made a preliminary commitment to sponsor the 2002 games? If you were a member of a committee from another city that was in the process of organizing a bid for a future Olympic Games?

On July 16, 1997, hundreds of federal and state law enforcement agents descended on dozens of Columbia/HCA hospitals. Their target was evidence of Medicare fraud. Armed with 35 separate search warrants, the government investigators moved with military precision through medical offices, seizing documents and computer files. At Columbia Hendersonville Hospital, near Nashville, agents told employees to back away from their desks, then began hauling away boxes of laboratory billing records. At the headquarters of Columbia's home care division in Winter Park, Florida, investigators brought in rented U-Haul trucks to carry off seized papers. These scenes were repeated in community after community, in seven states. The raid involved a coordinated effort by the FBI and the criminal investigative units of the Department of Health and Human Services, Defense Department, U.S. Postal Service, and various state Medicaid agencies. An attorney specializing in health care fraud told the press in awe, "This is as big a case as the government's ever done."

The target of this massive government probe, Columbia/HCA Corporation, was at the time the largest health care company in the world. With more than 340 hospitals under ownership, Columbia/HCA ran about 7 percent of all U.S. hospitals, and close to half of all investor-owned hospitals, as well as hundreds of surgery centers, rehabilitation centers, and home health care programs. With 285,000 employees, Columbia/HCA was the ninth-largest employer in the country—bigger, for example, than either McDonald's or General Electric. The health care titan brought in nearly $20 billion in revenue in 1996, 36 percent of it from Medicare reimbursements. In *Fortune*'s survey that year, Columbia/HCA had ranked as the most admired health care company; and the magazine had referred to its founder and CEO, Richard L. Scott—then just 43 years old—as a "boy wonder."

The federal agents were closed-mouthed about their operation, saying only that it was part of an ongoing probe. But the basic purpose of the investigation was well known to Columbia managers and to those both inside and outside the company who had followed the events of the previous few months. In April, the government had conducted a similar, although much more limited, raid on one of Columbia's hospitals in El Paso, Texas; and over the past few months grand juries in several states had interviewed current and former Columbia employees. At issue were allegations that Columbia had encouraged its managers to defraud Medicare, the federal health insurance program for the

This is a slightly abridged version of Anne T. Lawrence, "Columbia/HCA and the Medicare Fraud Scandal," *Case Research Journal* 20, no. 1 (Winter 2000), pp. 137–53. Abridged by the author and reprinted by permission of the *Case Research Journal*. Sources include articles appearing in the *New York Times, The Tennessean, Washington Post,* and other daily newspapers, and Columbia/HCA's annual reports. Book sources include Sandy Lutz and E. Preston Gee, *Columbia/HCA: Health Care on Overdrive* (New York: McGraw-Hill, 1998); Sandy Lutz, Woodrin Grossman, and John Bigalke, *Med Inc.: How Consolidation Is Shaping Tomorrow's Health Care System* (San Francisco: Jossey-Bass, 1998); Regina Herzlinger, *Market-Driven Health Care: Who Wins, Who Loses in the Transformation of America's Largest Service Industry* (Reading, MA: Addison-Wesley, 1997); and Malcolm K. Sparrow, *License to Steal: Why Fraud Plagues America's Health Care System* (Boulder, CO: Westview Press, 1996). A full set of footnotes is available in the *Case Research Journal* version. Copyright © 2000 by the *Case Research Journal* and Anne T. Lawrence. All rights reserved jointly to the author and the North American Case Research Association (NACRA).

elderly and disabled. Sources close to the investigation reported evidence that Columbia had, for example, inflated the seriousness of patients' illnesses to increase reimbursements and shifted costs to programs that were more generously compensated by Medicare. Columbia had also been criticized for providing various inducements to doctors to refer patients to its hospitals, in violation of federal law.

In the face of the unfolding crisis, Columbia publicly maintained a stance of business as usual. Samuel A. Greco, vice president of financial operations, when asked about the company's Medicare billing practices, simply said, "We hold ourselves to the highest standards." Other than that, Columbia had no official comment. On the evening of July 16, CEO Scott went ahead with a scheduled appearance on the Cable News Network show *Moneyline*. Questioned about the raids, Scott dismissed the subject with the comment, "It has not been a fun day. But as you know, government investigations are matter-of-fact in health care." But investors were not buying it. In the first day of trading after the news, Columbia's stock dropped 12 percent, losing over $3 billion in market value. Behind the scenes, members of the company's board urgently traded phone calls, trying to determine how best to respond to what promised to become the biggest health care fraud scandal in U.S. history.

Richard L. Scott

Richard L. "Rick" Scott, Columbia's founder and chief executive, was born in 1953 in Kansas City, Missouri, into a working-class family. His father drove a truck; his mother clerked at J.C. Penney's and sold encyclopedias door to door. As a child, Scott was highly competitive. His mother later recalled that "if Rick didn't win a game, he didn't enjoy it." Scott showed an early aptitude for entrepreneurship. While majoring in business at the University of Missouri, Scott, along with his mother and brother, purchased and successfully turned around two struggling doughnut shops. Scott went on to law school at Southern Methodist University. He then took a position as an attorney for a large Dallas law firm, where he developed a specialty in health care acquisitions.

But Scott wanted more from his career. In his work in the health care industry, Scott had come to the conclusion that with effective management, hospitals could be operated much more efficiently. He longed to acquire his own hospitals and turn them around, just as he had the two doughnut shops in college. With almost no capital and no experience in health care management, however, he had little credibility as a buyer. An early effort with two partners to buy a group of hospitals failed. In 1987, however, Scott got a break. Richard Rainwater, a Fort Worth financier and former adviser to the wealthy Bass brothers, was interested in starting a hospital company. Scott, then 34, was recommended to Rainwater by a mutual acquaintance as someone who was "young, smart, sharp, [and] aggressive." The two men hit it off. Both believed, they later recalled, that struggling hospitals could be picked up cheaply and returned to profitability with the right management. Both shared a vision of a multiservice health care chain. Rainwater set up Scott in an office on the twentieth floor of a building owned by the Bass brothers in Fort Worth and instructed him to start building a hospital company.

In November 1987, Scott wrote a thousand letters to prospective acquisitions. All rejected his overtures. "I tried everything. I called everybody. I flew all over the place," Scott later recalled. Finally, he made contact with a group of doctors in El Paso who wanted to own their own hospital. Scott and Rainwater each put up $125,000 of their own personal funds, 110 doctors bought shares, and the group borrowed $65 million from Citicorp. So financed, in July 1988 the partnership purchased two down-at-the-heel hospitals in El Paso, Texas, from Healthtrust, a hospital chain that was divesting properties. Scott picked the name Columbia Hospital Corporation for the fledgling chain because, he later recalled, it sounded "formidable."

The Rise of Medicare

The opportunity that Scott and Rainwater seized in 1987 was created, in large part, by transformations in the health care industry that had been wrought by government policy and, specifically, by Medicare.

In 1965, Congress created Medicare to provide health benefits to Americans over the age of 65 and for the seriously disabled. Medicare consisted of two parts. Part A, which provided hospitalization insurance, was funded through a 2.9 percent payroll tax, borne equally by employees and employers. Part B, which covered doctor bills and outpatient expenses, was funded through insurance premiums and government revenues. Between 1965 and 1980, expenditures on medical care in the United States rose from 6 to 9 percent of GNP. A number of factors were involved: growing numbers of people covered by both employer-sponsored and government insurance, the increasing use of expensive medical technologies, and a boom in hospital construction funded in part by the government. But perhaps the major factor was the lack of effective cost controls by either private or public health insurance providers.

At first, Medicare (like many other health insurers) had no effective cost controls. The program reimbursed doctors and other providers for any services deemed to be "usual, customary, and reasonable." Hospitals were reimbursed on a *cost plus* basis, meaning that Medicare paid for the cost of service plus a fee for administrative overhead. This system of third-party reimbursement lacked any of the normal checks on consumption. Patients had no incentive to shop for value, and they often were completely unaware of the cost of services. Both doctors and hospitals had incentives to perform more procedures and provide more services.

In 1983, Congress passed the first significant effort to constrain Medicare costs. The old system of cost plus reimbursement was abandoned. In its place, Congress adopted a payment system based on *diagnostic-related groups* (DRGs), that is, groups of related diseases. Each of around 480 DRGs was coded and an amount specified for reimbursement. Under the DRG system, hospitals would be paid *per admission,* with the amount determined by the diagnosis, rather than *per day* or *per service.* This reform for the first time introduced significant incentives for hospitals to control costs. Outpatient providers (such as home health care, ambulatory surgery centers, and the like) continued to be paid on a fee-for-service basis, on the theory that outpatient services were generally cheaper than hospitalization and should therefore be encouraged.

The new DRG system helped check runaway Medicare costs, but it also hurt hospitals' profitability. In 1984, Medicare margins were 14 percent. By 1987, they had dropped to 5 percent. Many hospitals were hemorrhaging money. There were simply too many hospitals. Many were managed by executives unused to operating in a cost-constrained environment. To their shareholders, communities, and customers, many of these hospitals represented a problem. To Scott and Rainwater, they represented an opportunity—to buy health care properties inexpensively and use modern business methods to turn them into profit-making enterprises.

Running a Marathon

In his Fort Worth office, Scott worked on building a hospital empire, sketching proposed deals on his white, vinyl walls with colored markers with the zeal of a general going into battle. At first, he and Rainwater acquired hospitals one by one, mainly in Florida and Texas. By 1990, Columbia owned 11 hospitals, with revenues of $290 million, and was reported to be the twelfth fastest growing company in the nation. That year, the company went public, for the first time selling shares of stock. As the company grew, its stock price rose quickly. After 1990, Columbia financed many of its deals through stock swaps in which it would trade its rapidly appreciating shares for the languishing stock of weaker hospitals. Columbia also raised capital by floating bonds.

By 1992, Columbia was buying, or trying to buy, almost everything in sight. A joke making the rounds among health care administrators at the time went like this: Have you gotten an acquisition letter from Columbia yet? It's the letter that starts out, *Dear Occupant*. Columbia's most notable acquisitions in the early 1990s included Basic American Medical (8 hospitals), Galen (75 hospitals), the Hospital Corporation of America (HCA) (97 hospitals), Medical Care America (a national chain of outpatient surgery centers and other outpatient facilities), and Healthtrust, Inc. (117 hospitals). In two years, 1994 to 1996, Scott nearly tripled Columbia's revenue, and profits were growing at close to 20 percent a year. But he did not feel the job was done. In 1995, Scott told a reporter, "I look at this as a marathon, and we're very early in it."

As a manager, Scott had a reputation for being extraordinarily hardworking. His habit was to rise at 5 o'clock and exercise on a treadmill; he was in the office by 6 o'clock. He was reputed to visit nearly 100 hospitals a year, send out scores of e-mails every day, and meet constantly with doctors, employees, and patients. Scott's lifestyle bordered on the ascetic. He did not smoke or drink. His office, even after the string of acquisitions of the early 1990s, remained modestly furnished with plastic laminated lamps and metal furniture. He was known to carefully save paper clips from his own mail. When asked by a reporter about his thrifty habits, Scott replied, "I don't like to spend money. I don't think I'm going to change."

"Health Care Has Never Worked Like This Before"

Scott's vision was to bring modern business practices to health care—a sector that had long been dominated by nonprofit institutions. The company's slogan was, "Health Care Has Never Worked Like This Before." In its mission statement, Columbia concisely stated its strategic objectives:

> Columbia's business strategy centers on working with physicians and other health care providers to develop comprehensive, integrated health care delivery networks in targeted markets. This strategy typically involves significant health care facility acquisition and consolidation activities.

The company's strategy had several key elements:

Physician Partnerships

One key element of Columbia's strategy was doctor ownership. Typically, doctors would be offered an opportunity to invest up to $150,000 each when Columbia took over a hospital. Up to 20 percent of the hospital could be physician-owned. Several thousand doctors were given this offer, and many accepted.

Columbia's practice changed the nature of the doctor–hospital relationship. Historically, physicians referred patients to hospitals, practiced medicine there, gave orders to staff, used supplies, and even ordered equipment. However, they were not employees, nor did they have an ownership stake. Consequently, they had little incentive to hold down costs or to comply with managerial directives. Columbia changed all this. As Columbia shareholders, physicians were motivated to consider cost before demanding expensive medical equipment or supplies. Moreover, they had an incentive to refer patients to Columbia hospitals, rather than to competitors. As Scott explained, "If someone has an ownership interest in something, they take pride in that, and so they will try to have whatever impact they can."

Consolidation within Regional Markets

A second element of Columbia's strategy was acquisition and consolidation, sometimes referred to as *horizontal integration*. The company might purchase two or three hospitals in a single market, close the weakest one or two, and consolidate operations in a smaller number of facilities. The goal was higher occupancy rates. "This industry's not any different than an airline industry or a ball bearing industry," David Vandewater, Columbia's president and chief operating officer, explained. "[If] you run at 40 percent of capacity or 60 percent of capacity, you're not getting the maximum value out of your assets." For example, in Miami, Columbia took over Victoria Hospital and Cedars Medical Center, merged their operations, and saved $3 million a year.

Vertical Integration

In Scott's vision, Columbia would become an integrated system of affiliated providers, offering a continuum of care, including general and acute hospital care, surgery, rehabilitation, physical therapy, mental health treatment, and home care. His objective was to offer managed care companies, preferred provider groups, and major employers "one-stop shopping"—a complete system of services within a regional market. Presumably, the arrangement would benefit patients as well, since continuity of care would improve. Many of Columbia's acquisitions of outpatient surgery centers, home health care programs, and rehabilitation and physical therapy facilities in the early 1990s were aimed at rounding out its networks within regional markets.

Strict Cost Controls

Within its system, Columbia implemented aggressive cost controls. One key tactic was to negotiate exclusive contracts with suppliers who were prepared to offer substantial discounts for the privilege of becoming Columbia's sole vendor for everything from sutures to soda. For example, Columbia negotiated a five-year contract with General Electric to become its exclusive provider of CT scanners and MRI units, at very substantial savings. Under Scott's direction, 95 percent of Columbia's purchasing agreements were regional or national in scope; many of them were exclusive deals. The company claimed to save $300 million a year through such arrangements.

Columbia also pushed to control labor costs, often through staffing cuts. By 1996, Columbia had reduced labor costs (salary and benefits) in its hospitals to 39.7 percent of total costs; the average in all investor-owned hospitals that year was 43.5 percent, and in nonprofit hospitals, 52 percent.

Brand Identification

A final element of the strategy was promoting the Columbia name as synonymous with quality care and efficient management. Managers and staff were expected to wear lapel pins with the Columbia logo (the letter C encased in two healing hands in a diamond shape). Scott insisted that all affiliated providers bear the Columbia name. In 1996, the company undertook an aggressive branding campaign, with the goal of becoming a household word "as familiar as Kellogg's and Campbell's soup." A multimillion dollar television advertising campaign featured a befuddled young man, trying to figure out where to find a quality hospital. The ads were humorous and edgy. In one, the fellow stopped to ask a farmer, standing by his tractor, whom he would call if he were going to have a baby in Denver. The farmer paused, then deadpanned: "The six o'clock news."

High Expectations

The management system Scott put in place was highly decentralized. Within each regional market, Columbia's network of health care providers was put under the control of a single manager. As Scott explained, "The key is to give decision-making power to local management teams [and have them] act like a small company." Columbia set an annual target for profit growth, typically 15 percent or higher. Regional administrators were given specific financial goals that integrated with the company's overall objectives. These were recorded on printed scorecards that were distributed to each manager.

The company's compensation system was structured to reward managers handsomely for meeting these goals. In general, executive compensation at Columbia was low, relative to the market. (Scott's own base salary, $858,000 in 1995, for example, was at least 20 percent lower than other health care executives at his level.) Bonuses, however, could be extremely generous; managers were able to as much as double their salaries by meeting or exceeding their financial targets. In 1995, 25 percent of Columbia managers received bonuses equal to 80 percent or more of their salaries; 30 percent, on the other hand, received no bonus. Explained one former Columbia vice president, "You have a highly decentralized system that grants a lot of autonomy to local and regional officers, and those officers have very significant monetary incentives tied to the net profitability of their markets."

Columbia's compensation system was quite unusual within the industry. Half of all hospitals at the time offered their managers no bonuses at all; most that did tied them to mortality rates and other measures of the quality of service rather than financial goals.

Columbia managers were under intense pressure, and not just from the carrot of attractive bonuses. The *New York Times* offered the following anecdote:

> Last August [1996], executives from Columbia's Midwest division ordered
> [manager Mark E.] Singer and 14 other department heads at Michael Reese
> Hospital and Medical Center in Chicago into the hospital boardroom to lambaste

them, one by one, for failing to cut costs aggressively enough, recalled Mr. Singer, administrative director for medicine at the time. (His job has since been eliminated.)

Mr. Singer was stunned by his treatment. "My father owned and operated a millinery factory in the garment district, and I never witnessed such an extent of demeaning, debasing, and devaluing behavior in the tough street environment as I personally experienced on 29 August," he wrote to the hospital's chief operating officer.

Managers who did not respond either to the inducements of a bonus or the humiliation of public criticism were summarily fired. In 1995, for example, 29 percent of Columbia administrators were replaced.

When asked about Columbia's methods of motivating its managers, Scott responded, "Do I believe that people feel like there's high expectations? Sure. But I'm not uncomfortable with that."

Health Care Fraud

At the time of the FBI raids on Columbia/HCA, no one in either the government or the private sector had a very good idea of the extent of fraud in the health care system. According to the Medicare carrier's manual, fraud was defined as "an intentional deception or misrepresentation which an individual or entity makes, knowing that the deception could result in some unauthorized benefit to the individual, the entity, or some other party." A 1992 Government Accounting Office (GAO) report estimated the percentage of the nation's health care budget lost to fraud to be around 10 percent, roughly $100 billion a year. The GAO acknowledged, however, that this figure was just a guess. An academic analysis of health care fraud published in 1996 concluded that there was no way to know the extent of fraud, because it had not been systematically measured.

Experts have argued that health care fraud was particularly difficult to control, for several reasons. One was the difficulty of determining what was fraud and what was not. Medicare rules were complicated and arcane; the regulatory manuals ran to upward of 45,000 pages. Many issues fell into a gray area. When was fraud actually fraud, and when was it merely aggressive billing or overzealous treatment by a well-meaning provider?

Moreover, unlike, for example, credit-card fraud, health care fraud was often not self-revealing. A person whose credit-card number was stolen would normally notice unusual charges on a monthly bill and promptly complain to the card issuer, who could then move to correct the problem. By contrast, under the Medicare program, patients normally received an *explanation of medical benefits* (EOMB) form itemizing charges only if a copayment was required or if a service was disallowed. In situations where a service was approved and paid, the patient normally never received an EOMB. Moreover, patients receiving an EOMB normally had little incentive to pay attention to specific charges, because they were rarely required to pay the full amount.

What happened when a beneficiary *did* complain—for example, that a service was billed that was not provided, or that a listed diagnosis was incorrect? According to an expert in health care fraud:

If a [Medicare] beneficiary says a service, reported on an EOMB, was not provided as billed, the investigative unit mails a form or letter to the provider asking them to confirm that the service was, in fact, provided. Depending on the practice of the Medicare contractor, providers may be asked to provide medical records; in other cases they merely have to sign a declaration that the service was provided. Assuming the provider confirms the service, the unit then sends the complainant a letter explaining that the service has been confirmed. That is the end of the matter, unless the beneficiary chooses to appeal the finding. To a complaining beneficiary this makes the government appear extraordinarily stupid. Most beneficiaries drop their complaint at that stage, many of them no doubt feeling the government does not deserve any help.

Medicare fraud, in addition to being difficult to identify, had traditionally suffered from weak enforcement efforts. In the 1980s, as the government focused on ways to trim skyrocketing Medicare costs, regulatory budgets were cut. The result was fewer inspections and fewer audits. Actual criminal prosecution of hospital administrators in the 1980s and early 1990s was extremely rare.

All this began to change in the early 1990s, however. A series of congressional hearings, held in connection with the debate over health care reform, cast a spotlight on the extent of health care fraud. The alarm was raised that Medicare might actually go broke. Many legislators saw fraud recovery as a way to cut costs or to protect or even expand government health coverage. Although the Clinton health care reform proposals failed, several antifraud initiatives moved forward. In 1995, a five-state pilot program called Operation Restore Trust was undertaken; and in 1996 the Health Insurance Portability and Accountability Act (the Kennedy-Kassebaum bill) provided generous funding for new fraud control programs, mainly aimed at Medicare. These efforts provided millions of new funding dollars for government investigators.

Another development that strengthened prosecutors' hands was new legal protections for whistle-blowers. In 1986, Congress amended the federal False Claims Act (originally passed in 1863 to deter fraud during the Civil War) to allow individuals who sued government contractors for fraud to receive up to 30 percent of any amount recovered by the government. The law also provided protections against retaliation by employers. These provisions for the first time provided substantial incentives for individuals to reveal fraud by their employers. The number of whistle-blower lawsuits rose from just 33 in 1987 to 530 in 1997. In 1997, the government recovered $625 million as a result of whistle-blower lawsuits.

At first, such lawsuits were directed primarily against defense contractors. Beginning in the early 1990s, however, the preferred target began to shift to health care. In 1996, for the first time the number of whistle-blower lawsuits in health care exceeded those in defense. "It has become a feeding frenzy," said one attorney who specialized in defending health care companies. Although details were under wraps, it was reported that more than a dozen whistle-blowers at Columbia/HCA had come forward and were cooperating with government investigators at the time of the raids of July 1997.

Investigating Columbia/HCA

By the spring of 1997, several government investigations of possible Medicare fraud by Columbia/HCA—aided in some cases by inside information provided by whistle-blowers—were moving forward. Grand juries were meeting in several states. The media was also looking into the story. On March 21 of that year, the *New York Times* published the first article in a series by the award-winning health care journalist Kurt Eichenwald. The *Times,* which had sources close to government investigators, provided important clues as to the issues that concerned Medicare regulators. The *Times* also reported the results of its own independent research into Columbia's practices.

At issue in the investigations were several different possibly fraudulent practices by Columbia/HCA and its managers. These included the following practices:

Upcoding

The term *upcoding* refers to the practice of inflating the seriousness of a treated illness to receive a higher payment from Medicare, or another insurer.

Under its DRG system, Medicare paid a fixed amount for each of about 480 covered illnesses. Of course, conditions that were more difficult to treat generally received higher reimbursements. For example, a hospital might be paid $6,800 for treating a case of complex respiratory infection (the most severe respiratory illness), but only $3,150 for simple pneumonia (the least severe respiratory illness). If a hospital reported to Medicare that it had treated a patient for complex respiratory infection, when in fact the illness had been less serious, this would represent upcoding. This practice was outlawed under Medicare regulations. If upcoding were found, Medicare would seek restitution. In the case of a pattern of behavior, the government might prosecute for fraud.

As part of its own investigation, the *New York Times* examined more than 30 million billing records of Columbia hospitals in Florida and Texas for 1995. Its analysis showed that 90 percent of the time, Columbia hospitals were more likely than other hospitals to bill for more highly compensated illnesses. One example was particularly striking. In 1992, as an independent hospital Cedars Medical Center in Miami had billed just 31 percent of its cases of respiratory illness at the highest rate. After its takeover by Columbia, this figure jumped to 76 percent.

In response to these charges, vice president David Manning stated Columbia's billing practices were "in complete adherence to all applicable federal laws." The discrepancies between Columbia's numbers and those of other hospitals simply reflected his company's greater accuracy, he asserted. "We believe that Columbia is more efficient in accurately billing the Medicare program than are our competitors," Manning stated.

Cost Shifting

Cost shifting occurs when a provider fraudulently shifts expenses from one program to another, for the purpose of increasing reimbursement.

One form of cost shifting allegedly committed by Columbia/HCA was reclassifying nonqualifying expenses so they would be covered by government insurance. For example, under federal rules, Medicare did not reimburse hospitals for sales, advertising, or promotional expenses. It did, however, reimburse providers for community education and patient care coordination, such as educating beneficiaries about available services or offering transitional support to patients newly discharged from the hospital. Federal investigators were looking into evidence that Columbia/HCA had routinely billed Medicare for the cost of "community educators" and "home care coordinators." In fact, the government alleged, these employees' actual duties were to act as sales representatives, promoting the company's services to physicians and the general public.

Another form of cost shifting was moving expenses from one program to another that was compensated at a higher rate. For example, under Medicare rules, hospital fees were capped. However, outpatient services, such as home health care, were not. Thus, an integrated health care provider, like Columbia, might have a financial incentive to shift costs billed to Medicare from its hospitals to its home health care units. Analysis of billing records from Texas by the *New York Times* showed that post-hospital care cost Medicare 23 percent more at Columbia hospitals than at other hospitals in the state, even after adjusting for the severity of the illness. The *Times* estimated the cost to the taxpayer of the Texas overcharges to be $48 million for one year alone. In 1997, Columbia owned 590 home health care units in 30 states; together, these provided 5 percent of the company's revenue.

Columbia defended its use of outpatient care, saying it cost Medicare less, not more. "It is not in any patient's interest to be served in an acute-care setting when less-intensive care is more appropriate," a spokesman said.

Unethical Tactics to Pressure Acquisition Targets

Federal prosecutors were also looking into charges that Columbia used illegal inducements to officials of hospitals the company was trying to acquire, violating antibribery laws. Hospital managers told government investigators that they had been offered Super Bowl tickets, jobs, and payments for consulting never performed.

Financial Relationships with Doctors

Finally, the investigation also focused on whether or not doctor ownership had led doctors to refer patients to Columbia facilities, even if another hospital was better equipped or could offer superior services for the patient's condition. In an independent investigation of referral patterns, the *Times* found that a group of doctors who had recently invested in Columbia increased their admissions to Columbia hospitals by 13 percent, while their referrals to non-Columbia hospitals dropped 22 percent. Columbia criticized this study for bias and defended itself by saying that investments were too small to influence doctors' decisions; and that in any case managed care plans, not doctors, were mainly responsible for choosing hospitals. Federal law barred doctors from referring patients to businesses such as home health care providers in which they had a financial interest, but law did not bar referral to *hospitals* in which they had an interest.

The Unfolding Crisis

Even before the events of July 16 transpired, the April raid on the company's El Paso hospital, the ongoing grand jury investigations, and the hard-hitting reporting of the *New York Times'* Kurt Eichenwald gave Columbia executives ample warning that prosecutions for fraud, and probably criminal indictments, were brewing.

One of the most concerned of Columbia's executives was Thomas F. Frist, Jr. Trained as an Air Force surgeon, Frist had founded the Hospital Corporation of America (HCA) in 1968 with his father, also a physician. Over the next two decades, HCA—headquartered in Nashville—gradually built an extensive chain of hospitals, becoming for a time the largest hospital chain in the country. Frist became president of HCA in 1977 and CEO in 1982. In a profile of leading corporate executives published in *Financial World,* Frist was described as a "mild-mannered" family man with a penchant for fiscal conservatism and efficient provision of medical services. He was also known for his moral righteousness. Frist, like his father before him, "ran the business like you were taught in Sunday school," recalled a former top executive of HCA. After HCA's merger with Columbia in 1994, Frist had stepped down from his day-to-day management role, becoming vice chairman of Columbia's board of directors and a member of the company's three-person executive committee.

Insiders reported that as the crisis unfolded at Columbia, Frist became increasingly disenchanted with Scott's leadership. Over a period of several months, he had urged Scott to tone down his aggressive management style, to little effect. In January 1997, according to one account, Frist had actually considered resigning from the board but had decided against doing so. Following the raid in El Paso in April, Frist and several other members of the board had expressed concern to Scott about the government investigation. Scott had responded, according to one insider, "by assuring the directors that the government had nothing on the company, that there were no problems, and that there had been similar investigations in the past that had simply fizzled."

A few weeks later, Frist had written a nine-page letter to Scott, outlining the company's problems and possible solutions. Scott never answered. "I didn't know what to do," Frist later recalled. "It was the most perplexing thing in my career." On the July 4 weekend, Frist cut short a vacation in Aspen, saying he was too upset to relax. Frist flew to California, where he met privately with Richard Rainwater and his wife, Darla Moore. Rainwater, Scott's original partner, and his wife were Columbia's largest shareholders, with shares worth around a quarter billion dollars. Before her marriage to Rainwater in 1991, Moore had been a vice president of Chemical Bank and one of the top-paid female executives in the country; she had served on Columbia's board between 1994 and 1996, when she resigned because of a potential conflict of interest.

According to a profile of Moore later published in *Fortune,* the threesome discussed several options for the troubled company and its chief executive. Rainwater later recalled his own position:

> Great executives make mistakes, and usually they recover. My hope was that Rick would alter his stance of righteous indignation. I felt he could carry on in the job.

Moore, however, was more troubled by Scott's apparently nonchalant response to the government investigation. "Rick was disdainful," she explained. "You don't spit on Uncle Sam." Moore advocated trying to negotiate a merger between Columbia and Tenet Healthcare, then the second-largest hospital chain. In this plan, Tenet's CEO, Jeffrey Barbakow, would be offered the chairmanship of the combined company, allowing Scott to leave with dignity. Moore agreed to initiate private talks with Tenet.

Before this plan could be carried out, however, the events of July 16 forced the board's hand. Columbia's board of 10 directors consisted mainly of close associates of Scott's, and the board had scant experience acting independently of management. In the past, board meetings had been limited to two hours. Typically, Scott would present a series of items and leave little time for debate. But this time, the directors agreed that something had to be done. Because it was mid-summer, however, it was difficult to assemble to entire group right away. Finally, almost two weeks after the government raid, on July 24 at 4 P.M., the full board assembled, with Scott present, at Columbia's Nashville headquarters. Everyone there knew that the board needed to respond without delay to the government's massive Medicare fraud investigation.

Discussion Questions

1. In your opinion, what causal factors contributed most significantly to the Medicare fraud crisis at Columbia/HCA? In your answer, please discuss both external and internal factors.
2. What do you think the board of directors of Columbia/HCA should do, as of the point the case ends?
3. What changes in hospital management practices, government regulation, or stakeholder behavior, if any, would help prevent this kind of problem from occurring in the future at other health care institutions?

On June 20, 1997, at a little after three in the afternoon, tobacco industry attorney Phil Carlton and Arizona attorney general Grant Woods emerged exhausted from a meeting room at the Park Hyatt Hotel in Washington, DC. From inside the room—where negotiators for the tobacco industry, public health organizations, and state attorneys general had been engaged in days of nearly around-the-clock talks—reporters waiting in the hall could hear applause, then whooping and whistling. Woods flashed a thumbs-up sign to the press corps. "We've got a deal," he announced.

For weeks, the outcome of the delicate tobacco negotiations had been in doubt. Observers had called the talks "chaotic" and "fractious." The talks had nearly broken down several times during the final few days, as negotiations foundered on the issues of document disclosure, government regulation, and whistle-blower protection. At one point, the attorney representing 20 of the 32 states at the table had simply walked out and flown off in his Lear jet. But at the last moment, both sides had made key concessions, and an agreement was reached.

In many respects, the deal struck at the Park Hyatt was astonishing. The big tobacco companies had agreed to pay *369 billion* dollars over the next quarter century and to submit to federal regulations and broad restrictions on cigarette advertising. In exchange, many state lawsuits would be settled, and the industry would be protected from most future litigation.

Never before had the tobacco giants been willing to make such vast concessions to their opponents. And never before had prominent public health advocates been willing to endorse limits on how much money smokers with lung cancer and heart disease could recover from the tobacco industry. The tobacco deal, said Mike Moore, Mississippi attorney general and a lead negotiator—with a bit of enthusiastic redundancy—was "the most historic public-health achievement in history." Many thought the agreement would herald a new era in the relationship between the tobacco industry and its critics in government and the public health community, as well as provide a model for the settlement of mass liability cases.

An earlier version of this case, Anne T. Lawrence, "The Tobacco Deal," was presented at the Western Casewriters Association Annual Meeting, Portland, Oregon, March 26, 1998. This case has been updated for this edition of *Business and Society*. The author would like to thank Carol Anderson, an MBA student at San Jose State University, for research assistance. This case was prepared from publicly available materials, including newspaper stories appearing in the *New York Times, Wall Street Journal, Washington Post, Arizona Republic, Louisville Courier-Journal, Business Week, U.S. News & World Report,* and *USA Today;* material published on the Internet by Center for Responsive Politics; a special issue of *Mother Jones* (June 1996); and three book-length studies: Philip J. Hilts, *Smokescreen: The Truth behind the Tobacco Industry Cover-Up* (Reading, MA: Addison-Wesley, 1996); Stanton E. Glantz, John Slade, Lisa A. Bero, Peter Hanauer, and Deborah A. Barnes, *The Cigarette Papers* (Berkeley: University of California Press, 1996); and David Kessler, *A Question of Intent: A Great American Battle with a Deadly Industry* (New York: Public Affairs, 2001). The Brown & Williamson papers are available on the Internet at www.library.ucsf.edu/tobacco.

Table 1 The big five tobacco companies, 1997, ranked by U.S. market share

Company	Subsidiary	Key Brands	Market Share (percent U.S./ percent global)	Market Value	Sales (in U.S. $ millions)	Profits	Assets
Philip Morris	—	Marlboro, Virginia Slims	43/16	$106,580	$54,553	$6,303	$54,871
RJR Nabisco	RJ Reynolds	Camel, Winston	28/6	8,758	17,063	611	31,289
BAT Industries	Brown & Williamson	Lucky Strike, Kool	18/13	27,767	25,721	2,536	76,630
Loews Corp.	Lorillard	Kent, Newport	7	11,188	19,964	1,384	67,683
Brooke Group	Liggett	L&M, Chesterfield	2	93	414	196	135

Note: Market value is the share price on May 30, 1997, multiplied by the latest available number of shares outstanding. Sales is annual net sales reported by the company. Profits is latest after-tax earnings available to common shareholders. Market value, sales, profits, and assets are worldwide.
Sources: "The Business Week Global 1000," *Business Week,* July 7, 1997, pp. 55–92; www.hoovers.com/quarterlies; www.sec.gov/archives/edgar/data.

The U.S. Tobacco Industry

In 1997, tobacco was one of the United States' most profitable businesses, as well as one of its most controversial.

The U.S. cigarette industry was dominated by five companies, as shown in Table 1. The industry leader was Philip Morris Companies, Inc. The world's largest tobacco company, Philip Morris controlled almost half of the U.S. market for cigarettes and owned the world's second most valuable brand, Marlboro (the most valuable brand was Coca-Cola). The company's market value in 1996 was slightly under $107 billion. Although over half the company's revenue came from the sale of tobacco products, Philip Morris also owned profitable real estate, financial services, and food and beverage businesses, including Kraft and Miller Brewing.

Second, ranked by U.S. market share, was RJR Nabisco Holdings Corp. The company's tobacco subsidiary, R.J. Reynolds, produced Camel, Winston, and Salem cigarettes, among others. The company's food subsidiary, Nabisco, was a major producer of cereals, crackers, cookies, candy, gum, and other packaged food products. Although sales were split about evenly between tobacco and food products, most of the company's profits came from cigarettes.

Bringing up the rear were three companies with smaller market shares. BAT Industries (formerly, British American Tobacco), based in Britain, was the owner of Brown & Williamson, maker of Lucky Strike and Kool cigarettes, with an 18 percent share. (BAT had acquired another U.S. company, American Tobacco, in 1995.) Loews Corporation, controlled by billionaire brothers Laurence and Robert Tisch, was a holding company that included CAN Financial (an insurance company) and the Loews Hotels. One of Loew's smaller holdings was the Lorillard Tobacco Company, maker of Kent, Newport, and True cigarettes.

The smallest of the big five was Brooke Group Ltd. Brooke's Liggett division (formerly Liggett & Myers) held about 2 percent of the U.S. market with its Chesterfield,

L&M, Lark, and some discount varieties of cigarettes. Brooke's chairman and CEO, Bennett LeBow, owned 57 percent of the company. (UST Holdings—formerly U.S. Tobacco—was normally not included in the big five because it manufactured chewing tobacco and snuff rather than cigarettes.)

In the United States in 1997, 26 percent of adults smoked. Slightly more men (28 percent) than women (23 percent) used cigarettes.

Domestic sales, however, were slipping, as they had for some time. At the peak of cigarette consumption in the United States in the early 1950s, fully half of American adults smoked; this percentage had been nearly halved in 40 years. All major tobacco companies had responded by moving aggressively to expand overseas sales, especially in the booming overseas markets of Asia, Eastern Europe, South America, Africa, and the Middle East, where American brands had status and consumption was rising. This strategy was to a large degree successful; in 1996, total international tobacco sales were $296 billion (the United States accounted for less than 40 percent).

The cigarette industry was phenomenally profitable. Warren Buffett, the well-known investor, explained the matter simply: "I'll tell you why I like the cigarette business," he said. "It costs a penny to make. Sell it for a dollar. It's addictive. And there's fantastic brand loyalty."

The tobacco industry was a major contributor to the U.S. economy. It added more than $55 billion annually to the gross domestic product. Federal, state, and local taxes collected from the sale of cigarettes and other tobacco products in the United States totaled $13.1 billion in 1996. The industry was also a major employer in some states. Of the approximately 700,000 people employed in growing, processing, transporting, marketing, and retailing tobacco and its products, most were concentrated in the southeastern states. These workers, of course, contributed to the economy through their spending and income taxes. Tobacco products, a major export, significantly improved the U.S. balance of trade. The industry spent $6.2 billion a year for advertising, a big boost to Madison Avenue, and kept legions of attorneys and public relations people employed.

The tobacco industry also imposed significant economic costs. The total annual costs of smoking-related illnesses were estimated by the Centers for Disease Control in 1996 to run around $50 billion. These costs included health care for persons with emphysema, lung cancer, heart failure, and other tobacco-related illnesses; and lost work time and reduced productivity of smokers. Some of these costs were borne by the federal government, and hence, indirectly, taxpayers, through Medicare and Medicaid. Annual state spending (through various state medical plans) on smoking-related health care varied by population, of course; to cite a few examples, the yearly tab was $250 million in Florida, $240 million in Massachusetts, and $500 million in West Virginia. Individuals also paid, both directly and through their insurance premiums. These figures did not include, of course, the incalculable costs of pain and grief suffered by victims and their families. On the other hand, one study—funded by the tobacco industry—argued that smoking actually *saved* the U.S. health care system money, for the simple reason that many smokers died early, sparing the system the cost of caring for them in old age.

Public Health Issues

The adverse health effects of cigarettes had been well known in the public health community since the early 1950s. Smokers are 10 to 20 times more likely to suffer from lung cancer than are persons who do not smoke. Among smokers, the number of cancers rise with the number of cigarettes smoked. Cigarette smoke has been linked with cancer in animal studies, and a specific chemical agent in tobacco tar, *benzo(a)pyrene,* has been found in experiments to cause cancerous mutations in human lung cells. In addition to causing lung cancer, cigarette smoking also causes a number of other ailments. Smokers are at higher risk for coronary heart disease, stroke, throat and bladder cancer, chronic bronchitis, and emphysema. Smoking by pregnant women retards fetal growth. Secondhand smoke can cause lung cancer and heart disease in healthy nonsmokers.

Smoking is the leading preventable cause of death in the United States. Each year, about 420,000 smokers and 53,000 nonsmokers die from tobacco-related illnesses; many more times as many as die from all other preventable causes of death (alcohol, auto accidents, AIDS, suicide, homicide, and illegal drugs) combined.

Nicotine, the pharmacologically active component of tobacco, is highly addictive. A member of the alkaloid family, nicotine is chemically related to other well-known addictive substances, including cocaine, heroin, and morphine. In any given year, about a third of smokers try to quit; only about 10 percent succeed, mainly because of the effects of nicotine addiction.

Smoking as a Pediatric Disease

Dr. David Kessler, commissioner of the Food and Drug Administration, frequently referred to smoking as a "pediatric disease," that is, a disease of children.

The reasons for Kessler's somewhat startling assertion is that most people take up the cigarette habit in their teens. Among lifelong smokers, 90 percent began smoking by the time they were 18, and over half by the age of 14. The percentage of U.S. high-school students in 1995 who said they had smoked in the past month was 35 percent, up from 28 percent in 1991.

The reasons that smokers start in their teens are complex. Although nicotine is highly addictive, it does not promote an immediate physiological dependence as do heroin and some other drugs. Rather, nicotine addiction takes on average one or two years of smoking to become fully established. At the same time, the act of smoking itself, for many people, is not particularly pleasurable initially; beginning smokers report that cigarettes burn their throats, make them cough, and don't taste particularly good. Who, then, sticks with the habit long enough to become hooked? The answer is: People in situations where peer pressures to smoke are strong and for whom peer influence is particularly compelling. Study after study has come to the same conclusion: Teens start smoking because their friends do. Once they've smoked regularly for a year or two, many find it extraordinarily difficult to quit, even if they want to.

Every day in the United States, 3,000 new young people take up the smoking habit. One out of three of them will die from tobacco-related illnesses, many in middle-age.

From the perspective of the tobacco companies, these facts about how people start smoking present a vexing problem. Sales of cigarettes to minors are illegal, and tobacco companies would prefer not to break the law or to face the public disapproval caused by peddling an addictive substance to youngsters. However, the industry is also well aware that it loses customers all the time; 1.3 million smokers quit every year, and 420,000 die. Most replacement smokers will be recruited, if they are recruited at all, from the ranks of the young.

Moreover, brand loyalty is exceptionally high among smokers, so the cigarette a smoker begins with often remains his or her brand for life. Cigarette makers thus have a strong financial incentive to market their products to teens, even though it is publicly awkward—not to mention illegal—to do so.

Lines of Defense

Although smoking was well known to cause death and disease, for many years the tobacco industry maintained a remarkable record of defending itself against both lawsuits and government regulation.

Until 1996, the tobacco industry never lost a lawsuit brought by a smoker. The tobacco companies were well funded, hired top attorneys, and defended all lawsuits extremely vigorously. The industry consistently maintained that tobacco had not been proven to cause cancer or other diseases. After warning labels were introduced in 1965, the industry was also able to argue that smokers had been informed of the risk and had assumed those risks and the consequences. Most juries blamed the smoker for not having the willpower to quit. "The American people know smokers can and do quit, and they still believe in individual responsibility," contended a press release distributed by R.J. Reynolds.

Moreover, the tobacco industry successfully used a variety of political strategies to block antismoking legislation and to thwart efforts to impose government regulation.

Table 2   *Tobacco industry soft-money political contributions, 1996 election year*

Company	Republican	Democrat	Total
Philip Morris	$2,520,518	$496,518	$3,017,036
RJR Nabisco	1,442,931	254,754	1,697,685
Brown & Williamson	635,000	7,500	642,500
U.S. Tobacco	556,603	118,362	674,965
Tobacco Institute	424,790	106,044	530,834
Total	$5,579,842	$983,178	$6,563,020

Note: Soft money refers to funds donated directly to political parties to support party-building efforts such as televised campaign commercials that do not support a specific candidate, get-out-the-vote drives, and other activities in connection with presidential and congressional races. Soft money was legal under U.S. election laws in 1996. Limiting, or banning, soft-money contributions has been a key element of many campaign finance reform proposals.
Source: Center for Responsive Politics, from Federal Election Commission data, based on year-end reports filed by political parties, January 31, 1997.

The big five and their political organization, the Tobacco Institute, consistently donated large sums of money both to political parties and, through their political action committees, to individual candidates. Historically, the industry had funneled funds more or less equally to both major parties, but in the mid-1990s—following the Clinton administration's stepped-up efforts to impose regulations on the industry—its support shifted notably to the Republicans. The industry's 1996 contributions to political parties are shown in Table 2. That year, Philip Morris was the top donor of "soft money" among *all* contributors. Collectively, the tobacco industry was responsible for $6.6 million to both parties, out of the $263 million total for soft money contributions that year.

In addition, the industry provided financial support to a variety of advocacy groups and think tanks with interests allied to its own—for example, those opposing FDA regulatory authority, promoting smoker's rights, and supporting free speech rights for advertisers. The industry's powerful corporate lobby, the Tobacco Institute, vigorously promoted its point of view. Individual firms also maintained their own lobbying efforts; in 1996, for example, Philip Morris spent $19.6 million on its Washington, DC, lobbying operation.

The industry-funded Council for Tobacco Research (founded in 1954 as the Tobacco Industry Research Committee) sponsored partisan research and publicized the industry's contention that there was no proof that smoking caused cancer and heart disease. Commented the attorney for the National Center for Tobacco-Free Kids: "While [the industry's] PR campaigns were a failure with the public, they accomplished something more important: They gave politicians cover for failing to act."

Tobacco's political and public relations efforts were remarkably successful. For many years, the industry succeeded in avoiding the regulation of nicotine, holding cigarette taxes to a moderate level, blocking many local antismoking ordinances, and retaining mildly worded warning labels. In instance after instance, the tobacco industry actually managed to turn apparent setbacks to its advantage. When Congress banned television advertising of cigarettes, it benefited existing brands because, without television, introducing new brands was prohibitively expensive. The TV ban also meant the end of mandated public interest antismoking television spots, ones that had been hurting sales. When Congress required warning labels on cigarette packs, the industry won a clause in the law that effectively blocked lawsuits, on the grounds consumers had been warned of the risks. When the government has levied taxes on cigarettes, tobacco companies have often raised prices and then blamed government intrusion. "Without exception, federal legislation designed to favor the public health has worked to the advantage of the industry," commented tobacco policy expert Kenneth E. Warner.

Chinks in the Industry's Armor

By the mid-1990s, however, tobacco's invincibility was weakening, leading some of its key strategists to consider negotiating an agreement with its adversaries. Several factors contributed to the industry's deteriorating position.

Congress Holds Hearings

In April 1994, the then-Democratic controlled House of Representatives opened hearings on the health effects of tobacco. In testimony under oath, top executives of the tobacco industry assured Congress that their companies did not manipulate nor independently control the level of nicotine in cigarettes and that cigarettes did not cause cancer or other illnesses. The hearings served to focus public attention on the industry. The tobacco industry executives' testimony was widely ridiculed; one survey later found that, when shown to the public, videotape of the tobacco chieftains swearing to tell the truth elicited "instant recognition and instant laughter." Grand juries later considered whether tobacco executives illegally conspired to obstruct a congressional investigation.

Industry Whistle-Blowers Come Forward

Just a few weeks later, an industry whistle-blower made public some highly damaging internal company documents. Merrell Williams was a paralegal working for a law firm in Louisville, Kentucky, that had been hired by Brown & Williamson to review thousands of pages of company documents in connection with its legal defense. Williams, a longtime smoker of Kools who was suffering from heart disease, was shocked at what he saw. Over a several-month period, Williams smuggled documents out of the office and secretly copied them before returning the originals.

In May 1994, Williams mailed these documents to a prominent antitobacco researcher at the University of California–San Francisco, Dr. Stanton Glantz. Glantz subsequently posted the documents on the Internet. In July 1995, Glantz and his colleagues published an initial review of the documents that provided strong evidence that Brown & Williamson was aware of the addictive nature of nicotine and of the health hazards of tobacco.

FDA commissioner Kessler later stated that the publication of the B&W documents was "a major moment, beyond which all went in one direction. It was the first time we had anyone saying, 'We are in the business of selling nicotine, which is an addictive drug.' Before that, it was all indirect evidence."

In November 1995, a second whistle-blower came forward. Dr. Jeffrey Wigand, chief of research for B&W from 1989 to 1993, gave a deposition in which he confirmed that the company had known that nicotine was addictive and had actively manipulated its levels in the final product.

FDA Moves to Regulate Tobacco

The B&W documents supplied the FDA with a new, and powerful, rationale for regulation. Under the Food, Drug, and Cosmetics Act, an article or substance is subject to regulation if it "affects the structure or function of the body." The industry had always maintained that, as a natural product—not a drug or device—tobacco should not be controlled by the FDA. The industry's apparent intent to cause addiction through the active manipulation of nicotine levels, however, seemed to qualify cigarettes as a drug-delivery device and hence subject to regulation.

In August 1995, using this reasoning the FDA proposed far-reaching new rules that called for eliminating cigarette vending machines, billboard advertising near schools, and many forms of promotion aimed at young people, such as ads in youth-oriented magazines. The proposed rules also banned brand-name sponsorship of sporting events, the sale of tobacco-branded merchandise, and the distribution of free samples.

Within days, the tobacco industry and its allies in the advertising industry filed suit in North Carolina, claiming the FDA had no legal authority to regulate tobacco and that the proposed restrictions on cigarette advertising violated First Amendment rights.

State Lawsuits Progress

Several states brought lawsuits against the tobacco companies to recover the costs of health care for citizens with smoking-related illnesses. Mississippi was the first in 1994; it was quickly followed by a slew of others. Eventually, 29 states mounted lawsuits. These cases gradually worked their way through the system, threatening the tobacco companies with the possibility of massive judgments and bad publicity. The Mississippi case was scheduled to go to trial in June 1997.

Brown & Williamson Found Liable

In August 1996, for the first time ever, the tobacco industry lost in court. Brown & Williamson Tobacco Corp. was ordered to pay a landmark $750,000 in a personal-injury case in Florida brought by a man who had contracted lung cancer after 25 years of smoking. The suit charged the tobacco industry with marketing a defective and dangerous product. Invoking the doctrine of strict liability, plaintiff's attorneys had argued that the company should be held liable for damage done by its products whether or not they were aware of the potential dangers. This landmark decision threatened the tobacco industry, for the first time, with a flood of personal-injury lawsuits.

Liggett Breaks Ranks

In March 1996, the Liggett Group Inc.—the smallest and financially weakest of the major tobacco companies—broke ranks, destroying the industry's longstanding united front. As part of an effort to make Liggett more attractive as a possible acquisition, Bennet LeBow, CEO of Liggett's owner, the Brooke Group, cut separate deals with class-action lawyers and states then suing the tobacco companies. As part of the settlement, LeBow acknowledged that cigarettes were addictive and carcinogenic and said manufacturers had targeted youths under age 18 in their marketing. He also agreed to drop opposition to FDA regulation and to turn over documents that the state attorneys general believed would assist them in their litigation against the tobacco industry.

Tobacco Becomes an Issue in the Campaign

In the 1996 presidential campaign, tobacco regulation became a campaign issue. The Clinton administration focused on protecting children from the dangers of smoking. Senator Robert Dole, the Republican nominee, committed an apparent gaffe when he stated during an interview that he did not believe nicotine was addictive. By some accounts, the tobacco issue helped the Democrats win the presidential election.

More Whistle-Blowers Come Forward

In March 1997, the FDA released affidavits from three former Philip Morris employees that confirmed earlier allegations that their employer had deliberately manipulated nicotine levels in its cigarettes to ensure smokers got a nicotine jolt. One former scientist for the company stated that, "Nicotine levels were routinely targeted and adjusted by Philip Morris . . . Knowledge about the optimum range for nicotine in a cigarette was developed as a result of a great many years of investigation." A former shift manager at a cigarette manufacturing plant in Richmond, Virginia, outlined for the FDA how Philip Morris carefully calibrated nicotine levels in a key production process.

Philip Morris responded to these allegations by denying that it manipulated the levels of nicotine in its tobacco products. To the contrary, the tobacco company described nicotine as a key component of taste: "At Philip Morris USA, we work hard to ensure the consistency and quality of our products—and quality control, no matter what the product or service, does not constitute 'manipulation.'"

FDA Jurisdiction Upheld

On April 25, 1997, a federal judge in North Carolina, acting in the industry's lawsuit, upheld the FDA's jurisdiction over tobacco. However, the court also ruled that the FDA had exceeded its authority when it banned certain forms of cigarette advertising, including billboard ads.

The Negotiations

The emergence of whistle-blowers and damaging internal documents, encroaching FDA regulation, successful smoker lawsuits, shifting public opinion, and a break in their own ranks combined to put great pressure on the tobacco companies. The industry was plainly concerned about the extent, and uncontrollability, of their liability for tobacco-related illnesses. For the first time, top executives of the leading tobacco companies began talking about a possible settlement. Cigarette makers "can't continue in public as kind of an outlaw industry," declared RJR Nabisco CEO Steven F. Goldstone. "A lot of forces are at work" favoring some broad settlement with industry adversaries, he noted. "In 1997, the most meaningful thing I can do is come to some solution [to] this problem."

From the industry's standpoint, a settlement held some attractions. Although any agreement would be extremely expensive, at least some of the costs could be passed on to consumers through higher prices. A deal would reduce the industry's legal fees, then running around $600 million a year. Stock prices could rise as tobacco shares, long depressed by investor concern over potential liability, emerged from under a cloud of uncertainty. And in the United States at least, a public admission of the hazards of tobacco would free the industry to produce a new range of "safer" products, such as smoke-free or low-smoke cigarettes, those with lower concentrations of carcinogens, or even those designed to help smokers quit.

In April 1997, a group of state attorneys general, plaintiff attorneys, and representatives of all of the big five (except for Liggett, which had already settled) began the negotiations that led to the June 1997 deal. Also included in the talks were a few representatives of the public health community, including Matthew Myers, general counsel for the National Center for Tobacco-Free Kids. The White House was not directly involved, but Bruce Lindsey, a key presidential aide, monitored the talks closely as they proceeded.

Terms of the Deal   The June 20, 1997, settlement included the following provisions:

- **Tobacco industry payments.** The tobacco industry would be required to pay $368.5 billion for the first 25 years and then $15 billion a year indefinitely. Most of this money would go to the states, to compensate them for the cost of health care for persons with tobacco-related illness. Of this, $25 billion would go toward health care for uninsured children. Some funds would also finance antismoking education and advertising and enforcement of the settlement. Some (the percentage was not specified) would pay the fees of attorneys who negotiated the settlement. Passing these costs along to consumers would, by some estimates, result in a 62-cents-a-pack increase in the price of cigarettes.

- **Advertising.** All billboard and outdoor advertising of tobacco products, the use of human and cartoon figures (such as "Joe Camel") in ads, Internet advertising, product placements in movies and TV, and brand-name sponsorship of sporting events, and brand-name promotional merchandise would be banned. Tobacco companies would be required to change their advertising to make it less appealing to children.

- **Warning labels.** Warning labels on cigarette packs would include the statements "Cigarettes Are Addictive," "Cigarettes Cause Cancer," "Smoking Can Kill You," and "Tobacco Smoke Causes Fatal Lung Disease in Non-Smokers" in white lettering on a black background over 25 percent of the top front of cigarette packs.

- **Government regulation of nicotine.** The Food and Drug Administration would be allowed to regulate the *quantity* of nicotine in cigarettes. However, the FDA could not *ban* nicotine from cigarettes until 2009. Even then, in order to reduce nicotine yield, the FDA would have to prove its action would result in a "significant" overall reduction of health risks, was technologically feasible, and would not create a "significant" demand for more potent black market cigarettes.

- **Cap on liability.** Tobacco companies would be protected from future litigation by a ban on punitive damages, class-action lawsuits, and consolidated litigation. The agreement would also settle the suits of 40 states and Puerto Rico, one class-action suit against the tobacco industry, and 16 others seeking certification. No money was given to plaintiffs in the 17 class-action suits. The agreement would ban class-action suits, consolidation of multiple suits, and punitive damages for past conduct. Medical bills and lost wages of individual claims would be paid from an annual $5 billion tobacco-company fund. Lawsuits by insurers to recover health care payouts linked to smoking would be restricted. Also, there would be a yearly cap on payments for settlements and judgments.

- **Access to children.** Sale of cigarettes through vending machines would be outlawed, and a nationwide licensing system for tobacco retailers would be required to enable regulators to enforce the prohibition on access to minors.

- **Youth smoking.** The tobacco industry would be subjected to fines if youth smoking did not drop 30 percent in 5 years, 50 percent in 7 years, and 60 percent in 10 years. There would be a penalty of $80 million per percentage point by which the target was missed. The annual fines would begin in 2002. The industry could petition for a 75 percent refund of a fine if it could show it had acted in "good faith" and in full compliance with the agreement, pursued all reasonable measures, and did nothing to "undermine achievement of required results."

- **Public smoking.** Smoking in public places and most workplaces without separately ventilated smoking areas would be prohibited. However, restaurants, bars, casinos, and bingo parlors would be exempt.

- **Smoker assistance.** Smokers would receive modest payments for smoking-cessation treatment and monitoring smoking-related illnesses.

The Agreement Goes Up in Smoke

The historic tobacco deal of 1997—perhaps the closest the tobacco industry would ever come to compromise with its adversaries—ultimately collapsed.

In order to go into effect, the tobacco deal required congressional approval, because in several critical respects it appeared on its face to contradict U.S. law. For one thing, the deal asserted FDA jurisdiction over tobacco. Although Commissioner Kessler had vigorously maintained that his agency had a mandate to regulate, on the grounds that nicotine was a drug and cigarettes were drug-delivery devices, the industry had disputed this in the courts. In addition, the immunity provisions of the settlement appeared to violate rights to due process by restricting the future rights of smokers to sue for damages. Enabling legislation was needed to clarify these important issues.

Congress, however, was unable to agree on the terms of the negotiated settlement. By the time a bill was introduced in early 1998, the amount of the payout had ballooned from $369 billion to more than $500 billion, and the protections against lawsuits sought by the industry had been removed. This package was unacceptable to the tobacco companies, which angrily withdrew their political support, and the deal promptly collapsed.

When the deal unraveled in Congress, the state attorneys general and the tobacco companies went back to the negotiating table, this time determined to craft a more modest settlement that would not require legislative approval. In November 1998, a group of 46 attorneys general announced a new deal under which the companies would pay a smaller, although still enormous, amount—$206 billion—and agree to limited marketing restrictions that did not require legislation. The 1998 settlement, however, neither granted the government the right to regulate nor granted the industry immunity from future lawsuits by individuals or groups. (Later, the remaining states reached their own, separate agreements with the companies.) The states began receiving payouts under this agreement in 1999.

With the failure of the 1997 tobacco deal, the industry remained vulnerable to product liability lawsuits. Many continued to wind their way through the court system, and a number produced multimillion dollar judgments against the tobacco makers. Most worrisome to the industry, however, was a class-action lawsuit brought on behalf of *all*

Florida residents who had been injured by smoking. In July 1999, a jury in Miami found the top cigarette companies liable for causing lung cancer, heart disease, and other illnesses and several months later slapped them with a stunning $145 *billion* punitive damage award. The companies, of course, immediately appealed. Several went on record as saying that the judgment, if allowed to stand, could lead to their bankruptcy. The case was likely to spawn similar class actions in other states.

In the meantime, the debate over the regulation of tobacco products continued. Commissioner Kessler's 1995 tobacco regulations were ultimately overturned by the Supreme Court in 2000 on a 5–4 vote, in what some called the most important public health case in decades. In early 2001, a commission appointed by President Clinton issued its conclusion that Congress ought to give the FDA the authority to regulate tobacco for health reasons and that the government should also compensate farmers who stopped growing the crop. Some in the industry, including Philip Morris, signaled a willingness to discuss the terms of possible government regulations. Incoming President Bush seemed receptive to the idea, saying during his campaign that the FDA should be given the authority to discourage teenage smoking. But in 2001, the quid pro quo at the heart of the original tobacco deal—that the industry would gain immunity from liability in exchange for submitting to tight government controls—remained illusory.

Discussion Questions

1. Who were the key stakeholders involved in, or affected by, the negotiations for a tobacco deal, and what were their central interests? To what degree were the interests of the various stakeholders met by the 1997 settlement? By the 1998 settlement?
2. Should the FDA regulate tobacco? What are the key arguments for and against involvement of the FDA in restricting or banning the sale or promotion of tobacco products?
3. What mechanisms of political influence had the tobacco industry historically used? Do you believe that the tobacco industry influenced the public policy process legitimately, or did it have too much influence?
4. Do you think it was ethical for the tobacco industry to continue to market cigarettes, even after evidence emerged that smoking caused lung cancer and other illnesses? Why or why not? In your answer, please refer to the three main methods of ethical analysis: utilitarianism, rights, and justice.
5. Do you think new tobacco legislation is needed? If so, what would be the key elements of such legislation?

THE ANTITRUST CASE AGAINST MICROSOFT

In June 2000, Judge Thomas Penfield Jackson issued a stunning decision in the landmark antitrust trial of Microsoft Corporation: he ordered the software giant broken up into two separate companies. This ruling followed Judge Jackson's findings of fact and findings of law, both of which strongly supported the government's charges that Microsoft had violated antitrust law. A panel of federal judges heard the company's appeal of Judge Jackson's decisions in February 2001; eventually, the case was expected to end up before the nation's highest court of appeal, the Supreme Court. The ultimate resolution of this ongoing dispute, many believed, would be a critical test of antitrust law in the new knowledge economy, where dominance of cyberspace and the computer desktop was as important as dominance of oil supplies and rail lines had been a century earlier.

Microsoft Corporation was one of the great business success stories of the information age. Founded in 1975 by Bill Gates, a computer whiz who had dropped out of Harvard, the company first made its mark by developing MS-DOS, an operating system that directs a computer's inner workings. When IBM adopted MS-DOS for use in its personal computers (PCs), the program quickly became the industry standard. Microsoft later introduced an improved operating system, Windows, and branched out into applications software, developing word processing, spreadsheet, and other desktop programs, as well as its web browser, Internet Explorer. The company also diversified into electronic commerce, interactive TV, and various Internet content ventures. By the late 1990s, Microsoft controlled over 90 percent of the market for all PC operating systems and was pulling in revenues of $19 billion a year. Its market cap, nearly $470 billion at the time the trial began, made it the world's second most valuable company, trailing only General Electric. Gates himself, with a net worth of approximately 100 billion dollars in 1999, was the wealthiest person in the world.

The government's antitrust case against Microsoft had begun in 1990 with a Federal Trade Commission investigation of allegations of collusion between Microsoft and IBM. The case was later taken over by the Department of Justice, which began looking into other possibly anticompetitive practices by the software company. In 1994, Microsoft signed a consent decree with the government that, among other things, prohibited the company from requiring computer makers licensing Windows also to buy other Microsoft software. The investigation heated up again in 1997 when antitrust

This is an updated version (2001) of an earlier case by the same title by Anne T. Lawrence, presented at the annual meeting of the Western Casewriters Association, Waikoloa Beach, Hawaii, April 6, 2000. This case was written on the basis of publicly available information solely for the purpose of stimulating student discussion. The full texts of various legal documents and decisions in the case are available online at www.usdoj.gov/atr/cases/ms and www.microsoft.com/presspass/legalnews.asp. Secondary sources consulted include Michael A. Cusumano and David B. Yoffe, *Competing on Internet Time: Lessons from Netscape and Its Battle with Microsoft* (New York: Free Press, 1998); Ken Auletta, *World War 3.0: Microsoft and Its Enemies* (New York: Random House, 2001); John Heilemann, *Pride before the Fall: The Trials of Bill Gates and the End of the Microsoft Era* (New York: HarperCollins, 2001); and Joel Brinkley and Steve Lohr, *U.S. v. Microsoft: The Inside Story of the Landmark Case* (New York: McGraw-Hill, 2001). © Copyright 2001 by Anne T. Lawrence and the North American Case Research Association. Used by permission.

regulators charged that Microsoft had violated the consent decree by requiring computer makers to install Internet Explorer on their computers as a condition of licensing Windows 95. After several futile attempts to resolve the matter out of court, in May 1998 the Department of Justice, joined by 20 state attorneys general, brought a major antitrust case against Microsoft in federal court. The trial began in October 1998 and concluded in June 1999. The appeals process was not expected to conclude until 2002 at the earliest.

Strategic Importance of the Browser

The core argument in the government's case was that Microsoft had attempted to use its dominance in the market for PC operating systems to leverage the competitive success of its web browser, Internet Explorer. It had done so, even at considerable cost to itself in lost revenue and goodwill, because Gates and other top executives had become convinced that control of the browser was critical to Microsoft's continued success.

Why was the browser of such strategic importance to Microsoft? By the mid-1990s, the Internet revolution was underway. The Internet referred to a global network of interconnected computers. This network enabled computer users to exchange electronic mail, files, and other documents. It also enabled them to access the World Wide Web, or simply web for short, a massive collection of digitally stored information residing on servers throughout the world. As word of the Internet spread, more and more users wanted access to the information superhighway.

In December 1994, Netscape Corporation, a new company founded just months earlier by James Clark and Mark Andreesen, released its first product—a graphical browsing program called Navigator. Netscape Navigator was the first fully functional software that enabled PC users to access and view content on the World Wide Web. Navigator took off like a meteor. Within a year, around 40 million copies of Navigator had been downloaded. By contrast, Microsoft was caught somewhat off guard by the booming popularity of the Internet. Although the company began work on its own browser in 1994, it did not release its first version of Internet Explorer until July 1995. By all accounts, IE was an inferior product. By mid-1996, Navigator had captured 87 percent of the market for web-browsing software; IE, by contrast, had less than 10 percent.

Microsoft viewed the success of Navigator as a serious challenge. Up until that point, most applications software was written for Windows, because it was the leading operating system. Developing new applications was very expensive. If a competing operating system, such as OS/2, did not have a large base of users, it was hard to write applications for it profitably. Because Windows ran on about 90 percent of all PCs, it attracted the attention of most software developers. This, in turn, tended to reinforce Windows' market position, because most PC users wanted an operating system that ran available software. In technical language, this was called an *applications barrier to entry,* or ABE. It was difficult for other operating systems, like OS/2, to mount a credible challenge to Windows, for the simple reason that fewer applications were written for it. The ABE was a kind of charmed circle that tended to reinforce the dominance of an already dominant product.

The success of Navigator posed a serious threat to this charmed circle. The browser was designed to run "on top of" the operating system. In the process, it became a kind of middle-level platform on which applications software could run. As the usage of

Navigator increased, Microsoft feared it would become increasingly popular as a platform for software developers, who would write directly for Navigator, bypassing Windows. Since Netscape could be used with any operating system, not just Windows, this would undermine the applications barrier to entry and, potentially, Microsoft's dominance.

Evidence presented at the trial suggested that by early 1995 Microsoft was becoming increasingly worried about Netscape. In an important May 1995 internal memo, titled "The Internet Tidal Wave," Gates stated that "a new competitor 'born' on the Internet is Netscape. . . . [They are] pursuing a multiplatform strategy where they move the key API [applications programming interface] into the client to commoditize the underlying operating system." In lay terms, this meant that software written directly for Navigator could run on any operating system, so PC users were less likely to need Windows to run the software applications they wanted. Gates, and other top Microsoft executives, were deeply concerned that they might be facing an inflection point, a critical moment when the entire basis of competition in the industry shifted, as it had earlier with the rise of personal computers. Microsoft did not want to be left behind.

The Government's Argument

The government's central argument in the trial was that from 1995 on Microsoft had in effect used its monopoly power in operating systems to protect its applications barrier to entry. It did this by using its dominance in the market for PC operating systems to leverage the competitive success of its browser product, Internet Explorer, at Navigator's expense. In his written decision, Judge Jackson found that Microsoft had taken three key anticompetitive actions:

- Microsoft had attempted to divide the market with Netscape. This effort was unsuccessful.

- Microsoft had used its operating system monopoly to compel its business partners to promote Internet Explorer, to restrict their ability to promote Navigator, and had taken other measures to increase use of IE at Navigator's expense.

- Microsoft had integrated Internet Explorer into Windows, made it difficult to uninstall, and made using Windows with Navigator inherently unstable.

All three of these actions were potential violations of the Sherman Antitrust Act, the law under which the case had been brought. Passed in 1890, the Sherman Act was the earliest and most important of U.S. antitrust laws. Sections 1 and 2 of the act prohibited monopolies, combinations, or conspiracies to restrain commerce. The main goals of the law were to promote open and fair competition and to protect consumers.

Microsoft as a Monopoly

Judge Jackson's first finding was that Microsoft did, in fact, enjoy monopoly power in the relevant market. Factual evidence showed, the judge said, that Microsoft supplied the operating systems for at least 95 percent of all Intel-compatible PCs worldwide and that this market share was "dominant, persistent, and increasing." In a key test, Jackson found that Microsoft was able to charge any price it wanted for Windows without fear of reducing demand.

Dividing the Market with Netscape

The government alleged, and the judge agreed, that Microsoft had tried to divide the market for web-browser software with Netscape in 1995. At a critical meeting on June 21 at Netscape's offices in California, executives of the two companies met to discuss their business relationship. According to government witnesses, Microsoft made an illegal offer to divide the market for browsers. If Netscape restricted Navigator to Macintosh, UNIX, and earlier versions of the Windows operating systems (leaving Windows 95 and subsequent versions to IE), Microsoft would give Netscape access to technical information and status as a preferred vendor. Netscape, seeing a threat to its self-interest, refused the offer. Microsoft subsequently withheld technical information Netscape needed to develop a version of Navigator for Windows 95 until October, two months after its release, delaying the availability of the Navigator upgrade during the critical holiday selling season.

Restrictive Contracts with Business Partners

The judge also found that Microsoft had used its operating systems monopoly to force computer makers, chip makers, Internet service and content providers, and other business partners to sign restrictive contracts. These contracts required them to support Microsoft products, or shun others' products, in order to obtain licenses for Windows or other benefits from Microsoft. Among the anticompetitive actions cited by the judge were the following.

Intel

Intel was the largest maker of chips—microprocessors for personal computers—in the world. Its relationship with Microsoft was so close that the most commonly configured PC, running Windows on an Intel chip, was referred to as a "Wintel" computer. In early 1995, Intel was in the process of developing a technology called native signal processing (NSP), designed to enhance the video and graphics performance of its microprocessors. Microsoft was concerned that NSP could be used by other software developers as a platform for writing their own multimedia programs, which could then be ported to different operating systems, making consumers less dependent on Windows. In August 1995, Microsoft threatened to withdraw technical support for Intel's next generation of chips unless it halted development of NSP technology. Intel quickly acceded to Microsoft's demand.

Compaq

Microsoft threatened some computer makers—called original equipment manufacturers, or OEMs—that it would terminate their license to install Windows if they removed Microsoft programs from or added others' programs to the desktop or Start menu. For example, in late 1995 Compaq began to ship its Presario PCs with the icons for Microsoft Network (MSN) and Internet Explorer removed and with icons for America Online and Spry (an Internet service provider that came with Navigator) on the desktop. Compaq's reason was that it believed these products were more popular with its customers. In May 1996, after lodging several complaints, Microsoft notified Compaq that it intended to terminate Compaq's license for Windows if it did not restore MSN and IE to their original positions on the desktop. Compaq immediately capitulated and agreed to install IE as the default browser. The judge concluded, "In its confrontation with Compaq,

Microsoft demonstrated that it was prepared to go to the brink of losing all Windows sales through its highest-volume OEM partner in order to enforce its prohibition against removing Microsoft's Internet-related icons from the Windows desktop."

Apple

In June 1997, Microsoft threatened to cancel Mac Office, Microsoft's office suite written for Apple computers, unless Apple agreed to bundle IE with its operating software and to make it the default browser. Apple complied. The judge concluded that Apple had switched its allegiance from Navigator to IE not because Microsoft's product was superior or its customers preferred it but out of fear of losing Mac Office, critical software for many of its customers.

IBM PC Company

The IBM PC Company, a division of IBM, made and sold its own line of personal computers, including some that ran on Windows. Other divisions of IBM developed software, including some programs—like OS/2 and SmartSuite—that competed with Microsoft products. The judge found that in an effort to pressure IBM to back off from promoting its own competing software, Microsoft charged the IBM PC Company higher prices for Windows, delayed granting a license for Windows 95, refused to endorse IBM PCs, and withheld key technical support. At one point, Microsoft had also offered an inducement—settlement of a disputed outstanding royalties audit—if IBM complied with its wishes. IBM estimated that it had lost hundreds of millions of dollars in business because of Microsoft's actions.

America Online

Microsoft offered to feature AOL in a folder on its desktop, if AOL adopted Internet Explorer and limited the distribution and promotion of Netscape. In March 1996, AOL agreed to these terms.

Hewlett Packard

Many OEMs developed splash screens that appeared when a new PC was turned on for the first time. These screens displayed the computer maker's own brand and then proceeded to a series of introductory programs that helped the user register their computer, choose desired configurations, and learn how to use their new system, before the Windows desktop was displayed. According to evidence presented at trial, some Microsoft licenses prohibited OEMs from modifying the initial Windows boot sequence. One of the OEMs most severely impacted by these restrictions was Hewlett-Packard, which experienced an increase in returns and customer support calls after removing its splash screen. In March 1997, HP's manager of research and development sent a letter to Microsoft, demanding, "We must have more ability to decide how our system is presented to our end users. If we had a choice of another supplier, based on your actions in this area, I assure you [that you] would not be our supplier of choice."

Evidence showed that Microsoft made use of the carrot, as well as the stick, in its dealings with its business partners. For example, when Compaq agreed to promote IE exclusively, Microsoft rewarded the company with a price for Windows significantly lower than the price charged other OEMs. The company paid AOL for every user who converted to access software that included IE. Microsoft also gave away for free to Internet access providers (IAPs) both Internet Explorer and a set of programs that made it easy for IAPs to provide IE to their subscribers. A condition of the license was that the IAP would make IE its preferred browser.

Linking Products

The judge found that another key strategy used by Microsoft was to bundle Internet Explorer with Windows for sale as a single product. It did this initially by refusing to license Windows 95 without IE and, later, by developing Windows 98 as an integrated product that included both the operating system and the browser. Linking the two programs made computer makers less likely to preinstall Navigator, since it would be redundant with a browser already on the system. Some evidence also suggested that Microsoft had tried to design Windows so that it would not work smoothly with Navigator. In an internal memo from late 1995, Brad Chase, a top Microsoft executive, had said, "We will bind the shell [operating system] to the Internet Explorer, so that running any other browser is a jolting experience."

Under antitrust law, linking products or services illegally is called *tying*. For example, if an automobile manufacturer required a car buyer to purchase a long-term service contract as a condition of the purchase, this would be an illegal tie. Generally, tying occurs when a company bundles a less popular product with a more popular product for the sole purpose of increasing its sales. In his findings of fact, the judge argued that the browser and the operating system were separate products with distinct functions, and there was no technical justification for integrating them. Moreover, he argued, integration hurt customers who wanted Windows without a browser, such as businesses that needed the operating system but did not want their employees surfing the Web at work, or simply those who wished to use less computer memory.

Microsoft's Success

Microsoft's efforts to increase the market share of IE, at Netscape's expense, by all accounts were almost completely successful. By early 1998, only 4 out of 60 OEM "subchannels" (computer configurations) carried Navigator as the default browser; the rest carried Internet Explorer. Although the absolute numbers of Navigator users continued to rise (since the total number of people browsing the Web was going up), Navigator's share of the market fell from close to 90 percent in early 1996 to the mid-50s by July 1998. During the same period, IE's share rose to between 45 and 50 percent. Within a two-year period, Microsoft had in effect turned the tide on Netscape. The judge opined that the main reason for Microsoft's success was not the superiority of Internet Explorer but rather that the company had "devoted its monopoly power and monopoly profits to precisely this end." The effect of all this on consumers, the judge concluded, was "that some innovations that would truly benefit consumers never happen for the sole reason that they do not coincide with Microsoft's self-interest."

Microsoft's Defense

In a statement issued immediately after Judge Jackson announced his findings of fact, Gates said, "We respectfully disagree with a number of the court's Microsoft findings, and believe the American legal system ultimately will affirm that Microsoft's actions and innovations were fair and legal, and have brought tremendous benefits to consumers, our industry and to the United States economy."

Throughout the trial and in the subsequent appeal, Microsoft vigorously defended itself against the government's charges. The central points in the company's defense were these:

- *Microsoft's actions did not harm consumers—a key test in antitrust law. On the contrary, consumers benefited from falling prices and continual technical innovation.*

Contrary to behavior expected of a monopolist, Microsoft had not raised prices on most of its products. During the 1990s, the price of Windows had remained low (an upgrade to Windows 98, for instance, retailed at $89) and relatively stable, at the same time that the product's functionality had greatly improved. The prices of Microsoft applications software, such as MS Office, had fallen sharply. In some cases, software had been given away for free—as in the case of IE, which was essentially provided as a free enhancement in Windows 98. The 1990s had also witnessed a stream of innovative new products and services, including interactive TV, electronic commerce sites, web-portal MSN, and business productivity software.

- *Microsoft did not possess monopoly power. Market dominance in an intellectual property industry, like software, was inherently unstable.*

Although Windows had a dominant share of the market for PC operating systems, Microsoft did not possess monopoly power—that is, the power that could be expected to flow from its market share. The reason, the company argued, was that high technology was different in important ways from old-line brick-and-mortar industries. Barriers to entry were few. Good ideas, unlike oil reserves or railroad tracks, could not be monopolized. All that was needed to compete in software was brains and entrepreneurial zeal. "In the computer software industry," Gates once noted, "rapid and unpredictable changes constantly create new market opportunities and threaten the position of existing competitors." In addition, unlike, say, a car or a washing machine, software did not wear out. Thus, in order to continue to sell products, Microsoft had to innovate continually, to give its existing customers reason to purchase an upgrade.

Moreover, the rapid evolution of technology constantly threatened Microsoft's dominance. For example, by the late 1990s, the rise of information appliances, such as smart phones and palm-held computers, promised a time when users would not have to use a desktop PC to access the Internet. Rival operating systems—like Linux, a variant of Unix that had 16 percent of the computer server market by 1998—threatened some day to supplant Windows. Sun Microsystem's Java had potential to become a platform for developing software that could run on any system, not just Microsoft's. Microsoft particularly pointed to AOL's acquisition of Netscape in November 1998 as evidence of the inherent instability of market dominance in the technology sector. William Neukom, Microsoft's attorney, said at the time, "This . . . deal pulls the rug out from under the government. It proves indisputably that no company can control the supply of technology."

- *The company had a right to compete vigorously. Much of the behavior described in court was standard practice in the industry and not a violation of antitrust law.*

Microsoft contested the government's interpretation of its interactions with various business partners. For example, the company viewed its meeting with Netscape in June 1995 as "a standard meeting between two companies exploring the possibility of forging a strategic partnership in some areas of their business, while continuing to compete in others." It asserted that its agreements with various Internet service providers and content providers, such as AOL, were "cross-promotional agreements ... [in which] Microsoft helps promote and distribute the other company's products and services, while the other company helps promote and distribute Microsoft's products and services." Microsoft maintained that its exclusive contracts with OEMs were perfectly legal and that in any case Netscape had many other distribution channels for Navigator, including free downloads off the Internet for anyone who wanted to use the product.

- *The purpose of bundling Internet Explorer with Windows was not to thwart Netscape but rather to enhance the operating system for the benefit of the user.*

Microsoft argued that integration benefited the user. An integrated product ran faster, and the parts worked better together. It avoided the redundancy and waste of memory that would result from a browser installed on top of a separate operating system. It kept the price down. It enabled users to view local data (on a hard drive or local network) and remote data (on the Internet) consistently. Moreover, Microsoft maintained that it began designing the browser into the operating system well before it even became aware of Netscape as a potential competitor.

- *Internet Explorer's increasing market share, relative to Navigator's, was the result not of anticompetitive practices but of the technical merits of the Microsoft product.*

Over the period of time analyzed in the trial, Microsoft worked assiduously to make Internet Explorer more competitive by improving the product. From 1995, the company invested large sums—more than $100 million a year—to upgrade its browser. By 1999, more than 1,000 programmers were working full-time on the product. Around $30 million a year was spent to market the program. By late 1997, many reviewers thought IE was as good as, if not better than, Navigator. The improvement in Microsoft's browser led many Internet service and content providers to switch from Navigator to IE. For example, America Online adopted IE in 1996 not because Microsoft offered AOL placement on the desktop, as the government claimed, but because AOL preferred IE's modular architecture.

- *Any government effort to restrict Microsoft would be poor public policy.*

The software industry was a major provider of jobs, growing two-and-a-half times faster than the U.S. economy overall in the 1990s. Microsoft products had improved business productivity across the entire economy. The company's dominance in operating systems software had helped the U.S. balance of trade and contributed to the emergence of the United States as a world technology leader. For the U.S. government to punish Microsoft would be self-destructive.

Possible Remedies

Judge Jackson's order that the company be broken up was just one of several possible outcomes. The appeals court had the authority to overturn this remedy and to replace it with another, if it found a breakup was not justified by the evidence. (It could also throw out the government's entire case, but this was considered unlikely.)

The remedy that Judge Jackson proposed was *structural:* the government would order Microsoft broken up into several smaller entities. In a *horizontal* breakup, which Judge Jackson favored, the company would be split into two separate businesses, with operating systems in one company and software applications and Internet products and services in the other. This kind of breakup would prevent Microsoft from leveraging its monopoly in operating systems to benefit its other products like IE, a key issue in the antitrust case. However, it would not end the Windows monopoly, which gave rise to the suit in the first place. Moreover, informal collaboration among the new companies, based on their long shared history, might compromise their independence. Presumably, many shares of stock would have to be liquidated or converted by employee shareholders, possibly roiling the markets.

In a *vertical* breakup, another possible option, the company would be divided into several "Baby Bills," smaller companies of equal stature, each launched with the same properties and functions. (The term "Baby Bills" was a sly reference both to Gates's name and to the Baby Bells, regional telephone operating companies spun off when the AT&T monopoly was broken up by government regulators in 1982.) A vertical breakup would produce competing products in each category, presumably leading to greater innovation and lower prices. This solution had a number of drawbacks, however. It would lead to incompatible operating systems, undermining the advantage of a single industry standard. Unlike AT&T, which was split on the basis of geographic region, Microsoft had no obvious basis on which to make a vertical division. Teams would have to be broken up, destroying valuable long-term working relationships. The division of assets, such as contracts with OEMs, among the Baby Bills would inevitably be messy and disputatious.

A *hybrid* structural remedy, would combine elements of both horizontal and vertical breakups. For example, Microsoft could be split into two or three operating systems companies and one other company that would retain all other assets. This solution would generate competition in operating systems while avoiding the problems of dividing the applications and Internet businesses.

Another set of solutions focused on *intellectual property rights.* In one scenario, Microsoft would be forced to auction rights to the Windows source code to other companies, such as Sun Microsystems or IBM. This would generate competition in operating systems, without the problems inherent in a Microsoft breakup. The key drawback to this solution was that, by all accounts, none of the possible bidders were interested. "We wouldn't bid on it," said the general counsel of Sun, noting that the all the programmers who understood the code lived in Seattle, "their average salary is $400,000 and they don't want to move."

In another scenario, the government would require Microsoft simply to publish either the entire Windows code or parts of it, enabling other firms to develop competing versions of Windows or to hook their applications onto Microsoft's platform. But even a free giveaway seemed problematical. Steven Salop, an antitrust expert, commented, "The source code is not well documented. It's not like the recipe for New Coke." Without technical support from Microsoft, many companies would be unable to put the code to good use, even if it were free.

A final set of solutions clustered under the heading of *conduct,* or behavioral, remedies. In this approach, the government would write and enforce rules of conduct for Microsoft. For example, the government could prohibit any contracts with OEMs that conditioned a Windows license on anything other than price. If Microsoft tried to withhold a license from an OEM that installed Netscape or devised its own splash screen, for instance, it would be in violation and subject to fines or other sanctions. Such a remedy could block specific anticompetitive behaviors, while avoiding the difficulties of a breakup. Some commentators criticized this approach, however. For one thing, it had been tried earlier and had failed. For another, it would require ongoing government intervention in the relations between Microsoft and its business partners, setting a bad precedent for intrusive regulation of high-technology industry. Even Eric Schmidt, CEO of Novell, a frequent competitor, commented, "I don't think anyone's in favor of a [government] Department of Microsoft Management."

One remedy that was out of bounds was a monetary penalty, not permitted in a government antitrust case of this type. However, in the wake of the judge's rulings, many attorneys stepped forward to file suit against Microsoft on behalf of private clients, claiming that the company's actions had injured customers and competitors. These suits potentially threatened Microsoft with billions of dollars in damages.

The Case Proceeds

In 2001, some observers thought that the tide had turned in Microsoft's favor in the long-running antitrust case. The new Republican administration in Washington hinted that it might take a softer line on antitrust enforcement. Many observers thought that the hearing before the court of appeals had not gone well for the government, and that the judges seemed sympathetic to Microsoft's arguments and disinclined to uphold Judge Jackson's breakup order. If the appeals court ruled largely or even partly in Microsoft's favor, this might create an opening for a negotiated settlement between the company and the government. But, others thought this unlikely. Even if the Department of Justice was disposed to settle the case, the federal government had been joined in the suit by 18 states and the District of Columbia. Some of the states were bound to press on all the way to the Supreme Court, with or without the support of the Department of Justice. As for Microsoft, the company was unlikely to agree to any settlement that undercut what one top company executive called its "core value, the soul of our company, and that is the freedom to innovate and design products as we see fit."

Discussion Questions

1. The U.S. government charged that Microsoft had violated antitrust law. Microsoft disagreed. Do you agree with the U.S. government, or with Microsoft? In answering this question, you may wish to address two issues. Was Microsoft a monopoly? Did it use its monopoly to compete unfairly against other companies?
2. Examine the various remedies possible in this case. In light of the strength of the various parties' positions in the case, what remedy would you advocate, and why?
3. Do you believe that contemporary antitrust law is appropriate to today's economy? Why or why not? If not, in what ways should the law be changed to better fit contemporary society?

Case Study
DOW CORNING AND THE SILICONE BREAST IMPLANT CONTROVERSY

The corporate jet lifted off from Washington's National Airport, en route to Dow Corning Corporation's headquarters in Midland, Michigan. February 19, 1992, had been a grueling day for Keith R. McKennon. Named chairman and chief executive officer of Dow Corning less than two weeks earlier, McKennon had just testified before the Food and Drug Administration's Advisory Committee on the safety of the company's silicone gel breast implants. Although not the only manufacturer of breast implants, Dow Corning had invented the devices in the early 1960s and had been responsible for most of their medical testing. Now, the company was faced with the task of defending the product against numerous lawsuits and a rising tide of criticism from the FDA, Congress, the media, and many women's advocacy organizations.

The company's potential liability was large: as many as two million American women had received implants over the past three decades, perhaps 35 percent of them made by Dow Corning. In December 1991, a San Francisco jury had awarded a woman who claimed injuries from her Dow Corning implants an unprecedented $7.3 million in damages. Although the company believed its $250 million in product liability insurance was adequate to meet any possible claims, some felt that the company's liability exposure could be much, much larger.

The hearings had been contentious. Critics had repeated their allegations, heard often in the press in recent weeks, that the implants could leak silicone into the body, causing pain, scarring, and, most seriously, debilitating autoimmune diseases such as rheumatoid arthritis and scleroderma. The silicone prostheses could also interfere with detection of breast cancer by mammography, they charged. In response, McKennon had testified that implants served an important public health need and did not pose an unreasonable risk to users. On the job less than a month, however, McKennon had had little time to sort through the thousands of pages of relevant documents or to talk with the many managers who had been involved with the product's development over the past 30 years.

The breast implant controversy would surely be a litmus test of McKennon's crisis management skills. Recruited from Dow Chemical Corporation, where he had been executive vice president and head of domestic operations, McKennon came to his new position with a reputation as a seasoned troubleshooter. At Dow Chemical (which owned 50 percent of Dow Corning), McKennon had earlier managed his firm's response to

This is an abridged version of a longer case: Anne T. Lawrence, "Dow Corning and the Silicone Breast Implant Controversy," *Case Research Journal* 13, no. 4 (Winter 1993), pp. 87–112. Abridged by the author and reprinted by permission of the *Case Research Journal*. Sources include articles appearing in the *New York Times, Wall Street Journal, Business Week, Newsweek, Time, Chemical and Engineering News, American Bar Association Journal, Journal of the American Medical Association, New England Journal of Medicine,* the Public Citizen Health Research Group *Health Letter,* the Command Trust Network *Newsletter,* press reports of the *Federal News Service,* and U.S. congressional hearings. The history of Dow Corning and the development of silicones is based on Don Whitehead, *The Dow Story: The History of the Dow Chemical Company* (New York: McGraw-Hill, 1968); and Eugene G. Rochow, *Silicon and Silicones* (Berlin: Springer-Verlag, 1987). The case also draws on internal Dow Corning documents released to the public in February 1992. A full set of footnotes is available in the *Case Research Journal* version. © Copyright 1993 by the author and the North American Case Research Association.

charges that its product Agent Orange, a defoliant widely used during the Vietnam War, had caused lingering health problems for veterans. Later, he had managed Dow Chemical's problems with Bendectin, an antinausea drug alleged to cause birth defects. At the time of his appointment as chairman and CEO, McKennon had served on Dow Corning's board of directors for nearly six years.

The unfolding breast implant crisis showed every sign of being just as difficult, and potentially damaging, as any McKennon had confronted in his long career. Would Dow Corning become known as another Johnson & Johnson, renowned for its skillful handling of the Tylenol poisonings in the 1980s? Or would it become another Manville or A. H. Robins, companies that had declared bankruptcy in the wake of major product liability crises? McKennon was well aware that the future of the company, as well as his own reputation, might well hinge on decisions he and his top managers would make within the next weeks and days.

Dow Corning, Inc.

Dow Corning was founded in 1943 as an equal joint venture of Dow Chemical Company and Corning Glass Works (later known as Corning, Inc.) to produce silicones for commercial applications. The term *silicone* was coined to describe synthetic compounds derived from silicon, an abundant element commonly found in sand. In the 1930s, Corning researchers working on possible applications of silicone in glassmaking developed a number of resins, fluids, and rubbers that could withstand extremes of hot and cold. In 1940, Corning approached Dow Chemical with a proposal for a joint venture, and by 1942 a small plant in Midland, Michigan (Dow's hometown), had begun production of silicones for military applications. At the close of World War II, Dow Corning moved successfully to develop multiple commercial applications for silicone. Within a decade, the company had introduced more than 600 products and doubled in size three times, making it one of the fastest-growing firms in the booming chemical industry. Its varied product line included specialty lubricants, sealants, and resins as well as a variety of consumer items—ranging from construction caulk, to adhesive labels, to Silly Putty.

Although most uses of silicone were industrial, by the mid-1950s Dow Corning scientists had become interested in possible medical applications and developed several implantable devices. In the early 1960s, Dow Corning engineers developed the first prototype of a breast implant by encapsulating a firm-density silicone gel within a silicone rubber bag. First marketed in 1963, this device—known as the Cronin implant—was used initially almost exclusively in reconstructive surgery performed on breast cancer patients following mastectomies (surgical removal of the breast).

When Dow Corning first developed and marketed breast implants (as well as its other medical products), the company was operating with virtually no government oversight. Unlike pharmaceutical drugs, regulated since 1906 under the Pure Food and Drug Act and its several amendments, medical devices—even those designed for implantation in the body—were for all practical purposes unregulated. Under the Food, Drug, and Cosmetics Act of 1938, the FDA had the authority to inspect sites where medical devices were made and could seize adulterated or misbranded devices. The agency could not require premarket approval for the safety or effectiveness, however, and could remove a product from the market only if it could demonstrate that the manufacturer had broken the law.

Although not required to prove its implants safe by law, Dow Corning—in accord with standard "good manufacturing" practices at the time—attempted to determine the safety of its own medical products before releasing them for sale. In 1964, Dow Corning hired an independent laboratory to undertake several studies of the safety of medical-grade silicones, including those used in breast implants. No evidence was found that silicones caused cancer, but two studies found that silicone fluid injected in experimental animals spread widely—becoming lodged in the lymph nodes, liver, spleen, pancreas, and other organs—and created persistent chronic inflammation. The company appeared unconcerned, noting that it did not advocate the direct injection of silicone fluid.

In the early 1970s, Dow Corning's breast implant business for the first time experienced a serious competitive threat. In 1972, five young men—all scientists or salesmen at Dow Corning—left the company to work for Heyer-Schulte, a small medical devices company in California, where they used their experience with silicones to develop a competing breast implant. Two years later, the group left Heyer-Schulte to form their own company, McGhan Medical Corporation. Their idea was to modify the basic technology developed over the past decade by Dow Corning to make a softer, more responsive implant that more closely resembled the natural breast. By 1974, both Heyer-Schulte and McGhan Medical had competing products on the market.

The Heyer-Schulte and McGhan implants quickly gained favor with plastic surgeons, and Dow Corning's market share began to erode. By 1975, Dow Corning estimated its market share had declined to around 35 percent, as plastic surgeons switched allegiance to products offered by the small company start-ups. Dow Corning managers became alarmed.

The Mammary Task Force

In January 1975, responding to the challenge from its California competitors, Dow Corning dedicated a special cross-functional team, known as the mammary task force, to develop, test, and bring to market a new generation of breast implants. The group's main goal was to reformulate the silicone gel to create a softer, more pliable implant competitive with the new products recently marketed by McGhan and Heyer-Schulte. The group of about 20, all men, hoped to have the new implants ready for shipment by June 1975. The company believed it was justified in bringing the new implant to market quickly, without extensive medical testing, because the new product would be based on materials substantially similar to those used in the older Cronin implants. The safety of the existing line, management maintained, had already been satisfactorily documented on the basis of earlier studies and the history of their use.

One of the questions that quickly arose in the task force's deliberations, as reported in the minutes of its January 21, 1975, meeting, was: "Will the new gel . . . cause a *bleed through* which will make these products unacceptable?" (emphasis in original). Dow Corning scientists clearly recognized that a more watery gel (dubbed *flo-gel*), while softer to the touch, might also be more likely to permeate its envelope and bleed into surrounding tissue. Two product engineers were assigned to investigate this issue. Three weeks later they reported that their experiments "*to date* indicate that the bleed with new gel is no greater than what we measure from old gel controls." They also added, however, that they viewed their earlier results as inconclusive, and they remained concerned about "a possible bleed situation."

Biomedical tests were contracted out to an independent laboratory, which proceeded with tests in which the new gel was injected into experimental rabbits. Earlier reports back from the lab on February 26 showed "mild to occasionally moderate acute inflammatory reaction" in the test animals around the injected gel, but the pathologist concluded it was probably due to the trauma of insertion, not the product itself. The task force also ordered biomedical testing of migration of gel into the vital organs of monkeys. The laboratory results showed "some migration of the [flo-gel] formulation." However, the task force agreed that the bleed was still not any more or less than standard gel.

Development proceeded so rapidly that, by March 31, 10,000 new flo-gel mammaries were ready for packaging. The task force minutes reported that the products were "beautiful, the best we have ever made." Now six weeks ahead of schedule, the company was able to ship some samples of the new product to the West Coast in time for the California Plastic Surgeons meeting on April 21. However, earlier demonstrations did not go flawlessly. The task force got back the following report: "In Vancouver, and elsewhere on the West Coast introduction, it was noted that after the mammaries had been handled for awhile, the surface became oily. Also, some were bleeding on the velvet in the showcase." The task force ordered samples from the West Coast for examination, but no further discussion of this issue appeared in the subsequent minutes.

As the flo-gel implants came on line, the focus of the task force's discussion shifted from production issues to marketing strategy. The task force debated various aggressive marketing approaches, such as rebates, distribution by consignment, price breaks for big users, and free samples for surgeons known to perform breast enlargement operations. Noting that June and July were the peak months of the "mammary season," managers called for a big push to regain some of Dow Corning's eroding market share. The group felt that their market share, which they estimated had eroded to around 35 percent, could be lifted back to the 50 to 60 percent range if they moved aggressively.

By September, Dow Corning was producing 6,000 to 7,000 units per month and aimed to phase out the older models by early 1976. However, many bugs in the production process remained to be ironed out. The reject rate at inspection was high, as high as 50 percent on some lots. Among the problems: floating dirt, weak bags, and thin spots in the envelopes. Doctors had returned some unused mammaries, citing breakage and contamination. Overall, however, plastic surgeons liked the product. One task force member later recalled that when plastic surgeons saw and felt the new material, "their eyes got big as saucers." Besides feeling more natural to the touch, the new softer devices were easier to insert and were more suitable for small-incision, low-trauma cosmetic procedures.

A Boom in Busts

Although breast implants first became available in the 1960s, it was only in the late 1970s and 1980s that the rate of implant surgery took off. The increase was due entirely to a fast rise in the number of so-called cosmetic procedures; by 1990, fully 80 percent of all implant surgeries performed in the United States were to increase the size of normal, healthy breasts rather than for reconstruction following mastectomy.

One cause of the rise in cosmetic augmentations, of course, was the availability of the softer, more pliable implants, which could be inserted through smaller incisions with less trauma to the patient in less expensive outpatient procedures. In 1990, 82 percent of all breast augmentation procedures were performed on an outpatient basis. Other, broader trends within the medical profession and the wider culture also played important roles, however.

One factor behind the boom in breast augmentation surgery was the growth of the plastic surgery profession. Although procedures to graft tissue from a healthy part of the body to another that had been damaged or multilated were developed early in the century, plastic surgery as a distinct subdiscipline within surgery did not emerge until the 1940s. During World War II, military surgeons struggling to repair the wounds of injured soldiers returning from the front pioneered many valuable reconstructive techniques. Many of these surgeons reentered civilian life to start plastic surgery programs in their home communities. Within a couple of decades, plastic surgery had become the fastest-growing specialty within American medicine. Between 1960 and 1983, the number of board-certified plastic surgeons quintupled, during a period when most other medical specialities were growing much less quickly (and the U.S. population as a whole grew by just 31 percent). The draw for the newly minted MDs was regular hours, affluent customers, and high incomes, averaging $180,000 per year after all expenses in 1987.

As their numbers soared, plastic surgeons faced an obvious problem—developing a market for their services. Demand for reconstructive surgery was not fast growing, and cosmetic procedures were often elective and typically not fully covered by medical insurance. In 1983, following approval by the Federal Trade Commission, the American Society for Plastic and Reconstructive Surgery (ASPRS), a professional association representing 97 percent of all board-certified plastic surgeons, launched a major advertising (or, as the society called it, "practice enhancement") campaign. Other ads were placed by individual surgeons. In one appearing in *Los Angeles* magazine, a seductive, well-endowed model was shown leaning against a sports car. The tag line: "Automobile by Ferrari, Body by [a prominent plastic surgeon]."

Plastic surgeons also campaigned to redefine female flat-chestedness (dubbed *micromastia* by the medical community) as a medical disease requiring treatment. In July 1982, the ASPRS filed a formal comment with the FDA that argued:

> There is a substantial and enlarging body of medical opinion to the effect that
> these deformities [small breasts] are really a disease which in most patients
> results in feelings of inadequacy, lack of self-confidence, distortion of body
> image and a total lack of well-being due to a lack of self-perceived femininity.
> The enlargement of the under-developed female breast is, therefore, often very
> necessary to insure an improved quality of life for the patient.

The ASPRS later officially repudiated this view.

By 1990, breast augmentation had become the second most common cosmetic procedure performed by plastic surgeons, exceeded only by liposuction (fat removal). Since it was a more expensive procedure, however, breast augmentation was the top money maker for plastic surgeons in 1990. That year, ASPRS members collected almost $215 million in fees from women for breast implant surgery.

Another factor contributing to the rise in cosmetic augmentation may have been changing cultural standards of feminine beauty in the 1980s, a decade characterized by social conservatism and, according to some commentators, by a backlash against feminism and female liberation. In the 1970s, women appearing in the glossy pages of fashion magazines were often tall and lanky, with long, straight hair tied at the nape of the neck, menswear dress-for-success suits, and distinctly boyish figures. The 1980s ideal woman was very different: the typical fashion model by this time was more likely to sport 1940s retro-look fashions, thick, full curls, sweetheart lips—and lots of bosom. In a special 100th anniversary edition, published April 1992, *Vogue* magazine summed up current standards of female beauty in this sentence:

> And in women's bodies, the fashion now is a combination of hard, muscular stomach and shapely breasts. Increasingly, women are willing to regard their bodies as photographic images, unpublishable until retouched and perfected at the hands of surgeons.

Ironically, the same issue also ran an ad, placed by trial attorneys, in which "silicone breast implant sufferers" were invited to come forward with legal claims.

A Stream of Sick and Injured

As the rate of implant surgeries rose in the 1980s, so did the number of women who were sick, injured, and in pain from their breast surgery. Their stories began to be told at medical conferences, in legal briefs, and by women's and consumer's advocacy organizations. As they were, Dow Corning and other implant makers were forced to respond to a growing crisis of confidence in their products.

The most common adverse side effect of implant surgery was a phenomenon known as *capsular contracture,* a painful hardening of the breast that occurs when the body reacts to the implant by forming a wall of fibrous scar tissue around it. The FDA estimated that severe contracture occurred in about 25 percent of all patients; some hardening may have occurred in up to 70 percent. Implants could also rupture, spilling silicone gel into the body and often necessitating repeat surgery to replace the damaged implants. Dow Corning's data, based on voluntary reporting by surgeons, showed a rupture rate of only 1 percent. These figures were challenged by researchers who pointed out that ruptures often did not show up on mammograms; some individual doctors reported rupture rate as high as 32 percent. Once the device had broken, silicone could and did travel via the lymphatic system throughout the body, lodging in a woman's spleen, liver, and other internal organs. Also worrisome was the tendency of silicone implants to obscure cancerous tumors that otherwise would be revealed by mammography.

More controversial and less well documented were allegations that silicone implants could lead to so-called autoimmune disorders—diseases in which the body's immune system attacks its own connective tissues. According to the FDA, by 1991 around 600 cases of autoimmune disorders, such as rheumatoid arthritis, scleroderma, and lupus erythematosus, had been reported in women with implants. Some scientists speculated that some women were, in effect, allergic to silicone and that their bodies had attacked their own tissues in an attempt to rid itself of the substance. Such reactions were most likely in the presence of ruptures, but even small amounts of gel bleeding through the envelope, or silicone in the envelope itself, could provoke an autoimmune response.

Other physicians believed, however, that the appearance of autoimmune disorders in women with implants was wholly coincidental. In any substantial population—and 2 million women with implants was clearly substantial—a certain number would develop autoimmune disease purely by chance. In an interview published in the *Journal of the American Medical Association,* one prominent plastic surgeon called the association between autoimmune disorders and breast implants a "crock of baloney. . . . People get immunological diseases and they just happen to have breast implants."

Unfortunately, no long-term controlled studies of the incidence of autoimmune disorders in populations of women with and without implants were initiated or even contemplated until 1991. In fact, no comprehensive registries of women with implants existed. The question about the relationship between implants and autommune disease was, on the basis of existing data, wholly unanswerable. Representative Ted Weiss (Democrat, New York), who reviewed data submitted to the FDA in 1991, later angrily concluded; "For 30 years, more than one million women have been subjects in a massive, uncontrolled study, without their knowledge or consent."

Victims Seek Redress

Some women who had suffered from breast implants sued. In 1984, a Nevada woman was awarded $1.5 million by jurors in a San Francisco court, who concluded that Dow Corning had committed fraud in marketing its implant as safe; the case was later settled for an undisclosed amount while on appeal, and the court records were sealed. In a post-trial ruling, a federal judge who had reviewed the case records called Dow Corning's actions "highly reprehensible." In the wake of this case, Dow Corning changed its package insert to include a warning that mentioned the possibility of capsular contracture, silicone migration following rupture, and immune system sensitivity.

As other cases slowly made their way through the courts, victims began to speak out publicly and to organize. Sybil Goldrich and Kathleen Anneken founded the Command Trust Network, an advocacy organization that became instrumental in providing information, support, and legal and medical referrals to implant victims. Other women's and public health advocacy groups also played a role in publicizing the risks of breast implants. One of the most active was the Health Research Group (HRG), a Washington, DC–based spin-off of Ralph Nader's Public Citizen. The HRG in 1988 began a systematic effort to pressure the FDA to ban silicone breast implants. The group petitioned the FDA, testified before Congress and other government agencies, issued regular press releases, and distributed information to consumers. The HRG also initiated an information clearinghouse for plaintiffs' attorneys. Another active advocacy organization was the National Women's Health Network, a public-interest group that widely distributed information on silicone-related issues.

Devising Regulation for Devices

The agency in charge of regulating implants—and thus the object of these and other advocacy organizations' pressure—was the Food and Drug Administration. In 1976, the year after Dow Corning's mammary task force developed its new generation of flo-gel implants, Congress passed the Medical Amendments Act to the Food and Drug Act. Enacted in the wake of the

Dalkon Shield controversy, in which thousands of women claimed they had been injured by a poorly designed intrauterine device, the amendments for the first time required that manufacturers of new, implantable medical devices be required to prove their products safe and effective before release to the public. Devices already on the market were ranked by risk, with the riskiest ones, designated Class III, being required to meet the same standards of safety and effectiveness as new devices.

In January 1989, after an extensive internal debate, the FDA identified silicone breast implants as Class III devices and gave their manufacturers 30 months, until January 1991, to submit safety and effectiveness data to the agency. Four breast implant manufacturers submitted the required documents to the FDA: Dow Corning, INAMED (formerly McGhan Medical), Mentor (formerly Heyer-Schulte), and Bioplasty. Surgitek, a unit of Bristol-Myers Squibb, withdrew from the implant business, saying it was unable to meet the FDA's deadline. On August 12, the head of the FDA Breast Prosthesis task force submitted a review of Dow Corning's studies, stating that they were "so weak that they cannot provide a reasonable assurance of the safety and effectiveness of these devices."

Finally, on November 13, the FDA convened an advisory panel of professionals to consider the most recent evidence and to take further testimony. The hearings were highly contentious. The panel heard, once again, arguments concerning the dangers of implants. But the hearings also generated intense support for implants from plastic surgeons, satisfied implant recipients, and breast cancer support and advocacy organizations. Among the most vocal defenders of the implants were women who had experienced successful reconstruction following mastectomies, including representatives of such peer support organizations as Y-Me and My Image after Breast Cancer. Several spoke of the positive psychological benefits of reconstruction and warned that if the FDA took implants off the market, some women, knowing that reconstrutive surgery was unavailable, would delay regular checkups for breast cancer, endangering their lives. Other witnesses argued that women should be free to choose implants, so long as they were fully informed of the benefits and risks of the devices.

The advisory panel debate was, by all accounts, heated. In the final analysis, the panel split hairs: It voted that although breast implants "did not pose a major threat to the health of users," the data submitted by manufacturers was "insufficient to prove safety." However, citing "a public health need," the panel recommended that the devices be left on the market.

The regulatory decision, at this point, passed to the FDA commissioner, Dr. David A. Kessler. Appointed just a few months earlier, Kessler had brought a new commitment to regulatory activism to an agency marked by what some viewed as a pattern of weak government oversight during the Reagan administration. Now, the fledgling commissioner had two months, until mid-January, to rule on the panel's recommendation on breast implants.

Unauthorized Leaks

Unfolding events, however, forced Kessler's hand sooner. In December, a San Francisco jury returned a verdict in *Hopkins* v. *Dow Corning*, awarding Mariann Hopkins $7.3 million, by far the largest victory ever for a plaintiff in a breast implant suit. Hopkins' attorney claimed that his client's implants (made by Dow Corning in 1976) had ruptured and spilled silicone gel—causing severe joint aches, muscle pain, fatigue, and weight loss—and told the jury that "this case is about corporate greed and outright fraud." Dow Corning immediately moved to have the legal records in the case—which included hundreds of pages of internal company memos Hopkins' attorney had subpoenaed—sealed.

Somehow, however, the documents from the Hopkins trial ended up in Commissioner Kessler's hands. Their contents evidently alarmed him. On January 6, 1992, Kessler abruptly reversed the FDA's November decision and called for a 45-day moratorium on all sales of silicone gel breast implants, pending further study of their safety, and he recalled the advisory panel to consider "new evidence." Both the plastic surgeons and Dow Corning were furious. The president of the American Society of Plastic and Reconstructive Surgeons took the unusual step of calling a press conference to brand Kessler's action as "unconscionable—an outrage" and called on Kessler to reconstitute the advisory panel, which he called unqualified to judge the safety of the devices. For its part, Dow Corning demanded publicly to know what new evidence Kessler had obtained and restated the company's intention to block any release of "nonscientific" internal memoranda. The chief of Dow Corning's health care business called a press conference to repeat the company's contention that "the cumulative body of credible scientific evidence shows that the implants are safe and effective."

Dow Corning's efforts to block release of the Hopkins documents, however, failed. On January 13, *New York Times* reporter Philip J. Hilts, saying only that he had obtained the material from several sources, broke the Hopkins case memos in a page-one article, under the headline "Make Is Depicted as Fighting Tests on Implant Safety." In a summary of the contents of several hundred internal company memos, Hilts charged that Dow Corning's safety studies were inadequate and that serious questions raised by its own scientific research and by doctors' complaints had not been answered.

More damaging revelations were yet to come. Over the next several weeks, newspaper readers learned of the following incidents, drawn from the company's internal documents:

- In a 1980 memo, a Dow Corning sales representative had reported to his marketing manager that he had received complaints from a California plastic surgeon who was "downright indignant" because the implant envelopes were "greasy" and had experienced "excessive gel bleed." "The thing that is really galling is that I feel like I have been beaten by my own company instead of the competition. To put a questionable lot of mammaries on the market is inexcusable," the sales representative wrote his manager. "It has to rank right up there with the Pinto gas tank."

- A marketing manager had reported in a memo that he had "assured [a group of doctors], with crossed fingers, that Dow Corning had an active study [of safety issues] under way." (The marketing manager later angrily disputed the interpretation given his remarks by the media, saying in a letter to the Associated Press that he had meant the term *crossed fingers* in a "hopeful" rather than a "lying" sense.)

- A Las Vegas plastic surgeon had had an extensive correspondence with the company reporting his dissatisfactions with the product. In one letter, he charged that he felt "like a broken record" and told of an incident in which an implant had ruptured and spilled its contents—which he described as having the "consistency of 50 weight motor oil"—onto the operating room floor.

Whether wholly justified or not, the memos created a strong impression that Dow Corning had been aware of safety concerns about its implants for many years and had failed to act on this knowledge. The press moved in aggressively, attacking Dow Corning for its "moral evasions"; a widely reprinted cartoon depicted a Dow Corning executive apparently deflating as silicone gel oozed from his body.

A Model Ethical Citizen

That Dow Corning was being labeled publicly as "a company adrift without a moral compass," as one *New York Times* columnist put it several days after the internal memos broke in the press, struck many in and around the company as deeply unjust. Ironically, Dow Corning Corporation was widely regarded in the business community as a model for its efforts to institutionalize ethical behavior.

At the center of Dow Corning's efforts was a formal code of conduct and an unusual procedure for monitoring compliance. In 1976, the first full year of sales for its new generation of breast implants, the company's board of directors had appointed a three-person Audit and Social Responsibility Committee and charged it with developing a corporate code of ethical conduct. Top managers were motivated, in part, by a breaking scandal at that time in which several large companies had been accused of questionable payments to foreign heads of state to secure contracts. With a substantial portion of its operations overseas, Dow Corning wanted its behavior to be above reproach.

In 1977, the company published its first corporate code of conduct, laying out a comprehensive statement of ethical standards. In order to ensure compliance, the company initiated a series of annual audits, in which top managers would visit various cities around the globe to evaluate corporate performance against code standards. In addition, the company held training programs on the code, and its semiannual employee opinion survey included a second on business ethics.

Yet, for whatever reason, the company's widely admired procedures had failed to flag the safety of breast implants as an ethical concern. A routine 1990 ethics audit of the Arlington, Tennessee, plant that manufactured silicone implants, for example, did not reveal any concerns about the product's safety. When later questioned about the apparent failure of the audit procedure, the chairperson of the conduct committee pointed out that normally product safety issues would come before the relevant management group, not the ethics review.

A Hardball Strategy

As the controversy widened, Dow Corning's response, in the words of one *Wall Street Journal* reporter, was to "play hardball." On January 14, eight days after the FDA had announced its moratorium on implant sales and one day after the first leaked documents appeared in the press, Dow Corning took a $25 million charge against fourth quarter, 1991, earnings to cover costs of its legal liability, unused inventory, and efforts to prove implants safe. The company also suspended implant production and placed workers at the company's manufacturing facilities on temporary layoff, with full pay and benefits. Investors, apparently alarmed by this turn of events, knocked down the stock price of both Corning, Inc., and Dow Chemical as they contemplated the parent firms' potential liability.

Implant recipients and trial lawyers also were contemplating the liability question. By March, as many as 600 lawsuits had been filed against Dow Corning and other breast implant makers, according to a representative of the Association of Trial Lawyers of America. The National Products Liability Database estimated that Dow Corning had been sued at least 54 times in federal court and possibly more than 100 times in state courts. Dow Corning's attorney disputed these figures, saying that there were far fewer than 200 cases pending against his client.

The unauthorized leaks created tremendous pressure on Dow Corning to release its own documents to the public. The FDA publicly called on the company on January 20 to release the material so that women and their doctors could evaluate the new evidence for themselves, rather than simply relying on news reports. (The agency, although in possession of the documents, could not release them because they were still protected under court order.) The company responded two days later by releasing a group of scientific studies—but not the infamous Pinto memo and other internal materials that the company dubbed unscientific.

Suspension of breast implant sales and release of the scientific studies did not slow down the crisis engulfing the company. On January 29, in an apparent acknowledgment of the severity of the situation, the company hired former attorney general Griffin B. Bell—who had performed a similar role at Exxon Corporation following the *Valdez* oil spill and at E. F. Hutton following the check-kiting scandal—to investigate its behavior in making implants.

Finally, on February 10, following a top-level intervention by the chairmen of Corning, Inc., and Dow Chemical, both of whom sat on Dow Corning's board, the board of directors executed a stunning management shakeup. Dow Corning demoted chief executive Lawrence A. Reed to the position of chief operating officer and forced longtime board chairman John S. Ludington to retire. Keith R. McKennon was named chairman and CEO. Simultaneously, the board announced that it would release to the public 15 scientific reports and 94 nonscientific memos or letters from company files, including the Pinto and "crossed fingers" memos, as well as other potentially damaging materials that had not yet been reported by the media.

Several top executives of Dow Corning met the press the same day to present the company's perspective. One defended the company's decision not to release the documents earlier, saying:

> Our motives are simple. First and foremost, these memos do not answer fundamental questions and concerns that women have about breast implants. And by focusing attention on the memos rather than the science that supports the device, we do nothing but further raise the anxiety level of women and physicians and scientists.

He added that "while we are not happy with the memos, we have nothing to hide, and we believe that each memo put in its proper context can be understood and explained." Many of the memos, he said, were best understood as part of the normal give and take that occurs within a technical organization, "one part of a multifaceted dialogue or communication or discussion that goes on," and did not reflect fundamental problems. By pulling various statements out of context, he implied, the press had misrepresented questions scientists might legitimately raise in the course of their inquiry as final conclusions. The Dow Corning executives closed the press conference by denying categorically that implants could cause autoimmune disease or cancer.

Facing a Crucial Decision

On February 20, the day after his testimony before the FDA, McKennon received word from Washington. After three hours of tense debate, the FDA advisory panel had voted just after 5:00 P.M. to recommend that implants be taken off the market, except for women needing reconstruction following mastectomies or to correct serious deformities. All implant recipients would be required to enroll in clinical studies. Cosmetic augmentations would be strictly limited to those required by the design of the clinical trials. Commissioner Kessler would have sixty days to rule on the panel's recommendation.

McKennon would have to lay a plan of action before his board soon—he certainly could not wait another two months for the FDA's next move. The breast implant business, he had learned, had not made any money for Dow Corning for the past five years. Even in its heyday, it had contributed no more than 1 percent of the company's total revenues. Some of his top executives had urged him just to get out of the implant business altogether and let the attorneys mop up the liability problems. Many in the company felt that the huge settlement in the Hopkins case would be greatly reduced on appeal, and the company's $250 million in insurance would be sufficient to cover their liability. McKennon reflected on these issues as he contemplated his next actions. Certainly, he needed to act decisively to stem Dow Corning's financial losses. But, he pondered, did the company not also have, as he had put it to a reporter a few days earlier, an "overriding responsibility . . . to the women who have our implants"? And what of the company's reputation, so carefully nurtured, for always upholding the highest standards of ethical behavior?

Discussion Questions

1. What internal and external factors contributed to the emergence of the silicone breast implant crisis for Dow Corning?
2. What should CEO McKennon do as of February 20, 1992?
3. What steps can Dow Corning, or other companies, take to prevent this kind of situation from occurring in the future?

On April 24, 2000, Philip H. Knight, CEO of athletic shoe and apparel maker Nike Inc., publicly announced that he would no longer donate money to the University of Oregon (UO). It was a dramatic and unexpected move for the high-profile executive. A former UO track and field star, Knight had founded Nike's predecessor in 1963 with his former coach and mentor, Bill Bowerman. Over the years, Knight had maintained close ties with his alma mater, giving more than $50 million of his personal fortune to the school over a quarter century. In 2000, he was in active discussion with school officials about his biggest donation yet—millions for renovating the football stadium. But suddenly it was all called off. Said Knight in his statement: "[F]or me personally, there will be no further donations of any kind to the University of Oregon. At this time, this is not a situation that can be resolved. The bonds of trust, which allowed me to give at a high level, have been shredded."

At issue was the University of Oregon's intention, announced April 14, 2000, to join the Worker Rights Consortium (WRC). Like many universities, UO was engaged in an internal debate over the ethical responsibilities associated with its role as a purchaser of goods manufactured overseas. Over a period of several months, UO administrators, faculty, and students had been discussing what steps they could take to ensure that products sold in the campus store, especially university-logo apparel, were not manufactured under sweatshop conditions. The University had considered joining two organizations, both of which purported to certify goods as "no sweat." The first, the Fair Labor Association (FLA), had grown out of President Clinton's Apparel Industry Partnership (AIP) initiative and was vigorously backed by Nike, as well as several other leading apparel makers. The second, the Worker Rights Consortium, was supported by student activists and several U.S.-based labor unions that had broken from the AIP after charging it did not go far enough to protect workers. Knight clearly felt that his alma mater had made the wrong choice. "[The] University [has] inserted itself into the new global economy where I make my living," he charged. "And inserted itself on the wrong side, fumbling a teachable moment."

By Rebecca J. Morris and Anne T. Lawrence. This is an abridged version of a full-length case, "Nike's Dispute with the University of Oregon," *Case Research Journal* 21, no. 3 (Summer 2001). Abridged and reprinted by permission of the *Case Research Journal*. Sources include articles appearing in the *New York Times, The Oregonian, Washington Post,* and other daily newspapers, and material provided by Nike at its website, www.nikebiz.com. Book sources include J.B. Strasser and L. Becklund, *Swoosh: The Unauthorized Story of Nike and the Men Who Played There* (New York: HarperCollins, 1993); D. R. Katz, *Just Do It: The Nike Spirit in the Corporate World* (Holbrook, MA: Adams Media Corporation, 1995); and T. Vanderbilt, *The Sneaker Book* (New York: New Press, 1998). Websites for the Fair Labor Association and the Worker Rights Consortium may be found, respectively, at www.fairlabor.org and www.workersrights.org. Ernst & Young's audit of Nike's subcontractor factories in Vietnam is available at www.corpwatch.org/trac/nike/ernst. Coverage of Nike and the WRC decision in the University of Oregon student newspaper is available at www.dailyemerald.com. A U.S. Department of Labor study of wages and benefits in the footwear industry in selected countries is available at www.dol.gov/dol/ilab/public/media/reports/oiea/wagestudy. A full set of footnotes is available in the *Case Research Journal* version. Copyright © 2001 by the *Case Research Journal* and Rebecca J. Morris and Anne T. Lawrence. All rights reserved jointly to the authors and the North American Case Research Association (NACRA).

The dispute between Phil Knight and the University of Oregon captured much of the furor swirling about the issue of the role of multinational corporations in the global economy and the effects of their far-flung operations on their many thousands of workers, communities, and other stakeholders. In part because of its high-profile brand name, Nike had become a lightening rod for activists concerned about worker rights abroad. Like many U.S.-based shoe and apparel makers, Nike had located its manufacturing operations overseas, mainly in Southeast Asia, in search of low wages. Almost all production was carried out by subcontractors rather than by Nike directly. Nike's employees in the United States, by contrast, directed their efforts to the high-end work of research and development, marketing, and retailing. In the context of this global division of labor, what responsibility, if any, did Nike have to ensure adequate working conditions and living standards for the hundreds of thousands of workers, mostly young Asian women, who made its shoes and apparel? If this was not Nike's responsibility, then whose was it? Did organizations like the University of Oregon have any business pressuring companies through their purchasing practices? If so, how should they best do so? In short, what were the lessons of this "teachable moment"?

Nike, Inc.

In 2000, Nike, Inc., was the leading designer and marketer of athletic footwear, apparel, and equipment in the world. Based in Beaverton, Oregon, the company's "swoosh" logo, its "Just Do It!" slogan, and its spokespersons Michael Jordan, Mia Hamm, and Tiger Woods were universally recognized. Nike employed around 20,000 people directly, and *half a million* indirectly in 565 contract factories in 46 countries around the world. Wholly owned subsidiaries included Bauer Nike Hockey Inc. (hockey equipment), Cole Haan (dress and casual shoes), and Nike Team Sports (licensed team products). Revenues for the 12 months ending November 1999 were almost $9 billion, and the company enjoyed a 45 percent global market share. Knight owned 34 percent of the company's stock and was believed to be the sixth-richest individual in the United States.

Knight had launched this far-flung global empire shortly after completing his MBA degree at Stanford University in the early 1960s. Drawing on his firsthand knowledge of track and field, he decided to import low-priced track shoes from Japan in partnership with his former college coach. Bowerman would provide design ideas, test the shoes in competition, and endorse the shoes with other coaches; Knight would handle all financial and day-to-day operations of the business. Neither man had much money to offer, so for $500 apiece and a handshake, the company (then called Blue Ribbon Sports) was officially founded in 1963. The company took the name Nike in 1978; two years later, with revenues topping $269 million and 2,700 employees, Nike became a publicly traded company.

From the beginning, marketing had been a critical part of Knight's vision. The founder defined Nike as a "marketing-oriented company." During the 1980s and early 1990s, Nike aggressively sought out endorsements by celebrity athletes to increase brand awareness and foster consumer loyalty. Early Nike endorsers included Olympic gold medalist Carl Lewis, Wimbledon champion Andre Agassi, and six members of the 1992 Olympic basketball "Dream Team." Later endorsers included tennis aces Pete Sampras and Monica Seles, basketball great Michael Jordan, and golf superstar Tiger Woods.

An important element in Nike's success was its ability to develop cutting-edge products that met the needs of serious athletes, as well as set fashion trends. Research specialists in Nike's Sports Research Labs conducted extensive research and testing to develop new technologies to improve the performance of Nike shoes in a variety of sports. For example, research specialists studied the causes of ankle injuries in basketball players to develop shoes that would physically prevent injuries, as well as signal information to the user to help him or her resist turning the ankle while in the air. Other specialists developed new polymer materials that would make the shoes lighter, more aerodynamic, or more resistant to the abrasions incurred during normal athletic use. Findings from the Sports Research Labs were then passed on to design teams that developed the look and styling of the shoes.

Although it was the leading athletic footwear company in the world, Nike never manufactured shoes in any significant number. Rather, from its inception, the company had outsourced production to subcontractors in Asia, with the company shifting production locations within the region when prevailing wage rates became too high. In the early years, it had imported shoes from Japan. It later shifted production to South Korea and Taiwan, then to Indonesia and Thailand, and later yet to Vietnam and China.

The reasons for locating shoe production mainly in Southeast Asia were several, but the most important was the cost of labor. Modern athletic shoes were composed of mesh, leather, and nylon uppers that were hand-assembled, sewn and glued to composite soles. Mechanization had not been considered effective for shoe manufacturing due to the fragile materials used and the short life spans of styles of athletic shoes. Therefore, shoe production was highly labor-intensive. Developing countries, primarily in Southeast Asia, offered the distinct advantage of considerably lower wage rates. For example, in the early 1990s, when Nike shifted much of its shoe production to Indonesia, daily wages there hovered around $1 a day (compared to wages in the U.S. shoe industry at that time of around $8 an hour).

Along with lower labor costs, Asia provided the additional advantage of access to raw materials suppliers. Very few rubber firms in the United States, for example, produced the sophisticated composite soles demanded in modern athletic shoe designs. Satellite industries necessary for modern shoe production, plentiful in Asia, included tanneries, textiles, and plastic and ironwork moldings. A final factor in determining where to locate production was differential tariff rates. In general, canvas sneakers were assessed higher tariffs than leather molded footwear, such as basketball or running shoes. As a result, shoe companies had an incentive to outsource high-tech athletic shoes overseas, because tariffs on them were relatively low.

Many of Nike's factories in Asia were operated by a small number of Taiwanese and South Korean firms that specialized in shoe manufacturing, many owned by some of the wealthiest families in the region. When Nike moved from one location to another, often these companies followed, bringing their managerial expertise with them.

Nike's Subcontractor Factories

In 2000, Nike contracted with over 500 different footwear and apparel factories around the world to produce its shoes and apparel. Although there was no such thing as a typical Nike plant, a factory operated by the South Korean subcontractor Tae Kwang Vina (TKV) in the Bien Hoa City industrial zone near Ho Chi Minh City in Vietnam provided a glimpse into the setting in which many Nike shoes were made.

TKV employed approximately 10,000 workers in the Bien Hoa City factory. The workforce consisted of 200 clerical workers, 355 supervisors, and 9,465 production workers, all making athletic shoes for Nike. Ninety percent of the workers were women between the ages of 18 to 24. Production workers were employed in one of three major areas within the factory: the chemical, stitching, and assembly sections. Production levels at the Bien Hoa City factory reached 400,000 pairs of shoes per month; Nike shoes made at this and other factories made up fully 5 percent of Vietnam's total exports.

Workers in the chemical division were responsible for producing the high-technology outsoles. Production steps involved stretching and flattening huge blobs of raw rubber on heavy-duty rollers and baking chemical compounds in steel molds to form the innovative three-dimensional outsoles. The chemical composition of the soles changed constantly in response to the cutting-edge formulations developed by the U.S. design teams, requiring frequent changes in the production process. The smell of complex polymers, the hot ovens, and the clanging of the steel molds resulted in a working environment that was loud and hot and had high concentrations of chemical fumes. Chemicals used in the section were known to cause eye, skin, and throat irritations; damage to liver and kidneys; nausea; anorexia; and reproductive health hazards through inhalation or in some cases through absorption through the skin. Workers in the chemical section were thought to have high rates of respiratory illnesses, although records kept at the TKV operations did not permit the tracking of illnesses by factory section. Workers in the chemical section were issued gloves and surgical-style masks. However, they often discarded the protective gear, complaining that it was too hot and humid to wear them in the plant.

In the stitching section, row after row of sewing machines operated by young women hummed and clattered in a space the size of three football fields. One thousand stitchers worked on a single floor of the TKV factory, sewing together nylon, leather, and other fabrics to make the uppers. Other floors of the factory were filled with thousands of additional sewing machines producing different shoe models. The stitching job required precision and speed. Workers who did not meet the aggressive production goals did not receive a bonus. Failing to meet production goals three times resulted in the worker's dismissal. Workers were sometimes permitted to work additional hours without pay to meet production quotas. Supervisors were strict, chastising workers for excessive talking or spending too much time in the restrooms. Korean supervisors, often hampered by language and cultural barriers, sometimes resorted to hard-nosed management tactics, hitting or slapping slower workers. Other workers in need of discipline were forced to stand outside the factory for long periods in the tropical sun. The Vietnamese term for this practice was *phoi nang,* or sun-drying.

In the assembly section, women worked side by side along a moving line to join the uppers to the outersoles through the rapid manipulation of sharp knives, skivers, routers, and glue-coated brushes. Women were thought to be better suited for the assembly jobs because their hands were smaller and more capable of the manual dexterity needed to fit the shoe components together precisely. During the assembly process, some

120 pairs of hands touched a single shoe. A strong, sweet solvent smell was prominent in the assembly area. Ceiling-mounted ventilation fans were ineffective since the heavy fumes settled to the floor. Assembly workers wore cotton surgical masks to protect themselves from the fumes; however, many workers pulled the masks below their noses, saying they were more comfortable that way. Rows and rows of shoes passed along a conveyor before the sharp eyes of the quality control inspectors. The inspectors examined each of the thousands of shoes produced daily for poor stitching or crooked connections between soles. Defective shoes were discarded. Approved shoes continued on the conveyor to stations where they were laced by assembly workers and finally put into Nike shoeboxes for shipment to the United States.

Despite the dirty, dangerous, and difficult nature of the work inside the Bien Hoa factory, there was no shortage of applicants for positions. Although entry-level wages averaged only $1.50 per day (the lowest of all countries where Nike manufactured), many workers viewed factory jobs as better than their other options, such as working in the rice paddies or pedaling a pedicab along the streets of Ho Chi Minh City (formerly Saigon). With overtime pay at one and a half times the regular rate, workers could double their salaries—generating enough income to purchase a motorscooter or to send money home to impoverished rural relatives. These wages were well above national norms. An independent study by researchers from Dartmouth University showed that the average annual income for workers at two Nike subcontractor factories in Vietnam was between $545 and $566, compared to the national average of between $250 and $300. Additionally, workers were provided free room and board and access to on-site health care facilities. Many Vietnamese workers viewed positions in the shoe factory as transitional jobs, a way to earn money for a dowry or to experience living in a larger city. Many returned to their homes after working for Nike for two or three years to marry and begin the next phase of their lives.

The Campaigns against Nike

In the early 1990s, criticism of Nike's global labor practices began to gather steam. *Harper's Magazine,* for example, published the pay stub of an Indonesian worker, showing that the Nike subcontractor had paid the woman just under 14 cents per hour, and contrasted this with the high retail price of the shoes and the high salaries paid to the company's celebrity endorsers. The Made in the U.S.A. Foundation, a group backed by American unions, used a million dollar ad budget to urge consumers to send their "old, dirty, smelly, worn-out Nikes" to Phil Knight in protest of Nike's Asian manufacturing practices. Human rights groups and Christian organizations joined the labor unions in targeting the labor practices of the athletic shoes firm. Many felt that Nike's anti-authority corporate image ("Just Do It") and message of social betterment through fitness were incompatible with press photos of slight Asian women hunched over sewing machines 70 hours a week, earning just pennies an hour.

By mid-1993, Nike was being regularly pilloried in the press as an imperialist profiteer. A CBS news segment airing on July 2, 1993, opened with images of Michael Jordan and Andre Agassi, two athletes who had multimillion dollar promotion contracts with Nike. Viewers were told to contrast the athletes' pay checks with those of the Chinese and Indonesian workers who made "pennies" so that Nike could "Just Do It."

In 1995, the *Washington Post* reported that a pair of Nike Air Pegasus shoes that retailed for $70 cost Nike only $2.75 in labor costs, or 4 percent of the price paid by consumers. Nike's operating profit on the same pair of shoes was $6.25, while the retailer pocketed $9.00 in operating profits. Also that year, shareholder activists organized by the Interfaith Center on Corporate Responsibility submitted a shareholder proposal at Nike's annual meeting, calling on the company to review labor practices by its subcontractors; the proposal garnered 3 percent of the shareholder vote.

A story in *Life* magazine documented the use of child labor in Pakistan to produce soccer balls for Nike, Adidas, and other companies. The publicity fallout was intense. The public could not ignore the photographs of small children sitting in the dirt, carefully stitching together the panels of a soccer ball that would become the plaything of some American child the same age. Nike moved quickly to work with its Pakistani subcontractor to eliminate the use of child labor, but damage to Nike's image had been done.

In October 1996, CBS News *48 Hours* broadcast a scathing report on Nike's factories in Vietnam. CBS reporter Roberta Baskin focused on low wage rates, extensive overtime, and physical abuse of workers. Several young workers told Baskin how a Korean supervisor had beaten them with a part of a shoe because of problems with production. A journalist in Vietnam told the reporter that the phrase "to Nike someone" was part of the Vietnamese vernacular. It meant to "take out one's frustration on a fellow worker." Vietnamese plant managers refused to be interviewed, covering their faces as they ran inside the factory. CBS news anchor Dan Rather concluded the damaging report by saying, "Nike now says it plans to hire outside observers to talk to employees and examine working conditions in its Vietnam factories, but the company just won't say when that might happen."

The negative publicity was having an effect. In 1996, a marketing research study authorized by Nike reported the perceptions of young people aged 13 to 25 of Nike as a company. The top three perceptions, in the order of their response frequency, were (1) athletics, (2) cool, and (3) bad labor practices. Although Nike maintained that its sales were never affected, company executives were clearly concerned about the effect of criticism of its global labor practices on the reputation of the brand they had worked so hard to build.

The Evolution of Nike's Global Labor Practices

In its early years, Nike had maintained that the labor practices of its foreign subcontractors, like TKV, were simply not its responsibility. "When we started Nike," Knight later commented, "it never occurred to us that we should dictate what their factor[ies] should look like." The subcontractors, not Nike, were responsible for wages and working conditions. Dave Taylor, Nike's vice president of production, explained the company's position: "We don't pay anybody at the factories and we don't set policy within the factories; it is their business to run."

When negative articles first began appearing in the early 1990s, however, Nike managers realized that they needed to take some action to avoid further bad publicity. In 1992, the company drafted its first Code of Conduct, which required every subcontractor and supplier in the Nike network to honor all applicable local government labor and environmental regulations, or Nike would terminate the relationship. The subcontractors were also required to allow plant inspections and complete all necessary paperwork. Despite the compliance reports the factories filed every six months, Nike insiders acknowledged that the code of conduct system might not catch all violations. Tony Nava, Nike's country coordinator for Indonesia, told a *Chicago Tribune* reporter, "We can't know if they're actually complying with what they put down on paper."

In 1994, Nike tried to address this problem by hiring Ernst & Young, the accounting firm, to independently monitor worker abuse allegations in Nike's Indonesian factories. Later, Ernst & Young also audited Nike's factories in Thailand and Vietnam. A copy of the Vietnam audit leaked to the press showed that workers were often unaware of the toxicity of the compounds they were using and ignorant of the need for safety precautions. In 1998, Nike implemented important changes in its Vietnamese plants to reduce exposure to toxics, substituting less harmful chemicals, installing ventilation systems, and training personnel in occupational health and safety issues.

In 1996, Nike established a new Labor Practices Department, headed by Dusty Kidd, formerly a public relations executive for the company. Later that year, Nike hired GoodWorks International, headed by former U.S. ambassador to the United Nations Andrew Young, to investigate conditions in its overseas factories. In January 1997, Good-Works issued a glossy report, stating that "Nike is doing a good job in the application of its Code of Conduct. But Nike can and should do better." The report was criticized by activists for its failure to look at the issue of wages. Young demurred, saying he did not have expertise in conducting wage surveys. Said one critic, "This was a public relations problem, and the world's largest sneaker company did what it does best: it purchased a celebrity endorsement."

Over the next few years, Nike continued to work to improve labor practices in its overseas subcontractor factories, as well as the public perception of them. In January 1998, Nike formed a Corporate Responsibility Division under the leadership of former Microsoft executive Maria S. Eitel. Nike subsequently doubled the staff of this division. In May of that year, Knight gave a speech at the National Press Club, at which he announced several new initiatives. At that time, he committed Nike to raise the minimum age for employment in its shoe factories to 18 and in its apparel factories to 16. He also promised to achieve OSHA standards for indoor air quality in all its factories by the end of the year, mainly by eliminating the use of the solvent toluene; to expand educational programs for workers and its microenterprise loan program; and to fund university research on responsible business practices. Nike also continued its use of external monitors, hiring PricewaterhouseCoopers to join Ernst & Young in a comprehensive program of factory audits, checking them against Nike's code.

Apparel Industry Partnership

One of Nike's most ambitious social responsibility initiatives was its participation in the Apparel Industry Partnership. It was this involvement that would lead, eventually, to Knight's break with the University of Oregon.

In August 1996, President Clinton launched the White House Apparel Industry Partnership on Workplace Standards (AIP). The initial group was comprised of 18 organizations. Participants included several leading manufacturers, such as Nike, Reebok, and

Liz Claiborne. Also in the group were several labor unions, including the Union of Needletrades, Industrial, and Textile Employees (UNITE) and the Retail, Wholesale and Department Store Union; and several human rights, consumer, and shareholder organizations, including Business for Social Responsibility, the Interfaith Center on Corporate Responsibility, and the National Consumers League. The goal of the AIP was to develop a set of standards to ensure that apparel and footwear were not made under sweatshop conditions. For companies, it held out the promise of certifying to their customers that their products were "no sweat." For labor and human rights groups, it held out the promise of improving working conditions in overseas factories.

In April 1997, after months of often-fractious meetings, the AIP announced that it had agreed on a Workplace Code of Conduct that sought to define decent and humane working conditions. Companies agreeing to the code would have to pledge not to use forced labor, that is, prisoners or bonded or indentured workers. They could not require more than 60 hours of work a week, including overtime. They could not employ children younger than 15 years old, or the age for completing compulsory schooling, whichever was older—except they could hire 14-year-olds if local law allowed. The code also called on signatory companies to treat all workers with respect and dignity; to refrain from discrimination on the basis of gender, race, religion, age, disability, sexual orientation, nationality, political opinion, or social or ethnic origin; and to provide a safe and healthy workplace. Employees' rights to organize and bargain collectively would be respected. In a key provision, the code also required companies to pay at least the local legal minimum wage or the prevailing industry wage, whichever was higher. All standards would apply not only to a company's own facilities but also to their subcontractors or suppliers.

Knight, who prominently joined President Clinton and others at a White House ceremony announcing the code, issued the following statement:

> Nike agreed to participate in this Partnership because it was the first credible attempt, by a diverse group of interests, to address the important issue of improving factories worldwide. It was worth the effort and hard work. The agreement will prove important for several reasons. Not only is our industry stepping up to the plate and taking a giant swing at improving factory conditions, but equally important, we are finally providing consumers some guidance to counter all of the misinformation that has surrounded this issue for far too long.

The Fair Labor Association

But this was not the end of the AIP's work; it also had to agree on a process for monitoring compliance with the code. Although the group hoped to complete its work in six months, over a year later it was still deeply divided on several key matters. Internal documents leaked to the *New York Times* in July 1998 showed that industry representatives had opposed proposals, circulated by labor and human rights members, calling for the monitoring of 30 percent of plants annually by independent auditors. The companies also opposed proposals that would require them to support workers' rights to organize independent unions and to bargain collectively, even in countries like China where workers did not have such rights by law. Said one nonindustry member, "We're teetering on the edge of collapse."

Finally, a subgroup of nine centrist participants, including Nike, began meeting separately in an attempt to move forward. In November 1998, this subgroup announced that it had come to agreement on a monitoring system for overseas factories of U.S.-based companies. The AIP would establish a new organization, the Fair Labor Association (FLA), to oversee compliance with its Workplace Code of Conduct. Companies would be required to monitor their own factories, and those of their subcontractors, for compliance; all would have to be checked within the first two years. In addition, the FLA would select and certify independent external monitors, who would inspect 10 percent of each firm's factories each year. Most of these monitors were expected to be accounting firms, which had expertise in conducting audits. The monitors' reports would be kept private. If a company were found to be out of compliance, it would be given a chance to correct the problem. Eventually, if it did not, the company would be dropped from the FLA and its termination announced to the public. Companies would pay for most of their own monitoring. The Clinton administration quickly endorsed the plan.

Both manufacturers and institutional buyers stood to benefit from participation in the Fair Labor Association. Companies, once certified for three years, could place an FLA service mark on their brands, signaling both to individual consumers and institutional buyers that their products were "sweatshop-free." It was expected that the FLA would also serve the needs of institutional buyers, particularly universities. By joining the FLA and agreeing to contract only with certified companies, universities could warrant to their students and others that their logo apparel and athletic gear were manufactured under conditions conforming with an established code of fair labor standards. Both parties would pay for these benefits. The FLA was to be funded by dues from participating companies ($5,000 to $100,000 annually, depending on revenue) and by payments from affiliated colleges and universities (based on 1 percent of their licensing income from logo products, up to a $50,000 annual cap).

Although many welcomed the agreement—and some new companies signed on with the FLA soon after it was announced—others did not. Warnaco, a leading apparel maker that had participated in the Partnership, quit, saying that the monitoring process would require it to turn over competitive information to outsiders. The American Apparel Manufacturing Association (AAMA), an industry group representing 350 companies, scoffed at the whole idea of monitoring. "Who is going to do the monitoring?" asked a spokesperson for the AAMA, apparently sarcastically. "Accountants or Jesuit priests?" Others argued that companies simply could not be relied upon to monitor themselves objectively. Said Jay Mazur, president of UNITE, "The fox cannot watch the chickens . . . if they want the monitoring to be independent, it can't be controlled by the companies." A visit from an external monitor once every 10 years would not prevent abuses. And in any case, as a practical matter, most monitors would be drawn from the major accounting firms that did business with the companies they were monitoring and were therefore unlikely to seek out lapses. Companies would not be required to publish a list of their factories, and any problems uncovered by the monitoring process could be kept from the public under the rules governing nondisclosure of proprietary information.

One of the issues most troubling to critics was the code's position on wages. The code called on companies to pay the minimum wage or prevailing wage, whichever was higher. But in many of the countries of Southeast Asia, these wages fell well below the minimum considered necessary for a decent standard of living for an individual or family. For example, the *Economist* reported that Indonesia's average minimum wage, paid by Nike subcontractors, was only two-thirds of what a person needed for basic subsistence. An alternative view was that a code of conduct should require that companies pay a *living wage,* that is, compensation for a normal workweek adequate to provide for the basic needs of an average family, adjusted for the average number of adult wage earners per family. One problem with this approach, however, was that many countries did not systematically study the cost of living, relative to wages, so defining a living wage was difficult. The Partnership asked the U.S. Department of Labor to conduct a preliminary study of these issues; the results were published in 2000.

The code also called on companies to respect workers' rights to organize and bargain collectively. Yet a number of FLA companies outsourced production to nondemocratic countries, such as China and Vietnam, where workers had no such rights. Finally, some criticized the agreement on the grounds it provided companies, as one put it, "a piece of paper to use as a fig leaf." Commented a representative of the needle trades unions, "The problem with the partnership plan is that it tinkers at the margins of the sweatshop system but creates the impression that it is doing much more. This is potentially helpful to companies stung by public condemnation of their labor practices, but it hurts millions of workers and undermines the growing antisweatshop movement."

The Worker Rights Consortium

Some activists in the antisweatshop movement decided to chart their own course, independent of the FLA. On October 20, 1999, students from more than 100 colleges held a press conference to announce formation of the Worker Rights Consortium (WRC) and called on their schools to withdraw from, or not to join, the FLA. The organization would be formally launched at a founding convention in April 2000.

The Worker Rights Consortium differed radically in its approach to eliminating sweatshops. First, the WRC did not permit corporations to join; it was comprised exclusively of universities and colleges, with unions and human rights organizations playing an advisory role. In joining the WRC, universities would agree to "require decent working conditions in factories producing their licensed products." Unlike the FLA, the WCA did not endorse a single, comprehensive set of fair labor standards. Rather, it called on its affiliated universities to develop their own codes. However, it did establish minimum standards that such codes should meet—ones that were, in some respects, stricter than the FLA's. Perhaps most significantly, companies would have to pay a living wage. Companies were also required to publish the names and addresses of all of their manufacturing facilities, in contrast to FLA rules. Universities could refuse to license goods made in countries where compliance with fair labor standards was "deemed impossible," whatever efforts companies had made to enforce their own codes in factories there.

By contrast with the FLA, monitoring would be carried out by "a network of local organizations in regions where licensed goods are produced," generally nongovernmental organizations, independent human rights groups, and unions. These organizations would conduct unannounced "spot investigations," usually in response to worker complaints; WRC organizers called this the "fire alarm" method of uncovering code violations. Systematic monitoring would not be attempted. The consortium's governance structure reflected its mission of being an organization by and for colleges and universities; its 12-person board was composed of students, university administrators, and human rights experts, with no seats for industry representatives. The group would be financed by 1 percent of licensing revenue from participating universities, as well as foundation grants.

Over the course of the spring semester 2000, student protests were held on a number of campuses, including the University of Oregon, to demand that their schools join the WRC. By April, around 45 schools had done so. At UO, the administration encouraged an open debate on the issue so that all sides could be heard on how to ensure that UO products were made under humane conditions. Over a period of several months, the Academic Senate, the student body, and a committee of faculty, students, administrators, and alumni appointed by the president all voted to join the consortium. Finally, after concluding that all constituents had had an opportunity to be heard, on April 12, 2000, University of Oregon president David Frohnmayer announced that UO would join the WRC for one year. Its membership would be conditional, he said, on the consortium's agreement to give companies a voice in its operations and universities more power in governance. Shortly after the University's decision was announced in the press, Phil Knight withdrew his philanthropic contribution. In his public announcement, he stated his main disagreements with the Worker Rights Consortium:

> Frankly, we are frustrated that factory monitoring is badly misconstrued. For us one of the great hurdles and real handicaps in the dialogue has been the complexity of the issue. For real progress to be made, all key participants have to be at the table. That's why the FLA has taken so long to get going. The WRC is supported by the AFL-CIO and its affiliated apparel workers' union, UNITE. Their main aim, logically and understandably, however misguided, is to bring apparel jobs back to the U.S. Among WRC rules, no company can participate in setting standards, or monitoring. It has an unrealistic living wage provision. And its "gotcha" approach to monitoring doesn't do what monitoring should— measure conditions and make improvements.

Discussion Questions

1. Who do you believe has a social and ethical responsibility for the wages and working conditions of the employees who produce Nike's shoes and apparel, Nike or its subcontractors? Why do you think so?
2. The Fair Labor Association and the Worker Rights Consortium differed on how to establish and enforce fair labor standards. Which approach, if either, do you favor, and why? Consider how you would answer this question if you were representing the following: Nike shareholders, a human rights organization, a U.S. labor union, or the government of a developing country.
3. If you were the CEO of Nike, what would you do next in this situation? If you were the president of the University of Oregon, what would you do next?

On November 10, 1995, world-renowned Nigerian novelist and environmental activist Ken Saro-Wiwa was executed by hanging in a prison courtyard. Just 10 days earlier, he had been convicted by a military tribunal on charges that he had ordered the murder of political opponents. Throughout his trial, Saro-Wiwa had vigorously maintained his innocence. Despite protests by many world leaders and human rights organizations, the Nigerian military regime had quickly carried out the death sentence.

Saro-Wiwa's execution provoked a profound crisis for the Royal Dutch/Shell Group of Companies. In its wake, some environmentalists and political leaders called for an international boycott of Shell's gasoline and other products. The World Bank canceled a promised $160 million combined loan and investment in Shell's liquefied natural gas project in Nigeria. In Canada, the Toronto city government refused a large gasoline contract to Shell Canada, despite its low bid—an event that received wide press coverage. Some even called for the oil company to pull out of Nigeria altogether.

Alan Detheridge, Shell's coordinator for West Africa, told a reporter in February 1996, "Saro-Wiwa's execution was a disaster for us."

Just what was the connection between Saro-Wiwa's execution and Shell? Why did the company find itself suddenly, in the words of the *New York Times,* "on trial in the court of public opinion?" Had the company done anything wrong in Nigeria? What, if anything, could or should it do in the face of an escalating chorus of international criticism?

The Royal Dutch/Shell Group

The Royal Dutch/Shell Group was the world's largest fully integrated petroleum company. "Upstream," the conglomerate controlled oil and gas exploration and production; "midstream," the pipelines and tankers that carried oil and gas; and "downstream," the refining, marketing, and distribution of the final product. The company also had interests in coal mining, forestry, chemicals, and renewable energy. In all, the Anglo-Dutch conglomerate comprised over 2,000 separate entities, with exploration and production operations, refineries, and marketing in scores of countries. Royal Dutch/Shell was, in both its ownership and scope, perhaps the world's most truly transnational corporation.

In 1994, Royal Dutch/Shell made more money than any other company in the world, reporting annual profits of $6.3 billion. The same year, the company reported

This is an abridged and revised (2000) version of a longer case, Anne T. Lawrence, "Shell Oil in Nigeria," *Case Research Journal* 17, no. 4 (Winter 1997), pp. 1–21. Abridged by the author by permission of the *Case Research Journal.* Sources include articles appearing in the *Wall Street Journal, New York Times, Economist, Fortune, Guardian, Independent,* and *Village Voice;* U.S. congressional hearings; reports by Amnesty International, Greenpeace, and the World Bank; and material provided by Royal Dutch/Shell and by Shell Nigeria and posted on their websites at www.shell.com and www.shellnigeria.com. The history of Royal Dutch/Shell is based on Adele Hast, ed., *International Directory of Company Histories* (Chicago: St. James Press, 1991) and *World Class Business: A Guide to the 100 Most Powerful Global Corporations* (New York: Henry Holt, 1992). Ken Saro-Wiwa's story is drawn primarily from his memoir *A Month and a Day: A Prison Diary* and other writings. A full set of footnotes in available in the *Case Research Journal* version. Copyright © 1998 by the *Case Research Journal* and Anne T. Lawrence. All rights reserved.

revenues of $94.9 billion, placing it tenth on *Fortune*'s Global 500 list. Assets were reported at $108.3 billion, and stockholders' equity at $56.4 billion. With 106,000 employees worldwide, it had the largest work force of any oil company in the world.

This highly successful global corporation traced its history back over more than a century and a half. In the 1830s, British entrepreneur Marcus Samuel founded a trading company to export manufactured goods from England and to import products, including polished seashells (hence, the name "Shell"), from the Orient. In the early 1890s, Samuel's sons steered the company into the kerosene business, assembling a fleet of tankers to ply the fuel through the Suez Canal to Far Eastern ports. At about the same time, a group of Dutch businessmen launched the Royal Dutch Company to drill for oil in the Dutch East Indies. In 1907, Royal Dutch and Shell merged, with Royal Dutch retaining a 60 percent interest and Shell, 40 percent. The resulting organization came to be known as the Royal Dutch/Shell Group of Companies, or simply the Group.

Over the years, Royal Dutch/Shell developed a highly decentralized management style, with its far-flung subsidiaries exercising considerable autonomy. The company believed that vesting authority in nationally based, integrated operating companies—each with its own distinctive identity—gave it the strategic flexibility to respond swiftly to local opportunities and conditions. The corporation was governed by a six-person committee of managing directors. Reflecting its dual parentage, the Group maintained headquarters in both London and The Hague. The chairmanship rotated periodically between the chairman of Shell and the president of Royal Dutch. Decision making was by consensus, with no dominant personality.

Shell Nigeria

The Shell Petroleum Development Company of Nigeria (SPDC), usually called Shell Nigeria, was a wholly owned subsidiary of Royal Dutch/Shell. The company stated its corporate objective simply. It was "to find, produce, and deliver hydrocarbons safely, responsibly, and economically for the benefit of our stakeholders."

The Royal Dutch/Shell Group began exploring for oil in West Africa in the 1930s, but it was not until 1956 that oil was discovered in the Niger Delta in southeastern Nigeria. In 1958, two years before Nigeria's independence, Shell was the first major oil company to commence oil production there. Nigerian oil was of very high quality by world standards; in the industry, it was referred to as "light, sweet crude," meaning that it had a low sulfur content and produced a higher proportion of gasoline after refining than heavier crude oil. Of all the multinational oil companies in Nigeria, Shell had by far the most visibility, because of the extent of its land-based operations. Other major players in the Nigerian oil industry, including Mobil and Chevron, mainly operated offshore.

Shell Nigeria was a participant in a joint venture with the Nigerian government and two other private firms. In 1995, the Nigerian National Petroleum Corporation (NNPC), the state-owned oil company, owned a 55 percent stake in the joint venture. Royal Dutch/Shell owned a 30 percent stake; Elf and Agip, both European oil companies, owned the remaining 15 percent. Shell was the joint venture operator; that is, it built and ran the oil operations on the ground. The other owners, although not involved in day-to-day management, had a say in the development of budgets and new projects. Investments in the business were made by the joint venture partners in proportion to their holdings. As operator, Shell issued "cash calls" to its partners to provide monthly payments. Shell executives were often frustrated by the NNPC's failure to pay their share on time. In 1995, the government was $300 million behind in its payments.

Shell Nigeria's operations were huge, not only by Nigerian standards, but even by those of its parent firm. In 1995, Shell Nigeria produced an average of almost one million barrels of crude oil a day, about half of Nigeria's total output, from 94 separate fields spread over 31,000 square kilometers. It operated 6,200 kilometers of pipelines and flow lines, much of it running through swamps and flood zones in the Niger Delta. In addition, the company operated two coastal export terminals. The company reported that the Nigerian operation provided about 12 percent of Royal Dutch/Shell's total world oil production and 7 percent of its profits.

Shell Nigeria employed about 5,000 people. Ninety-five percent of all employees, and about half of executive directors, were Nigerian. Fifty-seven percent of its staff was drawn from the oil-producing states.

The company's financial arrangements with its host country were highly beneficial to the Nigerian government. For every barrel of oil sold at between $12.50 and $23.00 a barrel, 70 cents went to Shell, 30 cents went to Elf and Agip, and $4.50 went to cover costs. The Nigerian government received the rest. At a per-barrel price of $15, for example, the government would receive $9.50, or about 90 percent of net revenue after expenses. The Nigerian government's take, at the time, was the highest of any government in the world with which Shell did business.

Nigeria: The Giant of West Africa

Nigeria, the Group's sometimes-troublesome partner, has been called the "giant of West Africa." Located on the Gulf of Guinea between the republics of Benin and Cameroon, Nigeria was slightly more than twice the size of California and, with over 100 million people, the most populous country on the continent. Nigeria's gross domestic product of $95 billion placed its economy second, smaller only than South Africa's. The economy was heavily dependent on petroleum; oil and natural gas sales produced 80 percent of the federal government's revenue, and more than 90 percent of the country's foreign exchange. Forty-one percent of oil exports went to the United States, more than to any other single country.

Nigeria was a land of stark socioeconomic contrasts. The nation's military and business elites had grown wealthy from oil revenues. Yet most Nigerians lived in poverty. The annual per capita income was $250, less than that of Haiti or China, and in the mid-1990s economic distress in many parts of Nigeria was deepening.

A legacy of colonialism, in Nigeria as elsewhere in Africa, was the formation of countries that had little historical basis other than common colonial governance. In the Nigerian case, the modern nation was formed from what had been no less than 250 disparate ethnic groups, many with few cultural or linguistic ties. The nation was comprised of three main ethnic groups: the Hausa-Fulani, the Yoruba, and the Ibo. Together, these three groups made up 65 percent of the population; the remaining 35 percent was made up of hundreds of smaller ethnic groups, including Saro-Wiwa's people, the Ogoni.

Since its independence from Britain in 1960, Nigeria had been ruled by military governments for all but nine years. Several efforts, all eventually unsuccessful, had been made to effect a transition to permanent civilian rule. In June 1993, then-military dictator Ibrahim Babangida annulled the presidential election, suspended the newly created national assembly, and installed an unelected civilian as president. Just five months later, yet another military man, General Sani Abacha, took power in a coup. The Abacha regime quickly developed a reputation as "indisputably the cruelest and most corrupt" government in Nigeria since independence. A specialist in African politics summarized the situation in Nigeria before the United States Senate Foreign Relations Committee in 1995:

> [The] current government appears indifferent to international standards of conduct, while dragging the country into a downward spiral of disarray, economic stagnation, and ethnic animosity. . . . [It] has curtailed political and civil rights to an unprecedented degree in Nigerian history, magnified corruption and malfeasance in an endemically corrupt system, and substantially abandoned responsible economic management.

In 1993, inflation was running around 50 percent annually, foreign debt was growing, and the country's balance of payments was worsening. A succession of governments had arguably wasted vast amounts of money on unnecessary projects such as the construction of a massive steel mill and a new capital city, Abuja. Agriculture was in decline, and a proliferation of states had produced a complex and inefficient bureaucracy. Corruption was so rampant in Nigeria, the *Economist* concluded in an editorial that "the parasite . . . has almost eaten the host."

The Ogoni People

The Ogoni people, Saro-Wiwa's ethnic group, lived in the heart of the Nigerian oil fields. Numbering about half a million in the mid-1990s, the Ogoni spoke four related languages and shared common religious and cultural traditions. Prior to the arrival of the British in 1901, a stable Ogoni society based on fishing and farming had existed for centuries in a small area (a mere 12 by 32 miles) in the Delta region near the mouth of the Niger River.

Production of oil in Ogoniland began in 1958. The value of the oil that had been extracted from Ogoniland was a matter of dispute. According to Shell's figures, $5.2 billion worth of oil had been pumped from the region's five major oil fields since 1958. Ogoni activists claimed the amount was much higher, $30 billion.

Although Ogoniland was the site of great mineral wealth, the Ogoni people had received little benefit from its development. Under revenue-sharing arrangements between the Nigerian federal government and the states prior to 1992, only 1.5 percent of the government's revenues from oil was returned to the Delta communities for economic development, and much of this went to line the pockets of officials.

Ogoniland, like much of the Delta area, was very poor and very densely populated. No modern sanitation systems were in place; raw sewage was simply buried or discharged into rivers or lakes. Drinking water was often contaminated, and water-related diseases such as cholera, malaria, and gastroenteritis were common. Housing was typically constructed with corrugated tin roofs and cement, or more commonly, dirt floors. A British engineer who later returned to the Delta village near Ogoniland where oil was first discovered commented, "I have explored for oil in Venezuela, I have explored for oil in Kuwait, [but] I have never seen an oil-rich town as completely impoverished as Oloibiri."

In 1992, in response to pressure from the Ogoni and other Delta peoples, the Nigerian government established a commission, funded with 3 percent of the government's oil revenues, to promote infrastructure development in the oil producing regions. In 1993, the group spent $94 million, with about 40 percent going to the Rivers State, in which Ogoniland was situated. Shell Nigeria also gave direct assistance to the oil-producing regions. In 1995, for example, the company's community development program in Nigeria spent about $20 million. Projects included building classrooms and community hospitals, paying teacher salaries, funding scholarships for Nigerian youth, operating agricultural stations, and building roads. However, Shell was criticized for making little effort to involve local residents in determining how its community development funds would be spent.

Ken Saro-Wiwa

Ken Saro-Wiwa, who became a leader of the Ogoni movement, was in many respects an unlikely activist. A businessman who later became a highly successful writer and television producer, he had a taste for gourmet food, sophisticated humor, and international travel. Yet in the final years of his life he emerged as a world-famous advocate for sustainable development and for the rights of indigenous peoples who was honored by receipt of the Goldman Environmental Prize.

Saro-Wiwa was born in 1941 in an Ogoni village. A brilliant student, he was educated first at government-run schools and later, with the aid of a scholarship, at the University of Ibadan, where he studied literature. After a brief stint as a government administrator, Saro-Wiwa left public service to launch his own business. After four years as a successful grocer and trader, he took the proceeds and began investing in real estate, buying office buildings, shops, and homes. In 1983, with sufficient property to live comfortably, Saro-Wiwa turned to what he called his first love, writing and publishing. He proved to be a gifted and prolific writer, producing in short order a critically acclaimed novel, a volume of poetry, and a collection of short stories.

In 1985, Saro-Wiwa was approached by a university friend who had become program director for the state-run Nigerian television authority. The friend asked him to develop a comedy series. The result, "Basi & Co.," ran for five years and became the most widely watched television show in Africa. Reflecting Saro-Wiwa's political views, the program satirized Nigerians' desire to get rich with little effort. The show's comic protagonist was Basi, "a witty rogue [who] hustled on the streets of Lagos and was willing to do anything to make money, short of working for it."

By the late 1980s, Saro-Wiwa had become a wealthy and internationally known novelist and television scriptwriter. His wife and four children moved to London, where his children enrolled in British private schools. Saro-Wiwa joined his family often, making many friends in the London literary community who would later work doggedly, although unsuccessfully, for his release.

In 1988, Saro-Wiwa undertook a nonfiction study of Nigerian history, later published under the title, *On a Darkling Plain.* This work reawakened his interest in politics and in the plight of his own Ogoni people. In a speech in March 1990, marking the study's publication, Saro-Wiwa laid out a theme from the book that was to become central to the rest of his life's work:

> The notion that the oil-bearing areas can provide the revenue of the country and yet be denied a proper share of that revenue because it is perceived that the inhabitants of the area are few in number is unjust, immoral, unnatural and ungodly.

On a Darkling Plain, not surprisingly, ignited a storm of controversy in Nigeria, and "Basi & Co." was canceled shortly after its publication, as was a column Saro-Wiwa had been writing for the government-owned weekly *Sunday Times.*

Movement for the Survival of the Ogoni People

The cancellation of his TV series and newspaper column seemed to propel Saro-Wiwa further into political activism. In August 1990, he met with a group of Ogoni tribal chiefs and intellectuals to draft an Ogoni Bill of Rights. This document called for political autonomy; cultural, religious, and linguistic freedom; the right to control a "fair proportion" of the region's economic resources; and higher standards of environmental protection for the Ogoni people.

Shortly thereafter, drafters of the bill of rights met to form an organization to press their demands. The group chose the name Movement for the Survival of the Ogoni People (MOSOP). From its inception, MOSOP adopted a philosophy of nonviolent mass mobilization. The group's earliest organizational efforts focused on educational work and appeals to the military government and to the oil companies. The organization published the Ogoni Bill of Rights and organized a speaking tour of the region to present it to the Ogoni. Saro-Wiwa traveled abroad—to the United States, Switzerland, the United Kingdom, the Netherlands, and Russia—where he met with human rights and environmentalist groups and government officials to build support for the Ogoni cause. MOSOP also issued a propagandistic "demand notice" calling on Shell to pay "damages" of $4 billion for "destroying the environment" and $6 billion in "unpaid rents and royalties" to the Ogoni people.

Environmental Issues

A central plank in the MOSOP platform was that the oil companies, particularly Shell, were responsible for serious environmental degradation. In a speech given in 1992 to the Unrepresented Nations and Peoples Organization (UNPO), Saro-Wiwa stated MOSOP's case:

> Oil exploration has turned Ogoni into a waste land: lands, streams, and creeks are totally and continually polluted; the atmosphere has been poisoned, charged as it is with hydrocarbon vapors, methane, carbon monoxide, carbon dioxide and soot. . . . Acid rain, oil spillages and oil blowouts have devastated Ogoni territory. High-pressure oil pipelines crisscross the surface of Ogoni farmlands and villages dangerously. The results of such unchecked environmental pollution and degradation include the complete destruction of the ecosystem.

Shell disputed these charges, saying that they had been "dramatized out of all proportion." Shell argued that the land it had acquired for operations comprised only 0.3 percent of the Niger Delta. Three-quarters of Shell's operations were constructed before 1973 and were in full compliance at the time they were built. The company maintained a regular program of upgrading and replacing its pipelines and other infrastructure, including a program to bury above-ground flow lines. The company asserted that it was in compliance with all relevant laws and regulations and that it attempted to remediate all oil spills. Moreover, Shell charged, many of the oil spills in the area had been caused by sabotage, for which it could not be held responsible.

One of the most hotly contested oil spills in the area had occurred in Ebubu (near Ogoniland), around a quarter century earlier. By all accounts, this was a major spill, with severe ecological and economic consequences. Crude oil had spread over 10 hectares (about 25 acres), penetrated deeply into the soil, and contaminated nearby waterways. The oil had burned and crusted over, leaving the land useless. Ogoni activists blamed Shell for the spill and vigorously criticized the company for failing to clean it up adequately. Shell, however, maintained that the Ebubu spill had been caused by retreating Biafran troops, during a period when the company had temporarily withdrawn from the area because of the civil war.

The relationship between human population and oil development in the region was complex. Ogoni activists claimed that Shell had insensitively located its pipelines and other infrastructure too close to human settlements. Shell pointed out, however, that the population of the Niger Delta had more than doubled during the 40 or so years that the company had operated there. In many cases, people had been drawn to the oil facilities in search of jobs, settling near pipelines and flow stations.

The Niger Delta was one of the world's largest wetlands, a vast floodplain built up by sedimentary deposits at the mouths of the Niger and Benue Rivers. In a comprehensive study of environmental conditions in the Niger Delta completed in 1995, the World Bank found evidence of significant environmental problems, including land degradation, overfishing, deforestation, loss of biodiversity, and water contamination. The study did find evidence of air pollution from refineries and petrochemical facilities and of oil spills and poor waste management practices at and around pipelines, terminals, and offshore platforms. Most of the Delta's environmental problems, however, the World Bank concluded, were the result not of oil pollution but rather of overpopulation coupled with poverty and weak, poorly enforced environmental regulations.

One of the worst environmental problems associated with the oil industry was gas flaring. Natural gas is often produced as a by-product of oil production. In most oil-producing regions of the world, this ancillary gas is reinjected into the ground or captured and sold. In Nigeria, however, gas was routinely simply burned off, or "flared," in the production fields. In 1991, over three-quarters of natural gas production in Nigeria was flared—compared with, say, less than 1 percent in the United States or a world average of less than 5 percent. In 1993, Nigeria flared more natural gas than any other nation on earth. Gas flaring had several adverse environmental consequences. The flares produced large amounts of carbon dioxide and methane, both greenhouse gases and contributors to global warming. Residents in the immediate vicinity of the flares experienced noise, heat, and soot contamination. The flares, which burned continuously, lit up the night sky nearby with an orange glow.

During the early 1990s, Shell Nigeria became involved in a joint venture known as the Nigeria Liquefied Natural Gas (LNG) project. The aim of this project, in which Shell was a 26 percent shareholder, was to pipe natural gas to a liquefaction plant and from there to ship it abroad in special ships at supercooled temperatures. In late 1995, plans were underway for construction of an LNG processing facility that would be fully operational by 1999; all flaring was scheduled to cease by 2008.

Contrary to charges made by some of Shell's critics, Nigeria did have some environmental regulations in place, dating from 1992. These laws, which were enforced by the federal Department of Petroleum Resources, set emissions standards, restricted toxic discharges, required permits for handling toxic wastes, and mandated environmental impact studies for major industrial developments. Regulatory institutions were poorly developed, however, and government authorities had little incentive to vigorously enforce the country's environmental rules.

Civil Disturbances in the Niger Delta

During the early 1990s, civil disturbances in Ogoniland and other Delta communities, many directed at Shell, escalated. In one typical incident, as reported by Shell,

> A gang of youths . . . stormed . . . a drilling rig in the Ahia oil field . . . looting and vandalizing the facility and rig camp. Rig workers were held hostage for most of the first day while property worth $6 million was destroyed or stolen. The rig was shut down for 10 days and the Ahia flow station was also shut down. . . . [A protest leader] raised the issue of [distribution] . . . of oil revenues to the oil producing communities by the government, the need for a new road, and rumours of bribery by Shell of a [local] chief.

Most of the civil disturbances followed a similar pattern. A group of young men, armed with whatever weapons were readily available, would attack one of Shell's many far-flung oil installations in the Delta. Employees would be attacked, equipment would be sabotaged, and the group would make demands.

Shell's own data on patterns of community disturbances in the Niger Delta revealed a pattern of escalating violence throughout the early 1990s, peaking in 1993. Shell estimated that the company sustained $42 million in damage to its installations in Ogoniland between 1993 and the end of 1995, as a direct result of sabotage.

One of the most highly publicized of these incidents occurred at Umeuchem, about 30 miles from Ogoniland. Shell later posted on the Internet a description of this event:

> [This] incident happened when armed youths invaded and occupied a rig location and nearby flow station, chasing off staff who were not given the opportunity to make the location safe. The youths demanded N100 million [*naira,* the Nigerian currency, at that time worth about $12.5 million], a new road, and a water scheme. Attempts to talk with the youths, who were armed with guns and machetes, failed.

In response, Shell staff called the Nigerian authorities, who sent in a Mobile Police unit. The Mobile Police were widely known in Nigeria as the "Kill-and-Go Mob" because of their undisciplined behavior. In the ensuing riot, at least one policeman and seven civilians in the local village were killed. Shell concluded its posting, "The Shell response to the threatening situation was made with the best intentions and what happened was a shock to staff, many of whom had friends [in the village]."

The relationship between these community disturbances and MOSOP was complex. Saro-Wiwa's group explicitly rejected violence and repeatedly disavowed vigilante attacks on Shell or other companies, and Saro-Wiwa himself frequently toured Ogoniland to restore calm. Yet publication of the Ogoni Bill of Rights and MOSOP campaigns focusing attention on injustices suffered by the Ogoni clearly had the effect of boosting expectations within Ogoni society. In this context, many young unemployed Ogoni men simply took matters into their own hands.

The escalation of violence against the company posed a difficult dilemma for SPDC executives. Shell Nigeria officials stated that the company did not want military protection, preferring dialogue with local communities. When it was impossible to operate safely, the company's practice was simply to withdraw its personnel. (The one exception was the two coastal terminals; considered strategic areas by the government, the harbors' oil-loading areas were protected by military troops.) The company's own personnel were not armed. However, Nigerian police officers known as *supernumerary police* were routinely assigned to protect oil facilities, including Shell's. The company paid these officers directly and was responsible for supervising, training, and equipping them. In one instance in 1982, Shell purchased 107 handguns for use by supernumeraries protecting its facilities. Shell defended these practices, saying it was normal in Nigeria to retain police protection in areas where violent crime was a daily occurrence.

Several human rights organizations claimed that as civil unrest escalated in Ogoniland, Shell began to work more and more closely with the authorities to coordinate security. The Nigerian Civil Liberties Organization reported that Shell-owned cars, buses, speedboats, and helicopters were regularly used to transport police and military personnel to the site of civil disturbances. Human Rights Watch reported that Shell met regularly with representatives of the Rivers State police to plan security operations. Shell denied this, stating that these practices would violate company policy; the company also stated that after the Umeuchem incident, in particular, it had been anxious to avoid any unnecessary dealings with the Mobile Police.

On January 3, 1993, MOSOP held a massive rally to mark the start of the Year of the Indigenous Peoples. Held at successive locations across Ogoniland, the rally was attended by as many as 300,000 people, three-fifths of the Ogoni population. Protestors carried twigs, a symbol of environmental regeneration. Two weeks later, after three attacks on its staff there, Shell abruptly announced that it would withdraw from Ogoniland. It evacuated all employees and shut down its operations. Company officials gave a terse explanation: "There is no question of our staff working in areas where their safety may be at risk."

Taking a Hard Line

After General Abacha took power in November 1993, he apparently decided to take a hard line with the Ogoni. Whether this was an effort to crush the Ogoni movement, to keep other ethnic groups from following their example, or to make the area safe for the resumption of commercial oil operations, or all three, was not clear. One of his first acts as a head of state was to dispatch a special paramilitary force, comprised of selected personnel from the army, navy, air force, and police, to restore order in Ogoniland and elsewhere in the Rivers State. Paul Okuntimo, a notorious military officer who publicly boasted of his proficiency in killing people, headed the special force.

According to an alleged government memo, dated May 12, 1994, the purpose of Okuntimo's force was to ensure that those "carrying out business ventures in Ogoniland are not molested." The memo also noted, "Shell operations still impossible unless ruthless military operations are undertaken for smooth economic activities to commence." It advised the governor of Rivers State to put "pressure on oil companies for prompt regular inputs as discussed." Shell challenged the authenticity of this document and adamantly denied making any direct payments to the military authorities for this purpose.

In May and June 1994, intense violence erupted in Ogoniland. Amnesty International, which collected eyewitness accounts, reported that the government's paramilitary force entered Ogoniland, where it "instigated and assisted" interethnic clashes between previously peaceful neighboring groups. The units then "followed the attackers into Ogoni villages, destroying houses and detaining people." In May and June, the force attacked 30 towns and villages, where its members "fired at random, destroyed and set fires to homes, killing, assaulting, and raping, and looting and extorting money, livestock, and food," according to the Amnesty International report. As many as 2,000 civilians may have been killed.

In 1995, despite Okuntimo's efforts, Shell had still not returned to Ogoniland. Claude Ake, a well-known Nigerian political economist, described the situation in the Delta in December 1995: "the flow stations, that is the operational bases of the oil industry, operated under armed presence. This is a process," he added, in a chilling phrase, "of the militarization of commerce."

The Arrest, Trial and Execution of Saro-Wiwa

On May 21, 1994, just over a week after the "smooth economic activities" memo, Saro-Wiwa was en route to a MOSOP rally where he was scheduled to speak. On the way, his car was stopped at a military roadblock, and he was ordered to return home. He never attended the rally. Later that same day, a group of Ogoni chiefs, founders of MOSOP who had resigned in 1993 and become political opponents of Saro-Wiwa, held a meeting. Their gathering was interrupted by a crowd of several hundred youths, who denounced the men as "vultures" who had collaborated with the military government. Four of the chiefs were assaulted and bludgeoned to death.

Later that day, Saro-Wiwa and several other leaders of MOSOP were arrested. In a televised press conference, the governor of Rivers State blamed the MOSOP leaders for the murders. Saro-Wiwa and his colleagues were detained in a secret military camp, where they were chained in leg irons and denied access to medical care. It would be eight months before they were formally charged.

During Saro-Wiwa's imprisonment, his brother, Owens Wiwa, met on at least two occasions with Shell Nigeria's managing director Brian Anderson to seek his help in securing Ken's release. Wiwa and Anderson's later accounts of these conversations differed sharply. Wiwa said that Anderson had told him that it would be "difficult but not impossible" to get his brother out of prison. Anderson allegedly said that if MOSOP stopped the international campaign against Shell, he might be able to intervene. Wiwa refused, he said. For his part, Anderson acknowledged that he had met with Wiwa as part of an effort at "quiet diplomacy," but he denied his specific allegations as "false and reprehensible." Anderson reported that Wiwa had offered to stop the campaign against Shell if the company intervened to help his brother. Anderson said that he was not willing to make that kind of deal and that Shell could not have stopped the executions in any case, because the company had very little influence with the military government.

In November, General Abacha appointed a Civil Disturbances Special Tribunal to try the case of the MOSOP leaders. Established by special decree, this tribunal was empowered to impose the death penalty in cases involving civil disturbances. The decision of the court could be confirmed or disallowed by the military government, but defendants had no right of judicial appeal. Amnesty International and many other human rights organizations denounced the tribunal for violating standards of due process guaranteed by Nigeria's own constitution and by international treaties.

Saro-Wiwa's trial for murder began in February 1995. Prosecution witnesses testified that Saro-Wiwa had relayed a message to his youthful supporters, after the roadblock incident, to "deal with" his opponents. Saro-Wiwa's defense attorneys countered that Saro-Wiwa had been at home at the time and had had nothing to do with the killings.

On October 31, the tribunal found Saro-Wiwa and eight other MOSOP leaders guilty of murder and sentenced them to death. Six defendants were acquitted. On November 2, Royal Dutch/Shell chairman Cor Herkströter sent a letter to General Abacha, appealing for mercy for Saro-Wiwa and his codefendants. In Nigeria, Brian Anderson spoke out publicly for clemency on humanitarian grounds. Around the world, many political leaders and human rights organizations also called on the Nigerian government to spare Saro-Wiwa.

The military authorities, however, moved swiftly to carry out the sentence. On November 10, Saro-Wiwa and eight MOSOP associates were hanged in prison. His last words on the gallows were: "Lord, take my soul, but the struggle continues."

With Deep Regret

Shell issued a statement on the executions that read, in part, "It is with deep regret that we hear this news. From the violence that led to the murder of the four Ogoni leaders in May last year through to the death penalty having been carried out, the human cost has been too high." Earlier, Shell had told reporters that it would have been inappropriate to have intervened in the criminal trial. "A commercial organization like Shell cannot and must never interfere with the legal processes of any sovereign state. . . . Any government, be it in Europe, North America, or elsewhere, would not tolerate this type of interference by business."

The company also defended its actions in the months leading up to Saro-Wiwa's arrest and trial. Shell representatives stated that it would have been wrong to have tried to influence government policy on Ogoni autonomy or other political issues of concern to MOSOP. An executive told the news media, "Our responsibility is very clear. We pay taxes and [abide by] regulation. We don't run the government." Shell also vigorously resisted demands by some human rights activists and environmentalists that the company withdraw from Nigeria. If the company withdrew its 250 or so expatriate managers, the government or another oil company could easily take over the operation and continue to run it, very possibly with lower environmental, safety, and human rights standards.

Shell's public disclaimers did little to slow down the controversy swirling around the company. By mid-1996, the company was facing calls for an international gasoline boycott, external pressure to abandon plans for its liquefied natural gas project, and persistent demands that it withdraw from Nigeria altogether. The crisis threatened the company's reputation and relations with stakeholders, not only in Nigeria, but throughout the world.

Discussion Questions

1. What arguments did Shell make in defending its actions in Nigeria? How would Shell's critics counter these arguments? Do you believe Shell could or should have done anything differently in Nigeria?
2. What internal or external factors contributed to the emergence of this crisis for Shell?
3. Evaluate Shell's actions in Nigeria with reference to an existing code of conduct for multinational organizations. Do you believe Shell was in compliance with the code you have selected? If not, how not? Do you believe the code you have selected is appropriate and adequate?
4. In your opinion, is it possible to develop a universal set of ethical standards for business, or do cultural differences make universal standards impractical, if not impossible?
5. What, if anything, should Shell do next?

In the late 1990s, Shell International underwent a remarkable transformation. Variously termed by observers a "sea change," a "mid-life crisis," and a "dramatic overhaul," the company undertook a deep and systematic effort to remake itself. In the process, Shell radically changed its organizational structure, its culture, its relationship with stakeholders (including its most vocal critics), its reporting practices, and indeed, even its very business principles. In the end, it set out to become an organization in which financial, social, and environmental performance were equally valued and fully integrated.

A cover story in *Fortune* in 1997 was pointedly titled, "Why Is the World's Most Profitable Company Turning Itself Inside Out?" To some, this transformation represented wrongheaded New Age tampering with a proven management formula. To some, it was nothing more than a sophisticated public relations offensive to repair a reputation badly tarnished by human rights abuses in Nigeria, the controversy over the disposal of the oil rig Brent Spar, and struggles with shareholder activists over corporate governance. To others, though, it represented more. To them, Shell's multileveled struggle to transform itself was the most ambitious effort ever by a major multinational corporation to define a new relationship between business and society in a world of rapidly changing public expectations.

The Campaigns against Shell

The early to mid-1990s were a period when international environmentalist, human rights, and shareholder campaigns directed against Shell gathered intensity. Three separate but related campaigns—opposing at-sea disposal of old offshore oil facilities, alleging human rights abuses in Nigeria, and backing shareholder resolutions for reforms in corporate governance—focused a spotlight of often negative publicity on the world's most profitable multinational corporation.

The Brent Spar Incident

A watershed event in Shell's transformation was what came to be known at the Brent Spar incident. The Brent Spar was an oil storage and loading buoy in the North Sea, about 100 miles off the coast of Scotland. Although a unique structure, it was one of several hundred North Sea installations, many nearing the end of their useful lives.

In 1991, Shell took the Brent Spar out of service and began looking at options for disposing of it. According to international and British law, operators were required to determine the best practical environmental option for disposal. This could involve either sinking the platform in the deep sea or removing and dismantling it on land. Government approval was required. In April 1995, after extensive consultations with outside experts about possible options, Shell announced its intention to dispose of the Brent Spar at sea, and British authorities agreed.

The plan quickly ran into resistance from Greenpeace, however. At the time, Greenpeace was the largest environmental organization in the world, with a full-time staff of 120, a budget of about $50 million, and a penchant for confrontational tactics. Greenpeace believed that toxic residue in the Brent Spar's tanks would harm the marine environment and that its disposal at sea would set a precedent for other, soon-to-be decommissioned oil installations.

On April 30, 1995, Greenpeace activists boarded and occupied the abandoned buoy. After a three-week standoff, Shell personnel, aided by local law officers, evicted the protesters nonviolently. The company defended its decision to sink the Brent Spar in full-page newspaper advertisements and began towing the rig toward the open sea. However, the Greenpeace occupation and resulting media coverage had galvanized public opinion, especially on the Continent. By mid-June, government officials of Belgium, Denmark, Sweden, the Netherlands, and Germany had asked Shell to postpone sinking the Brent Spar. Meanwhile, a consumer boycott had gathered steam. In Germany, Shell franchise owners reported a 50 percent decline in sales over a two-week period. Several Shell gas stations, also in Germany, were anonymously firebombed. The British prime minister continued to support Shell, however; and the boycott was less successful in Britain.

On June 20, Shell abruptly changed course, announcing that it had decided to abandon its plan to dispose of the Brent Spar at sea and to seek a permit for onshore disposal. In a statement, the company said, "The European Companies of the Royal Dutch/Shell Group find themselves in an untenable position and feel that it is not possible to continue without wider support." The company moved the buoy to a Norwegian fjord, while it considered further actions. Greenpeace later acknowledged that it had seriously erred in its estimate of the amount of toxic residue in the Brent Spar's tanks and apologized.

Human Rights in Nigeria

Just a few months later, the execution of Ken Saro-Wiwa and his colleagues in Nigeria on November 10, 1995 (described in the preceding case, "Shell Oil in Nigeria") led to what *Fortune* referred to as a "global uproar." Much of it was directed at the government of Nigeria, which was summarily suspended from the Commonwealth of Nations at the urging of President Nelson Mandela of South Africa. Other countries called for an arms embargo, sports boycott, and freezing the foreign bank accounts of the pariah nation's military leaders.

But much outrage was also directed at Shell, which was perceived by many as not acting forcefully to prevent Saro-Wiwa's execution. Environmentalist organizations, particularly, spoke out. The chairman of Greenpeace UK told the press, "There is blood on Shell's hands. Ken Saro-Wiwa was hanged for speaking out against Shell. He was trying to secure the most basic of human rights—the right to clean air, land, and water." The Sierra Club promoted a boycott of the company under the slogan "(S)hell no, corporate accountability yes," and urged its supporters to cut up their Shell credit cards, boycott Shell products, and participate in protest demonstrations.

One of the organizations most involved in the protests against Shell was The Body Shop International (BSI), the beauty products retailer chaired by social activist Anita

Roddick. BSI initiated a major protest campaign against Shell, which included the perhaps unprecedented event of one corporation publicly accusing another of murder. Greenpeace, The Body Shop International, and Friends of the Earth ran a full page advertisement with a photograph of a gas flare under the heading, "Dear Shell, This is the Truth. And it Stinks." Protest demonstrations featured hooded dummies dangling from nooses.

Shareholder Activism

Against the backdrop of the controversies over Brent Spar and Nigeria, a coordinated campaign by shareholder activists critical of Shell moved forward, placing into public debate issues that had previously been solely the prerogative of management.

Although less developed than in the United States, the movement to promote ethical investing was gaining ground in the UK in the early 1990s. A central player in this movement was a nonprofit organization called Pensions and Investment Research Consultants (PIRC). PIRC's goal was to use shareholder leverage to raise standards of corporate governance and to promote socially responsible management. With a staff of 25, the organization worked primarily with public employee pension funds. It also worked with religious organizations with stock holdings, some of which were members of the Ecumenical Council on Corporate Responsibility (ECCR), and with individual investors concerned with the ethics of companies in which they held stock. PIRC's chief tactic was to introduce and organize support for shareholder resolutions at corporate annual meetings.

In 1995, in response to the Nigeria and Brent Spar controversies, PIRC requested the first of what was to be a series of meetings with Shell officials. There, it made the first of several proposals to Shell reflecting its members' concerns with ethics, environmental policy, and corporate governance generally.

Initiating Organizational Change

In early 1994, more than a year before the Brent Spar, Nigeria, and shareholder campaigns erupted, Shell management had initiated a process of internal organizational change, aimed at improving the Group's financial performance relative to its competitors.

At the time, Shell's return on average capital employed (ROACE), a common measure of performance in the petroleum industry, showed that the company lagged behind many of its competitors. Although Shell remained very profitable (in fact, in 1994 it earned more profit than any other company in the world), other big oil companies, including rivals British Petroleum, Exxon, and Mobil, were enjoying significantly higher ROACE. Of particular concern to Shell executives were hypercompetition from discount retailers and weak sales of nonfuel products, such as food and convenience items, at the retail level. To help improve the company's profitability, the company engaged the services of management consultants McKinsey & Company to lead an extensive internal review. McKinsey quickly focused its attention on the company's organizational structure.

Since the 1950s, Royal Dutch/Shell had used a matrix form of organization. Under this structure, the chief executive of the national operating companies reported simultaneously to two superiors: a regional manager and a product manager. For example, the managing director of Shell Nigeria would report both to a regional coordinator for Africa and to the coordinator for exploration and production. In addition, staff at Shell's headquarters in London and The Hague provided functional expertise in finance, legal matters, human resources management, and external affairs. (Shell U.S., the largest of the Group companies, maintained its own staff of functional specialists and operated for most purposes independently.) At the time, it was believed that this matrix organization benefited Shell by devolving power and balancing interests.

In March 1995, Shell concluded the first phase of its internal review by announcing a plan to reorganize into five worldwide business units. These were exploration and production, oil products, chemicals, gas and coal, and central staff functions. The five units would be overseen by committees of senior executives, who would report to the committee of managing directors (CMD). Under this plan, managers of the operating companies would report only to their business unit superiors, in a single line of command, thus eliminating the matrix, which was perceived as unnecessarily complicated. Excess staff at the center was also cut. The restructuring was intended to enable the company to focus more efficiently on the needs of its business and retail customers.

Talking about a "New Shell"

Even as Shell announced its intended organizational redesign, however, external pressures on the company, as well as internal debate, had the effect of shifting the focus of the transformation process to the softer issues of the company's reputation and relations with stakeholders. The key events took place in a series of retreats for top executives held in late 1995 and early 1996.

In 1995, Shell had engaged the services of a group of private management consultants to lead the next phase of the transformation process. In a series of exercises, conducted at retreats in 1995 and early 1996, these consultants asked directors and a selected group of top executives from the operating companies to "hold up a mirror" to reflect their own practice. Their objective was to develop a "diagnosis of current reality" that could serve as a starting point for further changes aimed at improving corporate profitability.

To the apparent surprise of both the consultants and Shell's top leaders, discussion began to shift, seemingly spontaneously, from strictly business matters to Shell's social and environmental performance. Many participants at the retreats wanted to talk not about profitability but about the fact that Shell was being pilloried in the press as a corporate murderer. At first, the top leaders present tended to dismiss the relevance of Brent Spar and Nigeria to the business problems the company faced. But as the discussion proceeded, the attitude of the leadership appeared to change. One of the consultants present, Philip H. Mirvis, later recalled:

> The leadership stepped up. . . . Cor [Herkströter, chairman of the CMD] was essentially saying, "We own this problem. It is not a technical problem, if only we had had a better analysis with the Brent Spar. This is not a relationship problem, if only we had had a better relationship with the government, or if we had had a different government in Nigeria, this wouldn't have happened. We as leaders are responsible for this result." Quite frankly, Cor had a sense of shame over his own leadership and the leadership of the CMD. This sent a gasp through the organization. This was an organization that was Teflon, bulletproof, apologized

for nothing, admitted to nothing, and so on. To see the leadership taking on responsibility and expressing a deep sense of remorse over this opened the gates for a dialogue about what are we doing, what are we responsible for, what is the role of our company around the globe, and so on.

The willingness of Shell's leaders to take responsibility for what had happened, Mirvis later wrote, "legitimated expressions of guilt and anger over past wrongs and, in effect, assigned some blame to the corporate culture." The consultants used this opening to ask executives to write personal stories that expressed their vision of where they had been and where they wanted to go and to share them with each other and their staffs. This process was then repeated at lower levels of the organization.

Mark Moody-Stuart, a member of the CMD (and later Herkströter's successor as chairman), framed Shell's problem as the need for a new mind-set that paid greater attention to societal expectations. In Mirvis's words:

Mark Moody-Stuart should be credited with the intellectual framing of this. Shell was an engineering-type company . . . a very technical organization and essentially a very bureaucratic organization. . . . What Mark said was that the technical mind-set, our rational, logical approach, is blinding us to a world out there of human rights activists, of environmentalists, of governments with different wants and interests and changing customer tastes, expectations of the public, et cetera. We are so internally focused, so technical, that we are missing a whole set of opportunities and a whole new reality out there. . . . We are not talking any more about a structural change in the organization; we are not even talking about new leadership per se. We are talking about a new Shell.

Evaluating Society's Changing Expectations

Once the CMD became convinced that it had failed to meet the "new reality" of changing expectations, the directors quickly undertook a series of interrelated initiatives to improve Shell's social and environmental performance and the public's perception of its corporate citizenship. These involved a study of society's perceptions of the company, revision of the company's business principles, and a new approach to reporting and verifying its social and environmental performance to stakeholders.

One of Shell's first actions was to commission a report, entitled *Society's Changing Expectations*. Research, conducted over a year and a half, involved extensive roundtable discussions with Shell executives, stakeholders, academics, and journalists; a review of previous surveys; young person focus groups; and consultations with public relations professionals in all regions of the world. The central finding of the study, delivered in November 1996, was that Shell's reputation had suffered because the company's behavior had not kept pace with society's changing expectations. The report found that a number of factors had combined to make many people both more cynical about multinational corporations and more demanding of them. These factors included new communications technology (particularly the rise of the Internet), population growth and migration, growing nationalist and fundamentalist sentiment in some regions, and increasing public concern for the environment.

As might be expected, patterns varied by region and by stakeholder. For example, Shell enjoyed a better reputation in Latin America, where it was widely perceived as an effective provider of jobs, products, and services, than in Africa, where it was not. In developing countries, stakeholders expected Shell to encourage government concern for the environment; in developed countries, the opposite was true. Overall, however, the consultant's conclusion was that "economic, social, and technological changes have created a more cynical, questioning, indeed challenging attitude toward institutions, not the least, MNCs."

Revision of the Statement of General Business Principles

A second initiative was to take a fresh look at Shell's *Statement of General Business Principles (SGBP)*. First developed in 1976, the SGBP sought to define the Group's core values. Now, the directors believed, the SGBP needed to be revisited in light of the changing environment in which the company operated. Accordingly, in 1996 the directors asked Integrity Works, an ethics consultancy, to carry out a review of the SGBP. The process included distribution of hundreds of questionnaires and scores of interviews with managers in 80 operating companies, aimed at identifying areas in the SGBP that needed change. Most managers felt that the principles remained largely valid, but they flagged several areas in need of revision.

In March 1997, Shell published a revised Statement of General Business Principles. Although similar in most respects to the earlier document, the revision included three significant changes recommended by Integrity Works. First, the company declared its support for "fundamental human rights in line with the legitimate role of business." (Shell did not explicitly endorse the Universal Declaration of Human Rights in the revised business principles, although it did do so later in other documents.) Second, the company committed itself "to contribute to sustainable development." Finally, the revisions clarified the company's stand on political activity. The earlier formulation, which emphasized abstention from politics, was replaced with language stating the company's intention to abstain from *party politics,* while emphasizing its right and responsibility to make its position known to governments on matters affecting the company or its stakeholders.

All operating companies were instructed to adopt the revised principles as their own policy. Beginning in 1998, these companies' chief executives were required to confirm in writing annually to the CMD that they were in compliance with the revised principles or, if not, where they fell short. The compliance letter requirement focused the attention of operating managers on the changes and ways in which their actions were consistent, or inconsistent, with the company's values.

With the assistance of Amnesty International, Shell also developed a primer, *Business and Human Rights,* explaining what the commitment to human rights meant in practical terms.

Resolution 10

In early 1997, the Pensions and Investment Research Consultants (PIRC) decided that Shell, despite its efforts, had still not addressed its concerns satisfactorily. The investor activists therefore decided to place a resolution before the shareholders at the May annual general meeting (AGM) of Shell Transport and Trading. Resolution 10, as it came to be known, was jointly sponsored by 18 institutional investors.

The resolution called on Shell to take three actions. These were to place a director (board member) in charge of environmental and corporate responsibility; to monitor, externally audit, and report to shareholders on its environmental and social policies; and to issue a report by the end of the year on the company's operations in Nigeria. Resolution 10 generated intense media and shareholder interest.

The company recommended a vote against the resolution and issued a statement in response that stated, in part:

> Your Directors, and all Royal Dutch/Shell Group of Companies, consider that environmental and corporate responsibility policies are an integral part in the proper conduct of the Group's business activities. Your Directors reject the implication in this resolution that the Group does not have effective policies in place.

In spite of the company's opposition, of the 46 percent of shares that were voted, 10.5 percent supported the resolution and 6.5 percent abstained. Although the resolution failed, support for it was much higher than support for virtually any other such social responsibility resolution introduced that year by shareholder activists in Europe or the United States.

Although Shell opposed Resolution 10, it moved quickly to institute some organizational changes requested by its shareholder critics. In late 1997, Shell established a social accountability team, consisting of six members of the committee of managing directors and one representative each from Shell and Royal Dutch. Herkströter was given overall responsibility for environmental and corporate responsibility policies. A new position, manager for social accountability, was created.

Social and Environmental Reporting

Shell considered that an important element in its corporate responsibility initiative was to be publicly accountable not only to its shareholders but to its other stakeholders and society at large. Accordingly, it began publishing a series of reports that went well beyond traditional annual financial reports.

In April 1998, the company published its first annual *Shell Report,* subtitled *Profits and Principles—Does There Have to Be a Choice?* This unusual document reported on Shell's commitment to human rights, environmental protection, and corporate citizenship. It also invited others to join with the company in a global debate on the responsibilities of multinational corporations. In its introduction, the report stated:

> This Report is about values. It describes how we, the people, companies, and businesses that make up the Royal Dutch/Shell Group, are striving to live up to our responsibilities—financial, social, and environmental. It is also an invitation to you to tell us what you think of our performance.

The report described the revised SGBP in detail, gave examples of each principle, and explained the company's efforts to make sure they were honored by the operating companies and Shell's joint venture partners and contractors. It presented a series of challenging ethical questions and invited readers to share their reactions. Many of these questions had already been the subjects of extensive public debate, in connection with Nigeria and Brent Spar. For example, one question was: Under what circumstances, if any, should a major company use its economic power to deliver, or at least influence, political change—especially in nations with undemocratic governments and poor human rights records? The report presented Shell's approach to a number of difficult issues, such as climate change.

The report also included an essay by John Elkington, chairman of SustainAbility, a consultancy specializing in advising corporations on sustainable development. In this essay, Elkington presented his concept of the *triple bottom line,* arguing that companies had a duty to provide audited reports not only of their financial performance but of their social and environmental performance as well. The report concluded with a road map for the future. Shell followed up *Profits and Principles* with a *Health, Safety, and Environment Report* and *Shell's Investment in Society,* reporting specifically on its environmental and social performance. All three reports were intended to be annual publications.

Although Shell had opposed PIRC's 1997 shareholder resolution calling for external auditing of its environmental performance, it now undertook to provide independent verification of its social and environmental reports. This goal presented unique challenges. The scope of practices to be audited was worldwide and complex. Moreover, unlike financial reporting, where auditing practices were well established, meaningful measures of social and environmental performance were not generally accepted. The company set out to work with its auditors, KPMG and Price Waterhouse, and others to develop social and environmental accounting and assurance standards. In *Profits and Principles,* the company set out a timetable leading to integrated, externally verified reporting for its financial, social, and environmental performance by 2002.

The company's July 1998, *Health, Safety, and Environment Report* was the first independently verified audited environmental report ever published by a multinational oil company. The auditors, KPMG and Price Waterhouse, acknowledged that the job had "proved to be a considerable challenge" because of the "absence of established generally accepted international standards for the verification of HSE data." The initial cost to audit Shell's health, safety, and environmental data in 30 entities worldwide in 1998 was around $2 million.

To bring the message of these reports to a wider public, Shell in 1999 initiated a $25 million "profits and principles" advertising campaign. Its purpose, in the words of Mark Moody-Stuart, was "to keep all of our stakeholders informed, both about the issues themselves and the work we at Shell are doing to address those issues."

Dialogue with Stakeholder Organizations

During this period, Shell also maintained an ongoing dialogue with stakeholders, including some of its most vocal critics. It called this process *engagement.* In part, this was accomplished through tear-off "Tell Shell" cards in various reports, such as *Profits and Principles,* which readers were invited to fill out and mail back to the company. In part, it was accomplished through an interactive feature on Shell's website, which permitted anyone to submit comments for all to see. Scores of people did, including many that were morally outraged at Shell's behavior. Their comments were posted, without censorship, creating the unusual spectacle of a corporate website peppered with negative remarks, which activists could use to find each other and create a community of anti-Shell interest.

In addition to opening itself up for freewheeling public comment, Shell also engaged in written and face-to-face dialogue with stakeholders, including community activists and human rights, environmentalist, and corporate governance organizations. The engagement process was coordinated by Shell's Department of External Affairs, but it involved managers at many levels throughout the Group.

The Human Rights Dialogue

One such dialogue occurred with two human rights organizations, Amnesty International and Pax Christi. In December 1995, in the wake of Ken Saro-Wiwa's execution, Pax Christi—a Catholic lay organization devoted to promoting world peace, human rights, and economic justice—wrote Shell asking the company to speak out on the issue of human rights in Nigeria. Herkströter replied, responding to specific points in the letter and inviting Pax Christi to engage in further discussions.

Pax Christi asked Amnesty International, with which it shared many concerns, to join it in this process. At that time, Amnesty International was probably the best-known human rights organization in the world, with more than a million members worldwide. Over the following three years, these two organizations engaged in an ongoing dialogue with Shell, involving an exchange of position papers, public forums, and face-to-face meetings.

In these discussions, Pax Christi and Amnesty International focused on several issues. They argued that it was imperative that the company incorporate explicit support for the Universal Declaration of Human Rights in its Statement of General Business Principles. The two human rights organizations urged Shell to appoint a director for human rights and to institute better training in human rights for its staff, particularly its security personnel. They recommended independent auditing of the company's human rights practices. Other portions of the discussion focused specifically on the situation in Nigeria and on Shell's role during the Saro-Wiwa trial and its relationship to the Nigerian military authorities.

In some cases, the company made specific changes in response to the NGOs' recommendations. For example, the NGOs raised questions about the adequacy of the guidance provided to police assigned to protect Shell's property and for failing to require accountability for possible police misconduct. In response, Shell reviewed its policies and made specific changes to bring them into compliance with United Nations standards. The company also updated the plastic wallet-sized cards distributed to police assigned to Shell facilities, summarizing the company's revised human rights policies. In other situations, by contrast, Shell declined the NGOs' recommendations. For example, the company declined to appoint a director of human rights, saying that its current corporate governance procedures were sufficient.

The Brent Spar Dialogue

After reversing its initial decision to seek deep-sea disposal of the Brent Spar, Shell initiated a two-year long dialogue with its environmental critics, including Greenpeace. In October 1995, the company announced an international competition to solicit innovative solutions to the problem of what to do with the decommissioned rig. It also sponsored open meetings in the UK, Germany, Denmark and the Netherlands to discuss various options. These gatherings were facilitated by an independent organization, the Environmental Council, which worked with groups to find common ground in environmental disputes. After winnowing the list of possible options, in 1997 Shell held yet another round of public meetings in all four countries, accompanied by a CD-ROM describing the short-listed options.

Finally, in January 1998 Shell announced its selection of a solution: to recycle the Brent Spar as a ferry quay near Stavanger, Norway. So-called Ro/Ro (roll-on, roll-off) ferries, which carried both cars and people, were widely used in Norway, with its mountainous terrain and miles of coastline. Under the plan, the Spar would be disassembled, and its flotation tanks and other parts reused to construct a Ro-Ro dock. The ferry quay solution appealed to environmentalists, who liked the idea of putting the old rig to good use. The British government quickly approved the plan, and construction began in late 1998.

Shell later commented that the Brent Spar experience "taught us the value of dialogue with our critics and other interested parties. . . . This unique consultation exercise has helped promote a different approach to decision making in the Group, and has shown new ways in which Shell companies can be more open and accountable." In a speech, a Shell executive later described this new approach as a switch from DAD—decide, announce, and defend, to DDD—dialogue, decide, and deliver.

In addition to its dialogues with human rights organizations and environmentalists, Shell also continued to meet with shareholder activists, religious leaders, and other stakeholders during this period.

Continuing Challenges of Corporate Responsibility

Over a four-year period, Shell had undergone a major transformation. It had undertaken a revision of its business principles, an internal structural reorganization, a survey of its global reputation, and externally audited reports on its social and environmental performance. It had conducted hundreds of meetings with stakeholders, and changed its corporate policies in many areas.

What did the "new" Shell's proclaimed environmental and social commitments mean in practice? What changes did managers and employees on the ground in the Group's scores of operating companies do differently, if anything, as a result of the transformation of Shell? In its far-flung worldwide operations, the company continued to face daily challenges to act in a manner consistent with its support for human rights, sustainable development, and social responsibility. To some, the company was making marked progress toward meeting society's changing expectations. To others, it continued to fall short, focusing more on changing the public's perception than on changing its actual practice.

In an interview in July 1999, chairman Mark Moody-Stuart reflected on Shell's transformation process:

> I think that the main goals [of the transformation] were to make sure that we
> were internally effective, that we made best use of our resources, our assets, our
> people. . . . But, also, that we had this connection to society and to the

customers. . . . [It] is the society that commercial organizations have to serve, no matter what you do. Even if you are a baker making bread, you had better know what the trends are on bread in the society. If people are going to give up eating bread, you had better know about it. If they like chocolate bread, you had better know about that. . . . You can't divorce the two. People sometimes try to do that. They say, all this societal stuff is woolly, we should stick to commerce. The two are absolutely linked. . . . These soft issues are really business issues because we are part of society, and members of society are our customers. So, our impact on society really matters commercially.

Discussion Questions

1. In the late 1990s, Shell underwent a transformation. What were the key changes that Shell made in the areas of organizational structure and culture, relationships with stakeholders, reporting practices, and business principles? What additional changes, if any, do you believe Shell should have made?
2. In your opinion, what was the most important cause of Shell's transformation? Do you believe the company was motivated more by external pressures or by internal pressures? Why do you think so?
3. Some people believe that Shell was sincere in the changes it made, and others believe that the company's transformation was mainly an effort to manipulate public opinion. What is your opinion? How could you best determine the answer to this question?

Glossary

This glossary defines technical or special terms used in this book. Students may use it as a quick and handy reference for terms that may be unfamiliar without having to refer to the specific chapters where they are used. It also can be a helpful aid in studying for examinations and for writing term papers where precise meanings are needed.

Acid rain.   Rain that is more acidic than normal; occurs when emissions of sulfur dioxide and nitrogen oxides from utilities, manufacturers, and vehicles combine with water vapor in the air.

Administrative costs.   The direct costs incurred in running government regulatory agencies, including salaries of employees, equipment, supplies, and other such items. (See also *compliance costs*.)

Administrative learning.   A stage in the development of corporate social responsiveness during which managers and supervisors learn new practices necessary for coping with social problems and pressures.

Advocacy advertising.   A strategy used by companies to promote their social, political, or economic viewpoint through the media.

Affirmative action.   A positive and sustained effort by an organization to identify, hire, train if necessary, and promote minorities, women, and members of other groups who are underrepresented in the organization's workforce.

Affluenza.   A term used to describe the "illness" of having too much material wealth and too little sense of how to use it wisely.

Air pollution.   When more pollutants, such as sulfur dioxide or particulates, are emitted into the atmosphere than can be safely absorbed and diluted by natural processes.

Alternative dispute resolution.   A method for resolving legal conflicts outside the traditional court system, in which a professional mediator (a third-party neutral) works with the two sides to negotiate a settlement agreeable to both parties.

Altruism.   Acting for the benefit of others at the risk of sacrificing one's self-interest.

Annual meeting.   A yearly meeting called by a corporation's board of directors for purposes of reporting to the company's stockholders on the current status and future prospects of the firm.

Anticompetitive merger.   A merger of two or more companies that reduces or eliminates competition in an industry or region; usually illegal under U.S. antitrust laws.

Antitrust laws.   Laws that promote competition or that oppose trusts, monopolies, or other business combinations that restrain trade.

Balanced scorecard.   An approach to accounting for an organization's short-term and long-term accomplishments in financial and nonfinancial terms.

Biodiversity.   The variety of living organisms and the range of their genetic makeup.

Blowing the whistle.   (See *whistle-blowing*.)

Board of directors.   A group of persons elected by shareholder votes to be responsible for directing the affairs of a corporation, establishing company objectives and policies, selecting top-level managers, and reviewing company performance.

Bribery.   A questionable or unjust payment often to a government official to ensure or facilitate a business transaction.

Brick-and-mortar operations.   Traditional businesses that operated out of buildings made of brick or mortar, as opposed to electronic commerce, or virtual, operations.

Business and society.   The study of the relationship between business and its entire social environment.

Business ethics.   The application of general ethical ideas to business behavior.

Business legitimacy principle.   The view that a company must comply with the law and conform to the expectations of its stakeholders in order to be a corporate citizen in good standing.

Carrying capacity.   The maximum population that an ecosystem can support. (See also *limits to growth hypothesis*.)

Cause-related marketing. A form of philanthropy in which contributions to a nonprofit organization are tied to the use of the donor organization's products or services by the recipient organization's members.

Charity principle. The idea that the wealthier members of society or profitable businesses should give voluntary aid and support to those less fortunate or to organizations that provide community services.

Chief information officer. A manager who has been entrusted with the responsibility to manage the organization's technology with its many privacy and security issues.

Child care. The care or supervision of another's child, such as at a day care center; offered as a benefit by some employers to working parents.

Chlorofluorocarbons (CFCs). Manufactured chemicals, used as refrigerants, insulation, solvents, and propellants in spray cans, that are believed to react with and deplete ozone in the upper atmosphere. (See also *Montreal Protocol; ozone.*)

Civic engagement. A phrase that describes the active involvement of individuals and organizations in changing and improving communities.

Civil society. A term that refers to nonprofit and nongovernmental organizations that are committed to activities that will improve life for all citizens in a community or society.

Cloning. The process of genetically creating an identical cell or organism.

Coalitions. Groups of organizations or corporate stakeholders who work together to achieve a common goal. (See *stakeholder coalitions.*)

Collaborative partnerships. Partnerships between and among businesses and their key stakeholders to respond to complex social problems.

Command and control regulation. A regulatory approach in which the government "commands" companies to meet specific standards (such as amounts of particular pollutants) and "controls" the methods (such as technology) used to achieve these standards. This approach is often contrasted with market-based regulatory approaches in which the government establishes general goals and allows companies to use the most cost-effective methods possible to achieve them.

Common law. A system of law in which judges make decisions based on prior legal decisions, called precedent.

Commons. Traditionally, an area of land on which all citizens could graze their animals without limitation. The term now refers to any shared resource, such as land, air, or water, that a group of people uses collectively. (See also *global commons.*)

Community. A company's area of local business influence. This includes the people and other stakeholders residing near a business operation.

Community advisory panels (CAPs). Groups of citizens from a local community that meet with corporate officials to discuss issues of common interest about a company's operations, such as plant safety, traffic patterns, and emergency planning.

Community Reinvestment Act (CRA). A federal law requiring banks to reinvest a portion of their depositors' money back into the local community.

Community relations. The involvement of business with the communities in which it conducts operations.

Competition. A struggle to survive and excel. In business, different firms compete with one another for customers' dollars.

Competition policies. A term used to describe antitrust laws or policies in some nations and trading groups.

Compliance costs. The costs incurred by business and other organizations in complying with government regulations, such as the cost of pollution control machinery or the disposal of toxic chemical wastes. (See also *administrative costs.*)

Comprehensive Environmental Response, Compensation, and Liability Act (CERCLA). (See *Superfund.*)

Computer hackers. Individuals often with advanced technological training who, for thrill or profit, breach a business's or government agency's information security system.

Concentration (corporate, economic, industrial, market). When relatively few companies are responsible for a large proportion of economic activity, production, or sales.

Conglomerate merger. The combination, or joining together, of two or more companies in unrelated industries into a single company. (See also *horizontal merger; vertical merger.*)

Consumer bill of rights. Four rights of consumers outlined in a well-known speech by President John F. Kennedy. The four consumer rights Kennedy discussed were the right to safety, the right to be informed, the right to choose, and the right to be heard.

Consumer hot lines.   Telephone lines or interactive websites that provide consumers with direct access to companies.

Consumer movement.   A social movement that seeks to augment the rights and powers of consumers. (Also known as *consumerism.*)

Consumer privacy.   A person's right of privacy in his or her role as a consumer; for example, a customer's right to prohibit an online retailer from sharing with other businesses information collected from that customer during an electronic sales transaction. (See also *right of privacy.*)

Consumer protection laws.   Laws that provide consumers with better information, protect consumers from possible hazards, or encourage competitive pricing.

Consumer rights.   The legitimate claims of consumers to safe products and services, adequate information, free choice, a fair hearing, and competitive prices.

Consumerism.   (See *consumer movement.*)

Corporate citizenship.   Business practices that involve proactively building stakeholder partnerships, discovering business opportunities through social strategic goals, and creating a vision of corporate financial and social performance.

Corporate crime.   Illegal behavior by company employees that benefits a corporation.

Corporate culture.   A blend of ideas, customs, traditional practices, company values, and shared meanings that helps define normal behavior for everyone who works in a company.

Corporate employee volunteerism.   A program where employees engage in community service as a way to improve the company's image as well as serve the communities in which the business operates.

Corporate foundations.   Organizations chartered as nonprofits and funded by companies for the purpose of donating money to community organizations, programs, and causes.

Corporate giving.   (See *corporate philanthropy.*)

Corporate governance.   Any structured system of allocating power in a corporation that determines how and by whom the company is to be governed.

Corporate legitimacy.   Public acceptance of the corporation as an institution that contributes to society's well-being.

Corporate merger.   The combination, or joining together, of two or more separate companies into a single company. (See also *conglomerate merger; horizontal merger; vertical merger.*)

Corporate philanthropy.   Gifts and contributions made by businesses, usually from pretax profits, to benefit various types of nonprofit community organizations.

Corporate political agency theory.   A theory that holds that politicians are the agents of those who elect or appoint them to office.

Corporate political strategy.   Those activities taken by organizations to acquire, develop, and use power to achieve a political advantage or gain.

Corporate power.   The strength or capability of corporations to influence government, the economy, and society, based on their organizational resources and size.

Corporate restructuring.   The reorganization of a corporation's business units and activities, which often involves the closing of current facilities and reduction of workforce.

Corporate social involvement.   The interaction of business corporations with society.

Corporate social policy.   A policy or a group of policies in a corporation that defines the company's purposes, goals, and programs regarding one or more social issues or problems.

Corporate social responsibility.   The idea that businesses are accountable for their actions and should seek socially beneficial results as well as economically beneficial results.

Corporate social responsiveness.   How a firm addresses social demands initiated by corporate stakeholders or in the actions taken by the firm that affects its stakeholders.

Corporate social strategy.   The social, political, and ethical parts of a company's plans and activities for achieving its goals and purposes.

Corporate stakeholder.   A person or group that affects, or is affected by, a corporation's policies and actions. Stakeholders may be voluntary or involuntary and either bear risks or share benefits.

Corporate strategic management.   Planning, directing, and managing a corporation for the purpose of helping it achieve its basic purposes and long-term goals.

Corporate strategic planning.   A process of formulating a corporation's basic purpose, long-term goals, and programs intended to achieve the company's purposes and goals.

Corporate takeover.   The acquisition, usually by merger, of one corporation by another.

Corporation.   Legally, an artificial legal "person," created under the laws of a particular state or nation. Socially and organizationally, it is a complex system of people, technology, and resources generally devoted to carrying out a central economic mission as it interacts with a surrounding social and political environment.

Cost-benefit analysis.   A systematic method of calculating the costs and benefits of a project or activity that is intended to produce benefits.

Council of Institutional Investors.   An organization founded in 1985 that represents the interests of institutional investors.

Crisis management.   The strategic process companies use to respond to unexpected and high consequential shocks, such as accidents, disasters, catastrophes, and injuries.

Crisis management team.   The use of a special team to help a company cope with an unusual emergency situation that may threaten the company in serious ways.

Cross-media pollution.   Pollution that migrates across several different media, such as air, land, or water. For example, hazardous wastes disposed in a dump might leak out, contaminating groundwater, or evaporate, causing air pollution. (Also known as *multimedia pollution.*)

Culpability score.   Under the U.S. Corporate Sentencing Guidelines, the degree of blame assigned to an executive found guilty of criminal wrongdoing.

Cultural distance.   The amount of difference in customs, attitudes, and values between two social systems.

Cultural shock.   A person's disorientation and insecurity caused by the strangeness of a different culture.

Cyberspace.   A virtual location where information is stored, ideas are described, and communication takes place in and through an electronic network of linked systems.

Debt relief.   The idea that the world's richest nations should forgive the poor nations of the obligation to pay back loans.

Deceptive advertising.   An advertisement that is deceptive or misleading; generally illegal under U.S. law.

Defense industry conversion.   The process of transforming businesses that once specialized in military production

into businesses capable of producing goods and services for civilian or nonmilitary use.

Deflation.   A decline in the economic value (price) of goods or services.

Deregulation.   The removal or scaling down of regulatory authority and regulatory activities of government.

Design for disassembly.   Designing products so that they can be disassembled and their component parts recycled or reused at the end of their useful life.

Digital divide.   The gap between those that have technology and those that do not.

Digital certificates.   Encrypted computer files that can serve as both identification cards and signatures online.

Digital Millennium Copyright Act.   The United States law that made it a crime to circumvent antipiracy measures built into most commercial software agreements between the manufacturers and their users.

Directors.   (See *board of directors.*)

Discrimination (in jobs or employment).   Unequal treatment of employees based on non-job-related factors such as race, sex, age, national origin, religion, color, and physical or mental handicap.

Diversity.   Variation in the characteristics that distinguish people from one another, such as age, ethnicity, nationality, gender, mental or physical abilities, race, sexual orientation, family status, and first language.

Diversity council.   A group of managers and employees responsible for developing and implementing specific action plans to meet an organization's diversity goals. (See also *diversity.*)

Divestment.   Withdrawing and shifting to other uses the funds that a person or group has invested in the securities (stocks, bonds, notes, etc.) of a company. Investors sometimes have divested the securities of companies doing business in countries accused of human rights abuses.

Dividend.   A return-on-investment payment made to the owners of shares of corporate stock at the discretion of the company's board of directors.

Downsizing.   The reduction of a company's workforce; often part of a corporate restructuring program designed to reduce costs.

Drug testing (of employees).   The testing of employees, by the employer, for the presence of illegal drugs, sometimes by means of a urine sample analyzed by a clinical laboratory.

Earth Summit. An international conference sponsored by the United Nations in Brazil in 1992 that produced several treaties on global environmental issues. (Also known as the *Conference on Environment and Development.*)

Eco-efficiency. Occurs when businesses or societies are simultaneously economically efficient and environmentally responsible.

Ecologically sustainable organization (ESO). A business that operates in a way that is consistent with the principle of sustainable development. (See also *sustainable development.*)

Ecology. The study, and the process, of how living things—plants and animals—interact with one another and with their environment.

E-commerce. Electronic business exchanges where the buying and selling of goods and services is done electronically via the Internet.

Ecosystem. Plants and animals in their natural environment, living together as an interdependent system.

Egoist. (See *ethical egoist.*)

Elder care. The care or supervision of elderly persons; offered as a benefit by some employers to working children of elderly parents.

Electronic monitoring (of employees). The use by employers of electronic technologies, such as e-mail, voice mail, Internet browsing, and digitally stored video, to gather, store, and monitor information about employees' activities.

Electoral politics. Political activities undertaken by business and other interest groups to influence the outcome of elections to public office.

Emissions charges or fees. Fees charged to business by the government, based on the amount of pollution emitted.

Employee assistance programs. Programs provided by the employer to prevent or treat problems that interfere with employee job performance, such as alcohol or drug abuse.

Employee stock ownership plan (ESOP). A benefit plan in which a company purchases shares of its own stock and places them in trust for its employees.

Employment-at-will. The principle that workers are hired and retained solely at the discretion of the employer.

Encryption. A type of software that scrambles e-mails and files, preventing eavesdroppers from seeing information sent across the Internet and stored in databases.

Enlightened self-interest. The view that a business can be socially aware without giving up its own economic self-interest.

Entitlement mentality. A view that a person or group is guaranteed an economic or social benefit by virtue of being a member of the designated group. (See also *rights [human].*)

Environmental audit. A company audit, or review, of its progress toward meeting environmental goals, such as pollution prevention.

Environmental justice. A movement to prevent unfair or inequitable exposure to environmental risk, such as from exposure to hazardous chemicals; or a situation where exposure to such risk is fair and equitable.

Environmental partnership. A voluntary, collaborative partnership between or among businesses, government regulators, and environmental organizations to achieve specific environmental goals.

Environmental protection. A term that describes efforts by individuals or organizations to prevent damage or destruction to natural resources such as land, water, and air.

Environmental Protection Agency (EPA). The United States federal government agency responsible for most environmental regulation and enforcement.

Environmental scanning. Examining an organization's environment to discover trends and forces that could have an impact on the organization.

Environmental standards. Standard amounts of particular pollutants allowable by law.

Equal-access rule. A legal provision that requires television stations to allow all competing candidates for political office to broadcast their political messages if one of the candidates' views are broadcast.

Equal employment opportunity. The principal that all persons otherwise qualified should be treated equally with respect to job opportunities, workplace conditions, pay, fringe benefits, and retirement provisions.

Equal Employment Opportunity Commission (EEOC). An agency of the U.S. government, created in 1964, that is responsible for enforcing equal employment opportunity laws and executive orders.

Ergonomics.   Adapting work tasks, working conditions, and equipment to minimize worker injury or stress.

Ethical charismatic leader.   A leader who exhibits strong moral character and is therefore capable of positively influencing an entire department or organization.

Ethical climate.   An unspoken understanding among employees of what is and is not acceptable behavior.

Ethical egoist.   A person who puts his or her own selfish interests above all other considerations, while denying the ethical needs and beliefs of others.

Ethical principles.   Guides to moral behavior, such as honesty, keeping promises, helping others, and respecting others' rights, that are essential for the preservation and continuation of organized life everywhere.

Ethical relativism.   A belief that ethical right and wrong are defined by various periods of time in history, a society's traditions, the specific circumstances of the moment, or personal opinion.

Ethics.   A conception of right and wrong conduct, serving as a guide to moral behavior.

Ethics audit.   An assessment used by an organization to target the effectiveness of their ethical safeguards or to document evidence of increased ethical employee behavior.

Ethics codes.   Written sets of rules used to guide managers and employees when they encounter an ethical dilemma.

Ethics committee.   A high-level group of executives who provide ethical guidance for employees and are often empowered to investigate and punish ethical wrongdoing at the firm.

Ethics hot line.   A program providing employees access to an independent or business resource to report some ethical concern.

Ethics officer.   A manager designated by an organization to investigate breaches of ethical conduct, promulgate ethics statements, and generally promote ethical conduct at work.

Ethnocentric business.   A company whose business standards are based on its home nation's customs, markets, and laws.

Ethnocentric perspective.   The view that a company is an extension of its home country and owes its loyalty to the home country.

European Union (EU).   The political and economic coalition of European countries.

Executive compensation.   The compensation (total pay) of corporate executives, including salary, bonus, stock options, and various benefits.

Export of jobs.   A loss of jobs in a business firm's home nation, and a creation of new jobs in a foreign nation, caused by relocating part or all of the business firm's operations (and jobs) to the foreign nation.

Expropriation.   (See *nationalization*.)

Fair labor standards.   Rules that establish minimum acceptable standards for the conditions under which a company's employees (or the employees of its suppliers or subcontractors) will work. For example, such standards might include a ban on child labor, establishment of maximum work hours per week, or a commitment to pay wages above a certain minimum level.

Fairness and balance issue.   Raises the question of whether the media reports business activities impartially, showing both sides of a controversy.

Fairness Doctrine.   A U.S. law, repealed in 1987, that required television and radio broadcasters to cover both sides of important or controversial issues and to give the opportunity for contrasting viewpoints to be aired.

Family-friendly corporation.   A company that removes sex discrimination from all aspects of its operations and that supports both men and women in their efforts to balance work and family responsibilities.

Family leave.   A leave of absence from work, either paid or unpaid, for the purpose of caring for a family member.

Fiduciary responsibility or duty.   A legal obligation to carry out a duty to some other person or group in order to protect their interest.

Fiscal policy.   The patterns of spending and taxation adopted by a government.

Flextime.   A plan that allows employees limited control over scheduling their own hours of work, usually at the beginning and end of the workday.

Foreign direct investment (FDI).   The investment and transfer of funds by investors in one nation into business activities or organizations located in another nation.

Foreign investment review board.   A national government body that is empowered to review and approve or disapprove proposed investments by foreign owners in a nation.

Fraud.   Deceit or trickery due to the pursuit of economic gain or competitive advantage.

Free enterprise ideology.   A set of beliefs about one way to organize economic life that includes individualism, freedom, private property, profit, equality of opportunity, competition, the work ethic, and a limited government.

Free enterprise system.   A socioeconomic system based on private ownership, profit-seeking business firms, and the principle of free markets.

Free market.   A model of an economic system based on voluntary and free exchange among buyers and sellers. Competition regulates prices in all free market exchanges.

Free speech issue.   Presents the challenge of finding a balance between the media's constitutional right to free expression and business's desire to be fairly and accurately depicted in media presentations, as well as to present its views on controversial public issues.

Functional-area ethics.   Ethical problems that typically occur in specialized operational areas of business, such as accounting, finance, marketing and information technology.

Functional regulation.   Regulations aimed at a particular function or operation of business, such as competition or labor relations.

Future shock.   A human reaction to rapid technological change whereby individuals experience difficulty in coping with new conditions of life brought on by new technology.

Genetic engineering.   The altering of the natural makeup of a living organism, which allows scientists to insert virtually any gene into a plant and create a new crop or an entire new species.

Genetically modified foods.   Food processed from genetically engineered crops. (See *genetic engineering*.)

Genetically modified organism.   Any organism that has been modified through the alteration of its genetic structure. Includes animals, plants, and cells of human beings.

Geocentric business.   A company whose business standards and policies are worldwide in outlook including multinational ownership, management, markets, and operations.

Geocentric perspective.   The view that businesses are global citizens that should behave and respect the laws and culture of every country in which they do business.

Glasnost.   A Russian term used to describe "openness" during the late 1980s and early 1990s when the Soviet Union began to collapse as a political entity.

Glass ceiling.   A barrier to the advancement of women, minorities, and other groups in the workplace.

Glass wall.   A barrier to the lateral mobility of women, minorities, and other groups in the workplace, such as from human resources to operations.

Global commons.   Natural resources, such as the earth's atmosphere and oceans, that the world's people use collectively.

Global corporate citizenship.   A phrase that describes the efforts of some companies to provide leadership on key social issues wherever they do business in the world.

Global locations.   The business practice of establishing and operating plants or other facilities in many nations. A global location strategy refers to the deliberate decision to place facilities in locations where they can serve important segments of the company's customers.

Global market channels.   Systems by which goods and services are sold in more than one country through international marketing and distribution.

Global supply chains.   Systems by which the components of complex goods and services are created in more than one country and assembled for worldwide sale.

Global village.   The most remote places on earth are linked together—like a single village—through technological advances that allow faster and more widespread communications.

Global warming.   The gradual warming of the earth's climate, believed by some scientists to be caused by an increase in carbon dioxide and other trace gases in the earth's atmosphere resulting from human activity, mainly the burning of fossil fuels.

Globalization.   The process by which more of the world's commercial and noncommercial interaction is influenced by global business and global trends.

Government and business partnership.   A subtype of socioeconomic system in which government and business work cooperatively to solve social problems. (See also *public–private partnerships; environmental partnership*.)

Grassroots politics (programs).   Political activity directed at involving and influencing individual citizens or constituents to directly contact government officials on a public policy issue.

Green management.   An outlook by managers that emphasizes the importance of considering ecological factors as management decisions are made.

Green marketing.   A concept that describes the creation, promotion, and sale of environmentally safe products and services by business.

Greenhouse effect. The warming effect that occurs when carbon dioxide, methane, nitrous oxides, and other gases act like the glass panels of a greenhouse, preventing heat from the earth's surface from escaping into space.

Hackers. (See *computer hackers.*)

Hazardous waste. Waste materials from industrial, agricultural, and other activities capable of causing death or serious health problems for those persons exposed for prolonged periods. (See also *toxic substance.*)

Home country. The country in which a multinational corporation has its headquarters.

Honesty tests. Written psychological tests that seek to predict employee honesty on the job.

Honeypot. A system used to lure hackers to a fabricated website to track their activities. (See *computer hackers.*)

Horizontal merger. The combination, or joining together, of two or more companies in the same industry and at the same level or stage of production or sales into a single company. (See also *conglomerate merger; vertical merger.*)

Host country. A foreign country in which a multinational corporation conducts business.

Human capital. A term that refers to the value of employee knowledge, expertise, and ability as an asset of the organization; it is similar to natural capital, financial capital, and intellectual capital.

Human genome. Strands of DNA developing a unique pattern for every human.

Human rights. An ethical concept emphasizing a person or group's entitlement to something or to be treated in a certain way, such as the right to life, safety, or to be informed.

Human rights code of conduct. An organization's statement regarding acceptable and unacceptable types of behavior with respect to people's rights to life, liberty, and well-being.

Ideology. A set of basic beliefs that define an ideal way of living for an individual, an organization, or a society.

Image issue. How the media projects or reinforces images of various groups in society, such as ethnic groups or women.

Individualism. A belief that each individual person has an inherent worth and dignity and possesses basic human rights that should be protected by society. Each person is presumed to be a free agent capable of knowing and promoting his or her own self-interest.

Industrial ecology. Designing factories and distribution systems as if they were self-contained ecosystems, such as using waste from one process as raw material for another.

Industrial policy. Government action to encourage the growth and development of specific industries.

Industrial resource base. The minerals, energy sources, water supplies, skilled labor force, and human knowledge necessary for industrial production.

Industrial society. A society in which the building and mechanical processing of material goods dominates work and employs the largest proportion of the labor force.

Industry-specific regulation. Regulations aimed at specific industries, such as telephone service or railroad transportation, involving control of rates charged, customers served, and entry into the industry.

Inflation. Decline in the purchasing power of money.

Information society. The current phase of technology; emphasizes the use and transfer of knowledge and information.

Insider trading. The illegal practice of buying or selling shares of corporate securities based on fiduciary information that is known only to a small group of persons, such as executives and their friends ("insiders"), and that enables them to make profits at the expense of other investors who do not have access to the inside information.

Institutional investor. A financial institution, insurance company, pension fund, endowment fund, or similar organization that invests its accumulated funds in the securities offered for sale on stock exchanges.

Institutionalized activity (ethics, social responsiveness, public affairs, etc.). An activity, operation, or procedure that is such an integral part of an organization that it is performed routinely by managers and employees.

Intangible assets. Nonphysical resources of the organization that enable it to achieve its goals and objectives, including intellectual property and corporate reputation.

Intellectual property. Ideas, concepts, and other symbolic creations of the human mind that are recognized and protected under a nation's copyright, patent, and trademark laws.

Interactive model of business and society. The combined primary and secondary interactions that business has with society.

Intergenerational equity. A term describing the unfairness of one generation's accumulation of debt and tax burdens that will have to be borne by future generations.

Interlocking directorate. A relationship between two corporations that is established when one person serves as a member of the board of directors of both corporations simultaneously.

International regulation. A form of regulation in which more than one nation agrees to establish and enforce the same rules of conduct for international business activities.

Internet (or World Wide Web). A global communications network linking individuals and organizations everywhere.

Intranet. Private or limited information network systems cordoned off from public access by software programs called firewalls.

Intrusion-detection systems. Acting like a virtual motion detector, these systems monitor computer networks to sense specific activities.

Iron law of responsibility. The belief that those who do not use their power in ways that society considers responsible will tend to lose their power in the long run.

Issues management. The systematic method of identification, analysis, priority setting, and response to public issues.

Justice. An ethical approach that emphasizes whether the distribution of benefits and burdens is fair among people, according to some agreed-upon rule.

Knowledge economy. An economy in which new knowledge, in its many forms, is reshaping and transforming old industries and creating new ones.

Labor force participation rate. The proportion of a particular group, such as women, in the paid workforce.

Labor standards. Conditions affecting a company's employees or the employees of its suppliers or subcontractors.

Labor union. An organization that represents workers on the job and that bargains collectively with the employer over wages, working conditions, and other terms of employment.

Laissez faire. A French phrase meaning "to let alone," used to describe an economic system where government intervention is minimal.

Laws. Society's attempt to formalize into written rules the public's ideas about what constitutes right and wrong conduct in various spheres of life.

Legal obligations. A belief that a firm must abide by the laws and regulations governing the society.

Leveraged buyouts (LBOs). The acquisition of a corporation by a group of investors, often including top executives, that relies on debt financing to pay the purchase price. The value of the company's assets is used as a "lever" to borrow the necessary amount for the purchase.

License to operate. The idea that an organization cannot operate unless it has permission (i.e., a "license") from society to do so.

Life-cycle analysis. Collecting information on the lifelong environmental impact of a product in order to minimize its adverse impacts at all stages, including design, manufacture, use, and disposal.

Limits to growth hypothesis. The idea that human society is now exceeding the carrying capacity of the earth's ecosystem and that unless corrective action is taken soon, catastrophic consequences will result. (See also *carrying capacity*.)

Line manager involvement. The extent to which line managers are involved in the organization's socially responsive strategies.

Lobbying. The act of trying to directly shape or influence a government official's understanding and position on a public policy issue.

Macroenvironment. All of the factors, forces, and institutions outside of a firm's immediate operating environment that affect or are affected by its operations.

Market failure. Inability of the marketplace to properly allocate costs to the parties responsible (e.g., of air pollution emissions) or to achieve the benefits associated with free market economics.

M-commerce. Commerce conducted by using mobile or cell telephones.

Media. A means of communication that widely reaches or influences people. Media businesses include broadcast technology, broadcasting business, and service delivery.

Media training. A media strategy in which executives and employees who are likely to have contact with the media are educated in how to effectively communicate with the press.

Merger. (See *corporate merger*.)

Microenvironment of business. The interrelated social, economic, political, and technological segments of society that influence and are affected by a company's actions.

Monetary policy. Government actions to control the supply and demand of money in the economy.

Monoculturalism. The idea that the world is becoming "one culture," as evidenced in language, entertainment, goods, and services.

Montreal Protocol. An international treaty limiting the manufacture and use of chlorofluorocarbons and other ozone-depleting chemicals. (See also *chlorofluorocarbons; ozone.*)

Moral development, stages. (See *stages of moral development.*)

Morality. A condition in which the most fundamental human values are preserved and allowed to shape human thought and action.

Most favored nation (MFN). The foreign policy term used to describe any nation with which the United States has a relationship that is designed to encourage trade by minimizing trade barriers.

Multimedia pollution. (See *cross-media pollution.*)

Multinational corporation. A company that conducts business in two or more nations, usually employing citizens of various nationalities.

National competitiveness. The ability of a nation to compete effectively with other nations in international markets through the actions of its privately and publicly owned business firms.

National sovereignty principle. A nation is a sovereign state whose laws, customs, and regulations must be respected by people, organizations, and other nations.

Nationalization. Government taking ownership and control of private property with or without compensation. (Also known as *expropriation.*)

New social contract. An evolving view of how a corporation and its stakeholders should act toward one another in light of modern economic and social changes. (See also *social contract.*)

New world order. The phrase used to describe relationships among nations following the end of the Cold War in the late 1980s.

Nongovernmental organizations (NGOs). Nonprofit organizations that are created and work to advocate on behalf of particular causes, issues, and interests.

Nonpoint source. A source of water or air pollution that cannot be easily identified, such as the source of toxic runoff from urban storm drains. (See also *point source.*)

Nonrenewable resources. Natural resources, such as oil, coal, or natural gas, that once used are gone forever. (See also *renewable resources.*)

Occupational crime. Illegal activity by a business employee intended to enrich the employee at the expense of the company.

Occupational Safety and Health Administration (OSHA). An agency of the U.S. government, created in 1970, that is responsible for enforcing government safety and health standards in the workplace.

Occupational segregation. The inequitable concentration of a group, such minorities or women, in particular job categories.

Opportunity costs. The various opportunities that cannot be realized because money is spent for one purpose rather than for others.

Ozone. A gas composed of three bonded oxygen atoms. Ozone in the lower atmosphere is a dangerous component of urban smog; ozone in the upper atmosphere provides a shield against ultraviolet light from the sun. (See also *chlorofluorocarbons; Montreal Protocol.*)

Parental leave. A leave of absence from work, either paid or unpaid, for the purpose of caring for a newborn or adopted child.

Paternalistic. Caring for others in need, as a father cares for a child.

Patriarchal society. A society in which men hold the dominant positions in organizations, the society's values reflect and reinforce male-oriented privileges, and women tend to hold subordinate positions.

Pay gap. The difference in the average level of wages, salaries, and income received by two groups, such as men and women (the *gender pay gap*) or whites and persons of color (the *racial pay gap*).

Perestroika. A Russian term used to describe economic reform and reconstruction during the late 1980s and early 1990s when the Soviet Union began to collapse as a political entity.

Performance-expectations gap. The perceived distance between a corporation's actual performance and the performance that is expected by the corporation's stakeholders.

Perpetual political campaign. The continuous process of raising money, communicating with constituents, and running for reelection.

Personal spirituality. A personal belief in a supreme being, religious organization, or the power of nature or some other external, life-guiding force.

Philanthropy. (See *corporate philanthropy.*)

Plant closing laws. Legislation that requires employers to notify employees in advance of the closing of a facility in order to allow time for adjustment, including negotiations to keep the plant open, to arrange an employee buyout, to find new jobs, and so forth.

Pluralism. A society in which numerous economic, political, educational, social, cultural, religious, and other groups are organized by people to promote their own interests.

Point source. A source of water or air pollution that can be easily identified such as a particular factory. (See also *nonpoint source.*)

Policy decision. A stage in the public policy process when government authorizes (or fails to authorize) a course of action, such as by passing (or failing to pass) a law, issuing a court opinion, or adopting a new regulation.

Policy evaluation. The final stage in the public policy process when the results of a public policy are judged by those who have an interest in the outcome.

Policy formulation. A stage in the public policy process when interested groups take a position and try to persuade others to adopt that position.

Policy implementation. A stage in the public policy process when action is taken to enforce a public policy decision.

Political action committee (PAC). A committee organized according to election law by any group for the purpose of accepting voluntary contributions from individual donors and then making contributions on behalf of candidates for election to public office.

Political cynicism. A climate of public distrust of politics and politicians.

Polluter pays principle (PPP). A principle that states that a polluter should be responsible for paying for the full costs of its pollution, such as through taxes.

Pollution charge. A fee levied on a polluting source based on the amount of pollution released into the environment.

Pollution prevention. (See *source reduction.*)

Polygraph. An operator-administered instrument used to judge the truth or falsity of a person's statements by measuring physiological changes that tend to be activated by a person's conscience when lying.

Populism. A political philosophy that favors grassroots democracy and an economy based on small businesses and farms that opposes big business concentration.

Precautionary principle. An ethical principle that holds a company or person responsible to behave in a way that prevents harm to people and the environment if there is a significant risk of harm.

Predatory pricing. The practice of selling below cost for the purpose of driving competitors out of business; usually illegal under U.S. antitrust laws.

Preferential hiring. An employment plan that gives preference to minorities, women, and other groups that may be underrepresented in an organization's workforce.

Price-fixing. When two or more companies collude to set, or "fix," the price of a product or service; usually illegal under U.S. antitrust laws.

Primary interactions or involvement. The direct relationships a company has with those groups that enable it to produce goods and services.

Primary stakeholders. The people and groups that are directly affected by a corporation's economic activities and decisions.

Principle of national sovereignty. The idea that the government of each nation is legally entitled to make laws regarding the behavior of its citizens and citizens of other nations who are acting within the nation.

Priority rule. In ethical analysis, a procedure for ranking in terms of their importance the three ethical modes of reasoning—utilitarian, rights, and justice—before making a decision or taking action.

Privacy. (See *right of privacy.*)

Privacy policy. Business policies that explain what use of the company's technology is permissible and how the business will monitor employee activities.

Private property. A group of rights giving control over physical and intangible assets to private owners. Private ownership is the basic institution of capitalism.

Privately held corporation. A corporation that is privately owned by an individual or a group of individuals; its stock is not available for purchase by the general investing public.

Privatization. The process of converting various economic functions, organizations, and programs from government ownership or government sponsorship to private operation.

Product liability.   A legal responsibility of a person or firm for the harmful consequences to others stemming from use of a product manufactured, sold, managed, or employed by the person or firm.

Product recall.   An effort by a business firm to remove a defective or sometimes dangerous product from consumer use and from all distribution channels.

Productivity.   The relationship between total inputs and total outputs. Productivity increases when the outputs of an organization increase faster than the inputs necessary for production.

Profit maximization.   An attempt by a business firm to achieve the highest possible rate of return from its operations.

Profit optimization.   An attempt by a business firm to achieve an acceptable, rather than a maximum, rate of return from its operations.

Profits.   The revenues of a person or company minus the costs incurred in producing the revenue.

Proxy.   A legal instrument giving another person the right to vote the shares of stock of an absentee stockholder.

Proxy statement.   A statement sent by a board of directors to a corporation's stockholders announcing the company's annual meeting, containing information about the business to be considered at the meeting, and enclosing a proxy form for stockholders not attending the meeting.

Public affairs function.   An organization's activities intended to perceive, monitor, understand, communicate with, and influence the external environment, including local and national communities, government, and public opinion.

Public affairs management.   The active management of an organization's external relations with such stakeholders as legislators, government officials, and regulatory agencies.

Public expectations.   The idea that the public, as a stakeholder, has legitimate expectations of what a business will do and how it will behave.

Public issue.   A problem or concern of corporate stakeholders that has the potential to become a politicized matter, leading to legislation, regulation, or other formal governmental action.

Public issue life cycle.   The sequence of phases through which a public issue may pass.

Public policy.   A plan of action by government to achieve some broad purpose affecting a large segment of the public.

Public policy agenda.   All public policy problems or issues that receive the active and serious attention of government officials.

Public policy process.   All of the activities and stages involved in developing, carrying out, and evaluating public policies.

Public–private partnerships.   Community-based organizations that have a combination of businesses and government agencies collaborating to address important social problems such as crime, homelessness, drugs, economic development, and other community issues.

Public referendum.   A citizen's initiative to place a question or resolution on the election ballot for a popular vote.

Public Relations Society of America.   A professional association of public relations officers committed to maintaining individual dignity and the free exercise of human rights within the media industry.

Public trustee.   A concept that a business owner or manager should base company decisions on the interests of a wide range of corporate stakeholders or members of the general public. In doing so, the business executive acts as a trustee of the public interest. (See also *stewardship principle*.)

Publicly held corporation.   A corporation whose stock is available for purchase by the general investing public.

Questionable payments.   Something of value given to a person or firm that raises significant ethical questions of right or wrong in the host nation or other nations.

Quotas (job, hiring, employment).   An employment plan based on hiring a specific number or proportion of minorities, women, or other groups that may be underrepresented in an organization's workforce.

Racial harassment.   Harassment in the workplace based on race, such as ethnic slurs, derogatory comments, or other verbal or physical harassment based on race that creates an intimidating, hostile, or offensive working environment or that interferes with an individual's work performance. (See also *sexual harassment*.)

Rain forest.   Woodlands that receive at least 100 inches of rain a year. They are among the planet's richest areas in terms of biodiversity.

Reengineering.   The concept of redesigning work systems and organizations in ways that enhance productivity and efficient work activities.

Regulation.   The action of government to establish rules by which industry or other groups must behave in conducting their normal activities.

Reinventing government.   A phrase used to describe efforts to reengineer, restructure, and reduce the cost of government.

Relational capital.   Organizational resources that are of value and flow from the organization's relationships with key stakeholders.

Relationship investing.   When large stockholders, usually institutions, form a long-term committed link with a company.

Renewable resources.   Natural resources, such as fresh water or timber, that can be naturally replenished. (See also *nonrenewable resources*.)

Reregulation.   The imposition of regulation on activities that were deregulated earlier.

Reverse discrimination.   The unintended negative impact experienced by an individual or group as a result of legal efforts to overcome discrimination against another individual or group.

Rights (human).   (See *human rights*.)

Right of privacy.   A person's entitlement to protection from invasion of his or her private life by government, business, or other persons.

Rule of cost.   The idea that all human actions generate costs.

Sanctions.   The political action of nations, through economic pressure, to punish countries for violations of international law and agreements.

Secondary interactions or involvement.   The relationship a company has with those social and political groups that feel the impact of the company's main activities and take steps to do something about it. These relationships are derived from the firm's primary interactions.

Secondary stakeholders.   The people and groups in society who are indirectly affected by a corporation's economic activities and decisions.

Sexual harassment.   Unwanted and uninvited sexual attention experienced by a person, and/or a workplace that is hostile or threatening in a sexual way. (See *racial harassment*.)

Shareholder.   (See *stockholder*.)

Shareholder resolution.   A proposal made by a stockholder and included in a corporation's notice of its annual meeting that advocates some course of action to be taken by the company.

Shareholders' lawsuit.   A lawsuit initiated by one or more stockholders to recover damages suffered due to alleged actions of the company's management.

Social accountability.   The condition of being held responsible to society or to some public or governmental group for one's actions, often requiring a specific accounting or reporting on those activities.

Social auditing.   Systematically studying and evaluating an organization's social and ethical performance. (See also *social performance audit*.)

Social capital.   The degree of "connectedness," or mutual support, among members in an organization or community. This commitment is a basic aspect of the corporation's role in the community.

Social Charter.   Social policy developed by countries in the European Union.

Social contract.   An implied understanding between an organization and its stakeholders as to how they will act toward one another. (See also *new social contract*.)

Social forecasting.   An attempt to estimate major social and political trends that may affect a company's operations and environment in the future.

Social overhead costs.   Public and private investments that are necessary to prepare the environment for effective operation of a new business or other major institutions.

Social performance audit.   Measuring a firm's corporate activities on an ideal socially responsible scale or comparing the resulting rating of a firm's actions against those of other, similar organizations.

Social regulation.   Regulations intended to accomplish certain social improvements such as equal employment opportunity or on-the-job safety and health.

Social responsibility.   (See *corporate social responsibility*.)

Social responsibility shareholder resolution.   A resolution on an issue of corporate social responsibility placed before stockholders for a vote at a company's annual meeting, usually by social activist groups.

Social responsiveness.   (See *corporate social responsiveness*.)

Socially responsive strategy.   Socially responsive businesses tend to emphasize a collaborative and problem-solving approach in dealing with their stakeholders.

Socially responsive structure.   How a firm changes its structure to be more responsive to external social challenges and better able to implement socially responsive strategies.

Society.   The people, institutions, and technology that make up a recognizable human community.

Socioeconomic system.   The combined and interrelated social, economic, and political institutions characteristic of a society.

Soft money.   Funds donated to a political party to support party-building activities such as televised commercials that do not specify a candidate, get-out-the-vote drives, and opinion polling. Soft money is often criticized as a loophole in the political campaign finance laws.

Software piracy.   The illegal copying of copyrighted software.

Solid waste.   Any solid waste materials resulting from human activities, such as municipal refuse and sewage, industrial wastes, and agricultural wastes.

Source reduction.   A business strategy to prevent or reduce pollution at the source rather than to dispose of or treat pollution after it has been produced. (Also known as *pollution prevention.*)

Special economic zones.   Industrial areas in the People's Republic of China that are reserved for foreign companies to establish business operations.

Specialized learning.   A stage in the development of corporate social responsiveness within a company during which managers and supervisors, usually with the help of a specialist, learn the new practices necessary for coping with social problems and pressures.

Stages of moral development.   A sequential pattern of how people grow and develop in their moral thinking, beginning with a concern for the self and growing to a concern for others and broad-based principles.

Stakeholder.   (See *corporate stakeholder.*)

Stakeholder analysis.   An evaluation of the relationships between a business and individuals or groups that are affected by or affect the firm.

Stakeholder coalitions.   Temporary unions of a company's stakeholder groups in order to express a common view or achieve a common purpose on a particular issue.

Stakeholder power.   The ability of one or more stakeholders to achieve a desired outcome in their interactions with a company.

State-owned enterprise.   A government-owned business or industry (e.g., a state-owned oil company).

Stateless corporation.   A multinational corporation whose activities are conducted in so many nations as to minimize its dependence on any single nation and enable it to establish its headquarters' activities virtually anywhere in the world.

Stewardship principle.   The idea that business managers, as public stewards or trustees, have an obligation to see that everyone, particularly those in need, benefits from the company's actions.

Sticky floor.   When women, minorities, or other groups are unable to advance in the workplace because they become "stuck" in entry-level, low-paying jobs.

Stockholder.   A person, group, or organization owning one or more shares of stock in a corporation. (Also known as *shareholder.*)

Strategic philanthropy.   A form of philanthropy in which donor organizations direct their contributions to recipients in order to achieve a direct or indirect business objective.

Strategic rethinking.   The process of reconsidering critical business assumptions about what an organization does, business activities it conducts, and in which markets and how it will compete.

Strategies of response.   Reactive, proactive, and interactive patterns of corporate behavior toward stakeholders.

Streaming.   A customized, on-demand radio service developed by music distributors to protect their copyrights to music.

Strict liability.   A legal doctrine that holds that a manufacturer is responsible (liable) for injuries resulting from the use of its products, whether or not the manufacturer was negligent or breached a warranty.

Subliminal advertisements.   Advertising tactics that direct messages to the viewers' subconscious rather than conscious mind.

Superfund.   A U.S. law, passed in 1980, designated to clean up hazardous or toxic waste sites. The law established a fund, supported mainly by taxes on petrochemical companies, to pay for the cleanup. (Also known as the *Comprehensive Environmental Response, Compensation, and Liability Act [CERCLA].*)

Sustainability.   The idea that a business must pursue economic results, plus sound environmental results, plus social well-being for its stakeholders.

Sustainable development.   A concept that describes current economic development that does not damage the ability of future generations to meet their own needs.

Sweatshop.   Factories where employees, sometimes including children, are forced to work long hours at low wages, often under unsafe working conditions.

Technology.   The application of science, especially in industry or commerce.

Technology cooperation.   Long-term cooperative partnerships between companies in developed and developing countries to transfer advanced technologies.

Technology superpowers.   Businesses that built and controlled the global information technology system.

Telecommunications.   The transmission of information over great distances via electromagnetic signals.

Telecommuting.   Performing knowledge work and transmitting the results of that work by means of computer terminal to an organization's central data bank and management center, while the employee works at home or at some other remote location.

Term limits.   Limits on the maximum number of terms in office that an elected official can serve.

Third world nations.   Developing nations relatively poorer than advanced industrial nations.

Tissue engineering.   The rejuvenation or replication of healthy cells or tissues to replace failing human organs and aging cells.

Top management philosophy.   Top management's values focusing on the role of the organization in society.

Total quality management (TQM).   A management approach that achieves high quality and consumer satisfaction through teamwork and continuous improvement of a product or service.

Toxic substance.   Any substance used in production or in consumer products that is poisonous or capable of causing serious health problems for those persons exposed. (See also *hazardous waste.*)

Tradable allowances.   A market-based approach to pollution control in which the government grants companies "rights" to a specific amount of pollution (allowances), which may be bought or sold (traded) with other companies.

Trade association.   An organization that represents the business and professional interests of the firms or persons in a trade, industry, or profession, such as medical doctors, chemical manufacturers, or used-car dealers.

Trade-offs, economic and social.   An attempt to balance and compare economic and social gains against economic and social costs when it is impossible to achieve all that is desired in both economic and social terms.

Trade policy.   Actions by government to encourage or discourage commerce with other nations.

Transparency.   The degree of openness or visibility surrounding a government's, or other organization's, decision-making process.

Triple bottom line.   The idea that an organization should be measured on the basis of its economic results, environmental impact, and contribution to social well-being.

Unanimity rule.   In ethical analysis, a procedure for determining that all three modes of ethical reasoning—utilitarian, rights, and justice—provide consistent and uniform answers to an ethical problem or issue.

United Nations Global Compact.   Voluntary agreement of business, labor, and nongovernmental organizations to work for sustainable development goals.

U.S. Corporate Sentencing Guidelines.   Standards to help judges determine the appropriate penalty for criminal violations of federal laws and provide a strong incentive for businesses to promote ethics at work.

U.S. Foreign Corrupt Practices Act.   Federal law that prohibits businesses from paying bribes to foreign government officials, political parties, or political candidates.

Utilitarian reasoning.   An ethical approach that emphasizes the consequences of an action and seeks the overall amount of good that can be produced by an action or a decision.

Utility (social).   A concept used in ethical reasoning that refers to the net positive gain or benefit to society of some action or decision.

Value chain.   The idea concept that all products are the result of a chain of economic activities, from raw materials to finished goods, with economic value for customers.

Values.   Fundamental and enduring beliefs about the most desirable conditions and purposes of human life.

Values issue.   How the media contributes to the shaping of social attitudes and values, influencing the basic determinants of human behavior and social attitudes.

Venture philanthropy. A new form of giving associated with entrepreneurial businesses in which the wealthy donor commits personal efforts plus money to achieve program goals.

Vertical merger. The combination, or joining together, of two or more companies in the same industry but at different levels or stages of production or sales into a single company. (See also *conglomerate merger; horizontal merger.*)

Virtue ethics. Based on a way of being and what is considered valuable rather than focusing on rules for correct behavior.

Volunteerism. The uncompensated efforts of people to assist others in a community.

Wall Street. A customary way of referring to the financial community of banks, investment institutions, and stock exchanges centered in the Wall Street area of New York City.

Warranty. A guarantee or assurance by the seller of a product or service.

Water pollution. When more wastes are discharged into waterways, such as lakes and rivers, than can be naturally diluted and carried away.

Whistle-blowing. An employee's disclosure to the public of alleged organizational misconduct, often after futile attempts to convince organizational authorities to take action against the alleged abuse.

White-collar crime. Illegal activities committed by corporate managers, such as embezzlement or fraud.

Women's movement. A social movement for the rights of women.

Workforce diversity. Diversity among employees. (See also *diversity.*)

Workplace safety team. A group of workers and managers who seek to minimize the occurrence of workplace accidents.

World Business Council for Sustainable Development (WBCSD). A group of more than 125 companies from several nations formed in 1995 to encourage high standards of environmental management and to promote cooperation among businesses, governments, and other organizations concerned with sustainable development.

World Trade Organization (WTO). An organization of member nations committed to advancing free trade and open markets in all countries.

Bibliography

Part One *Chapters 1–2*

Academy of Management Review. Special Topic Forum on Shifting Paradigms: Societal Expectations and Corporate Performance, vol. 20, no. 1, January 1995.

Dennis, Lloyd B., ed. *Practical Public Affairs in an Era of Change.* Lanham, MD: Public Relations Society of America and University Press of America, 1996.

Dertouzas, Michael L. *The Next Revolution.* New York: Harper, 2001.

Dertouzas, Michael L.; Richard K. Lester; and Robert M. Solow. *Made in America: Regaining the Productivity Edge.* Cambridge, MA: MIT Press, 1989.

Drucker, Peter. *The New Realities.* New York: Harper and Row, 1989.

Etzioni, Amitai. *The New Golden Rule.* New York: Basic Books, 1996.

———. *The Spirit of Community.* New York: Crown Publishers, 1993.

Frederick, William C. *Values, Nature, and Culture in the American Corporation.* New York: Oxford University Press, 1995.

Freeman, R. Edward. *Strategic Management: A Stakeholder Approach.* Marshfield, MA: Pitman, 1984.

Heath, Robert L., ed. *Strategic Issues Management.* 2d ed. San Francisco, CA: Jossey-Bass, 1996.

Kennedy, Paul. *Preparing for the Twenty-First Century.* New York: Vintage/Random House, 1994.

Kessler, David. *A Question of Intent: A Great American Battle With A Deadly Industry.* New York: Public Affairs, 2001.

Krugman, Paul. *The Age of Diminished Expectations.* Cambridge, MA: MIT Press, 1994.

Post, James E., ed. *Research in Corporate Social Performance and Policy.* "The Corporation and Public Affairs," vol. 14. Greenwich, CT: JAI Press, 1994.

Post, James E.; Lee E. Preston; and Sybille Sachs. *Redefining the Corporation: Stakeholder Management and Organizational Wealth.* Palo Alto, CA: Stanford University Press, 2002.

Putnam, Robert D. *Bowling Alone: The Collapse and Revival of American Community.* New York: Simon and Schuster, 2000.

Werhane, Patricia H. *Adam Smith and His Legacy for Modern Capitalism.* New York: Oxford University Press, 1990.

Wolfe, Alan. *One Nation, after All.* New York: Viking, 1998.

Part Two *Chapters 3–4*

Ackerman, Robert. *The Social Challenge to Business.* Cambridge, MA: Harvard University Press, 1975.

Academy of Management Journal. Special Research Forum on Stakeholders, Social Responsibility, and Performance, vol. 42, no. 5, October 1999.

Bollier, David. *Aiming Higher.* New York: American Management Association, 1996.

Bowen, Howard R. *Responsibilities of the Businessman.* New York: Harper, 1953.

Business and Society Review. Special Issue: Corporate Citizenship, vol. 105, no. 1, Spring 2000.

Chamberlain, Neil W. *The Limits of Corporate Social Responsibility.* New York: Basic Books, 1973.

Clarkson, Max B. E., ed. *The Corporation and Its Stakeholders: Classic and Contemporary Readings.* Toronto: University of Toronto Press, 1998.

Domini, Amy L. *Socially Responsible Investing: Making a Difference and Making Money.* Chicago: Dearborn Trade, 2001.

Forward, David C.; and Richard F. Schubert. *Heroes after Hours: Extraordinary Acts of Employee Volunteerism.* San Francisco: Jossey-Bass, 1994.

Himmelstein, Jerome. *Looking Good and Doing Good.* Bloomington, IN: Indiana University Press, 1997.

Levy, Reynold. *Give and Take: A Candid Account of Corporate Philanthropy.* Cambridge, MA: Harvard Business School, 1999.

McIntosh, Malcolm, et al. *Corporate Citizenship: Successful Strategies for Responsible Companies.* Upper Saddle River, NJ: Prentice Hall, 1998.

Sagawa, Shirley; Eli Segal; and Rosabeth Moss Kanter. *Common Interest, Common Good: Creating Value through Business and Social Sector Partnerships.* Cambridge, MA: Harvard Business School, 1999.

Scott, Mary; and Howard Rothman. *Companies with a Conscience: Intimate Portraits of Twelve Firms That Make a Difference*. New York: Citadel Press Book/Carroll Publishing Group, 1994.

Svendsen, Ann. *The Stakeholder Strategy: Profiting from Collaborative Business Relationships*. San Francisco: Berrett-Koehler, 1998.

Part Three   *Chapters 5–6*

Allegretti, Joseph G. *Loving Your Job, Finding Your Passion: Work and the Spiritual Life*. New York: Paulist Press, 2000.

Cavanaugh, Gerald F. *American Business Values: With an International Perspective*. 4th ed. Englewood Cliffs, NJ: Prentice Hall, 1998.

Ciulla, Joanne B., ed. *Ethics, the Heart of Leadership*. Westport, CT: Quorum Books, 1998.

Colby, Anne; and Lawrence Kohlberg. *The Measurement of Moral Judgment: Volume I, Theoretical Foundations and Research Validations*. Cambridge, MA: Harvard University Press, 1987.

Donaldson, Thomas; and Thomas W. Dunfee. *Ties That Bind: A Social Contracts Approach to Business Ethics*. Cambridge, MA: Harvard Business School Publishing, 1999.

Jackall, Robert. *Moral Mazes: The World of Corporate Managers*. New York: Oxford University Press, 1988.

Kidder, Rushworth M. *How Good People Make Tough Choices*. New York: William Morrow & Co., 1995.

Nash, Laura L. *Believers in Business*. Nashville, TN: Thomas Nelson Publishers, 1994.

Petrick, Joseph A.; and John F. Quinn. *Management Ethics: Integrity at Work*. Thousand Oaks, CA: Sage Publications, 1997.

Rawls, John. *A Theory of Justice*. Cambridge, MA: Harvard University Press, 1971.

Rosenthal, Sandra B.; and A. Rogene Buchholz. *Rethinking Business Ethics: A Pragmatic Approach*. New York: Oxford University Press, 1999.

Sethi, S. P.; and Oliver F. Williams. *Economic Imperatives and Ethical Values in Global Business: The South African Experience and International Codes Today*. Boston/Dordreecht/London: Kluwer, 2000.

Solomon, Robert C. *A Better Way to Think about Business*. New York: Oxford University Press, 1999.

Stone, Christopher D. *Where the Law Ends: The Social Control of Corporate Behavior*. Prospect Heights, IL: Waveland Press, 1975.

Velasquez, Manual G. *Business Ethics: Concepts and Cases*. 4th ed. Upper Saddle River, NJ: Prentice Hall, 1998.

Werhane, Patricia H. *Moral Imagination and Management Decision-Making*. New York: Oxford University Press, 1999.

Werhane, Patricia H.; and R. Edward Freeman. *The Blackwell Encyclopedic Dictionary of Business Ethics*. Malden, MA: Blackwell, 1997.

Part Four   *Chapters 7–9*

Ayres, Ian; and John Braithwaite. *Responsive Regulation: Transcending the Regulation Debate*. New York: Oxford University Press, 1992.

Berry, Jeffrey M. *The Interest Group Society*. Boston: Little, Brown, 1985.

Derber, Charles. *Corporation Nation: How Corporations Are Taking over Our Lives and What We Can Do about It*. New York: St. Martin's Press, 1998.

Dewey, Donald. *The Anti-Trust Experiment in America*. New York: Columbia University Press, 1990.

Epstein, Edwin M. *The Corporation in American Politics*. Englewood Cliffs, NJ: Prentice Hall, 1969.

Fugate, Wilbur L.; assisted by Lee Simowitz. *Foreign Commerce and the Anti-Trust Laws*. 4th ed. Boston: Little, Brown, 1991.

Galambos, Louis; and Joseph Pratt. *The Rise of Corporate Commonwealth: United States Business and Public Policy in the Twentieth Century*. New York: Basic Books, 1988.

Garvey, George E.; and Gerald J. Garvey. *Economic Law and Economic Growth: Anti-Trust, Regulation, and the American Growth System*. New York: Greenwood Press, 1990.

Judis, John B. *The Paradox of American Democracy: Elites, Special Interests, and the Betrayal of the Public Trust*. New York: Pantheon, 2001.

Lipset, Seymour Martin; and William Schneider. *The Confidence Gap: Business, Labor, and Government in the Public Mind*. Baltimore: Johns Hopkins University Press, 1987.

Lodge, George C. *The New American Ideology*. New York: Alfred A. Knopf, 1978.

———. *Comparative Business-Government Relations*. Englewood Cliffs, NJ: Prentice Hall, 1990.

———. *Perestroika for America: Restructuring Business-Government Relations for World Competitiveness*. Boston: Harvard Business School Press, 1990.

Mahon, John F.; and Richard A. McGowan. *Industry as a Player in the Political and Social Arena: Defining the*

Competitive Environment. Westport, CT: Quorum Books, 1996.

Maitland-Walker, Julian, ed. *Toward 1992: The Development of International Anti-Trust*. Oxford, England: ESC Publishing, 1989.

Marcus, Alfred A.; Allen M. Kaufman; and David R. Beam. *Business Strategy and Public Policy: Perspectives from Industry and Academia*. Westport, CT: Quorum Books, 1987.

McGowan, Richard. *State Lotteries and Legalized Gambling: Painless Revenue or Painful Mirage*. Westport, CT: Quorum Books, 1994.

———. *Business, Politics, and Cigarettes: Multiple Levels, Multiple Agendas*. Westport, CT: Quorum Books, 1995.

———. *Government Regulation of the Alcohol Industry: The Search for Revenue and the Common Good*. Westport, CT: Quorum Books, 1997.

Porter, Michael. *The Competitive Advantage of Nations*. New York: Basic Books, 1991.

Reich, Robert B. *The Work of Nations*. New York: Free Press, 1991.

Reich, Robert B., ed. *The Power of Public Ideas*. Cambridge, MA: Ballinger, 1988.

Scherer, F. M. *Competition Policies for an Integrated World Economy*. Washington, DC: The Brookings Institution, 1994.

Schier, Steven E. *By Invitation Only: The Rise of Exclusive Politics in the United States*. Pittsburgh, PA: University of Pittsburgh Press, 2000.

Vietor, Richard H. K. *Strategic Management in the Regulatory Environment*. Englewood Cliffs, NJ: Prentice Hall, 1989.

Vogel, David. *Kindred Strangers: The Uneasy Relationship between Politics and Business in America*. Princeton, NJ: Princeton University Press, 1996.

Weidenbaum, Murray. *Business, Government and the Public*. 4th ed. Englewood Cliffs, NJ: Prentice Hall, 1990.

Wolf, Charles. *Markets or Government: Choosing between Imperfect Alternatives*. Cambridge, MA: MIT Press, 1988.

Part Five   *Chapters 10–11*

Anderson, Ray C. *Mid-Course Correction: Toward a Sustainable Enterprise*. Atlanta, GA: Peregrinzilla Press, 1998.

Arnold, Matthew B; and Robert M. Day. *The Next Bottom Line: Making Sustainable Development Tangible*. Washington, DC: World Resources Institute, 1998.

Brown, Lester R., et al., eds. *State of the World 2000*. New York: W.W. Norton, 2000.

Collins, Denis; and Mark Starik, eds. *Research in Corporate Social Performance and Policy*. "Sustaining the Natural Environment: Empirical Studies on the Interface between Nature and Organizations," vol. 15, supp. 1. Greenwich, CT: JAI Press, 1995.

Daly, Herman E. *Beyond Growth: The Economics of Sustainable Development*. Boston: Beacon Press, 1996.

Easterbrook, Gregg. *A Moment on the Earth: The Coming Age of Environmental Optimism*. New York: Viking, 1995.

Ehrlich, Paul R.; and Anne H. Ehrlich. *The Population Explosion*. New York: Simon & Schuster, 1990.

Fischer, Kurt; and Johan Schot, eds. *Environmental Strategies for Industry: International Perspectives on Research Needs and Policy Implications*. Washington, DC: Island Press, 1993.

Foreman, Christopher H., Jr. *The Promise and Perils of Environmental Justice*. Washington, DC: The Brookings Institution, 2000.

Frankel, Carl. *In Earth's Company: Business, Environment, and the Challenge of Sustainability*. Gabriola Island, British Columbia: New Society Publishers, 1998.

Friedman, Frank B. *Practical Guide to Environmental Management*. 8th ed. Washington, DC: Environmental Law Institute, 2000.

Gore, Al. *Earth in the Balance: Ecology and the Human Spirit*. Boston, MA: Houghton Mifflin, 1992.

Hammond, Allen. *Which World? Scenarios for the Twenty-First Century*. Washington, DC: Island Press, 1998.

Hawken, Paul; Amory Lovins; and L. Hunter Lovins. *Natural Capitalism: Creating the Next Industrial Revolution*. Boston: Little Brown, 1999.

Hertsgaard, Mark. *Earth Odyssey: Around the World in Search of Our Environmental Future*. New York: Broadway Books, 1998.

Hoffman, Andrew J. *Competitive Environmental Strategy: A Guide to the Changing Business Landscape*. Washington, DC: Island Press, 2000.

Hoffman, Andrew J., ed. *Global Climate Change: A Senior Level Debate at the Intersection of Economics, Strategy, Technology, Science, Politics, and International Negotiations*. San Francisco: New Lexington Press, 1997.

Hoffman, W. Michael; Robert Frederick; and Edward S. Petry, eds. *The Corporation, Ethics and the Environment*. Westport, CT: Quorum Books, 1990.

Mann, Charles C.; and Mark L. Plummer. *Noah's Choice: The Future of Endangered Species*. New York: Alfred A. Knopf, 1995.

Nattrass, Brian; and Mary Altomare. *The Natural Step for Business: Wealth, Ecology and the Evolutionary Corporation.* Gabriola Island, British Columbia: New Society Publishers, 1999.

Poltorzycki, Steven. *Bringing Sustainable Development Down to Earth.* New York: Arthur D. Little, 1998.

Postel, Sandra. *Pillar of Sand.* New York: W.W. Norton, 1999.

Schmidheiny, Stephan. *Changing Course: A Global Perspective on Development and the Environment.* Cambridge, MA: MIT Press, 1992.

Stead, W. Edward; and Jean Garner Stead. *Management for a Small Planet.* Newbury Park, CA: Sage Publications, 1992.

Stone, Christopher. *The Gnat is Older than Man: Global Environment and Human Agenda.* Princeton, NJ: Princeton University Press, 1993.

Part Six *Chapters 12–13*

Barbour, Ian G. *Ethics in an Age of Technology.* San Francisco: Harper, 1993.

Brin, David. *The Transparent Society.* Reading, MA: Addison-Wesley, 1998.

Castells, Manuel. *The Rise of the Network Society.* Malden, MA: Blackwell, 2000.

Compaine, Benjamin M. *The Digital Divide Companion: Facing a Crisis or Creating a Myth?* Cambridge, MA: MIT Press, 2001.

Davies, Kevin. *Cracking the Genome: Inside the Race to Unlock Human DNA.* New York: Free Press, 2001.

Dhillon, Gurpreet, ed. *Information Security Management: Global Challenges in the New Millennium.* Hershey, PA: Idea Group Publishing, 2001.

Dorf, Richard C. *Technology, Humans, and Society: Toward a Sustainable World.* San Diego: Academic Press, 2001.

Hawkes, Nigel. *Genetically Modified Foods (Saving Our World).* Brookfield, CT: Millbrook Press, 2000.

Heinberg, Richard. *Cloning the Buddha: The Moral Impact of Biotechnology.* San Juan Capistrano, CA: Quest Books, 1999.

Johnson, Steven. *Interface Culture: How New Technology Transforms the Way We Create and Communicate.* New York: Basic Books, 1999.

Kass, Leon R.; and James Q. Wilson. *The Ethics of Human Cloning.* Washington, DC: AEI Press, 1998.

Lane, Frederick S. *Obscene Profits: The Entrepreneurs of Pornography in the Cyber Age.* London: Routledge, 1999.

Mannion, Michael. *Frankenstein Foods: Genetically Modified Foods and Your Health.* London: Welcome Rain, 2001.

McHughen, Alan. *Pandora's Picnic Basket: The Potential and Hazards of Genetically Modified Foods.* New York: Oxford University Press, 2000.

Nichols, Randall K.; Daniel J. Ryan; and Julie J. C. H. Ryan. *Defending Your Digital Assets against Hackers, Crackers, Spies, and Thieves.* New York: McGraw-Hill, 1999.

Reich, Robert B. *The Future of Success.* New York: Knopf, 2001.

Reiss, Michael J. *Improving Nature? The Science and Ethics of Genetic Engineering.* New York: Cambridge University Press, 1996.

Zilinskas, Raymond A.; and Peter J. Balint, eds. *The Human Genome Project and Minority Communities: Ethical, Social, and Political Dilemmas.* Westport, CT: Prager, 2000.

Part Seven *Chapters 14–17*

Blair, Margaret M. *Ownership and Control: Rethinking Corporate Governance for the Twenty-First Century.* Washington, DC: The Brookings Institution, 1995.

Brancato, Carolyn Kay. *Institutional Investors and Corporate Governance: Best Practices for Increasing Corporate Value.* Burr Ridge, IL: Irwin Professional, 1996.

Crystal, Graef S.; Ira T. Kay; and Frederic W. Cook. *CEO Pay: A Comprehensive Look.* New York: American Compensation Association, 1997.

Jennings, Marianne. *The Board of Directors: 25 Keys to Corporate Governance.* New York: Lebhar-Friedman Books, 2000.

Lorsch, Jay William. *Pawns or Potentates: The Reality of America's Corporate Boards.* Boston: Harvard Business School Press, 1989.

Monks, Robert A. G. *The Emperor's Nightingale: Restoring the Integrity of the Corporation in the Age of Shareholder Activism.* Reading, MA: Addison-Wesley, 1998.

Monks, Robert A. G.; and Nell Minow. *Watching the Watchers: Corporate Governance for the Twenty-First Century.* Oxford: Blackwell Publishers, 1996.

Rubach, Michael J. *Institutional Shareholder Activism: The Changing Face of Corporate Ownership.* New York: Garland Publishers, 1999.

Useem, Michael. *Investor Capitalism: How Money Managers Are Changing the Face of Corporate America.* New York: Basic Books, 1996.

Van Den Berghe, L.; and Liesbeth DeRidder. *International Standardisation of Good Corporate Governance: Best Practices for the Board of Directors.* Dordrecht, The Netherlands: Kluwer Academic Publishers, 1999.

Varley, Pamela, ed. *The Sweatshop Quandary: Corporate Responsibility on the Global Frontier.* Washington, DC: Investor Responsibility Research Center, 1998.

Whitman, Marina, V. N. *New World, New Rules: The Changing Role of the American Corporation.* Boston: Harvard Business School Press, 1999.

Part Eight   *Chapters 18–20*

Alder, Nancy; and Dafna N. Israeli, eds. *Competitive Frontiers: Women Managers in the Global Economy.* Cambridge, MA: Basil Blackwell, 1995.

Caplan, Lincoln. *Up Against the Law: Affirmative Action and the Supreme Court.* New York: Twentieth Century Fund Press, 1997.

Edley, Christopher F. *Not All Black and White: Affirmative Action, Race and American Values.* New York: Hill and Wang, 1996.

Elkington, John. *Cannibals with Forks: The Triple Bottom Line of Twenty-First Century Business.* London: Thompson, 1997.

Fagenson, Ellen A., ed. *Women in Management: Trends, Issues, and Challenges in Management Diversity.* Newbury Park, CA: Sage, 1993.

Faludi, Susan. *Backlash: The Undeclared War against American Women.* New York: Doubleday, 1991.

Fombrun, Charles. *Reputation.* Boston: Harvard Business School Press, 1996.

Friedman, Thomas L. *The Lexus and the Olive Tree.* New York: Anchor Books, 2000.

Goldin, Claudia. *Understanding the Gender Gap: An Economic History of American Women.* New York: Oxford University Press, 1990.

Hattiangadi, Anita U. *The Changing Face of the Twenty-First Century Workforce: Trends in Ethnicity, Race, Age, and Gender.* Washington, DC: Employment Policy Foundation, 1998.

Hudson Institute. *Workforce 2020: Work and Workers in the Twenty-First Century.* Indianapolis: Hudson Institute, 1999.

Kaplan, Robert; and David Norton. *The Balanced Scorecard.* Boston: Harvard Business School Press, 1996.

Kennedy, Paul. *The Rise and Fall of the Great Powers.* New York: Random House, 1987.

Kidder, Rushworth M. *How Good People Make Tough Choices.* New York: William Morrow & Co., 1995.

Kittrie, Nicholas N. *The War against Authority: From the Crisis of Legitimacy to a New Social Contract.* Baltimore, MD: Johns Hopkins University Press, 1995.

Korten, David. *When Corporations Ruled the World.* San Francisco, CA: Berrett-Kochler, 1996.

Leana, Carrie; and Denise Rousseau, eds. *Relational Capital.* New York: Oxford University Press, 2000.

Levine, Marvin J. *Worker Rights and Labor Standards in Asia's Four New Tigers: A Comparative Perspective.* New York: Plenum Press, 1997.

Loden, Marilyn. *Implementing Diversity.* New York: McGraw-Hill, 1995.

Massie, Robert Kinloch. *Loosing the Bonds.* New York: Doubleday, 1998.

Morrison, Ann M.; Randall P. White; and Ellen Van Velsor. *Breaking the Glass Ceiling: Can Women Reach the Top of America's Largest Corporations?* Updated ed. Reading, MA: Addison-Wesley, 1992.

Post, James E. *Managing the Challenge of Global Corporate Citizenship.* Policy Paper Series. Chestnut Hill, MA: Boston College Center for Corporate Community Relations, 1999. (Available through the Center website at www.bc.edu/cccr.)

Powell, Gary N. *Women and Men in Management.* 2d ed. Newbury Park, CA: Sage Publications, 1993.

Rosen, Jeffrey. *The Unwanted Gaze: The Destruction of Privacy in America.* New York: Random House, 2000.

Sethi, S. P.; and Oliver F. Williams. *Economic Imperatives and Ethical Values in Global Business: The South African Experience and International Codes Today.* Boston/ Dordreecht/London: Kluwer, 2000.

Sonnenshein, William. *The Diversity Toolkit.* Chicago: Contemporary Books, 1997.

Tavis, Lee. *Power and Responsibility: Multinational Managers and Developing Country Concerns.* South Bend, IN: University of Notre Dame Press, 1997.

Tichy, Noel M.; Andy R. McGill; and Linda St. Clair. *Global Corporate Citizenship: Doing Business in the Public Eye.* San Francisco: New Lexington Press, 1997.

Waddock, Sandra. *Leading Corporate Citizens: Meeting the Business in Society Challenge.* New York: McGraw-Hill, 2002.

Williams, Oliver F., ed. *Global Codes of Conduct: An Idea Whose Time Has Come.* South Bend, IN: University of Notre Dame Press, 2000.

Name Index

A

Abacha, General Sami, 584, 589-591
Abrams, Frank W., 63n
Ackerman, Frank, (exh.) 265n
Ackerman, Robert W., (fig.) 84, 85n
Adams, W., 237n
Agle, Bradley R., 70n
Ake, Claude, 590
Akers, John, (exh.) 9
Albrecht, W. Steve, 121
Allen, Lisa Wimberly, 487n
Allen, Paul, (exh.) 90
Alsop, Ronald, (exh.) 294n
Altman, Barbara W., 81n, 384n, 410n
Altomare, Mary, (exh.) 238n
Anderson, Brian, 589
Anderson, Carol, 535n
Anderson, John, 194
Anderson, Sarah, 345n
Anderson, Ray C., 275, 275n
Andreas, Dwayne, 349-350
Andreas, G. Allen 350
Andreesen, Mark, 549
Andrews, Edmund, 19n
Annan, Kofi, 19, 499, 501
Anneken, Kathleen, 564
Aquinas, Thomas, 129
Aristotle, 128, 129
Armstrong, Susan J., (exh.) 249n
Arnold, Matthew B., 253n, 277n
Arrow, Kenneth, 243n
Auletta, Ken, 546n
Auster, Ellen R., (fig.) 274n
Avolio, Bruce J., 128n

B

Bagdikian, Ben, 231
Bahrenberg, Jeff, 291
Baird, Bruce, 518
Baker, Norman, 322
Bansal, Pratima, 274n
Baralengwa, Edward, 80
Barbakow, Jeffrey, 534
Barksdale, James, 346
Barnes, Deborah A., 535n

Baron, Barnett, 74n
Baskin, Roberta, 575
Bassett, Bonnie, 504
Bauer, Raymond A., (fig.) 84
Baum, B., 403n
Beam, Henry H., 227n
Bear, Larry Alan, 109n
Beauchamp, Tom L., 113n
Becker, Regis, 149n
Becklund, L., 568n
Bell, George, 230
Bell, Griffin B., 568
Bell, Rodger, 53
Bender, Joyce, 57
Bentley, Zachary, 115
Berenbeim, Ronald C., 140n, 142n
Berger, Samual R., 486n
Berman, Steven, 35
Bero, Lisa A., 535n
Bhat, Rishi, 290n
Bigalke, John, 523n
Blair, Margaret M., 338n
Blanch, Paul, 115
Blomstrom, Robert, 60n
Bluestone, Barry, 368n
Bluestone, Irving, 368n
Boatright, John R., 109n, 136n
Boggs, Carl, 214n
Boone, Rolf, 24n
Botzler, Richard G., (exh.) 249n
Bowe, Gerald, 77
Bowen, Howard R., 61n, 93n
Bowerman, Bill, 570, 571
Bowie, Norman E., 113n
Bradbury, Hilary, (exh.) 238n
Brancato, Carolyn Kay, 338n
Brinkley, Joel, 546n
Briscoe, Forrest, 275n
Brockovich, Erin, 14, 453
Broder, David S., 41n, 193n, 202n
Brooks, Leonard J., 107n
Brown, Lester R., 236n
Brownstein, Andrew, 345n
Bruni, Frank 396n
Bruyn, Severyn T, 17n

Bryant, Bunyan, 264n
Buchanan, Pat, 194
Buchholz, Rogene A., 129n
Buffett, Warren, 538
Bulkeley, William M., (fig.) 297n
Bullock, Ken, 521
Burke, Edmund M., (fig.) 376n
Burke, James E., 468
Burnett, Jason K., 156n
Bush, George, 175, 194, 396, 396n, 488
Bush, George W., 161, 194, 198, 497, 497n, 499, 547

C

Cantoni, Craig, 57
Cantrell, Calvin, 311
Carlton, Phil, 535
Carnegie, Andrew, 60, 62
Carney, James, 220
Carroll, Archie B., 86n
Carter, Jimmy, 175, 194, 396
Casabona, Patrick, (fig.) 311n
Case, Jean, 300
Case, Stephen M., 230, 300, 375
Caton, Greg, 323
Cauvin, Henri E., 476n
Chase, Brad, 551
Chavez, Cesar, 38
Chen, Zhangliang, 323
Chonko, Lawrence B., 111n
Clair, Judith A., (exh.) 238n
Clark, James, 549
Clark, Jr., Lindley H., 22n
Clemens, Will, 285
Clinton, William, 161, 194, 200, 311, 313, 314, 388, 396, 547, 576-577
Coalter, Terry, 128n
Cobb, Roger, 189, 189n, 190n
Cochran, Philip L., (fig.) 139n
Colby, Anne, 132n
Cole, George, 484n
Coleman, Robin, (exh.) 386
Connerly, Ward, 440n
Cook, Frederic W., 344n
Correy, Paul, 76

Corrothers, Andra L., 74n
Corzine, John, 198
Cotter, Bill, 77
Cotter, Nancy, 77
Crystal, Graef S., 344, 344n
Cullen, John B., (fig.) 133n
Cusumano, Michael A., 546n

D

Daft, Douglas, 451
D'Allesandro, David, 522
Dalton, Dan R., 105n, 416n
Daly, Herman E., 243n
D'Amico, Carol, 430n
Dangel, Justin, (exh.) 201
Davenport, Kim, (exh.) 82, 94, 94n
Davis, Keith, 60n
Day, Robert M., 253n
Deal, Terrence E., 133n
DeButts, John, 10, 10n
DeGeorge, Richard T., 120n, 419n
Dell'Apa, Frank, 219n
Denton, Elizabeth, 130n
DePalma, Anthony, 476n
Derber, Charles, 213n
De Ridder, Liesbeth, 342n
Dertouzos, M., 163n
Deshpande, Satish P., 128n
Detheridge, Alan, 580
Deyin, An, 323
Dietz, Tracy L., 457n
Dill, William, 10n
Dinin, Paul, 290n
Dole, Robert, 543
Donaldson, Thomas, 8n, 16n, 120, 120n
Donovan, Jim, (exh.) 386
Dowd, Maureen, 46n
Druge, Matt, 200
Dunfee, Thomas, 16n

E

Easterbrook, Gregg, 243n
Edelman, Marion Wright, 38
Edelman, Murray, 189, 189n
Eichenwald, Kurt, 531, 533
Eisner, Robert, 167n
Eitel, Maria S., 576
Elkington, John, 495, 495n, 600
Ellos, SJ, William J., 120n
Ells, Richard, 63n
Engberg, Karen, 435n
Epstein, Edwin, 187n, 214n
Erdener, Carolyn B., 128n
Erickson, Scott, 294
Ermann, M. David, 112n

Eron, Leonard, 458
Essomba, Rene, 515
Essomba, Sonia, 515
Estes, Ralph, 345n
Etzioni, Amitai, 5n
Evans, Paul, 499
Evenett, Simon J., 229n

F

Fackler, Martin, 483n
Fahey, Liam, 32n
Falbe, Cecilia M., 71n
Fanning, Shawn, 324
Feuerstein, Aaron, 10, 76-78
Fienberg, Bob, 469n
Fiet, James O., 127n
Flavin, Christopher, 236n
Fogerty, Patricia, (exh.) 390
Fombrun, Charles J., 18n, 493n
Forbes, Steve, 198
Ford, Gerald, 396
Ford, Henry, 61, 153
Ford, II, Henry, 153
Ford, William Clay, 153, 278, 278n, 343n, 473
Foreman, Christopher H., 264n
Frank, Robert H., 230
Frankel, Martin 113
Frederick, William C., 8n, 93n, (fig.) 119n, 179n
Freeman, R. Edward, 8n, 63n
Friedan, Betty, 38
Friedman, Frank B., 270n
Friedman, Milton, 22, 22n, 67n, 68n
Friedman, Thomas, (fig.) 480n, 480n
Frist, Jr., Thomas F., 534
Frohnmayer, David, 580
Frooman, Jeff, 70n
Furdyk, Michael, 290
Fussler, Claude, 251n

G

Gaebler, Ted, 177n
Galambos, Louis, 154n, 216n
Galef, Barry, 272n
Galvin, Christopher B., 477
Ganga, Jean-Claude, 519-520
Garff, Robert, 521
Garnett, Laurie, 164n
Gates, Bill, (exh.) 90, 293, 548-557
Gates, Melinda, (exh.) 90
Gee, E. Preston, 523n
Geesink, Anton, 519
Gelbspan, Ross, (exh.) 248n
George, Elizabeth, 128n

Gerstner, Jr., Louis V., (exh.) 9, 345, 375, 375n, 387
Getz, Kathleen A., (fig.) 119n, 179n
Gibeaut, John, (exh.) 367n
Gillespie, Janet, 132n
Gineste, Isabelle, 322
Gingrich, Newt, 38, 194, 200
Glantz, Stanton E., 535n, 542
Glaser, Rob, 301
Goldrich, Sybil, 564
Goldstone, Steven F., 544
Goodstein, Laurie, 396n
Googins, Bradley K., 83n, 384n, 398n
Gorbachev, Mikhail, 21
Gordon, Robert A., 338n
Gore, Al, 177n, 194, 198, (exh.) 461
Gorlin, Rena A., 140n
Goss, Martha Clark, 140
Gould, Edwin, 306
Goyder, George, 93, 93n
Grabowski, Gene, 322
Grant, Kenneth, 272n
Graves, Samuel B., 332n
Gray, Rob, 93n
Greco, Samuel A., 525
Greenfield, Karl Taro, (exh.) 90n
Griffin, Jennifer J., 41n, (exh.) 42, 70n, 378n
Griffin, Patricia, 514
Grode, George, 388
Grossman, Woodrin, 523n
Guerard, Jr., John B., 332n
Guirandou-N'Diaye, Louis, 519

H

Haggerty, Mike, 470n
Hahn, Robert W., 156n
Hamanaka, Yasuo, 104
Hamilton, Suzy, 458
Hammond, Allen, 243n
Hanauer, Peter, 535n
Hanifan, L.J., 377n
Hanson, Kirk, 94
Hardin, Garrett, 236n
Harp-McGovern, Lore, (exh.) 90
Harrison, Jeffrey S., 127n
Hart, Stuart L., 279n
Hartzel, Kathleen, 303n
Haseltine, William A., 319
Hast, Adele, 579n
Hattiangadi, Anita U., 429n
Hawken, Paul, 243n
Hawkins, Gregory J., 310
Hayibor, Sefa, 70n
Heald, Morrell, 61n
Heilemann, John, 546n

Helsin, Sheila N., 21n
Herkstroter, Cor, 591, 596, 599, 601
Hershman, Michael J., (exh.) 118n
Hertsgaard, Mark, 242n
Herzlinger, Regina, 523n
Hill, John W., 105n
Hilts, Philip J., 417n, 535n, 566
Hindrey, Leo, 314
Hodler, Marc, 515
Hoffman, Andrew J., 23n, 246n
Hoffman, W. Michael, 142
Hofmeister, Sallie, 400n
Hogarth, Meg, (exh.) 455n
Hopkins, Mariann, 564
Hosmer, LaRue Tone, 101n
Houck, John W., 17n, 410n
Howell, Jane M., 128n
Hoy, Frank, 86n
Hubka, Rachel, 86
Huffington, Michael, 198
Hughes, Catherine, 436
Hunt, Christopher B., (fig.) 274n
Huntsman, John, (exh.) 90
Huus, Kari, 256n
Hyde, Henry, 458

I

Ingram, Martha R., (exh.) 90
Ivester, M. Douglas, 450-451
Izraeli, Dove, 105n

J

Jackson, Jesse, 389
Jackson, Thomas Penfield, 548-557
Jacob, Mark, 306
Jaffe, Adam B., 272n
Jager, Durk, 329
Jennings, Marianne, 57, 335n
Janofsky, Michael, 400n
Jensen, Michael C., 337n, 345n
Jeurissen, R.J.M., 128n
Jobs, Steve, 507
Johnson, Cameron, 290n
Johnson, Dave, 519, 521
Johnson, Haynes, 41n, 193n, 202n
Johnson, Michael O., 467
Joseph, Joshua, 106n, 139n, 146n
Josephson, Matthew, 61n
Joy, Bill, 286n, 305, 305n, 306, 318, 318n
Judy, Richard W., 430n

K

Kahn, R., 163n
Kaikati, Jack G., 117n
Kaizaki, Yoichiro, 472-473

Kalleberg, Arne L., 436n
Kaltenheuser, Skip, (exh.) 118n
Kaplan, Robert, 495n
Kapp, Jack, 400
Karras, Nolan, 518
Katz, D.R., 568n
Kay, Ira T., 344n
Kelly, Aundrea, (exh.) 248n
Kelly, Pat, 124
Kelvie, William E., 312
Kennedy, Allan A., 133n
Kernisky, Debra A., 468, 468n
Kessler, David, 535n, 539, 542, 546-547,
    565-566, 569
Kidd, Dusty, 576
Kile, Daniel, 144
Kimmelman, Gene, 231
King, Andrew A., 277n
King, Larry, 200
King, Jr., Martin Luther, 38
Klein, Jerry, 460
Knight, Philip H., 570-571, 574-577
Kohlberg, Lawrence, (fig.) 131n, 132n
Koogle, Timothy, 336
Koppel, Seth, 124
Koppel, Ted, 199-200
Korten, David C., 60n, 214n, (fig.) 480n
Krigsner, Miguel, (exh.) 491
Kurschner, Dale, 105n
Kuttner, Robert, 406n

L

Labaton, Stephen, (exh.) 171n
Laczniak, Gene R., 111n
Lagomasino, Maria Elena, 442
Lake, Robert, 182-183
Lampe, John, 472-473
Larson, Andrea, (exh.) 238n
Lawrence, Anne T., 275n, 504n, 523n,
    535n, 546n, 556n, 568n, 580n,
    591n
LeBow, Bennett, 538, 543
Lee, Pamela, 313
Leicht, Kevin T., 436n
Lenox, Michael J., 277n
Lenway, Stefanie, 163n
Leopold, Aldo, (exh.) 249
Lepore, Dawn, 312
Lerner, Michael, 189n
Lester, R., 163n
Levin, Gerald, 375
Levy, David L., (exh.) 248n
Lewinsky, Monica, 200
Li, Cheng, 128n
Liebig, James E., 63n

Limbaugh, Rush, 200
Lindsey, Bruce, 543
Little, Arthur D., 253n
Lodge, George, 154n
Lodin, Marilyn, 429n
Logan David, 384n
Lohr, Steve, 23n, 546n
Long, Frederick J., 277n
Lovins, Amory, 243n
Lovins, L. Hunter, 243n
Ludington, John S., 568
Lutz, Sandy, 523n

M

Mace, Myles, 338n
Mahon, John F., 70n, 190, (fig.) 190n,
    191n
Mainiero, Lisa A., 444n
Makower, Joel, 278n
Maldonado-Bear, Rita, 109n
Mandela, Nelson, 594
Manning, David, 532
Marcus, Alfred, 275n
Markovitz, Mark, 126
Matthews, Chris, 22
Matthews, Jessica, 481
Maxwell, James, 275n
Mayhew, David, 194n
Mazur, Jay, 578
McCain, John, 38
McCarthy, Brian, 121
McGill, Andy R., 489n, 490n
McGovern, Patrick J., (exh.) 90
McGowan, Richard A., 37n, 169n, 190,
    (fig.) 190n, 191n
McKaughan, Molly, 380n
McKennon, Keith R., 558-559, 568-569
Meadows, Dennis L., 243n
Meadows, Donella, 243, 243n
Meares, Richard, (exh.) 222n
Metzger, Michael B., 105n, 416n
Mfume, Kweisi, 456
Miles, Robert, 87, 87n
Miller, Robert Steve, 145
Milman, Claudio, 128n
Minow, Nell, 340n
Mirvis, Philip H. 596-597
Mitchell, George, 522
Mitnick, Barry M., 202n
Mitroff, Ian, 130n, (fig.) 469n
Moeller, Albert, 144
Monks, Robert, A.G., 340, 340n
Moody-Stuart, Mark, 597, 600, 602
Moore, Mike, 536
Moorthy, R.S., 120n

Moran, Jon, (exh.) 118n
Morrell, David, 275n
Morris, Dave, 52-54
Morris, Rebecca J., 568n
Morrison, Ann M., 435n
Moseley, Ray, 54n
Moynihan, Patrick, 154
Mujica, Amanda, 296n
Mukora, Charles Nderitu, 519
Murphy, Kevin J., 345n
Murphy, Patrick E., 111n, 140n
Murray, John D., 458, 458n
Myers, Matthew, 544
Myerson, Allen R., (exh.) 390n

N

Nader, Ralph, 38, 38n, 81, 194, 356, 356n
Naess, Arne, (exh.) 249
Narayanan, V.K., 32n
Nash, Roderick, (exh.) 249n
Nasser, Jacques, 375, 473
Nattrass, Brian, (exh.) 238n
Nava, Tony, 576
Neal, Alfred C., 214n
Nerland, Rick, 518
Neukom, William, 554
Newman, Paul, 63
Nightingale, Jennifer, 303n
Norton, David, 495n
Novak, Michael, 62n
Nunes, Maria de Lourdes, (exh.) 492n

O

O'Bannon, Douglas P., 70n
O'Boyle, Thomas F., 126n
Ogden, Brad, 290n
Okuntimo, Paul, 589-590
Olson, Elizabeth, 500n
Ono, Masatoshi, 472-473
Oreskes, Michael, (fig.) 206n
O'Rourke, Ray, 468n
Osborne, David, 177n
O'Toole, James, 93n

P

Packard, Vance (exh.) 461
Paine, Lynn, (exh.) 141, 141n
Panner, Morris J., 345n
Parente, Steven E., 166n
Peace, A. Graham, 303n
Percy, Gerry, 504
Perlmutter, Felice Davidson, 388n
Perot, Ross, 194, 198
Petersen, George, 398n

Peterson, Steven R., 272n
Petry, Edward, 296n
Phillips, David, 458
Plastrik, Peter, 177n
Poltorzycki, Steven, 254n
Porter, Michael E., 279n
Portney, Paul R., 272n
Post, James E., 10n, 17n, 21n, 38n, 41n, (exh.) 42, 51n, 179n, 203n, 378n, 410n, 489n, (exh.) 490n, (fig.) 494n
Postal, Sandra, 239n
Pound, Dick, 518, 521
Powell, Colin, 396, 396n
Powers, Dennis M., 413n
Pratt, Joseph, 154n, 216n
Preijono, Onny, 74n
Preston, Lee E., 8n, 10n, 17n, 21n, 38n, 51n, 70n, 93n
Priem, Richard, 128n
Putin, Vladmiri, 21
Putman, Robert D., 5n, 187n, 193, 193n, 377, 377n

R

Rabe, Barry G., 267n
Rainwater, Darla Moore, 534
Rainwater, Richard, 525-527, 534
Rampton, Richard, 53
Ramus, Catherine A., 276n
Randers, Jorgen, 243n
Rands, Gordon P., 275n
Rappaport, Alfred, (exh.) 72
Rasmussen, Wallace, 470n
Rather, Dan, 575
Reagan, Ronald, 175, 192, 194, 396
Reed, Lawrence, A., 568
Rehbein, Kathleen, 94n, 163n
Reihart, Joel E., (exh.) 238n
Reiner, Gary, 312
Repetto, Robert C., 251n
Revkin, Andrew, 15n
Rifkin, Jeremy, 250n
Roback, Steven, 484n
Robert, Karl-Henrik, (exh.) 238
Roberts, Julia, 14, 453
Robertson, Pat, 314
Robertson, Tim, 314
Rochlin, Steven A., 83n, 384n, 398n
Rochow, Eugene G., 556n
Rockefeller, John D., 62
Roddick, Anita, 18, 18n, 594-595
Rolston, Holmes, (exh.) 249
Roman, Ronald M., 70n

Romero, Simon, 477n
Rosen, Jeffrey, 353n
Rosenthal, Sandra B., 129n
Rosler, Lora, (exh.) 381n
Ross, Marc Howard, 189, 189n, 190n
Roth, Kendall, 274n
Rothenberg, Sandra, 275n
Rubach, Michael J., 340n
Rubin, David, 231
Rubin, Robert, 389
Runyan, Curtis, 481n

S

Sachs, Sybille, 10n, 17n, 21n, 38n, 51n
Salisbury, Lois, 456
Salop, Steven, 555
Samaranch, Juan Antonio, 516-517, 521
Samuel, Marcus, 582
Samuelson, Robert J., 17n
Santander, Sergio, 519
Saponara, Anthony, 279n
Saro-Wiwa, Ken, 581-592, 594, 601
Schattschneider, E.E., 189, 189n
Schlesinger, Arthur M., 193n
Schmidheiny, Stephan, 251n, 254n
Schmidt, Eric, 555
Schwartz, Ann, (exh.) 92
Schwartz, Mark, 105n
Scott, Richard L., 524-535
Seger, Julie E., 515n
Sethi, S. Prakash, 71n 179n
Sever, Joy, (exh.) 294
Sharfman, Mark, 392n
Shauf, Michele S., 112n
Shepard, Jon M., 74n
Shigeta, Yasumitsu, 293
Shiva, Vandana, 499
Shortliffe, Edward H., 163n
Shrivastava, Paul, 275n, (fig.) 469n
Sikora, Michael, 225n
Singer, Andrew W., 143n, 144n, 145n
Singer, Mark E., 529
Slade, John, 535n
Slovik, Peter, 312
Smith, Craig, (exh.) 390n, 483n
Socolow, R.H., 253n
Solomon, Robert C., 120n, 129n
Solow, Robert, 163n, 243n
Sommer, Ron, 297
Son, Masayoshi, 293
Sonnenschein, William, 443n
Soros, George, (exh.) 90
Sotira, Angelo, 290n
Sparrow, Malcolm K., 523n

Sperry, Laura, 144n
Spinello, Richard, 112n
Spitzner, Lance, 312
Stahl, Jack, 450
Starik, Mark, 275n
Starks, L., 156n
Starr, Kenneth, 200
Starr, Paul, 166n
Stasch, Julia, 92
Stavins, Robert N., 272n
St. Clair, Linda, 489n, 490n
Steel, Helen, 52-54
Steele, Shelby, 440n
Steger, Ulrich, 276n
Steinem, Gloria, 38
Stella, Mary Anne, 375
Steltenpohl, Greg, 504-514
Stevens, Betsy, 140n
Stowers, Jr., James E., (exh.) 90
Stowers, Virginia, (exh.) 90
Strasser, J.B., 568n
Sullivan, Leon, 119
Sundblad, Dana, 398n
Suryatna, Estie W., 74n

T

Tagliabue, John, 484n, (exh.) 485n
Talner, Lauren, 342n
Tavis, Lee A., 483n
Taylor, Dave, 575
Tetlock, Paul C., 156n
Textor, Robert B., 120n
Thomas, Tom, 203n, 204
Tichy, Noel M., 489n, 490n
Tillman, Audis, 392n
Tisch, Laurence, 536
Tisch, Robert, 536
Toffler, Alvin, 286n
Travolta, John, 13
Trevino, Linda Klebe, (fig.) 139n, 141n

Truell, Peter, 389n
Turner, Ted, (exh.) 90

U

Udwadia, Firdaus E., (fig.) 469n
Useem, Michael, 340n

V

Valenti, Jack, 458
Van Den Berghe, L., 342n
Vanderbilt, T., 568n
van der Linde, Claas, 279n
Vandewater, David, 528
van Luijk, H.J.L., 128n
Van Velsor, Ellen, 435n
Velasquez, Manual G., 129n, 136n
Venter, J. Craig, 321
Verschoor, Curtis C., 105n
Vickery, Dianne, 296n
Victor, Bart, (fig.) 133n
Vidal, John, 54n
Vidaver-Cohen, Deborah, 81n
Vitousek, P.M., 236n
Vogel, David, 342n
Votaw, Dow, 214n

W

Waddock, Sandra, 332n
Wallach, Lori, 500
Walsh, Ekaterina, 300
Walters, Bruce, 128n
Walton, Clarence C., 66n, 129, 129n
Walton, Sam, 383
Ware, Carl, 450
Warren, Kim, 518
Warren, Melinda, 174n
Watson, Jr., Thomas J., (exh.) 9
Watson, Sr., Thomas J., (exh.) 9
Weaver, Gary R., (fig.) 139n, 141n
Weber, James, 94n, (fig.) 127n, 132n, 134n, 303n, 515n

Weidenbaum, Murray L., 94, 170n
Weiss, Ted, 564
Welch, Jack, 126
Welch, Thomas, 518-519, 521
Whitcomb, Laura L., 128n
White, Randall, P., 435n
Whitehead, Don, 556n
Wigand, Jeffrey, 417, 542
Wilgoren, Jodi, 387n
Wilkins, Roger, 439, 439n
Williams, Mary B., 112n
Williams, Merrell, 542
Williams, Oliver, 17n, 179n, 410n
Williamson, Stephen, 504-514
Wilmut, Ian, 320
Wilson, Edward O., 247, 247n
Wilson, William Julius, 167n
Winfrey, John C., 388n
Wiwa, Owens, 590-591
Wokutch, Richard E., 74n
Woods, Grant, 535
Worrell, Dan, 128n
Wyden, Ron, 299

Y

Yamamoto, Tadashi, 74n
Yeltsin, Boris, 21
Yoffe, David, 546n
Young, Andrew, 576
Yu, Songmei, (fig.) 311n

Z

Zander, Edward J., 293
Zebich-Knos, Michele, 250n
Zhiranovsky, Vladimir, 21
Zich, Arthur, 256n
Zimbalist, Andrew, 219n
Zorraquin, Federico J.L., 251n
Zuniga, Jose, 80

Subject Index

A

Abbott Laboratories, (exh.) 386, 391
Acid rain, 262, (exh.) 263
Acquired immune deficiency syndrome
    (AIDS), 80
Adam's Mark, (exh.) 361
Adult-oriented information, the manage-
    ment of, 313-314
Advocacy advertising, 199
Aetna, 446
Affirmative action, 439-440
AFL-CIO, 405, (www) 423
Aid to minority enterprise, 389
AIDS (*See* Acquired immune deficiency
    syndrome)
Air pollution, 260-262, (fig.) 261
Air Transport Association, 369
Alcohol abuse, 415-416
Alternative dispute resolution (ADR), 367,
    (exh.) 368
Amazon.com, (exh.) 308
America Online (AOL), 230-232,
    375, 552
American Electric Power (AEP), 144
American Institute for Certified Public Ac-
    countants (AICPA), 107, (exh.) 108
American Lung Association, (www) 280
American Marketing Association (AMA),
    (exh.) 110, 111
American politics:
    campaign financing, 194-198,
        (exh.) 195, (fig.) 196, (fig.) 197
    coalitions, 193-194
    lobbying, 186-187, 198-204, (exh.) 201
    political cynicism, 192-193
American Red Cross, 375-376
Americans with Disabilities Act (ADA),
    437-438, (fig.) 437, (exh.) 438
Amnesty International, 601
Antitrust:
    and global competition, 226-229
    key issues, 220-222, (exh.) 222
    major laws, enforcement of, 216-220,
        (exh.) 217, (fig.) 218
    objectives of, 214-216

Antitrust Improvements Act, 218-219,
    (fig.) 218
Apple Computers, 552
Archer Daniels Midland (ADM),
    349-351
Association for Computing Machinery
    (ACM), (exh.) 110-11
Association for Investment Management
    Research (AIMR), (exh.) 108-109
AT & T, 85, 314, 454

B

Balanced scorecard, 494-495
Barlow et al. v. A.P. Smith Manufacturing,
    65-66, 66n
Bell Atlantic, 6-7
Better Business Bureau, (www) 371
Bidder's Edge, 220
Big Dig Project, 160
Biodiversity, 247-250
Biometrics, 24
Body Shop, 94, 594-595
Boeing, 57
Boston College Center for Corporate
    Community Relations, (www) 399
Brent Spar incident, 593-594, 601-602
Bribery, 116-120, (exh.) 118
Bridgestone/Firestone (*See* Firestone)
Brown & Williamson, 417, 543
Burma, 487
Business Enterprise Trust, 91-93
Business for Social Responsibility, Cana-
    dian (CBSR), 58-59
Business for Social Responsibility, U.S.
    (BSR), 58-59, (www) 76,
    (www) 96, (www) 498
Business-government-society relations:
    systems perspective, 5-8, (fig.) 6, 15
Business Software Alliance (BSA), 316,
    (www) 324
By Us International Company, 370

C

CalPERS, 341, 345, 350
Calvin Klein, 462-463, (exh.) 463

Carnival Cruise Lines, 453
Cause-related marketing, 393
Caux Roundtable, (exh.) 72, 120
Celera Genomics Group, 318
Cendant Corporation, 145-146, (exh.) 418
Center for Media and Democracy,
    (www) 471
Chief Information Officer (CIO), 312
Child & Family Canada, 455, (www) 471
Child care, 444-445
Child Guidance, 35
Chiquita Brands International, 476
Clayton Act, 217-218, (fig.) 218
Coalition for Environmentally Responsible
    Companies (CERES), 94-95,
    (exh.) 95
Coca-Cola, 207-209, 449-451, 453,
    468-469
Collaborative partnerships, 83
Columbia/HCA, 524-535
Command and control regulation, 267
Common law, 155
Community:
    definition of, 376
    partnerships, 397-398
    strengthening the, 383-391, (exh.) 386,
        (exh.) 390
Community advisory panels (CAPs), 390
Community Reinvestment Act
    (CRA), 386
Community relations, 376-383, (fig.) 376,
    (fig.) 379, (exh.) 381, (fig.) 382
Compaq, 551-552
Comprehensive Environmental Response
    Compensation Liability Act (CER-
    CLA) (*See* Superfund)
Consumer affairs departments, 369-370
Consumer bill of rights, 354-355
Consumer Federation of America,
    (www) 371
Consumer hot lines, 369
Consumer movement, 354
Consumer privacy, 362-365, (exh.) 363
Consumer Products Safety Commis-
    sion, 370

Consumer Product Safety Commission, 359, (fig.) 360, (www) 371

Consumer protection laws, 357-359, (fig.) 358

Consumerism:
advocacy groups, 356
anatomy of, 354-355
business responses to, 368-370
government protection, 356-362, (fig.) 358, (fig.) 360, (exh.) 361
in the Internet age, 362-365, (exh.) 363
pressures to promote, 353-354
product liability, 365-368, (exh.) 367
reasons for, 355-356

Cooper Industries, 89

Corporate Citizenship, 81, (exh.) 82, (fig.) 83

Corporate culture, 132-133

Corporate employee volunteerism, 90-91

Corporate giving, 391-396, (fig.) 392, (fig.) 394, (fig.) 395

Corporate governance, 334-337, (fig.) 336
current trends in, 339-344
process of, 338-339, (fig.) 339

Corporate mergers, 223-225
consequences of, 225-226

Corporate philanthropy, 89-90, (exh.) 90, 391 (See Corporate giving)

Corporate political agency theory, 202

Corporate power, 211-214, (exh.) 212, (exh.) 213

Corporate social audits, 93-95
standards, 94-95, (fig.) 95

Corporate Social Climate, 80-83

Corporate Social Responsibility, 59-61, (fig.) 61, (fig.) 83
balancing multiple responsibilities, 69-72, (fig.) 69
charity principle, 61-63, (fig.) 61
debate, 64-69, (fig.) 65
stewardship principle, 63-64, (fig.) 61
two views, (exh.) 72
around the world, 73-75

Corporate Social Responsiveness, 81, (fig.) 83
becoming a responsive firm, 87-89
framework for, 86-87
implementation, 83-87, (fig.) 84
model of, 83-86, (fig.) 83
in practice, 89-93, (exh.) 90, (exh.) 92

Cost-benefit analysis, 173

Council for Better Citizenship, Japan's (CBCC), 58-59

Council of Institutional Investors, (www) 349

Council on Economic Priorities (CEP), 91, (exh.) 92, (www) 96

Council on Foundations, (www) 399

Crisis management, 47, 467-470, (fig.) 469

Cross-media pollution, 267

D

De Beers, 476

Debt relief, 486

Deceptive advertising, 357-358

Defense Industry Initiative on Business Ethics and Conduct, (www) 122

Deregulation, 174-177, (fig.) 175, (exh.) 176

Design for disassembly, 253

Diamond Multimedia Systems, 317

Digital divide, the, 299-301, (www) 302

Digital Millennium Copyright Act, 316

Disaster relief, 391

Diversity, 429 (See Workplace diversity)

Diversity Council, 444

Domestic partner benefits, 447-448, (exh.) 448

Doubleclick, 353

Dow Chemical, 44, 47, 277, 468

Dow Corning, 558-569

Drug testing, 414, (fig.) 415

E

Earth Summit, 235

Eastman Kodak, 4

E. coli bacteria, 504-514

Ecological challenges, 236-243, (exh.) 238, (fig.) 241, (fig.) 242

Ecologically Sustainable Organization (ESO), 274

Ecology, 236

E-commerce, 289-292, (www) 302, 302-303

Economic competition, 15-19

Economic development, 384-385

Ecosystem:
forces of change to, 240-242, (fig.) 241
limits to growth of, 242-243
threats to, 238-240

Education reform, 387

EG & G, 179

Elder care, 445

Electronic Communications Privacy Act, 412-413

Electronic monitoring, 412-413

Employee assistance programs (EAPs), 415-416

Employee Stock Ownership Plan (ESOP), 343

Employment-at-will, 409-411

Employment relationship, 403-404, (fig.) 404

Emulex Corporation, 306

Enlightened self-interest, 69-70

Entitlement mentality, 167

Environmental ethics, (exh.) 249
international codes, (exh.) 252

Environmental justice, 264

Environmental partnerships, 277

Environmental protection, 22-23

Environmental Protection Agency (EPA), (www) 255, 260, (www) 280, 280-282, 370

Environmental regulation:
alternative policy approaches, 267-270, (fig.) 270
costs and benefits of, 271-273, (fig.) 271, (fig.) 272
greening of management, 273-279, (fig.) 274
major areas of, 260-267, (fig.) 261, (exh.) 263, (exh.) 265, (exh.) 266

Environmental scanning, 33-34

Environmental standards, 267

Equal employment opportunity, 437-439, (fig.) 437

Equal Employment Opportunity Commission (EEOC), (fig.) 437, 438, 440, (www) 449

Ergonomics, 407

Ethical character, core elements of, 126-134

Ethical charismatic leader, 128

Ethical climate, 133-134, (fig.) 133

Ethical egoist, 112-113

Ethical principles, 102

Ethical problems in business, 112-116, (fig.) 113

Ethical reasoning, 134-139
priority rule, 137-139, (fig.) 138
unanimity rule, 137, (fig.) 138

Ethical relativism, 102-103

Ethical safeguards, 140-147, (fig.) 139, (exh.) 141

Ethics:
in accounting, 106-107, (exh.) 108
and law, 120-122
audits, (fig.) 139, 145-146
awards, 146-147
codes, (fig.) 139, 140-142
committees, (fig.) 139, 142
in finance, 107-109, (exh.) 108-109
in functional areas, 112

global, 116-120, (exh.) 118, (fig.) 119
hot lines, (fig.) 139, 144
in information technology, (exh.)
        110-111, 111-112
in marketing, 109-111, (exh.) 110
meaning of, 102-106, (fig.) 103,
        (fig.) 104
officers, (fig.) 139, 142-143
ombudspersons, 143
training programs, (fig.) 139, 144-145
Ethics Officers Association, 143,
        (www) 147
Ethics Resource Center, (www) 26
Ethnocentric perspective, 482
Executive compensation, 344-346

F

Fair Labor Association, 570, 577-580
Fair labor standards, 419-420
codes of conduct, 420-422
Fairness and balance issue in the media,
        459-460
Fairness Doctrine, 460
Family and Medical Leave Act
        (FMLA), 445
Family-friendly corporation, 446-448,
        (exh.) 447, (exh.) 448
Fannie Mae, 442-443
Federal Communications Commission
        (FCC), 460, (exh.) 461
Federal Election Commission, (www) 207,
        (www) 230, 359, (fig.) 360,
        (exh.) 363
Federal Trade Commission, (www) 230,
        359, (www) 371, 457-458,
        (www) 471
Federal Trade Commission Act, 218,
        (fig.) 218
Firestone, 49, 472-474
Fiscal policy, 160
Food and Drug Administration (FDA),
        123, 359-362, (fig.) 360, 370, 462,
        511, 513, 539, 542-547, 564-569
Ford Motor Company, 30-31, 49, 153-154,
        278, 292, 375, 472-474
Free speech issue in the media, 460-463,
        (exh.) 461, (exh.) 463

G

General Electric (GE), 126, 369
General Electric Power Systems, 279
Genetic engineering, 321
Genetically modified foods (GM foods),
        321-323, 353
Geocentric perspective, 482

Glass ceiling, 434-435
Glass walls, 435
Global commerce:
        dominant trends in, 477-478
        globalization, 477
        models of, 479-480
        scope and scale in, 478
Global commons, 236-237
Global corporate citizenship, 488-489
        business strategies, 489-492, (fig.) 490,
                (exh.) 491-492
Global market channels, 479
Global political issues:
        international cooperation, 486
        repressive political regimes, 486-488
Global social issues:
        affluenza, 484-485, (exh.) 485
        anti-Americanism, 483-484
        cultural distance, 482-483
        non-governmental organizations
                (NGOs) 481-482
        pros and cons of globalization,
                480-481, (fig.) 480
Global Sullivan Principles, 119
Global supply chains, 479
Global tools for a new century:
        quest for sustainability, 496-497
        reputation management, 493-494,
                (fig.) 493
        stakeholder communication, 495-496
        triple bottom line, 494-495, (fig.) 496
Global warming, 245-247, (fig.) 245,
        (exh.) 248
Government regulation:
        costs of, 173-174, (fig.) 174
        effectiveness of, 174-177, (fig.) 175,
                (exh.) 176
        goals and objectives, 167-168
        international, 177-179, (fig.) 178
        types of, 168-173, (fig.) 172
Government relations:
        corporate political strategy, 190-191,
                (fig.) 190, (fig.) 191
        managing the political agenda, 189-190
        political involvement, 188-189,
                (fig.) 188
        strategic management of, 185-186
        techniques of political action, 186-188,
                (fig.) 186
Grass roots programs, 199
Green marketing, 278

H

Habitat for Humanity, 385, (exh.) 386
Hackers, computer, 310-311, (fig.) 311

Health Care Compliance
        Association, 143
Helene Curtis, (exh.) 92
Herman Miller, 278
Hewlett-Packard, 133, 291, 552-553
Home Depot, 443
Honda, 116
Honesty tests, 416
Housing, 385-386, (exh.) 386
Human capital, 17
Human rights, 135-136, (fig.) 135

I

IBM, (exh.) 9, 88, 375, 552
Image issue in the media, 455-457,
        (exh.) 455
Industrial ecology, 253
Industrial policy, 163
Information security, management of, 310-
        313, (fig.) 311
Information society, 287
Inland National Bank, 26-28
Insider trading, 346-348
Institute of Social and Ethical Account-
        ability (ISEA), 94-95, (fig.) 95
Intangible assets, 493, (fig.) 494
Intel, 280-282, 551
Intellectual property:
        and copyrighted music, 317-318
        protection of, 314-315
        software piracy, 315-317, (fig.) 315
Interactive Digital Software Associa-
        tion, 120
Interface, 275
Interfaith Center on Corporate Responsi-
        bility (ICCR), 342
International Monetary Fund, 486
International Olympic Committee (IOC),
        515-523
International Organization for Standard-
        ization (ISO), 94-95, (fig.) 95
Internet, (exh.) 7, 296
Investor Responsibility Research Center
        (IRRC), (www) 76, (www) 349
Iron law of responsibility, 60
Issues analysis, 33-34
Issues management, 44-48, (fig.) 45,
        (fig.) 48

J

Japan External Trade Organization,
        JETRO, 74
Job training, 388
Johnson & Johnson, 66
Justice, 136-137, (fig.) 135

K

Knowledge economy, 24-25

L

Labor unions, 405-406
Land pollution, 264-266, (exh.) 265
Legal obligations, 71
Leo Burnett Worldwide, 459
License to operate, 380-382
Life-cycle analysis, 252-253
Liggett Group, 543
Line manager involvement, 89
Lockheed-Martin, 145
Lucent Technologies, 84, 490
Luman Foods, 323

M

Macroenvironment of business, 31-33, (fig.) 32
    economic segment, 32, (fig.) 32
    political segment, 32-33, (fig.) 32
    social segment, 32, (fig.) 32
    technological segment, 33, (fig.) 32
Malden Mills, 10, 76-78
Maquiladoras, (exh.) 390
Market-based mechanisms, 268
Market failure, 167
Marriott International, 429
Mattel Toy Company, 94, 370, (exh.) 421
McDonald's, 52-54, 365-366
MCI Communications, 106
MCI/WorldCom, 3
M-commerce, 296-297
Media:
    businesses' influence of the, 465-471
    definition of, 453-454
    ethical and social responsibilities, 455-463
    industry, 453-454
    role of, 199-202, (exh.) 201
Media training, 470-471
Merck & Company, 141-142, 329
Mergers, corporate (See Corporate mergers)
Microsoft, 288, 315-316, 548-555
Minorities at work, 431-432, (fig.) 431
Mitsubishi Motor Manufacturing of America, 440
Monetary policy, 161
Monoculturalism, 484
Monsanto, 322
Montreal Protocol, 244-245
Moral development, stages of, 130-132, (fig.) 131
Motorola, 476-477

N

Napster, 324-326
National Association of Attorneys General (NAAG), 464-465
National Football League (NFL), 121
National Highway Traffic Safety Administration (NHTSA), 359-360, (fig.) 360, 370
NBS of South Africa, (exh.) 381
New social contract, 17
New York Times, 412
Nigeria, 583-584, 594
Nike Corporation, 403, 458, 570-580
Nissan, 89
North American Free Trade Agreement (NAFTA), 162
Novo Nordisk, 64

O

O Boticario, (exh.) 491-492
Occupational Safety and Health Administration (OSHA), 407-408, (exh.) 408, (www) 423
Occupational segregation, 432-433
Odwalla, 65, 504-514
Ogoni people, 584-586
Orange and Rockland Utilities, 142
Ozone depletion, 244-245

P

Pacific Bell, 143
Pacific Gas & Electric (PG & E), 453
Parental leave, 445
Pax Christi, 601
Pensions and Investment Research Consultants (PIRC), 595-598, 600
Performance-expectations gap, 34-35, (fig.) 35
Perpetual political campaign, 196
Personal spirituality, 129-130
Pinnacle Worldwide, 460
Points of Light Foundation, (www) 96, (www) 400
Political action committees (PACs), 196-198, (fig.) 196, (fig.) 197
PPG Industries, 148-149
Predatory pricing, 215-216
PricewaterhouseCoopers, 107, (www) 76, 311-312
Prince of Wales Business Leaders Forum, 63-64, 64n
Privacy:
    in the workplace, 411-416, (fig.) 415
    protecting businesses', 306-309, (fig.) 307, (exh.) 308

Privacy policy, 307-309, (exh.) 308
Proctor & Gamble, 329
Product liability, 365-368, (exh.) 367
Product recall, 370
Proxy, 333
Prudential Insurance, 104
Public Affairs Council, 185
Public affairs function, 41-48
Public affairs management, 41-44, (fig.) 42, (fig.) 43, 466-467
Public Citizen, 356
Public expectations, 19
Public issues:
    emergence of, 34
    life cycle, 35-41, (fig.) 36
    strategic approach to, 48-51, (fig.) 49
Public policy, 154-155
    and business, 158-163, (fig.) 158
    elements of, 155-157
    role of government, 154-155
Public-private partnerships, 397-398
Public referendum, 203
Public Relations Society of America (PRSA), 466, 471

R

Racial harassment, 441
Radio One, 436
Recording Industry Association of America (RIAA), 317, 325-326
Reengineering, 16
Reinventing government, 177
Relational capital, 494
Relationship investing, 340
Responsible business politics, 204-206, (exh.) 205-206, (fig.) 206
Reverse discrimination, 439-440
Rocky Mountain Steel, 406
Royal Dutch Shell, 21 (See Shell Oil)
Rule of cost, 173
Russia, 21

S

Salt Lake Organizing Committee (SLOC), 515-523
Sanctions, political and economic, 487
Scientific breakthroughs:
    biotechnology, 319
    cloning, 320-321, (exh.) 320
    genetically engineered foods, 321-323
    human genome, 318-319, (www) 324
Scott Paper, 14-15

Securities and Exchange Commission (SEC), 107, (www) 181, 346-347
SEMATECH, 227
Sexual harassment, 440-441
Shell Oil, 487, 581-592, 593-603
Sherman Act, 216-217, (fig.) 218
Silicone breast implant, 558-569
Small Business Administration, U.S., (www) 449
Smith & Wesson, 372-373
Social capital, 377
Social contract, 16-17, 410
Social Investment Forum, (www) 349
Social welfare policies, 163-164
    entitlements, 167
    health policy, 164-166, (fig.) 165
    social security, 166
Socially responsive strategy, 88
Socially responsive structure, 88-89
Soft money, 198
Sprint Corporation, 143
Stakeholder:
    analysis, 34
    coalitions, 14-15
    concept of, 8-10
    interests and power, 13-14
    primary, 10-11, (fig.) 11
    secondary, 11-13, (fig.) 12
State Farm, 353
Stockholders:
    and corporate governance, 334-344, (fig.) 336, (fig.) 339
    and employee ownership, 343-344
    government protection of, 346-348
    institutional investors, 339-341
    legal rights and safeguards, 333-334, (fig.) 333
    objectives of ownership, 330-332
    and shareholder resolutions, 342-343
    types of, 330, (fig.) 331
Strategic philanthropy, 393, (fig.) 394
Strategies of response, 50-51, (fig.) 50
Streaming, 317
Strict liability, 365-366
Subliminal advertisements, 461
Sumitomo Corporation, 104
Superfund, 265-266, (exh.) 266
Sustainability, 496-497
Sustainable development, 237-238, (exh.) 238
Sweatshops, 419

T

Technology:
    and business innovations, 292-293
    defined, 286
    digital divide, the, 299-301
    and e-commerce, 289-292
    and global participation, 293-296, (fig.) 295
    new knowledge, 23-25
    phases of, 287-289, (fig.) 287
    superpowers, 293, (exh.) 294
    in our daily lives, 296-299, (fig.) 297
Telecom Italia, 329
Telecommunications, 286
Telecommuting, 446
Term limits, 203
Texaco, 438-439
Three Gorges Dam, 255-257
TIAA-CREF, 329
Time Warner, 230-232, 375
Timekeeping systems, 403
Tissue engineering, 319
Tobacco advertising, government regulation of, 464-465
Tobacco industry, U.S., 37, 39-40, 536-547
Top management philosophy, 87-88
Total quality management (TQM), 368-369
Toyota, 384
Toysmart.com, (exh.) 363
Tradable allowances, 268
Trade policy, 162
Transparency International, 116
Trend analysis, 33
Triple bottom line, 494-495, (fig.) 496
TRUSTe, 309, (www) 324

U

United Airlines, 3, 343
University of Oregon, 570-580
U.S. Chamber of Commerce, 187
U.S. Corporate Sentencing Guidelines, 105
U.S. Department of Justice, (www) 230
U.S. Federal Trade Commission (See Federal Trade Commission)
U.S. Foreign Corrupt Practices Act (FCPA), 117
Utilitarian reasoning, 134-135, (fig.) 135

V

Value chain, 495, (fig.) 496
Values issue in the media, 457-459
Values, manager's, 127-128, (fig.) 127
Vancouver City Savings Credit Union (VanCity), 96-98
Ven-A-Care, 115
Venture philanthropy, 395
Viagra, 123-124
Virtue ethics, 128-129
Volunteerism, 396-397

W

Wal-Mart, 383
Walt Disney Company, (www) 399, 400-401, 467
Warner-Lambert, 3
Water pollution, 262-264
Welfare Reform Act, 388
Weyerhaeuser, 142
Whistle-blowing, 416-419, (exh.) 418, 542, 543-544
Worker Rights Consortium, 570, 579-580
Workforce diversity, 429-430
    and business ownership, 435-436
    businesses' policies and practices, 442-444
    gender and race at work, 430-432, (fig.) 431
    gender and racial pay gap, 432-433, (fig.) 433
    glass ceiling, 434-435
    and management, 433-434, (fig.) 434
Workplace rights:
    to a safe and healthy workplace, 406-409, (exh.) 408
    to a secure job, 409-411, (exh.) 411
    to organize and bargain collectively, 405-406
Workplace romance, 413
World Bank, 486, (www) 498
World Business Council for Sustainable Development (WBCSD), 250-251, (www) 255
World Economic Forum, (www) 498
World Trade Organization, 69, 179, (www) 498, 498-501

Y

Yahoo!, 336, (exh.) 485